W9-CNX-868

Management

3rd Edition

Don
Hellriegel
College of Business,
Texas A&M University

John W.
Slocum, Jr.
College of Business
Southern Methodist University

Addison-Wesley Publishing Company
Reading, Massachusetts □ Menlo Park, California
London □ Amsterdam □ Don Mills, Ontario □ Sydney

Management

3rd Edition

Sponsoring Editor:	*Janis Jackson Hill*
Production Editor:	*Herbert A. Merritt*
Designer:	*Marie McAdam*
Illustrator:	*Phil Carver and Friends*
Cover Design:	*Nason Design Associates, Inc.*

Library of Congress Cataloging in Publication Data
Hellriegel, Don.
   Management.

   Bibliography: p.
   Includes index.
   1. Management.   I. Slocum, John W.   II. Title.
HD31.H447 1982   658.4   81-3641
ISBN 0-201-04070-0   AACR2

ISBN 0-201-04070-0
ABCDEFGHIJ-DO-898765432

To Lois and Gail
Never say never

PREFACE

In the study of chemistry, biology, or physics, the real world is carried into the laboratory. The science student need not rely on verbal explanations, past records, or pictures to describe events in the real world. In such settings, students can learn how to do scientific experiments, practice those skills, and ultimately acquire the knowledge needed to attain a degree in science.

A major problem in teaching management lies in finding a counterpart to the laboratory. Firsthand experience in many organizations is hard to come by. We can not always find a company, union, church, hospital, school, or other organization that will allow students to observe the behavior of its managers. Therefore, management is a difficult subject to teach and study, in part because many of the concepts appear as abstractions to the students. Although a great deal of research has been done since the second edition, it was not our sole purpose to critically examine it. Rather, we have attempted to integrate research findings into the text only when they are relevant. As a result, we feel that the explanations of concepts and theories are clear and meaningful.

SPECIAL FEATURES

To help the student understand the concepts of effective management, we have included in the third edition of this text numerous lively, firsthand examples of problems facing managers and how they were solved. We have emphasized the actual behavior and thinking that went into numerous decisions and have not dwelled on abstract concepts or models. Each chapter opens with a *Preview Case* that serves to highlight the focus of the chapter. In addition, *Case Studies* of over 100 companies are used in the text to demonstrate how a concept or approach was applied in the real world to aid managers in performing their jobs. Some of the companies used to illustrate the management concepts and models include Burger King, National Can, Radio Shack, American Telephone & Telegraph, Westinghouse, Sambo's, Dow

Chemical, General Mills, the Columbus Ohio Police Department, Miller Brewing, Lockheed, McDonald's, and Coca-Cola. *Management Incidents and Cases* are presented at the end of each chapter to further explore the materials presented in the chapter.

A second major goal of this edition has been to include topics and illustrations of high interest to students and practicing managers. Several of the new topics included are office politics, corporate social responsibility, Japanese business practices, government-business relations, and women in management.

A third goal of this edition is to be very student oriented. It is designed to be used in the first course in management. Readers without any prior management experience can learn about and gain appreciation of the functions of a manager. As a further aid to students, important terms are set in boldface italics in the text, are highlighted as key words at the end of each chapter, and are defined in the glossary. Discussion questions are found at the end of each chapter. These are designed to help the reader think about critical issues posed in the chapter.

NEW IMPROVEMENTS

This third edition contains some very significant changes. The major revisions are as follows:

1. Broader coverage of management topics. Five new chapters have been added and the rest have been significantly revised. A chapter on the "Development of Management Thought" has been added so that students will be able to trace how modern management concepts developed from earlier practitioners and are still important today. The chapter on "Planning Aids and Techniques" has been extensively rewritten and a new chapter on "Strategic Planning Concepts and Approaches" has been added. Chapters on "International Environments" "Decision-Making in Operations Management," and "Communication in Organizations" have been added to present additional coverage of important management concepts.

2. Improved organization of topics. We have organized the topics in this edition in six basic parts. Each part reflects one of the basic functions performed by managers. The first part discusses what managers do, the roles they play in their organizations, and the history of management. The second part focuses on how the environment affects managers' decision-making and company performance. The third part addresses the importance of planning and how it affects the organizing function of the company. The fourth part addresses decision-making and the control strategies managers use to increase the effectiveness of their organizations. The fifth part covers the behavioral side of the firm, including chapters on leadership, communication, motivation, conflict, and groups. The sixth part discusses the ways managers can change organizations and some of the challenges that they will have to manage in the 1980s.

3. *More industry applications.* In order to motivate readers and give them an appreciation for management, we have provided actual cases of company successes and failures in each chapter. These cases pertain to the topics covered in the chapter and highlight the concepts or models being discussed. Applications from the literature and the authors' consulting experience are presented in the text as well as in the Management Incidents and Cases at the end of each chapter.

4. *Expanded, more accessible cases.* In this edition, there are usually two cases or management incidents at the end of each chapter. The solutions to these cases are presented in the Instructor's Resource Guide.

5. *Expanded problems and discussion questions.* There are approximately 50 percent more problems and discussion questions provided at the end of the chapters. These span the public and private sectors as well as service and manufacturing companies.

6. *New Supplementary Aids.* A unique workbook, entitled *Management Ideas: Study Guide and Exercises,* has been prepared by James Schreier, of Marquette University. By combining self-study and assessment, and experiential exercises, it gives students valuable experience that will lead to successful and satisfying management career decisions. An extensive Instructor's Resource Guide, test bank, and set of transparency masters are also available. Customized test preparation and computerized testing service are provided.

7. *Improved readability and appearance.* Our objective in this third edition was to provide a quality book that is highly readable and interesting. The use of color, open space, and illustrations enhance its appeal to readers.

We continue to be grateful for the intellectual stimulation and guidance provided by the reviewers for this edition of the book. We would like to thank them for their comments and suggestions that led to an improved manuscript:

**ACKNOWLEDG-
MENTS**

Gerald Allen, Mary Kay Cosmetics
Carl Anderson, University of North Carolina
Lloyd Baird, Boston University
Otis Baskin, University of Houston, Clear Lake City
Arthur Bedeian, Auburn University
David Blevins, University of Mississippi
John Castellano, Suffolk University
Grahame Clark, Banctec Corporation
Joyce Crawford, DBG&H Unlimited
John Daniels, Pennsylvania State University
Robert German, Bonanza International Corporation
Giovanni Giglioni, Mississippi State University
Mark Hammer, Washington State University

Richard Huseman, University of Georgia
Gopal Joshi, Central Missouri State University
Raymond Lesikar, North Texas State University
Vincent Luchsinger, Texas Tech University
Mick McGill, Southern Methodist University
Susan Mohrman, University of Southern California
William Muhs, Washington State University
James Necessary, Ball State University
James Overstreet, Appalachian State University
Barbara Pelletier, McDonald's Corporation
Kenneth Ramsing, University of Oregon
Robert Rasberry, Southern Methodist University
Diana Reed-Mendenhall, Western Michigan University
Mark Rigg, Southland Corporation
Robert Rosen, University of South Carolina
James Rothe, G. D. Searle & Company
Chester Schriesheim, University of Southern California
John Sheridan, Texas Christian University
Robert Stokes, University of Southwestern Louisiana
Ed Sweet, Sweet Engineering
Kenneth Thompson, University of Notre Dame
Jeffrey Wood, Arthur Anderson & Company
April Vitale, Coca-Cola Company
Carl Zeithaml, Texas A&M University

We would like to provide our special thanks to Donald Campbell, Bowling Green State University, for his significant help with the entire manuscript through several phases of development.

For prompt and accurate typing, we thank these superb secretaries: Jane Bell, Edith Benham, Bonnie Campion, Janet Coonrad, Arelia Jimenez, Joyce Kennedy, Laurie Lang, Pam Ross, and Bess Vick. Without them, it is doubtful that this manuscript could have ever been completed.

Appreciation is also expressed to Dean Alan B. Coleman and Mike Wooton, The Edwin L. Cox School of Business, Southern Methodist University, as well as Dean William V. Muse and William H. Mobley, Texas A&M University, who were most helpful in providing assistance and other needed resources.

We would like to acknowledge the special contribution made by Kenneth Ramsing for writing the chapter on "Decision-Making in Operations Management."

College Station, Texas
Dallas, Texas
December 1981

D.H.
J.W.S., Jr.

CONTENTS

Chapter 4
INTERNATIONAL ENVIRONMENTS

Chapter 5   **Part III**
STRATEGIC PLANNING CONCEPTS AND APPROACHES

Chapter 6
PLANNING AIDS AND TECHNIQUES

Chapter 7

ORGANIZATIONAL DESIGN: BASIC CONCEPTS

Chapter 8

ORGANIZATIONAL DESIGNS: MODERN APPROACHES

Part IV

Chapter 9

DECISION-MAKING CONCEPTS AND CONTINGENCIES

Chapter 10
DECISION-MAKING: MODELS AND TECHNIQUES

Chapter 11
DECISION-MAKING IN OPERATIONS MANAGEMENT

Chapter 12
CONTROL CONCEPTS AND STRATEGIES

Chapter 13
MOTIVATION

Part V

Chapter 14
THE LEADERSHIP PROCESS

Chapter 15
COMMUNICATION IN ORGANIZATIONS

Chapter 16
MANAGING GROUPS

Chapter 17
CONFLICT PROCESS

Part VI

Chapter 18
ORGANIZATIONAL CHANGE

Chapter 19
CHALLENGES TO MANAGEMENT IN THE 1980s

Glossary

Index

Part I consists of two chapters that serve to introduce you to problems and opportunities facing managers. Chapter 1 defines management as a process of working with and through people to reach the goals of the organization. The process of managing includes the activities of planning, organizing, deciding, controlling, and motivating. We identify three levels of managers, how managers spend their time, and what roles they play to assist the organization in reaching its goals. The point is also made that managers must strive to develop their human-relations, technical, and administrative skills to be effective. This chapter further introduces the point that there is "no one best way" to do a job well.

Chapter 2 further explores the various approaches that managers can use to reach the organization's goals: the classical approach, the behavioral approach, the quantitative approach, and the contingency approach. The classical approach stresses that managers manage by emphasizing certain principles. The behavioral approach supports the ideas that people are the most important part of the organization. It is how employees react to managers' styles that influences behavior. The quantitative approach suggests that through the use of mathematical models and other quantitative aids, managers can improve their effectiveness. The main theme of the contingency approach is one of integration between these three approaches. Managers should assess the situation and manage on the basis of the knowledge they have gained from the traditional, behavioral, and quantitative approaches. This integrative approach is the theme of the entire book.

Part 1

THE IMPORTANCE OF MANAGEMENT AND MANAGERS

After reading this chapter, you should be able to:

1. Define the term "management."

2. Identify three levels of management.

3. Define the term "manager" and give examples of managers in several organizations.

4. Explain the importance of managers in today's organizations.

5. Describe the basic characteristics of managerial work.

6. Explain the roles managers play in organizations.

7. Identify the three basic skills of an effective administrator.

8. Describe a general framework for studying management.

During the last 50 years, every developed country has become a society of organizations. We are no exception. At various times in our lives, each of us will become a member of an organization — school, college, church, fraternity or sorority, sport team, armed forces, homeowner's association, or a business. These organizations differ from one another in numerous ways. Some, like the armed forces or large corporations, spend thousands of dollars recruiting members and developing highly sophisticated control methods to assure that members conform to the organization's rules and regulations. Others, like the neighborhood homeowner's association and PTA, spend relatively little money attracting members, and they impose few controls on their members' behavior. Each of us could write our own biography as a series of encounters with organizations. Consider your life and the organizations you will meet or have met from birth to death.[1]

You're born in a hospital.

Your birth is registered by a city or county bureau of records.

You're educated in a school system, assigned to a variety of teachers in your 13 years in the system.

When old enough, you're licensed to drive by a state agency.

You're loaned money for your first car or house by a financial institution.

If you travel abroad, you'll be required to carry a passport issued by an agency of the national government.

Your marriage is registered by the bureau of records.

Home furnishings and food are purchased from businesses whose owners you do not know.

By the time you're 30 years old, you'll have moved at least twice, relying upon a moving company to transport your belongings from dwelling to dwelling.

Quite likely, you or someone you know will be granted a divorce by state courts, with the aid of a law firm.

At your death, you'll be ministered to by representatives of at least three organizations — a law firm, the church, and the undertaker!

Organizations are all around us, and we sometimes take them for granted. Some make our lives more varied and exciting than would otherwise be possible. Others enslave us and make us feel powerless to fight back. All organizations we encounter, however, have at least three common elements. First, they have *goals*. The goal of a football team is to win games and the league title. The goals of Ray Kroc, founder and Senior Chairman of the Board of McDonald's, are to serve quality food with fast service in clean surroundings and to earn a profit. Second, to reach these goals, McDonald's has devised *certain methods* — uniformity in menu and service, product consistency, heavy advertising, locations primarily in suburban areas, and community service. Without these methods, it is unlikely McDonald's would be one of the most successful billion-dollar-a-year companies. Third, organizations have *managers* who are responsible for helping the organization reach its goals. Each McDonald's manager is sent to Hamburger University in Elk Grove Village, Illinois, where, in addition to getting work experience in a restaurant, the manager learns about business management, accounting, marketing, community relations, and personnel management. Without this training, Kroc's goal of selling a billion hamburgers every four months would not be reached.[2]

This book is about how organizations are managed and how managers set and achieve their goals. **Managers** give directions to the organizations they manage. They have to think through the organization's goals, set objectives, and organize resources to achieve results. In performing these functions, managers everywhere face the same types of problems. They have to organize work for productivity, lead employees toward productivity and achievement, and be responsible for the social impact of their organization on society. Helping you understand how managers accomplish these tasks is the purpose of this book. It is not our intention to include every problem a manager might face, but just those with which all managers can be expected to deal, regardless of their background, goals, and size of their organizations.

**WHAT IS
MANAGEMENT?**

Management is the art of getting things done through other people. Managers achieve the organization's goals by arranging for others to do things, not by performing all the tasks themselves. In fact, most employees do nonmanagerial work. Receptionists, file clerks, secretaries, security guards, janitorial staffs, and bank tellers are all nonmanagers.

The importance of good management can be seen everywhere. Look at the success of McDonald's, K-Mart, Radio Shack, Seven-Up, Miller Brewing Company, and W. R. Grace and Company, to name a few. On the other hand, look at the management failures of W. T. Grant, World Football League, Chrysler Corporation, Lockheed Aircraft Corporation, and Amtrak, among others. Good management is the difference between success and failure of an organization. Management guides the organization. When Philip Morris, the nation's second largest cigarette manufacturer, purchased Miller Brewing Company in 1969, it was Philip Morris' management team that turned Miller around. With its creative marketing strategies and new production facilities, Miller beer increased its market share from four percent in 1972 to 20 percent in 1979, second only to Anheuser-Busch.[3]

**Levels of
Management**

Now that we can see the importance of management, it is time to look at the types of managers typically found in organizations. Harry Cunningham is the president of K-Mart and is called a manager. He is responsible for supervising thousands of employees and the operations of over 1500 K-Mart Stores. Don Bolger is the manager of five waitresses at the local Dairy Queen. Both are managers, but their jobs are not the same. Managerial jobs differ according to how high the manager is in the organization. Managers are classified by their level in the organization and by the range of organizational activities for which they are responsible.

First-line managers

Directly responsible for the actual production of goods and services (Fig. 1.1), *first-line managers* have various titles: section chief, lead person, supervisor. The employees, who report to them, perform the operations of the organization. For example, first-line managers in a steel manufacturing plant are in charge of the employees making the steel, operating machines, shipping orders, and performing the maintenance. This level of management is the link between managers and nonmanagers. It is the "firing line" where the action is.

Studies of first-line managers show that they spend little time with top managers and people from other organizations. Most of their time is spent with subordinates. The topics of conversation and the time spent on each by first-line managers are shown in Table 1.1. The topics of conversation indicate

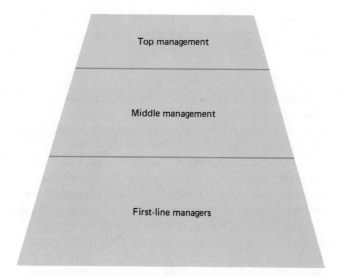

Topic	Percent of Time
	1.1 *Average Amounts of* *Time Spent by Foremen* *on Each Topic*

Topic	Percent of Time
Quality	18.2%
Work progress	13.2
Personnel administration	11.2
Personal relations and other non-job-related topics	10.2
Performance of an operation	8.1
Tools, jigs, and fixtures	8.1
Materials	8.0
Employee job performance	7.6
Production schedule	5.2
Grievances	2.0
Injury, illness	1.2
Housekeeping	0.5
Work standards	0.4
Safety	0.2
Meeting	0.1
Miscellaneous	2.4
Topic unknown	2.4

From R. Guest, "Off Time and Foreman." *Personnel* **32,** 1955–1956. Reprinted, by permission of the publisher, from PERSONNEL, May 1956, © 1956 by American Management Association, Inc., p. 481.

that first-line managers often lead hectic, interrupted work lives, spending most of their time communicating and caring for problems in their own work areas.

Middle managers   As organizations get bigger and more complex, so do the problems, especially those of coordinating the activities of people, determining which products the first-line managers should make, and how to market these products to potential customers. These problems are dealt with by **middle managers,** who receive the broad, overall strategies and policies from top managers and translate them into specific action programs that can be implemented by first-line managers. Therefore, middle managers spend most of their time analyzing data, preparing reports, and helping first-line managers do their job. For example, the head of the payroll department does not determine how much salary a particular manager gets, but wants to make sure that payroll checks are issued on time and for the correct amount. The parent who is dissatisfied with a teacher goes to the principal to complain. The principal is a member of middle management: The teacher is the first-line manager.

The job of many middle managers is to act as a buffer between top and first-line managers. Thus, they spend about 80 percent of their time talking on the phone, in committee meetings, and preparing reports. The rest of the time is spent reading. The following self-report highlights the duties of a middle manager:*

> I have a terrible time trying to explain what I do at work when I get home. My kids think of a manager in terms of someone who has authority over those people who work for him and who, in turn, get his job done for him. You know, they think of those nice, neat organization charts, too. They also expect that when I get promoted, I'll have more people working for me.
>
> Now, all of this is unrealistic. Actually, I only have eighteen people directly reporting to me. These are the only ones I can give orders to. But I have to rely directly on the services of seventy-five or eighty other people in this company if my project is going to get done. They, in turn, are affected by perhaps several hundred others, and I must sometimes see some of them, too, when work is being held up.
>
> So I am always seeing these people, trying to get their cooperation, trying to deal with delays, work out compromises on specifications, etc. Again, when I try to explain this to my kids, they think that all I do all day is argue and fight with people.

---

* Adapted from L. Sayles, *Leadership: What Effective Managers Really Do . . . and How They Do It.* pp. 14–15. Copyright © 1979 by McGraw-Hill. Used with permission.

Although I am an engineer, trained to do technical work in the area encompassed by this project, I really don't have to understand anything about the technical work going on here.

What I do have to understand is how the organization works, how to get things through the organization — and this is always changing, of course — and how to stop trouble, how to know when things aren't going well.

As for doing a lot of planning ahead, well, it's foolish. In fact, I usually come to my office in the morning without any plans as to what I am going to do that day. Any minute something can happen that upsets the works. Of course, I keep in mind certain persisting problems on which I haven't been able to make much headway.[4]

Managers who are responsible for the overall operations of the organization are *top executives*. Typical titles of top managers are "chief executive officer," "president," "chairman," or "executive vice-president." **Top managers** establish policies and represent the organization in community affairs, business deals, and government negotiations. They spend most of their time with peers, people outside the company, and, to a lesser extent, subordinates. William Sneath, Chairman of the Board for Union Carbide Corporation, spends approximately 25 percent of his time dealing with governmental agencies and Congress in behalf of Union Carbide by attempting to tell Carbide's story with respect to energy, health, safety, capitalism, and tax reform.[5]

Top managers

Clearly, distinguishing among these three levels can help us understand the jobs different managers perform at different levels in the organization. In large organizations there is also a distinction between managers that depends on the scope of the activities managed. The *functional manager* is responsible for a specialized area of operations, such as accounting, personnnel, finance, marketing, and production. Such a manager will have people reporting to him or her who specialize and have skills in one area. A *general manager* is in charge of more than one specialized area, such as a company, a subsidiary, or plant. This manager is responsible for people from the various functions. Lloyd Haldeman, of Inovision, a wholly owned subsidiary of Electronic Data Systems, is a general manager in charge of all functional personnel of this subsidiary. Haldeman's goal is to capture a part of the rapidly expanding video-cassette-disc and home computer market.

Functional and general managers

The word "manager" is a broad one. It covers people who are first-line supervisors as well as chief executive officers of multinational corporations. We have tried to illustrate what typical categories are used by organizations to differentiate among their managerial personnel. We also recognize that, in some organizations, there is no clear-cut separation among the three levels.

BASIC
CHARACTERISTICS
OF MANAGERIAL
WORK

Among the thousands upon thousands of books written about managers, relatively few have been devoted to examining what managers actually do. From these studies and articles, one gets the impression that managers spend most of their time reading reports in their air-conditioned offices, trying to get to the airport to catch the 5:30 plane, entertaining important customers, and solving complicated problems. Studies of chief executives suggest that they seldom stop thinking about the job. Four out of five nights are spent working for the company. One night is spent at the office and another entertaining business associates. On the two other "working" nights, the chief executive goes home, not to rest but to use it for a branch office. Such an approach to time management succeeds in freeing some time at work, but it creates stresses on most families. Tightly scheduled workdays, heavy travel, and simultaneous demands exert considerable pressures. Work weeks of 60 hours or longer are not uncommon in management positions. During a typical day, a chief executive opens 36 pieces of mail, handles five telephone calls, and attends eight meetings. A true break seldom happens. Coffee is taken during meetings, and lunchtime is often devoted to informal meetings with other managers in the company's executive dining room. When free time occurs, eager subordinates quickly try to see the manager.

One reason managers work at such a fast pace is that managerial work is open-ended. The manager is responsible for the success or failure of the organization. There are no times when a manager can say, "My job is finished." An engineer can say the project is designed, or the computer programmer can say the system is operational, but a manager's job is perpetual motion. Managerial work has five basic characteristics: (1) hard work in a variety of activities, (2) preference for nonroutine tasks, (3) face-to-face verbal communications, (4) involvement in a series of communications networks, and (5) blending of rights and duties.[6]

**Hard Work in a
Variety of Activities**

Many jobs require specialization and concentration. A machine operator may require 40 hours to machine a part, a computer programmer may need a month to design a system to handle the materials flow of the purchasing department, and a certified public accountant may need a month to audit the books of a large customer. But a manager's job is characterized by *variety*, *brevity*, and *fragmentation*. One study found that first-line managers average 583 different job problems a day (about one every 48 seconds). As a result, they have little time to plan. A general manager's day might include processing mail, listening to a subordiate tell about a consumer group boycotting their product, attending a luncheon for an employee who is retiring after 45 years with the company, discussing the loss of an $8-million contract with the marketing manager, and discussing how to buy another plant so production might be more efficient. Throughout the day, the manager's activities are interrupted constantly. The effective manager must be able to shift gears quickly and frequently. One financial vice-president told the authors, "I change hats every 10 minutes. I act as a tax specialist for a while, a manager for the next few minutes, then a banker, a personnel specialist, and so on." Constant and seemingly endless telephone calls, sudden meetings, and personnel problems seem designed to ruin the manager's schedule.

The actions a manager takes are brief. Most activities take less than nine minutes. Telephone calls average about six minutes (brief and to the point), unscheduled meetings about 12 minutes, and routine desk work takes about 15 minutes. When dealing with long reports and memos, few managers do more than skim them.

The activities managers engage in are fragmented. That is, there are few common patterns. Frequently managers leave meetings before they are over. Many times they interrupt subordinates to request a chat about a problem. One study found that in 35 days there were only 12 occasions when a manager worked undisturbed in the office for an interval of at least 23 minutes.

CASE STUDY

W. R. Grace and Company*

A description of a top manager will help you understand what the job can be like. J. Peter Grace, Jr., President and Chief Executive Officer of W. R. Grace and Company (1979 sales, $4 billion), has worked for the family firm for 34 years.[7] Grace's operations include specialty chemicals, consumer products, and natural resources. Those of you who live in the far West might have eaten at Del Taco, a restaurant catering to the growing demand for Mexican food at moderate prices. Sporting enthusiasts in the New York City area probably know of Herman's World of Sporting Goods. These are two examples of Grace's program for expanding its consumer product lines. How does Grace do it? He regularly works 80 hours per week, putting in 112 hours per week during the two annual budget months. One observer had the following to say about Grace.

J. Peter Grace, President and Chief Executive Officer of W.R. Grace & Co., an international firm with balanced interests in chemicals, natural resources, and consumer services.

No one says it's easy to work for Peter Grace. Except for infrequent breaks for his beloved horseplay, Mr. Grace hates to waste a single minute that could be used for work. Colleagues say he carries a special key that makes the elevator to his 48th floor office move faster by skipping stops; that saves a minute for work. Mr. Grace spends the 35-minute limousine ride between his Long Island estate and his Manhattan office dictating memos to a secretary (he has eight) who rides with the chauffeur. On frequent business trips via corporate jet, Mr. Grace becomes so absorbed in his work that he sometimes forgets to eat — so underlings don't eat either. (In many ways a softhearted man, Mr. Grace has been known to apologize for such carelessness.)

Subordinates are expected to have instant answers to Mr. Grace's numerous questions. "Peter will call me up to ask me the price of corn," says James J. Galvin, a vice president and group executive for agricultural products. "He'll know damn well what the price of corn is, but he'll be checking to see if I do." What's more, Grace executives routinely compile massive statistical reports that Mr. Grace scrutinizes from cover to cover (it is said that he rejected one such report because a single punctuation mark was misplaced) ...

His colleagues say Peter Grace has changed remarkably little over three decades and that he appears to enjoy every minute of his job. Says Mr. Griswold: "Peter gets a hell of a kick out of being a big businessman; he likes the recognition that he isn't just a rich playboy." Mr. Grace himself says that as long as he holds his job he'll continue to work as hard as he does now. There's no point, he says, in working less hard than one is able. Adds D. Walter Robbins, Jr., an executive vice president and long-time associate: "Peter once told me that when he dies, they can just put on his tombstone, 'I did my best.'"

**Preference for
Nonroutine Tasks**

Managers move toward the active elements in their work. Routine jobs, such as handling the mail or previewing long reports, are delegated to subordinates. Managers constantly seek new and "hot" information, which is picked up from unscheduled meetings, telephone calls, gossip and speculation. Such hearsay forms an important part of a manager's informational diet. When the manager receives this type of information, it is given top priority.

Because of a manager's desire for the most current information, routine reports receive little, if any, serious attention. Although most managers write reports, few top managers take the time to read them. Top managers are concerned with today and tomorrow.

The avoidance of routine does not suggest that managers establish dates and deadlines that are easily missed. When an appointment is made, it is kept. An unspecified meeting time, "sometime next Friday," does not generate much interest. Unless a time is specified and written down, something else will take priority.

Managers work in a stimulus-response environment. They do more than reflect. They must have the ability to shift gears and handle anticipated snags. The problems associated with nonroutine tasks can be illustrated by a conversation with Tom Krebs, a manager for Babcock and Wilcox.

I can't tell you how many hours I wasted handling the water problem in the mill. There was water coming into the mill's floor, threatening our boring equipment. The maintenance department said that they couldn't fix the problem because the local water company had to give its permission to dig up the street. When we finally got the water company's permission to dig, the maintenance crew still couldn't do it because they found a nearby electric cable was causing the copper water lines to disintegrate through moisture in the ground. The electric utility company said that it wasn't their fault and they would not send a crew to fix a water company problem.

Managers communicate in five ways: mail (documented communication), telephone (verbal), unscheduled meetings (informal person-to-person), scheduled meetings (formal person-to-person), and tours (visual). There are fundamental differences among these means of communication.

**Face-to-Face Verbal
Communications**

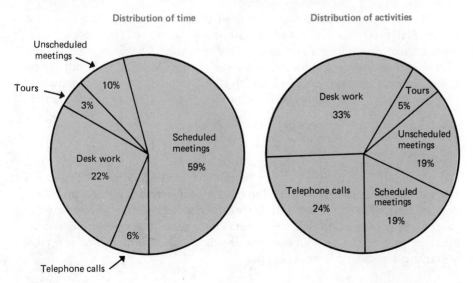

Distribution of time

Unscheduled meetings

Tours

10%

3%

Desk work
22%

Scheduled meetings
59%

6%

Telephone calls

Distribution of activities

Desk work
33%

Tours
5%

Unscheduled meetings
19%

Telephone calls
24%

Scheduled meetings
19%

1.2

Distribution of managerial
time and activities

Figure 4, "Distribution of Time and Activities by Media," from *The Nature of Managerial Work*, by Henry Mintzberg. Copyright © by Henry Mintzberg. Reprinted by permission of Harper & Row, Publishers, Inc.

Mail requires the use of formal communication and is hampered by long delays in feedback. There is little opportunity for give-and-take and none at all for nonverbal gestures. Mail processing is a chore, something to be done but not enjoyed. Managers can process more than 30 pieces per hour just by skimming over inconsequential matters — solicitations, acknowledgements. Their treatment of mail is explained by the fact that nearly 90 percent of mail communication does not deal with "live" action. Managers prefer verbal communication. As shown in Fig. 1.2, 78 percent of all managerial time is spent using verbal communication. Generally, telephone calls and unscheduled meetings are short, but together they account for nearly two-thirds of the executive's verbal communications. The telephone and unscheduled meetings are used when the parties know each other and have to transmit information quickly or to make a request. It is through these contacts that the manager gives or obtains a great deal of "live" information quickly. When problems arise suddenly, unscheduled meetings can be called and telephone calls can be made to "straighten out the mess."

Scheduled meetings tend to be held when a large amount of information needs to be communicated, when the individuals are relatively unknown to the manager, or when scheduling a meeting is the only way to bring a lot of people together.

Tours give the manager a unique opportunity to get out of the office and chat informally with employees. While it is used infrequently, managers use this time to see individuals and extend congratulations on a recent marriage, birth, graduation, or other honor.

To summarize, managers like verbal communication. Informal telephone conversations and unscheduled meetings are important to maintain "live" action. Formal, scheduled meetings are used to deliver communications or for events that involve a large number of people, such as ceremonies, labor-management negotiations, and stockholder meetings. The point needing emphasis is that *communication is a manager's work.* Managers do not do research, admit emergency patients to the hospital, or write computer programs. Rather, managers are communicators and receivers of information.

**Involvement in a
Series of
Communications
Networks**

Managers not only prefer verbal communications; they are the center of a series of communications networks. These networks include subordinates and superiors. Approximately one-third to one-half their time is spent with subordinates and only 18 percent with their superiors. The same percentage appears to hold true for middle and upper managers. And when a lower-level manager communicates with the boss, much of the communication is formal — status requests and formal reports.

another and how changes in one part can affect all the others; (3) knowing how to diagnose and assess different types of management problems.

The development of conceptual skill involves thinking in terms of the following: relative emphasis and priorities among conflicting objectives and criteria; relative tendencies and probabilities (rather than certainties); and rough correlations and patterns among elements (rather than clear-cut, cause-and-effect relationships). A strong thrust throughout this book is the goal of developing your conceptual skill. This is often more difficult than learning concrete technical skills. Thus, to avoid confusion, we have made extensive use of examples and cases to illustrate the concepts and models discussed throughout the book.

Katz suggests that all three of these skills are important to effective management, but the relative importance of each depends on the manager's level in the organization. In Fig. 1.4, we indicate the relative skill mix for the three management levels. Technical skills are most important to first-line management, and decrease in importance with the move up the organization's hierarchy. The supervisor in Mrs. Baird's bakery, for example, is likely to need more technical skill than the company president because the problems brought to the supervisor are primarily technical in scope. Human-relations skills are important at every level in the organization. They may be most important for middle-level managers whose often hectic, active days are spent mostly in communicating and caring for problems brought to them by subordinates, peers, and superiors.

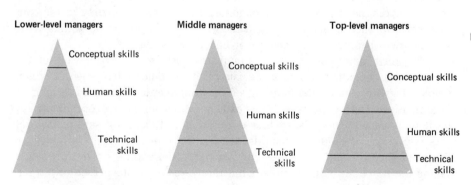

Lower-level managers   Middle managers   Top-level managers

Conceptual skills

Human skills

Technical skills

1.4
Relative skill emphasis for
different management
levels

The importance of the conceptual skill varies across the three management levels. The higher the manager is in the organization, the more he or she will be involved in long-term decisions affecting the profitability of the entire system. Managers at this level need enough conceptual ability to recognize how the important factors in the situation interrelate and to choose the decision that will be in the best interest of the entire organization.

GENERAL FRAMEWORK FOR UNDERSTANDING MANAGEMENT

It is obvious that no single management textbook can, by itself, teach you enough to become a successful manager. Learning how to be an effective manager requires not only knowledge and personal ability but actual experience. When people join organizations, the first task usually is to learn to be successful subordinates. In order to become a successful manager, most people have to prove themselves as subordinates. Individuals who acquire a good basic understanding of how organizations are run and how managers make decisions are moving toward an understanding of management. One of the purposes of this book is to assist you in developing an awareness of what management is all about.

There are four major interrelated parts of this book. The first consists of the three basic viewpoints toward management and organizations. These viewpoints are particular ways of looking at and dealing with different aspects of management. The three — traditional, systems, and behavioral-sciences — viewpoints can be integrated and/or used by themselves to solve management problems. The *traditional* viewpoint emphasizes stable, orderly management through the application of principles. The *systems* viewpoint emphasizes relationships and the interdependencies among the parts of the organization and the external environment. The *behavioral science* viewpoint emphasizes the organization's key resource — people.

The *contingency approach*, the second part of our general framework, enables us to draw upon the strengths and contributions by the traditional, systems, and behavioral-science viewpoints. Moreover, it shows how the three viewpoints can complement one another and provides a comprehensive means for diagnosing specific management problems. According to the contingency approach, the processes, strategies, and techniques for dealing with management problems will vary according to the situation.

The third major component in our framework is the *territory*, or subject areas of the book. The territory consists of three major parts, each of which helps integrate your understanding of the management and functioning of organizations. These parts are the external environment of organizations; basic managerial processes, such as organizing and planning; and behavioral processes, such as motivation and leadership. Each of these parts emphasizes the need for different strategies and practices, depending on the problems facing the manager. For example, what motivates a counterperson at Burger King is vastly different from what motivates lawyers, dentists, and managers. The causes and probable solutions for motivational problems are likely to vary for these groups.

For many years, a set of universal management principles existed. These principles were presumed to hold under all conditions. But the more we learn about management, the less universal these principles become. This development parallels the experiences in other professional fields, such as medicine, law, and education.

Words such as "concept," "theory," "process," and "function" have little
meaning unless they can be related to something "real." To overcome this
problem, *management examples* and case studies of organizations are used as
the fourth part of our general framework. The actual managerial problems
presented may be diagnosed and solved with your knowledge of the materials
presented in this book. The general framework for the study of management
used in this book is summarized in Fig. 1.5.

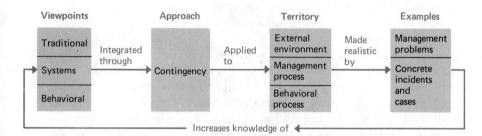

An examination of the traditional, systems, and behavioral-science viewpoints
of the study of management and organizations shows that they can be complementary and interdependent. Keep in mind that we will be presenting only
some of the basic, common threads in each of these viewpoints.

Viewpoints

The ***traditional viewpoint*** refers to a body of knowledge managers can use
to create order and stability within an organization. The emphasis is on formal management processes, such as organizing, decision-making, planning,
and controlling. The treatment of these management processes tends to focus
on finding the one best way and the establishing of universal principles. The
emphasis on the organizational point of view is illustrated in the definitions of
the planning and organizing processes:

*Planning is working out in a broad outline the things that need to be done
and the methods for doing them to accomplish the purpose set for the enterprise;*

*Organizing is the establishment of the formal structure of authority through
which work subdivisions are arranged, defined, and coordinated for the
defined objective.*

***Traditional
viewpoint***

Implicit in these definitions is a relatively simple assumption about the organization's key resource — people. Traditionalists tend to write about planning and organizing processes as though working people, especially non-managers, are interested only in money and/or job security. This may be true in some cases; in others, it is not. This "sometimes-yes-sometimes-no" approach is the essence of the contingency approach. The key to the contingency approach is that it provides a way of diagnosing situations and of knowing when the application of a principle is likely to result in high performance. Rather than concluding that a particular way of organizing is bad, we suggest that it may be effective in certain situations, depending on the type of tasks, the customers, and the employees who accept this form of organization.

Systems viewpoint   Drawing on the work from many fields, systems theorists analyze the total organization in terms of systems — inputs, processes, and outputs — with a view toward improving operations. Compared to the traditional and behavioral-science viewpoints, the ***systems viewpoint*** is less a body of knowledge about management and more a way of considering management problems and issues. The systems viewpoint is a way of observing, thinking, and solving problems.

Every individual, group, or organization can be viewed as a subsystem of a larger system and as interdependent with other subsystems. You may recall, for example, a time when you were under considerable pressure and soon thereafter experienced a severe headache or nausea. In simplified terms, your psychological subsystem triggered reactions in your physiological subsystem. Similarly, any business organization is a system composed of various subsystems. Subsystems might include the impersonal aspect of the control, planning, and decision-making subsystems of the organization. Furthermore, a business organization can be viewed as a subsystem of the parent corporation, which itself is a subsystem of the nation's economic system.

The type of system studied depends on the problems faced. The economist trying to forecast the national level of unemployment, for example, would not need an analysis of a single work group. Similarly, gate personnel for TWA must balance the value of holding a flight to receive passengers and baggage from delayed connecting flights with the desirability and passenger demand for on-time departure. For them there is little value in a study of the national economy.

The systems approach to the study of management is useful because it keeps us from snatching at simple cause-and-effect relationships.[13] It also cautions us against a false sense of certainty about the definition of the problem, as well as about having the ultimate answer to any given management problem. Although the systems viewpoint constantly directs our attention to complex relationships, it does not provide us with concrete answers for dealing with such relationships. In any event, managers may experience many feelings — joy, frustration, achievement, and sometimes ambiguity — in their efforts to understand the relationships among key subsystems in their organization. We feel that the struggle is worthwhile if the end result is more effective management of the organization.

Behavioral science is a body of knowledge about how people behave and why they act as they do. The importance of the **behavioral-science viewpoint** to the study of management becomes apparent when one realizes only people act and have goals. Organizations act and have goals only as a result of decisions made by people. The need for a behavioral science viewpoint in developing managerial (especially the human) skills has been expressed forcefully as follows:[14]

Behavioral-science viewpoint

> *Of all the subjects which he might undertake to study formally, none is more appropriate for the businessman-to-be than human behavior. It is not the general or liberal values alone that justify the inclusion of this topic in the business curriculum. The very nature of the firm and of the manager's role in the firm suggests that every person anticipating a responsible position in a modern enterprise needs a substantial amount of knowledge about human behavior. Thus, we stress human behavior as an element in the undergraduate business curriculum, more for its professional implications than for its general educational significance, although the latter is far from unimportant.*

The application of behavioral-science insights, although applied generally from a systems point of view, is more limited than a totally integrated approach. For example, a behavioral-science approach would be concerned with the design of jobs used by organizations to reach their objectives. Our interest, on the other hand, focuses on the interpersonal and problem-solving behavior occurring within organizations. In addition, concepts, techniques, and problems that represent the core of personnel and industrial relations are considered as secondary and supportive in a behavioral-science approach. Thus, a behavioral scientist's concern with compensation essentially is limited to the general forms of rewards on individual motivation. A personnel book, taking a broader, more integrated view, would also be concerned with the elaborate flow of events in allocating rewards, e.g. job analysis, job descriptions, and job evaluation.

We use behavioral science in this book to apply concepts from a wide range of disciplines — anthropology, economics, political science, psychology, and sociology — to enhance your understanding of the what, where, and why of management, people, and organizations. From anthropology, managers learn of the wide-ranging differences among societies and how organizations, even though different, can operate effectively. From psychology, managers learn to understand and deal with differences among individuals, as well as understand their own goals, needs, and motives. From sociology, managers learn the importance of values and the various ways of relating to groups or organizations whose values differ from their own. From political science, managers learn about the sources and uses of power in achieving objectives.

Summary

The systems viewpoint emphasizes a way of thinking about the complex relationships involved in the management of organizations. The traditional viewpoint comprises a body of knowledge and skills that have been recommended historically for dealing with specific management issues. Finally, the behavioral-science viewpoint provides additional dimensions and depth for realizing the objectives of describing, understanding, predicting, and controlling that are so necessary for effective management. Through the contingency approach, it is possible to use these three viewpoints independently or in combination for dealing with different situations that confront managers. Let's now consider the contingency approach more carefully.

Contingency Approach

The *contingency approach* means that there is no one best way of managing all situations. [15] It also means that managers are not free to manage in any way that might fit their personal biases. Given certain combinations of situations, one can specify general approaches and practices to management that are likely to be more effective than others. In other words, the contingency approach requires the manager to diagnose the situation and then make a decision. The contingency approach is based on the development of a manager's conceptual skills — diagnosing and understanding the various types of situations likely to face the manager before proposing a solution.

The contingency approach suggests that the effectiveness of various managerial styles, guidelines, techniques, or approaches will vary according to the situation. Neither the contingency approach nor the state of management knowledge is developed sufficiently to offer detailed prescriptions as to the one best way to manage in all situations. Rather, the essence of the contingency approach is that management practices generally should be consistent with the tasks being performed by the individuals, the external environment, and the relative needs of the employees.

Use of contingency variables

The contingency variables and their relative emphasis that need to be considered by a manager will depend on the type of managerial problem being considered. For example, in designing the structure of an organization, considerable emphasis should be placed on the nature of the external environment. In Chapter 7 we learn that managers must determine whether their firm is competing with many others for the same customers and whether the customers' buying habits are stable or changing. The structure on the Internal Revenue Service is vastly different than the structure of Braniff Airlines. Braniff has many competitors and a changing set of passengers, while the IRS has no competitors and a stable set of customers who generally pay taxes on April 15 each year.

On the other hand, the contingency variables to be considered in designing jobs are the psychological makeup of the workers and the jobs they are to perform. As we note in Chapter 13, the differences in workers' personalities are likely to influence their interest in redesigning their jobs to give them more meaningful work, greater reponsibility, and feedback on how well they are performing.

1.6
Three key contingency variables

Figure 1.6 identifies three of the key contingency variables discussed throughout the book. As the diagram shows, a contingency variable normally has a range. This range enables you to identify and measure differences either within or between departments and/or organizations. In Fig. 1.6 for example, the external environment of an organization may be anywhere from highly stable and certain to highly unstable and uncertain. Similarly, the tasks to be performed by a person might range from highly routine to highly nonroutine. A routine task is one performed repeatedly in a well-defined manner, e.g., an assembly line task. Nonroutine tasks, on the other hand, are those in which there is a lot of variety and no one best way. Individuals, the third variable, have varying degrees of tolerance for dealing with uncertainty in their positions; their motivations, abilities, and personalities may result in various levels of effectiveness in different types of positions.

One of management's goals in using the contingency approach is to create an appropriate match among the external environment, task, and the individual. For example, McDonald's, Burger King, and Roy Rogers operate in environments that appeal to similar customers, e.g., those who want fast service and low prices. The employees perform tasks that are relatively routine, and most want to be told what to do. Under these conditions, a bureaucratic organization is likely to be highly successful.

Implications for development of managerial skills

The contingency approach should serve as an aid in developing the technical, human, and conceptual skills needed by all managers. All of these skills are based on your diagnostic ability.

The contingency approach helps you to develop the technical skills for determining the techniques and methods likely to be effective for different circumstances. Human-relation skills are needed for dealing with various "people" problems and issues. For example, in Chapter 17 we present a basic conflict model that suggests the need for different conflict-management strategies and styles, given different managerial problems. Finally, the emphasis on diagnosis and complex relationships should contribute directly to the development of your conceptual skills.

In summary, the contingency approach focuses on: (1) the idea that, although there is no one best way to manage, not all ways are equally effective; (2) action guidelines for determining the most likely form of effective management, given the situation; and (3) the development of diagnostic ability. The contingency approach will be applied to a range of managerial issues, topics, and problems, presented throughout the book.

SUMMARY

Organizations are needed for societies because they can accomplish things individuals cannot do. Dealing with and working within organizations occupies a great deal of time and attention throughout your lifetime.

Organizations reach goals through people. Managers are people who perform a wide variety of roles in order that the organization can reach its goals. There are three basic levels of managers, and each level of management performs different jobs. As indicated in this chapter, all managers use their technical, conceptual, and human-relations skills, but the amount and type of skill needed varies, depending upon the level of management and the role the manager is performing. The major roles a manager performs are interpersonal, informational, and decisional.

Finally, we examined the current approaches to management. The traditional approach emphasizes the orderly application of management principles. The systems approach emphasizes the relationship between departments in the organization and how the organization responds to its environment. The behavioral approach emphasizes people and how the organization's success depends upon the people. The contingency approach provides a way of diagnosing the situation before you give an answer. The three major contingency variables discussed were the task, personnel, and organization's environment.

KEY WORDS

behavioral-science viewpoint
conceptual skill
contingency approach
decisional roles
first-line managers
functional managers
general managers
human-relations skill
informational roles

interpersonal roles
management
managers
middle managers
systems viewpoint
technical skill
top managers
traditional viewpoint

DISCUSSION QUESTIONS

1. What is management?

2. What are the major differences in jobs between a first-line manager and an accountant?

3. What are the major differences in how various managers spend their time?

4. Name a successful top-level manager and describe this person's working patterns.

5. How do managers play their roles? Give examples of the three major roles managers play.

6. What are the three types of management skills identified by Katz?

7. How does level in the organization affect the skill mix of the successful executive?

8. Give an example of the contingency approach as it applies to your study habits.

9. The consulting firm of Heidrick and Struggles, Inc. recently surveyed top managers and compiled profiles of the Mobile Manager and Woman Officer. What are the differences and similarities in their work activities?

Profile of a Mobile Manager

Age Under 44, 34.8%; 45–49, 23%; 50–54, 21.3%; 55 and older, 20.2%
Race White, 98.8%
Religion Proestant, 61.9%
Marital Status Married to first spouse, 83.8%
Spouse Employed No, 90%
Education Undergraduate degree, 45.1%; MBA, 23.5%
Cash Compensation $90,000–$119,000, 25.9%; Over $160,000, 25.2%
Average Compensation $134,500.
Hours Devoted to Business/Week 50–59, 43.8%; 60–69, 38.5%
Average Hours Devoted to Business 57.5
Satisfaction with Career High, 50%; Very high, 40.9%
Reasons for Mobility Challenge, 69.6%; Scope of responsibility, 69.1%
Geographic Mobility Willing to move, 59.3%; Reluctant to move, 35.3%

Source: Profile of a Mobile Manager, Heidrick & Struggles, Inc., Dallas, TX, 1980.

Profile of a Woman Officer

Age Under 44, 48.7%; 45–49, 13.7%; 50–54, 14.1%; 55 and older, 23.5%
Race White, 98%
Religion Protestant, 58.2%
Marital Status Single, 29.5%; Married to first spouse, 35.8%; Divorced, 18.5%; Remarried, 10.3%; Widowed, 5.9%
Husband's Occupation Executive, 31.3%; Professional, 33.9%; White collar, 11%; Self employed, 1.7%; Retired, 10.2%
Education Attended college, 28.5%; College graduate, 22.1%; Graduate degree, 26.5%
Cash Compensation $20,000–$29,000, 28.2%; $30,000–59,000, 40%; Over $60,000, 31.8%
Geographic Mobility Willing to move, 31.6%; Reluctant to move, 52.6%
Hours Devoted to Business/Week 41–50, 54.3%; 51–60, 25.6%; Over 60, 8.3%
Satisfaction with Career High, 47.2%; Very high, 32.7%

Source: Profile of a Woman Officer. Heidrick & Struggles, Inc., Dallas, TX, 1980.

Management Incidents and Cases

It may not have seemed to be the time when most people would start a business, but for Mary Kay Ash, bored with retirement, it was the right answer. Since its founding in 1963, Mary Kay Cosmetics, Inc., has grown from a local Dallas, Texas, firm with a 10 member sales force into an international organization selling over $16 million dollars of cosmetics in 1980. It has a sales force of 12,000 independent beauty consultants.

Mary Kay, President and founder of Mary Kay Cosmetics.

Mary Kay didn't just start a company in one day. She thought about it quite awhile first and wrote down all her ideas about running a company that dealt with direct sales. She had plenty of ideas, too, because she had spent 13 years working in direct sales with Stanley Home products and the World Gift Company. At World Gift Co., she began at the sales level and moved up to national training director in a relatively short period. Her suggestions often were passed off by the men she worked for as simply her "thinking like a woman again." By taking all these ideas and finding answers for all the problems she'd encountered at Stanley Products and World Gift, Mary Kay believed she had the marketing plan for what could become a successful company.

In the early days of the company, she made final approval on everything. She hired experts to guide her decisions concerning the business and cosmetic sides of the company, areas she professed little knowledge of. She also instilled the personnel policies that are still working today.

The company sells their products to beauty consultants who are considered to be independent businesswomen. Sales are handled on a cash-and-carry basis, since Mary Kay feels there should be no credit extended. Thereby when the consultant makes her sale to the customer, she recognizes her profit and is solvent. Consultants are trained in the cosmetic's history, use, and how to give a beauty show in the home demonstration technique used by the company.

* Prepared by Joyce Crawford, Cox School of Business, Southern Methodist University, Dallas, Texas, 1981. Used by permission of Mr. Gerald Allen, Mary Kay Cosmetics, Dallas, Texas.

Mary Kay also returned to her saleswomen the highest commission in the direct-sales field. No fixed territories were assigned. She instituted a system of incentives whereby bonuses were awarded for individual achievement in sales and recruiting. These bonuses included diamonds, gold, mink, vacations, and the coveted pink Cadillac that was specially designed for Mary Kay Cosmetics.

Her main focus from the beginning was that the company would not threaten the family structure of the beauty consultants. "God first, family second, career third," was what she felt the company should stress. Mary knew that many women wanted to work, but were reluctant to leave their home and/or children. This is the labor force she went after to sell her products.

As time passed, she moved further away from day-to-day operations, directing her time on Public Relations and communicating with the sales force. Her son, Richard Rogers, who had been with the company from its start, was made president in 1968 and now runs the business side of the organization. She had full confidence in her executives to continue the business as she started it, especially since many of them were with her from the beginning and have acquired her professional tastes and managerial skills as they grew with the company.

A usual day for Mary Kay will begin with reading the mail and dictating replies, a job she starts at 5:15 a.m. and usually finishes around 8:30 or 9:00 a.m. She dictates at home over the phone, and it is picked up by a machine at the office. This leaves her some time to do things around her house before she comes to the office at 10:30 a.m.

Upon arrival, she will already have had calls and her secretary will have transcribed much of the earlier dictation. Most of Mary Kay's day is spent in conversation with her sales directors. Beauty consultants advance to sales directors through a combination of selling and recruiting. The directors form a unit that reports to her, and that she advises and controls.

Mary Kay also reviews sales directors' monthly newsletters, taking their best ideas so they can be compiled and used as part of the weekly sales suggestions, which she writes and sends to all the directors. The directors in turn pass the ideas on to their units during their weekly sales meetings where they discuss sales progress and new methods. There is also a monthly magazine, "Applause," which is the main print communication to the sales force and includes an article Mary Kay writes.

Much of her time is spent in building the Mary Kay image. The company spends very little on advertising, preferring to rechannel the money back to the consultants as bonuses. The time Mary Kay spends with Public Relations is beneficial to all. Time spent here includes being a company spokesman through the media — TV, newspapers and magazines — as well as making personal appearances at Mary Kay sponsored events, like the 1981 LPGA Mary Kay Classic Golf tournament held in Dallas.

She is also available to talk with her "girls" (the directors and consultants) when they call. Not only does she relate well to people, but she believes it is important to the company as well as to herself to keep in contact with directors. To this end, she spends much time traveling across the country attending meetings and training sessions. Her day ends at six or seven o'clock when she leaves the office with that day's mail ready to start the process over again early the next morning.

Questions

1. Describe Mary Kay's work activities.
2. What managerial roles does she play?

MANAGERIAL PROBLEM — JIM FLOWERS

The Place: The director of marketing research's office at a large tire company in Dallas, Texas on Monday morning. Jim Flowers, a member of the marketing group, has submitted his plans for a new tire to Don Donaldson, his immediate supervisor.

Don: Jim, have a chair while I quickly look at the sales promo for the new tire.

Jim: Thanks, Don. I have been running all last week and this will give me the opportunity to collect my thoughts on another project that is still sitting on my desk.

Don: From a quick look, this new tire ad seems to be a winner. With the Firestone's '721' Jimmy Stewart ad, Goodyear's blimp, and Goodrich's no-blimp ad campaigns, this promotional piece looks excellent.

Jim: Thanks, Don. I appreciate the comment.

Don: Jim, the report looks fine, but it is late again. You know that it was due last Monday and I needed it for a meeting at headquarters on Thursday. Why wasn't it ready on time?

Jim: Sorry about that, Don, but let me tell you about last week. On the previous weekend, my kids were playing soccer, the Cowboys were playing home, SMU was playing Baylor, and the Longhorns were playing the Sooners. My wife invited friends from out of town to spend Friday and Saturday with us. They decided to fly to Houston just before the SMU game. You know what the traffic is like after the Texas-Oklahoma game. After driving them to the airport, I ran to catch the last part of my son's soccer game. He won. We drove home and on the way we picked up the baby sitter. We left for the game and got some dinner at a tailgate party. After the game, we drove home and my son said that he heard water running in the house. I drove the sitter home and Gail looked for the water. When I got home, she had found the leak. A water pipe had broken and the carpeting in the bathroom was soaked. I had to shut off the water at 11:45 p.m. and call the plumbing serivce. Did you ever try to get a plumber at that time of night, especially on a Saturday? The answering service finally located someone and he called. We chatted briefly and he told me to have another beer and go to bed. Our middle son has another boy sleeping over when all this is going on. On Sunday, no water. The plumber calls again and said that he would be over at 11:00 a.m. Naturally, he doesn't show until 12:00. By this time, the kids are running around, etc. He finds the leak, but has to cut through the wall to fix it. The carpeting is still wet, but at least we had water. We pulled up the carpeting and cut it off to dry. I had brought home all the data to work on the ad campaign on Sunday, but just couldn't get to it.

Don: Sorry about your problems, but why didn't you call me?

Jim: I still thought that with a super effort on Monday and Tuesday, I could do it. On Monday, I was pulling out of the drive and the Mazda's oil pump broke. Oil was going all over. Gail had already taken the little one to nursery school, and the Mazda was in trouble. After calling for a tow truck, Gail got home and I took her car. I arrived to work at 10:30 and there was a message from June saying that Todd was sick and that the new girl's husband decided to take that job in Houston and she wasn't coming in again. I had thought about the ad on the way to the office, but nothing was down on paper. I called Mike and by the time we had a rough draft, it was 4:30 and I had to rush home to get the kids to soccer practice. That evening, Mike called me and said that his wife's mother had died in Los Angeles and that he was leaving on the next plane to handle the funeral arrangements. Did I mind? Naturally, I said no. As it was, I was working my tail off and finally got it to June on Friday. She typed it Friday and then I polished it on Saturday. She came to the office on Sunday and made the final copy you have now. Don, you know last week was a zoo. Not only the house, car, but the treasurer's report was supposed to be in last

Monday and that was Mike's task. I had to finish that report also and have Lisa type it. Bill was out until Friday with the flu.

Don: I know that you work hard, Jim. Please don't interpret my comments to suggest that you don't. This looks terrific, but you shouldn't have done it. You've had this assignment for two weeks. Just last Monday we discussed the status of it and you said nothing about the house, car, or secretary leaving.

Jim: I know, but you really didn't need the report until Thursday.

Don: Not really, I needed the report on Monday so that I could have looked it over and had the opportunity to discuss it with you. We needed copies made and our presentation rehearsed before taking it to the top. Why can't we get things out on time?

Jim: Don, I really worked hard on this report; I was here until 9:30 Tuesday night and worked home until midnight Wednesday trying to get this ready. The production problem that Bill was to handle also became my problem Thursday. You know that I can't get along well with production foremen. It took me all day to straighten out that mess. I probably should have called Bill at home, but I didn't think it would take all day.

Don: I don't want you to work too hard. I want you to organize your department and job so that jobs are completed on time.

Jim: I understand what you're telling me, but last week was an exception.

Don: Let's go to lunch and talk about it.

Jim: I can't go for lunch. My desk is piled high with papers, and I must pick up the Mazda from the shop. Gail is screaming that she needs the car, and I can understand her point. I'll probably stay here until the Monday night football game comes on and then go home. (Jim gets up and walks toward the door, muttering that he works harder than anyone else and no one really cares.)

Questions

1. Why is Jim having so much trouble meeting deadlines?

2. How does Jim define his responsibilities as a manager?

3. How can Don help Jim?

4. What do you think it would be like to have a subordinate like Jim?

REFERENCES

1. H. Aldrich, *Organizations and Environments*. Englewood Cliffs, NJ: Prentice-Hall, Inc., 1979, p. 3.

2. J. Clark, *Businesses Today: Successes and Failures*. New York: Random House, 1979, pp. 7–13.

3. Ibid., pp. 32–42.

4. L. Sayles, *Leadership: What Effective Managers Really Do . . . and How They Do It*. New York: McGraw-Hill, 1979, pp. 14–15.

5. *Fortune*, September 15, 1978.

6. Much of this section is drawn from H. Mintzberg, *The Nature of Managerial Work*. New York: Harper & Row, 1973. M. Le Boeuf, "Managing Time Means Managing Yourself." *Business Horizons* **23** (1), 1980, 41–46.

7. P. Bernstein, "Grace's Long Search for Security." FORTUNE, May 8, 1978, p. 127.

8. P. Drucker, *Management: Tasks, Responsibilities and Practices*. New York: Harper & Row, 1973, p. 398.

9. H. Mintzberg, *The Nature of Managerial Work*. New York: Harper & Row, 1973. J. Paolillo, and K. Chung, "An Empirical Assessment of the Manager's Job." Unpublished manuscript, Wichita State University, Wichita, KS., June 1980. P. Allan, "Managers at Work," *Academy of Management Journal*, **24,** 1981, 613–619.

10. *Time Magazine*, August 27, 1979.

11. "Harry Cunningham Didn't Play for Safety." *Fortune*, July 1977.

12. R. Katz, "Skills of the Effective Administrator." *Harvard Business Review* **52,** 1974, 90–101.

13. For a greater discussion of the systems approach, see: F. Kast and J. Rosenzweig, "General Systems Theory: Applications for Organization and Management." *Academy of Management Journal* **15,** 1972, 447–465, and D. Katz and R. Kahn, *The Social Psychology of Organizations* (rev. ed.), New York: John Wiley & Sons, 1978.

14. R. Gordon and J. Howell, *Higher Education for Business*. New York: Columbia University Press, 1959, p. 166.

15. R. Dewar and J. Werbel, "Universalistic and Contingency Predictions of Employee Satisfaction and Conflict." *Administrative Science Quarterly* **24,** 1979, 426–448.

Chapter 2

DEVELOPMENT OF MANAGERIAL THOUGHT

After reading this chapter, you should be able to:

1. Describe the three major schools of management thought and how they evolved.

2. Identify how principles developed in the three schools can be used by today's managers.

3. List the differences between the three schools.

4. Discuss the contributions and limitations of each school.

5. Discuss how the contingency approach attempts to blend the contributions of the three schools.

OUTLINE

PREVIEW CASE

**The Great
Pyramid of
Cheops***

The Great Pyramid was built as a tomb for Cheops, a Pharaoh of Egypt, about 2000–3000 B.C.[1] It has been studied perhaps more intensively than any other building in history. Extensive management skill was required to plan, schedule, and coordinate its building. For example, the rock base is less than half an inch from being perfectly level. Exactly how the construction was managed still is uncertain and subject to a great deal of debate.

When built, originally, the pyramid measured 755 feet on each side at the base and was 482 feet high. It covers thirteen acres and contains about 2.5 million stone blocks, each weighing from about 2.5 to 15 tons. The blocks were cut to size from quarries along the Nile River and moved by barge or raft to the construction site. The specifications were such that each block could be fitted into place with only slight adjustments. The blocks were fitted together so well that a knife cannot be inserted in the joints.

Cheops commissioned the project. The architect, probably after a number of conferences with Cheops, selected the specific site and drew up the plans. Many problems had to be overcome. For example, a number of changes were made in the design during the course of construction. A well coordinated schedule had to be developed to ensure that each individual stone arrived at the construction site at the proper time. Too many blocks would be in the way; too few would slow construction.

The planning and coordination involved many different activities. These included quarrying the stone, moving the stone to the Nile, loading and unloading barges or rafts, transporting the stone to the construction site, building ramps, building the pyramid itself, building and decorating the inside galleries and funeral chamber, making and maintaining timber tracks and rollers, making clay bricks, making baskets for the transport of the fill to the ramps, baking, cooking, and supplying sanitary services.

Scholars disagree as to where the stone was quarried, how it was moved, how it was put into place, how long the project lasted, and how many workers were involved. Some scholars have suggested that a ramp was built to the top of the pyramid. Engineers argue that a ramp could be built only about halfway up. How could blocks weighing up to 15 tons be lifted hundreds of feet into the air? Block and tackle, cranes, and similar lifting devices had not yet been invented.

This case shows early problems in management. Were the Great Pyramid to be built today, the approach would undoubtedly be different, but many of the problems of planning, coordination, and decision-making would still be present. In this chapter, we will examine some of the ways in which management thought has evolved over the centuries. As with other types of knowledge, there has been an explosion of ideas and thoughts about management in recent years. Nevertheless, the same basic management problem exists today as in Cheops' time: What is the best way to manage an organization?

To help you understand current management concepts and thinking, this chapter traces the history of management thought. A look at the history of management is important. We must know where we have been before we can determine where we are or where we want to go. The manager who is up-to-date on existing theories and practices can form a personal perspective on management. Too often, managers retain management principles out of step with current organizational and managerial realities. Intuition, hunches, and hope are of limited use in today's managerial world. Each year, thousands of

Contingency school

Quantitative school

Human relations school

Classical school

| 1890 | 1910 | 1920 | 1930 | 1940 | 1950 | 1960 | 1970 | Present |

managers attend management development programs in an attempt to keep in step with the latest management practices.

This chapter reviews the major theories and three well-established schools of management thought – the classical, the behavioral, and the quantitative schools. We also will briefly discuss the contingency approach. These schools and approaches differ in their assumptions as to how individuals behave in organizations, as to what are the key objectives of the organization, as to the problems they emphasize, and in the solutions they seek. Figure 2.1 indicates an overview of these schools and when they started. The lines indicate that all schools are still influencing managers' thinking. Because of these various schools of thought, managers are sometimes confused as to what advice to follow. The major purpose of this chapter is to indicate how these schools of thought have contributed to our understanding of modern management.

THE CLASSICAL SCHOOL OF MANAGEMENT

Although various approaches to management have been developed over the years, the oldest and perhaps most widely accepted among practitioners is called the classical or traditional school of management. Since the beginning of recorded history, people have been managed in groups. Even the rural villages in Indonesia have a recognized leader who performs the basic functions of management – organizing, planning, controlling and directing. The ***classical school*** focuses on managers and how they should plan and direct the efforts of employees towards the accomplishment of organizational goals. There are three main branches to the classical school – bureaucracy, scientific management, and administrative management.

Bureaucracy

Bureaucracy refers to a system of management characterized by rules and regulations, hierarchy, division of labor, and procedures. Max Weber, a German social historian who lived at the turn of the twentieth century, is the individual most closely associated with the bureaucratic model. Writing in the early 1900s, he was one of the first persons to systematically deal with problems of organization. He discussed not only the structure of complex organizations, but also the broad economic and social issues facing society. Thus, his ideas on bureaucracy represent only a part of his total contributions.

One of the first to deal with the problems of organizational complexity, Weber developed the bureaucratic model in an attempt to analyze the structural relationships in complex organizations.[2] He regarded proper staffing and structure as essential ingredients of organizational efficiency. Efficiency was to be achieved through the use of authority based on the manager's position in the organization. Managers were to have more authority and greater expertise than their subordinates. Each member of the organization was to occupy a position that had specific amounts of power, salary, and expertise (determined by technical competence). There was to be a set of rules and regulations specifying the relationships between positions. This would permit appointment of experts to a position and establishing rules and regulations for activities. Motivation was to be achieved by providing higher salaries and patterns of career advancement. According to Weber, the main reason for the advancement of bureaucratic organizations was their purely technical superiority over other forms of organizations.

There are seven characteristics that are usually associated with a bureaucratic organization: a formal system of rules and regulations, impersonality, division of labor, hierarchical structure, life-long career commitments, a legal authority structure, and rationality.[3] These dimensions will be described briefly.

Characteristics

Rules and Regulations A formal system of rules and regulations controls the decision-making behavior of all employees. ***Rules and regulations*** specify courses of action that employees must follow. Bureaucracies are based on the idea that rules and regulations help provide the order needed to reach the organization's goals. Adherence to these rules and regulations ensures uniformity of procedures and operations regardless of the individual manager's personal desires. Managers may come and go, but the rules and regulations ensure the organization's stability over time.

Rules and regulations also provide a means by which top management can coordinate the efforts of various employees. The typical "red tape" that each student must go through to register for course work in many colleges, for example, has remained the same for years, even though registrars have come and gone. This red tape gives the college a stable registration procedure. Thus, we should not assume all rules and regulations are bad for the organization.

Impersonality Reliance on rules and regulations leads to impersonality. ***Impersonality*** refers to the idea that all managers were subject to the

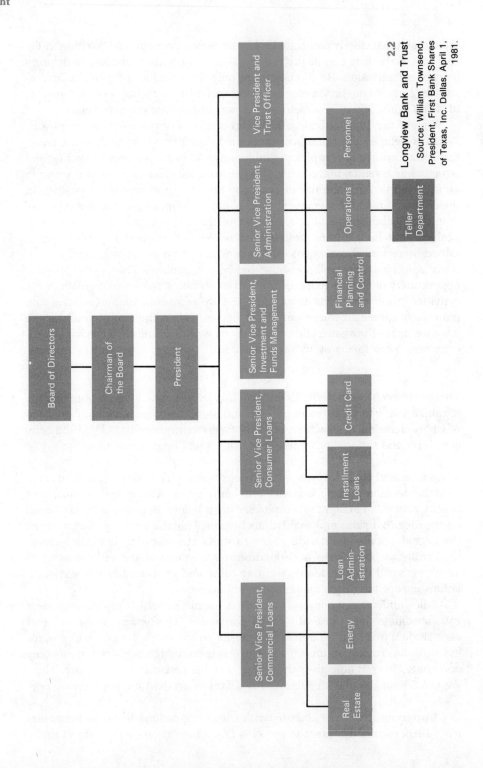

2.2
Longview Bank and Trust
Source: William Townsend,
President, First Bank Shares
of Texas, Inc. Dallas, April 1,
1981.

same rules and regulations and were thus saved from the personal whims of the manager. Although this term often has negative connotations, Weber believed that impersonality guaranteed managers' job security. Superiors rated subordinates on performance and expertise rather than on personal and/or emotional considerations. In other words, impersonality was designed to preserve objectivity and the individuality of the bureaucrat.

Passage of equal opportunity legislation in the 1960's strengthened impersonality. Today employers cannot ask potential employees about their sex or race on the application form. The purpose of this rule is to protect candidates from the personal whims of managers who might screen out applicants on the basis of sex or race.

Division of Labor   The manager must perform official duties that are assigned on the basis of specialization and expertise. ***Division of labor*** is the actual dividing of a task into specialized parts. This enables the organization to take advantage of individuals who are experts in a particular area. A person develops these skills through repetition and practice. When the tasks are divided into simpler ones, the individual can be assigned to perform these simpler tasks which are easier to do and more repetitive than the complex task. The individual is able to learn the tasks and the necessary skills quickly. These steps lead to increased efficiency by the individual and, therefore, less reliance by the organization on the skills of any particular person. For example, personnel replacement is eased and relatively simple on an assembly line. When a job opens, the person to fill the position can be chosen solely on the basis of an ability to do the work. At a Frito-Lay chip plant in the Dallas area, turnover on the packaging line is more than 90 percent a year. According to Ben Dowell, a manager for Frito-Lay, this does not present a problem because replacements can be trained in 30 minutes how to correctly place a bag of chips in a box.

There are a number of consequences of specialization. It permits managers to become experts in one area. At Longview Bank and Trust, for example, the senior vice president for consumer loans is an expert in this area. If there is a problem in this area of the bank, the president knows who to go to for answers. As indicated in Fig. 2.2, the senior vice president for consumer loans is in charge of staffing only that area of the bank.

Hierarchical Structure   Most organizations have a pyramid-shaped hierarchical structure, as in Fig. 2.2. Each level of the hierarchy represents a different degree of authority. Typically, power and authority increase with level in the hierarchy. Each lower-level position is under the control and direction of a higher-level position.

According to Weber, a well-defined hierarchy controls the behavior of employees. In Fig. 2.2, the relationships between the six hierarchical levels are clearly defined. For example, bank tellers are responsible and accountable for their activities to the person in charge of operations. The operations officer reports to the Senior Vice President for Administration. Through this structure, all teller activities can be coordinated to achieve the goal(s) of the bank.

Life-Long Career   According to the bureaucratic model, employment is a life-long career commitment. Managers should be appointed to positions in accordance with their technical qualifications. They should regard the position as their primary occupation. In essence, the individual's technical qualifications alone are sufficient for continued employment; job security is guaranteed as long as the individual is qualified. Entrance requirements, such as a level of education or past experience, ensure technical qualification rather than reliance on "pull" or patronage.

Job security, tenure, incremental salaries, and pensions are used to ensure the devoted performance of official duties, without regard to external political pressures. Promotion is granted on the passage of examinations to determine the individual's technical competence to handle the demands of the next job. For example, promotion through civil service ranks is determined by technical qualifications and seniority. Technical qualification can often be determined by examination results, amount of formal education, and previous work experience. Thus a GS-7 position in the federal government requires less education, experience, and technical skill than does a GS-8. The assumption is that there is a close correspondence between organizational level and expertise.

Authority   The system created by rules, regulations, impersonality, division of labor, and the hierarchical structure is tied together by authority. *Authority* is the right to make a decision. Weber identified three types of authority structures. The first type, ***traditional*** authority, carries the force of tradition or custom. The divine rights of kings and the authority of the tribal witch doctor are examples of traditional authority; it rarely occurs in modern organizations.

Charismatic authority, the second type, occurs when subordinates comply voluntarily with the supervisor and suspend their own judgment because of the extraordinary personal capacities, strengths, or powers perceived in the leader. Often social movements are headed by charismatic leaders, e.g., Jesus Christ, Adolf Hitler, and Martin Luther King.

Rational-legal authority is the only type based in law. A superior is obeyed not because of his or her personal or charismatic qualities but because of the individual's position in the organization's hierarchy. This system of authority is most appropriate in a bureaucracy. Authority is based on rules accepted by the members of the organization. A manager's behavior should be consistent with the rules and regulations of the firm.

Rationality   Rationality brings order to a system of activities. ***Ratio-nality*** is the process of making decisions that serve to maximize the firm's goals. The organization should be ordered on the basis of "logic" and "science." The activities of employees should be directed toward the organization's goals. If activities are goal-directed, financial and human resources can be used more effectively. Organizations have general goals which are then separated into subgoals for each department. At Motorola, the corporate goals are to serve the needs of the community by providing products and services of superior quality at a fair price to customers while earning an adequate profit required for the growth of the firm. The goal of the research and development (R&D) department is to pursue and transform technological breakthroughs that will result in high quality products and services. If all of Motorola's departments reach their goals, the general goal is reached. It is assumed that individuals in the organization accept the goals when they accept their job. Members have an obligation to achieve the goals set by the organization.

The seven characteristics of bureaucracy can be used to place organizations along a continuum from high to low bureaucratic orientation. As indicated in Fig. 2.3, organizations may not fall at either extreme of this continuum. Rather, they vary in the degree to which they exhibit the various characteristics.

Degree of bureaucracy

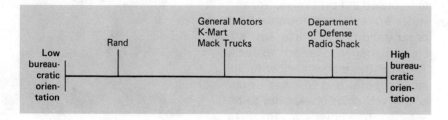

2.3
Continuum of bureaucratic characteristics.

One of the problems in transforming these seven dimensions into an overall rating is that of measurement. For example, one organization may be highly bureaucratic on division of labor and low on structure, whereas in another organization these characteristics are reversed. Are these two organizations equally bureaucratic?

In general, government agencies, such as the Department of Defense, rank high on these dimensions and can therefore be placed near the bureaucratic end of the continuum. On the other hand, most research and development laboratories, such as the RAND Corporation, rank low on these characteristics and thus can be placed at the other end of the continuum.

But ranking organizations is more complex than this. An organization's departments can vary considerably in their degree of bureaucracy. For example, General Motors, K-Mart, and Mack Trucks are centrally located on the continuum (see Fig. 2.3). Their research and development departments, however, are likely to be less bureaucratic than the organization as a whole. Similarly, the companies' production departments, concerned with producing standardized goods, such as automobiles and refrigerators, would be more bureaucratic. Thus, only in the broadest sense can an organization be "placed" on this continuum. Therefore, Fig. 2.3 is best suited for making comparisons in assessing the degree of bureaucracy in an organization. It suggests important variables and the relationships to look for among the dimensions.

CASE STUDY

Radio Shack*

John V. Roach, President of
Tandy Corporation

Large, bureaucratic organizations have many rules and regulations. This, as well as other characteristics of a bureaucracy, is seen easily in the Radio Shack division of the Tandy Corporation, based in Fort Worth, Texas.[4] Rules are evident throughout the organization, and rules at the store manager level are explicit. They tell the manager how to file store reports and in what order, and which color copies are to be sent to headquarters. Prior to opening a store, the manager receives a large binder notebook with instructions on the steps to be taken while opening the store and procedures to use in its day-to-day operations. These instructions cover topics from inventory methods to finances to how to fill out daily reports to how to keep the front window clean.

* From S. Wilson, "The Tandy Corporation: A Study of Organization Design." Unpublished manuscript, Edwin L. Cox School of Business, Southern Methodist University, Dallas, June 1980, and *Tandy Corporation Annual Report,* June 30, 1980.

Individual store managers do not have the authority to make large purchases but can submit a capital expenditure request form for proper approval. If the request is approved, the form is forwarded to the accounting department and charged against that store's profits. With just the district manager's approval, a store manager can not incur an expense of more than $100. In this case, the *original* invoice would be sent to central accounting office in Fort Worth for payment. The accounting department only accepts and pays on an original invoice. This policy may seem stringent, but it does safeguard against making duplicate payments since vendors have many copies of invoices but only one original.

The feeling of impersonality can be seen in the stores. All managers receive the same binder and, therefore, are required to run all stores the same way. Although this allows the manager no room for innovation, it does supply structure for possibly weak managers. If they have a question, they can look in the book. This also gives the customer confidence that the store in Atlanta is exactly like the store in Dallas. The customer feels comfortable knowing what to expect once inside.

Each manager has a signature card on file in the accounting department. This ensures that only properly approved expenses are paid. Only store managers can sign for invoices, refunds, petty cash payments, attendance records, and daily reports. A manager's other responsibilities include making nightly deposits, hiring and firing sales personnel with district manager approval, doing inventory checks every three months, and assigning the responsibility for store operations to another individual while they are out of the store. The "temporary manager" must have a temporary signature card on file for the period he or she is in charge.

Each Radio Shack store is operated as a profit center. The Radio Shack division of Tandy is divided into eight broad, functional areas. Each function is headed by a Radio Shack vice president. These officers and all the managers down through the hierarchy are responsible for, and rewarded on the basis of, the profits their respective functions earn. For example, the manager of a store showing a 10 percent increase in sales would receive a bonus based on this increase. If a 10 percent reduction occurs, the manager's bonus is cut by twice the percent decline, or 20 percent in this example.

District managers, regional managers, and division managers all receive bonuses based on profits in their geographic areas. For top executives, the formula is based on yearly trends in profits for the entire Radio Shack Division. Managers at the store level do not have a fixed salary. They have a fixed hourly wage that is set when they join the company. It is revised every six months, depending on the store's sales volume.

This policy was established by President John V. Roach, who stated: "I want people who live for and will die for this work. If they don't want to do that, then beat it." Tandy's wish is to have employees make a career with Radio Shack. Even though the turnover at the store manager level is high (52 percent per year), the 27 Radio Shack officers have an average length of service of 17 years, and 12 of them began by managing retail stores.

Each officer works in a clearly defined area, whether it be Tandy Electronics, which designates in-house manufacturing operations, or U.S. Retail Store Operations, which manages the 3600 company-owned stores. Managers in Retail Store Operations send directives down through the division to the regional level to the district level and finally to the store managers. Tandy management does not want to leave anything to chance, which is why they maintain such tight inventory and financial control on store managers.

Store managers follow these directives because they are handed down by those having more authority. Similarly, they use their authority to direct the behavior of their salespeople. The manager is subject to strict and systematic discipline when any policies are violated or when there is any misconduct in the operation of the store.

Possible negative effects of bureaucratic behavior   The same organizational and managerial practices that make bureaucracy potentially superior to other forms of organization can be used in ways that impair organizational efficiency.[5] As shown in Table 2.1, although a bureaucracy is intended to be highly efficient, in practice its characteristics may give rise to five unanticipated harmful effects.

Rigid Rules and Red Tape   Robert McLaughlin was a mail sorter in Des Moines, Iowa for 11 years. His supervisor docked him $400 in wages because he did not follow a rule. According to the Postal Service's Manual

Characteristics	Anticipated Benefits	Unanticipated Effects
Rules and regulations		
Impersonality		Rigid rules and red tape
Life-long career commitments		Protection of authority
		Slow decision-making
Division of labor	Efficiency	
Hierarchical structure		Incompatibility with technology
Detailed authority structure		Incompatibility with values
Rationality		

Operations Methods Improvement Program that tells sorters how to sit on their stools and sort letters, the right way to hold a letter is at a 45-degree angle. McLaughlin held his letters at a 90-degree angle. In the Manual, there is a drawing showing the right and wrong way. According to his supervisor, McLaughlin violated the rule and, therefore, was fined.

Rigid adherence to rules and regulations for their own sake is a major complaint of employees in most companies. In the case of the mail sorter, they permit little individual freedom and creativity. For most people, bureaucracy means routinization, task specification, and red tape. An ever-increasing number of rules, procedures, and programs to control individual behavior usually accompanies a bureaucracy. This can lead to reduced motivation to perform, higher turnover, and shoddy work. Rules and regulations are often-times seen as setting the minimum level of performance, but, practically, they define the maximum level. Anything an employee does above that which is required is perceived as giving the organization "free" work. Minimum-level performance can lead to close supervision, which generates resentment among subordinates and an even further unwillingness to perform above that minimum. Similarly, clients may become dissatisfied because the bureaucrat will not "bend" the rules to fit the situation. If the client is dissatisfied and goes over the manager's head, it could lead to criticism or a reprimand for the manager. This unwanted attention from superiors can result in an even greater reliance on rules and regulations. The following passage provides one person's view of bureaucracy.

The Bureaucrat's Prayer

Oh, Thou, who seest all things below
Grant that thy servants may go slow;
That we may study to comply
With regulations til we die.

Teach us, O Lord, to reverence
Committees more than common-sense;
Impress our minds to make no plan
And pass the baby when we can.

And when the Temper seems to give
Use feelings of initiative,
Or when, alone, we go too far,
Recall us with a circular.

'Mid fire and tumult, war and storms,
Sustain us, Blessed Lord, with forms,
Thus may thy servants ever be
A flock of perfect sheep for Thee.

— Anonymous

Protection of Authority   A study of the Tennessee Valley Authority (TVA) revealed that a central problem was the need for delegation of power and decision-making rights to lower-level managers. This need emerged from the increasing complexities of managing the numerous projects sponsored by the TVA. Lower-level managers, however, chose to neglect the organization's goals in favor of more limited personal goals that would maximize their own self-interest and prestige within the organization. Several of these individuals became "empire builders," valuing power, status, and pay. These people brought in unneeded subordinates, added more space and physical facilities, and used work projects to build up their value to the organization. This suggests that bureaucracies may encourage employees to perform at minimum productivity and to be lukewarm toward reaching the organization's goals.

Slow Decision-Making   Large complex organizations are highly dependent on decisions being made on time. Delays in reaching one decision may cause delays in reaching others. In a highly bureaucratic organization, adherence to rules, regulations, and procedures may be regarded as more important than high-quality, timely decisions. In such cases, adherence to rules and regulations becomes a value in and of itself. Formalism and ritualism ensue. Decisions are delayed until all red tape has been cleared and the petty insistence on the privileges of power and status has been played out.

Incompatibility with Technology   Differences in technology also may make the universal application of the bureaucratic model impossible.[6] For example, in the automobile industry, each work station along the assembly line contributes its own small part to the total car. In this context, bureaucracy has worked fairly well for most American automobile manufacturers. However, workers making Mercedes cars are not on a highly automated assembly line but rather are grouped in teams; a team assembles each car and places its stamp of approval on each car it assembles. Here the technology is more of a craft, which simply does not fit the assumptions of the bureaucratic model.

Incompatibility with Values   Professional values, such as science, service to professional organizations, and innovation, may be incompatible with the bureaucratic values of efficiency, order, and stability. Since professionals are being increasingly hired by bureaucratic organizations and assuming more important decision-making positions in organizations, this criticism is very important. For example, to the bureaucrat, authority is related to hierarchical position; to the professional, authority derives from personal competence or technical expertise that resides outside of the formal organization. For example, a doctor's prestige in the field depends upon his or her contributions to medicine and not on how to get the budget approved at the next meeting. Routinization of work and standardization of procedures are of prime importance to the bureaucrat; by contrast, the professional stresses the uniqueness of the problem and advocates change through research and development.[7]

The modern view is that although bureaucracy is not dead, managers must recognize its limitations and negative effects. James Webb, former administrator for the National Aeronautics and Space Administration (NASA), used a bureaucratic organizational structure, but relied on real-time feedback rather than on position-based authority.[8] Under this plan, four levels of hierarchical authority — frequently working simultaneously with a variety of information networks — were used in launching the Apollo projects. This adaptation of the model was made to meet the particular needs of NASA.

Today's view of bureaucracy

Another view is that bureaucracy functions best when large amounts of routine work are to be done. Lower-level employees handle the bulk of the work by simply following rules and regulations. It is only the exceptional case, one to which the rules do not apply, that must be called to the attention of supervisors, who decide whether to change the rules, make exceptions to the rules, or ignore the case. Lower-level employees are not expected to use discretion and can be evaluated on the basis of how well they conform to the rules.

**Scientific
Management**

At the beginning of the twentieth century, industries were becoming larger and more complex. Haphazard management, previously sufficient, was now inefficient. Managers were no longer involved with the production process; they had to spend more of their time on administrative planning, scheduling, and staffing problems. Managers also had difficulty in keeping abreast of the technical methods of production and, therefore, no longer had a basis for judging a fair day's work from the increased number of employees. **Scientific management,** one approach to the solution of these problems, emphasizes the one best way to perform a task through the use of time and motion studies.

Frederick Taylor

The changing technology had created a need for specialists who understood production operations and who were well versed in the solution of common problems that threatened operating efficiency. Frederick Taylor, a mechanical engineer, focused on the human aspect of the new machine-oriented production system. To expand productivity, ways had to be found to increase the efficiency of the workers. The goal was to define precisely all aspects of the worker-machine relationship.

Taylor believed there was only one best way to perform a given task. Like Weber, Taylor believed that an organization should be governed by definite, predictable methods, logically determined and written into laws. Efficiency could be increased by having workers perform repetitive tasks that did not require problem-solving activities; furthermore, performance should be described in behavioral terms (e.g., number of units produced per shift).

**Time-and-motion
study**

The nature of the task was determined by time-and-motion study. **Time-and-motion studies** measure all movements made by a worker and try to eliminate those that do not lead to increased productivity. Productivity was measured in terms of time and costs.[9]

Another objective of the time-and-motion study was to make the job highly routine and efficient. Eliminating wasted effort and detailing a specific sequence of activities would minimize the amount of time, money, and effort needed to produce a product. A standard method and time for task accomplishment could not be stated unless other factors, such as machine speeds and feeds and supplies of raw materials, were standardized as well. Thus, Taylor undertook an analysis of work flows, supervisory techniques, worker fatigue, and inventory storage.

Taylor's idea of functional foremanship was based on his principle of specialization. To Taylor, who viewed expertise as the only source of authority, the gap between authority and managerial expertise was a problem. Since one foreman could not be expected to have expertise in all of the tasks supervised, the foreman's particular area of specialization was the same as the area of authority. This, of course, created the need for multiple foremen for each worker. This led to the concept of *functional foremanship.* Workers would have eight foremen — one each for planning, production scheduling, time-and-motion studies, and discipline, as well as four on the shop floor to deal with such matters as maintenance of machinery, speeds and feeds of materials in the machines, etc.

Functional foremanship

Taylor's view of the worker was a logical extension of his methods and the tasks studied. The only relevant behavior was the worker's physical capacity. The worker's production capability, muscle durability, and fatigue were the major factors Taylor examined. Speed in task performance was assumed to be related to skill, manual dexterity, and effort expended. According to Taylor, workers should be selected and receive job training on the basis of these physical characteristics and not on psychological ones, such as emotions, personality, or on physical appearance.

View of worker

Taylor believed the workers' underlying motivation was money. Scientific management was based on the assumption that workers would be rational and follow management's orders in order to gain extra money. A piece-work system was recommended as the primary pay system. If a worker met a quota, he or she was paid a standard wage rate. A worker who produced more than his or her quota was paid a higher rate for all pieces produced, not merely those exceeding the standard. Clearly, employees would work harder if they could double their wages. It was assumed that management would be most receptive to this because increases in productivity would more than compensate for the higher labor costs. For example, a worker who produced 100 automobile tires was paid $100. A worker who produced 110 tires would be paid $120. The 100 tires was the standard for which the company paid $1.00/tire. Because the 10 extra tires were in excess of the standard, the worker's rate was adjusted for all 110 tires produced. Under this rate system, workers were encouraged to surpass previous performance standards and earn more money. Taylor believed that because companies benefited from the increased productivity in terms of sales and profits, there would always be work.

CASE STUDY

Burger King

Burger King's executives like to say that theirs is a company run by 50,000 teenagers, and those kids are getting more expensive each day.[10] To fight labor costs, Burger King has got hamburger making down to a "science" through the application of scientific management principles. In this industry, an increase in production means extra sales. According to Donna Nicol, Burger King's communication director, "Nobody cares how many hamburgers we can make between 11:00 p.m. and 6:00 a.m. What counts is production at peak times."

To increase productivity at these peak times, every movement of each employee has been calculated and readjusted by the use of time-and-motion studies. For example, at drive-in windows, just moving the bell hose — which triggers a loud ring when cars drive over it — has made a big difference. Through time-and-motion studies, it was discovered that order-takers needed 11 seconds to react to the ring. The time-and-motion people moved the hose back 10 feet, so that by the time a car had stopped at the order machine, the order-taker was waiting to check off what the customer wanted. This change permitted Burger King to save 30 seconds per customer. That means the drive-in window can handle an extra 30 orders an hour.

To serve those extra orders, Burger King had to increase its production inside. Engineers installed computerized french-fry machines and put television terminals in the kitchen. This enabled the chef to read incoming orders off the screen. Time-and-motion engineers have visions of machines that will mix, pour, and cap soft drinks automatically.

Managers and employees who suggest ways to improve productivity get cash rewards. All employees are constantly encouraged to fine-tune what goes on within the restaurant to bring Burger King neck-and-neck with its archrival, McDonald's. As one Burger King executive said, "The new attention to productivity amounts to nothing more than getting back to the basics."

Companies such as Burger King, Corning Glass, B.F. Goodrich, United States Steel, and General Motors, have used Taylor's principles to make finished products probably better and faster than Taylor could have dreamed. The methods of scientific management have been applied to a variety of problems. For example, the emphasis that Taylor placed on the scientific selection of workers has made many companies realize that without proper ability and training, employees cannot be expected to do their jobs properly. The importance of Taylor's work caused managers to seek the "one best way to do things" in a given situation. What Taylor did was not to simply take one answer and apply it to every situation; instead, he scientifically studied each situation to find out what unique characteristics it had before he recommended a solution.

Unfortunately, the proponents of scientific management misread the human side of the problem. When Taylor formulated his theory, it was popular for managers to believe that people were rational. Workers would be motivated primarily by a desire to earn money to satisfy economic and physical needs. Thus Taylor overlooked the social needs of the workers as members of a group and never considered the tensions created when these needs were not satisfied. To many workers, job satisfaction means more than money. Workers have gone on strike to protest poor working conditions, the speed-up of an assembly line, or harassment by management. Modern managers should not assume that workers are interested only in higher wages. As we shall discuss in the chapter on motivation, dividing jobs into their simplest tasks does not always ensure a quality product, high morale and organizational effectiveness.

Scientific management focuses on the shop level and worker-machine relationships. **Administrative management** focuses on the similarities of managers in performing their basic functions of organizing, planning, and controlling. This model evolved during the early 1900s and is most closely identified with Henri Fayol, a French industrialist whose most famous work on management was not translated into English until 1949.[11] Fayol believed his success as a manager was due not to his personal qualities but to the methods used. He believed managers could be taught to become successful once they understood the basic functions and principles of management.

Fayol claimed that similarities in structure and processes among organizations could be identified. For example, he believed an organization's structure can be viewed both vertically and horizontally. *Vertical structure* is the hierarchy created by delegation of authority and responsibility from the top downward; *horizontal structure* is the variety of functions carried out, e.g., finance, marketing, production.

Henri Fayol

This model focuses on the formal aspects of the organization's structure and minimizes the effects of the human factor. Management's main tasks are to: (1) discover a set of functions necessary for the organization to reach its goal, and (2) group tasks so as to maximize productivity and efficiency and minimize cost.

Management functions

Management's functions are to organize, plan, command, coordinate, and control. Planning is the responsibility of top management and involves forecasting and preparing to meet the future. Command — the directing and structuring of subordinates' tasks — is based on authority and the level of the manager in the organization's hierarchy. Like command, coordination is an essential aspect of the control process and is closely related to the formal authority structure of the organization. Coordination, the most important function, is the means by which the organization and its managers achieve goals. Coordination gives hierarchical form to the organization. Through control managers could check the actual performance of subordinates against the organization's rules, regulations, and standards. You might recall that in Chapter 1, we discussed characteristics of managerial work. Some of the activities performed by successful managers today were similar to Fayol's.

Principles of management

Fayol developed 14 principles of management. He believed that through formal training in these principles, managers could become more effective than relying on their seat-of-the-pants practices. His principles are:

1. *Division of labor.* The more people specialize, the more efficiently they can perform their work. As we have already suggested, this principle is epitomized by the modern assembly line.

2. *Authority.* Managers need to be able to give orders so that they can get things done. While their formal authority gives them the right to command, managers will not always compel obedience unless they have personal authority (such as intelligence) as well.

3. *Discipline.* Members in an organization need to respect the rules and agreements that govern the organization. To Fayol, discipline will result from good leadership at all levels of the organization, fair agreements (such as reasonable provisions for salary increase) and judiciously enforced penalties for infractions.

4. *Unity of command.* Each employee must receive his or her instructions about a particular operation from only one person. Fayol believed that if an employee was responsible to more than one superior, conflict in instructions and confusion of authority would result.

5. *Unity of direction.* Those operations within the organization that have the same objective should be directed by only one manager. For example, the personnel department in a company should not have two directors, each with a different hiring policy.

6. *Subordination of individual interest to the common good.* In any undertaking, the interests of employees should not take precedence over the interests of the organization as a whole.

7. *Remuneration.* Compensation for work done should be fair to both employees and employers.

8. *Centralization.* Decreasing the role of subordinates in decision-making is centralization; increasing their role is decentralization. Fayol believed that managers should retain final responsibility but that they also need to give their subordinates enough authority to do their jobs properly. The problem is to find the best amount of centralization in each case.

9. *The hierarchy.* The line of authority in an organization — often represented today by the neat boxes and lines of the organization chart — runs in order rank from top management to the lowest level of the enterprise.

10. *Order.* Materials and people should be in the right place at the right time. In particular, people should be in the jobs or positions best suited for them.

11. *Equity.* Managers should be both friendly and fair to their subordinates.

12. *Stability of staff.* A high employee turnover rate is not good for the efficient functioning of an organization.

13. *Initiative.* Subordinates should be given the freedom to conceive and carry out their plans, even when some mistakes result.

14. *Esprit de corps.* Promoting team spirit will give the organization a sense of unity. To Fayol, one way to achieve this spirit is to use verbal communications instead of formal written communications whenever possible.

Today's view of
Fayol

Many of the principles discussed by Fayol are used in organizations today. In Chapters 7 and 8 you can see why many of these principles are important in the everyday running of a company. What you should remember about these principles is that the same principle is seldom applied in exactly the same way. Situations change and so too must the application of a principle. In large companies, too much specialization sometimes has led to a point where lines of authority are unclear. At one steel corporation, for example, the maintenance superintendent took orders from the plant manager, chief engineer, and production manager. In this case, we have a violation of Fayol's principle of the unity of command.

General
Characteristics of
Classical School

The bureaucratic, scientific, and administrative management models are still used and referred to by current management practitioners and writers.[12] Therefore, it is useful to pinpoint the similarities and differences.

1. All three models emphasize the formal aspects of the organization. That is, role relationships, authority, and hierarchy. All three emphasize the rationality of the worker to follow management's directives, organization, and the science of management. The classical writers of management were concerned with the formal relations among departments, task, and structural elements of organizations. Seat-of-the-pants management practices were replaced with theoretical and scientific concepts.

Although it was surely recognized that people had feelings and were influenced by their friends in the organization, the overriding focus was on job performance. For example, Taylor was concerned with eliminating the senseless antagonism between workers and management. His wage-incentive system was intended to provide workers with a monetary reward for their work. Similarly, the bureaucratic model gave attention to job security, career progression, and protection of the worker from the manager's arbitrary whims. This suggests that Weber was concerned with the individual in the organization. However, none of these models dealt with informal or social relationships and the psychological aspects of work. Rather, they all assumed that sound job analysis and well-written rules and regulations would help ensure efficient performance.

2. All three models were concerned primarily with efficiency — the cost-benefit ratio. The principles of scientific management, administrative management, and bureaucracy were seen as fostering efficiency as the major standard against which to judge employees' performance.

3. All three models highlighted the role of the manager. The bureaucratic model suggested that a strong relationship exists between expertise and organizational level. A superior was to be obeyed by subordinates on the basis of

I. Structure
1. focus on
   a) division of labor
   b) hierarchical and functional processes
   c) structure
   d) span of control
2. assumptions are implicit
3. emphasize principles

II. People
1. machines
2. economic or job security motives only
3. must adjust to job
4. can be hired and fired as need arises

III. Leadership
1. single leader
2. chosen on merit
3. chosen by superiors
4. relies on authority in position
5. leader's task to achieve organizational (rather than subordinates') goals
6. unitary goal

IV. Decision-making
1. consciously rational
2. efficiency sole value criterion
3. maximizing decisions

not only his or her higher position but also presumed greater expertise. A similar inference can be drawn from the emphasis on structure in the administrative-management model.

These similarities may be seen in Table 2.2. Division of labor, hierarchical arrangements of positions, and rules and regulations were the chief ingredients in these models. Decisions were made to maximize the economic benefits to the firm. Profit was the major criterion. Employees were thought of as instruments of production. Their behavior was influenced primarily by economic rewards. Even today, time-and-motion studies prescribe the movements most appropriate for performing a task most efficiently.

4. An important difference among the three models was the part of the organization emphasized. Taylor studied production workers and how their productivity could be improved through time-and-motion studies. Fayol developed principles for managers to follow. He believed a structure was needed to make sure all important functions were performed. If people are organized to work together, then it was necessary to define clearly what they were trying to accomplish and to make sure that everybody saw how their work related to the achievement of the organization's goals. His 14 principles were intended to do this. Weber's bureaucratic model was designed to be a rational blueprint of how an organization should work, with emphasis on rules and regulations. The clear specification of authority and reponsibility made it easy to evaluate a manager's performance and distribute rewards fairly.

THE BEHAVIORAL SCHOOL OF MANAGEMENT

In the 1920s and 1930s, there was some concern among managers that the classical school was shortsighted and incomplete because it largely ignored the feelings of employees. Managers still encountered difficulties with workers because they did not always follow what management thought was "rational" behavior. Workers were not performing up to their physical capabilities as predicted by Taylor, and effective managers did not consistently follow the 14 principles of Fayol. The **behavioral school** increased interest in helping managers deal more effectively with the "people side" of their organizations. The behavioral school emerged from the work of Elton Mayo and his associates at the Hawthorne plant of the Western Electric Company from 1927 to 1932.[13]

Elton Mayo

Fritz Roethlisberger

The Hawthorne Experiments

Mayo was called in by Western Electric when other researchers, who had been experimenting with work-area lighting, reported some puzzling results. They had divided the employees into a test group that was subject to deliberate changes in lighting, and a control group whose lighting remained constant throughout the experiment. When the test group's lighting conditions improved, productivity increased, just as expected. But what mystified the researchers was a similar jump in productivity when lighting was reduced to the

Hawthorne Experiment

point of twilight. To compound the mystery, the control group's output kept rising with each change in the test group's lighting conditions, even though the control group experienced no such changes.

In a new experiment, Mayo and his Harvard co-worker, Fritz Roethlisberger, placed two groups of six women each in separate rooms. In one room the conditions were varied and in the other they were not. A number of variables were tried: salaries were increased; coffee breaks were shortened; the researchers, who now acted as supervisors, allowed the groups to choose their own rest periods and to have a say in other suggested changes.

Once again, output went up in both the test and control rooms. The researchers felt they could rule out financial incentives as a cause, since the control group was kept to the same payment schedule. Mayo concluded that a complex emotional chain reaction was behind the productivity increases. Because the test and control groups had been singled out for special attention, they developed a group pride that motivated them to improve their work performance. The sympathetic supervision they received had further reinforced their increased motivation.

The result of this experiment gave Mayo his first important discovery. When special attention is given to workers by management, productivity is likely to change regardless of actual changes in working conditions. This phenomenon became known as the *"Hawthorne effect."*

One question, however, remained unanswered. *Why* should special attention and the formation of group bonds elicit such strong reactions? To find the answer, Mayo interviewed workers. This led to his most significant finding: that informal work groups — the social environment of employees — have a great influence on productivity. Many of the employees found their lives inside and outside the factory dull and meaningless. But their work-place friends, chosen in part on a basis of mutual antagonism toward the "bosses," imparted some meaning to their working lives. For this reason, group pressure, rather than management demands, had the strongest influence on how productive they would be.

To maximize output, Mayo concluded that management must recognize the employees' needs for recognition and social satisfaction. It had to turn the informal group into a positive, productive force by providing employees with a new sense of dignity and a sense of being appreciated. To Mayo, then, the concept of *social man* — motivated by social needs, wanting on-the-job relationships, and more responsive to work-group pressures than to management control — had to replace the concept of *economic man.* Economic man was motivated largely by incentives and bonus systems that encouraged the worker to produce a high quantity and quality of work.

The basic assumptions of the human relations model are:

1. Workers basically are motivated by *social needs* and obtain a sense of identity through association with others.

2. Workers are more responsive to the social forces of the *peer group* than to the incentives and controls of management.

3. Workers are responsive to management to the extent that a supervisor can meet a subordinate's social and acceptance needs.[14]

CASE STUDY

National Can

Putting people before profits may not sound like the way to become number one in business, but it is exactly what Frank W. Considine, president and CEO of the National Can Corp., has done.[15]

A true follower of the human-relations model, he believes that a worker who can interact with others on the job and be happy on the job will be motivated about doing that job — and doing it well. Production is valued. Considine believes, "If you give people pride in their jobs, you are really giving them something better than wages. You are giving them status, recognition, and satisfaction." This belief also can be seen after hours at plant dedications where such things as picnics, concert performances, and open-air circuses turn company activities into family affairs for customers and employees. For example, when National opened its plant in Oklahoma City, Oklahoma, there were 2000 applications for the 100 jobs. When the plant was dedicated, the families of all employees were invited and entertainment was provided by the Up With People group. National was also one of the pioneers in setting up a cardiopulmonary resuscitation program that trained employees to respond to heart attack emergencies. Two lives were saved in 1979 because of this program. Even using the most up-to-date computer system to make cans, the production of the plant has far surpassed the expectations of National's managers and employee turnover is still near zero.

National Can is a big company with a typical amount of red tape. Considine has minimized this to some extent by operating an on-the-floor policy, which means everyone is cross-trained. When problems arise you go to the person who can solve it. Sometimes this means going across formal channels, not following them. Small company advantages are held on to as much as possible by giving managers the autonomy to use their own operating style on their level. Considine feels that the more autonomy there is, the closer managers can get to their subordinates and the better productivity will be. "We capitalize on autonomy and minimize bureaucracy wherever possible," he said.

This approach has worked well for National Can, whose sales were at $1.4 billion in 1979. It was the consistency of the policy that did it for them, too. Not only was it a day-in-and-day-out consideration of the individual, but all managers and supervisors were living by the policy. This in turn generated an atmosphere in which the everyday problems and gripes are communicated and kept in the open where they can not fester and grow. All this shows that while profits are important as they would be for any company, people at National Can are equally as important. It is through people the job gets done and the questions get answered.

It is from a company like this that an employee would say, "I think the company cares about its people and wants to keep them. National Can is no different than any other company; it has to be productive and profitable. But there is good morale here and solid loyalty to the company."

The **human-relations** movement stressed the social needs of the employees, and how the social environment of an organization influences the quality and quantity of the work produced. Indeed, the behavioral school highlighted the importance of a manager's leadership style and group dynamics. From the works of Mayo and his colleagues, later behavioral scientists, such as Argyris, Likert, Maslow, and McGregor, formulated theories that would more accurately explain the behavior of people at work. (In Part V of this book, we will be discussing the contributions of these people in much greater detail.)

*Today's view of the
human-relations
school*

A limitation of the human-relations movement was that results often ran counter to what Mayo had expected. Improving working conditions and the human-relations skills of managers did not result in higher productivity. Economic aspects of work still were important, as predicted by Taylor. While employees enjoy co-workers who are friendly, low salaries usually lead to absenteeism and turnover. The structure of the organization and the assignment of an employee to routine and boring tasks were not likely to contribute to a worker's motivation, regardless of the social environment. Thus, human behavior was more complex than originally thought by Mayo.

THE QUANTITATIVE SCHOOL OF MANAGEMENT

During World War II, the British developed a team of mathematicians, physicists and other professionals to solve wartime problems. This team of professionals formed the first operational research (OR) group and were able to analyze complex problems, such as convoy makeup and submarine locations. The team was able to achieve significant technological and tactical breakthroughs because of their ability to handle complex problems that could not be handled by intuition or experience.[16] The focus of the **quantitative school** is the development of mathematical models to simulate problems. The models showed, in symbolic terms, how all the revelant factors of a problem were interrelated.

With the aid of the computer, models have been constructed to simulate possible conditions facing today's manager. The development of the computer greatly increased the ability of managers to perform complex quantitative studies of business problems, since the large number of computations necessary in many types of these analyses cannot be handled easily without computers. Imagine trying to simulate an inflation rate of 15 percent per year on the U.S. economy without the aid of the computer. It would be impossible. By changing the value of a variable (such as the unemployment rate from 15 to 10 percent) and analyzing different equations of the model with the computer, the OR team can determine the effects of each change. Eventually, the OR team presents its findings to management so a rational decision can be made.

The range of quantitative decision-making tools useful to management is becoming broader. Present-day management makes use of inventory decision models, statistical decision theory, linear programming and many other tools. (See Chapters 10 and 11 for a further discussion of how quantitative techniques can be applied to management problems.) The methods have been applied to problems found within marketing, production, finance, and personnel management. In the largest companies, groups of managers, called *management scientists*, tackle a broad range of important business problems using highly sophisticated mathematical models.

The techniques of management science and operations research are a well-established part of the decision-making tools of most companies. In spite of widespread use of these techniques in many problem areas, however, management science has not yet reached the stage where it can deal effectively with the human side of the firm. The contributions from this school have been greatest in the planning and decision-making areas. At the present time, however, variables related to behavioral considerations and human values cannot be built into a mathematical model. Since these subjective variables must be considered by a manager before making a decision, managerial judgment remains important in arriving at a final decision.

Today's view of the quantitative school

The classical, behavioral, and quantitative schools offer different viewpoints of how to manage. Each school serves to highlight the important functions of a manager. In Chapter 1 we stated that the ***contingency approach*** attempts to integrate the various contributions from these three schools. The theme of the contingency approach is: *It all depends.* A principle may work well in one situation and terribly in others. How the manager diagnoses the differences in the situation is important. As managers in the contingency school, it is important that you realize how the solution fits in with the organization's structure, resources, goals, and people.

THE CONTINGENCY APPROACH

The managers of Rath Packing Company proposed a novel solution to solve its financial problems. The shareholders of Rath Packing Company voted to permit employees to convert their wages into shares of Rath common stock. They did so to allow the firm to be eligible for federal and local loans that will keep the firm in business. The pork processing company in Waterloo, Iowa has been facing fierce price competition from Swift, Armour, and Oscar Mayer. In 1979, Rath lost $1.5 million. Through this plan, the employees will eventually gain 60 percent control in the company. While the jobs of the workers have not changed, bosses no longer intimidate workers, and an easygoing atmosphere permits workers a voice in the decisions that affect them. Rath executives believe this plan will make workers more effective. By taking all factors into consideration before making a decision, the Rath executive team hopes it has made the best decision.[17]

Throughout this book, we want you to take into account not only the situation, but how you can influence the situation. By its very nature, being an effective manager requires that you take into account the realities of the situation when applying a theory or principle. Essentially, the contingency approach is a *situational* one.

SUMMARY   Three well-established schools of management thought — classical, behavioral, and quantitative — have contributed to managers' understanding of organizations and how to run them. Each school offered a different set of solutions to managerial problems. The classical school attempts to solve managers' problems through the application of logic and well-designed organizational structures. Weber's bureaucratic model dealt with how a manager can structure specialized jobs for subordinates to ensure predictable results. Rules and regulations helped managers make rational decisions. Taylor attempted to arrive at the one best way to do a job. Once the best method had been determined and taught to all workers, a standard time could be used for motivational purposes. This scientific approach to management leads to the development of the time-and-motion study. Fayol thought a manager's job consisted of distinct functions: planning, controlling, organizing, commanding, and coordinating. Fayol's emphasis was on what a manager should do. He developed a set of principles to prescribe how managerial functions should be performed.

When Burger King wanted to increase the number of hamburgers it produced during peak times, it diagnosed the problem as productivity. A behavioral scientist might diagnose the same problem as a people problem. To tackle the problem, the behavioral scientist will try to create a climate that leads to increased productivity. Such a climate might require managers to go to human-relations classes, the development of group incentives, or a job-enrichment program. A manager trained in the contingency school will ask: Which method will work best here? In the Burger-King example, the application of time-and-motion principles seemed most appropriate to solve that problem.

The behavioral school started with the human relations movement carried out in the Hawthorne plant of the Western Electric Company. Whereas the classical school focused primarily on the rational decision-making plan of a manager, the human-relations movement gave major consideration to the feelings of the worker and the work group. The finding of the Hawthorne experiment was that social and human factors were often much more important than physical factors in influencing productivity.

The quantitative school stressed the application of mathematical models to the solution of management decisions. With the development of the computer, many management decision-making analyses came under quantitative examination. Management science techniques described later in this book are used in such activities as planning for manpower development programs, aircraft scheduling, inventory control, and production scheduling.

The contingency approach offers the manager the ability to draw from all three schools, depending on the problem. The contingency approach requires the manager be aware of the complexity of the situation before choosing the best alternative. Since there is no one best theory of management, managers using the contingency approach will find many theories useful.

administrative management
authority
behavioral school
bureaucracy
charismatic authority
classical school
contingency approach
division of labor
functional foremanship
Hawthorne effect
Hawthorne experiments

human relations
impersonality
management functions
quantitative school
rational-legal authority
rationality
regulations
rules
scientific management
time-and-motion studies
unity of command

1. Why is it important for you to understand the history of management?

2. Describe Weber's contributions to management theory.

3. What are some of the negative results of using the bureaucratic approach to management?

4. What methods did Taylor indicate should be used to increase productivity? Give some examples.

5. Which of Fayol's principles do you believe are still used by today's managers? Why?

6. What are some similarities between the three approaches in the classical school?

7. What happened at the Hawthorne plant?

8. Compare and contrast the assumptions of Mayo to those of Taylor.

9. What is the quantitative approach to management? Give an example.

10. What is the major task of a manager according to the contingency approach?

11. McKinsey & Company, a management consulting firm, studied the management practices of the 10 best-managed companies in the United States. The outstanding performers had these characteristics:

A bias toward action.

Simple and lean organization form.

Stress on one key business value.

Simultaneous loose-tight management controls.

As a potential manager, can you trace these characteristics to a school of thought? If so, which one? If not, why? (The entire article can be found in *Business Week,* July 21, 1980, 196–201.)

Management Incidents and Cases

CRAWFORD
AUTOMOTIVE

An analysis of the accident records at Crawford Automotive revealed one job to be responsible for the majority of lost-time accident cases. It was a punch press operation involving a 30-second cycle as follows:

1. Left hand picks up 4-inch square, 1-inch thick piece of metal.
2. Left hand places metal on drill press.
3. Right hand presses button activating press.
4. Hydraulic press punches 1-inch hole through center of metal.
5. Right hand removes metal and places it in box to right of press.

Since employees were paid on a piece rate, William Gerlach, an industrial engineer, believed they were tempted to work fast, and in their haste often failed to remove the left hand before activating the machine with the right hand. The result was severed or badly mashed fingers. In order to eliminate such accidents, Gerlach installed a safety device requiring each punch press operator to attach a strap to his wrists in such a way that movement of the right hand to activate the press pulled the left hand free of the punch area.

Immediately after installation of this safety device, such accidents were eliminated completely. After several months, however, an increased frequency of the same type of accident was noted again. An investigation revealed that employees incurring such accidents had no safety device attached to their wrists at the time of their accident. Apparently, employees were avoiding the attachment when they thought they could do so without detection. While they were unlikely to admit it, it was suspected that attaching the safety device to their wrists caused them to be less productive, thereby affecting their piece-rate compensation.

Questions

1. Using the concepts of Taylor, explain what happened.
2. If you were Bill Gerlach, what would you do?

NORTHWOOD
ELECTRONICS

Some years ago, an electronics company in Dallas experienced a major reorganization. The president, Robert Price, had become acquainted with the writings of many authorities on contemporary management and organization. He became convinced that for this small company, there was a potential benefit both in human and business terms to change the form of organization.

Northwood Electronics was in the business of making electronic instrumentation products and test systems. The products were protected by patents. The company was owned by Price, who controlled all of the stock. Annual sales in 1980 amounted to about $7 million. The market was quite competitive. One day, Price announced a change to his employees. He discontinued the use of time cards, disbanded the assembly line, introduced a salary base for everyone, and indicated to the employees that they were free to organize their work as they saw fit. With one specialist on electronics acting as team leader, 16 production teams were established. Under its team leader, each group of six employees was able to decide how to organize its effort.

The company's organization incorporated the traditional functions of sales and finance, as well as supporting staff functions such as engineering and accounting. The accounting department was eliminated and the accountants were reassigned to areas such as personnel, shipping, and purchasing. The departments now kept their own books and reported to the treasurer. An attempt also was made to get rid of the drafting room. Teams were created for engineering and research, consisting of an engineer, a draftsman, a designer, and a technician. However, the need for a central drafting department became too strong and the pooling of drafting talent turned out to be a better use of this resource. For the salespeople, the requirement of filing expense reports with the office was eliminated, and each salesperson was given an allowance to cover selling expenses. This plan also was scrapped as selling expenses became higher than under the old system.

The executives reporting to Price were given new titles indicating functional responsibilities for such matters as "productivity," "profitability," "performance and development," "market standing," "physical and financial resources," and "public responsibility." These members of the executive council of Northwood Electronics were uneasy about their new titles. They desired more specific definition of their responsibilities. Confusion also was created because the next level of executives now had to report to each member of the executive council. Discussions carried out under a specialist in sensitivity training were unsuccessful. The executives reverted to their old titles after a year.

1. What principles of management were violated in this change process?

2. How would Weber's bureaucratic model explain the behavior of the members of the executive council?

3. What is Price's model of management?

Questions

Two pharmaceutical companies — Millman and Snow — are among the most successful companies in the industry. Both are very large and spend large amounts of money on research and development.

Millman — the oldest company and the leader in the industry since the end of World War II — spends a great deal of research money on one carefully selected product at a time. It picks this research when researchers at a university first indicate that a genuine breakthrough has occurred. Long before commercial production begins, it hires the best people in the field and puts them to work. Its aim is to gain early leadership in a major area, acquire the widest market share, and then maintain it for years to come. To accomplish this leadership, the president, Mr. Lynn Trent, ran the company by the book. All decisions had to be cleared through channels. There were numerous rules and regulations to follow and employees who did not follow these were usually not promoted or given good salary increases. To ensure that the company hired the most qualified people, each employee was asked to take a battery of tests. These tests not only measured an individual's character and personality, but his or her managerial beliefs and style. Those who did not pass the test were not hired.

The strategy of Snow was different. Its research lab, perhaps the most famous in the world, works in a wide variety of fields, such as tranquillizers, microbiology, antibiotics, and vitamins. It enters a new field when the idea is first thought of and then works with the idea until it has been proven in the lab to offer significant advances to medical practice. When it becomes reasonably clear that an effective drug will be marketed, it begins production and contacts doctors. Phyllis Jones, the president of the company, believes that people and teamwork are the essential ingredients that make Snow successful. Weekly management briefings are held to inform managers of important decisions and how these will influence their areas of responsibility. There is a bonus system that encourages all employees to make suggestions on how to run a company better. When an employee's suggestion is used, that person is taken to lunch by a vice-president, his or her picture is displayed in the company cafeteria and newspaper, and his or her spouse is sent flowers. Phyllis visits with all employees once a year, even though this means that she has to get up in the middle of the night to go to talk to the people working the night shift.

Questions

1. Analyze the Millman Company using the principles of classical management.

2. What human relations concepts is Phyllis Jones using in her management style?

3. From a contingency approach, why are both companies so successful?

1. E. Huse, *The Modern Manager.* St. Paul, MN: West Publishing Co., 1979, pp. 44–45.

2. A. Bedeian, *Organizations: Theory and Analysis.* Hinsdale, IL: Dryden Press, 1980, pp. 46–51. M. Weber, *The Theory of Social & Economic Organization*, trans. by A. Henderson and T. Parsons. New York: The Free Press, 1947.

3. P. Grinyer, and M. Yasai-Ardekani, "Dimensions of Organizational Structure: A Critical Replication." *Academy of Management Journal* **23,** 1980, 405–421. N. Toren, "Bureaucracy and Professionalism: A Reconsideration of Weber's Thesis." *Academy of Management Review* **1,** 1976, 36–46.

4. S. Wilson, *The Tandy Corporation: A Study of Organization Design.* Unpublished manuscript, Edwin L. Cox School of Business, Southern Methodist University, Dallas, TX, June 1980, and *Tandy Corporation Annual Report*, June 30, 1980.

5. M. Crozier, *The Bureaucratic Phenomenon.* Chicago, IL: University of Chicago Press, 1964; J. March and H. Simon, *Organizations.* New York: John Wiley and Sons, 1958, 12–32. *Dallas Morning News*, December 12, 1980, 18A.

6. J. Ford and J. Slocum, "Size, Technology, Environment and the Structure of Organizations." *Academy of Management Review* **2,** 1977, 561–575. J. Kimberly and M. Evanisko. "Organizational Technology, Structure and Size." In S. Kerr, (ed.) *Organizational Behavior.* Columbus, OH: Grid Publishing Company, 1979, pp. 263–288.

7. Y. Vardi, "Organizational Career Mobility: An Interpretive Model." *Academy of Management Review* **5,** 1980, 341–355; R. Merton, "Bureaucratic Structure and Personality." In *Social Theory and Social Structure* (rev. ed.), Robert Merton (ed.). New York: Free Press, 1957. P. Selznick, *TVA and the Grass Roots.* Berkeley, CA: University of California Press, 1949.

8. J. Webb, *Space-Age Management.* New York: McGraw-Hill, 1969.

9. C. Wrege and A. Perroni, "Taylor's Pig-Tale: A Historical Analysis of Frederick W. Taylor's Pig Iron Experiment." *Academy of Management Journal* **17,** 1974, 6–27. F. Taylor, *Scientific Management.* New York: Harper & Row, 1947.

10. E. Meadows, "How Three Companies Increased Their Productivity." *Fortune*, March 10, 1980, 93–101.

11. N. Mouzelis, *Organization and Bureaucracy: An Analysis of Modern Theories.* Chicago, IL: Aldine, 1968, pp. 79–96.

12. H. Koontz, "The Management Theory Jungle Revisited." *Academy of Management Review* **5,** 1980, 175–188.

13. E. Mayo, *The Social Problems of an Industrial Civilization.* Boston, MA: Harvard University, Graduate School of Business, 1945.

14. G. Homan, *The Human Group.* New York: Harcourt, Brace and World, 1950, pp. 48–81.

15. P. Schwab, "How a Nice Can Company Can Finish First." *Nation's Business*, March 1980, 60–68.

16. P. Carlson, *Quantitative Methods for Managers.* New York: Harper & Row, 1967.

17. *Business Week*, June 30, 1980, 52.

Part II focuses on the external environments of organizations — both here and abroad. The two chapters in this part emphasize the broad environmental trends that serve to shape and reshape organizations over time. Both domestically and abroad we highlight the impacts of value-system and political-system influences on the management of organizations.

Chapter 3, "Organizational Environments," describes the types of task environments that may face organizations — ranging from simple/stable to complex/changing. The environments of organizations are described as becoming increasingly complex and changing. The impacts of value systems and political systems in creating this complexity and change, especially within the United States, are developed. The chapter concludes with a discussion of the corporate social responsibility concept — including the pressures and controversy surrounding this concept.

Chapter 4, "International Environments," develops an awareness of how the whole world has increasingly become the "stage" for the operations of major multinational corporations. Global trends shaping the creation and methods of operation of multinational corporations are developed. The chapter highlights several international environmental influences on U.S. multinationals and provides some sensitivity of how management practices can differ in other countries from that in the United States. This is achieved by noting the differential impact of value- and political-system influences on management in Japan as compared to America. For example, an overriding value in Japanese society is "collectivism" versus "indi-

Part II

vidualism" in the United States. This and other value differences influence the practice of management in the two countries. For example, in Japan there is a greater emphasis on lifelong employment with a firm, group decision-making, and managerial concern for the personal problems of employees.

Chapter 3

ORGANIZATIONAL ENVIRONMENTS

After reading this chapter, you should be able to:

LEARNING
OBJECTIVES

1. Describe and assess the different types of environments facing organizations.

2. Describe your values and those of others.

3. Indicate how values influence the decisions and behavior of managers.

4. Identify the political strategies used by organizations in dealing with groups in their environments.

5. Describe the concept of corporate social responsibility.

6. List the sources of environmental turbulence for organizations.

PREVIEW CASE

American Telephone and Telegraph Co.

American Telephone and Telegraph Co. is now trying to change its service-oriented operation to give equal weight to marketing new services and products. Past attempts to do so ignored the corporate culture and failed. For example, in 1961, AT&T set up a school to teach managers how to coordinate the design and manufacture of data products for customized sales. But when managers completed the course, they found that the traditional way of operating — making noncustomized mass sales — was what counted in the company. They were given neither the time to analyze individual customers' needs nor rewards commensurate with such efforts. The result was that 85 percent of the graduates quit, and AT&T disbanded the school.

AT&T takes pride in its service, and with good reason. It provides the most efficient telephone system in the world. It reacts to disaster with a speed unknown anywhere.

Costs for AT&T's service have been readily passed to customers through rate increases granted by public service commissions. Keeping costs down, therefore, was never a major consideration. Since the Federal Communications Commission has decided to allow other companies to sell products in AT&T's once-captive markets, AT&T must now change the orientation of its 1 million employees. In numbers alone, such a change is unprecedented in corporate history. Still, to survive in its new environment, Bell must alter its plans, strategies, and employee expectations of what the company wants from them, as well as their belief in the security of their jobs and old way of doing business.

To make these changes Bell has analyzed its new requirements in minute detail filling thousands of pages. It acknowledges its lack of skills in certain crucial areas; marketing, cost control, and administrative ability to deal with change. The company had rewarded managers who followed policies by the book. Today, it is promoting innovators with advanced degrees in business administration. Once it measured service representatives by the speed with which they responded to calls; today they are measured by the number of problems they solve.

Instead of its traditional policy of promoting from within, people have been hired from outside the company. Archie J. McGill, a former executive of International Business Machines Corp., was made vice-president of business marketing. McGill is described by associates as an innovator who is the antithesis of the traditional "Bell-shaped man" because of his "combative adversarial style." Just as IBM's slogan, "Think," encouraged employees to be problem-solvers, McGill is hammering a new slogan, "I make the difference," into each of his marketers, encouraging them to become entrepreneurs. That idea is reinforced by incentives that pit salespeople against each other for bonuses — an incentive system unknown at Bell before McGill's arrival.

Even so, the changes have been slow. Learning to become solution-sellers has produced "a tremendous amount of confusion" among Bell marketing people, reports one large corporate customer. For example, AT&T is "absolutely trapped" if a customer requests an extra editing part for its standard teletype system, he says. "If you want something they don't have, they tend to solve the problem by saying, 'Let's go out for a drink'."

Even McGill concedes that "anytime you have an orientation toward servicing established products as opposed to marketing, change doesn't happen overnight." Bell's director of planning, W. Brooke Tunstall, estimates it will take another three to five years to attain an 85 percent change in the company's orientation. Still, he insists, there has already been "a definite change in the mindset at the upper levels." Arguments heard around the company now concern the pace of change rather than its scope. Says Tunstall, "I haven't run into anyone who doesn't understand why the changes are needed."[1]

The interplay between environmental influences and organizations is well illustrated in the AT&T case. Major internal changes have become necessary at AT&T, particularly in its marketing. This is a result of a combination of powerful environmental influences. These environmental influences include new electronic technologies for communicating, new firms that are exploiting these new technologies in direct competition with AT&T, and new "rules of the game" from the Federal Communications Commission. The changes by the Federal Communications Commission eliminated AT&T's monopoly over long distance communications and encouraged competition in several other service areas. For example, American Satellite Corporation provided Bank of America with 80 telephone circuits via an all-satellite system between San Francisco, Los Angeles, and New York. The bank estimates the 80 circuits cost about half the approximately $1700 a month AT&T would charge.[2]

The AT&T case also illustrates how employee values and attitudes can serve as a source of resistance to change. Of course, the values and attitudes of the society may represent environmental influences that create the need for internal organizational changes. For example, changes in the values and attitudes in society lead to new laws, programs, and government agencies concerning equal employment opportunity and affirmative action. In a landmark 1973 court judgment resulting from a lawsuit based on this legislation, AT&T was ordered to pay $15 million in back wages to women and minorities plus about $50 million each year to adjust wages and accelerate promotions for those groups.[3]

The AT&T case reveals the primary thrust to this chapter. We will outline some of the broad environmental trends facing managers within the United States, review how values and political systems impact on the management of organizations, and conclude with some commentary on the concepts and controversies associated with the social responsibilities of managers and businesses. The international influences and issues of increasing importance to managers are highlighted in Chapter 4. Chapter 5, which focuses on strategic planning, will zero in on the role of market and competitor influences.

ENVIRONMENTAL TRENDS

Drucker's Views

In 1939 Peter Drucker wrote his first book, *The End of Economic Man.* In 1980 he published *Managing in Turbulent Times.* A **turbulent environment** is complex, changing, and erratic. Between 1939 and 1980 Drucker produced 16 other books, as well as numerous speeches and articles to managers. A theme running through all of his efforts is the importance of trends in economics, politics, and society for practicing managers. Because of his profound impact on contemporary management, it is fitting to share a sample of Drucker's views of the turbulent environment facing many managers of today and of the future. The following excerpts are provided from *Managing In Turbulent Times.**

> *Some time during the 1970s, the longest period of continuity in economic history came to an end. At some time during the last ten years, we moved into turbulence.*
>
> *In three related facets of its environment — the economic, the social, and the political — management faces new realities, new challenges, and new uncertainties. Economically, the world has become integrated and interdependent as never before. There is now a true world economy which is moving toward a transnational money that is increasingly independent of — or at least "uncoupled" from — any national currency. There is no more "key currency." While the world economy is increasingly integrated, the world polity is, however, increasingly fragmented, and the process of political disintegration has clearly not run its course.*
>
> *The political system in every developed country has become pluralistic. Society in all developed countries has become a society of institutions. The political process in every developed country — probably even in totalitarian ones — is moving from integration to confrontation. This makes every institution, including business enterprise, into a political institution that has to attract and to satisfy a number of "constituencies" (i.e., groups accepted as entitled to a say, or at least a veto, even though they may have little or no stake in the institution's primary mission and purpose). Managers, therefore, have to add a political dimension to their task. They must become activists in politics who take the initiative, set goals, and create vision rather than being content to cooperate, respond, and react.*[4]

The themes expressed by Drucker have significance for all managers. Of course, the relative importance and form of these themes will vary in terms of small- versus large-scale organizations, supervisors versus executives, and firms operating in relatively simple and stable environments versus firms operating in dynamic and complex environments. Drucker's turbulent times do not strike all employees, managers, or organizations with equal force nor in the same form. For example, the turbulence being experienced by AT&T appears to have had much greater impact on top management and the mar-

---

keting divisions at all levels than on other areas of the firm, such as the residential installation and service departments.

Basic Types of Environments

The ***task environment*** includes all those factors and forces external to the organization that are important to managerial decision-making.[5] Some of these factors and forces are likely to include customers, suppliers, competitors, political groups (i.e., government regulatory agencies), and technical developments.

As mentioned in Chapter 1, the task environment is an important contingency variable that needs to be evaluated by managers in considering a wide variety of problems. Some of these problems include the processes used in decision-making and planning, how to structure the organization, the types of control techniques to use, the best leadership styles, etc. Throughout the book, we will be suggesting how different types of task environments can influence solutions to problems. Thus, our intent here is simply to present the basic framework used throughout the book for looking at task environments for firms as a whole or their various departments and divisions.

Figure 3.1 provides a classification of organizational task environments. The *simple–complex dimension* refers to whether the factors in the task environment are few in number and similar to each other or many in number and different from each other. A construction firm that builds standardized residential homes would have a simple environment relative to a firm that builds

3.1

Basic types of task environments

Adapted from Robert Duncan, "What Is The Right Organization Structure: Decision Tree Analysis Provides The Answer," *Organizational Dynamics*, Winter 1979 (New York: AMACOM: a division of the American Management Associations, 1979), p. 63.

	Stable	Changing
Simple	Factors in environment are: 1. Few in number 2. Quite similar to each other 3. Basically the same over time Example: Soft drink distributors	Factors in environment are: 1. Few in number 2. Somewhat similar to each other 3. Continually changing Example: Fast food outlets
Complex	Factors in environment are: 1. Many in number 2. Not similar to each other 3. Basically the same over time Example: Basic food products firms	Factors in environment are: 1. Many in number 2. Not similar to each other 3. Continually changing Example: Commercial airline firms

customized homes, office buildings, and shopping centers. The *stable–changing dimension* refers to whether the factors in the task environment remain the same or vary over time. For example, for decades, AT&T could count on the Federal Communications Commission (FCC) for well-defined and stable regulations that gave AT&T a virtual monopoly in interstate telephone services. When the FCC deregulated some of these service areas, AT&T was faced with major changes in regulations and competitors. This created the need for significant changes in their organizational structure and marketing practices.

By combining the simple-complex and stable-changing dimensions, Fig. 3.1 identifies four basic task environments — simple/stable, simple/changing, stable/complex, and changing/complex. Drucker's comments on managing in turbulent times fit the changing/complex task environment. Drucker and others suggest many managers are increasingly facing task environments that are becoming more changing and complex.[6] In contrast, a relatively simple/stable environment might be illustrated by soft drink distributors. A soft drink distributor may have many customers, but the services provided are quite standardized. It is simply a matter of how many bottles to deliver to each customer. Most soft drink distributors only deal with a couple of national firms, such as Pepsi Cola or Coca Cola, and distribute the types of products they provide to them. Moreover, most of the marketing efforts are undertaken by the franchiser. Thus, this type of environment is relatively simple and stable over time.

The stable/complex and simple/dynamic environments fall in between the two extremes. Fast-food outlets like McDonald's and Burger King seem to exist in a relatively simple/changing environment. They have limited menus with standardized and simple procedures for preparing and serving the food. The customers don't expect and cannot receive much personal treatment. However, the menus, restaurant decor, and marketing techniques are constantly being "tinkered with" to adjust to changes in consumer preferences and to keep up with competition. Basic food products firms seem to operate in a relatively stable/complex environment. For example, the basic line of Campbell soups; such as chicken noodle, tomato, and bean; have not changed for decades. However, the production and distribution processes for getting these soups to the grocery shelf are quite complex and involved.

For purposes of this chapter, the value and political systems within the United States represent two major areas that have been changing at a relatively rapid rate, while also becoming more complex. As will be seen, the value and political systems affect the management of organizations in a variety of ways. The importance of the systems to managers on a worldwide basis are addressed in the following chapter, International Influences. Within the United States, changes in the value system and political systems have led some groups to demand new social responsibilities of managers and organizations. In the last section of this chapter, we examine this controversial issue.

VALUE-SYSTEM INFLUENCES

Values and value systems are important for understanding similarities and differences in the actions by groups and individuals within one nation or between nations. A ***value*** is a basic concept that has considerable importance and meaning to the individual and is relatively stable over time.[7] Terms such as "competition," "individualism," "equality," and "cooperation" are basic value concepts. A ***value system*** is the sum of an individual's or group's values that normally fits into a pattern of relative importance and meaning. A value system usually consists of value concepts that are compatible and supportive of one another. Of the four value concepts mentioned previously, "competition" and "individualism" are more compatible with each other than are "equality" and "cooperation."

Importance of Values to Managers

Managers need to appreciate the significance of values and value systems. Let's consider the significance of personal values to managers. Personal value systems influence a manager's:

1. view of other individuals and groups of individuals, thus influencing interpersonal relationships;

2. perceptions of situations and problems;

3. decisions and solutions to problems;

4. determination of what is and is not ethical behavior; and

5. acceptance or resistance of organizational pressures and goals.[8]

Of course, value systems influence all individuals, not just managers, in similar ways. We now turn to the types of concepts that can go into a value system. Variations in the "importance" and "meaning" assigned to value concepts show differences in value systems.

Value Framework

Our value framework is drawn from the work of George England and his associates.[9] We highlight only major aspects of this value framework.

Identifying and assessing values

England and his associates identified 66 value concepts for assessing managers' personal value systems. These 66 value concepts were then grouped into five classes: goals of business organizations, personal goals of individuals, groups of people, ideas associated with people, and ideas about general topics. The 66 concepts and their grouping into each class are shown in Fig. 3.2.

To assess the managers' values, a questionnaire listing the 66 concepts was developed. Managers were asked to react to each value concept in terms

3.2

Value concepts within five
groupings

(From: G. England, O.
Dhingra, and N. Agarwal, "The
Manager and The Man: A
Cross-Cultural Study of
Personal Values."
*Organization and
Administrative Sciences* 5,
1974, p. 9. Used with
permission.)

**Goals of business
organizations**

____ Employee welfare
____ High productivity
____ Industry leadership
____ Organizational efficiency
____ Organizational growth
____ Organizational stability
____ Profit maximization
____ Social welfare

**Personal goals of
individuals**

____ Achievement
____ Autonomy
____ Creativity
____ Dignity
____ Individuality
____ Influence
____ Job satisfaction
____ Leisure
____ Money
____ Power
____ Prestige
____ Security
____ Success

Groups of people

____ Semiskilled workers
____ Highly skilled workers
____ Customers
____ All employees
____ Government
____ Unskilled workers
____ Labor unions
____ Managers
____ Me
____ My boss
____ My company
____ My coworkers
____ My subordinates
____ Owners
____ Stockholders
____ Technical staff
____ White-collar employees

**Ideas associated
with people**

____ Ability
____ Aggressiveness
____ Ambition
____ Compassion
____ Conformity
____ Cooperation
____ Honor
____ Loyalty
____ Obedience
____ Prejudice
____ Skill
____ Tolerance
____ Trust

**Ideas about
general topics**

____ Authority
____ Caution
____ Change
____ Competition
____ Compromise
____ Conflict
____ Conservatism
____ Emotions
____ Equality
____ Force
____ Liberalism
____ Property
____ Rational
____ Religion
____ Risk

of its *importance* and *meaning.* The *importance* of a concept was determined by having the manager rate it as high, average, or low. For *meaning,* the manager rated each concept as being successful, right, or pleasant. Managers might view the same concepts as important, but for different reasons.

You will find it useful to make a general diagnosis of your own values. You could then compare yourself with some of the findings to be presented or use the diagnosis as a basis for discussion with your classmates. On a separate sheet of paper, rate each of the 66 concepts' *importance* (high, average, or low) and *meaning* (successful, right, or pleasant) to you. Underscore the concepts you indicated as having high importance. Then, for those concepts indicated as highly important within each class, look for a pattern to the meaning you assigned to them. The three patterns of meaning are explained in the next section.

*Three value
orientations*

Normally, one of three value orientations emerges from a person's responses on the questionnaire. A ***pragmatic value orientation*** exists if the individual tends to respond to highly important concepts as "successful." This type of individual is guided primarily by a concern for whether a certain course of action will work and how successful it is likely to be. There tends to be an emphasis on practicality versus idealism. American managers tend to have a pragmatic value orientation.

An ***ethical-moral value orientation*** exists if the individual tends to respond to highly important concepts as "right." This type of individual is guided primarily by a concern for whether a certain course of action is right or wrong, moral or immoral. The debates in the United States over the practice of giving bribes to obtain foreign business are partly based on conflicts between pragmatic vs. ethical-moral value systems. Some American executives have stated off the record: "Although we don't like to give bribes, it is necessary to get the orders, and this is an established way of doing business in certain countries." Other executives have stated: "It's wrong, that's why we don't and won't do it, so there's no other issue to consider."

A ***self-satisfaction value orientation*** exists if the individual tends to respond to highly important concepts as "pleasant." This type of individual is guided primarily by a concern for whether a certain course of action will maximize his or her own self-interest. There tends to be an emphasis on increasing personal pleasure and decreasing pain.

While managers can give different *meanings* to the 66 value concepts, they also differ in the relative *importance* assigned to these value concepts. Let's consider some patterns for successful vs. nonsuccessful managers and business managers vs. labor leaders.

*Values of highly
successful vs. less
successful
managers*

Twenty-one of the 66 value concepts were related to the relative success of managers. Success is defined in terms of factors such as salary level, organizational level, and rate of promotions. We recognize that this represents a value judgment regarding what is or is not success. Given this definition of success, the most successful managers tend to emphasize the values shown on the left in Fig. 3.3. They deemphasize those value concepts shown on the right. The pattern is reversed for less successful managers in business firms.

How did you rank the importance of each of the value concepts shown in Fig. 3.3? Do you think the value profile of successful managers is changing and will continue to change? You need to recognize that these profiles are based upon studies of managers in the early 1970s. Because of changing society values and the need for "team play" in complex organizations, we suspect that the more successful managers of the future will have somewhat higher ratings of trust, tolerance, and compromise. They may also have more moderate ratings of aggressiveness, competition, and conflict.

Values Highly Rated by Successful Managers	Values Highly Rated by Less Successful Managers
1. Profit Maximization	1. Social Welfare
2. Customers	2. Laborers
3. Aggressiveness	3. Obedience
4. Individuality	4. Conformity
5. Ability	5. Trust
6. Achievement	6. Loyalty
7. Creativity	7. Tolerance
8. Competition	8. Security
9. Conflict	9. Equality
	10. Compromise
	11. Emotions
	12. Religion

3.3
Value concepts related to success for American managers
(From: G. England, O. Dhingra, and N. Agarwal, *Ibid*, p. 54.)

Values of managers vs. labor leaders

Individuals' values are influenced, over time, by the requirements and expectations of their positions and organizations. Individuals are also likely to apply for and remain in positions consistent with their values. Striking differences have been found in the values of American managers and union leaders.[10] One major difference is that union leaders emphasize an ethical-moral orientation and managers a pragmatic value orientation.

The two groups were asked to indicate the relative importance of organizational goals; including employee welfare, organizational efficiency, high productivity, organizational stability, industry leadership, organizational growth, social welfare, and profit maximization. The union leaders considered employee welfare the most important and profit maximization the least important organizational goal. The managers ranked these goals the other way around. Ambition, ability, and skill were important values for business managers, whereas trust, loyalty, and honor were much less important. Just the reverse was found for union leaders.

These contrasting value patterns help explain why managers and union leaders approach various issues from different and even conflicting directions. You might want to take another moment to see how you compare with the union leaders and managers on the values just outlined.

Philosophies About Employees

Managers' values determine their philosophy about the basic nature of people in organizations, especially subordinates. Differences in philosophies are determined by the assumptions and beliefs managers make about subordinates. These assumptions and beliefs define a managerial philosophy and the probable strategy for dealing with subordinates.

Before reading further, take a couple of minutes to complete the managerial assumptions and beliefs questionnaire shown in Table 3.1.

Instructions. There are 15 *pairs* of statements shown below. You have 5 points to allocate between each pair of statements. The points assigned to each pair of statements must always total 5 points. For example, you might strongly agree with 1a while strongly disagreeing with 1b. Thus, you would assign 1a 5 points while assigning 1b 0 point weighting. On the other hand, you might agree slightly more with 1a than 1b. In this case, you would assign 3 points to 1a and 2 points to 1b. You may *not* split ratings equally between pairs of statements, i.e., 2½ points for 1a and 2½ for 1b. This questionnaire is *not* a test. There are *no* right or wrong responses. For purposes of this survey, employees do *not* include managers and professionals in organizations. You might want to record your point values on a separate sheet of paper.

1. a_____ Employees are naturally lazy; they prefer to do nothing.
   b_____ Employees are naturally active; they set goals and enjoy striving.

2. a_____ Employees work mostly for money and status rewards.
   b_____ Employees seek many satisfactions in work: pride in achievements, enjoyment of process, sense of contribution, pleasure in association, stimulation of new challenges, etc.

3. a_____ The main force keeping employees productive in their work is fear of being demoted or fired.
   b_____ The main force keeping employees productive in their work is desire to achieve their personal and social goals.

4. a_____ Employees are somewhat like children; they are naturally dependent on leaders.
   b_____ Employees normally mature beyond childhood; they aspire to independence, self-fulfillment, responsibility.

5. a_____ Employees expect and depend on direction from above; they do not want to think for themselves.
   b_____ Employees close to the situation see and feel what is needed and are capable of self-direction.

6. a_____ Employees need to be told, shown, and trained in proper methods of work.
   b_____ Employees who understand and care about what they are doing can devise and improve their own methods of doing work.

7. a_____ Employees need supervisors who will watch them closely enough to be able to praise good work and reprimand errors.
   b_____ Employees need a sense that they are respected as capable of assuming responsibility and self-correction.

The scoring of this questionnaire should be done as follows:

1. Theory X orientation. Add the point values for all "a" response ratings for items 1 through 15. The maximum score for "a" ratings is 75 points and the minimum is 0 points. Total points for Theory X orientation is _____.

2. Theory Y orientation. Add the point values for all "b" response ratings for items 1 through 15. The maximum score for "b" ratings is 75 points and the minimum is 0 points. Total points for Theory Y orientation equals _____.

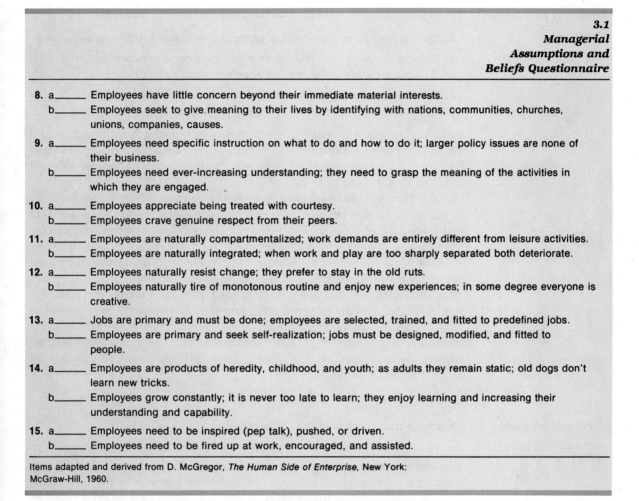

3.1
*Managerial
Assumptions and
Beliefs Questionnaire*

8. a_____ Employees have little concern beyond their immediate material interests.
   b_____ Employees seek to give meaning to their lives by identifying with nations, communities, churches, unions, companies, causes.

9. a_____ Employees need specific instruction on what to do and how to do it; larger policy issues are none of their business.
   b_____ Employees need ever-increasing understanding; they need to grasp the meaning of the activities in which they are engaged.

10. a_____ Employees appreciate being treated with courtesy.
    b_____ Employees crave genuine respect from their peers.

11. a_____ Employees are naturally compartmentalized; work demands are entirely different from leisure activities.
    b_____ Employees are naturally integrated; when work and play are too sharply separated both deteriorate.

12. a_____ Employees naturally resist change; they prefer to stay in the old ruts.
    b_____ Employees naturally tire of monotonous routine and enjoy new experiences; in some degree everyone is creative.

13. a_____ Jobs are primary and must be done; employees are selected, trained, and fitted to predefined jobs.
    b_____ Employees are primary and seek self-realization; jobs must be designed, modified, and fitted to people.

14. a_____ Employees are products of heredity, childhood, and youth; as adults they remain static; old dogs don't learn new tricks.
    b_____ Employees grow constantly; it is never too late to learn; they enjoy learning and increasing their understanding and capability.

15. a_____ Employees need to be inspired (pep talk), pushed, or driven.
    b_____ Employees need to be fired up at work, encouraged, and assisted.

Items adapted and derived from D. McGregor, *The Human Side of Enterprise*, New York: McGraw-Hill, 1960.

The *combination* of your Theory X and Theory Y scores must equal 75 points. A Theory X philosophy may be indicated by a score of 46 to 75 points on the "a" responses to the questionnaire. In contrast, you may have a Theory Y philosophy if you scored between 46 and 75 points on the "b" responses. Finally, you may have a mixed philosophy if you scored between 30 to 45 points on the Theory X scale and 30 to 45 points on the Theory Y scale.

Douglas McGregor first presented these two contrasting management philosophies — Theory X versus Theory Y — in his 1960 book, the *Human Side of Enterprise*.[11] His writings best fit into the behavioral school of management. This school focuses on helping managers deal more effectively with the people-side of organizations.

Theory X philosophy

Theory X managers hold the following assumptions and beliefs.

1. The average employee dislikes work and will avoid it if possible.

2. Because employees dislike their work, they must be coerced, controlled, and directed to achieve the organization's goals.

3. The average employee wishes to avoid responsibility, has relatively little ambition, and desires security above everything else.

By observing the way many organizations were managed in the 1950s and 1960s, McGregor concluded that numerous managers believe employees must be directed and controlled — primarily through such devices as external rewards, threats, and close supervision.

The Theory X philosophy assumes that employees are motivated basically by money and fringe benefits. Theory X managers tend to: (1) strictly interpret and apply policies, rules, and regulations; (2) design highly specialized jobs for subordinates; and (3) emphasize economic incentives to motivate employees.

Individual and career development under Theory X assumes that employees are like young children and should be treated accordingly. Children are often dependent on and submissive to their parents. Parents represent authority figures with the power to give and withhold rewards. The responses to authority figures learned at home become further developed and reinforced in schools, churches, scouting, Little League Baseball, and many other organizations. Theory X assumes that most employees do not advance much beyond this "child" stage of development.

Theory Y philosophy

Theory Y managers hold the following assumptions and beliefs.

1. The expenditure of physical and mental effort is as natural as play or rest. The average human being does not inherently dislike work. Depending on conditions, work may be a source of satisfaction and will be performed voluntarily or it may be a source of punishment and will be avoided if possible.

2. External control and the threat of punishment are not the primary means for directing effort toward performance. Employees will exercise self-direction and self-control in the service of objectives to which they are committed.

3. Commitment to objectives depends on the rewards associated with their achievement. The most significant of such rewards — e.g., the satisfaction of esteem and personal growth needs — can be direct products of efforts directed toward organizational objectives.

4. Under proper conditions, the average human being accepts and seeks responsibility. Avoidance of responsibility, lack of ambition, and emphasis on security generally are a result of experience, not inborn human characteristics.

5. The ability to show imagination, ingenuity, and creativity in the solution of organizational problems is widely, not narrowly, distributed in the population.

6. Under the conditions of modern industrial life, the abilities of most employees are used only partially.[12]

The Theory Y philosophy suggests that it is management's responsibility to establish a work environment promoting employee development and cooperation. If the employees are lazy and produce shoddy products, it is management's responsibility to change the work and control systems to achieve better performance. Theory Y assumes workers are motivated to achieve organizational goals and are self-directed adults. Employee commitment to performance goals is strongly influenced by management practices.

Under Theory X, employees' needs are ignored or suppressed by management. Thus, employees are more likely to:

1. Fight the organization and try to gain more control by joining a union, sabotaging the work, being absent, and so on.

2. Leave the organization.

3. Become apathetic toward their work and the organization.

4. Downgrade the importance of their work and substitute higher pay as a reward for having to perform meaningless work.[13]

As suggested by the procedures for scoring responses to the questionnaire in Table 3.1, some managers may be neither extremely Theory X nor Theory Y. Situational factors, such as the day-to-day experiences with employees and the organization, may tilt the managers' natural leanings toward a more or less Theory X or Y orientation over time. Individuals can and do change as a result of experiences in organizations.

Situational assessment of Theories X and Y

Theory Y managers assume that employees want the freedom and the opportunity to fully use their talents. This may overemphasize the desire of some employees for freedom and underestimate their desire for security. It also is possible that not all people want to achieve highly on the job; be helped, counseled, and nurtured; and derive satisfaction from their job. One author suggests:

> *Work, for probably a majority of workers, and even extending into the ranks of management, may represent an institutional setting that is not the central life interest of the participants. . . . Thus, the industrial worker does not feel imposed upon by the "tyranny" of organizations, companies or unions.*[14]

Company and Manager differences   There are substantial differences between companies and managers in terms of the relative dominance of the Theory X versus Theory Y philosophies in American industry. Employee surveys suggest that there have been significant shifts over the past 30 years in the attitudes and values of the U.S. work force. Employees increasingly desire to work in firms where management leans toward a Theory Y philosophy. There is growing discontent among hourly and clerical employees working in firms dominated by Theory X managers. Clerical and hourly employees are beginning to express their needs for achievement, recognition, and job challenge.[15]

Survey of Young Adults   A survey of 17,000 high school seniors suggests that while work is important to them, for many it does not represent their central interest in life. Nearly four out of five of these young adults ranked "having a good marriage and family life" as extremely important and ahead of all other goals. "Having strong friendships" was rated extremely important by about two-thirds of the respondents, making it their second most important goal. Three-fourths of both the college-bound and noncollege groups agreed or mostly agreed with the statement, "I expect work to be a very central part of my life." Only about 15 percent of college freshmen agreed with the statement, "To me, work is nothing more than making a living" (compared with almost twice as many of their noncollege peers). While the work ethic is far from dead among young adults, it does have limits. For example, half the college freshmen and two-thirds of the noncollege group said they would like a job they could forget after the workday is over.[16] These attitudes and values, along with those presented in Table 3.2, indicate young adults generally desire to work in organizations with a tilt toward the Theory Y managerial philosophy.

In 1979 a survey asked 17,000 young adults graduating from high school 10 questions about what they plan to look for in work. Table 3.2 reports the percentages of college-bound and noncollege-bound individuals who rated each characteristic as being "very important." The other possible ratings were "pretty important," "somewhat important," and "not important." In reviewing Table 3.2, you might want to rate each of these characteristics for yourself. Interesting work and the opportunity to use skills and abilities were ranked as "very important" by more than 70 percent of all the young adults. These two characteristics are central to the assumptions and beliefs about employees under the Theory Y philosophy.

Workers increasingly desire to be employed in an organization with a Theory Y philosophy. A slight majority of managers probably tilt toward a Theory X philosophy, but not nearly to the same degree as 20 or more years ago.[17] The values and attitudes of employees toward work seem to have

| | % Who Rated Characteristic as | | 3.2 What 17,000 Young Adults Rated as "Very |
Job Characteristics	"Very Important"		Important" in a Job
	College-Bound	Non-College Bound	
1. Interesting to do	93%	87%	
2. Uses skills and abilities	74%	70%	
3. Good chances for advancement	64%	66%	
4. Predictable, secure future	63%	66%	
5. See results of what you do	61%	58%	
6. Chance to make friends	57%	56%	
7. Worthwhile to society	48%	40%	
8. Chance to earn a good deal of money	47%	60%	
9. A job most people look up to, respect	37%	35%	
10. High status, prestige	26%	24%	

From J. G. Bachman and L. D. Johnston, "The Freshmen, 1979." Reprinted from *Psychology Today* Magazine **13**, 4, p. 82. Copyright © 1979 Ziff-Davis Publishing Company.

changed more rapidly than the reduction in the Theory X philosophy and the movement toward a Theory Y philosophy.[18] While the nature and conditions of work have improved dramatically over the past 25 years, the values of employees and their expectations of their jobs may have shifted even more dramatically.

We think there is a clear overall movement in the United States away from an extreme Theory X philosophy. The majority of managers probably have not yet accepted the Theory Y philosophy totally. Young adults and professionals generally desire jobs and work environments consistent with a Theory Y philosophy. These shifts have resulted in organizations with value differences among managers as well as value differences among employees. Such differences indicate clearly how value-system influences have become increasingly complex and changing. On a *comparative* basis, value-system influences probably fit the stable/complex cell in Fig 3.1 up to about 25 years ago. Today, value-system influences probably fit the changing/complex cell, especially for large organizations such as General Motors, Exxon, and AT&T.

The current turbulence in America's values has influenced organizations directly through the changing values managers and employees carry into the workplace. The changes, complexity, and diversity of values have also been expressed through the political system.

**POLITICAL-SYSTEM
INFLUENCES**

Conflicts in values often are expressed through political processes. Business, education, and religious organizations, among others, typically try to influence the political system to improve the likelihood of their own survival and the attainment of the values they cherish. This means that business and other organizations use direct or indirect political processes to influence the behavior and even the survival of other organizations. Consumer groups, for example, have tried to influence business organizations primarily through government agencies.

**What Is the Political
System?**

The *political system* includes the components in a business firm's environment that can influence its decisions, survival, or growth. An organization's political environment extends beyond governmental institutions. It includes the whole complex of groups, institutions, and individuals possessing power to influence an organization. For the business firm, the important components in the political environment include trade associations, major customers, and government agencies, among others.

Figure 3.4 identifies the diverse components of the external business environment — especially of large corporations with which political processes often occur. These components can both influence and be influenced by or-

3.4
Major components of a
business firm's task
environment

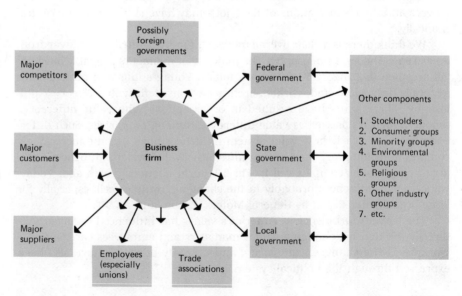

ganizations. The need for managers to deal with each component will vary over time as issues come and go. Customers, suppliers, and employees commonly are regarded as key components in the economic system. They are included in the political environment because of the interaction that often occurs among economic, social, and political forces.

Figure 3.4 also suggests that the influences business firms have on other groups are as diverse as the contemporary values in America. One author claims, "Although the political power of business firms and their managers is very real and pervasive, it does not presently constitute a danger to the American pluralistic democracy."[19] This is because legislation, court rulings and decisions, and programs that are contrary to the desires of significant corporate interests continue to be made. Nonetheless, some are concerned that large organizations may exert excessive political power on society in general.[20]

Political strategies are the general approaches used by firms in dealing with important and powerful components in the environment. There is no single political strategy for responding to or influencing the task environment. In discussing some of the major political strategies managers have used, we will focus on "what is" rather than on "what ought to be." Since what-ought-to-be questions often create pressures for change, you may want to think about them as each strategy is examined. Here are three examples of what-ought-to-be questions:

Political Strategies

1. How much influence should an organization exert or be permitted to exert on its environment?

2. What forms of influence are appropriate?

3. Under what conditions is it acceptable for the manager to choose particular strategies and tactics?

For example, there may be widespread agreement that business firms should have the right to lobby government agencies. There is considerable disagreement over the tactics they should be permitted to use.

Figure 3.5 identifies six of the major political strategies organizations and managers use to influence and respond to environmental components. As suggested in Fig. 3.5, these strategies are not mutually exclusive. They usually are used in some combination. Our examples of each strategy often contain elements of the others. The bargaining strategy probably is the most important political strategy. The other five strategies almost always contain some degree of bargaining. Accordingly, bargaining is shown in the center of Fig. 3.5 and overlaps with the other five political strategies — including cooptation, lobbying, coalitions, representation, and socialization.

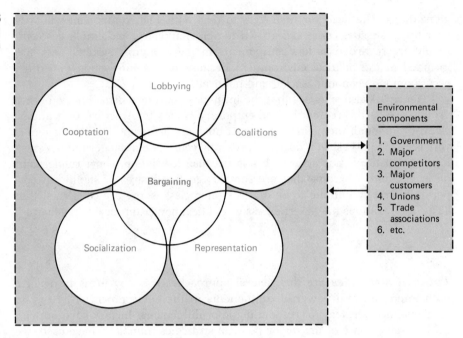

3.5
Organizational political
strategies

Bargaining Strategy

Bargaining is used extensively within an organization to resolve differences or reach accommodation among its members. Here, we focus on bargaining with external groups. **Bargaining** is the negotiation of an agreement between two or more organizations or individuals about the exchange of goods, services, or expected behaviors. Bargaining means that each organization, individual, or group decides what it must do to satisfy the other party or parties.[21] Bargaining normally occurs as a result of disagreements, but it can happen *only* when the parties believe that some form of agreement is both possible and beneficial to them.

Types of bargaining relationships

The types of bargaining relationships between a business firm and groups in its task environment can be classified in many ways. Table 3.3 identifies four basic types of bargaining relationships. The "power" bargaining relationship is normally characterized by the most intense conflict and bitter feelings between the parties. In contrast, the "cooperation" relationship is characterized by bargaining and negotiation in which there is mutual concern between the parties and a strong effort by them to reach an agreement pleasing to everyone.

Types of Relationships	Characteristics
■ Power	At least one of the parties attempts to obtain the very maximum benefits or advantages from the other party. At least one party is very unwilling to compromise.
■ Deal (collusion)	Two or more parties negotiate secretly and arrive at agreements which are unknown to others. This is usually done to maintain some mutual advantage over other parties.
■ Accommodation	Extreme expressions of power are usually avoided. The parties are tolerant of one another's demands and usually accept the spirit of compromise.
■ Cooperation	The parties show strong mutual concern over the others' well-being and are concerned about how their action affects the welfare of the other parties. Extreme expressions of power are avoided.

Adapted from: B. M. Selekman, S. K. Selekman, and S. H. Fuller, *Problems in Labor Relations*, 2nd ed. New York: McGraw-Hill, 1958.

*Union/management
bargaining*

The most widely recognized bargaining relationship is that between management and labor. One study found that 75 percent of the bargaining relationships examined involved a moderate form of joint participation.[22] This was often characterized by:

1. The practice of union and management to work together on a continuing basis.

2. Union influence limited to jobs, work conditions, wages, and fringe benefits.

3. Bargaining and grievance settling with little inclination to strike.

4. A moderate degree of joint problem-solving.[23]

Bargaining between management and labor in the United States is generally one of accommodation (see Table 3.3). This accommodation tendency can shift rather dramatically in specific situations. Given the diversity in the value patterns of managers and labor leaders, this isn't very surprising. To give an example, an accommodating relationship can change dramatically if management makes a surprise announcement that it is going to relocate a plant during the coming year.

Government/ business bargaining

One hundred and sixteen federal governmental agencies now regulate business. Twenty new federal regulatory agencies sprang up during the 1970s. To name a few, they include the Environmental Protection Agency, the Consumer Product Safety Commission, the Occupational Safety and Health Administration, the Council on Wage and Price Stability, and the Department of Energy. Federal regulatory expenditures grew nearly sixfold during the decade to an estimated $4.8 billion in 1980. The number of people to staff these agencies nearly tripled.[24] These changes led to increased use of bargaining between federal government agencies and business firms. One executive described the process used by his firm in bargaining with regulatory agencies as follows:

> *In dealing with the agencies, you must yield on minor matters in order to get fair treatment on the ones that are most important to the company. Yielding is calculated to build goodwill and avoid antagonizing agency staffers. This principle causes executives to go along with what they believe are a number of bad ideas. As a businessman who spends much of my time negotiating with the Environmental Protection Agency: "You bite your lip a lot, and it gets pretty swollen."*[25]

Cooptation Strategy

Cooptation occurs when the organization formally brings individuals from environmental components into its managerial decision-making groups. These environmental components are believed to have the power to influence the organization's stability, survival, or growth.[26]

Paradoxically, the process of cooptation influences the organization's autonomy. On the one hand, the coopted individuals or groups can influence and shape the organization's future course of action. From this perspective, the organization's freedom and flexibility may be reduced, at least in the short run. On the other hand, cooptation is one way for an organization to adapt to its environment. Individuals or groups which were previously outside of the organization are now in a position to influence its stability, growth, and chances of survival. For example, bankers are often given positions on the board of directors of corporations after loaning them significant amounts of money. The bankers may gain a voice and possibly a veto in decisions concerning additional borrowing or other long-term obligations.

CASE STUDY

U.A.W's Fraser on Chrysler's Board

Douglas Fraser, president of the United Auto Workers Union, was elected to the board of directors of the Chrysler Corporation in 1980. Never before has a representative of a major union joined the board of a major U.S. company. In the fall of 1979, the United Auto Worker's Union had agreed to defer over $200 million in wages and benefits in exchange for Fraser's appointment to the board of directors. Fraser's appointment drew little support from either corporate executives or other labor union leaders. General Motors' former Chairman, Thomas A. Murphy, said: "It makes as much sense as having a member of GM's management sitting on the board of an international union." Most union leaders supported AFL-CIO President Lane Kirkland, who said that workers are best represented "through the collective bargaining process and the adversary system that it represents."

In a statement to Chrysler's stockholders, Fraser said that he plans an active part in discussions on nearly all topics, including worker health and safety, plant closings, new products, and major investments. He says he will not participate in any company discussions on pay negotiations. Says Fraser: "I believe my activities will advance the interests of the broad Chrysler community—shareholders, workers, suppliers, dealers, consumers, and the public." In Delaware, however, where Chrysler is registered as a corporation, the law requires directors to have undivided loyalty to the corporation and its stockholders. It remains to be seen if this example of cooptation sets a precedent for union-management relations in American industry."[27]

Lobbying Strategy

Lobbying is attempting to influence decisions of an administrative or legislative branch of government through persuasion and the provision of information. Congress and regulatory agencies (such as the Civil Aeronautics Board, the Federal Communications Commission, and the Interstate Commerce Commission) are the targets of continual lobbying efforts by organizations affected by their decisions. Business organizations whose survival, stability, and growth are influenced by the decisions of these groups typically use high-ranking officials in their organizations as lobbyists.

For example, every major airline and the three leading broadcast networks (ABC, CBS, and NBC) are represented by corporate vice-presidents in Washington D.C.

Role of associations
The most common form of lobbying is carried out by associations representing the interests of a group of individuals and organizations.[28] Only the very largest corporations, such as AT&T and General Motors, can afford to lobby on behalf of their own interests. There are approximately 4000 national lobbying organizations with some representation in Washington, D.C. An additional 75,000 state and local associations and organizations occasionally call on Washington decision-makers. Two of the largest associations representing business interests are the National Chamber of Commerce, with about 36,000 business and organizational members, and the National Association of Manufacturers, with about 16,000 member corporations.[29]

CASE STUDY

AT&T's Lobbying Failure

At the beginning of this chapter, we discussed the several sources of environmental turbulence for AT&T. One of these sources was the deregulation of portions of AT&T's markets. When deregulation was proposed and introduced initially, the management of AT&T did *not* welcome this change with open arms. In fact, in 1976 and 1977, AT&T led the major telephone companies in an all-out lobbying effort in Washington, D.C. The objective was to reverse decisions by the courts and the Federal Communications Commission opening up some parts of AT&T's multibillion dollar industry to competition. The telephone companies lobbied Congress to pass a law that would forbid competition in long-distance services. The telephone companies sought legal authority to acquire the companies that would be put out of business. Lastly, the companies sought to eliminate the Federal Communications Commission's jurisdiction over technical and operating standards affecting terminal and accessory equipment attached to telephone company facilities. These proposals were not passed by Congress.

The positions taken by the major telephone companies (AT&T and GTE) and the intense opposition to them by the Federal Communications Commission and many other private companies created a heated political struggle. It appears AT&T has accepted deregulation. As outlined in this chapter's preview case, the company is implementing many organizational and managerial changes to compete in a deregulated environment. At the state and federal levels, there generally has been a widespread movement to decrease the use of rules and regulations by the regulatory agencies serving to protect firms from competition.[30]

In sum, lobbying is a political strategy managers often use in dealing with government agencies. Lobbying becomes quite complex when organizations form coalitions — another political strategy for influencing a firm's environment.

A ***coalition*** is the combination of two or more organizations to obtain common goals and increase their influence over their environment.[31] Economic self-interest is typically the main reason coalitions are formed, especially when they are created to influence government actions. Three broad categories of economic issues motivate the formation of coalitions. They are government policy (control of raw materials and taxes), foreign relations (control of foreign sales and investment in overseas plants), and labor relations (strike and arbitration procedures).

Coalition Strategy

There are a variety of uses for the coalition strategy. For example, coalition enables its members to:

Use of coalitions

1. oppose or support legislation or proposed heads of regulatory agencies;

2. promote particular products or services (such as oranges and railroads);

3. construct facilities beyond the resources of any one firm (such as generating plants for electric utilities);

4. represent the interests of particular groups (such as women, the elderly, minorities, particular industries); and/or

5. secure higher prices for goods or services (such as the Organization of Petroleum Exporting Countries — OPEC).

A coalition, like cooptation, both broadens and limits the power of management. It is broadening when it makes possible the attainment of objectives that would otherwise be unattainable. It is limiting when it requires a commitment to making certain joint decisions in the future. For example, the OPEC coalition engages in bargaining to try and reach some degree of agreement over the range of prices for their different grades of oil and the amount of oil each country will supply to the market.

Case Example: Business Roundtable   The Business Roundtable is a coalition of 196 big companies (as of 1980). The member companies can be represented at Roundtable activities only by their chief executives. The Roundtable was formed in the 1970s as the voice of big business in Washington, D.C.[32] The Roundtable develops positions on issues concerning big business and then lobbys the administrative and legislative branches of the federal government. The Roundtable uses the chief executive officers of major business corporations as lobbyists. These include chief executive officers of Exxon, AT&T, General Motors, General Electric, and DuPont.

During the 1970s, the Roundtable played an important role in eliminating or modifying proposals by environmental and consumer coalitions. For example, the Roundtable joined the United States Chamber of Commerce and National Association of Manufacturers in helping defeat a bill for a federal consumer protection agency. In 1979 and 1980, the Roundtable helped defeat bills that would have: (1) permitted a single striking union to picket an entire construction site; (2) made it easier for unions to organize nonunion corporations: and (3) created central planning for the national economy.

Representation Strategy

Representation involves encouraging or requiring members of one organization to form or join other groups or organizations. The primary purpose of this political process is to serve the interests of the representatives' organization or group. This is a subtle and indirect strategy. School administrators, for example, often are given paid time off and the use of school resources to participate in voluntary community associations which might support the school system. Some of these organizations include the Chamber of Commerce, Elks, Kiwanis, Moose, Rotary, and United Appeal.

Another form of representation is to have individuals serve on behalf of some group. This form of representation, such as boards of directors, usually is based on some legal requirement.

Corporate boards of directors

Corporate boards of directors are legally required to represent the interests of stockholders. This is supposed to be done by having the boards review (or initiate) and approve all major policies and decisions. Recent disclosures about corporate price fixing, bribing, and polluting have made it appear that the boards of a few major organizations could be characterized as "nobody knowing from nothing." Several suggestions for alleviating this problem include the following:

1. Clearly separate the board from operating management.

2. Have a fulltime board chairperson.

3. Have the chief operating executive report to the whole board, not just to the board chairperson.

4. Pay active board members for their efforts.

5. Have boards take initiative and not just react to proposals or other matters brought to their attention by management.[33]

It remains debatable whether such proposals will result in better representation of stockholders. However, the domination of boards of directors by members of management appears to be on the way out. "Insider" dominated boards have been criticized by shareholders and regulators for representing the interests of management more than the interests of the stockholders. Because of external pressures for accountability and independence, outside directors were in the majority on 88 percent of the boards of major U.S. corporations in 1980 — up from 64 percent in 1971. The proportion of companies with at least one woman director rose to 40 percent in 1980 — up from about 20 percent in 1976. About 19 percent of the firms surveyed had at least one minority group director in 1980 compared with 15 percent in 1976.[34]

The changes in the membership of boards of directors is a direct result of pressures and demands from the firm's environmental components. Of course some, such as consumer advocate Ralph Nader, would contend that these changes are still too cosmetic and have not gone far enough.

CASE STUDY

Cleveland Electric Illuminating Company

One form of representation involves encouraging members of an organization to join other organizations. This form of representation was used by the Cleveland Electric Illuminating Company. The utility was located in a large metropolitan area and was privately owned. The city of Cleveland also owned and operated an electric utility company less than one-tenth the size of the Illuminating Company. Ironically, the part of the city served by the city-owned utility also was served by the Illuminating Company. Some streets had two columns of poles and power lines. The city claimed the duplicate system provided a means of evaluating rate increase requests from the Illuminating Company. The city also claimed its experience in the power business could be useful if the private utility became "unreasonable" and the city decided to purchase it. As a result, the private ownership of the Illuminating Company was threatened continuously.

To combat this threat, the Cleveland Electric Illuminating Co. encouraged its employees to be active in the community. Employees were "loaned" out to work on public causes, such as United Appeal (Community Chest) campaigns, while continuing to receive full salary. Employees were encouraged to run for elective offices (such as city council, school board, and the like) and were allowed to be absent or leave work early for this purpose. Finally, employees were encouraged to gain membership and leadership positions in important community and civic groups. These groups often influence government decision-making.

**Socialization
Strategy**

Socialization is the attempt to indoctrinate people in beliefs or values consistent with the interests of the organization or the broader society. It is assumed that if people accept and support these basic values, they are less likely to be sympathetic toward positions that threaten the organization or the political system in which it operates.

***Societal
socialization***

The so-called "American business creed" advances the idea that a decentralized, privately owned, free, competitive system in which the price mechanism is the major regulatory or control system is desirable and should be continued. The creed holds that governmental actions interfering with or threatening this system should be opposed and stopped. During the campaign of 1980, President Reagan frequently expressed his belief in this creed.

Tactics used for societal socialization vary widely. For example, the National Association of Manufacturers and the United States Chamber of Commerce have provided materials for elementary and secondary schools to use in teaching about the American economic system. Milton Freidman, the Nobel Prize-winning economist, believes in the "American business creed." One tactic he uses is to spread this creed through speeches and appearances on television.

***Organizational
socialization***

Organizational socialization refers to the formal or informal attempts to "mold" employees into having certain desired attitudes and ways of dealing with others and their jobs. Of course, the socialization attempted by top management can be offset or reinforced by the expectations and pressures exerted by an employee's fellow workers.

Role of the First Supervisor. For new employees, the first supervisor often plays a crucial role in the socialization process. The first supervisor can be a major source of support and help by assisting new employees in "learning the ropes," being tolerant of initial errors, and serving as a source of reassurance and security. In contrast, there is the danger that the first boss and others will feel the need to "straighten new employees out," "show them what life is really like," or "put them through initiation rites." This approach to socialization often comes across to new employees as a way of being put down and may turn them away from rather than toward the organization.[35]

Women in Management. The increased number of women moving into managerial roles, as well as the changing societal and legal expectations toward women in general, has resulted in the need for new organizational socialization practices. Table 3.4 provides a summary of the dos and don'ts for three areas of organizational socialization: (1) women's status as managers; (2) their competence as managers; and (3) their behavior as managers.

			3.4 Samples of Organizational Socialization

Recommen-dations	Managers		
	Women	*Men*	
Do	Plan your career and take risks.	Be as supportive or critical of a woman as of a man.	
	Stress your ambition. Ask: "What can I do to get ahead?"	Practice talking to her if you are self-conscious.	
	Speak at least once every ten minutes in a meeting.	Let her open the door if she gets there first.	
	Take the chip off your shoulder.	Tell your wife casually about a woman peer.	
Don't	Say: "I worked on . . ." when you wrote the entire report.	Make a fuss when appointing the first woman.	
	Imitate male mannerisms or do needlepoint at meetings.	Tune her out at meetings.	
	Hang on to the man who trained you.	Say: "Good morning, gentle-men—and lady."	
	Leap to serve coffee when someone suggests that it's time for a break.	Apologize for swearing.	

From "How to Get Along in the Corporate Office": *Business Week*, March 22, 1976, pp. 107–110.

The recommendations in Table 3.4 suggest new types of social behavior for both men and women managers when dealing with each other. These recommendations are attempts to resocialize and change certain sex-role stereotypes.[36] Due to pressures from various groups and government agencies, many organizations have changed their formal practices and policies in terms of equal employment opportunity applied to women and minority groups.

Overview

All organizations function within a larger environment which influences their stability, survival, and growth. In the political environment, conflicts over topical issues and fundamental values are worked out. Business firms must deal with the components of their environment. To do so, they use several political strategies — bargaining, cooptation, lobbying, coalitions, representation, and/or socialization.

PRESSURES FOR CORPORATE SOCIAL RESPONSIBILITY

Changes in societal values and the political system have increased the pressures and demands for corporate social responsibility. The controversy surrounding the social responsibility concept is consistent with the diverse values and interest groups in America. As will be seen, there have been powerful arguments raised against the concept of social responsibility for business organizations, even though it might appear to be attractive on the surface.[37]

Concept of Social Responsibility

Social responsibility is corporate behavior which is consistent with current social norms, values, and performance expectations of society.[38] The major dimensions and types of corporate behavior prescribed under the concept of social responsibility are highlighted in Table 3.5.

Dimensions of Corporate Behavior	Examples of Corporate Behavior	3.5 *Concept of Corporate Social Responsibility*
Search for legitimacy	Willingness to consider and accept broader—extra-legal and extra-market—criteria for measuring corporate performance and social role.	
Social norms	Definition of norms in community related terms, i.e., good corporate citizen. Avoids taking moral stand on issues which may harm its economic interests or go against prevailing social norms (majority views).	
Operating strategy	Maintain current standards of physical and social environment. Compensate victims of pollution and other corporate-related activities even in the absence of clearly established legal grounds. Develop industry-wide standards.	
Response to social pressures.	Accepts responsibility for solving current problems; will admit deficiencies in former practices and attempt to persuade public that its current practices meet social norms; attitude toward critics conciliatory; freer information disclosures than the law requires.	
Legislative and political activities	Shows willingness to work with outside groups for good environmental laws; concedes need for change in some status quo laws; less secrecy in lobbying.	

Adapted and modified from: S. P. Sethi, "A Conceptual Framework for Environmental Analysis of Social Issues and Evaluation of Business Response Patterns," *Academy of Management Review* 8, 1979, 63–74. Used with permission.

On the basis of our definition and the concept of social responsibility outlined in Table 3.5, "socially responsible" managers must consider and respond to the possible economic and social impacts of their decisions and the firm's operations on environmental components. To be socially responsible, managers presumably must take action in three areas.[39] First they must be aware of the firm's obligations to solve some of the problems facing society. This awareness of social problems has to exist in the firm's relationships with its customers, owners, employees, creditors, community, government, and society in general. Second, the managers must be willing to help solve social problems. Not all problems can be solved by business organizations. But the managers must be willing to tackle some of society's problems (e.g., inflation, drug and alcohol addiction). Third, and more specifically, managers must attempt to make decisions and actually commit resources in some of the following problem areas: pollution (air, water, solid wastes, land noise), poverty and racial discrimination (minority groups, black capitalism, and urbanization), and consumerism (product safety, misleading advertising, customer complaints).

**Business
Applications**

A number of large corporations have adopted programs and philosophies that mirror the major characteristics of the social responsibility concept. These programs are usually influenced by the corporation's chief executive. A few examples illustrate this point.

Cornell C. Maier, chairman and chief executive officer of Kaiser Aluminum and Chemical Corporation in Oakland, California, sees social responsibility as a big concern. He devotes considerable time to community projects while encouraging his managers to become personally involved in their community. In a program dubbed "Lady of the Lake" by Kaiser employees, Maier helped get a boat for a group of elderly women who rowed around Lake Merritt across the street from the Kaiser building. The club had grown so large that the one boat they had was not enough. His other programs included Adopt-a-Park, where an inner city park was revitalized; Summer on the Move, a work-learn program for Oakland high school students; and money donations to local groups, education and charity.[40]

Thornton Bradshaw, president of Atlantic Richfield Company, believes his company has a substantial responsibility to improve the quality of the products and services it manufactures while attempting to alleviate negative effects the firm might have upon the public. These effects include pollution, inflation, and minority hiring. He agrees that it is tough to tackle programs in all social areas of national concern. Atlantic Richfield employees in Dallas and Houston receive time off with pay to tutor public school students. Dealers frequently donate tools, uniforms, and advice to school hobby clubs. The Sierra Club received a $100,000 grant from Atlantic Richfield for a study of caribou herds in the Arctic.[41]

Thomas Murphy, the former chairman of General Motors, wrote the foreword to the report entitled *1980 General Motors Public Interest Report*. This 120 page report serves to document General Motors' efforts at corporate social responsibility. It covers topics ranging from the marketplace to being a good corporate neighbor. Murphy comments in this annual report:[42]

> *1980 is a milestone for the Public Interest Report. Ten years ago, mindful that interest in General Motors was not limited to its stockholders, the Corporation decided to supplement its Annual Report with a published account of its goals, programs and "progress in areas of public concern." Through a politically and economically turbulent decade, during which GM has responded to growing challenges in the marketplace, its managers have also participated more and more in the so-called "marketplace of ideas." Now an annual tradition, the Public Interest Report is part of GM's participation in this once unfamiliar marketplace, which forms and informs public opinion.*

As indicated in Table 3.6, General Motors seems to have a more pragmatic and enlightened self-interest view of social responsibility. This is relative to the concept of social responsibility presented in Table 3.5. While GM still feels that their primary long-term responsibility is to the stockholders, it does formally claim responsibilities to other groups.

It is beyond the scope of this book to assess the effectiveness of social responsibility programs by business firms. Neither can it evaluate what happens when managers are faced with conflicting demands and pressures from environmental components. Such conflicts are inevitable in the American pluralistic society with its organizations and groups which have conflicting goals, values, and interests.

Corporate Social Audits

A corporate **social audit** is a systematic study and assessment of the social performance of a business.[43] This is in contrast to its economic performance, as measured in the financial audit. The social audit normally results in a report of social performance, such as the *1980 General Motors Public Interest Report*.

Conducting social audits

Table 3.7 presents a model for corporate social auditing and reporting. The trend in recent years has been for large corporations to assess the social impacts of their actions. Ninety-two percent of the companies in *Fortune* maga-

3.6
General Motors View of
Corporate Social
Responsibility

Selected comments by Thomas A. Murphy (Chairman and Chief Executive Officer, retired effective January 1, 1981):

If business people have learned one overriding lesson from the '70s, it is that economic success alone is not enough. Important as they are, superior products are not enough; nor are innovations in manufacturing, marketing, or service. And certainly, returning a profit on our stockholders' investment, although absolutely necessary, is no longer sufficient by itself to ensure a firm's acceptance. All of these traditional marketplace measures of success fall short of fully explaining General Motors to the public at large.

This larger constituency most often uses other scales to weigh performance in nonproduct, even nonbusiness, areas. These gauge the way we respond to society at large. They evaluate the way we relate to our society, its economy, and its physical and social environment. Because today's public relies heavily upon the broad marketplace of ideas to form its opinion, any business which chooses not to enter this arena does so only at its own risk. . . .

Our financial statements report on our primary responsibility as a business — the obligation to return a fair profit on stockholders' investment. Without profits, our economic system would not long permit General Motors to fulfill its wider social responsibilities.

In the past decade, this basic fiscal responsibility has sometimes become subordinated, in the public mind, to other worthy and popular goals; yet, any firm which fails to achieve its investors' goals cannot survive to pursue other goals, no matter how worthy. Conversely, public opinion will not permit a firm to succeed in business unless it also lives up to the laws of the land and, beyond that, to the accepted standards of good corporate citizenship.

Business and society enter the new decade with heavy mutual responsibilities. No single interest can be permitted to upset the economic and social balance of the whole. No goal can be appraised blindly, or isolated from others equally essential. Only goodwill and hard work can solve our economic and social problems. Institutions and individuals alike must contribute their particular talents to ensure that we continue the growth which has made this society great. . . .

We emerge from the tests of the last decade, however, even more dedicated to meeting new challenges — be they economic, environmental, technological, or social.

1980 General Motors Public Interest Report. Detroit: General Motors Corporation, April 3, 1980, p. 1.
Used with permission.

zine's top 500 list undertake a social audit. Several corporations have tried to measure these impacts in quantitative terms, as recommended in Table 3.7 but it is often difficult to measure how much a particular social action is worth in dollars and cents. For example, William Buckley, president of Allegheny Ludlum Steel, asks: "How much is it worth to those downwind to have emis-

		3.7 *A Model for Corporate* *Social Auditing and* *Reporting*
Parts	**Explanations**	
1. A list of social expectations and the corporation's response	A candid summary of what is expected for each program area (e.g., consumer affairs, employee relations, physical environment, local community development). A statement of the corporation's reasoning as to why it has undertaken certain activities and not undertaken others.	
2. A statement of the corporation's social objectives and the priorities attached to specific activities	For each program area, the corporation's report on what it will try to accomplish and what priority it places on the programs and activities it will undertake.	
3. A description of the corporation's objectives in each program area and of the activities it will conduct	For each priority activity and program, the corporation's statement of a specific objective (in quantitative terms when possible), describing how it is striving to reach that objective (e.g., in the community, making available 10 qualified employees from members of its staff for a total of 400 man hours).	
4. A statement indicating the resources committed to achieve objectives and goals	A summary report, by program area and activity, of the costs — direct and indirect — assumed by the corporation.	
5. A statement of the accomplishments and/or progress made in achieving each objective	A summary describing the extent to which each objective has been achieved. (When feasible, the description should be in quantitative terms. Objective, narrative statements should be used when quantification is not possible.)	

Adapted from J. J. Carson, and G. A. Steiner, *Measuring Business Social Performance: The Corporate Social Audit.* New York: Committee for Economic Development, 1974, 61. Used with permission.

sions removed from the exhaust of a steelmill? Is it the cost of cleaning or replacing dirty clothes, rotting window sills, hospital expenses, or lost income of those injured physically? Does it also include the aesthetic and economic impacts on those directly affected?"

The American Institute of Certified Public Accountants and the model in Table 3.7 recommend the use of qualitative descriptions where quantitative measurements are unavailable. This approach does not put a dollar sign on everything, but aims at providing a reasonable profile of the corporation's performance in important environmental, cultural, and economic sectors. While measurement problems still are great and this process involves less than total accuracy, a basic profile of activities and achievement in the social areas probably can be developed. The social audit focuses on actual experiences and not on intentions.

Assessment of social audits

Corporate social auditing practices are widespread and increasing. The impact of this activity on performance is difficult to pin down. In a study of consumer-oriented food processing companies, the most profitable companies made no mention of a social audit in their annual reports. Another study found that 71 high-performance firms were more socially conscious than 200 low-performance firms. We must remember there are many other factors (i.e., size, location, type of industry, and the like) probably affecting the association between profitability and social auditing practices.[44] It may be that the higher performing firms simply had the resources to conduct social audits and engage in "social responsibility" activities.

Criticisms of Social Responsibility

Despite the arguments for the social-responsibility concept by some individuals and groups, there also are some powerful arguments against it. Some question whether public problems should be placed on the shoulders of business managers. Critics argue that business people are not held responsible to the voters for their decisions. In assessing what is best for society, business managers could turn into paternalistic rulers. Many people believe that business may suffer serious profit losses by accepting a heavy burden of social responsibility. Capital and managerial talent may be drained by those activities, counter to the profit motive of the firm and its stockholders.

Friedman's views

Milton Friedman, the Nobel Prize-winning economist, believes that a corporate manager is an agent of the stockholders. Any movement of resources from maximizing stockholder profits and interests amounts to spending the stockholders' money without their consent.[45] He argues that government, rather than business, is the institution best suited for solving social problems. Friedman's point is that managers' actions are constrained by the economic needs of their companies. Profit and positive cash flow are still the bottom lines for all firms. Friedman stresses that no executive can or should jeopardize the firm's financial position in the name of social involvement. Boise Cascade Corporation, for example, promoted a minority enterprise in the heavy-construction industry. The venture resulted in a pre-tax loss of approximately $40 million to Boise Cascade. As a result, the corporation's stock fell 60 points, and the stockholders demanded the resignation of the corporation's officers.

Horns of a dilemma   Managers may find themselves on the horns of a dilemma. When they attempt to become involved in society's problems, they may face angry stockholders who maintain that companies have no right to use earnings for such purposes. Since the stockholders are the legal owners of the company, only they can make such decisions. On the other hand, when managers attempt to achieve maximum profits for stockholders, they may face the wrath of some groups who claim that managers have no respect for the needs of society as a whole. By failing to adequately consider environmental components, they are accused of threatening the survival, stability, and growth of the entire free-enterprise system.[46] The horns of this dilemma for managers mirror the contrasting and conflicting values apparent in the pragmatic value orientation versus the ethical-moral orientations. Those pressing for the social-responsibility concept appear to be representing the ethical-moral value orientation. Opponents to this concept for business firms appear to have a more pragmatic value orientation.

It is our speculation that the pressure on business firms to fully implement the social responsibility concept in the United States will not increase or may even be reduced in the 1980s, relative to the 1970s. The changes in the political environment in Washington, D.C., the increased level of foreign and domestic competition, the widespread recognition of the need to improve productivity and innovation, and the scarcity of capital to invest in new plant and equipment seem to have come together as the major issues requiring the attention and energies of corporate managers in the 1980s.

SUMMARY   This chapter has focused on developing your skills to function more effectively in the liaison, monitor, disturbance handler, and leadership roles. The *liaison role* involves dealing with people outside of the organization — government officials, suppliers, unions, etc. The purpose of this role is for the manager to gather information from environmental components that can influence the organization's success. Much of our discussion on environmental trends and changing values should help in understanding what types of environmental information to look for and how to assess this information.

In the *monitor role*, the manager scans the environment for information that may affect the department's or organization's performance. In a sense, the entire chapter represents an attempt to scan some of the broad themes and characteristics of organizational environments as they are likely to influence managerial decision-making today and in the future.

The *disturbance-handler role* depicts the manager as responding to situations beyond his or her immediate control — such as strikes, rulings by regulatory agencies, and major suppliers who go bankrupt. Disturbances may arise because managers ignore developments in the environment until crisis proportions are reached. Through this chapter's discussion of developments in the environment, you should have a better understanding of the nature of environmental disturbances for organizations and an improved ability to anticipate disturbances. Even good managers cannot possibly anticipate all environmental disturbances. Thus, our discussion of political strategies suggests useful *means* for avoiding, reducing, or responding to environmental disturbances. You will recall that the political strategies included bargaining, cooptation, lobbying, coalitions, representation, and socialization.

During the 1970s, a major environmental disturbance for the managers of business firms was the pressure to adopt the social responsibility concept. Given the changing and pluralistic values in contemporary America, many managers are on the horns of a dilemma in assessing whether — or the degree to which — they should apply this concept. The social-responsibility concept and especially the Theory X versus Theory Y managerial philosophies bear upon the *leadership role*. This role involves responsibility for directing and coordinating the activities of subordinates to accomplish organizational goals. Certainly, the particular managerial philosophy — such as Theory X versus Theory Y — and the other values considered to be important and meaningful to managers influence *how* they lead subordinates.

The United States and the other industrialized nations have literally become part of a worldwide economy which affects every consumer, employee, and manager. The following chapter touches on some of the international influences on managers and organizations. These international influences have been even more turbulent than the environmental influences within the United States.

KEYWORDS

bargaining strategy
coalition strategy
cooptation strategy
ethical-moral value orientation
lobbying strategy
organizational socialization
political strategies

political system
pragmatic value orientation
representation strategy
self-satisfaction value orientation
social audit
social responsibility
socialization strategy

task environment	*turbulent environment*
Theory X	*value*
Theory Y	*value system*

1. Do you agree or disagree with some or all of Drucker's views of the turbulent environment facing managers? Explain.

2. Through the use of Fig. 3.1, how would you classify the task environments of a local movie theatre, a research and development department, a local real-estate agent's office specializing in home sales, and the president's office at General Electric? Defend your classifications.

3. What value concepts will be highly rated by successful managers of the future? Why? (Choose from the value concepts shown in Fig. 3.2.)

4. Describe a manager you worked for who seemed to have either a Theory X or Theory Y philosophy.

5. How would you describe yourself relative to the pragmatic value orientation versus the ethical-moral value orientation?

6. Do you think business groups such as the Business Roundtable, the U.S. Chamber of Commerce, and the National Association of Manufacturers should be allowed to lobby for their interests before Congress or administrative agencies? Explain.

7. If a community claims that a firm has polluted a nearby river, what political strategies might management use to deal with this pressure?

8. Do you agree with the social-responsibility concept? Defend your response.

9. What problems do you think women and minority college graduates will have in their first supervisory roles?

10. Describe the approach used by your college or a firm you have worked for in trying to socialize you.

Management Incidents and Cases

PRECISION
DYNAMICS
CORPORATION*
Precision Dynamics Corporation is a manufacturer of military and commercial aircraft, missiles, radar, and related equipment. About one-third of Precision's sales are to foreign countries, divided, as are domestic sales, about equally between commercial and military orders. Precision's fortunes have

* From *The Media and Business,* edited by Howard Simons and Joseph A. Califano, Jr. Copyright © 1979 by Howard Simons and Joseph A. Califano, Jr. Reprinted by permission of Random House, Inc.

improved dramatically over the past three years, due largely to increases in foreign military orders. One important recent foreign sale by Precision was to Mlay, an oil-rich country in the Middle East, which bought 50 Panthers, supersonic fighter aircraft which are also purchased in substantial numbers by the United States Air Force. Each Panther fighter costs ten million dollars. Precision has also benefited from very large development contracts with the Pentagon for a top-secret, long-range, air-launched missile capable of such course changes and elusive maneuvers that it would be virtually invulnerable to existing Soviet air defense and antiballistic missile technologies. If this new missile becomes operational, the United States could drastically reduce other offensive missile systems, such as the cruise missile. Such reductions could produce dramatic progress in SALT negotiations with the Soviets. A prototype missile has been built, and in extensive testing it has met all specifications.

Code-named "Broken Field," the new missile depends on highly sophisticated airborne guidance systems, which are separate from the missile itself and code-named "Hydra," and which can read defenses deployed against the Broken Field missile and instruct it to take diversionary action. For the guidance process to work, it is necessary that at least two Hydra surveillance and computer systems be airborne along geographical vectors north and south of the general target area. These systems are highly complex, utilizing recent breakthroughs in surveillance, data processing, and transmission technologies. Each Hydra system is housed in a large aircraft, an adaptation of a long-range bomber which Precision manufactures for the United States Air Force.

The Pentagon has adopted plans to deploy Broken Field missiles on 50 aircraft in various parts of the United States, and to keep two Hydra systems airborne in each vector north and south of the Soviet Union at all times. Aircraft based at SAC airfields in the United States can easily maintain the vector position to the north of the Soviet Union. However, the vector south of the Soviet Union (roughly the area from the Philippines to Saudi Arabia) presents strategic problems. The guidance aircraft are to be camouflaged as SAC bombers. These bombers regularly occupy airspace to the north, east, and west of the Soviet Union, but not to the south. Thus, even disguised, the Hydra aircraft would excite Soviet curiosity along the southern vector.

To meet the need for airborne southern guidance systems, the Pentagon has proposed an ingenious solution: a country located along the southern vector should be induced to purchase six or more guidance systems on the supposition that the systems are to be used solely for its own defense. The buyer-country would not be aware of the additional Hydra guidance function

Pentagon's Plans

in relation to the Broken Field missile. Rather, other equipment would be included and the systems would appear to the buyer-country to be advanced surveillance and communications systems, useful for spotting land or air incursions into largely uninhabited border areas. The highly sophisticated devices necessary to guide the Broken Field missiles would be hidden. Only routine surveillance systems would normally be operational. On a signal from the United States during testing sequences or during an actual launching of the Broken Field missiles, the Hydra systems would be activated to provide guidance for the Broken Field missiles. Even when activated, however, the Hydra function would not be apparent to the buyer-country.

Andrew Josephs With this plan in mind, the Assistant Secretary of Defense for International Security Affairs called on Andrew Josephs, the president and chief executive officer of Precision, to discuss the possibilities of persuading Mlay, which is located south of the Soviet Union, to purchase the guidance systems. Mlay seemed a logical choice not only because of its strategic location, but also because of its recent purchase from Precision of the Panther fighters. The Assistant Secretary suggested to Josephs that Mlay be induced to buy six (disguised) Hydra systems. The United States was also planning to purchase six systems. If the Pentagon approved the sale to Mlay, and endeavored to persuade Mlay that the disguised Hydras would be useful for Mlay's security, the Assistant Secretary inquired, would Precision use its contacts among Mlay's military leaders to try to make a sale? The Assistant Secretary pointed out that successful deploying of Hydra systems in the airspace over Mlay would make it possible for the United States to give up several missile systems that have been stumbling blocks in SALT negotiations with the Soviet Union.

For Josephs, the matter of Precision's contacts in Mlay currently happens to be one of acute sensitivity. Josephs took over as head of Precision about 12 months ago, after the former president of the company resigned under pressure due to disclosures of widespread questionable payments in several foreign countries. One of Joseph's first steps as the new president of Precision was to order a confidential audit by outside counsel of all payments and commissions paid by Precision to foreign consultants. He has just received a report on payments made in connection with the sale of Panthers to Mlay which disclosed that two million dollars was paid about 18 months ago to an unnamed "high official" of the Mlay Defense Ministry. The Panther sale was finally closed about six months ago, although negotiations had been in the works for more than a year before the deal was closed. At present, about half of the 50 Panthers have been delivered to Mlay; the remainder are to be delivered within the coming six months. Precision's chief sales agent in Mlay has said that he will not disclose the identity of the recipient of this money to anyone other than Josephs in person, claiming that the official could be executed if his receipt of money from Precision is revealed. Josephs has summoned the agent to meet with him. He is due to arrive in two days.

Questions for Josephs

1. If Josephs learns the identity of the Mlay official to whom the two-million-dollar payment was made, should he reveal that fact, or the questionable payment generally, to the outside counsel conducting the investigation, to the board, to the company's general counsel, to his personal lawyer? Does it matter if any of these lawyers is also a member of the board?

2. Should Josephs notify the SEC, the Justice Department, or any other agency of the federal government? How much should he reveal?

3. Suppose Precision proceeds with a public offering of a $250 million bond issue in order to tool up for production of the Broken Field/Hydra program. How much should Josephs disclose in the prospectus about the Broken Field/Hydra project? Should he disclose the prospects for sale of Hydras to Mlay? Should Josephs disclose the possibility that a bribe in Mlay might be revealed which might threaten the sale of Hydras to Mlay?

4. How should Josephs respond if a reporter calls and asks whether Precision is planning to sell advanced airborne surveillance-computer systems to Mlay?

*SOUTHERN REALTY INVESTORS, INC.**

In the late 1940s a northern industrialist came to the shores of southeast Florida and recognized what he believed to be an area for future growth and investment in real estate. Subsequently, he formed Southern Realty Investors, Inc., a wholly owned Florida based corporation. From wealth accumulated in his worldwide business interests, he purchased $700 million in Florida property. Through this massive land investment strategy the Southern Realty Investors, Inc. became the largest single property owner in the state.

Conflicts over Growth

As the years passed the reputation of Florida as a retirement area flourished and the population of the state grew astronomically, especially along the coast of the Atlantic Ocean. The obvious result of the land rush was soaring property values. Cities whose populations in 1960 were 8000 residents had

* Case developed by Paul Preston (University of Texas at San Antonio) and Thomas Zimmer (Clemson University). Used with permission.

surpassed the 50,000 resident population mark by the early 1970s. Such rapid growth caused a backlash against the feared overbuilding by developers, and in 1973 the residents of San Remo, gem of the gold coast, enacted the rights of property owners in the use of their land. The most radical adversary of the growth "cap," as it became known, was Southern Realty Investors, Inc. As proposed (and subsequently adopted by the people), the growth cap law uses zoning to reduce the allowed density (number of dwelling units per acre) of underdeveloped land. Fully implemented, the city of San Remo would reach a maximum population of 105,000 persons. This number was considered by some experts to be the optimal population after accounting for the availability of water resources and essential public services.

Opponents of the move to limit growth included such community elements as the land developers (including Southern Realty Investors, Inc.), the Chamber of Commerce representing local businesses, the building and construction trades, and other related groups. Their arguments were centered around the proposition that growth in a desirable region such as San Remo is inevitable. Orderly growth is desirable but an outright limit on growth within the city itself will have the effect of "building a wall" around San Remo. This in turn would force the overflow population into the surrounding county-controlled lands and result in exactly the kind of undesirable overcrowded sprawl the antigrowth forces sought to prevent. As the largest land owner in both San Remo and the surrounding area, Southern Realty Investors pointed out in a well-financed publicity campaign that such actions by the community would result in economic and social strangulation.

Strategies and Tactics by Southern Realty Investors

Southern Realty Investors land developments, in the opinion of most unbiased observers, are noted for low density and high property values. An outstanding example exists within the limits of San Remo itself. The San Remo Yacht and Country Club features very low density individual housing. The values of the homes built by Southern Realty Investors in this section have tripled in price since being developed in the mid-1960s. The most prestigious section of town, it is the home of most of the community's social, political, and business leaders.

The company's officers acted as informal speakers for the progrowth and anticap forces. They were aided in their opposition by Jim Donner, a local attorney and former minority leader in the State House of Representatives. During Donner's years in the legislature, he was an outspoken advocate of restricting population growth. On leaving the legislature and resuming his law practice, he began to represent many of the land developers in South Florida and ultimately was retained as the chief counsel for Southern Realty Investors. With his knowledge of the law (having written most of the laws concerning the rights of the local communities to regulate growth), he was an eloquent and forceful speaker for the position of Southern Realty Investors and its allies.

Present and previous members of the city council received membership in the internationally known resort located in San Remo. They also were owners in Southern Realty Investors. In addition, Southern Realty Investors' community activities and involvement in local affairs were well known, with the company supporting financially and in other ways several of the community charities and local organizational projects. In the course of this involvement, the company came to develop close ties to most of the business and political leaders, including the members of both the city and county councils.

The situation in San Remo came to a dramatic head the night of the city council debate over putting the question of limiting the number of allowed dwelling units in the town (the growth cap) to a vote of the people. On one side with Southern Realty Investors was an impressive array of business people, political leaders (including sympathetic members of the city council), and local legal talent retained by Southern and other developers. Against these forces was the coalition of the Audubon Society, local environmentalists and ecology buffs, citizens fearful of the disadvantages of higher density, and a host of interested citizens and citizen groups. The initiative for the growth cap grew out of a severe water shortage three years before, when water was rationed and severe economic and personal hardships were suffered throughout South Florida. Arising from the fears that such a catastrophe could happen more easily with uncontrolled growth, the citizens groups circulated petitions that ultimately forced the issue of the "cap" on the ballot.

Southern Realty Investors was careful, in the heated debate, to align itself not only with the interests of "big business," but also to show that the small, individual landowner could be most hurt by adoption of the cap. The company spokesperson pointed out that if the cap was adopted, the city would, in effect, be able to destroy the value the small investor had earned in the land by refusing to permit the land to be used to the fullest extent. This was a persuasive and quite realistic position. While the company was the largest landowner in town, and several other developers owned large parcels of land, the bulk of the underdeveloped land in San Remo and the surrounding community was owned by small, individual investors with, at most, an acre of land apiece.

Emotional arguments intimated that these landowners would someday not be permitted to even build a home for themselves on their small lot (if the 40,000 units had already been reached). Foes replied that this was sheer emotional fantasy, designed to stir up a "smokescreen" for the profiteering of the large landowners and developers. The cap proponents noted that their proposal would achieve the 40,000 unit ceiling through remedial zoning, so that at least one dwelling unit would be permitted on each standard building lot now defined within the city.

Polarization of the City

In that council meeting, and in the weeks before the referendum, the city polarized, with each side accusing the other of political subterfuge, and with charges and countercharges going far beyond the actual issues under consideration. Southern Realty Investors company spent thousands of dollars in an expensive publicity campaign, while donations from the citizens financed a strong (although more limited) procap effort. San Remo became the rallying point for environmentalists from across the country, with personal appearances and much publicity for the "brave efforts of the citizens' groups." San Remo was billed nationwide as the "test case," the forerunner for other efforts to restrict local growth. In the process of publicizing the need for the cap, Southern Realty Investors company's previously lauded accomplishments and community-minded actions were ignored, and the company was painted as an irresponsible "environmental rapist" and a political manipulator for corporate profits. Advocates of the cap defied the corporate giant to trample on the rights of individual citizens.

The Outcome

In the January election the cap was victorious, with 60 percent of the vote. The city council began actions to implement the cap, and Southern Realty Investors, Inc., filed suit in Federal District Court to overturn the cap as unconstitutional, claiming it deprived the company and other individuals from their right to dispose of their land as they see fit.

Questions

1. What value concepts seemed to be given high priority by the "growth" advocates and the "nongrowth" proponents? You might draw from Figs. 3.2 and 3.4 to identify the values held by each of these groups.

2. What were the political strategies and tactics used by the managers of Southern Realty Investors? Do you think they used the best political strategies and tactics available, given the circumstances?

3. How would managers who accept the social-responsibility concept, as outlined in Table 3.5, have handled this situation?

4. Do you feel the passage of the cap referendum excessively violates the rights of the owners to the use of their property? Explain.

5. If Southern Realty Investors is not successful in their suit to overturn the "cap" as unconstitutional, what should the managers of this firm do next?

1. "Corporate Culture: The Hard to Change Values That Spell Success or Failure." *Business Week*, October 27, 1980, 148–160.

2. "Bell System's Long-Distance Service Faces Loss of Business To Host of Competitors." *The Wall Street Journal*, October 14, 1980, 31.

3. K. Davis, W. C. Frederick, and R. L. Blomstrom, *Business and Society: Concepts and Policy Issues.* New York: McGraw-Hill, 1980, p. 361.

4. P. F. Drucker, *Managing In Turbulent Times.* New York: Harper and Row, 1980.

5. R. Duncan, "What Is the Right Organization Structure?" *Organizational Dynamics* **7,** 1979, 59–80. For a more complex model of the environment see: R. L. Tung, "Dimensions of Organizational Environments: An Exploratory Study of Their Impact on Organization Structure." *Academy of Management Journal* **22,** 1979, 672–693.

6. A. Toffler, *The Third Wave.* New York: William Morrow, 1980. W. H. Newman (ed.), *Managers For the Year 2000.* Englewood Cliffs, NJ: Prentice-Hall, 1979.

7. G. England, "Organizational Goals and Expected Behavior of American Managers." *Academy of Management Journal* **10,** 1967, 107–117.

8. G. England, O. Dhingra, and N. Agarwal, "The Manager and The Man: A Cross-Cultural Study of Personal Values." *Organization and Administrative Sciences* **5,** 1974, 1–97.

9. Ibid.

10. G. England, N. Agarwal, and R. Trerise, "Union Leaders and Managers: A Comparison of Value Systems." *Industrial Relations* **10,** 1971, 211–226.

11. A. McGregor, *The Human Side of the Enterprise.* New York: McGraw-Hill, 1960.

12. Ibid., pp. 47–48.

13. C. Argyris, "Personality and Organization Theory." *Administrative Science Quarterly* **18,** 1973, 141–168.

14. R. Dubin, "Industrial Research and the Discipline of Sociology." *Proceedings of the 11th Annual Meeting*, Madison, WI: Industrial Relations Research Association, 1959, 161.

15. M. R. Cooper, B. S. Morgan, P. M. Foley, and L. B. Kaplan, "Changing Employee Values: Deepening Discontent?" *Harvard Business Review* **57,** 1979, 117–125.

16. J. G. Bachman and L. D. Johnston, "The Freshmen, 1979." *Psychology Today* **13,** 4, 1979, 79–87.

17. P. A. Renwick and E. E. Lawler, "What You Really Want From Your Job." *Psychology Today* **11,** 12, 1978, 53–65, + 118.

18. L. E. Davis, "Individuals and the Organization." *California Management Review* **22,** 2, 1980, 5–14.

19. E. Epstein, *The Corporation in American Politics*. Englewood Cliffs, NJ: Prentice-Hall, 1969, p. 303.

20. W. G. Scott and D. K. Hart, *Organizational America*. Boston: Houghton Mifflin, 1979.

21. J. Thompson and W. McEwen, "Organizational Goals and Environment: Goal Setting as an Interaction Process." *American Sociological Review* **23,** 1958, 23–31.

22. M. Derber, W. Chalmers, and M. Edelman, *Plant-Union Management Relations: From Practice to Theory*. Urbana, IL: Institute of Labor and Industrial Relations, 1965.

23. M. Van De Vall, *Labor Organizations*. Cambridge, England: Cambridge University Press, 1970.

24. V. Pappas, "More Firms Upgraded Government-Relations Jobs Because of Sharp Growth in Federal Regulations," *The Wall Street Journal*, January 11, 1980, 32.

25. A. F. Ehrbar, "Pragmatic Politics Won't Win For Business." *Fortune* **99,** 11, 1979, 76–80.

26. P. Selznick, *TVA and the Grass Roots*. New York: Harper Torchbook, 1966, pp. 13–16.

27. "Blue Collars in the Board Room." *Time* **115,** 20, 1980, 78.

28. J. C. Alpin and W. H. Hegarty, "Political Influence: Strategies Employed By Organizations to Impact Legislation In Business and Economic Matters," *Academy of Management Journal* **23,** 1980, 438–450.

29. O. Hall, *Cooperative Lobbying — The Power of Pressure*. Tuscon: University of Arizona Press, 1969.

30. J. E. Post and J. F. Mahan, "Articulated Turbulence: The Effect of Regulatory Agencies on Corporate Responses to Social Change." *Academy of Management Review* **5,** 1980, 399–407.

31. S. B. Bacharach and E. J. Lawler, *Power and Politics In Organizations*. San Francisco: Jossey-Bass, 1980.

32. W. A. Guizzardi, Jr., "New Public Face for Business." *Fortune* **120,** 1, 1980, 48–52.

33. C. Brown, *Putting the Corporate Board to Work*. New York: Macmillan 1976. W. R. Boulton, "The Evolving Board: A Look at the Board's Changing Roles and Information Needs." *The Academy of Management Review* **3,** 1978, 827–836.

34. L. Ingrassia, "Outsider-Dominated Boards Grow, Spurred by Calls for Independence." *The Wall Street Journal* **66,** 88, 1980, 29.

35. E. H. Schein, *Career Dynamics: Matching Individual and Organizational Needs*. Reading, MA: Addison-Wesley, 1978, pp. 94–111. J. Van Maanen and E. H. Schein, "Toward a Theory of Organizational Socialization." In B. M. Staw (ed.), *Research in Organizational Behavior*. Greenwich, Conn., JDI Press, 1979 (Vol. 1), 209–264.

36. B. D. Stead (ed.), *Women In Management*, Englewood Cliffs, NJ: Prentice-Hall, 1978.

37. G. D. Keim, "Corporate Social Responsibility: An Assessment of the Enlightened Self-Interest Model." *Academy of Management Review* **3,** 1978, 32–39.

38. S. P. Sethi, "A Conceptual Framework For Environmental Analysis of Social Issues and Evaluation of Business Response Patterns." *Academy of Management Review* **4,** 1979, 63–74.

39. N. Churchill and D. Toan, "Reporting on Corporate Social Responsibility: A Progress Report." *Journal of Contemporary Business* **7,** 1, 1978, 7.

40. *Industry Week,* October 29, 1979, 56.

41. T. Bradshaw, "One Corporation's View of Social Responsibility." *Journal of Contemporary Business* **7,** 1, 1978, 19–24.

42. *1980 General Motors Public Interest Report.* Detroit: General Motors Corporation, April 7, 1980, 1.

43. V. Barry, *Moral Issues In Business.* Belmont, CA: Wadsworth, 1979, 367–369.

44. For reviews of the relevant research see: W. Abbott and R. Monsen, "On the Measurement of Corporate Social Responsibility: Self-Reported Disclosures as a Method of Measuring Corporate Social Involvement." *Academy of Management Journal* **22,** 1979, 501–515. J. Grunig, "A New Measure of Public Opinions on Corporate Social Responsibility." *Academy of Management Journal* **22,** 1979, 738–764.

45. M. Friedman, "The social responsibility of business is to increase profits." *New York Times Magazine,* September 13, 1970, 122–126.

46. S. Payne, "Organization Ethics and Antecedents to Social Control Process." *Academy of Management Review* **5,** 1980, 409–414.

Chapter 4

INTERNATIONAL ENVIRONMENTS

LEARNING OBJECTIVES

After reading this chapter, you should be able to:

1. Describe some of the differences in the environments facing firms abroad.

2. Compare and contrast multinational corporations with international corporations.

3. List how the differences in values have influenced the general characteristics of American vs. Japanese organizations.

4. Identify the forces leading to the passage of the Foreign Corrupt Practices Act.

5. List the dimensions of political risk in foreign investments.

PREVIEW CASE

**Westinghouse
Corporation***

John Marous will long remember the day, shortly after New Year's, 1979, when he was summoned to the office of Douglas Danforth, vice chairman and chief operating officer of Westinghouse. Danforth startled Marous by asking him to head an exhaustive study of Westinghouse's international operations.

Westinghouse was not performing horribly abroad. But Danforth wanted it to do better. He was also worried that the big electrical-equipment maker was gaining a reputation abroad for being internally disorganized and, at times, downright arrogant. The company could ill afford that reputation, because demand for most of its 8000 products was expected to grow faster overseas than in the United States in the years ahead. Danforth wanted Marous's report, along with recommendations for rectifying the situation, on his desk in a mere 90 days.

The report was delivered on time. Now John Marous has the title of President–International and is attempting to transform Westinghouse from a basically domestic company, albeit with substantial foreign business, to a full-fledged multinational.

---

* From H. Menzies, "Westinghouse Takes Aim at the World." FORTUNE magazine. Copyright ©
1980, Time Inc. All rights reserved.

If Westinghouse does not hold its own worldwide, Marous argues, "we will not be able to spread our costs and generate the necessary R. and D. This worries us, even in the nuclear field, where we are No. 1." Danforth wants 35 percent of Westinghouse's sales to be coming from abroad by 1984.

Although the company has been a presence on the world scene since the late nineteenth century, two previous attempts to establish major international empires ended up in shambles. Prior to 1914, the company had a dozen subsidiaries overseas, most of them in Europe. But World War I and the Russian Revolution caused the destruction and sale of those plants. For the next 50 years, Westinghouse restricted its international activities largely to manufacturing in Canada, to exporting through a New York-based operation called Westinghouse Electric International, and to licensing technology.

Then, in the late 1960s, Westinghouse got worried about being left behind in the American corporate invasion of Europe, and began buying several companies in Italy, Belgium, and France, hoping to merge them into a single operation that would start life with $1 billion in sales. French President Charles de Gaulle dealt that plan a blow in 1969, when he vetoed the acquisition of the keystone company — the French engineering concern, Jeumont-Schneider.

Donald Burnham, then Westinghouse's chief executive, reacted to this defeat by doing a complete about-face, abandoning an overall strategy for tackling world markets in favor of a piecemeal approach. In 1971, he gave Westinghouse's 125 division managers responsibility for foreign as well as domestic business. That meant the end of Westinghouse Electric International.

By 1976, Westinghouse's foreign business had soared to 31 percent of total sales, nearly three times the volume five years earlier. But that was the high-water mark. Two years later, the foreign-sales component had slumped to 24 percent.

Both Danforth and Robert Kirby, Westinghouse's chairman and chief executive, got a message from that foreign profit performance: they had better starting paying more attention to global matters. Danforth had been interested all along. He had joined Westinghouse as a general manager of the Mexican subsidiary in 1955 and later had overseen Canadian operations. After he was appointed chief operating officer in July 1978, he traveled abroad extensively. What he heard bothered him. "Our own people were telling me we could do better," he says. "We were turning down projects because the job needed six of our business units and only three were interested."

Even more telling, foreign customers and governments were complaining that Westinghouse was difficult to do business with. That is the way it still appears to Kim Ki Soo, executive director of Hyosung Heavy Industries, a South Korean company with annual sales of about $100 million. Westinghouse licensed Hyosung to make a line of heavy electrical equipment back in 1962, and has been happily banking the royalties ever since. But Hyosung is not so pleased. "That company is too aloof when dealing with small fry like us," Kim said recently. "When we ask for new technology, they say come and get it in the United States. Our guys went there and got shifted around from one business unit to the next and came home dizzy and empty-handed."

To Kim, the American giant compares poorly with Hitachi, one of its Japanese rivals. "The day after we sent a message to Tokyo, Hitachi came right back with an answer," says Kim. "Two days later, a Hitachi delegation empowered to make a decision turned up at our offices. In all the years of close association with Westinghouse, Hyosung has never been graced with such quick action." Hyosung may not renew the Westinghouse license when it expires in 1982.

Marous presented his team's report to Danforth in mid-April, and within a month the management committee had bought it, virtually in toto. In July 1979, he was tapped for the international job. Marous is on a level with the presidents of the three major internal groups. He has divided the entire overseas world into three parts — the Far East, Latin America, and a third region that takes in Europe, the Mideast, and Africa — and appointed a president to head each region. A fourth regional president, who heads Canadian operations, now reports to Marous as well.

Marous's staff will develop foreign strategies based upon the plans of the in-country managers. These strategies will then have to be meshed with the product-oriented plans drawn up by the business-unit managers. "We'll have to make our strategic plan fit," explains Harry Weingarten, manager of the switchgear unit. "The country manager can't say, 'I'm going to expand switchgear in Brazil by 40 times,' while I say, 'I'm going to expand by 50 percent.' "

The business units retain control of technology, product pricing, and capital budgets. When the unit and country managers disagree, which is likely to happen a lot in the early years, the matter will move to a higher level. The country manager will be able to appeal his case all the way up through Marous to Westinghouse's management committee.

Quite apart from developing strategies for foreign markets, the country managers will centralize staff functions in order to eliminate the duplication that existed in the past. The business-unit managers will continue to have profit-and-loss responsibility for their units in each country, but the country manager will have such responsibility for the country as a whole.[1]

This case shows the changing and complex international influences on one organization over time and the strategies used by managers to cope with these environmental influences. The basic driving forces for Westinghouse and all private corporations engaging in worldwide commerce are the opportunities provided for economies in production and/or increased sales. Westinghouse is one of a number of U.S. firms who are now more dependent on international sales and profits. With more sales and assets located outside of the familiar U.S. market, American managers have faced new uncertainties as to how to operate and organize their firms for worldwide business.

Throughout the Westinghouse case, we see the impact of the political influences: the losses resulting from World War I; the Russian Revolution; and Charles de Gaulle's decision forbidding Westinghouse from acquiring a French engineering firm. The French decision resulted in a complete change in the overall corporate strategy for dealing with the international environment. Westinghouse was missing business opportunities and facing the loss of foreign customers to competitors. The historical and evolutionary story provided in the Westinghouse case shows how managers' decisions will change over time. These decisions were influenced by changes in the environment as well as changes in the attitudes and values held by the key managers. Danforth's experience as a general manager of a Mexican subsidiary and his extensive travels abroad probably increased the degree of high-level attention given to Westinghouse's international environment.

Westinghouse is only one of a number of major U.S. organizations which have developed into multinational corporations. The organization changes made by Westinghouse will not be effective for all firms. (The specifics of organization design are considered in the next two chapters). For example, oil companies with fairly limited product lines (compared to Westinghouse's 8000 products) have been very successful at incorporating foreign operations within functional divisions. There are a variety of ways to successfully organize and operate as a multinational firm. Our point is that the key managers of multinational firms spend a good deal of time and thought as to how their products, services, and production operations fit into world markets — not just the United States.

EMERGENCE OF THE MULTINATIONAL CORPORATION

What Is a Multinational Corporation?

A *multinational corporation* is one in which: (1) the key managers try to take a worldwide view in assessing problems and opportunities; (2) there are one or more subsidiaries operating in at least several countries; and (3) there is a willingness to consider a variety of locations in the world to make sales, obtain resources, and produce goods. The Westinghouse case suggests it has only recently created the organization consistent with this definition. A variety of large organizations headquartered in the United States and Western Europe have a long record of operating as multinational corporations. Major U.S.-based firms serving as examples of multinational corporations include General Motors, Ford Motors, General Electric, Eastman Kodak, DuPont, Exxon, Coca Cola, Singer, and Standard Oil.

It has been typical for most U.S. firms to operate more as Westinghouse has done — as international corporations. An *international corporation* is one with business interests that cut across countries, often focusing on the import or export of goods or services, with one or more subsidiaries operating in other countries. In their initial expansion overseas, American corporations typically followed the same pattern. First, they would create a foreign marketing department or branch abroad. Second, they would build some factories abroad because of lower taxes, transportation costs, or labor costs. Third, once production and marketing were brought together in a foreign country, the purchasing of raw, semifinished, or other materials were often obtained locally at less cost. This coordinated effort saved money.[2] During the past ten years, many major U.S. corporations have evolved into the multinational form of organization. This has been accelerated by important environmental trends which are global, rather than limited to a particular country.

Global Trends

A variety of global environmental trends are shaping the creation and methods of operation of multinational corporations. A few of these global trends have been identified as follows:

1. The internationalization of political and economic institutions is increasing in other than the large industrialized nations. The less developed countries, such as India and Indonesia, are bargaining more vigorously with the developed countries.

2. There is a growing dependence of developed nations on the availability of basic resources obtainable mainly in less developed countries. The balance of physical survival and economic health vs. political relationships is shifting between developed and less developed countries.

3. A political explosion in the formation and reformation of new nations increases the number of nations on the global stage. A rapid increase in sophistication of these participants is occurring; whether they are new governments, political aggregations, cartels, culture groups, new private enterprises, new suppliers, or consumers.

4. Basic value systems are changing. There is a strong drive toward "egalitarianism," resulting from the growth and affluence of developed nations. This increases interdependence among nations.

5. The impacts of technology will affect industries, social-economic maturity, and the relations between nations. This will be a continuing cause of future turbulence.[3]

These global trends suggest that the international environment of multinational corporations will continue to be complex and changing for years to come. Moreover, multinationals are one of the conduits through which different countries influence and affect one another. For many years, countries and firms from around the world have sent their students, managers, and technicians to the United States to learn about management practices and technologies. In other cases, the foreign operations of U.S. multinationals served to transfer these technologies and management practices into other countries. After World War II, Japanese firms studied and adopted many U.S. management practices and technologies. For a number of years after World War II, Japanese products were considered to be shabby and of low quality by U.S. consumers. Japanese management came to recognize this as a major problem. They called on W. Edwards Deming, an American expert in statistical quality control procedures. Deming spent considerable time in Japan teaching Japanese management and specialists the quality control techniques he learned and developed in the U.S. His impact has been so great that the Deming Award is given annually to the Japanese firm which best represents the standards of quality control he set forth. Deming's efforts are generally regarded as a major factor in the high quality now found in many Japanese products.

Since 1970, Japanese multinationals have literally exploded in world markets and there appears to be no let-up in sight. In 1970 Japanese investment in plant and equipment in the United States was less than $1 billion. This figure increased to about $9 billion in 1980, and estimates are that it will be $22

**Japanese
Multinationals**

billion in 1985. The total overseas investment by Japanese companies was only about one-fifth of the over $180 billion in foreign investment by U.S. multinationals in 1980. However, the trend and momentum of Japanese foreign investment is accelerating relative to U.S. multinationals.[4] One can hardly pick up a newspaper or business magazine without reading about Japanese investments within the United States or the skyrocketing sales of Japanese made goods in the United States and other countries. For example, between 1975 and 1980, Japanese companies sold about $100 billion worth of goods to American firms and individuals, the equivalent of $1800 for each family in the United States.[5] The U.S. industries particularly affected by Japanese competition are autos, motorcycles, steel, television, watches, machine tools, and electronics.[6] For the 1980s, the Japanese government has set a high priority national policy objective of becoming the global leader in the computer industry as well as in the whole range of advanced electronic products.[7] This represents a direct challenge to U.S. based firms like IBM, Xerox, and Texas Instruments.

A 1980 report from a trade subcommittee in the U.S. House of Representatives concluded:

It may be that the most important action we can't take to compete with Japan is outside the realm of government action and lies strictly with improved management by American businessmen, which can result in major improvements in the quality of production and the morale of workers.[8]

Given the importance of Japanese multinational corporations and their management practices, this chapter makes a number of comparisons between Japanese and U.S. management. Our limited space prevents a comprehensive treatment of the complexities and scope of international management throughout the world.

John Opel, president of International Business Machines Corporation, has recognized the important role of the Japanese values and political system in contributing to the growth and competitiveness of its multinational corporations. Opel states: "In the past two decades, the Japanese nation has repeatedly shown the rest of the world the effectiveness of prudent planning and specialization — plus the application of the most advanced techniques in every phase of business and, most of all, pure and simple dedication and hard work."[9]

VALUE-SYSTEM INFLUENCES

In the previous chapter, we noted that the values operating within the United States are diverse and changing. On a world-wide basis, the complexity and changes of value systems in different countries are even more difficult to understand and appreciate. This is one of the reasons multinational corporations often give some flexibility and freedom to their managers operating foreign subsidiaries. These managers need some freedom to change policies, procedures, and management processes in response to local conditions.

In Fig. 3.3 we identified a variety of value concepts rated high by successful U.S. managers. Studies of Japanese managers suggest a somewhat different value profile. For example, U.S. managers tend to rate the value concepts of aggressiveness, individuality, and conflict quite high. Just the opposite is found for Japanese managers. We will discuss these and other value differences as they relate to the management of organizations.

Relative to the United States, the societal value system in Japan is less diverse. Severe conflicts due to underlying differences in values are fewer in Japanese society than in the United States. The overriding common value in Japanese society has been identified as "collectivism."[10] In contrast, the concept of "individualism" is highly rated and valued by many of us in America.

Collectivism means that individuals are submerged by the groups they belong to — ranging from the family to the total society. Individuals are regulated by the code of each group. Groups and organizations are not thought of as being made up of individuals. Rather, the organization or group exists first and absorbs individuals within itself. The Japanese form of collectivism leads to group cohesion based on the sacrifice or denial of the individual's wants. Collectivism emphasizes group goals and a dependency on others. Japan's high levels of achievement are group-oriented. In contrast, the need for achievement in the United States is relatively individualistic.[11] The value concepts of collectivism in Japan vs. individualism in the United States shows up in differences in management processes and practices. Let's consider these differences.

In identifying differences in Japanese and American management, you need to recognize that we are painting with a broad brush. The differences between U.S. firms and managers are much greater than the differences you are likely to find between Japanese firms and managers. This is simply because the values and philosophies of managers within the United States are more diverse and pluralistic than those in Japan.

Table 4.1 compares and summarizes eight basic characteristics of Japanese and American organizations. These characteristics are strongly influenced by contrasting values between the two nations. The theme of relative individualism in America vs. collectivism in Japan is apparent in the eight dimensions in Table 4.1. For most Japanese, the company is not only a place of

Japan's "Collectivism"

Japanese and American Organizations

work, but a sharing and caring group. It is a place where one is treated like a member of a family. Japanese employees are often proud of their company's success and frequently identify themselves with their company: one becomes

4.1
*Characteristics of
Japanese and
American
Organizations
Influenced by
Differences in Values*

Dimensions	American Organizations	Japanese Organizations
1. Employment	On average, short term, but varies widely. Unstable and uncertain.	Lifetime, relatively secure and stable.
2. Attitude Toward Work	Individual responsibilities.	Collective responsibilities, group loyalty, duty oriented.
3. Decision-Making	Individual oriented, relative top-down emphasis.	Consensus and group oriented, bottom up emphasis.
4. Relationship with Employees	Depersonalized, emphasis on formal contracts. Employee resents organization intrusion into personal affairs.	Personalized. Employees like family members. Paternalism, lifelong employment. Employee expects organization to show concern for personal affairs.
5. Evaluation and Promotion	Rapid.	Slow.
6. Salary	Merit pay based on individual contribution.	Heavy emphasis on seniority.
7. Controls	Detailed within rules and regulations.	Informal rules and regulations.
8. Competition	Relatively free and open between individuals.	Very low between individuals within groups. Very high between groups, such as with other organizations.

Adapted and modified from: W. G. Ouchi and A. M. Jaeger, "Type Z Organization: Stability In the Midst of Mobility." *Academy of Management Review* **3**, 1978, 305–314. Used with permission.

Mr. Yamada of Sony, Mr. Tanaka of Toyota, Ms. Ogawa of Honda, and so on.[12] The characteristics of Japanese organizations fit into a general pattern known as the "Nenko" system.

The **Nenko system** is the general pattern of management commonly used in large-scale Japanese organizations. The characteristics of the Nenko system are summarized in Table 4.1. The Nenko system is a natural outgrowth of the broader Japanese culture and economy.[13] It cannot easily be transferred to organizations in other cultural and economic environments, such as America with its relatively high emphasis on the value of individualism.

Nenko System

The Nenko system stresses *life-long employment* with a particular firm. After completing one's formal education, the individual joins an organization and is expected to remain until retirement — normally at about 55 years of age. Of course, the obligation is mutual. The large Japanese employer is not supposed to fire or lay off an employee, except in an extreme emergency.

Employment security

In practice, there has been some loosening up of this pattern of mutual life-long commitment. Some employers have successfully "raided" highly skilled employees from other firms. Employers also use a higher percentage of "temporary" employees who can be laid off. Even with these exceptions there is considerable job security. This is one of the reasons Japanese employees are probably more accepting of change, especially technological change, than American employees.

The amount of compensation and opportunities for promotion are heavily based on *seniority*, i.e., the length of an employee's service. This Nenko practice is widely accepted because many employees believe that competence (within a job) increases automatically with seniority. Many managers are compensated almost entirely on the basis of seniority. After a manager has reached about 45 years of age, heavier weight is given to performance and merit.

Emphasis on seniority

The possible implications of these contrasts between American and Japanese firms were noted by Morita Akio, President of the Sony Corporation. Akio observed:

> *Fortunately Japan has a lifetime employment system, which encourages the long-range view even among lower and middle management levels. For example, a member of our company may be stationed in some far-off land, struggling to learn in a country with entirely different customs and charac-*

teristics. But he realizes that with the knowledge he has gained in five years or so, he might become chief of the department in our head offfices that deals with this area, and that in ten years he may become director in charge of our international operations, and later have the chance of becoming a top executive of our company. He, therefore, is keenly interested in how strong the company will be in five or ten years from now, at the same time that he gives his attention to the business at hand. He is thus not only working constantly to achieve today's objectives but also paying close attention to what should be accumulated over the years ahead.[14]

Group loyalty

There is an intense sense of group loyalty and shared obligations under the Nenko system. Cooperation and working as a team is the standard. Individuals tend to think of themselves in terms of the groups to which they belong. This results in a strong feeling of duty and loyalty to the groups. Performance assessments for determining promotability (for people who meet the seniority test) give heavy weight to criteria such as flexibility, group support, and company loyalty. Japanese managers see their companies and its employees as an extension of their families. Long-term commitments by managers and employees to their organizations also encourage the long-term training and development of employees.

Group decision-making

Extensive use is made of a form of group decison-making leading to a group consensus. This consensus is aimed at *defining the questions* needing attention rather than at deciding what should be done. This process of group decision-making is much more time consuming than other methods, such as simply letting one person decide. However, implementation tends to be quicker, since people are more familiar with reasons why something is being done and the merits of doing it.

In Japanese organizations ideas often flow from the bottom up rather than just from the top down. The hierarchial chain of command is not nearly as clear cut as in U.S. firms. Anyone with a stake in a major problem or decison is consulted. A consensus is almost always reached by those involved before the decision is implemented. Even though there is a strong seniority system, anyone who is affected by a decision and has the ability to make a contribution is consulted. This means that younger employees are not cut out of the decision-making process simply because they don't have as much seniority as the older workers.

Notable exceptions

There are notable exceptions to the Nenko system in Japanese society. Highly capable and assertive individuals *do* leave their firms and start businesses of their own or join smaller organizations. Firms started by individualistic enterpreneurs include Honda Motor, Sony, and Matsushita, among others.

Moreover, the numerous small-scale Japanese enterprises (300 or fewer employees) do not and cannot afford to offer fringe benefits as extensive as those of the giants. They also offer less job security because these firms are less secure in their markets.

Some American workers appear to have a "what's-in-it-for-me?" attitude. This is sometimes a severe problem in dealing with workers who are members of labor unions. Some of this attitude probably stems from the belief and possible experience that management views its workers as mere "labor inputs" to be used in the most cost-efficient manner. The "what's-in-it-for-me?" attitude is unusual among Japanese workers because they are integral parts of their companies. Their attitude is more likely to be, "How can I help?"

James Hodgson, a former U.S. ambassador to Japan, captured the basic differences in the American and Japanese societies.

> American society is first and foremost underpinned by that venerable Judeo-Christian objective of individual justice. The Japanese, however, spurn individual justice as a priority goal. Instead they seek something in many ways the opposite; they seek group harmony. We American justice-seekers speak proudly of our rights. The harmony-minded Japanese stress not rights but relations. They reject our emphasis on individual rights as being divisive and disruptive.
>
> The distinction that emerges from all this may be capsulized simply. In American life the individual strives to stand out. The Japanese citizen, however, seeks to fit in. And fit in he does — into his family, his schools, his company, his union, his nation. Japan is a nation where the parts fit.
>
> We Americans make our national policy decisions and settle our many differences largely through adversary proceedings — we compete, we sue, and we vote. In Japan "adversarism" is out. Consensus is in, and it has been for centuries. The Japanese do not consider 51 percent a "majority," at least not a workable majority.[15]

These fundamental differences in broader societal values show themselves through the many differences in American and Japanese organizations. A number of these differences were highlighted in Table 4.1. Does this mean that American managers cannot transfer to their organizations any of the ideas that have worked so well in Japanese management? No! In fact, with appropriate changes, some of the processes of group decision-making have been successfully used in American firms. For example, as of 1980, 65 American firms (up from 15 firms in 1970) have adopted the use of "quality circles" from the Japanese.

Quality circles are small groups of employees that meet regularly and are trained to spot and solve production problems in their areas. Companies using quality circles include General Motors, Ford, Rockwell International, and American Airlines, among others.

The basic idea of the quality circle is quite simple. A plant steering committee, composed of labor and management, decides which area of a company could benefit from a circle. Eight to 10 workers are asked to serve in a circle. They meet once a week on company time with their immediate supervisor and with a person trained in personnel or industrial relations. This specialist trains the workers in data-gathering and in statistics. The circle members learn how to talk the language of management and to present their ideas to executives. In the motivation chapter, we will discuss why the circles motivate employees to perform better.

General Motors has over 100 quality circles operating in the plants of its Buick, Chevrolet, Fisher Body, Cadillac, and Oldsmobile divisions. "This isn't a fad," says Delmar L. Landen, GM's director of organizational research and development. "It's part of a fundamental shift toward a new outlook on worker participation in decision-making."[16]

The circle at a GM plant in Michigan decided it should do something about the large number of automobiles leaving the assembly line with flat tires. Their analysis eventually traced the problem to a defective tire stem. The part was replaced, and the company's annual saving turned out to be $225,000.

Competitive threats have motivated American firms to study the Japanese management practices that might be adapted. While quality circles are one type of useful adaptation, we doubt that the more fundamental characteristics of Japanese organizations (see Table 4.1) can be "plugged" into American operations. This is partly a result of the strong value of collectivism in Japan while America still has a comparatively strong value of individualism. These and other differences in values spill over to influence the character and form of political system influences.

In the previous chapter, the political environment of business firms, both in the U.S. and abroad, was characterized as turbulent, changing, and complex. A recent survey of U.S. corporate executives indicates that they see themselves on the *defensive*. They are struggling to maintain their company's position in America and the other countries in which they operate. Executives increasingly believe that they need to be trained to work in the political arena. This should help reduce their anxiety about political risk-taking. The interest in developing managerial skills for coping with the political environment is a natural outcome of the overwhelming support for future political action by American business. Over 88 percent of the responding executives agreed with the statement: "Since the institutions of government are the most important arenas within which social issues are resolved, corporations must seek access to these formal and informal structures in the same manner as do claimants with competing interests."[17]

One of the significant examples of political-system influences on American multinational and international corporations was the Foreign Corrupt Practices Act of 1977, passed by the United States Congress and signed into law by President Carter.

All of the political strategies identified in Chapter 3 for coping with powerful environmental components are used by firms operating in other countries. As you may recall, these political strategies include bargaining, lobbying, coalitions, representation, socialization, and cooptation. The discussions and negotiations leading up to the passage of the Foreign Corrupt Practices Act was accompanied by an extensive use of the bargaining and lobbying strategies. This legislation is an example of how businesses must deal with conflicting pressures from domestic vs. foreign political environments.

In 1975 and 1976, it was disclosed that some of the largest multinational business firms in the United States had paid millions of dollars in bribes to foreign politicans and government officials. The resulting furor and conflicting positions in the United States suggest the differences between a pragmatic value orientation and an ethical-moral value orientation. A person with a pragmatic value orientation is guided by a concern for whether a certain course of action will work and how successful it is likely to be. These individuals noted that people in certain other countries appear to accept bribery and "influence peddling" as a normal standard of conduct. For U.S. multinationals to compete, they needed to engage in these types of activities, even though it might be personally distasteful. The "pragmatists" are likely to say, "Who are we to say they are wrong for allowing this type of activity and we won't play by their rules in their country?" In contrast, a person with an ethical-moral value orientation is guided by a concern for whether a certain course of action is "right" or "wrong," "moral" or "immoral." These are defined by the commonly accepted values and standards of behavior within one's own society. Cliffton Garvin, Jr., chairman of Exxon, seemed to echo the ethical-moral value orientation in his statement:

> An overly ambitious employee might have the mistaken idea that we do not care how results are obtained, as long as he gets results. He might think it best not to tell higher management all that he is doing, not to record all transactions accurately. . . . He would be wrong on all counts. . . . We don't want liars for managers.[18]

**Foreign Corrupt
Practices Act of
1977**

The pluralistic (diverse) values within the United States resulted in much controversy and conflicting pressures in Congress over the desirability and form of legislation to "control" the acts of multinational and international corporations concerning bribes and influence peddling abroad. This controversy was settled, at least temporarily, with the passage of the Foreign Corrupt Practices Act of 1977. The provisions of this act suggest that the ethical-moral value orientation was the dominant force in the political arena in 1977.[19] One of the U.S. corporations receiving front page attention for bribing foreign officials was Lockheed Aircraft Corporation. The pragmatic value orientation of the individuals representing Lockheed's interest comes through loud and clear in the following case description.

CASE STUDY

Lockheed Aircraft Corporation*

In September of 1975, Daniel Haughton, president of Lockheed Aircraft Corporation, in testimony before the Senate Foreign Affairs Subcommittee on Multinational Corporations, stated that his company paid over $202 million in agent's commissions between 1970 and 1975. At least $22 million of these "commissions" were earmarked for bribes to foreign officials. Over half of total commissions went to one Saudi Arabian businessman, Adwan M. Khashoggi. Khashoggi reportedly was paid the sum of $106 million between 1970 and 1975. Much of his "commission" was forwarded to Saudi officials to win approval for aerospace sales in that country.

Commenting on the payments, Haughton stated, "Lockheed does not defend or condone the practice of payments to foreign officials. We only say that the practice exists, and that in many countries it appeared, as a matter of business judgment, necessary in order to compete against both U.S. and foreign competitors."

On October 9, 1975, the Securities and Exchange Commission (SEC) asked a federal court to order Lockheed, the nation's largest defense contractor, to produce documents which the agency said may show the "possible falsification of Lockheed corporate records and disbursement of millions of dollars of Lockheed funds through conduits, nominees, and by other means, to foreign governmental officials in connection with the acquisition of foreign business."

*Adapted from "Lockheed Aircraft Corporation." In R. Hay and E. Gray (eds.), *Business and Society: Cases and Text*. Cincinnati: South-Western Publishing Co., 1981, pp. 134 – 137. Used with permission.

On October 21, Lockheed admitted in a Washington federal district court to making "under-the-table payments" to promote sales in 15 foreign countries including at least one major nation in Western Europe.

On February 4, 1976, Senator Frank Church, chairman of the Senate Subcommittee on Multinational Corporations, released 146 pages of Lockheed internal documents. After the release of the information, an aide reportedly said to Senator Church, "Senator, in two hours you brought down more governments than Lenin did in a lifetime" The aide's remark, while obviously exaggerated, highlighted the political significance of the disclosures. In Japan for example, a parliamentary committee was established to investigate the alleged payoffs. The investigation, which ousted former Prime Minister Kakuei Tanaka, among others, concentrated attention on the 1972 governmental decision to switch from a plan to produce antisubmarine patrol planes domestically and instead import the Lockheed P3C.

There was a strong feeling among some Lockheed executives and industrial analysts that the company was "being made to pay for the sins of all the multinationals." One member of the Board stated that Lockheed was being treated unfairly because "foreign payoffs are too common and old" a practice to get very excited about. Many of Lockheed's 58,000 employees became angry over what they felt was unfair treatment of their company for what was considered to be common practice for many major corporations. Lockheed kept the workers informed of developments through inhouse newspapers, talks on public-address systems, and a special eight-page memo explaining rules governing foreign agents. At Lockheed, Gerald Sklarsky, president of the Engineers and Scientists Guild, said "We'll take our chances in the marketplace and win, if everybody plays by the same rules." Clyde Isham, a 49-year-old dispatcher, stated that he supported the company completely. "If I could spend $1 million to make $100 million, I'd do it, and if it brings jobs to us, I don't see any problem."

On February 13, 1976, Daniel Haughton, Lockheed board chairman, and A. Carl Kotchian, board vice-chairman, resigned at a special meeting of the Lockheed Board of Directors. The men, however, were retained as consultants and advisors for ten years at a "fair and generous amount although less than they were drawing." The board then named Robert Haack, a former president of the New York Stock Exchange, as temporary head of the company.

On March 3, 1976, Lockheed announced that the firm's future international activities would be directed from the home office. According to a

Lockheed spokesperson, "Lockheed International reported to the corporate organization, but it was a separate company. Now the international operations will come under the newly established vice-president for international marketing and will become a part of the corporate organization instead of being a separate company."

The investigations of Lockheed and several other multinationals influenced the provisions written into the Foreign Corrupt Practices Act of 1977.[20]

Basic provisions

On December 20, 1977, President Carter signed into law the Foreign Corrupt Practices Act. This act makes it a crime for American corporations to offer or provide payments to officials of foreign governments for the purpose of obtaining or retaining business. The act established record-keeping requirements for publicly held corporations. This is to make it difficult to conceal political payments prohibited by the Act.[21] Violators of this law, both corporations and managers, face stiff penalties. A company may be fined up to $1 million. Any of its managers who directly participated in violations of the Act or had reason to know of such violations, face up to five years in prison and/or $10,000 in fines.

The Act prohibits corporations from paying the fines imposed on their directors, managers, employees, or agents. The Act does not prohibit "grease" payments to foreign government employees whose duties are primarily ministerial or clerical. These payments are sometimes required to persuade the foreign government employees to perform their normal duties.[22]

Continuing controversy

Since its passage, this Act has been subjected to much critical analysis.[23] Many practical arguments have been advanced in favor of its repeal. An Export Disincentives Task Force was created by President Carter in 1978 to recommend ways of improving exports from the United States. This Task Force identified the Foreign Corrupt Practices Act as a major contributor to economic and political losses in the United States. Economic losses were claimed to come from a reduced ability of American corporations to do business abroad. Political losses were claimed to come from the creation of a "holier-than-thou image" in relation to other countries.[24] With the shifts in the political environment in Washington, D.C. in 1981, we would not be surprised to see revisions in this Act.

The Foreign Corrupt Practices Act of 1977 is only one of many possible illustrations of the strain and tension that often exists between U.S. managers in their relations with the federal executive and legislative branches of government. Quite a different picture emerges in Japan. The Japanese government believes in taking a more "pragmatic" view in dealing with its multinationals and other societies. In contrast, the United States government is claimed to be more "idealistic" in its worldwide dealings and attempts to force this idealism on the way U.S. multinationals operate abroad.[25]

While the relations between the business and government sectors have been more harmonious in Japan than those in the United States, they have not been without tension and conflict. The Japanese government restricted overseas investments by Japanese firms until 1971. Of course, the government has long supported and encouraged exports. Large and small firms successfully lobbied the Japanese government to permit greater expansion abroad by lifting the ceilings on the size of foreign investments.[26] There was considerable conflict between the Japanese business managers and government bureaucrats who feared increased foreign investment would not be in the national interest. The Japanese businessmen claimed the national interest, not their own welfare, as the overriding justification for increased foreign investment. They sensed other nations would not tolerate the political situation of the Japanese simply sending exports to their shores as well as importing needed raw materials from them.

The leaders of Japan's business and government are members of a relatively unified elite. They come from a society with a dominant value of collectivism. They believe strongly in the importance of the group and discount the significance of individualism as we know it. They often graduate from the same universities that further socialize them into a common set of values. The group-oriented Japanese leaders in business and government follow a spirit of consensus and compromise.[27]

Japan must import 99.7% of its oil, as well as almost all the coal, iron ore, and other raw materials. To soften the blow of rising commodities prices, business and government have pursued a policy of slowing the growth of resource-intensive industries such as steel and petrochemicals. The government's plan is to channel more of the nation's capital into "knowledge-intensive" industries such as microelectronics and computers. When the government decides to encourage an industry, the state-owned Japan Development Bank makes low-interest loans to manufacturers and suppliers in the field. Private bankers know that the government also expects them to give easy credit. Companies working on a new technology can get a 50 percent government subsidy, provided they turn over the basic patents to the Ministry of International Trade and Industry (MITI). MITI then offers the technology, for a small royalty, to any Japanese manufacturer.[28]

Assessing Political Risk

An issue of increasing concern to all multinational corporations is the political risk associated with their present or proposed investments in foreign countries. **Political risk** is the probability of occurrence of some political event that will change the profitability of a given investment. One aerospace executive expressed his perceptions of increasing political risks for managers, both in the United States and abroad, in these pessimistic words:

> *Restrictions on the activities of multinational companies are being proposed and will, to a serious degree, be adopted in almost every country. These take the form of increased taxation, restrictions on the transfer of technology, antitrust regulations, restrictions on foreign ownership, restrictions on repatriation of capital and earnings, restrictions on imports and exports (both tariff and nontariff barriers), and restrictions on the employment of expatriate personnel, to mention some important ones.*

> *Besides these specific problems, there are, of course, the general problems of rampant inflation, protectionism in the United States, economic nationalism almost everywhere, an outdated monetary system, a basic distrust of big business, a questioning of the validity of the profit motive of the system as a whole. In the United States, there is a basic absence of cooperation between business and government, and increasing curbs on mergers, acquisitions, financial activities, and management prerogatives.*

Political risk factors

Various techniques have been developed for assessing political risks. These techniques may involve the assessment of several hundred political, economic, and sociocultural factors in a particular country. The hundreds of variables that may be analyzed can generally be classified under four major factors. As suggested in Fig. 4.1, these factors include domestic instability, foreign conflict, political climate, and economic climate. These political risk factors are defined as follows:[29]

1. Domestic instability refers to the subversion, rebellion, and turmoil within the nation. Variables in this category are riots, purges, assassinations, guerilla wars, and government crises.

2. Foreign conflict refers to the degree a nation shows hostility toward other nations. This could range from diplomatic expulsions to outright war.

3. Political climate refers to the degree to which a government is likely to swing to the far left or far right. Typical variables in this category are size of the communist party, socialist seats in the legislature, and the role of the military in the political process.

4. Economic climate refers to the degree of market and financial risks associated with investments. Included in this category are the government's thoughts about clamping regulatory and economic controls on the firm (such

4.1
Factors influencing the
political risk of investments

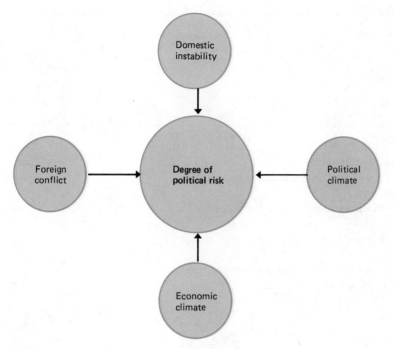

as wage and price controls) as well as the ability to manage its own economic affairs (such as inflation and debt levels).

In sum, political risks and economic concerns with foreign investments often show themselves through a wide range of restrictions, controls, and threats. Some of the specific categories of restrictions, controls, and threats are highlighted in Table 4.2.

U.S. multinationals consider political risks, not just economic risks, in their investment and other managerial decisions. For example, Gulf Oil was hard hit by the wave of nationalization of its assets in the Arab countries in 1975. Gulf then established a four person international studies unit. This unit evaluates the changing political risks where it has assets or is considering to invest. Gulf's international studies unit warned of the Shah of Iran's probable fall four months in advance and well before it was widely anticipated. Gulf was able to begin early planning to cope with the loss of Iranian oil. This amounted to 10 percent of Gulf's crude supplies.[30] U.S. and other multinational managers face fiercer competition abroad and their power to control the political environments of other nations have diminished. Thus, they have only one choice — to get wiser about the world.

*Management
implications*

4.2
Some Types of
Restrictions, Controls,
and Threats that may
be Encountered by
Foreign Operations of
U.S. Firms

■ Threat of nationalization and expropriation.

■ Limitations on the expansion of foreign operations.

■ Limitations on the percent of ownership of foreign operations by U.S. firms.

■ Nationality restrictions on who can serve as managers and directors of foreign subsidiaries.

■ Requirements to purchase needed materials and supplies from the host country, regardless of quality.

■ Restrictions on the amount of dividends from foreign operations that can be returned to the parent company.

■ Controls over the prices that can be charged.

■ Controls on the amount of imports and exports.

■ Restrictions on flows of capital into and out of host countries.

■ Threat of war or political upheaval within the country.

SUMMARY   This chapter had the goal of making you somewhat wiser about international influences on management. We lightly sampled several influences on U.S. multinationals and attempted to provide some sensitivity about how the practice of management in other countries can differ from that in the United States. This was achieved by showing how value and political system influences operate in Japan as compared to America. Of course, multinational corporations operate in many countries, each with its own traditions, values, and political patterns. The complex and changing international environment requires multinational managers to have a degree of flexibility and freedom in managing foreign subsidiaries to respond to subtle or major differences in various countries. Worldwide turbulence also requires managers to constantly monitor and assess the political risks in the countries with subsidiaries or with whom major import or export transactions take place.

This chapter focused on developing your skills to successfully fulfill the *liaison* and *monitor* managerial roles. The *liaison role* involves dealing with people outside the organization to gather information that can affect the organization's success. The opening case suggests the many changes made at Westinghouse to improve its liaison capabilities in world business. The explanation of Japanese values and patterns of management should improve your sensitivity in relating to those from countries with many different value systems, not just those of Japan. The *monitor role* is concerned with scanning the environment for information that may affect the organization's performance. The entire discussion of political system influences should increase your monitoring skills with respect to international business.

Management practices and the forces operating on organizations do vary widely from nation to nation. These differences are influenced by values, political considerations, and the economic circumstances of the particular country. Of course, similarities also exist.[31] Many of the concepts, models, and techniques presented in the following management-process chapters will be useful in most countries. However, the concepts and techniques in the behavioral-processes chapters must be carefully evaluated and adapted to the values and expectations of the specific foreign country. We hope this chapter has served to stimulate your interest in and appreciation of the rich and varied world of multinational management.

KEYWORDS

collectivism   *multinational corporation*
domestic instability   *Nenko system*
economic climate   *political climate*
foreign conflict   *political risk*
international corporation   *quality circles*

**DISCUSSION
QUESTIONS**

1. Should managers in your country try to adopt more of the characteristics identified for Japanese organizations in Table 4.1? Explain.

2. Would you like to see more of the "collectivism" value, as discussed for Japan, in this country?

3. What problems do you anticipate with the organizational changes made by Westinghouse?

4. Should the Foreign Corrupt Practices Act be eliminated or changed? Explain.

5. Should your government and business managers become more cooperative, similar to the way they are in Japan? Explain.

6. Would you like to work under the Nenko system? Explain.

7. Was Lockheed Aircraft Corporation wrong in giving bribes to secure orders from other countries? Explain.

8. What do you see as the major political risks for a foreign multinational firm considering the establishment of a subsidiary in your country?

9. Which of the global environmental trends do you think will be most important for multinational corporations over the next 10 years?

10. Evaluate the statement: "Multinational corporations care only about their own interests and really don't have loyalty to any country. Thus, we should do everything to control them and limit their growth."

Management Incidents and Cases

THE NEW BOSS*
"That little Jap is the boss?" Pete asked. "Him? With that broken English? Wow!"

Jason nodded. "He sure is. Mr. Noritake Kobayashi, general manager of the North American AKT Company. Remember, we got taken over by them last year. You've been out in the sticks at the Kokomo plant, so you haven't been around to see the takeover. He came in a month ago."

"I didn't see any announcement," Pete commented.

"Oh, it was very quiet. Our new owners aren't the least bit anxious to rock the boat. But Nori is the boss, just the same."

"Nori, huh. You seem to be on close enough terms with the little fellow."

Pete nodded. "He likes to run an informal office. He thinks that we Americans like it that way."

"Trying to be one of the boys, heh? Boy, Pete, I'm old enough to remember World War II — I was in it in the Pacific. The last Japs I saw were shooting at me."

"You're old, Jason. Nobody's been shooting for 30 years."

Jason nodded. "I know. But sometimes it's hard to change. If anyone had told me ten years ago that I'd be working for a Jap ... wow!"

"Don't sell Nori short, Jason. He's a very, very sharp manager. You know all the trouble we were in — that's why we got taken over. Losses mounting, inventories a mess, the whole works. Well, Nori has just about turned it around. Give him six more months, and this place will really be a profitable operation."

Jason nodded slowly. "I'll take your word for it. Lord knows, it was a mess before." He stared at Pete. "Hey, I may be an old has-been, but you were hoping to move up. I remember you talking about how some day you might even be president of this outfit. How about that now?"

---

*From: R. Farmer, *Incidents In International Business*. 2nd ed. Bloomington, IN: Cedarwood Press, 1975, pp. 60 – 62. Reproduced by permission of Cedarwood Press, Bloomington, Indiana. All rights reserved.

Pete shrugged his shoulders. "We're a Japanese outfit now, even though we operate in the United States. Do you know how many top managers of Japanese firms are Americans?"

"No."

"Just about none. Oh, I may make the top in the North American division — they brought over Nori and a couple of top level engineers. Boy, are those guys good! They really did some sensational things in the Newark plant, and they are just getting started. But I doubt very much that I'll ever get to Tokyo, at the top of the company. It just doesn't happen that way."

"Does it bother you, Pete?"

"It scares me, Jason. Nori is better than I am, and I thought I was pretty good. I used to think that all the good managers were Americans, but I sure found out differently. I sure have."

Questions

1. Would you work for a Japanese manager in the United States? Why or why not?

2. Would you work for a foreign-owned company in the United States, when you were 99 percent sure that you wouldn't make it to the very top of the company? Why or why not?

3. The North American AKT Company is now Japanese owned. What long-term North American personnel strategy should they follow, in terms of nationalities who manage this company? Why?

THE HYPER-
NATIONALISTS*

"We were planning to start a modest operation in X (naming an African country, recently made independent)," Mr. Thomas of the Westport Packing Company commented. "We have been expanding our pineapple production, and in searching for likely areas where we could produce the crop, we found that X had everything in its favor. The soil and climate were just right, and even the highway system in the area was quite good. We could have set up a packing and canning plant, contracted with local farmers and landowners for the crop, and given them good technical advice and assistance to help them over the rough early years. Our total investment would have been over $35 million.

"Of course, we would have come out all right, too — we estimated our rate of return at over 30 percent on equity. But local expenditures would have run at an annual rate of over $35 million, and virtually all of this would have

*From: R. Farmer, *Incidents in International Business*. 2nd ed. Bloomington, IN: 1975, pp. 26–28. Reproduced by permission of Cedarwood Press, Bloomington, Indiana. All rights reserved.

gone to local farmers, truckers, landowners, packing-plant workers and supervisors, and so on. X would have almost doubled its foreign exchange earnings as well, and we were to pay a 50 percent net profits tax to the local government, which would have given the government about $8.5 million a year in hard currencies.

"Last year, we were well along in our negotiations on this project. The local government was quite enthusiastic about its potential, and it was attempting to get a law through the local parliament which would give us what we needed, particularly in marketing arrangements. X has a very poor contract-law structure, and some clarifications were needed before we could sign proper contracts with growers."

Mr. Thomas tossed a batch of newspaper clippings on his desk. "When the project was made public, we began to see this sort of material (see Attachment). Within a month, the American Embassy was attacked by a mob, another American trading company in X was boycotted, and a major demonstration was mounted in the capital against the parliament. The new contract bill was quietly blocked in committee, and we decided not to go forward with the project.

"Since then, we've changed our plans, and we will expand in Hawaii." He sighed: "You have no idea of how expensive good pineapple land is now in Hawaii. Our costs will be much higher than they would be in X. However, at least we can be sure that our workers and managers will be safe, and that our operations will not be sabotaged by nationalist radicals."

Attachment: News Items From Magazines and Papers in X

From the New Leader!

"For over 100 years, we were subject to colonialism and neo-slavery. Only in the past three years have we been free to control our own destiny. Now our own government is trying to sell us back into slavery. The profit-mad, blood-sucking American capitalists will enslave us as surely as night follows day. While these plutocrats take our life blood from our land, we will get some pittance for our share. Even now, our parliament debates a new contract law which will make slaves of every poor farmer who will be ensnared by lavish promises. This law must be defeated!"

From Freedom:

"The only useful thing to do with the mad dog capitalist exploiters from the Westport Company is to kill them all, before they kill us over a few years. Any fool who cooperates with these monsters should also be shot like a dog. Our farmlands are ours, not the property of exploiters from abroad!"

"We are admittedly poor — our GNP per capita is among the lowest in the world. However, we prefer to starve before we will allow neo-colonialists the pleasure of destroying our economy by taking over our agriculture. It is far better to be poor and free than to gain wealth and lose our souls."

"Land reform is receiving a new setback in the pending contract-law changes before parliament. The Westport American company seeks changes which will make farmers slaves of their operations. Of course, they point glibly to huge profits to be made by landowners and farmers as a result of their plans. But we all know exactly what will happen — it is all so dreary, so very familiar. They promise much, and they will produce nothing. Our farmers will starve, while the monopoly capitalists squeeze the last penny from them. Of course, Westport will take millions home to the United States. And of course Europeans and Americans will enjoy the pineapples that will be produced by the sweat of our farmers' brows. And perhaps even a few of our own politicians will get a new Cadillac or Mercedes as a sop for allowing our wealth to flow abroad.

"We know these white men, and we know these Americans. We know how our very best young men have been discriminated against in Washington and New York for being black. We know how they have been sent to the worst colleges, the poorest in America, because they were Africans. We know all too well how white men have enslaved us for over a century. We know of broken promises, shoddy dealings, exploitation, and misery. We know that our educated young men are employed, while Westport intends to bring in more white Americans to manage their plants and farms. Now we are free — let us remain free! Go, demonstrate, fight for your freedom — now!"

1. Why do you think that citizens of a newly independent African state would react so strongly to Westport's proposal? Do you think that Westport could have done anything (in public relations) to soften their feelings? What?

2. If Westport wanted to establish an operation which did not involve agricultural land (such as a straight manufacturing operation), do you think that the reaction would have been so violent? Why or why not?

3. Suppose you had to advise the leaders of X, who are very anxious to develop their economy. What would you suggest as workable methods of convincing local citizens that foreign companies usually create more wealth and development? What arguments might be effective here?

REFERENCES

1. H. Menzies, "Westinghouse Takes Aim at the World," *Fortune* **101,** *1,* 1980, 48–53.

2. A. Chandler, *The Visible Hand: The Managerial Revolution In American Business.* Cambridge: Harvard University Press, 1977, pp. 368–369.

3. R. Mueller, "Thinking Internationally: The Importance of Being Strategic." in E. Curtiss and P. Untersee (eds.), *Corporate Responsibilities and Opportunities to 1990.* Lexington: Lexington Books, 1979, pp. 25–32.

4. "Japanese Multinationals: Covering the World with Investment," *Business Week* June 16, 1980, 92–102.

5. L. Curry and J. Hildreth, "Japan's Goods Hurting More," *Houston Chronicle*, September 24, 1980, 1, 10.

6. Ibid., 10.

7. W. Givins and W. Rapp, "What It Takes To Meet The Japanese Challenge," *Fortune* **99,** 12, 1979, 104–120.

8. Curry and Hildreth, *loc. cit.*

9. M. Tharp, "Tokyo, After Buying Technology for Years, Now Exports Its Own," *The Wall Street Journal* **65,** 122, 1980, 1, 12.

10. S. Uemura, *Japanese Business Organizations and Environmental Changes.* The Research Institute, Momoyama Gakuin University, 1979.

11. R. Rehder, "Japanese Management: An American Challenge," *Human Resource Management* **18,** 4, 1979, 21–27.

12. T. Ozawa, "Japanese World of Work: An Interpretive Survey. *MSU Business Topics* **28,** 2, 1980, 45–55.

13. T. Oh, "Japanese Management — A Critical Review," *Academy of Management Review* **1,** 1975, 13–25.

14. F. Gibney, *Japan: The Fragile Super Power.* Tokyo: Charles F. Tuttle Co., 1975, p. 206.

15. J. Hodgson, *The Wondrous Working World of Japan.* Washington, D.C. American Enterprise Institute, 1978, p. 3.

16. E. Gottschalk, Jr., "U.S. Firms, Worried by Productivity Lag, Copy Japan In Seeking Employees' Advice," *The Wall Street Journal* **65,** 3, 1980, 40.

17. "How Companies React to the Ethics Issue," *Business Week*, February 9, 1975, 155.

18. Ibid., 78.

19. N. Jacoby, P. Nehemkis, and R. Eells, *Bribery and Extortion In World Business.* New York: Macmillan, 1977.

20. "Lockheed Aircraft Corporation." In R. Hay, and E. Gray (eds.), *Business and Society: Cases and Text.* Cincinnati: South-Western Publishing Co., 1981, pp. 134–137.

21. M. Pastin and M. Hooker, "Ethics and The Foreign Corrupt Practices Act, *Business Horizons* **23,** 6, 1980, 43–47.

22. H. Baruch, "The Foreign Corrupt Practices Act," *Harvard Business Review* **57,** 1, 1979, 32–50.

23. D. Gustman, "The Foreign Corrupt Practices Act of 1977," *The Journal of International Law and Economics* **13,** 1979, 367–401.

24. Pastin and Hooker, *loc. cit.*

25. Y. Hara, "Cultural Roots of Japan–U.S. Economic Friction," *Japan Echo* **6,** 3, 1979, 23–31.

26. T. Yoshi, *The Japanese Are Coming.* Cambridge: Ballinger Publishing Co., 1976.

27. M. Yoshino, *Japan's Multinational Enterprises.* Cambridge: Harvard University Press, 1975.

28. "Capitalism in Japan," *Time* **115,** 16, 1980, 52–53.

29. D. Haendel, *Foreign Investments and The Management of Political Risk.* Boulder, CO: Westview Press, 1979.

30. L. Kraar, "The Multinationals Get Smarter About Political Risks," *Fortune* **101,** 6, 1980, 86–100.

31. J. Daniels, E. Ogram, Jr., and L. Radebaugh, *International Business: Environments and Operations* (2nd ed). Reading MA: Addison-Wesley, 1979.

*Part III presents two of the four basic management processes —
planning and organization design — developed in this book. Part III
flows naturally from the preceding part since planning and organization design are directly affected by the organization's environment.
Additional environmental influences are identified in the two planning chapters and the two organization-design chapters as appropriate.*

*Chapter 5, "Strategic Planning Concepts and Approaches," primarily
takes a top management view of planning. The nature of strategic
planning, operational planning, and strategies are explained. The
reasons for engaging in planning and the conditions under which
planning is likely to be effective are described. The chapter focuses
on the steps and key issues in the strategic planning process. The
roles of market, technological, and political influences on defining
the nature of the organization and setting basic goals are examined.
For example, the strategies and functional areas emphasized are
likely to change with different stages of the product/service life cycle
— introduction, growth, maturity, decline, and termination. The alternative market/investment strategies available to top management
are developed. These include: grow and penetrate, defend and hold,
rebuild, harvest, and divest and exit. Finally, the dominant thrusts
used by top-level managers for implementing the market/investment
strategies are described. The four top management strategies discussed are: executive dominated, innovation dominated, production
dominated, and marketing dominated.*

*Chapter 6, "Planning Aids and Techniques," develops four areas of
planning — forecasting, managing by objectives, scheduling, and*

152

Part III

budgeting — that are often of concern in both strategic and operating planning. Scenarios, the Delphi technique, and simulation models are examined as forecasting aids and techniques. Management by Objectives is presented as one philosophy, system, and process for integrating strategic planning, operational planning, and day-to-day decision-making into a unified whole. The Program Evaluation and Review Technique (PERT) is described as a common planning aid, especially for purposes of scheduling. The most noble or creative ideas or objectives must eventually come face-to-face with a basic economic question: What are the specific costs of the resources needed to achieve the stated objective(s)? Budgeting is the process for determining and assigning the required resources. Zero-base budgeting is presented as one approach for justifying activities and programs in terms of efficiency, effectiveness, and relative priorities.

Organization design is the management process that flows naturally out of planning. This is because organization designs provide a primary means for managers to put their strategic and operational plans into action.

Chapter 7, "Organizational Designs: Basic Concepts," puts forth the basic alternative ways for grouping tasks and personnel to achieve the organization's objectives. Four traditional strategies of departmentation are reviewed: by function, by place, by product, and by customer. Once the organization tasks and people are divided up into these different bases of departmentation, they must be pulled back together again. Thus, three traditional concepts of coordination are reviewed: unity of command, scalar principle, and span of control. These concepts of coordination are given concrete meaning through the authority structure. The authority structure is a function of the power, responsibility, and accountability for each position and level in the organization. Line and staff relationships are reviewed in terms of types of staff authority (advisory, compulsory advice, concurring authority, or command authority), line and staff conflicts, and the location of staff units in organizations.

Chapter 8, "Organizational Design: Contingency Approaches," builds on the previous chapter by explaining how differences in the technology and environment should influence the choice of organization designs. The contingency approach in this chapter identifies four types of task environments for the organization as a whole and its various divisions or subsidiaries. The task environments identified include: simple and stable, simple and changing, complex and stable, and complex and changing. The organization design appropriate to each of these task environments is described. For example, the managers of an organization with a complex and changing task environment may find an organic management system operating through a matrix organization design to be effective.

Chapter 5

STRATEGIC PLANNING CONCEPTS AND APPROACHES

After reading this chapter, you should be able to:

1. Define strategic planning, operational planning, and strategies.

2. Describe when planning is likely to be effective or ineffective.

3. List the critical issues that are normally a part of strategic planning.

4. Identify the step-by-step activities in strategic planning.

5. Describe alternative market/investment strategies used by firms.

6. List the four basic types of management strategies that can dominate top-level managerial decision-making.

PREVIEW CASE

Sambo's Versus Denny's*

Sambo's and Denny's are both similar-sized West-Coast-based restaurant chains. As of 1980 and early 1981, both were lagging behind the family restaurant/coffee shop segment of the restaurant industry in terms of sales per restaurant outlet, average sales per customer served, and average number of customers served per restaurant. Both had relatively new chief executive officers. Daniel Shaughnessy was appointed the chief executive officer of Sambo's in late 1979 and Vern Curtis was appointed CEO of Denny's in mid-1980. Shaughnessy was appointed from the outside; Curtis was promoted from the executive vice president's position. Sambo's had sales of about $600 million and 1120 units; Denny's had sales of $720 million and 1700 units (about 900 of which are Winchell's Donut Houses.)

Sambo's overall strategy has been to cut overhead and attempt to bring in new customers. However, its strategic plans have appeared to work

---

* Since this was written, "Sambo's" has changed the name of its restaurants in the northeastern United States to "No Place Like Sam's."

against each other and, at times, seemed to represent a scattershot approach. Let's review Sambo's strategic decisions and actions.

1. Shaughnessy slashed supervisory and management personnel. Five regional vice presidents and 55 territorial managers were replaced with 11 regional vice presidents, each with a small staff. Twenty-five hundred of some 4000 employees he considered unnecessary were also cut, but he backed off on eliminating the remaining 1500.

2. The level of management skill has been lowered by recruiting only high school graduates as management trainees at $12,000 per year plus bonus.

3. Incentive compensation for store managers has been changed from bonuses based on profits to bonuses based on gross store sales, then to bonuses based on sales improvement. Some store managers apparently believe these changes have been designed to make it more difficult for them to get bonuses. Turnover in restaurant managers has shot up, with some units having a half-dozen managers in 1980. A restaurant chain executive at another firm claims: "Building back morale at Sambo's is going to take years."

4. A scattershot approach has been taken to attract customers from other fast food restaurants. One of the basic strategic goals is to increase the average per-customer ticket of $2.20. This requires that Sambo's decrease the dependency on breakfast sales, which make up 60 percent of total sales. Yet, competitors have noted that Sambo's has been using its advertising dollars to promote 99¢ discount breakfasts and 20 percent discounts for senior citizens. Moreover, Shaughnessy claims that Sambo's wants to take on fast-food firms like McDonald's "head-to-head" by promoting a triple-decker hamburger called the Samburger. This appears to represent a shift from being a middle-market family restaurant. An executive at Denny's commented: "Nobody knows what Sambo's is trying to be."

As of early 1981, Sambo's had not made progress in dealing with its problems. Shaughnessy commented: "The condition of the company has surprised us." He claims it may take eight years before Sambo's is returned to financial health. This is generally regarded as a long time in this type of consumer market.

The overall strategy by Denny's is in stark contrast to Sambo's. Denny's strategy for coping with its problems was to: improve appeals to the broad middle segment of the family restaurant market by: (1) broadening its menu; (2) reducing planned expansions and closing down poor performers; (3) retaining and fine-tuning its operating strategies. Let's review Denny's strategic decisions and actions.

1. Curtis has only fine-tuned Denny's multiple levels of management, which are designed to insure consistency and quality. Denny's has 14 regional managers, 120 district managers, 825 managers, and 1500 assistant managers. Most Denny's have two assistant managers, where only the largest Sambo's have two assistants. Denny's assistant managers must complete a 10-week basic program. After a year, an assistant manager is eligible to become a store manager.

2. Incentive programs to encourage entrepreneurship by store managers and others have been improved.

3. Denny's has promoted specials such as a New York steak dinner for $5.95 and a Super Bird grilled turkey sandwich for $2.69. It is also adding beer and wine to the menu. The firm is evaluating and may experiment with a chicken concept. Curtis comments: "There may be room in this world for one more good chicken concept." All of their efforts have been designed to boost traffic and customer tickets. The average customer tab went from $2.52 in 1979 to $2.75 in 1980. But, it is still below the family restaurant industry average of $3.41.[1]

The Sambo and Denny case studies provide some insight into the nature of strategies and strategic planning in action. The cases suggest how market competition and declining profits can motivate top managers to reevaluate the firm's strategies. We also see the role top managers play in strategy formulation. Curtis has fine-tuned Denny's overall strategy and made decisions that were consistent with each other. In contrast, there appears to be confusion in the overall strategy at Sambo's and inconsistencies in decisions. Sambo's wanted to increase sales per customer but spent considerable advertising dollars in promoting discount 99¢ breakfasts.

These cases clearly suggest that the top executives are normally quite involved in the strategic planning process. The effectiveness of the specific strategies can have a dramatic impact on the organization. These impacts can range from growth to stagnation to possible failure. You might want to determine the current effects of the strategies at Denny's and Sambo's and possible changes in them.

INTRODUCTORY QUESTIONS

Planning refers to the formal process of making decisions that are intended to affect the future.[2] All planning is decision-making, but not all decision-making is planning. Planning, as an area of decision-making, incorporates several special characteristics: anticipatory decision-making, a system of decisions, and the creation of goals and objectives.[3] *Anticipatory decision-making* is deciding what to do and how to do it *before* action is required. Although this process can be highly informal, our focus is on formal planning which precedes action. The *system of decisions* refers to the interconnections between one decision and other decisions. The decision to obtain a college degree creates the need for dozens of other interrelated decisions: e.g., which college to attend, when to start, and where to live. The system of decisions has no simple beginning or ending point.

Many firms like General Electric encourage their managers to think of planning as a way of life on a year-around, day-to-day basis. This contrasts with the view that planning is simply the activity of preparing the annual plan a couple of months before the new year. The *creation of desired goals and objectives* is also a special characteristic of planning.

In the 1950s Kresge's set a goal to move into the discount business. The key managers of Kresge's forecast this to be a rapidly growing market and observed there were no national discount store chains. As a result of creating their new goal, K-Mart Stores literally blanket the United States today.

There are two major types of planning processes — strategic planning and operational planning.

Strategic planning refers to the process of: (1) analyzing the environment; (2) defining the nature of the organization; (3) formulating basic goals; and (4) identifying, evaluating, and selecting the fundamental courses of action for the organization.

Strategic planning is concerned with basic questions that define the organization's nature and purpose.[4] The management at Denny's stated that their firm's basic purpose and strategy is to serve the middle segment of the family restaurant market. A sampling of basic questions considered in the strategic planning process is suggested in Table 5.1. These include such questions as: (1) What business are we in? (2) What business should we be in? (3) What important fundamental changes are taking place in the firm's environment? (4) To what opportunities should the firm's resources be committed? As you read down the list in Table 5.1, the questions move from a focus on the current strategy to associated problems and missed opportunities to new possible strategies to the selection of a specific strategy.

The distinctions between strategic planning and operational planning are not always clear cut. **Operational planning** generally focuses on: (1) the detailed means of implementing the broader goals and strategies that have al-

5.1
*Sampling of Questions
and Issues Considered
in Strategic Planning*

1. *Record current strategy:*
- What is the current strategy?
- What kind of business does management want to operate?
- What kind of business does management feel it ought to operate?

3. *Identify problems with the current strategy:*
- Are trends discernible in the environment that may become threats and/or missed opportunities if the current strategy is continued?
- Is the company having difficulty implementing the current strategy?
- Is the attempt to carry out the current strategy disclosing significant weaknesses and/or unutilized strengths in the company?

3. *Discover the core of the strategy problem:*
- Does the current strategy require greater competence and/or resources than the company possesses?
- Does it lack sufficient competitive advantage?
- Will it fail to exploit opportunities and/or meet threats in the environment, now or in the future?

4. *Formulate alternative new strategies:*
- What possible alternatives exist for solving the strategy problem?
- To what extent do the company's competence and resources limit the number of alternatives that should be considered?
- To what extent do management's preferences limit the alternatives?

5. *Evaluate alternative new strategies:*
- Which alternative *best* solves the strategy problem?
- Which alternative offers the *best* match with the company's competence and resources?
- Which alternative offers the *greatest* competitive advantage?

6. *Choose a new strategy:*
- What is the *relative significance* of each of the preceding considerations?
- What should the new strategy be?

ready been determined; (2) the means for improving and coordinating current operations; and (3) the allocation of resources to established functions, especially through the annual budgeting process.[5] For example, the product manager of Crest Toothpaste must develop annual and quarterly operational plans concerning sales forecasts, advertising, production, and needed sales representatives.

Despite their different focuses, strategic and operational planning must be tied together to have a well-designed planning system.[6] Each type of planning provides the basis for the other. Bell and Howell has incorporated operational and strategic plans into one overall company plan. A 60-month (five-year) "moving" plan consists of both strategic and operational plans for all parts of the organization; the "moving" plans are reanalyzed and updated quarterly.[7]

Strategies are the patterns of important decisions that: (1) guide the organization in its environment; (2) influence the structure and processes of the organization; and (3) centrally affect the profitability, growth, and survival of the organization.[8] The key decisions in strategy formulation are referred to as strategies. When taken together, these strategies represent the overall organization strategy.[9] A strategy or set of strategies are outputs from the strategic planning process. Our discussion of Denny's and Sambo's referred to key decisions (specific strategies) that were made as part of each organization's overall strategy for dealing with the decline in profits and stagnant growth. With Denny's, we suggested that the specific strategies seemed to add up to a consistent organization strategy. With Sambo's, it appeared that some of the key decisions worked against each other and were not likely to improve their market or profit position.

What are strategies?

The concepts of strategy and strategic planning are relatively straightforward in firms with one or two products or services, such as Denny's and Sambo's. For firms operating in multiple markets, with numerous products or services, these concepts are much more complicated. In 1981, ITT had 250 separate companies and operating divisions. Its products and services are wide-ranging — including telecommunications equipment (ITT Telecommunications), baked goods (Continental Baking), insurance (Hartford Fire Insurance Co.) and hotel accommodations (Sheraton Hotels), among others. With so many firms and over $25 billion in sales, strategic planning and the development of strategies is far different for ITT's top executives from what it is for the top executives of Sambo's and Denny's. ITT's top executives have been contemplating the strategic questions of "How should we grow and by how much?" Up until about 1979, the overall goal was fast growth. ITT did this through the strategy of acquiring other companies. Since that time, there has been somewhat of a shift toward internal growth and divesting the corporation of the poorer performers. During 1979 and 1980, 34 companies and divisions were shut down or sold off.[10] These firms were sold for $638 million. The top executives of ITT spend much of their time determining what lines of business they should be in. Their strategic planning focuses on the assessment, modification, and approval of the strategic plans submitted to them by those heading up ITT's 250 or so companies and divisions.

In a large and diverse organization like ITT, the component companies and divisions are often called strategic business units.[11] A ***strategic business unit*** is a division or company within an organization that provides relqted products or services to a particular market. Several of the strategic business units at ITT include Continental Baking Company, Hartford Fire Insurance Company, and Sheraton Hotels. Denny's corporation actually has two strategic business units — the chain of Denny's restaurants and the chain of Winchell's Donut Houses. In contrast, Sambo's is in one line of business. For Sambo's, the strategic business unit and the whole corporation are one and the same. Much of this chapter focuses on strategies and strategic planning at the strategic business unit level.

5.1

Overview of planning

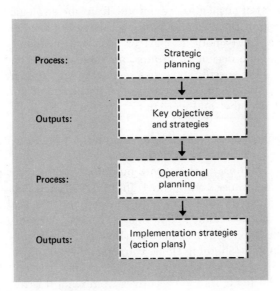

Figure 5.1 provides an overview of business planning. The process of strategic planning creates outputs in the form of key objectives and strategies. Operational planning is the process of translating general company or division strategies and objectives into detailed implementation strategies. The implementation strategies are also outputs. They can be in the form of detailed budgets, departmental action plans, proposed changes in organization design, control techniques, and the like.

Organizations can survive only if they are able to manage change. Organizations that manage change well will progress and grow. As the rate of change and complexity of the business world increases, new and better ways must be found to understand, anticipate, and respond to changes. Planning is a key management process for helping organizations to maintain stability, adapt to change, and create change.

Figure 5.2 suggests that the three primary objectives of planning are to: (1) identify opportunities that will occur in the future; (2) anticipate and avoid future problems; and (3) develop courses of action. If these planning objectives are achieved, there is a better chance that the organization will maintain its stability, will adapt to and create desirable changes, and will improve the effectiveness of employees and managers. All of these outcomes are desired because they should lead to the long-term growth, survival, and profitability of the organization.

Why Engage in Planning?

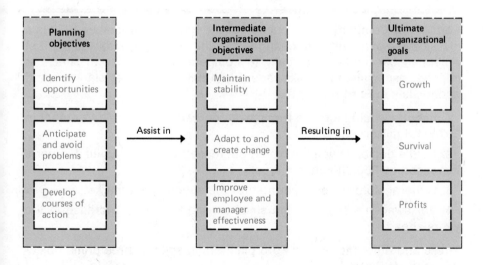

5.2
Planning objectives and organizational goals

Stability refers to the objective of creating a sense of predictability, control, and certainty in the organization. Coordinating the physical and human resources of an organization can contribute to its stability. The predetermined courses of action established through planning help determine and control the organization's future actions. For example, one of the purposes of operational plans is to enable one department to anticipate the actions of other departments with which it is interdependent.[12] Ford Motor Company develops monthly and quarterly plans with tire companies to deliver certain numbers and types of tires to its various production plants.

Maintain stability

Planning departments are used to help achieve internal coordination between the major divisions or departments of an organization. The need for coordination becomes especially actue when the departments are highly differentiated in terms of products, geographical areas, and clientele served. Planning departments are also used to help the firm adapt to and create desired changes.[13]

Adapt to and create change   Organizations' attempts to adapt and innovate are usually expressed in their strategic plans. These specify the basic goals and strategies, markets, and products or services. Key managers may spend considerable time on planning activities intended to develop alternative strategies for different business conditions.[14]

CASE STUDY

The Pinto

Ford Motor Company's introduction of the Pinto in September 1970 is a classic case of adaption to changed conditions.[15] The Pinto was the first American car made specifically to compete "head-on" with small-car imports, especially the Volkswagen. In 1968, the market planners and economists at Ford thought:

1. Imports would increase from seven percent in 1967 to 14 percent in 1975 (1.5 million units);

2. Ford's domestic volume would decrease by 240,000 units if imports increased by 750,000 units annually;

3. General Motors would soon enter the subcompact market;

4. Volkswagen's share of the small-car market would increase in the years ahead.

These and other factors led Ford planners to specify three prime objectives for the Pinto:

1. Its size was to be the same as the Volkswagen sedan.

2. Its cost of ownership was to equal that of the Volkswagen: competitive purchase price, equivalent fuel consumption, built-in durability and reliability, comparable serviceability, lower maintenance costs, and competitive parts prices.

3. Its comfort, convenience, and appearance were to be better than Volkswagen's: wider tread and lower height for better stability; better maneuverability, ventilation, and heating; easier front- and rear-seat entry and exit; more interior room; wider option availability; and distinctive styling.

These objectives provided criteria for evaluating the numerous operational plans and decisions needed to introduce the Pinto. By relating the objectives for the Pinto to Volkswagen, the Ford planners were also given a firm base of comparison. The success of the Pinto suggests that Ford adapted to change fairly well. When the energy crisis hit in 1973, Ford was able to make a further change in the Pinto by introducing the four-cylinder MPG model. However, some would claim that Ford was not very effective in anticipating or reacting to the numerous consumer and governmental problems associated with the tendency of Pinto gas tanks to explode when struck from the rear at high speeds.

The ability and willingness to engage in planning is generally believed to improve the effectiveness of employees and managers. Table 5.2 lists how your personal abilities to use planning concepts and aids can improve your own effectiveness.

Improve employee and manager effectiveness

5.2
How Planning Can Improve Your Effectiveness

- Increases the ability to be proactive in seeking out and creating new opportunities.
- Forces analytical thinking and evaluation of alternatives, thus improving your decisions.
- Establishs a framework for your decision making consistent with top management's objectives.
- Modifies your style from just day-to-day decisions to include future-focused thinking and decisions.
- Helps you to be reactive on a timely basis to uncontrollable events through the development of contingency plans.
- Provides a basis for measuring organizational and individual performance, thus determining how well you are doing.
- Increases your sense of involvement and motivation.
- Improves communications between you and others in the organization.

Adapted from D. German, "Techniques of Planning in Employee Relations." *Personnel Journal* **58,** 1979, 761–770. Reprinted with permission of Personnel Journal, Costa Mesa, California. Copyright © November 1979, all rights reserved.

The need to engage in planning can be summed up in these notable quotes:

- Any organization that doesn't plan for its future isn't likely to have one.
- The most effective way to cope with change is to help create it.
- Planning without action is futile; action without planning is fatal.
- When you don't know where you're going, any road will get you there.

When Is Planning Likely To Be Effective?

Consistent with the contingency theme of this book, planning needs to fit the purposes and situations it is intended to serve.

Mitchell's planning law states; "He who allows detailed trivia to smother clarity of purpose shall suffer the flames of hell."[16] This law was developed by J. Ernest Mitchell, Jr., a planning executive at Dow Chemical Company. The graphic form of this law is shown in Fig. 5.3. The numbers used on the vertical and horizontal scales are for illustrative purposes only. The line of this graph suggests that organizational effectiveness should increase quite rapidly with the effort expended on planning — up to a critical range. Beyond that narrow range, additional planning is likely to lose effectiveness rapidly — even to become counterproductive. At this point, the project being considered would be better off if formal planning stopped.

5.3

Mitchell's planning law

Adapted from "Corporate Planning: The Dow Chemical Company." Unpublished paper presented by J.E. Mitchell, Jr., Director of Corporate Planning, Dow Chemical Company, at the *Business Week* Strategic Planning Conference, Los Angeles, California, March 6–7, 1979, p. 26. Used with permission.

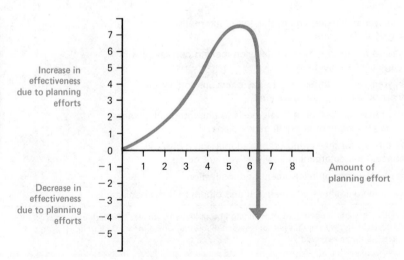

Mitchell's planning law recognizes that some managers have approached planning from two extreme patterns. At one extreme, there is the pattern of "extinction by instinct." This occurs when managers are so concerned with immediate problems and making quick decisions that they do not plan adequately for the organization's future. Firms operating in a simple/stable environment may use this approach for years without loss in profitability, but firms operating in a simple/changing or complex/changing environment are likely to fail or stagnate with little or no strategic planning. Exxon, Texas Instruments, General Electric, and similar large companies recognize the need for intensive strategic planning because of their complex and changing environments.

The other extreme planning pattern is "paralysis by analysis."[17] This occurs when managers try to plan for every detail and possibility. The planning process gets so bogged down that important decisions are not made when they are needed. Dow Chemical illustrates a firm which has gone through various patterns of planning.

CASE STUDY

Dow Chemical

J. Ernest Mitchell, an executive at Dow Chemical, comments on their patterns of planning over time, including "paralysis by analysis":

J. Ernest Mitchell, Jr., Dow Chemical Company

Let me trace the stages of development in planning in the Dow Chemical Company. Obviously, we started out with no formal activity. The first effort was a one-year profit plan. We then started to add a capital plan. Then we progressed to a five-year system and tightened things up considerably, adding much trivial detail. We soon found that the five-year perspective was not long enough for meaningful goals. So we extended to 10 years, still continuing with almost infinite detail. As you can imagine, everything bogged down, activities did not relate to people, line people seriously considered lynching the planners, the approach loaded the computers and created a lot of waste paper but little else. After this experience we have become wiser and have considerably reduced numbers pollution. We are now operating in stage 6, which I would characterize as segmented planning adapted to the needs of people and the corporation. We are continuing to work toward a real-time segmented planning system adapted to the needs of people and the corporation.[18]

Dow's philosophy is that planning systems must be designed for people, not for machines. Accordingly, Dow has developed six essentials for good planning, and they are summarized in Table 5.3. These six essentials are useful guidelines for any organization or manager. Of course, they cannot guarantee that the decisions made from planning activities will be effective.

5.3
***Dow's Essentials for
Good Planning***

- Planning must have the unqualified and open support of top management.
- Line management must be heavily involved and do a major part of the planning.
- The professional planning staff must supply the consistent framework. In Dow, planning people must have extensive line experience before they are candidates for planning.
- The planning process should be as nearly continuous as feasible . . . part of the corporate way of life.
- Strategic planning, which introduces flexibility, must be used to balance the inflexibilities introduced by budgeting and operational planning.
- If planning does not result in DECISIONS and ACTION, don't do it!

From J. Mitchell, Jr., "Corporate Planning: The Dow Chemical Company." Unpublished paper presented at the Business Week Strategic Planning Conference, Los Angeles, California, March 6–7 1979, pp. 23–24.

**Risk reduction and
understanding**   Planning is likely to be effective when it reduces risks or improves the understanding of risks associated with decisions and actions. Planning *cannot* eliminate risks and uncertainties! As one planning manager noted: "No amount of sophistication is going to dismiss the fact that all our knowledge is about the past and all of our decisions are about the future."[19]

The capability for responding to risks and uncertainties can be improved through contingency planning. **Contingency planning** refers to identifying alternative future possibilities and developing a plan of action for each of them. For example, a number of large companies have developed contingency plans for action in the event the flow of foreign oil is sharply reduced.

Planning can help competent and knowledgeable managers to make better decisions, but it cannot compensate for key managers who lack ability. H. Edward Wrapp, who serves on a number of boards of directors, comments:

Ability and outlook of key managers

> ... my argument is that a good general manager has to know a lot about the industry in which he is operating, and particularly the markets and product capabilities. He has to develop sensitivities to the marketplace to help him make those very difficult, razor-edge decisions on product development, market strategy, and such. You just don't pick that up overnight. I think some of the disasters in marketing and product decisions have been made by people who just did not understand the subtle things that were important in their particular industry. I have seen numerous instances where companies have undertaken expensive and extensive market research and have proceeded to introduce a product to the wrong customer, or have over- or under-priced a product, or have designed a product that does not meet the customer's needs. [20]

How key managers think, their motivations, and their assumptions about the business conditions also influence the effectiveness of a company's strategic planning. One study of firms demonstrated this point. [21] The themes and content of the annual reports for 82 food-processing firms were analyzed. This study revealed striking differences between the top 25 percent of the companies and the least successful 25 percent. Compared to the former, the latter:

1. Had more complaints about the weather.

2. Had vigorous complaints about price controls.

3. Talked less about the coming changes in their environment, product market portfolio, and their future direction.

4. Were less inclined to mention changes in their organization.

5. Were less clear in their plans to cope with the energy crisis.

6. Were less clear in their plans to respond to the worldwide demand for protein.

By contrast, the more successful food-processing companies focused on anticipating and avoiding problems, identifying opportunities, and developing courses of action.

There are also instances in which the key managers of all the firms in a particular industry were each so busy focusing on what the others were doing that they failed to consider and look for potentially important technological changes. Firms in the film and camera industry didn't develop the instant "finished" print film. Polaroid, which had not been involved with either film or cameras, invented and marketed such a system. Similarly, IBM, a computer company, was the first to develop the electric typewriter. Royal and Remington were working on ways to improve the manual typewriter.[22]

In sum, our position is that planning is more likely to be effective when:

1. the costs vs. benefits of planning efforts are explicitly considered;

2. certain essentials of planning, such as those in Table 5.2, are followed;

3. top management accepts the fact that planning can reduce risks or improve the understanding of risks, but it cannot eliminate them; and

4. planning cannot compensate or substitute for key managers whose abilities are lacking and outlooks are inappropriate.[23]

You should now be beginning to understand the nature of strategic and operational planning, the reasons for engaging in planning, and the conditions under which planning is most likely to be effective. We can now consider the basic steps in the strategic planning process.

STEPS IN THE STRATEGIC PLANNING PROCESS

The process of strategic planning focuses on the step-by-step activities for developing strategic plans.[24] The basic steps of strategic planning are highlighted in Fig. 5.4. This figure suggests the points of merger between strategic and operational planning. The directional steps in planning are not just one-way in practice. There is obviously much interaction and revision between the steps. A strategy proposed in the process of strategic planning might have to be abandoned if it is later discovered that it cannot be implemented.

Several of the aids and techniques used in the process of strategic and operational planning are covered in the next chapter. The critical issues in the strategic planning process are discussed in the next chapter part. Thus, we will only briefly review the steps of the process shown in Fig. 5.4.

Initial Data

Strategic planning typically begins with assessing the basic goals and nature of the organization and how these relate to the external environment. Environmental data is used to develop forecasts of probable future events or conditions of importance to the firm. Key components in such forecasts are the

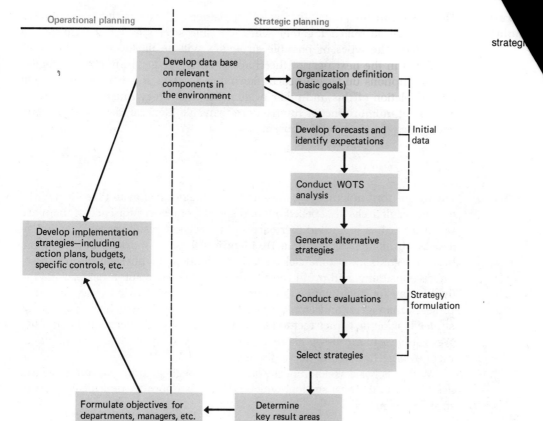

Operational planning | Strategic planning

Develop data base on relevant components in the environment

Organization definition (basic goals)

Develop forecasts and identify expectations

Conduct WOTS analysis

Initial data

Develop implementation strategies—including action plans, budgets, specific controls, etc.

Generate alternative strategies

Conduct evaluations

Strategy formulation

Select strategies

Formulate objectives for departments, managers, etc.

Determine key result areas

Developing means

present and changing expectations of powerful individuals or groups within and external to the firm. These forecasts and expectations are useful inputs to a WOTS analysis of the firm or strategic business unit. WOTS is simply the acronym for four of the factors most critical to an organization's functioning: Weaknesses, Opportunities, Threats, and Strengths. Many firms require the managers of each department to develop a WOTS analysis on a yearly basis. Accordingly, this step often takes place in both strategic and operational planning.

171

Steps in the Strategic
Planning Process

5.4
Steps in
...-to-operational
planning

...ntal data, forecasts, assessment of expectations, and WOTS
...pulled together when possible strategies for the future are
...pes of possible strategies will be illustrated by the cases
...xt part of the chapter. After the generation of strategies,
...erlying each alternative strategy must be evaluated. On
...of this and other evaluations, a strategy must be selected. In
...multiproduct or multiservice firms like General Electric, more than
...rategy is likely to be chosen.

...oping Means The means for implementing the selected strategies begins to take form when
the key result areas are spelled out and specific objectives for each of them are
set. Drucker has suggested there are eight basic key result areas for any business or strategic business unit. He identifies these as marketing, innovation,
human organization, financial resources, productivity, physical resources, social responsibility, and profit requirements.[25] The key result areas provide the
foundation for formulating specific objectives for divisions, departments,
projects, managers, and employees. This is the step in which the process of
strategic planning comes fact-to-face with the process of operational planning.
We will have more to say about this in the next chapter when the management-by-objectives approach is discussed.

With this basic skeleton of the steps of strategic planning in mind, we can
flesh it out in the next section, which addresses a number of critical issues in
strategic planning.

KEY ISSUES IN THE This part of the chapter zeroes in on the key issues and choices that are
STRATEGIC included in the strategic planning process. The key issues and choices are
PLANNING highlighted in Fig. 5.5, which also suggests the areas of merger and overlap
PROCESS between strategic and operational planning. The major parts in this figure are
reviewed in the following sections.

External The preceding two chapters focused on the importance of the external envi-
Environment ronment to the management of organizations. These chapters particularly developed the role of political and value system influences. Thus they need not be
developed here. We do need to develop, however, several issues with respect to
market and technological influences in strategic planning.

5.5
Key issues in
strategic-to-operational
planning

The key questions normally evaluated for each major market served are suggested in the following:[26]

Market influences

1. What is the size of the market (potential sales volume, number of customers, etc.)?

2. How competitive is the market (number of other suppliers of the good or service, management capabilities and financial strength of competitors, etc.)?

3. How profitable is the market likely to be in the future?

4. What is our market share and position in this market?

5. What are our strengths and weaknesses in this market?

6. What are the economic forecasts for the economy in general and this market in particular?

7. What political changes might take place to influence this market? (For example, deregulation in the airline industry has affected pricing, flights offered, and mergers.)

8. What shifts are taking place in consumer preferences that might affect this market?

9. What are the other possible risks and uncertainties in this market?

These questions are not intended to be exhaustive. They are simply intended to make more specific the important market influences. One of the other key questions in assessing the market is: At what point on the product/service life cycle are we for each of our products or services?

Product/Service Life Cycle   The *product/service life cycle* refers to the market phases for most products and services. One version of this life cycle is shown in Fig. 5.6. The vertical axis indicates the degree to which the industrial or consumer market demand for the product or service is increasing, on a plateau, or decreasing. The horizontal axis indicates the span of time. For fads like leisure suits and space war toys, the time period required to go through the five phases might be a year or less. For other products or services, the time period might be quite lengthy. Gasoline products for automobiles have been on the market for over 70 years and just now appear to be in the advanced maturity phase.

5.6

Product/service life cycle

(Adapted from S. Michael, "Guidelines for Contingency Approach to Planning." *Long Range Planning* **12**, 6, 1979, 63.) Reprinted with permission from *Long Range Planning*, copyright © 1979, Pergamon Press, Ltd.

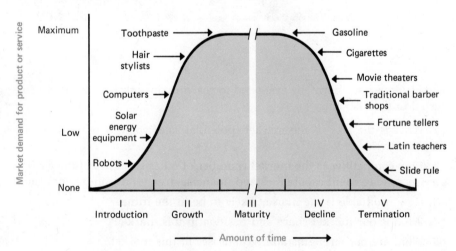

Figure 5.6 suggests the life cycle phases for a number of other products and services. Strategic planning for each product or service is influenced by the life cycle phase: introduction, growth, maturity, decline, or termination. Firms like Exxon, Gulf, and Standard Oil have rapidly diversified into alternative energy sources like coal, lignite, and uranium. They recognize that petroleum-based products appear to be in the maturity phase. The product/service life cycle has forced some firms to reassess what they are and what they want to become.

The strategies and functional areas focused on are likely to change with different stages of the product/service life cycle. During the growth phase, we might find dominant concerns to be those of expanding capacity and finding new customers. During the maturity stage, the dominant concerns might shift to improving the *efficiency* of production to reduce per unit costs and refining the marketing efforts to capture a greater share of the steady market demand.

***Technological
influences***

A number of large firms have established specialized departments to monitor technological changes. These firms may also actively participate in the creation of new technologies that will contribute to present strategies or provide the basis for new strategies.

Dr. Cutler, the director of corporate research at Whirlpool, identified the five basic missions of Whirlpool's corporate research with the corresponding general objectives:

1. Current product R&D — Extend and complement division engineering.

2. Manufacturing systems R&D — Apply new and improved technologies to manufacturing systems.

3. New opportunities — Identify and develop avenues for new growth opportunities.

4. Technological research — Seek, identify, and develop technologies to improve Whirlpool's competitive position.

5. Continuing support — Meet needs of the corporation for support and service.[27]

Statements 3 and 4 make Whirlpool's corporate research unit an integral part of its strategic planning process. Statements 1 and 2 focus on the role of corporate research in operational planning.

Technological developments and opportunities must be one of the central themes in a company's strategic planning.[28] The complexity and rate of technological changes can be so extreme in some industries (electronics, energy) that to ignore them may threaten the very survival of the firm.

**Organization
Definition**

Organization definition refers to the answers to the following types of questions: (1) Who are we? (2) What do we want to become? (3) What are our basic goals? In addition to marketing and technological influences, political influences play a key role in the current and possible changes in organization definition.

***External political
influences***

Political power groups — both within an organization and outside it — have an interest in the organization's definition.[29] The organization definition of firms like AT&T and Bank of America are influenced by state and federal regulatory agencies. Firms do attempt to influence and negotiate with powerful groups in their environment. The dashed line in Fig. 5.5 shows this. You might recall from Chapter 3 that AT&T initially followed a strategy and plan of lobbying in Washington, D.C. to have legislation passed prohibiting certain types of market competition. When this failed, AT&T went through the difficult experience of redefining what they are to become and what some of their basic goals would be. They made significant organizational changes in marketing. A top marketing executive from IBM was recruited to head up these changes.

***Internal political
influences***

The power of internal groups or individuals also influences the answers to questions of organization definition. The failure of W.T. Grant is an example of internal power struggles interacting with marketing influences.

Case of W.T. Grant The W.T. Grant Company is a good example of a firm which was unclear as to both its strategic and operational plans. Its failure was due to high-level power struggles and middle- and lower-level management which could not develop or implement operational plans. Grant's could not make up its mind what kind of store it was. "There was a lot of dissension within the company whether we should go the K-Mart route or go after the Ward and Penney position," says a former executive. "Ed Staley and Lou Lustenberger were at loggerheads over the issue, with the upshot being we took a position between the two and that consequently stood for nothing."

From 1963 to 1973 Grant opened 612 stores and expanded 91 others, with the bulk of the increase starting in 1968 under the guidance of President Richard W. Mayer and Chairman Edward Staley. "The expansion program placed a great strain on the physical and human capability of the company to cope with the program," says Chairman James G. Kendrick. "These were all large stores — 6 million to 7 million square feet per year — and the expansion of our management organization just did not match the expansion of our stores." Adds a former operations executive: "Our training program couldn't keep up with the explosion of stores, and it didn't take long for the mediocrity to begin to show."[30]

The influence of powerful figures on effectively or ineffectively defining "who we are" or "what do we want to become" cannot be underestimated. Consider the effective case of United Airlines.

Case of United Airlines   Eddie Carlson took over an ailing United Airlines (UAL) in 1970. He diagnosed UAL as a systems-choked bureaucracy that had lost touch with its customers — a bad state of affairs for a service business. Mr. Carlson undertook a program labeled as "visible management," "management by walking about," or "touching bases." He and his top team spent 65% of their time in the field for more than a year, directly instilling the customer service theme among UAL's over 1700 station managers.[31] Once the key power groups or individuals in the organization have defined what the organization is doing and why it exists, it is possible to develop the basic goals of the organization.

Organization goals normally specify the general directions and areas in which the accomplishments are desired. Sometimes these goal statements present the general future conditions desired without reference to a definite time period. This is illustrated by the statement of corporate goals shown for Hewlett-Packard in Table 5.4. For example, the profit goal of Hewlett-Packard states: "To achieve sufficient profit to finance our company growth and to provide the resources we need to achieve our other corporate objectives." At other times, specific objectives and time periods are tied to the key goal areas. This is illustrated by the statement of goals for the Robertshaw Controls Company in Table 5.4. For example, there are several specific profit-related objectives identified for Robertshaw Controls — including the objective that "10 percent profit before tax is necessary to assure adequate stockholder return reinvestment in corporate growth."

*Basic organization
goals*

There are four likely stages to organization growth: (1) single business firm; (2) dominant business firm; (3) related businesses firm; and (4) unrelated businesses firm.[32] These stages and their relationship to the relative complexity and scope of strategic planning are plotted in Fig. 5.7. As you would expect, a firm such as ITT, with its numerous products and services that serve unrelated markets, must have a wide-ranging and complex strategic planning system. In comparison, a firm like Sambo's, with its single business line of family restaurants, does not require nearly as elaborate a strategic planning system. This is not to suggest that strategic planning is an easy or simple matter in a firm like Sambo's.

A single-business firm is one which provides a limited number of products or services to a particular part of an overall market. Again, Sambo's has

*Stages of corporate
growth*

Hewlett-Packard's Corporate Goals

- *Profit.* To achieve sufficient profit to finance our company growth and to provide the resources we need to achieve our other corporate objectives.

- *Customers.* To provide products and services of the greatest possible value to our customers, thereby gaining and holding their respect and loyalty.

- *Field of interest.* To enter new fields only when the ideas we have, together with our technical, manufacturing and marketing skills, assure that we can make a needed and profitable contribution to the field.

- *Growth.* To let our growth be limited only by our profits and our ability to develop and produce technical products that satisfy real customer needs.

- *People.* To help our own people share in the company's success, which they make possible: to provide job security based on their performance, to recognize their individual achievements, and to help them gain a sense of satisfaction and accomplishment from their work.

- *Management.* To foster initiative and creativity by allowing the individual great freedom of action in attaining well-defined objectives.

- *Citizenship.* To honor our obligations to society by being an economic, intellectual and social asset to each nation and each community in which we operate.

Robertshaw Controls Company Corporate Goals 198—

- Minimize historical trends in sales and profits.
  (Objective: 10 percent profit before tax is necessary to assure adequate stockholder return and reinvestment in corporate growth.)

- Increase Robertshaw's sales and profits in the international market.
  (Objective: 10 percent minimum annual profit growth assures compounding profitability and established positive trend line.)

- Increase utilization of stockholders' equity through return on assets and return on investment justification.
  (Objective: 10-15 percent annual sales growth is required to double the sales of the corporation every five to eight years.)

- Review all product lines and products that cannot justify continuance based on ROA.
  (Objective: Within the broad parameters of sensors and associated controls, Robertshaw can develop adequate diversification and maximize inhouse abilities and expertise.)

- Establish corporate and divisional financial standards.
  (Objective: To evaluate and justify investments in new or old areas of opportunity to verify the potential for the corporation to achieve an industry position of no less than third.)

- Develop improved consumer awareness and recognition of Robertshaw.
  (Objective: The criteria for growth must include favorable corporate identity at the consumer and investor levels.)

Adapted from Y. Shetty, "New Look at Corporate Goals." © 1979 by the Regents of the University of California. Reprinted from *California Management Review* **22**, 2, p. 72 by permission of the Regents.

5.7
Stages of corporate
growth and strategic
planning

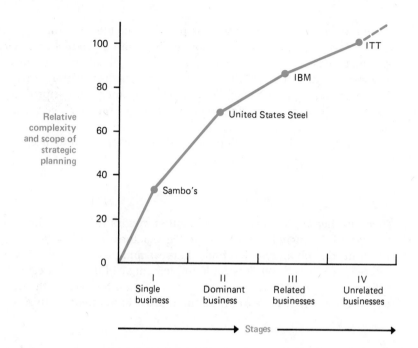

been positioned in the middle tier of the family restaurant industry. A dominant-business firm is one which tries to serve the various segments of a particular industry or market. For example, United States Steel has not significantly diversified out of the steel business. Within the steel business, there are numerous types of steel and markets for steel. The third possible growth stage is to become a related-businesses firm. In this stage, a firm may diversify into related products or services. IBM appears to function in this stage. It provides numerous products and services — ranging from typewriters to sophisticated computers — to businesses related to information processing.

Unrelated-businesses firms — like Westinghouse and ITT — provide diverse products and services to diverse markets and industries. These types of firms are often referred to as conglomerates. As you will recall, ITT operates an insurance company, hotel chain, and telecommunications firm, among others. In this type of firm, the executives of each strategic business unit have a key responsibility for the strategic planning of their unit. Their strategic plans are normally submitted to the corporate headquarters executives for review, approval, or modification. The headquarters executives are heavily involved in determining which firms they might acquire, divest themselves of, and reduce, maintain, or increase through capital investment decisions.

Key managers help define a firm by their choice of strategies, such as moving from one stage to another or remaining in a particular stage. Firms can be successful in all of these stages. A single-business or dominant-business firm needs to be very sensitive to its phase in the life cycle for its products or services (see Fig. 5.6). A single-business firm with a product or service in the declining phase of the life cycle may have a difficult time earning profits, surviving, or growing. This firm could ward off disaster for some period of time by capturing portions of competitors' customers and improving internal efficiency. Their strategy might be to get a larger relative piece of the shrinking "pie."

The organization definition of the firm is likely to influence the types of market/investment strategies pursued.

Market/Investment Strategies

There are five basic market/investment strategies that might be followed by managers in a single-line business. In Fig. 5.5, these are identified as grow and penetrate, defend and hold, rebuild, harvest, and divest and exit.[33] A firm with different products or services could implement all of these strategies. That is, a different market/investment strategy can be used for each of the major product or service lines. Let's examine the market investment strategies.

Grow and penetrate: case of K-Mart

The **grow-and-penetrate** strategy refers to active investment and marketing efforts to increase the size and sales of the firm. This could be achieved by increasing present market share (penetration), entering similar markets in other geographic areas (such as international expansion), or even entering entirely new industries (such as ITT). For a number of years, K-Mart has pursued a growth-and-penetration strategy. In 1976, with sales of $8.4 billion, K-Mart moved past J.C. Penney to take second place behind Sears and Roebuck in the non-food retail area. K-Mart has grown rapidly for years by changing their stores and merchandise lines to fit the market. It had no plans of resting in 1976. K-Mart found itself, however, faced with an unusual problem. All sales and profit forecasts showed that they would have more money than they could successfully put back into the company.

A Study Group on Corporate Strategy was organized by top management to analyze the problem of excess cash. The group was primarily composed of ten junior executives. Senior managers thought these younger executives would be implementing any suggestions in years to come. Several areas were explored and some decisions were made.

K-Mart's annual growth of 20 percent slipped to about 12 percent in 1980 for its 1900 stores. Most of the forecasted growth through 1983 is expected to come from new store openings. Top management believes that only 60 percent of its urban market potential has been reached. This is based on the new strategy of locating stores as close as three miles from each other. Previously, ten miles had been considered the optimum distance. K-Mart has already introduced some 400 scaled-down stores in smaller market areas. These smaller stores have 40,000 square feet, rather than the 84,000 square feet of larger K-Marts. These steps are designed to increase K-Mart's market penetration. Plans call for a total of 3000 K-Marts by 1989.

In addition to increasing its market penetration, K-Mart introduced plans to diversify in 1977. Controversies at the top levels occurred over the form and pace of diversification. Walter Teninga, the vice chairman and chief development officer, left K-Mart in May 1979 after 22 years of service. Presumably, other key executives were unwilling to diversify as aggressively as Teninga wanted. After his departure, K-Mart acquired Furr's 76 cafeterias for $70 million. This move was viewed as a logical outgrowth of the cafeterias K-Mart operates in its stores. This suggests that top management is moving cautiously toward diversification by first acquiring relatively small firms in related businesses.[34] It will be interesting to see if K-Mart's actions are effective in returning it to a 20 percent rate of annual growth.

The ***defend-and-hold strategy*** refers to investment and marketing efforts designed to maintain sales and profit levels from a particular service or product. If the overall market is growing, sales may continue to increase. But the firm's market share could decline. This strategy does not necessarily mean that managers can sit back and relax. Consider the case of Listerine.

Defend and hold: case of Listerine

Up until the mid-1960s, Listerine Antiseptic, marketed by Warner-Lambert, had virtually the entire mouthwash market. New mouthwash products began to be tested at this time by Colgate and Proctor and Gamble. Warner and Lambert set as an objective the maintenance of Listerine's profit contribution to the firm. Their strategy was to very aggressively promote Listerine in the growing market. The market growth for Listerine was actually greater than forecasted. There was, however, a loss in relative market share for Listerine, as expected.[35]

The ***rebuild strategy*** refers to investment and marketing efforts designed to increase or exceed sales, profits, or market share levels that were held at an earlier time. Rebuilding is often attempted when a complacent or inept management is replaced by new key executives. Consider the case of Volkswagen.

Rebuild: case of Volkswagen

In 1974, Germany's biggest carmaker, Volkswagen, appeared to be on the ropes. It had a loss of $313 million on sales of $6.6 billion. By 1980, it had sales over $14 billion and profits over $300 million. Toni Schmücker became the chief executive officer of VW in 1975. German investors in VW have called him a "hero." In 1972, 98 percent of the cars VW sold worldwide were traditional

Volkswagens, with over one-half of them Beetles. Today, VW offers a variety of cars that match different market niches—Rabbit, Scirocco, Dasher, Audi, etc. VW's key strategy is to produce a variety of high quality cars that can bring high prices. Sales of over $14 billion were generated by virtually the same number of vehicles (2.3 million to 2.4 million) that brought in $6.6 billion in 1971. Another key element in VW's new success has been its high-mileage-per-gallon diesel engines.

Schmücker has started to implement an international grand strategy. He wants the company to build regional production plants. North American VW plants will produce cars for the U.S. market; the Brazilian plant will supply much of South America and the Third World, etc. Investments are now being focused on plant expansion in North America, some nonautomotive acquisitions, diversification, and ways of increasing the efficiency of production. The rebuilding strategy at VW appears to have been a remarkable success. When Schmücker took over in February, 1975, he said his worst fears were confirmed. He commented: "The cash position was desperate and being made worse by huge stocks of unsold cars. The first task was to bring the payroll into line with expected output. That meant laying off 25,000 people. For about two months I was uncertain whether we would make it. I told them (the other top executives): 'You are my team and we are going to do this together.' "[36] And they did!

Harvest: case of Philip Morris tobacco business

The **harvest strategy** refers to investment and marketing efforts designed to draw excess cash and profits generated from a particular product or service line for use elsewhere. Firms with products or services in the mature or declining phases of their life cycles (see Fig. 5.6) may try to "harvest" them. The harvest strategy does not mean that the firm has surrendered or stopped investing in the product or service line. Consider the case of Philip Morris.

In 1970, Philip Morris, a major tobacco company, purchased the Miller Brewing Company. This and other diversification efforts by Philip Morris resulted from the U.S. Surgeon General's 1964 report. The Surgeon General's and subsequent reports linked cancer, heart disease, and other health problems with cigarette smoking. Miller was the seventh largest brewer in the industry when acquired in 1970. It is now the second largest. Philip Morris had the cash from profitable cigarette operations to purchase Miller. It launched an aggressive marketing program and expanded Miller's brewing capacity. Philip Morris brought to Miller the consumer product marketing techniques that had made Philip Morris a success in the cigarette industry. Joseph Coleman III, the chairman of the board of Philip Morris, commented, "We are a marketing organization—our success is related to our ability to market and merchandise using consistent and integrated themes aimed at the gross segments of the markets."[37]

Philip Morris forecasted in the 1960s that the cigarette industry was in for difficult times. Through technological developments, the industry has been able to introduce lower tar and nicotine brands—helping to reduce, but not eliminate, the health-related concerns with smoking. In retrospect, Philip Morris was correct! Cigarette sales became relatively flat. Sales grew by 1.3 percent in 1980. This was the biggest increase since 1974. James Morgan, executive vice president of marketing for Philip Morris, predicted that annual consumption through the 80's will vary between a 0.3 percent decline and a 0.7 percent gain. Other industry executives agree with this forecast.

While Philip Morris has harvested profits from its cigarette operations, it has not abandoned this major segment of its business. In 1980, the firm introduced the very successful nine mg. Lights, a version of Virginia Slims. Philip Morris' other brands include Marlboro, Benson & Hedges, Merit, and Parliament. They all are aggressively promoted. Marlboro was the number one selling brand in 1980, with 17.8 percent of the market. It had a 4 percent increase over 1979. Philip Morris raised its overall share of the cigarette market from 29 percent in 1979 to 30.8 percent in 1980.[38]

The ***divest-and-exit*** strategy refers to efforts designed to eliminate a product or service line by selling it to someone else or simply discontinuing it. Management may recognize that it has a "loser" on its hands or that its efforts and resources can be more productively employed elsewhere. Divestment is often used to generate cash for use in other lines. ITT has sold some subsidiaries to get the huge sums of capital needed in its telecommunications business. Subsidiaries or divisions are also sold to avoid further losses. Consider the case of RCA's computer business.

Divest and exit: case of RCA's computer business

RCA entered the computer business in 1957 and left it in 1971 — after losing somewhere between $400 and $500 million. A number of strategic errors by RCA have been identified. The specific strategy for the computer division was not well planned; it was simply to imitate IBM. RCA was the brunt of industry jokes like: "RCA computer manuals are just as good as IBM's — they even have the same spelling errors." The death blow took place in 1970 when RCA attempted to go "head on" with IBM by cutting prices. This failed because: (1) RCA did not have the trained sales force and systems engineers to deliver the goods; (2) IBM's customers were loyal because of past good results; and (3) RCA had developed a reputation for inferior marketing and service in comparison to IBM. At the time, one Honeywell executive commented: "This strategy doesn't seem credible in the long run."[39] And it wasn't!

In sum, a variety of market/investment strategies can be used by organizations. In large multiproduct or multiservice firms it may be desirable to use all of these strategies. This discussion has not yet suggested the different top management profiles or outlooks that may come to dominate an organization. These profiles serve to suggest the major thrust behind the market investment strategies.

**Top-Management
Strategies**

Top-management strategies refer to the dominant thrusts of key managers for implementing the various marketing/investment strategies. There is no required one-to-one relationship between each market/investment strategy and each management strategy. There are four basic top-management strategies: executive dominated, marketing dominated, innovation dominated, and production dominated.[40] As suggested in Fig. 5.8, a firm may have a predisposition or thrust toward one of these strategies. The strategy may consciously or unconsciously dominate in key planning and decision-making issues. We need to add our qualifier again. The strategic business units within a single firm could follow different management strategies. ITT's top management probably follows the executive-dominated strategy, its Sheraton chain of hotels the marketing-dominated strategy, and its telephone switching equipment division the production-dominated strategy.

5.8
**Types of top-management
strategies**

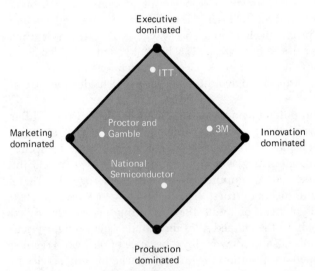

***Executive
dominated: case of
ITT***

The ***executive-dominated strategy*** refers to a focus of key managers on managing the portfolio of firms under its control. Attention is on acquisitions, divestures, joint ventures, mergers, allocation of capital between its various businesses, and the like. As suggested and described in previous sections of this chapter, the top management of ITT seems to mirror the executive-dominated strategy.

The **marketing-dominated strategy** refers to a focus of key managers on "managing" the consumer. Firms marketing soaps, detergents, cereals, cosmetics, men's and women's personal care products, and the like often use a marketing-based management strategy. Extensive advertising and point-of-sales promotion are common. This strategy may also focus on customer service or even price. Consider the case of Procter and Gamble.

Marketing dominated: case of Procter and Gamble

Procter and Gamble lives, eats, and sleeps the marketing-dominated management strategy. Its major lines include personal care products (Ivory soap, Crest toothpaste, Scope mouthwash, and Prell shampoo), laundry and cleaning items (Tide, Joy, and Comet), and traditional foods (Crisco shortening, Duncan Hines cake mixes, and Folger's coffee).

Its marketing prowess is the envy of many firms. Some have called P&G "Marketing U." This is because of the outstanding job it does in training and developing college graduates into superb marketers. Firms often lure these individuals away after several years at P&G.

P&G has also begun to diversify into such fields as prescription drugs, synthetic foods and food ingredients, and supplies for hospitals and nursing homes. These product lines serve primarily commercial and institutional markets. P&G is probably the leader and model in consumer marketing. The marketing skills and techniques acquired through their consumer marketing are directly applicable to their diversification activities. As of 1980, these new products only accounted for about $60 million of their $10 billion plus in sales. P&G has a goal of about 20 percent in sales from these new products by the late 1980s.[41]

An **innovation-dominated strategy** refers to a focus of key managers on the creation and/or implementation of new technologies, products, or services. A common outlook in such an organization is the creation and management of change. There may be a goal of anticipating and creating the firm's environment, not just responding to it. Such organizations try to upset the status quo and may represent sources of threat to other less innovative firms. Consider the case of 3M.

Innovation dominated: case of 3M

At 3M (Minnesota Mining and Manufacturing Company), every division is expected to get 25 percent of its sales each year from products that did not exist five years earlier. This goal encourages managers to constantly use and work with 3M's technical and scientific people to develop new products. Daniel

MacDonald, head of one 3M division, says: "Our top executives are never interested in what you've already got on the market. They want to know what's new. It's a way of life here. We take each segment of the market and try to develop products that fit. If somebody has an idea they believe in, we'll give them a chance."[42] Failures at 3M are accepted as part of the process of making risky entrepreneurial decisions. Managers and researchers who bring along winners are recognized and promoted. Those who develop losers are given second and even third chances. Ideas at 3M are sought out from everyone — executives, managers, researchers, employees, and customers. Through their successful innovation program, 3M has achieved substantial growth in sales and profits and has changed both itself and its markets.[43]

Production dominated: case of National Semiconductor

A ***production-dominated strategy*** refers to a focus of key decision-makers on manufacturing and processing know-how. The efficient use of plant and equipment is often crucial for success in capital intensive industries like paper making, electric power generation, and chemicals. The key managers using this strategy spend considerable time in developing plans to improve the efficiency and productivity of making mass-produced standardized products or services. Efficiency might also be increased by acquiring suppliers. For example, Dow Chemical, a major producer of standard raw chemicals used by other firms, now has under its control over half of its energy requirements. Dow is a major consumer of gas and petroleum based supplies. Dow began preparing for the energy shortages that hit in the 70s during the early 60s.[44] Firms in rapidly changing markets have also successfully used the production dominated management strategy. Consider the case of National Semiconductor.

National Semiconductor, headquartered in Santa Clara, California, follows the strategy of forcing down production costs for its broad range of microelectronic components — especially the computer chips going into computer memories. With lowered production costs, they slash prices to grab a bigger share of the market. From 1977 to 1980, sales doubled to almost $1 billion. As of 1981, National was regarded as the lowest-cost producer of many types of chips and had implemented a plan for similar dominance in quality.

National has a hard-nosed, frugal operating style. Overhead is kept down by using sales representatives and distributors rather than hiring its own salesmen. Labor intensive operations have been moved across the Pacific to Thailand, Indonesia, the Philippines, etc. A labor force of about 40,000 is located in these countries.

Top management has created a spartan working environment for employees at all levels. There are few potted palms. An executive from a competing firm observes: "National is the sweatshop of our industry — a piperack, low-cost, survival-oriented company. Those who survive develop great esprit de corps based on hard work." The production-dominated management strategy of National Semiconductor seems to be summed up by Charles Spock, its chief executive officer, in these words: "We are catching up to the Japanese (quality) faster than any other U.S. company. And in making high-volume products, nobody can match our costs. No one."[45]

We hope that our use of cases has helped you get a clear picture of each of the four major types of management strategies that can dominate a firm or one of its strategic business units. These strategies will influence the implementation strategies of a firm.

Figure 5.5 indicates that implementation strategies are a part of operational planning; thus they are not considered here. However, a number of implementation strategies are considered in future chapters. Implementation strategies focusing on organization design are developed in Chapter 7 and 8, and those concerning human resource management in Chapters 13 through 17. Operations management implementation strategies are developed in Chapter 11 and somewhat in Chapter 12.

Implementation strategies provide the detailed means for getting products and services to the market. To do so effectively, they are affected directly and indirectly by the external environment. Thus, Figure 5.5 shows the external environment as having a direct impact on both strategic and operational planning issues. For example, changing expectations for the management of human resources often work their way "up" to top-management through new employees — women, minorities, and young adults. Many operational managers work directly with outside groups (suppliers, customers, government agencies, etc.) in implementing strategic policies and plans.

Implementation Strategies

The strategic planning issues and processes covered in this chapter should assist in developing your abilities to successfully perform the managerial roles of *entrepreneurial and resource allocator*. It may be some time before you are in a position to actively participate in a strategic planning process. However, you are likely to soon be involved with operational planning. An appreciation of strategic planning should aid you in developing and understanding your operational plans. If you have a sense and understanding of the "larger picture", you are less likely to develop tunnel vision and are better able to make good, sound day-to-day decisions.

Throughout the chapter we introduced case examples so that the various concepts and frameworks might have more meaning. We described the strat-

SUMMARY

egies employed by Sambo's and Denny's in coping with stagnant sales and slipping profits. We went out on a limb by saying that Denny's strategies are more likely to be successful. You might want to go to current issues in *Business Periodicals Index* to seek out articles that update you on the status of Denny's and Sambo's.

The issues and process of strategic planning change with the times and the key decision-makers. Strategic planning requires the exercise of many judgments by key managers. This should be evident in the many company examples reviewed. Planning is a form of decision-making. The basic decision-making concepts and techniques used in strategic planning are developed in Chapters 9 and 10.

Strategic planning can be no better than the managers who engage in it. Charles Summer has spent a lifetime studying strategic planning and top-level managers. He concludes: ". . . one key factor that determines the life cycle of all organizations at each stage of development is the leadership pattern displayed by general managers or strategists. How these general managers formulate strategies and policies, and how they use strategy and policy as instruments of influence and power, will to a large extent determine whether the organization enjoys a long and successful life or whether it disintegrates in a shorter span of time."[46]

The first part of the chapter provided answers to a series of questions, such as: What is strategic planning? Why engage in strategic planning? When is planning likely to be effective? The second part of the chapter reviewed the step-by-step procedures that are normally a part of the strategic-planning process. Part three addressed key issues that are central to strategic planning. For example, the importance of market, technological, and political influences in strategic planning were highlighted.

KEYWORDS

contingency planning
defend-and-hold strategy
divest-and-exit strategy
executive-dominated strategy
grow-and-penetrate strategy
harvest strategy
innovation-dominated strategy
top-management strategies
marketing-dominated strategy
Mitchell's planning law
operational planning

organization definition
organization goals
planning
product/service life cycle
production-dominated strategy
rebuild strategy
stability
strategic business unit
strategic planning
strategies

1. Do you think any changes should be made in the strategies pursued by Sambo's or Denny's? Explain.

2. What concepts in this chapter are applicable for strategic planning that you might undertake for yourself?

3. Most of us have a strategy even if we are not consciously aware of it. What is your strategy for the next year? Two years? Four years?

4. How much planning do you do in relation to Mitchell's planning law?

5. When can planning serve to reduce risk for yourself or an organization?

6. When can planning serve to increase risk for yourself or an organization?

7. How would you characterize the "organization-definition" for a firm you are now with or have worked for?

8. Identify one firm with which you are familiar. Where does this firm seem to fall on the product/service life cycle? (See Fig. 5.6.)

9. Do you think that the firm identified in question 8 is pursuing the strategy appropriate to its phase in the product/service life cycle?

10. What do you perceive as the organization goals of the high school you attended? What seemed to be its strategy?

11. Since so much knowledge appears to have been developed about the steps and issues of strategic planning, why do firms still fail?

Management Incidents and Cases

THE COCA-COLA
COMPANY —
PART B: SHAPING
THE ROLE OF
CORPORATE
PLANNING*

It was Henry Norman's first day as Director of Corporate Strategic Planning for the Coca-Cola Company. He had selected the proper spot on the wall for his prize marlin and had decided to keep the chair which came with his new office instead of replacing it with the chair from his old office. Feeling more settled and at ease, he reflected on his objectives for his department and how he hoped to accomplish them.

The Corporate Strategic Planning Office at The Coca-Cola Company consisted of only three people, as opposed to that in General Electric for example,

* This case was prepared by James M. Higgins (Crummer Graduate School of Business, Rollins College). Source: J. Higgins, *Organizational Policy and Strategic Management: Text and Cases.* Hinsdale: The Dryden Press, 1979, pp. 421–425. The author, James M. Higgins, wishes to express his thanks to Marion B. Glover, Jr. of The Coca-Cola Company and to The Coca-Cola Company for assisting him in the development of this case. Copyright © 1979 by The Dryden Press, a division of Holt, Rinehart and Winston, Publishers. Reprinted by permission of Holt, Rinehart and Winston.

which had approximately 100 staff members. Yet, the Corporate Planner at The Coca-Cola Company and his staff wielded considerable influence within the company because this office was responsible for reviewing and advising the Chief Operating Officer (COO), the President of The Coca-Cola Company, as to the soundness of operating group and divisional strategic objectives and plans. In addition, Corporate Planning (CP) initiated investigations of strategic problem areas, areas of interest to the COO, and was responsible for coordinating the strategic issues management efforts of the firm. Reporting directly to the COO, CP helped shape the future direction of the company's organization. But as Henry considered the past activities of the department, he was convinced that CP needed to become more active in formulating corporate strategy and fulfilling its company defined role. He felt that his predecessor, who had just retired, had been very good at identifying problems, but that solutions to these problems had just not materialized. Henry felt that his most important task would be to provide the operating managers and the COO with solutions in terms of well defined strategies.

Under each of the three major operating groups — the American Group, the Pacific Group, and the Europe-African Group — were small planning staffs at the division level. Similar units existed in the Foods Division and the Aqua-Chem Division. For example, the Coca-Cola USA Division, a member of the American Group, had a seven-member planning department. It was from this department that Henry had been promoted to Corporate Planning. Henry had had seven years experience in this department. Upon completion of his MBA at Harvard University he spent two years as a lieutenant in a project office of the Army Material Command and joined The Coca-Cola Company as a District Manager in the Bottler Sales field force. His undergraduate degree had been in Industrial Management from the Georgia Institute of Technology. Henry had served as Director of the USA Planning Office for the past three years.

Henry's Objectives and Plan of Action	Henry's thoughts turned to the objectives which he hoped to accomplish. Some were immediate results that he felt were necessary; others were more long range in nature.

First, he felt that his most vital role was to assist the president in establishing objectives and in formulating strategies to reach those objectives. Since he was already familiar with domestic operations, he would concentrate on the major 10 to 20 foreign operations of the 135 countries in which the company operated. Once he was familiar with the total operation he would be better able to advise as to objectives and strategies.

Given the limited size of his department, he believed that providing planning direction to all of the company could best be accomplished through a planned course of action. First, he would establish a planning perspective throughout the company, including renewal of the annual strategic planning exercise. Second, he would need therefore to assist the group and division planners in strategic planning, on getting the numbers right and acceptable, but too little time on determining group and division direction, primarily strategic objectives and plans to reach those objectives. Third, where necessary, either because of strategic issues or as the result of COO interest or in order to further group and division interest in planning, he would institute a program of management by objectives throughout the company, just as he had assisted in establishing for Coca-Cola USA the previous year. Next, he concluded that he must establish and maintain a rapport with the group and division managers. He summarized that if he could be of genuine assistance to them, he could aid the corporation in accomplishing its objectives. He had already met with the three soft drink group vice presidents, and they had indicated a strong need for his assistance. He believed that they were sincere. Indeed, they did need his department's assistance because the company faced some severe challenges in the next few months.

Next, he noted to himself that he had to sell his programs, and teach others in the company how to sell their programs. Further, he would help sell to the COO those programs which he felt the company should adopt. The COO reserved the right to make all strategic decisions in conjunction with the CEO, the Chairman of the Board. As Henry recalled previous experiences in attempting to have programs implemented, he realized that where presentations were weak the subject programs were simply not adopted, no matter how good the proposed action might actually have been. He saw his function as assisting all the major parties involved, trying to get each to see the others' needs and perspectives.

His thoughts turned to the strategic planning process at the company. Traditionally there had been a bottom-up approach, with virtually all managers submitting strategic proposals for refinement by the CP. This program, known as the "Soft Approach" had been adopted at the recommendation of the Stanford Research Institute. Experience had proven the system to be unwieldy, and Henry was certain that the CP should request only a few strategic issues and objectives from the key profit centers. As part of the policy, the company was to have an annual planning exercise in which the various divisions, the CP, and eventually the groups submitted strategic plans for review by the COO and possibly the Operating Committee, which was composed of the three soft drink group presidents, the presidents of the Foods Division and Aqua-Chem, and the corporate vice presidents of Marketing, Finance, Personnel, Planning (CP), and Technical. In the last two years, this process had been set aside because of various crises which had occurred. The function of the Operating Committee was to recommend to the president what actions should be taken on strategic proposals. The COO retained the decision prerogative, however. Normally, decisions were made in separate meetings with only the operating manager involved. The Operating Committee did not concern itself with the detailed operations of groups and divisions. Intermediate and operational plans were left to the group and division managers. Only strategic decisions which involved several divisions and crossed group lines were brought before the committee.

Henry wanted to insure that the Operating Committee reviewed the Strategic Plans annually and was already planning for the spring's submissions. He felt that this process was vital on an annual basis because it allowed resource managers to vent their full feelings, to get them out in the open. By challenging proposals with all major parties present, the president and his staff were less likely to adopt unfavorable proposals or similarly less likely to adopt favorable strategic alternatives. Further, by placing planning on an annual basis as opposed to the sporadic and random pattern which had existed in the last two years, Henry felt the company would move more systematically toward its objectives.

Corporate Objectives and Planning

As Henry reflected on the company's desires to increase its profit each year, at least at the level of the past years (12 percent), the enormous challenge of his job became apparent. To accomplish this objective would require the addition of profits of a size equal to that of two major divisions. And it was he who must assist in putting into effect these objectives and others established by the COO and CEO.

The CEO preferred to personally pursue some of the actions necessary to increase profits. For example, he practiced personal diplomacy in efforts to gain access to the potentially lucrative markets of the Mideast, Russia, and China. The CP really had very little input to this strategic action. The CEO would also occasionally make other strategic decisions, for example, determining new businesses for the company. Henry thought that this was appropriate since the CEO had great vision with respect to these kinds of decisions. But for the current group heads and division managers, Henry knew that he must provide advice to the COO as to what could be accomplished and how, with the existing business.

Henry considered this an extremely difficult challenge. Because of the size of the firm, a 12 percent increase was of enormous proportion. And because of the increased competition and continual Federal intervention such

as that from the Food and Drug Administration on saccharin, the task was
not an easy one.

Having worked with Coca-Cola USA managers to establish numerous
objectives in the past, Henry concluded that this year the total MBO program
would be based on four to six key objectives for each of the managers at each
level and that they should determine what were the most important, subject
to corporate headquarters approval, of course. (It was the CPs responsibility
to summarize lower-level submissions for the COO's review.) Naturally, appropriate objectives would be necessary for sales, market share, and profits.
Other objectives relative to each individual situation would be considered.

Henry was concerned with reaching the 12 percent profit increase objective. He felt that selling the major product line, Coca-Coca, was absolutely
necessary in order to reach this objective. However, the strength of the USA
operation had to be the franchisees, the bottlers. Henry felt that it was the
bottlers who had made Coke the most successful consumer product of the
century. The bottlers had to sell the products. The Coca-Cola Company
through advertising pulls the customer in, but so does the local franchise.
Further, push strategies only work where bottlers support them. Henry had
determined that the central focus of the company domestic strategy should be
on supporting the bottlers in their efforts to sell Coke and in turn winning
their support. After all, Coke was the main product. It was the main source of
profits. But he felt that the company should also pursue new products, for
example, the conversion of Hi-C to a soft drink.

Turning his attention to the foreign situation, he had already concluded
from his previous meetings with the group vice presidents that many of their
problems were operational in nature, yet of such a size that they took on
strategic consequence. That is, he felt that if enough plants could be built and
financed, and distribution arranged, many foreign operations would have no
trouble meeting the profit objectives. However, the company would have to
develop a plan to insure that these events occurred. Foreign nations posed
special problems, and these would require a great deal of attention. Distribution, for example, was extremely difficult in many developing nations,
which often had inadequate transportation systems. Marketing posed another problem where communications media were not of the type that U.S.
corporations were used to employing. Furthermore, capital formation in developing nations was often a function of government and not in the realm of
free enterprise. Finally, the various political and social customs proved to be
obstacles in many situations. He was not sure exactly what his recommended
actions would be, but forthcoming visits to the major overseas operations
could hopefully provide some indications of appropriate measures.

Numerous strategic issues plagued the industry. Within the past few
months, the company had faced these problems: the acryonitrile plastic bottle

was reported to contain carcinogens; saccharin, the only artificial sweetener currently approved for diet drinks, the fastest growing segment of the market, was considered carcinogenic; the South African racial situation and the related social responsibility issues of selling soft drinks there was a matter of controversy; an FTC case attacked the validity of exclusive territories for bottlers; and state and federal bills were attempting to place deposits on nonreturnable containers.

Often, the company's plan had been to wait and see what developed, although certain contingency strategies had been prepared in the event, for example, that the federal government were to take any of several courses of action with respect to saccharin. Henry felt that this was appropriate. "You have to know what the government is going to do before you can comply," he thought.

Shaping the Future   Henry was as yet undecided on the exact actions he wanted to take and those he wanted the company to investigate, but he had formed objectives and a strategy for the near future in any event. He was pleased with his staff. Paul Smith had ten years of foreign experience and Ann Moss had five years in the financial aspects of planning; so he felt that among the three of them, they would have no problem with the technical aspects of their job. It was coming up with the right strategies to reach corporate objectives that concerned him. 1978 was going to be a challenging year.

Questions   *1.* Can you detect a primary market/investment strategy at Coca-Cola? What do you think this strategy ought to be? Why?

2. Can you detect a dominant management strategy at Coca-Cola? What do you think the management strategy ought to be? Why?

3. What would be your objectives and plan of action if you were Henry Norman? Why?

4. What do you think of Henry Norman's objectives and plans of action; i.e., what is your evaluation of them?

JEWEL COMPANIES*   The Jewel Companies, Incorporated, is headquartered in Melrose Park, Illinois. It has approximately $2 billion a year in sales. The company operates

---

* Reprinted by permission of the publisher from *Long Term Profit Planning*, by E. Weinwarm and G. Weinwarm. Copyright 1971 by American Management Association, Inc., pp. 126–127.

several hundred supermarkets. Many of these supermarkets are connected with drugstores opened by the company. Jewel Companies has also branched into self-service department stores, convenience food stores, restaurants, and the manufacturing of food products.

The planning process of Jewel was described by Howard O. Wagner, its executive vice president, as follows:

The organization has changed substantially in recent years. During the 1950s, the company operated with a five-year expansion plan. This planning was restricted to the corporate level. Since then the company has become widely decentralized. The operating companies have their own management staffs and largely operate independently.

All of the operating companies have short-term annual budgets, which are very detailed and extended to the store level. The operating companies submit their plans to corporate management for review. Long-range planning is done mainly at the operating-company level. Each company submits detailed statements of funds required, including inventories and other current requirements, and profit projections. Many of the stores are leased from corporate-controlled real estate companies.

A three- to four-day conference of top executives of the corporation and the subsidiaries is held annually, away from headquarters. At that time the long-range plan is reviewed and another year is added. The long-range plan now covers three years. Management feels that a longer period would be unrealistic in view of the number and rapidity of unforeseeable changes in this industry.

A capital planning committee makes the final allocation of available funds, and the operating companies then plan the use of their respective shares. A minimum return of 10 percent on investment is required and is considerably higher for riskier projects. The analysis is based on the discounted cash-flow technique.

There is no separate planning organization or staff. Top management of the corporation and the operating companies, with their staffs, do the planning. Management believes that this method is economical and works satisfactorily. The company has been highly successful in regularly exceeding the growth rate of the industry.

Special attention is given to recruitment and training of personnel and the development of the supervisory and executive personnel needed to support the planned expansion programs. There have been no problems in staffing new facilities from the available inventory of trained personnel.

1. What planning concepts seem to be illustrated in this description of the planning process at Jewel Companies?

Questions

2. How might you characterize the Jewel Companies' situation in terms of its apparent market/investment strategy?

3. On the basis of the limited description presented above, do you feel that there should be any changes in or additions to the planning process at the Jewel Companies? Explain.

REFERENCES

1. "Managing for Troubled Times," *Business Week,* 2667, December 15, 1980, 98–105; K. Farrell, "Sambo's: What Went Wrong?," *Restaurant Business* **79,** May 1, 1980, 158–160.

2. R. Ackoff, *A Concept of Corporate Planning.* New York: Wiley-Interscience, 1970.

3. Ibid., pp. 3–4.

4. M. Moskow, *Strategic Planning in Business and Government.* New York: Committee for Economic Development, 1978.

5. A. Schendel and C. Hofer (eds.), *Strategic Management: A New View of Business Policy and Planning.* Boston: Little, Brown, 1979.

6. W. Hall, "Corporate Strategic Planning — Some Perspectives for the Future." *Michigan Business Review* **24,** 1972, 16–21.

7. C. Percy and W. Roberts, "Planning the Basic Strategy of a Medium-Sized Business," In D. Ewing (ed.), *Long Range Planning for Management* (rev. ed.) New York: Harper and Row, 1964, pp. 106–114.

8. D. Hambrick, "Operationalizing the Concept of Business-Level Strategy in Research." *Academy of Management Review* **5,** 1980, 567–575.

9. J. Bracker, "The Historical Development of the Strategic Management Concept." *Academy of Management Review* **5,** 1980, 219–224.

10. "ITT: Groping for a New Strategy." *Business Week,* 2667, December 15, 1980, 66–80.

11. C. Hofer and A. Schendel, *Strategy Formulation: Analytical Concepts.* St. Paul, MN: West Publishing Co., 1978.

12. J. Emery, *Organizational Planning and Control Systems.* New York: Macmillan, 1971, p. 113.

13. C. Springer, "Human Resource Strategy." *Journal of Business Strategy* **2,** 1980, 78–83.

14. F. Gluck, S. Kaufman, and A. Walleck, "Strategic Management for Competitive Advantage." *Harvard Business Review* **58,** 1980, 154–161.

15. Adapted from: Ford Motor Company Case. In D. David, *Marketing Management.* New York: Ronald Press, 1972, pp. 547–568.

16. J. Mitchell, Jr., "Corporate Planning: The Dow Chemical Company." Unpublished paper presented at Business Week Strategic Planning Conference, Los Angeles, CA, March 6–7, 1979, 26.

17. G. Steiner, "Does Planning Pay Off?" *California Management Review* **5,** 1962, 37–39.

18. J. Mitchell, Jr., *Op. cit.,* 5.

19. Interview: "Does G.E. Really Plan Better?" *MBA* **9,** 1975, 42–45.

20. "Don't Blame the System, Blame the Managers." *Dun's Review* **116,** September 1980, 82–88.

21. E. Bowman, "Strategy and the Weather." *Sloan Management Review* **17,** 1976, 49–62.

22. L. Sayles, "Technological Innovation and the Planning Process," *Organizational Dynamics* **2,** 1973, 68–80.

23. Formal studies on the effectiveness of strategic planning have provided mixed results. For example, see: R. Kudla, "The Effects of Strategic Planning on Common Stock Returns." *Academy of Management Journal* **23,** 1980, 5–20; M. Leontiades and A. Tezel, "Planning Perceptions and Planning Results." *Strategic Management Journal* **1,** 1980, 65–75; D. Wood, Jr., and R. La Forge, "The Impact of Comprehensive Planning on Financial Performance." *Academy of Management Journal* **22,** 1979, 516–526.

24. G. Steiner, *Strategic Planning: What Every Manager Must Know.* New York: The Free Press, 1979.

25. P. Drucker, *Management: Tasks, Responsibilities, Practices.* New York: Harper and Row, 1973.

26. W. Lewis, "Planning for Change and Changes in Planning." (Unpublished paper.) Washington, D.C., Strategic Planning Associates, Inc. 1979.

27. W. Cutler, "Formulating the Annual Research Program at Whirlpool." *Research Management* **22,** 1, 1979, 23–26.

28. J. Quinn, "Technological Innovation, Entrepreneurship, and Strategy." *Sloan Management Review* **20,** 3, 1979, 19–30.

29. I. MacMillan, *Strategy Formulation: Political Concepts.* St. Paul, MN: West Publishing Company, 1979.

30. B. Tregoe and J. Zimmerman, Strategic Thinking: Key to Corporate Survival. *Management Review* **68,** 2, 1979, 7–14.

31. T. Peters, "The Planning Fetish." *The Wall Street Journal* **66,** 40, 1981, 10.

32. M. Leontiades, *Strategies for Diversification and Change.* Boston: Little, Brown, 1980.

33. W. Rothschild, *Strategic Alternatives: Selection, Development, and Implementation.* New York: AMACOM, 1979.

34. "Where K-Mart Goes Next Now That It's No. 2." *Business Week*, 2639 (June 2, 1980), 109–114.

35. G. French, "The Payoff from Planning." *Managerial Planning* **28,** 2, 1979, 6–12.

36. R. Ball, "Volkswagen Hops a Rabbit Back to Recovery." *Fortune* **100,** 3, 1979, 120–128; L. Behr, "Boom Times at Volkswagenwerk." *Automotive News*, 4813 (June 9, 1980), 17–26.

37. J. Higgins, "Miller Brewing Company." In J. Higgins, *Organizational Policy and Strategic Management: Text and Cases.* Hinsdale, IL: Dryden Press, 1979, pp. 361–375.

38. "Cigarette Sales Keep Rising." *Business Week*, 2667 (1980), 52, 57.

39. J. Ross and M. Kami, *Corporate Management in Crisis: Why the Mighty Fall.* Englewood Cliffs, NJ: Prentice-Hall, 1973.

40. W.E. Rothschild, *Ibid.*

41. "P&G's New/New–Product Onslaught." *Business Week*, 2605 (October 1, 1979), 76–81.

42. L. Ingrassia, "How Four Companies Spawn New Products by Encouraging Risks." *The Wall Street Journal* **66,** 56, 1980, 1, 20.

43. G. Sawyer, "Innovation in Organizations." *Long Range Planning* **11,** 6, 1978, 53–57.

44. L. Smith, "Dow Versus DuPont: Rival Formulas for Leadership." *Fortune* **100,** 5, 1979, 74–84.

45. B. Uttal, "The Animals of Silicon Valley." *Fortune* **103,** 1, 1981, 92–96.

46. C. Summer, *Strategic Behavior in Business and Government.* Boston: Little, Brown, 1980, p. 3.

Chapter 6

PLANNING AIDS AND TECHNIQUES

After reading this chapter, you should be able to:

LEARNING OBJECTIVES

1. Describe three interrelated forecasting techniques — scenarios, Delphi technique, and simulation models.

2. Use Management by Objectives (MBO) and describe the conditions under which it is most likely to be effective.

3. Apply Management by Objectives as an aid to your personal planning and career development.

4. List the four major elements in the Program Evaluation and Review Technique (PERT).

5. Identify the purposes and elements in Zero-Base Budgeting (ZBB).

PREVIEW CASE

Intel*

Robert W. Noyce, Vice Chairman of INTEL Corporation

In 1971, Intel Corporation invented the microprocessor, the specialized semiconductor chip that contains the "brain" of a computer. During the past 10 years, Intel has developed more than 20 innovative products in the semiconductor industry — making it one of the leaders. Intel has over 15,000 employees and sales of about $1 billion annually. The following are portions of an interview with Robert N. Noyce, the vice chairman of Intel, that appeared in the *Harvard Business Review.** [1] Noyce's comments are of interest to us because he conveys: (1) a sense of Intel's values and organization definition, (2) their strategies and processes of planning; and (3) their use of MBO (management by objectives) as a planning aid and management system for tying together strategic and operational planning. MBO as a planning aid and philosophy is developed later in the chapter.

HBR   From its beginning, Intel has had a spectacular record. What's the secret of your success? Did you have a specific management philosophy from the start?

Noyce   No, you didn't have to then. In a small organization there's enough communication so that the objectives are very clearly defined to begin with. If you can't communicate with only 25 people, your communication skills are pretty awful. So our organization was very sharply focused. We knew what product we were going after; everybody understood that very well. That was almost enough of a statement of objectives to last through the first couple of years.

HBR   What is the management style now?

Noyce   Now we've run out of the collective experience of everyone. There's only one member of the board who has ever worked for a company larger than Intel — as Intel is today. And consequently, we feel that we're plowing new ground in terms of how we organize, how we do things, how we keep focus.

HBR   How do you keep focus?

Noyce   Well, the thing that we've been concentrating on recently is the culture. What makes Intel *Intel?* A lot of it is what has evolved because of the personalities of the people around. It is MBO practiced all the way through. I think there's a lot of lip service given to MBO, and it's not practiced. But here everybody writes down what they are going to do and reviews how they did it, how they did against those objectives, not to management, but to a peer group *and* management. So that's also a communication mechanism between various groups, various divisions, et cetera.

HBR   Do you have a formal way to do that, then?

Noyce   Yes, and it's pretty well built into the system. There is an openness, a willingness to discuss problems, identify them, which is not confrontational but rather, "Hey, I've got a problem. Here's how it's going." The executive staff, which basically consists of all the division managers, is truly an executive staff. They worry about the whole business, not just their own business, although they have the primary responsibility for their own business. There is very little in the way of staffers as such. Staff work is done by line management as a secondary assignment.

HBR   You don't have a separate planning function, then?

Noyce   No, strategic planning is imbedded in the organization. It is one of the primary functions of line managers. They buy into the program; they carry it out. They're determining their own future, so I think the motivation for doing it well is high. Now that is not to say that we won't call on other resources. If we have a product area that we don't know much about, we certainly will call in a market research organization or whatever to give us more information to work on. But it is not a planning function that reports to the president, and it has no interaction with the organization.

HBR   How do you keep making this a challenging place to work?

Noyce   I think it's because people have the control of their own destiny, and they get measured on it. They get their M&M candies for every job, as one of our business instructors always said. It's now getting to be a real challenge because the billion-dollar company is clearly in view in the next year or so. The question is whether we can do it right. A great deal of effort goes into thinking about how we plan it, how we operate it, and how we build incentives into it. Where are we going? Are we going where we want to go? How do we win at this game called business? And, as I say, I think that our team is made of high achievers who really want to do that. They still see plenty of challenges.

HBR   Is there a lot of internal competition?

Noyce   Well, there isn't the political infighting that you often see in companies. The direction is very carefully and definitely set, and everybody understands that. It's partly because of the way it's set — for both the MBO system and the strategic planning system. There just isn't any room for politics in the organization. It is very quickly rooted out. Someone who's crawling over someone else's body just doesn't get very far.

HBR　How does it get weeded out, though? The culture's strong enough?

Noyce　No, I think the information is open enough so that what the individual manager is doing is put under a microscope once every six months by all his peers. His peers know all those games, too, so politics just doesn't work. He doesn't get any support from his peers if he's doing that. It's an interactive company. Most of the divisions are heavily dependent on another organization that will let them get their job done.

HBR　It's a good idea to know where your strength lies. Would you say that's one of the key things?

Noyce　Yes, and certainly in strategic planning, the analysis of where our strengths and weaknesses lie is an essential part. We build on strength and try to stay out of competition where we're weak. Our strength is clearly in the components manufacture, in the design capabilities there, so that's where we want to compete. That's where we want to do battle with our competition. We certainly don't want to compete with IBM, anymore than we want to compete with General Motors. Just because we make an engine control, we don't want to make an automobile.

HBR　How would you say Intel differs from other companies in your industry?

Noyce　I used to characterize our business as compared to others in the industry as working on the edge of disaster. We are absolutely trying to do those things which nobody else could do from a technical point of view. We measure everything that we do so that when something goes wrong we have some idea of what it was that went wrong — a very complex process. We've tried to extend that same philosophy to the running of the whole organization. You don't do something unless you know what you're doing. You don't change something unless you know that it's been done on a pilot basis, that it won't louse up something else.

HBR　What is your major concern right now?

Noyce　My major concern right now for all U.S. business is how we are going to compete with Japan. Because they're doing it right, and we're doing it wrong.

HBR　What can be done about it?

Noyce As a nation we can't let Japan win this competitive battle because of complacency. I think we're much more alert to the situation than the automobile industry was — or the steel industry,
the TV industry, the tape recorder industry, the ball-bearing industry, the bicycle industry, or the motorcycle industry. Just list
them all as they disappear out of American society because of
Japanese competition. It's a little frightening to think that this is
happening in this industry right now. Yes, the semiconductor
industry is healthy right now, but if we are to remain healthy,
some changes will have to be made.

This interview with Robert Noyce of INTEL captures a number of the
themes developed in the first five chapters of this book, and those to be developed in this and later chapters.

This chapter unfolds by presenting planning aids and techniques in four
areas — forecasting, managing by objectives, scheduling, and budgeting. The
forecasting discussion focuses on strategic planning. The managing-by-objec-
tives discussion shows how it can help tie together strategic and operational
planning. The scheduling and budgeting presentations are centered on operational planning aids and techniques.

FORECASTING   *Forecasting* refers to predicting, projecting, or estimating future events or
conditions in the organization's environment. Forecasting is an important part
of any planning process. It is concerned with possible events or conditions that
are outside of the *direct* control of management. Firms like General Electric
and Westinghouse develop forecasts for a variety of conditions — market,
technological, values, political, and international, among others.

The basis of all forecasting is some form of extrapolation. *Extrapolation*
is the projection of some tendency from the past or present into the future.[2]
The simplest, and at times most misleading, form of extrapolation is the linear
or straight line projection of a past trend into the future. In the early 1960s, for
example, several producers of baby foods assumed that birth rates would be a
simple projection of the past. They ignored information that there was an
increasing acceptance of the Pill and that women's values and attitudes were
changing.[3]

The available forecasting technologies are quite varied and can become
extremely complex. We briefly review scenarios, the Delphi technique, and
simulation models as examples of forecasting techniques.

The use of forecasting aids and techniques represents an effort to engage in the formal search for information that can be used to help develop plans. As suggested in Fig. 6.1, the forecasting aids of scenarios, the Delphi technique, and simulation models overlap and support each other.

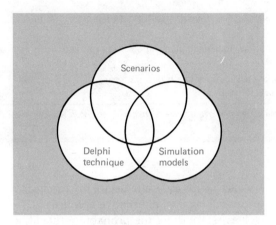

Scenarios

A **scenario** refers to a potential sequence of events and processes in a particular area of interest during a certain time period. Scenarios are descriptive narratives and/or "word pictures" of the future in some particular area. The word "scenario" became popular in 1967 with the publication of Kahn and Weiner's book, *The Year 2000*. Scenarios attempt to address two types of questions: (1) How might some potential (hypothetical) situation come about, step by step? (2) What alternatives exist at each step for preventing, diverting, or encouraging this process?[4] Table 6.1 suggests that scenarios can serve a variety of purposes as an aid to planning.

There are several types of scenarios.[5] One common type is the normative/anticipatory scenario. The *normative/anticipatory scenario* conveys the means that can be used to achieve certain desired goals. An illustrative scenario question follows: If the United States aims to lower its annual rate of inflation to 6 percent by 1987, what measures (in what combinations and sequences) can and should be used by the federal government? Many of us frequently develop the normative/anticipatory scenario in our minds as we think about the future — what we want to achieve and how we might get there.

- Provides a wide range of possibilities against which to evaluate strategies.
- Provides a broader vision of alternative events.
- Helps identify events that warrant the development of contingency plans.
- Expands the imagination and stimulates thinking about future environments.
- Improves the ability to conceptualize and see broad patterns, generalizations, and interrelationships.

Adapted from G. Steiner, *Strategic Planning: What Every Manager Must Know.* New York: The Free Press, 1979, pp. 237–238.

Scenarios are quite useful in "forcing" managers to evaluate their present proposals against alternative scenarios. Of course, part of this assessment involves establishing the probability (likelihood) of occurrence for the different possible scenarios.[6] The Delphi technique may be a useful aid in developing certain scenarios and evaluating the likelihood of their occurrence.

The Delphi Technique

The **Delphi technique** is a method for securing the consensus of experts regarding their predictions of the future or assessment of current needs.[7] This technique involves the step-by-step refinement of experts' opinions to reach a general consensus about the future. Since the Delphi technique relies on experts' opinions about the future, it is obviously not foolproof. However, by using a *consensus* of experts' opinions the Delphi technique has achieved a higher degree of accuracy than a single expert opinion could be expected to give.[8]

The Delphi technique has gained considerable recognition as a forecasting technique for use in strategic planning. It was developed at the Rand Corporation in the early 1960s. Rand used it to obtain expert opinions about urgent national defense problems.

Basic steps

The Delphi technique "provides for an impersonal anonymous setting in which opinions can be voiced without bringing the 'experts' together in any kind of face-to-face confrontation."[9] The basic steps in this process include the following:

1. A questionnaire is sent or given to the experts. It requests numerical estimates of specific technological or market possibilities — e.g., expected dates, volumes, and developments — as well as assigned probabilities of certain events occurring.

2. A summary of this first round is prepared. It may show the average, median, and quartile ranges of responses. This summary report is fed back to the anonymous experts. The second round may request them to revise their earlier estimates if they feel it appropriate or to justify their opinions.

3. Another summary report is prepared on the basis of responses to the second round. This report usually reports on the developing consensus. The experts are asked to indicate if they support this emerging consensus and the explanations which accompany it. Any minority opinions about the reasons for not joining the consensus are encouraged.

Three "rounds" with the experts are generally recommended. More rounds could be used, but there is generally a problem of the respondents dropping out after the third round because of other time commitments. The number of participants with the Delphi technique has ranged anywhere from a handful to 140 individuals. Fifteen to 20 experts are generally adequate.[10]

The heart of Delphi is a series of questionnaires. The first questionnaire may include broadly worded questions. With additional rounds, the questionnaires become more specific because they are built on responses to the preceding questionnaires.

Sample applications

In 1966, TRW, a major advanced technology firm, began to use the Delphi technique for planning studies in such diverse fields as space, transportation, and housing. In 1968, LTV, a large conglomerate, began to use it as a tool of technological forecasting. An application in a more basic industry was made by the Goodyear Tire and Rubber Company in its planning of future tire research.[11] In recent years, the Delphi technique has also been applied to help identify problems, set goals and priorities, and identify problem solutions. It has certainly become more than just a forecasting technique.

Delphi questionnaire

Figure 6.2 provides an example of one type of Delphi questionnaire that has been developed for student and classroom use. The questionnaire is concerned with future possible developments in the typical American business firm within the next 20 years. You might want to take a few minutes now and answer the questions in Fig. 6.2. The Delphi technique may generate insights that can be used to develop simulation models.

6.2

Delphi questionnaire of future developments in American business firms

(Prepared by Dr. Harvey Nussbaum, School of Business Administration, Wayne State University. Reprinted by permission.)

Introduction

Each of the following 10 questions is concerned with future possible developments in the typical American business firm within the next 20 years or so.

Instructions

In addition to giving your answer to each question, you are also being asked to rank the questions from 1 to 10. "1" means you feel that you have the best chance of making an accurate projection for this question relative to the others. "10" means you regard that answer as least probable. Please rank all questions such that every number from 1 to 10 is used exactly once.

Rank (1–10)	Questions	Answer* (year)
_____	1. In your opinion, in what year will women serve as presidents of at least five of *Fortune Magazine's* 500 largest corporations?	_____
_____	2. In what year will most board of directors of publicly held corporations contain members who represent primarily the consumer rather than the stockholders?	_____
_____	3. In your opinion, in what year will managers regularly be paid for working a 20-hour work week?	_____
_____	4. By what year will business have effectively reduced its pollution of the environment to a nondangerous level?	_____
_____	5. In what year will top management in half of the largest 100 manufacturing firms rely on computerized systems as their primary tool for planning?	_____
_____	6. By what year will the use of mind-stimulating drugs be employed by 10% of the chief executives as an aid in determining corporate policy alternatives?	_____
_____	7. In what year will energy prices make operations unfeasible for most American industrial corporations?	_____
_____	8. By what year will the M.B.A. degree be a minimum requirement for entry into the management training programs of most corporations?	_____
_____	9. In what year will prime interest rates make it totally prohibitive for corporations to expand their plant capacities?	_____
_____	10. In what year will most financial statements reflect a significant level of accounting for social costs and assets (e.g., pollution, welfare, and human resources)?	_____

*"Never" is also an acceptable answer.

Simulation Models

Simulation models forecast what effects environmental changes and/or management decisions will have on an organization or any of its departments. The objective of simulation models is to obtain the essential qualities of reality without actually experiencing reality. Simulation models are intended to let management take a contingency approach to the future by forecasting the effects of numerous "if-then" questions — such as the effects of different rates of inflation on sales and profits. *If* inflation is 8 percent and management continues its past decisions and policies, *then* profits might be forecasted to decline by six percent. Or: *If* inflation is 12 percent and management does so-and-so, *then* profits might be forecasted to increase by five percent.

These models often require the development of mathematical equations so that step-by-step computations can be performed. These computations are normally performed through the use of computers.

*Typical questions
and variables*

A simulation model could help top managers deal with three common questions.[12] First; what effects will a changed economy have on the organization if the key decisions and policies of management are not changed? Second; what will be the effect on the firm when a particular decision or policy is altered in anticipation of or response to certain changes in the economy (e.g., an increase in interest cost to 20 percent)? Third, are there combinations of management decisions and policies that can enable the firm to take advantage of changes in the economy?

The types of environmental variables used in a simulation model could include inflation rate, short-term interest rate, tax rate, and unemployment levels. Some of the management decisions and policies included in simulation could affect prices charged, growth rate of products sold, dividend policy, operating cash, depreciation, and capacity expansion plans. The performance measures included in a simulation model could be an income statement, financial ratios (such as debt/equity ratio, return on equity, and earnings per share), and balance-sheet statements.

Sample applications

Without worrying about the mechanics of simulation models, the important point is that management may be able to better forecast the effect of numerous "if-then" questions on profits, sales, earnings per share, etc. Simulation models can be used for virtually any problem or functional area (i.e., finance, marketing, personnel, and production) where there is a concern with forecasting. Let's consider two of these applications.

The IBM World Trade Corporation, which is responsible for IBM's international business, makes major use of computerized simulation models. The elements of its simulation models, expressed in mathematical equations, include: (1) present operational activities; (2) forecasts about changes in costs, prices, investments, labor productivity, etc.; and (3) extrapolation of past performance. The effects of planning alternatives and assumptions are obtained through predicted data on sales forecasts, revenue comparisons, income and expense accounts, etc.[13]

Managements and unions are also utilizing computer based simulation models for the development of their collective-bargaining plans and for anticipating the long-run effects of each other's proposals. The vice-president of corporate planning at American Airlines stated: "When our pilot contract was under negotiation recently, the union requested a new limitation on the number of flight hours each pilot would fly per month. We were able to feed this limitation into our computers and relate it to production levels we had planned over the next five years. We were able to determine exactly what our crew costs over the five-year period would be with new flight hours and to compare them with present costs."[14]

Limitations to Forecasting

Because the future is rarely the same as the past, managers can mislead themselves if they base forecasting models entirely on historical relationships and data. This would be like steering the ship by watching its wake. A high degree of judgment and skill is needed to construct forecasting models.

Even the most sophisticated forecasting and planning systems will not anticipate sudden changes and surprises. The "petroleum crisis," for example, created a discontinuity for many societies and major corporations that had modern forecasting and planning systems. Some of these firms simply weren't looking into this possibility. Others had forecasts of Arab action, but apparently felt that the probability was too low to justify planning for this possibility.

William Woodside, President of American Can, notes that there is a strong tendency to ignore, suppress, or reject forecasted warnings of crisis: "The roughest thing to get rid of is the Persian-messenger syndrome, where the bearer of bad tidings is beheaded by the king. You should lean over backwards to reward the guy who is first with the bad news. Most companies have all kinds of abilities to handle problems if they only learn about them soon enough."[15] In sum, while there has been tremendous progress in the development of forecasting techniques over the past 25 years, the future remains uncertain. In fact, over the past 25 years the increase in complexity and change in organizational environments may well have kept pace with improvements in the forecasting aids and techniques. When used in operational planning, forecasting aids and techniques have helped improve managers' "batting averages." Developments in computer technology, including simpler computer languages, have accelerated this progress.[16] Three quantitative forecasting techniques used in operational planning and day-to-day decision-making are developed in Chapter 11.

CASE STUDY

General Electric

General Electric is a pioneer in developing and implementing forecasting methods for assessing future environmental impacts and factoring them into their strategic planning. They use all of the forecasting aids mentioned plus others.

Assessing the Environment

G.E. divides the total environment into the following nine parts: (1) geopolitical and defense, (2) international, (3) economic, (4) social, (5) political, (6) legal, (7) technological, (8) manpower, (9) financial. They then use nine panels of experts (Delphi technique), each of which focuses on one of the environmental components. Each panel develops a list of

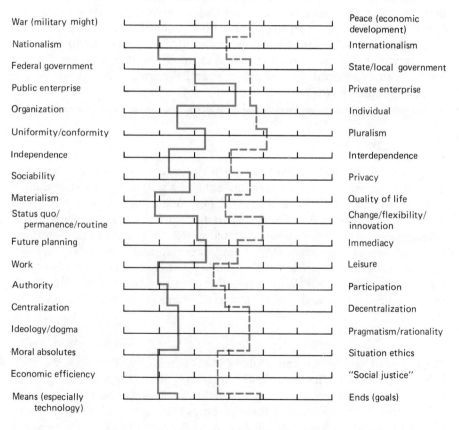

| 1969 Profile ———— | 1980 Profile ----- |

6.3
G.E.'s forecast of value-system changes: 1969–1980

(I. Wilson, "Socio-Political Forecasting: A New Dimension to Strategic Planning." *Michigan Business Review* **26** 4, 1974, 24. Used with permission of the Division of Research, Graduate School of Business Administration, University of Michigan.)

probable significant future events and trends, and the outputs from each panel are brought together by G.E. planners using cross-impact analysis.

Cross-impact analysis is a technique for examining all possible pairings of events[17] to determine the probability that each event may be affected by the others. Through this analysis, a manageable number of chains of events is developed into alternative scenarios. The key managers of each strategic business unit are given these scenarios, which they use to develop and assess alternative strategies.

Forecasting Value-System Changes
General Electric forecasts its environment in many areas. Figure 6.3 presents the profile of the general value system assessed in 1969 and forecasted for 1980. This forecast was developed around 1970 by General Electric's Business Environment Department. The profile in Fig. 6.3 is based on 18 sets of paired "opposite" concepts. The 1969 profile is the vertical solid line on the left, whereas the 1980 forecasted profile is the dashed line to the right. It is useful to reflect on this forecast. Do you think it was a reasonably accurate forecast? Where do you agree? Where do you disagree? Why?

MANAGEMENT BY OBJECTIVES

Management by Objectives (MBO) is a system and philosophy of management that can serve as both a planning aid and a way of organizational life.[18] The opening case on INTEL suggested how one company uses MBO as a philosophy of management and system for implementing planning tasks. Management by Objectives is one possible system for integrating the strategic planning process, operational planning process, and day-to-day decision-making into a unified whole.[19] As a planning system, MBO is most commonly used as a means for translating key corporate strategies into operational objectives and plans through the levels and functions of the organization.

Intended Philosophy and Goals

The intended philosophy and goals of Management by Objectives are highlighted in Table 6.2. The table clearly suggests that MBO is a positive philosophy and leans more toward Theory Y than the Theory X managerial philosophy.

In some situations, management becomes fascinated with the procedures of MBO without an adequate understanding or acceptance of the system's philosophy. There have been applications in which management became so fascinated by the logical and rational flow of its elements and steps that they

- Mutual problem-solving between organizational levels in the establishment of objectives.
- Formation of trusting and open communications.
- Creation of win-win relationships.
- Rewards and promotions are based on job-related performance and achievement.
- Minimize political games and the use of fear or force.
- Development of a positive, proactive, and challenging organizational climate.

continue to develop those steps in greater detail. The result was a paperwork monstrosity which was imposed on top of the already overloaded information and decision-making channels.[20]

This is just the opposite of the intended MBO philosophy. In larger bureaucratic organizations a good grasp of the philosophy should normally lead to a *reduction* in paperwork and a decreased concern for supervising nitty-gritty day-to-day activities. These all-too-frequent frustrating applications occur because the MBO system has been plugged into the firm without the precondition of analyzing the existing organizational climate and philosophy.

To be consistent with the MBO philosophy, management must first become aware of the changes which may be needed. An organization dominated by managers with theory X beliefs is likely to use MBO in a way that differs from one dominated by theory Y beliefs. Robert Noyce's description of the MBO system at INTEL suggests that their philosophy leans toward theory Y beliefs. (Chapter 3 explains theories X and Y). In a theory-X dominated organization, the setting of objectives is more likely to create power struggles than mutual problem-solving. Also, different levels of a theory X organization — or different units at the same level — may feel that other units or individuals will not exercise self-control over what had been agreed to. Let's review the elements in the MBO model.

Basic MBO Model

The basic Management by Objectives model (MBO) is presented in Fig. 6.4. There are five interconnected key steps in the MBO process, starting with the setting of objectives for the firm as a whole, for each of the departments (such as marketing, finance, production) and for as many individuals as possible.[21] Step 1 is based on the principle that *knowledge of what is expected* of individuals, departments, and the firm as a whole will increase the probability of improved performance. The planning step of setting objectives should clarify, provide shared information, and hopefully increase agreement about the expected results and priorities for departments and individuals.

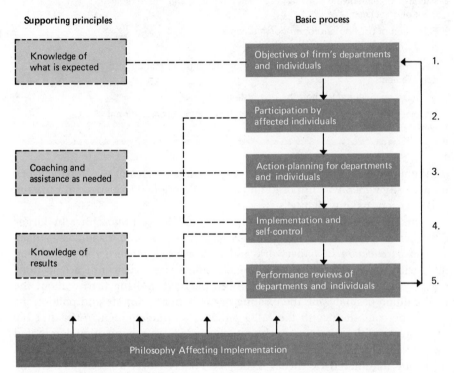

6.4
Basic MBO model

Step 2 in Fig. 6.4 suggests that those individuals who are directly affected by the objectives established for a particular individual or department should participate as much as possible in setting their objectives. Step 3 indicates that action plans would be developed by each department and individual for implementing their objectives. An **action plan** is a set of detailed steps and a combination of resources for implementing the departmental or individual objectives. Step 4 recognizes that these action plans must be implemented to have meaning. The individuals and departments should have as much self control as possible in implementing their action plans and making corrections as they proceed.

Steps 2, 3, and 4 are supported by the principle that *coaching and assistance will be provided* by superiors or others. This principle requires that management shift from a position of crisis to one of planning ahead; that managers shift somewhat from a judgmental position to one of helping subordinates and others to achieve objectives.

Step 5 recognizes that the performance of departments and individuals will be formally and objectively reviewed. This performance review step normally involves assessments for a particular time period, such as the last six months or year. This step and step 4 are based on the *knowledge-of-results principle*. This principle assumes that timely and appropriate feedback are necessary for correcting, maintaining, or improving performance. The performance-review step serves as a basis in setting new or revised objectives for future time periods. Thus there is a feedback loop shown in Fig. 6.4 from step 5 (performance review) to step 1 (objectives of departments and individuals).

The bottom "foundation" in Fig. 6.4 conveys the idea that the intended philosophy of MBO will affect its implementation, including the basic process from steps 1 through 5. With this overview of the basic MBO model, we can review the major steps in somewhat more detail.

1. Objectives of Departments and Individuals

The distinguishing feature of MBO is the establishment and linking of objectives (also called goals, targets, or purposes) for all departments and as many individuals as possible.[22] The objective-setting stage should provide clear answers to two basic questions: "Why are we here?" and "If this is why we are here, what should be accomplished?" The objective-setting step is likely to include the development of objectives at the following levels:

1. Top managers set long-range objectives that determine what the organization is and what it is trying to become.

2. Top- and middle-level managers develop more specific organizational objectives. They are often quantitative and include time periods, e.g., an objective to increase profits by 20 percent within three years.

3. Middle- and lower-level managers develop objectives for the various departments. For example, the production department may have an objective to reduce electrical energy consumption by 10 percent over the next 12 months.

4. Lower-level managers and workers develop individual job objectives. For example, a machine operator may develop an objective to reduce waste and spoilage from six percent to five percent within the next six months.

Characteristics of objectives

Objectives specify levels of achievement in quantitative and time-bounded terms. The quality and quantity of achievement expected within a defined period of time is defined for each division, department, and individual. The objectives are the standards for evaluating effectiveness. *Quantitative* objectives for a sales manager this year might be to: (1) increase sales by five percent; (2) maintain private-label sales at seven percent of total sales; and (3) keep expenses for advertising promotion at last year's level. The sales manager could also be accountable for such *qualitative* objectives as: (1) developing a sales quota system for all salespeople; (2) preparing and recommending an incentive-compensation system for area managers; and (3) shifting the advertising emphasis from wholesalers to consumers. This contrasts with traditional systems that claim to measure effectiveness by rating individual performance on factors such as health, judgment, ability to deal with others, cost consciousness, job knowledge, initiative, and so forth.

***Objectives of a
minimarket food
store***

Table 6.3 provides examples of objectives for one type of organizational unit — a minimarket food store. Note that all of these objectives have at least two important components. First, they clearly identify the areas (e.g., sales, waste, number of employees) in which the accomplishment should occur. Second, six of the eight objectives clearly specify a deadline when the objective is to be accomplished. All objectives specify a level of achievement. The desired achievement is the performance level defined within each objective. The third column in Table 6.3 is for inserting the dates when the actual level of achievement on each of these objectives should be reviewed. The last column is used for recording the actual or percent of actual achievement on each objective.

The process of setting objectives includes identifying specific areas of job or departmental responsibility and standards of performance. Two things should be kept in mind. First, objectives should not be stated in general terms that have little personal significance to the individual or department. A poor objective would be "your job is to maximize the welfare of the firm and of society." Second, objectives should not be stated in such detail that the worker or department must concentrate on dozens of day-to-day objectives. The underlying themes in the objective-setting process are noted in Table 6.4. Objective-setting can lead to disappointing outcomes if these themes are not taken to heart. The process of setting objectives under MBO requires participation.

**2. Participation by
Affected Individuals**

Participation in the establishment of objectives is generally recommended. When objectives are established and implemented only from the top downward, MBO is likely to be viewed by people as a means of measurement and control and not as a planning and motivational system.[23] If MBO is used to pressure people or departments into higher performance, it might be expected to fail or to have limited success. However, there are situations in which some

Objectives	Measurement Used	Review Dates	Evaluation (actual or percent of objective achieved)	6.3 Objectives of a Minimarket Food Store
1. Number of customers attracted to store monthly will be increased by a seven percent monthly average.	Actual count of sales tickets			
2. Cash outlay per customer will increase three percent quarterly	Sales tickets			
3. Promotion of new items will be emphasized by newspaper coupons so that 15 percent of these items sold are paired with coupons.	Newspaper coupons			
4. No more than two percent of customers will be kept waiting for more than three minutes at the check-out station.	Random sampling of stores during operations			
5. Operating costs will be increased by no more than 10 percent over the past year.	Accounting records			
6. Part-time employee turnover will be reduced by 20 percent in one year.	Personnel records			
7. The ratio of food costs to waste will be reduced by 10 percent as a monthly average.	Sales and food records			
8. The net profit margin will increase from four percent to four and one-half percent on the dollar volume of store sales over the past year.	Accounting records			

■ Forces managers and others to explicitly realize there is *no single
objective* for the organization, its departments, or its members.

■ Forces managers and others to explicitly recognize that objective
setting *involves risk* and *uncertainty* in balancing and making trade-
offs between objectives.

■ Forces managers and others to explicitly analyze and reach decisions
about relative *priorities*.

■ Forces managers and others to explicitly analyze and reach decisions
about the *relationships between objectives* of the organization, objectives of the departments within the organization, and the objectives
of the individuals within the departments.

objectives have to be given from the top downward;[24] The Environmental
Protection Agency has forced companies to achieve certain environmental objectives within a specified period of time or pay stiff fines.

***Superior-
subordinate
participation***
Under an MBO program, superior and subordinate participation attempts to
reach a consensus on: (1) what objectives the subordinate will attempt to
achieve in a specified period of time; (2) the general means by which the
subordinate will attempt to accomplish the objectives; and (3) how progress
toward objectives will be measured and the specific dates for such measurements.[25]

This process begins with intensive preparation, focuses on a face-to-face
objective-setting interview, and ends in specific written objectives. The joint
objective-setting process may also provide an opportunity for two other benefits. First, it can open a channel for effective two-way communications between a superior and subordinate. Second, it can provide a useful way to
identify training and development needs of subordinates. The key to the objective-setting interview is to get the active involvement of both superior and
subordinate. Distortions can occur if the supervisor dominates the interview
or conversely abdicates responsibility. The success of the MBO system depends
on how well both the objectives and plans are defined, communicated, and
accepted. Table 6.5 provides a brief summary of the possible benefits of objective-setting and participation for individual employees and the organization.

■ Helps individuals understand their responsibilities and define priorities for their jobs.

■ Helps stimulate constructive feedback from others, particularly the superior.

■ Helps provide individuals with a means for assessing their own progress on a day-to-day basis.

■ Helps develop and increase individuals' commitment to desired results and outcomes.

■ Helps individuals play a strong role in shaping their own career development and opportunities.

As individuals think about a possible objective, they often immediately proceed to thoughts about how this objective might be achieved – e.g. they engage in action-planning.

After the objectives have been established, action plans should be developed for accomplishing the desired objectives.

**3. Action-Planning
for Departments and
Individuals**

The comprehensiveness of action plans vary widely. In more stable and less complex environments, management needs less action-planning. This is because the means for accomplishing objectives are likely to be routine and standardized. In contrast, the activities that might be part of the action plan for a vice-president of marketing whose objective is to increase sales volume by 10 percent within 12 months might look like this:

Variations

1. Release the new product that has been developed to supplement the product line by _____.

2. Evaluate the feasibility of a reduction in price to stimulate demand for the existing product line (products X and Y).

3. Upgrade the effectiveness of sales personnel in selected geographical areas.

4. Increase the rate of delivery for products X and Y.[26]

The extent to which an individual will be involved in developing action plans will vary. For example, developing an action plan to achieve departmental objectives might involve group discussion by the departmental members and managers.[27] On the other hand, the action plan to achieve an individual's objectives might be developed by that individual alone and submitted to the superior for his or her information or possible comment. Let's consider General Mills' approach to action-planning and objective-setting.

CASE STUDY

General Mills For each manager at General Mills, a statement of "accountabilities" is included as part of the job description.[28] The statement sets forth, in general terms, the results that a specific position should produce. In preparing General Mills' "Action Plan," a manager consults the list of responsibilities and then writes, under each statement, specific objectives to be achieved during the year ahead to fulfill that responsibility. After all such responsibilities have been identified, the manager and subordinate discuss the action plan. This discussion can modify the specific objectives until both agree that they are meaningful, obtainable, and challenging.

General Mills advises its managers that the terms they select should be quantifiable (e.g., percents, ratios, number of, average number of, etc.). It is one thing to have an objective to "lower production costs," but quite another to have an objective to "lower the costs of producing the net weight 10 oz box of cereal 7 percent by April 30 by having operations 7, 8, and 9 done by one machine operator." Further, the more precise the statement, the more readily its contribution to successful operations can be anticipated. "To lower costs y percent" makes it possible to determine what changes in price or increases in profits can be planned for.

To have "bottom line" significance, the first three steps in the process of MBO must lead to action and a sense of "self-control" by organizational members.

4. Implementation and Self Control "Implementation" refers to translating the results from the objective-setting process into new day-to-day behaviors that lead to the attainment of desired objectives. It often means that superiors must give greater latitude and choice to subordinates, and discontinue managing subordinate's hour-by-hour and day-by-day activities. Superiors are to be available to coach and counsel the subordinates as needed. They take on less of a judgmental role and more of a helping or facilitating role.

"Self-control" means that employees will be given the responsibility and opportunity for controlling their own activities to achieve the objectives. It means that management trusts individuals to work effectively toward the desired objectives and discuss problems with their superiors or others. Of course, formal performance reviews of departments and individuals are conducted periodically.

This step means there should be systematic and scheduled reviews to: measure and assess progress; identify and resolve problems; and revise, drop, or add objectives. Although these reviews look to the past, there is considerable emphasis on determining the significance and lessons from the immediate past for dealing with the future.[29]

5. Performance Reviews of Departments and Individuals

The appraisal of an individual's or department's achievements during a performance review focuses on *mutual problem-solving* between the superior and subordinate. The mutual problem-solving approach requires that subordinates *participate* in reviewing their personal performance or that of their department. The superior encourages this by asking subordinates to identify obstacles, problems, and ways to improve performance. Since objectives have previously been developed and (hopefully) agreed on, the review process zeros in on actual achievements of the individual or department. This is in contrast to evaluating such personality traits or subjective characteristics as "conscientious," "enthusiastic," and "creative."[30] As suggested in Fig. 6.4, performance reviews should be a source of obtaining inputs to future objective-setting. Thus the MBO process recycles over time.

Distinguishing features

Performance reviews under MBO are to provide feedback to the employee or group of employees. This permits them to know how well they are achieving the objectives. *Knowledge of results* is essential to changes in job performance. It aids the development of new skills, attitudes, and knowledge. MBO emphasizes that subordinates must review their own performance and participate in evaluating it if they are to operate under self-control. By knowing our objectives and how these are measured, we should gain insight into our performance and the possible need for change. Two of the objectives of a furniture salesperson may be a 10 percent sales increase and a 40 percent average

Strengths and limitations

mark-up on goods sold during the next year. So long as there is informational feedback regarding these areas, the salesperson will be able to see just how he or she is progressing toward achievement of these objectives.

Unfortunately, the review process is not so simple. In the case of the salesperson, there may be factors other than the salesperson's own behavior that influence possible gaps between the stated objectives and actual results. Some of these factors could include the state of the economy, store hours, advertising campaigns, and the availability of credit. Significant parts of some managerial jobs may not lend themselves to the development of objective indicators of performance. Homer Wilson, the vice president of operations at Celanese Chemical Company, said that one of his objectives is to build morale and develop people's careers. This type of objective must be evaluated on the basis of judgment. We must decide *whether* the objective was achieved before we can ask *why* it was — or wasn't.[31]

While MBO does not recommend a passive role by superiors in the performance-review step, it does require that superiors shift from a judgmental and critical posture to a helping and mutual problem-solving role.[32] At times, we have found individuals interpreting this step and the whole MBO process as "soft." Quite the contrary! Individuals can be demoted and dismissed under this system. This is because the rationale and basis for such actions should be more apparent and it should be easier for the superiors to confront the need for making such decisions.[33] Of course, the MBO process is intended to reduce and prevent the need for such decisions.[34] Tenneco is one firm that has most of the qualities outlined in steps 1 through 5 and which is operating an MBO system for its managers and professionals.

CASE STUDY

Tenneco's PP&E System

Tenneco is a large, diversified company operating in eight major industries; some of which are oil, chemicals, and automotive equipment. The firm employs about 85,000 people, of which 15,000 are managers and professionals.

Tenneco has adopted a performance planning and evaluation (PP&E) system for its managers and professional employees — their version of an MBO system. We will review their system with special emphasis on its aspects of personal development and advancement. Their system consists of three major parts: performance planning; performance evaluation; and personal-development planning.[35]

Performance Planning and Evaluation

In the performance planning part, jobs and situations are diagnosed and employees state their job responsibilities and objectives for the year. The steps in this process include:

1. Broadly defining the key responsibilities in jobs.
2. Developing specific objectives for each key responsibility.
3. Assigning relative priorities to the desired objectives.

Discussions between superiors and subordinates to obtain agreed-upon objectives are encouraged. These objectives are recorded on a form and reviewed periodically in meetings between the superior and subordinate. The meetings are intended to check progress, discuss problems, and possibly agree on changes in the objectives because of changes in the economy or other things. The employee's performance is judged against the stated objectives and priorities. The steps in this part include:

1. The supervisor completes an evaluation of the subordinate's performance.
2. The supervisor's superior reviews the evaluation to assure consistency, equity, and quality.
3. The supervisor discusses the evaluation with the subordinate, with a focus on developing the subordinate.[36]

Note that this evaluation part gives the employee less opportunity to participate in self-evaluation than other versions of MBO do.

During their performance-evaluation sessions, subordinates are told how well they are doing and specific plans for development are made. These activities are based on a discussion of:

1. Strengths and weaknesses of past performance.
2. Potential performance improvement opportunities.
3. The subordinate's interest in development and aspirations for advancement.

Personal-Development Planning

After the performance-evaluation session, the superior completes an assessment of the employee's potential for development. The report includes:

1. Overall performance rating during the last period.
2. Development needs and mutually agreed-upon action plans.
3. Progress and achievement from previous development plans.
4. Individual interests and objectives.
5. Present promotability and potential for promotions.
6. Possible replacements.

This report is reviewed by the manager's superior. It is kept in each division and at corporate headquarters to serve as a source for locating employees with potential for advancement.

Figure 6.5 provides an outline in Tenneco's Performance Planning and Evaluation (PP&E) system. Special concern is given to the personal-development planning part. The PP&E system at Tenneco is designed to plan for good performance and assist managers and professional employees in developing their optimal skills through long-run career planning. The preliminary research results on the effectiveness of this system are positive and encouraging.[37]

6.5

Philosophy and basic process of Tenneco's PP&E system

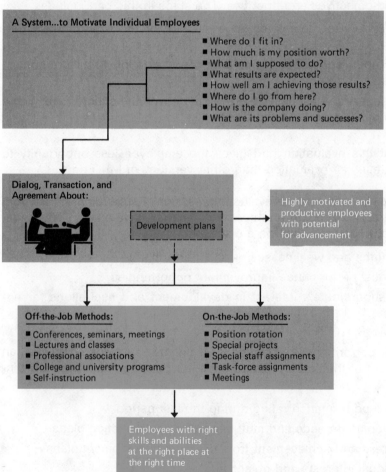

A System...to Motivate Individual Employees

- Where do I fit in?
- How much is my position worth?
- What am I supposed to do?
- What results are expected?
- How well am I achieving those results?
- Where do I go from here?
- How is the company doing?
- What are its problems and successes?

Dialog, Transaction, and Agreement About:

Development plans

Highly motivated and productive employees with potential for advancement

Off-the-Job Methods:

- Conferences, seminars, meetings
- Lectures and classes
- Professional associations
- College and university programs
- Self-instruction

On-the-Job Methods:

- Position rotation
- Special projects
- Special staff assignments
- Task-force assignments
- Meetings

Employees with right skills and abilities at the right place at the right time

Assessment of MBO
as a Planning Aid

The effectiveness of Management by Objectives is influenced by top management's values and philosophy. The research on the effectiveness of MBO is mixed. These research results are often difficult to interpret because neither the philosophy nor steps outlined were fully implemented. In any event, two contrasting views of Management by Objectives can be presented:

1. The MBO programs most likely to be successful include: (a) emphasis on objective setting; (b) frequent interaction and feedback between subordinates and superiors regarding progress toward objectives, stumbling blocks, or the need for revised objectives; and (c) opportunities for subordinates participation in setting their objectives, even though the final objectives may reflect the needs of the entire organization.[38]

2. When MBO is used as a top-down club to control people, it is likely to be ineffective.[39] If the values of organizational members are strongly antagonistic to the philosophy and systems of MBO, then MBO is probably doomed to failure.

A critical factor in the implementation of MBO programs is the organizational climate — political or achieving — of the organization. Top management cannot assume a passive role. They must explain, coordinate, and guide the program. Some firms begin to manage by objectives only to discover unsound organization structures or poor administrative practices. When top management is committed, changes will penetrate through the entire organization more easily. Lower-level management will also see that top management is really committed to the program.[40]

Management by Objectives is not offered as a cure-all for planning and motivational problems. It is an aid that justifies careful consideration by managers. MBO can link the different 'levels of the organization as well as its operational and strategic planning processes. The next planning aid to be considered — PERT — assumes that strategic objectives have been established. It is often used as a technique in operational planning.

SCHEDULING:
PROGRAM
EVALUATION AND
REVIEW
TECHNIQUE

Scheduling is a common planning aid and technique. *Scheduling* refers to the creation of timetables for communicating when certain things should occur or get done. Organizations and life in general are filled with schedules — class schedules, airline schedules, workweek schedules, and production schedules. One measure of managers' effectiveness is their ability to manage time and to achieve objectives within time limits. Managers' time may be the organization's scarcest resource. Scheduling is one way to improve managerial efficiency. If a million-dollar printing press that has been operating for eight hours a day is made to operate at the same capacity for ten hours a day, then

6.6
*Advantages to Effective
Scheduling*

■ Provides a time baseline for coordinating starts and stops of
various activities, tasks, projects, or programs.

■ Assists in planning and controlling the necessary steps or
tasks for reaching objectives on a timely basis.

■ Reduces dependence on personal relationships and "politics"
and increases emphasis on formal organizational links to gain
commitments.

■ Forms a basis for negotiating specific agreements on how and
when resources will be allocated.

■ Improves the ability to focus on the critical activities
or tasks and separate them from the trivial.

Adapted and modified from P. Mali, *Improving Total Productivity: MBO Strategies for Business,
Government and Not-For-Profit Organizations.* New York: John Wiley & Sons, 1978, p. 346.

the result is improved organization productivity. Better scheduling of the
items to be printed and better scheduling of maintenance might have been the
factors making this possible. The primary advantages to scheduling are highlighted in Table 6.6

To develop a schedule, one must start with well-defined objectives. The
action-planning element in MBO often includes schedules that are linked to
each of the key objectives.

One type of widely used schedule is the Program Evaluation and Review
Technique (PERT). The Program Evaluation and Review Technique is a special
type of flow diagram for planning and controlling nonrecurring projects or
programs. PERT uses a flow diagram to show the necessary activities and
events to reach an objective. It is normally used for projects that have not been
done before and will probably not be done again in exactly the same manner.
Examples include the Golden Gate Bridge in San Francisco, the Empire State
Building in New York, Disneyworld in Florida, and the construction of a particular house. PERT is a useful aid for dealing with a variety of nonrepetitive
planning and control problems. The purpose of PERT scheduling is to analyze
and specify in detail what is to be done, when is it to be done, and what is the
likelihood of achieving the objective on time.

Four Major Elements   PERT consists of four major elements: a network; resource allocation; time
and cost considerations; and the critical path.[41] Let's consider these elements.

A basic network is shown in Fig. 6.6. A ***network*** is a diagram of the sequence of activities that must be performed to complete a project. It consists of events, activities, and relationships. *Events* are points of decision or accomplishment of some activity. *Activities* occur between events and are the physical or mental efforts required to complete an event.

Activities are broken out to show when different individuals or departments are to be held responsible for them. The *relationships* between the basic tasks are indicated by the desired sequence of events and activities in the network. For example, event 3 cannot occur until activities A, B, and C have been accomplished. If these activities are the responsibility of different managers, these managers must coordinate their work.

Network

6.6
Basic PERT network

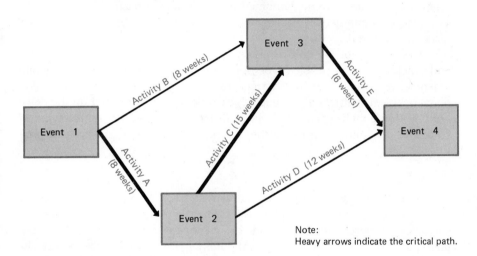

Note:
Heavy arrows indicate the critical path.

To undertake the activities needed, resource requirements — such as labor, material, equipment, and facilities — need to be estimated. The availability of these resources are a key influence on the length of time between events and the costs associated with each activity.

Resource allocation

PERT's principal value is its ability to aid management in reducing time and cost expenditures. The cost considerations are expressed in the form of sub-budgets, or estimated costs for each specified activity against which actual costs can be compared.

Given the available resources, time estimates for each activity can then be made. Figure 6.6 shows that the activity between events 1 and 2 should require eight weeks. Time estimates are normally developed after the activities and events have been defined. Four time estimates are often developed for each activity.

Time and costs

1. The *most likely time* is the estimated required time for an activity if normal problems and interruptions are considered. Figure 6.6 presents only the most likely times for each activity.

2. The *optimistic time* is the estimated required time for an activity if virtually no problems occur. In Fig. 6.6, we might estimate the optimistic time for the activity between event 2 and event 3 as 12 weeks.

3. The *pessimistic time* is the estimated required time for an activity if problems and interruptions of an unusual nature occur.[42] In Fig. 6.6, we might estimate the pessimistic time for the activity between events 2 and 3 as 18 weeks.

These three times may be combined to obtain an *expected time* for activity. The expected time usually represents some form of weighted average of the three time estimates.

Development of alternative time periods enables managers to anticipate and quickly react to problems or opportunities. If you are running behind schedule, you might find it advantageous to use overtime or hire some additional people. Or, if you are ahead of schedule, you might speed up the delivery dates on supplies that are needed in later activities. These two types of responses are quite common in the use of PERT on major construction projects.

Critical path A **path** is the sequence of events and activities that should be followed over the course of a project. A complex project like the construction of Disneyworld consists of hundreds and thousands of activities and paths. Of course, work takes place along each of the different paths separately and concurrently. The length of the entire project is determined by the *path with the longest elapsed time*. To shorten a project, activities in the longest path should be the focal point for managerial attention. The **critical path** is the longest time path through the network. Any delay of activities within the critical path will cause delay in reaching the ultimate objective — occupying the building, opening Disneyland, selling the new product, etc. Since the longest path determines the shortest possible completion time, it is called the *critical path*. The critical path in Fig. 6.6 requires a total elapsed time of 29 weeks and can be calculated by adding the number of weeks scheduled to complete the activities between events 1 and 2, events 2 and 3, and events 3 and 4.

Sample Applications The first major appliction of PERT occurred in 1958. It was used in the United States Navy's Fleet Ballistic Missile Program, more popularly known as the

Polaris Missile Program. PERT was credited as a major reason why this program was completed two years early.[43]

Some governmental agencies require companies with whom they have contracts to use PERT. This technique has far-ranging action planning applications — filming a movie, building a plant, diversifying into a new business, or introducing a product.

After a project is under way, PERT becomes less of a planning aid and more of a control mechanism. Through the periodic reporting system it can monitor the variances between actual and planned elapsed times and costs for each activity.

An underlying theme in the applications of PERT is that the projects are extremely *complicated* and require tight *coordination* between activities and events if the ultimate objective is to be reached on schedule. PERT is particularly helpful in developing a schedule that specifies what is to be done, when it is to be done, and what the likelihood is that it will be done. PERT is used as a planning technique to reduce time and cost requirements, for its full potential as a planning tool is increased when budgets are tied to each major set of activities or events.

Budgeting refers to determining and assigning the resources required to reach objectives. Most budgeting shows the allocation of resources in terms of dollars. In budgeting for completely new and uncertain activities, managers may assign dollar costs based on rough estimates, but budgets for established activities and objectives are usually easier to determine. In either case, though, the person making up the budget exercises his or her best judgment in the use of historical data and knowledge in combination with forecasts of changing costs for each resource category. Budgets are often developed for a one-year period and then broken down by month. This enables managers to track their progress in meeting the budget as the year unfolds. The major categories in budgets usually include labor (human effort), materials and supplies, and facilities (property, buildings, equipment, and the like).

Budgeting serves three main purposes. First, it aids managers in planning their work more effectively. Second, it aids managers at all levels in planning how best to allocate resources within their jurisdiction. When we put "dollars and cents" to the specific resources needed to achieve our plans, we sometimes realize that the objectives we were going to pursue aren't worth the costs. In this case, we might be saying to ourselves that the priorities for objectives aren't the same now that we have an understanding of what the objectives are likely to cost. Third, once budgets are established, they aid in controlling and monitoring the resources being used to achieve specific objec-

BUDGETING: ZERO BASE

Role and Purposes of Budgeting

tives. Strategic plans are often translated into operational plans through the use of capital budgeting. **Capital budgeting** refers to the financial planning necessary for allocating resources to major tangible projects often requiring a time horizon beyond one year.[44] Capital budgets are usually developed for new buildings, additions or revisions to present buildings, major purchases of new equipment, and the like. When Disneyworld was developed in Florida, the capital-budgeting process was very complex. The overall capital budget was developed into a series of component capital budgets. Each theme area, such as Frontierland, had a capital budget. Within a theme area, capital budgets were also developed for each building and entertainment activity.

Nature of Zero-Base Budgeting

For some types of ongoing activities in organizations, Zero-Base Budgeting has been used as a planning tool. **Zero-Base Budgeting** (ZBB) is a system of justifying activities and programs in terms of efficiency and organizational priorities and treating them as if they were entirely new.[45] The goal of Zero-Base Budgeting is to assist managers in allocating and moving resources to their most cost-effective uses. Thus, it is a planning technique for aiding in the achievement of strategic objectives in response to proven needs, perceived threats and risks, or perceived opportunities. ZBB apparently started in the U.S. Department of Agriculture in the early 1960s. It has since been refined and used in many firms and government agencies such as Texas Instruments, Eastern Airlines, Owens-Illinois, New York Telephone, and the U.S. Department of Agriculture.

Two major elements

ZBB is essentially a "bottom-up" system that includes two major elements. The first element is a *decision package* — a verbal description of what is needed to accomplish each major objective for a manager's unit. Developed by analyzing and describing discrete objectives, decision packages generally include the following:

1. Objective of the activity.

2. Description of the activity.

3. Alternative ways of achieving the objective.

4. Consequences of not performing the activity.

5. Advantages of retaining the activity.

6. The personnel, equipment, space, and other resources required during the current budget year.

7. The resources needed for the activity during the next budget period.[46]

PROGRAM NAME	Service Force Job Enrichment Program		Program No. 16

DESCRIPTION (objectives, target population, implementation schedule)

To extend the job enrichment program for the service force — as piloted in Spring Falls, Avon Hills, and Maplewood branches — to all branches between 1972 and 1976.

Is program legally required? ☐ Yes ☒ No

STATE OF THE ART	☒ High	☐ Medium	☐ Low
EASE OF IMPLEMENTATION	☐ High	☐ Medium	☒ Low
ECONOMIC BENEFITS	☒ High	☐ Medium	☐ Low

	Potential revenue impact	Probability of occurrence	Probable gross benefit (cost)
Identifiable benefits:			
Reduction in service force turnover of 1 point	$ 450,000	.2	$ 90,000
Extension of 1-2 point reduction in absenteeism, as demonstrated in pilot project	$ 2,132,500	.8	$ 1,706,000
Extension of 5% increase in service force productivity, as demonstrated in initial efforts	$85,500,000	.1	$ 8,550,000
Total benefits:	$88,082,500	.1175	$10,346,000
Tangible costs to Xerox of acting: Group personnel staff time to develop program, and line management time to implement program in all branches	($ 472,950)	.9	$ 425,655
Total costs:	($ 472,950)	.9	$ 425,655
Probable net benefits (cost):			$ 9,920,345

Intangible benefits

Increased morale in service force, with improved customer service and satisfaction.

"Contagious effect" of job enrichment to other groups, e.g., sales and clericals.

Improved service manager development with concurrent sharpening of their motivational skills. As an extreme example, one manager at Avon Hills increased his team's productivity 70%.

ECONOMIC RISKS	☒ High	☐ Medium	☐ Low

Possible consequences of not acting:
Continued escalation of service costs as a percent of revenue.

ASSUMPTIONS AND OTHER CONSIDERATIONS

Cost estimates assume 4.4 man years of group staff time, 26 man years of branch manager time, and 15.8 man years of service manager time to implement program in a population of 1,053 service managers.

Benefit estimates assume elimination of 3 days absenteeism per month for each of 1,053 service teams, favorable productivity, and that turnover experience in pilot branches can be cascaded to all branches.

6.7
Sample decision package with ZBB

Reprinted by permission of the Harvard Business Review, Exhibit from "Cost Effectiveness Comes to the Personnel Function" by Logan M. Cheek (May–June 1973). Copyright © 1973 by the President and Fellows of Harvard College; all rights reserved.

The second major element in ZBB involves the ranking of decision packages.[47] This may be accomplished through a variety of means — from complicated cost/benefit assessments right through to subjective evaluation by a superior. Sometimes the rankings include a voting process in which key managers rate activities on a scale.

Figure 6.7 provides a sample decision package for a service force job enrichment program. It is presented only as an example because there is no such thing as an ideal decision package format; formats will vary between and even within organizations.

Overall assessment   ZBB is quite consistent with Management by Objectives. In fact, ZBB serves as a particularly useful tool within the action-planning and objective-setting steps of an MBO system. The departments that can most easily use ZBB are legal, traffic, public relations, advertising, production control, personnel and human resources, credit and financial management, and the like. All of these departments provide service, advice, control, or information functions. ZBB has caught on in many government agencies because their primary objectives revolve around these types of functions. Departments for which profit-related objectives can be established may find other budgeting techniques to be better.[48] In the final analysis, strategic planning, operational planning, and day-to-day decision-making must be linked together as a system for maximum effectiveness.[49] MBO and ZBB are compatible aids in providing a means for making such linkages a reality.

SUMMARY   This chapter has barely tapped the many planning aids and techniques available to managers. We presented only a few of them. This was done to convey a clear understanding of those aids and techniques that were covered.

The forecasting discussion should be important in developing your abilities to perform the *monitor* managerial role. This role focuses on scanning the environment for signals and developments important to the department or organization. The discussions on Management by Objectives (MBO), scheduling through the use of the Program Evaluation and Review Technique (PERT), and budgeting through Zero-Base Budgeting (ZBB) should all serve to develop your ability to perform the *entrepreneur* and *resource allocator* managerial roles. The MBO presentation should also help you perform the *leadership* managerial role.

These planning aids and techniques are easiest to use in simple/stable task environments and most difficult to apply in changing/complex task environments. However, the potential benefits from these planning aids are likely to be greatest in the latter type of environment.

The relation of these planning aids and techniques to strategic and operational planning might be noted as follows: Through forecasting, we attempt to monitor the environment so that some sense of possible environmental futures can be developed. These possible environmental futures are a critical component in the strategic planning process. MBO serves as a system and philosophy for linking strategic planning, operational planning, and the day-to-day affairs of organizational life. Scheduling through PERT generally assumes that the basic objectives and strategies have been developed for new or one-of-a kind projects. It serves as an operational planning technique to reduce the time and costs for achieving a well-defined objective. Finally, budgeting through ZBB serves as a tool for evaluating ongoing activities against desired objectives.

The next three chapters on decision-making should deepen and broaden your understanding of this and the previous chapter on planning. This is because all planning is a form of decision-making.

KEYWORDS

action plan
budgeting
capital budgeting
critical path
cross-impact analysis
Delphi technique
extrapolation
forecasting
management by objectives
network
objectives
path
program evaluation and review technique
scenario
scheduling
simulation models
zero-base budgeting

DISCUSSION QUESTIONS

1. What is the difference between strategic planning and forecasting?

2. Explain the similarities and differences between the Delphi technique and simulation models.

3. Use the Management by Objectives model to develop an analysis of the experiences you had in your last job. You should assess this experience in terms of how consistent or inconsistent it was with the basic MBO model in Fig. 6.6.

4. Use the Program Evaluation and Review Technique (PERT) to develop an action plan for the successful completion of your college degree.

5. The opening case to this chapter was on INTEL. What do you like and/or dislike about the system of management described in this case? Explain.

6. Develop a likely scenario for your life over the next four years.

7. Do you agree or disagree with the philosophy of MBO? Explain.

8. Could you use Zero-Base Budgeting in your personal planning? Explain.

9. How does capital budgeting differ from ZBB?

Management Incidents and Cases

**FRANK JONES:
SUPERVISOR***

Frank Jones became supervisor of plant maintenance after 15 years as operator of a local electrical appliance repair shop. Spindle Rayon Mill had moved to the small Southern community in which Frank lived in 1958. Frank accepted a job on the construction crew and was later employed to install and maintain lights, air conditioning, generator, steam plant, and miscellaneous equipment.

By 1965, floor space had tripled and the work force increased by several hundred. Frank found that his responsibilities had grown commensurately. He was often required to work overtime and occasionally returned to the plant during the night to make necessary repairs. He performed his work in a conscientious manner and was considered to be a devoted and loyal employee. It was necessary to add men to his crew, and in late 1973 he found himself with a salary, a title as Director of Physical Plant, and responsible for the efforts of 16 men.

It was noted, however, that he still preferred to personally repair the machines rather than direct his subordinates to do so. The plant manager told him one man could no longer perform all the work required of his department and encouraged him to do less of the repair work himself, but instead to select, train, and direct capable subordinates.

Frank made an attempt to do so. He even dressed like the other supervisors and organized his crew in such a way that he could spend most of his time in the office. It was not long, however, before department heads were complaining that machinery needed repairs and work schedules were disrupted due to idle machines. It was reported that when physical-plant repairmen were summoned, more likely than not they were incapable of completing the repairs without calling Frank. After a brief interval Frank returned to his blue denims. One department complained to the plant man-

---

* Case developed by John M. Champion (University of Florida). In J. Champion and F. Bridges *Critical Incidents In Management* (rev. ed.). Homewood, IL: Richard D. Irwin, 1969, pp. 188–189. © Richard D. Irwin, Inc., 1969. Used with permission.

ager that Frank was possessive about the machinery and was deliberately not selecting and training qualified repairmen because he seemed to feel secure only if others regarded him as indispensable.

The plant manager took under advisement the action to be taken. He knew that Frank was not performing the supervisory function, yet he remembered the years and loyalty Frank had devoted to the company.

Questions

1. How would you describe Frank's problem or problems?
2. What should the plant manager do?
3. Would objective-setting help?
4. Who needs objectives and what are they?

CASUAL TOGS, INC.*

Casual Togs is a 20-year-old firm producing moderately priced women's apparel, headquartered in a midwestern city. About 80 percent of production is sold to large- and middle-sized department stores in cities throughout the country. The remaining 20 percent is sold to small women's specialty shops. All clothes carry the firm's well-known brand label. Products are principally shirts and blouses, with some knitted dresses making up the balance.

The owner and principal stockholder, Cy Geldmark, is an entrepreneur. Geldmark served a long apprenticeship in the New York garment district and saved part of his meager wages until he could open his own firm, staffed primarily with relatives and friends. An innovator, Geldmark pioneered in the "mix and/or match" coordinate idea of fashion ensembles, whereby a customer of moderate means could build a complete wardrobe of work and casual clothes. Designers with trend-setting styles and above-average quality (considering the semi-mass production methods employed) helped propel Casual Togs to a prominent position in the industry.

However, the mix-and-match coordinate idea was not patented and intense fashion competition has now developed from larger firms as well as from new, smaller companies with fresh fashion ideas. In Geldmark's words, price competition is "deadly." The company has rapidly expanded in the last five years, setting up production plants in eight southern states to capitalize on low wage rates in these areas.

---

* Developed by Paul J. Wolff, Associate Professor, Dundalk Community College, Baltimore, Md. Used with permission.

All facilities in these states are leased. Notwithstanding the use of the latest in large-capacity cutters and high-speed sewing machines, production hinges on a great expenditure of careful, personal effort by the individual worker. Many quality checks are necessary before a garment is finished.

In an attempt to coordinate production and delivery, the company is constructing a new multimillion-dollar central distribution plant at the present home office location, where all administrative and some production functions are performed. All production runs will be shipped to this new facility; then they will be dispatched by a computer-programmed delivery-inventory scheduling method. This facility is planned to help cope with an increasingly serious problem of merchandise returned from customers who refuse acceptance because delivery is later than promised.

The industry is characterized by five distinct selling fashion "seasons"; consequently garments must be ordered, produced, and delivered within a relatively short time period. This five-season cycle produces unusual production and forecasting problems. Based on pilot sales during the first two weeks of each season, forecasts are developed regarding the quantity and styles to be produced for the entire season. Once the bolts of cloth are cut into a particular season's patterns, there is no turning back. If pilot sales are not indicative of the rest of the season or if the sales forecast is in error, the company is saddled with stock that can be disposed of only through "off-price" outlets, usually at a loss.

In an effort to increase the accuracy of sales forecasting and to pinpoint specific reasons for late deliveries, Geldmark instituted a computer printout of each day's sales, as reported by telephone by field salesmen. This printout was, initially, distributed to the president, the vice-president of sales, the sales forecast manager, the treasurer, the production manager, and the eight regional sales managers. All of these people were located at the firm's headquarters offices. The printout was voluminous, often running one hundred or more pages.

Geldmark relied a great deal on his "feel of the situation" for making decisions. Although he made all final important operating and policy decisions, he said that all department heads should feel free to act as "you see fit"; he said that he would back any decision made without consultation with him. Despite Geldmark's exhortations that he need not be consulted, almost all vice-presidents and departmental managers conferred daily with him, usually regarding the progress of the then current fashion season's products. During each fashion season many style modifications and quantity-level changes were made. With rare exceptions Geldmark made all important daily decisions in these matters.

These daily decision sessions were marked by emotional outbursts by various management personnel. The meetings were informal and nonscheduled and different groups would meet at different times with Geldmark. The groups were not formal or even based on functional problem lines. If one individual felt that a daily printout indicated change "X," regardless of whether or not it affected his department, he would go to the president asking that the change be effected. If another department manager or even a vice-president were present and disagreed, inevitably a shouting match developed in the president's office. Usually Geldmark remained impassive during these interchanges, giving his decision after all participants had finished.

Some management personnel said that Geldmark was "too lenient" and should curb these emotionally charged sessions because they were disruptive and led to erroneous decisions. These same critics pointed to Geldmark's reputation as an easy mark for suppliers; e.g., if a supplier had some previous tie from the old days or was remotely related to someone in Geldmark's family, he would be assured of at least some orders despite the fact that his prices were higher than those of competing suppliers.

Often the president's sister, Judy, who was vice-president in charge of administration, would wander into these daily decision sessions. She would often object to proposed changes on the grounds that they were "too damned expensive." She often countermanded a department manager's instructions and would hire and fire personnel without the manager's knowledge. Geldmark always backed Judy's decisions once they were made. Although the formal organizational chart depicted Judy and the treasurer as being on the same level, the treasurer, Stan Seeburg (Geldmark's nephew), was not allowed to approve any expenditure over $1000 without Judy's informal approval. But several sources reported that if Judy and her brother had an argument in private, Judy always deferred to her brother's decision.

For many years Geldmark's chief source of sales data and forecasts was Andy Johnson, sales forecast-budget manager. Johnson prepared daily, handwritten recaps from telephone reports in the earlier years and from the printout in more recent years. Using intuition and a very thorough knowledge of the garment industry, Johnson would prepare the season's forecasts and modify them as the actual sales started coming in. He had rapport with Geldmark and was quite proud of the clearly evident esteem that the president had for him.

This rapport was important to Johnson for more than reasons of self-esteem. Johnson had been with the firm for 15 years but despite his knowledge had never been promoted. He resented this keenly. "At least," said Johnson once, "Cy listens to me more than to these shirt-tail relatives"; Johnson was one of the very few people who called the president by his first name in public.

In a recent change in office location, Johnson and his former co-worker, Sol Green, were moved from one large, shared office, which housed subordinates as well, to individual glass-partitioned offices. The subordinates were now located adjacent to Johnson's and Green's offices. After this move Green was promoted to manager-internal accounting and sales and was given control over all subordinates who previously had worked collectively for Johnson and Green.

Johnson was given one new man to help with sales forecasts and budgets; the new man had an MBA and was trained in statistical analysis. Johnson held a bachelor's degree in business. Smith, the new man, suggested several new methods of collating and analyzing the daily printout to Johnson, who abruptly rejected the ideas, saying, "Cy isn't used to getting data in that form; he would be confused by a change."

As the daily printouts began to be more detailed and more widely distributed, Johnson became more critical of them than ususal. He said that they didn't "really" show what styles were leading and that there were many errors. Johnson quoted personal conversation with field salesmen to prove his points. When Smith cited several instances in which, on the recap, Johnson was combining several new styles in what had previously been one category, Johnson replied that he was using horse sense to report data in a way that Geldmark and others would best understand. Johnson was away from his desk for long periods during this time, attending numerous management meetings that the president called. The pattern of these meetings was as before, or worse; there were loud, emotional arguments punctuated by fist-pounding and door-slamming.

The problem of returns was now most acute; on the average, 40 percent of all shipments were being returned. Although all management personnel agreed that the reason for returns was late delivery, there was no agreement as to what caused the late deliveries. Some managers argued that forecasting by style line was inaccurate and resulted in erroneous production scheduling; others said that there was no coordination betweeen the nine production centers and the shipping department which was located at the home office site. Still others said that shipping and/or production methods were not efficient. The production manager said that there was a disparity between the delivery dates given customers and those on the salesman's order, which served as the basis of a production run. The sales manager maintained that poor quality was the real reason for returns, customers did not want to become embroiled in arguments with home office personnel over quality questions and therefore they wrote "late delivery" on substandard merchandise because it was simpler.

In an effort to solve the dilemma, Geldmark hired an experienced market analyst who had a strong computer-oriented background, Stan Levin. Levin was given a private office and the authority to effect any changes he deemed necessary. Several events happened immediately: a supplemental recap of the printout was published every day by Levin — in addition to Johnson's handwritten recap; the printout format was changed. Green objected strongly to the new format, saying that it did not provide accounting with the categorizations necessary for their work. Johnson referred to Levin as "this egotistical, snot-nosed kid."

At this same time, several new designers were hired, salesmen's commissions schedules were changed, many regional vice-presidents were put on the road "temporarily," and Johnson, backed by Geldmark, cut all departments' budgets by 15 percent (the company was in the middle of a twelve-month budget period).

Approximately four weeks after all of these changes had occurred problems continued to arise. Returns had increased to an even higher level and many old customers had stopped ordering, saying that the poor quality and late deliveries made Casual Togs too undependable. Performance of the nine plant centers fell, on the average, 15 percent under previously established production goals. In addition, two of the new designers resigned. Johnson, Green, and Levin would not speak to each other. Johnson began distributing two daily sales recap reports to a select group of top managers; and the computer services department complained directly to Geldmark that their new work load was too great because Levin now required them to produce a daily selling forecast, by week, month, and season.

Questions

1. What are the primary reasons for this firm's problems?

2. Could any of the forecasting approaches discussed in this chapter be used by Casual Togs? How?

3. Could MBO help this firm? Explain.

4. Could PERT help this firm? Explain.

5. Could ZBB help this firm? Explain.

REFERENCES

1. L. Salerno, "Creativity by the Numbers: An Interview with Robert N. Noyce." *Harvard Business Review* **58,** 3, 1980, 122–132.

2. D. Bell, *The Coming of Post Industrial Society: A Venture in Social Forecasting.* New York: Basic Books, 1973.

3. I. Ansoff, "Managing Strategic Surprise by Response to Weak Signals." *California Management Review* **18,** 1975, 21–33.

4. H. Kahn and A.J. Wiener, *The Year 2000: A Framework for Speculation on the Next Thirty-Three Years.* New York: Macmillan, 1967.

5. C. Ducot, and G.J. Lubben, "A Typology for Scenarios." *Futures* **12,** 1, 1980, 51–57.

6. K. Nair and R.K. Sarin, "Generating Future Scenarios — Their Use in Strategic Planning." *Long Range Planning* **12,** 3, 1979, 57–61.

7. A. Delbecq, A. Van de Ven, and A. Gustafson, *Group Techniques for Program Planning: A Guide to Nominal Group, and Delphi Processes.* Glenview, IL: Scott, Foresman, 1975.

8. D. Roman, "Technological Forecasting in the Decision Process." *Academy of Management Journal* **13,** 1970, 127–138.

9. J. Pfeffer, *New Look at Education.* Princeton, NJ: Western, 1969, p. 155.

10. R. Bunning, "The Delphi Technique: A Projection Tool for Serious Inquiry." In J. Jones, and J. Pfeffer (eds.), *The 1979 Annual Handbook for Group Facilitators.* La Jolla, CA: University Associates, 1979, pp. 174–181.

11. A. Fusfeld and R. Foster, "The Delphi Technique: Survey and Comment." *Business Horizons* **14,** 1971, 63–74.

12. S. Wheelwright, "Management by Model During Inflation." *Business Horizons* **18,** 1975, 33–42.

13. H. Schollhammer, "Long-Range Planning in Multinational Firms." *Columbia Journal of World Business* **6,** 1971, 79–86.

14. G. Steiner (ed.), *Managerial Long-Range Planning.* New York: McGraw-Hill, 1963, p. 60.

15. A. Roalman, "Why Corporations Hate The Future." *MBA* **9,** 1975, 35–37.

16. T.H. Naylor, *Corporate Planning Models.* Reading, MA: Addison-Wesley 1979; G.R. Warner, "Things to Come in Planning Technology." *Financial Executive*, May 1980, 34–40.

17. I. Wilson, "Socio-Political Forecasting: A New Dimension to Strategic Planning." *Michigan Business Review* **26,** 4, 1974, 15–25.

18. G. Odiorne, *MBO II: A System for Managerial Leadership for the 80's.* Belmont, CA: Fearon Pitman Publishers, 1979.

19. W. Giegold, *Volume I: Strategic Planning and the MBO Process.* New York: McGraw-Hill, 1978.

20. J. Muczyk, "Dynamics and Hazards of MBO Application." *The Personnel Administrator* **24,** 5, 1979, 51–62.

21. W. Giegold, *Volume II: Objective Setting and the MBO Process.* New York: McGraw-Hill, 1978.

22. M. Richard, *Organizational Goal Structures.* St. Paul, MN: West Publishing Co., 1978.

23. H. Levinson, "Management by Whose Objectives?" *Harvard Business Review* **48,** 4, 1970, 125–135.

24. H. Weihrich, "An Uneasy Look at the MBO Jungle: Toward a Contingency Approach to MBO." *Management International Review* **16,** 3, 1976, 103–109.

25. D. Klinger, "Does Your MBO Program Include Clear Performance Contracts?" *The Personnel Administrator* **24,** 5, 1979, 65–74.

26. A. Raia, *Managing by Objectives.* Glenview, IL: Scott, Foresman, 1974.

27. H. Weihrich, "TAMBO: Team Approach to MBO." *University of Michigan Business Review* **31,** 3, 1979, 12–17.

28. L. Hrebiniak, "Power and Control." Unpublished paper delivered at Alabama A&M University, May 28, 1976.

29. P. Mali, *Improving Total Productivity: MBO Strategies for Business, Government, and Not-for-Profit Organizations.* New York: John Wiley and Sons, 1978.

30. W. Giegold, *Volume III: Performance Appraisal and the MBO Process.* New York: McGraw-Hill, 1978.

31. R. Babcock and P. Sorensen, Jr., "An MBO Checklist: Are Conditions Right for Implementation?" *Management Review* **68,** 6, 1979, 59–62.

32. W. Tips and H. Gysels, "The Structure of Goal Sets in Planning and The Environment." *Journal of Environmental Management* **10,** 1, 1980, 13–23.

33. M. McConkie, "A Clarification of the Goal Setting and Appraisal Processes in MBO." *The Academy of Management Review* **4,** 1, 1979, 29–40.

34. J. Quick, "Dyadic Goal Setting Within Organizations: Role-Making and Motivational Considerations." *The Academy of Management Review* **4,** 3, 1979, 369–380.

35. J. Ivancevich, J. McMahon, J. Streidl, and A.D. Szilagyi, Jr., "Goal Setting: The Tenneco Approach to Personnel Development and Management Effectiveness." *Organizational Dynamics* **6,** 3, 1978, 58–80.

36. Ibid., 69.

37. Ibid., 74–75.

38. J. Ivancevich, "Changes in Performance in a Management by Objectives Program." *Administrative Science Quarterly* **19,** 1974, 563–574.

39. S. Kerr, "Some Modifications in MBO as an OD Strategy." *Academy of Management Proceedings*, 1972.

40. R. Mayer, "The Secret Life of MBO." *Human Resource Management* **17,** 3, 1978, 6–11.

41. *New Uses and Management Implications of PERT.* New York: Booz Allen and Hamilton, 1964.

42. A. Laufer, *Operations Management.* 2nd ed. Cincinnati, OH: South-Western Publishing Co., 1979.

43. D. Boulanger, "Program Evaluation and Review Technique." *Advanced Management* **26,** 1961, 8–12.

44. R. Horwitz, "Corporate Planning — A Conceptual Critique." *Long-Range Planning* **12,** 1, 1979, 62–66.

45. P. Pyhrr, *Zero-Base Budgeting: A Practical Management Tool for Evaluating Expense.* New York: John Wiley, 1973.

46. G. Odiorne, *MBO II: A System of Managerial Leadership for the 80's.* Belmont, CA: 1979, pp. 210–217.

47. M. Dirsmith and S. Jablonsky, "Zero-Base Budgeting as a Management Technique and Political Strategy." *Academy of Management Review* **4,** 1979, 555–565.

48. L. Cheek, *Zero-Base Budgeting Comes of Age.* New York: AMACOM, 1977.

49. J. Camillus, and J. Grant, "Operational Planning: The Integration of Programming and Budgeting." *Academy of Management Review* **5,** 1980, 369–379.

Chapter 7

ORGANIZATIONAL DESIGN: BASIC CONCEPTS

After reading this chapter, you should be able to:

1. Name the three reasons why organizations divide up the work.

2. Identify and give examples of departmentalization practices.

3. List the basic concepts of coordination, and explain how they are used by managers.

4. List the contrast advantages and disadvantages of centralization versus decentralization.

5. Describe the relationship between line and staff personnel.

PREVIEW CASE

Burt Richardson

Burt Richardson's hobby of selling ceiling fans had grown gradually into a small-scale business after he retired from his job with a small electrical contractor. At the time of his retirement, he was selling 3000 fans per year simply by advertising in the *Ladies Home Journal*. From this he netted about $250,000 annually. His sales were growing because of OPEC's price raises in oil. Burt purchased fans from manufacturers, and he and his wife assembled and shipped them to buyers within a three-state area. His wife kept the books in her spare time.

Burt needed some additional money to move the operation from his garage to a local manufacturing site. He persuaded some neighbors to contribute money, incorporate, and create a national distribution system. His neighbors welcomed the opportunity and formed a firm.

Burt placed a few more ads in several other women's magazines. His sales volume grew rapidly. Within a short time, he had 20 production people, two foremen and three salespersons who called on building contractors. At this time, Burt decided not to buy fans from other manufacturers and assemble them but to manufacture all the parts. He hired 25 additional people to manufacture the fans and three foremen to supervise this process. In addition, he hired a young college graduate to assist his wife in keeping the books. Two others were employed to purchase parts from suppliers.

Shortly after this expansion, Burt noticed profits were off, orders were not being filled on schedule, employees were asking for a lot of overtime, absenteeism and turnover were higher than ever, and customers were returning fans because of damage or shoddy workmanship.

Burt's organization was suffering from low motivation and morale, late and inappropriate decisions, lack of coordination, and rising costs. When Burt examined the organization closely, he noticed several reasons for these problems. Motivation and morale were low because people perceived they had little responsibility, opportunity for achievement, and recognition of their worth. There was insufficient delegation of authority. Decision-making was delayed because there were no adequate procedures for evaluating the results. People were working out of step with each other and, therefore, the organization was becoming uncoordinated. Methods for coordinating the sales and production people had not been worked out. The sales force was promising fans which the production department could not make or deliver on time. Costs were rising because of excessive procedures and paperwork for the supervisors. This was distracting them from their productive work of supervising manufacturing personnel. Some of Burt's questions were:

1. How should my company be organized?

2. What kind of coordination mechanisms are there to choose from?

3. Should the overall structure of the organization be centralized or decentralized?

4. Is it appropriate to hire staff personnel?

5. Should the jobs be broken down into narrow areas of work and responsibility so as to secure additional benefits of specialization?

There was no single best answer to Burt's questions. The problems Burt faced are the focus of this chapter. This chapter provides some answers to these questions and alerts you to the alternatives Burt has available when redesigning the structure of the company. We caution you that organizational design is not as rational as indicated in this chapter. Organizations often evolve by change and by making changes to meet a particular problem at a given time. As described in the next chapter, there are other important determinants of structure; including the technology used by the organization, the environment in which it operates, and the values of its members. We present the basic concepts in this chapter.

BASES OF DEPARTMENTATION

The design of its organization is one of management's major problems. Any organizational structure should enable employees to work effectively toward accomplishing organizational goals. As Drucker points out, the function of an organization's structure is to assist managers in the attainment of the goals. This can be done in three ways.[1]

First, structure formally allocates people and resources to tasks that have to be done and provides the means for coordination. Job descriptions, organization charts, committees, and lines of authority assist the manager. Second, members of the organization understand more clearly what is expected of them when operating procedures spell out ways in which tasks are to be performed. Standards of performance can be established. Using criteria, such as output or quality of performance, enables the manager to plan and communicate effectively the organization's operating procedures to all employees. Third, the structure helps the manager know who has the information needed to make decisions. Procedures can be established whereby information is collated, evaluated, and made available to managers on a regular basis.

When designing an organization, a fundamental requirement is that people be allocated responsibilities in agreement with the tasks to be performed. Given the total range of tasks to be performed by the organization, the question arises as to how tasks should be grouped. Another way to put the question is: On what basis should the people in the organization be specialized? *Departmentation* is the process of establishing departments within the company. It can be accomplished in four general ways: function, place, product, and customer. Each way has advantages for management. The difficulty lies in the fact that tasks and people can be grouped differently at various levels in the organization's hierarchy. The choice of how to group people and their activities depends on which factors management feels to be most significant.

Departmentation by Function

Members of an organization who share a common expertise and draw upon the same set of resources are grouped by *function*.[2] Functional grouping of activities is a widely used and accepted managerial practice. It covers what the

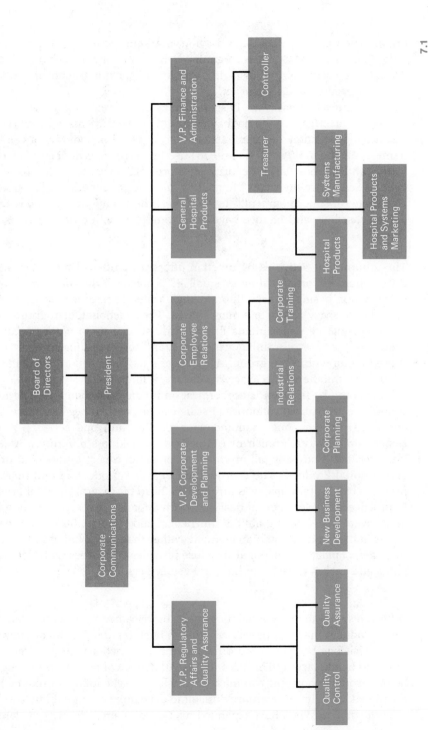

7.1

American Sterilizer Company

(From the abridged version of the American Sterilizer Business Review and Fact Book, 1981, p.3. Used with permission, Corporate Communications, February 1981.)

organization actually does — production, marketing, finance. American Sterilizer Company (AMSCO) is organized in this manner (see Fig. 7.1). In AMSCO's structure, specialists in separate departments contribute to the common product and its market.

Sometimes, however, the basic functions do not really appear on an organization chart. Hospitals do not have marketing departments, and churches do not have production departments. Rather, these functions are given other names. Airlines (TWA, KLM, Pan Am) use the terms operations (production), traffic, and finance; large department stores (Lazarus, May Company, J. C. Penney, Sears) use the terms "finance," "general merchandising," "publicity," and "general superintendent." In the latter, the traditional functions of productions, selling, and finance have been combined with other activities.

Advantages The grouping of activities by function offers a number of advantages, especially when the organization is small. It is particularly appropriate for an organization basing its growth on a single range of products or services sold almost exclusively within one market area. The functional form groups activities into separate departments that provide specialists to work on common problems. Methods of training, experience, and resources, for example, can be shared by all within the group. A manager's job satisfaction is enhanced by working with others who share similar work interests.

Grouping by function is economical on managerial manpower because it is a simple structure. Economies of scale can be reached because there is only one sales function, one manufacturing facility, and one set of managers. Hence, capital and administrative expenses are held to a minimum. At American Sterilizer Company, all production personnel report to the head of General Hospital Products. The coordination between production and marketing personnel is formally achieved through the head of General Hospital Products. In practice, however, a great deal of coordination is often accomplished informally over coffee, during golf, at luncheons, and so forth. Strategic coordination is in the hands of top management, rather than in the hands of lower-level managers. Finally, a functional structure provides employees with clear career paths and makes it easier to hire and retain personnel.

Disadvantages Difficulties with the functional form start to arise once the organization diversifies products, markets, or services. Just as Burt found in his fan organization, quick decisions become more difficult because functional managers have to report to headquarters. The sales representative may have to wait a long time before production people can make a decision on scheduling a product. In the functional form, it is often more difficult to determine accountability and levels of performance. When Burt expanded his fan company, who was to blame for the loss in profits, production, sales, personnel? While it might be a "people" problem, it was most likely because the organization wasn't designed to handle the increase in sales. Coordination between departments may become a problem for top management; functional departmentation tends to deemphasize the goals of the firm as a whole while departments concentrate on meeting their own costs and schedules without regard for the entire organization. Finance people are finance experts, and production people are production experts; experts often have difficulty seeing the firm as a whole, thus complicating coordination between activities. In other words, people develop loyalty to the department, thereby creating "walls" between departments instead of identifying with counterparts in other functions or the entire plant. Considerable effort is required by top management to promote coordination.[3]

Departmentation by Place

Departmentation by *place*—on the basis of geographic area — is a rather common method for organizing physically dispersed firms. On the assumption that efficiency will improve, all activities in a given territory are grouped and assigned to one manager. Place departmentation is used by the major companies. Southland's organization is based on regions (Eastern, Western, and Central) that are further subdivided into districts (Fig. 7.2). Other examples of place departmentation are large police departments that divide the city into precincts and department stores that assign floorwalkers, janitors, and window washers to various parts of the store. Similarly, many governmental agencies, such as the Internal Revenue Service, the Federal Reserve Board, the federal courts, and the Postal Service, adopt place departmentation as the basis of organization in their efforts to provide nationwide services. Many multinational firms use this basis of departmentation because of the differences in cultural and legal factors in each country. The lack of uniformity in market structure, differences in production methods, and divergent patterns of a nation's traditions and norms make geographical considerations important for the firm's success.

The Coca-Cola company operates in about 150 countries. Much of its annual sales of over $3 billion comes from foreign operations. Coca-Cola divides the world into three parts, each with an executive vice president in charge. The United States, Central and South America are one part. Another grouping is Europe, Africa, Southeast Asia, and India. The third is Canada, the Pacific, and the Far East.[4]

Advantages

The advantages of place departmentation are primarily those of economy and efficiency. For the production function of the organization, place departmentation involves establishing plants, refining or assembling the same product,

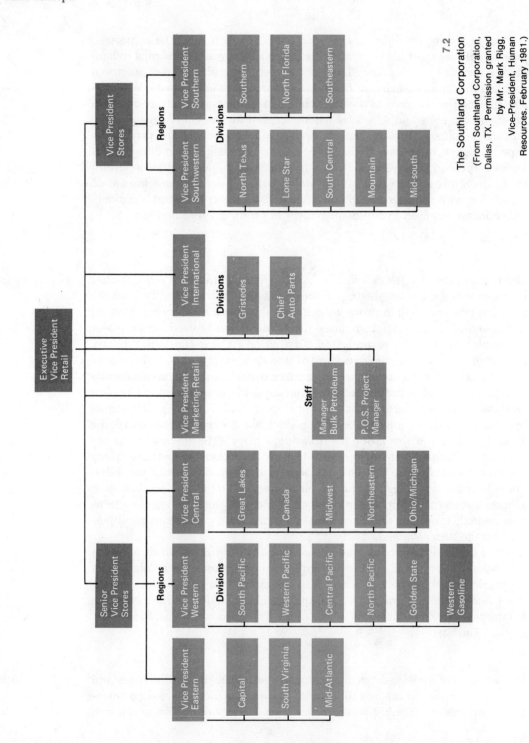

7.2 The Southland Corporation
(From Southland Corporation, Dallas, TX. Permission granted by Mr. Mark Rigg. Vice-President, Human Resources. February 1981.)

and distributing the product to a given area. By catering to local factors, the production activity can realize gains from providing jobs for local labor, lower freight rates, and (perhaps) lower labor costs. The marketing function can benefit from having sales personnel spend more time in sales and less time in travel. They can get to know the customer's needs and, in doing so, serve the customer better. Being closer to the customer may permit the salesperson to pinpoint the marketing strategy most likely to succeed.

Companies that serve international markets usually follow multiple strategies. Coca-Cola's organization by place recognizes that decisions and strategies vary considerably between countries. For example, when Coca-Cola gave an Israeli firm a franchise to bottle and sell Coke, Coke was boycotted in the Arab countries from 1967 until July of 1969. However, Coca-Cola also owns Aqua-Chem, a company that designs and manufactures equipment for desalting seawater. Saudi Arabia is planning to spend billions of dollars for desalting equipment. The decision to sell Coke to Israel, therefore, had far-reaching effects on Coca-Cola's operations.

Disadvantages

Place departmentation requires more personnel with managerial abilities, clearly increases control problems for central corporate staff, and leads to duplication of many services that could be performed centrally in a functional organization. District managers usually want some control over their own purchasing, personnel, accounting, and other services so they can truly be responsible for the profitability of the operation. As indicated in the disadvantages of functional departmentation, each manager can easily build his or her own "empire" at the expense of the entire firm's effectiveness. The decision to franchise Coke in Israel had a detrimental effect on the profits of Aqua-Chem. Finally, the reluctance of the district manager to rely on corporate headquarters for services could reflect a management attitude of "I'll show them it can be done without their help." To ensure proper controls, many activities are duplicated in each geographical area. Naturally, this leads to higher costs. For example, for the Internal Revenue Service to have several districts processing tax forms requires more personnel and expensive computer equipment than if there was just one central clearinghouse. To ensure uniformity of services, extensive rules and regulations are used by the IRS, Southland (7-Eleven stores), Steak and Ale, Searle Optical, and Zale Jewelry to coordinate the activities of their various districts.

Departmentation by Product

A ***product*** structure becomes a more appropriate way to group activities when an organization produces two or more products that are different in technical make-up, production process, and market distribution. This basis of grouping activities has been an emerging trend in large multiproduct companies, such as GM, Ford, Procter and Gamble, General Foods Corporation, Mack Trucks, and conglomerates. These organizations started with a functional structure, but their growth and subsequent management problems made functional departmentation uneconomical. Gulf and Western Industries, Inc., is engaged in eight totally different areas of business, e.g., leisure time, financial services, consumer and agricultural products, manufacturing, apparel, paper and building, natural resources, and automotive replacement parts. Each of these products groups operates as an individual business. The president of Gulf and Western believes the strength of the company lies in its ability to combine the best efforts of entrepreneurial drive for success and the strict central monitoring of planning budgeting and financial controls.[5] So far as Gulf and Western is concerned, the more rapid the change in the environment, the higher the rate of technological change. In general, the greater the pressures for rapid response to external pressures, the greater the advantage the product structure has over the functional form.

Advantages

The product form has the advantage of all employees making specialized contributions to a particular product line. At Gulf and Western, the leisure time group — producers of the movies *Grease, The Godfather,* and *Saturday Night Fever* — enjoyed a phenomenal increase in income. On the other hand, the agricultural products group, manufacturers of Dutch Masters Cigars and Schrafft Candy, reported a decline in income primarily because the price of sugar went too high and the market for premium cigars was down. Top management at Gulf and Western was then able to focus attention on the agricultural product group and make decisions to improve this group's ability to handle new responsibilities and challenges.

Disadvantages

The disadvantages of product grouping are very similar to those faced when people are grouped on the basis of place. That is, both require the firm to have a large number of personnel with the required managerial skills to staff the product lines. Most of the functional activities (e.g., marketing, finance, production, etc.) are duplicated in each product line, thus increasing the expense of doing business for the entire organization. While product organization appears to enhance each product line's adaptability, extensive communication lines and coordinating mechanisms between the product lines are required. At General Motors, for example, major decisions are made by the executive committee (see Fig. 7.3). This group coordinates the decisions made by the various product line managers and keeps the overall company goals in perspective. Too frequently top management may be drawn into day-to-day coordinating decisions between the products. This is detrimental because it detracts from strategic issues.

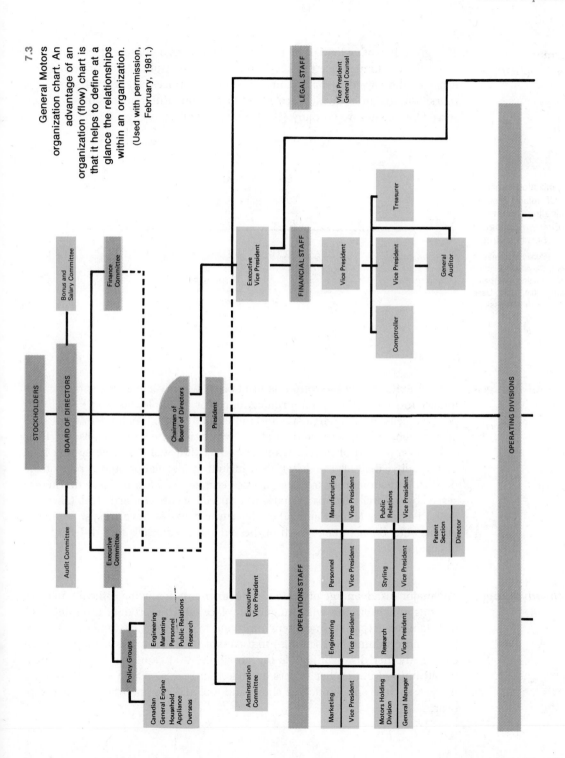

7.3

General Motors organization chart. An advantage of an organization (flow) chart is that it helps to define at a glance the relationships within an organization.

(Used with permission, February, 1981.)

Departmentation by Customer

The grouping of activities to reflect the interests of different customers is common. Customers are the key to the way many utilities are organized because of the varied demands on the utilities' services. Figure 7.4 shows the marketing group is divided according to the four different customer groups served by this utility company. The heads of all groups report to one manager.

7.4
Organization chart for Cleveland Electric Illuminating Company's Energy Application Services Group.

(Public Information Department, Cleveland Electric Illuminating Company, Cleveland, Ohio, 1981. Used with permission.)

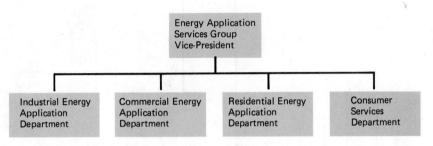

Advantages

Departmentation by ***customer*** is used often when various needs of the customers must be met by the organization. For example, Standard Steel Corporation sells to both wholesale and industrial buyers. Wholesalers want steel of a dependable quality and quantity which is suited for the use of their customers. Industrial buyers want a product that will save money and is of high quality; they also seek services, including installation and repair of the product and sometimes training of sales employees. Each of these markets is served by different groups of marketing specialists at Standard Steel. Likewise, Sears, Penney's, Macy's and other department stores have men's, women's, infants', etc. departments. Each of these departments sells to a different type of customer.

Disadvantages

The major disadvantage of customer departmentation is the difficulty in coordinating this grouping with functional, place, and/or product groupings. To maintain (or get) sales, managers may want to give some customers privileges (rates, entertainment, discounts) that cannot be given to all of the firm's clientele. Another disadvantage is the possibility that capital equipment might be left unused until other orders are filled. In recessions, an entire customer market, such as small machine shops and tool and die operations, may disappear.

Underlying our discussion so far has been the theme that people should be grouped in a way that eases the flow of communication and information. Departmentation is not an end in itself but simply a method of grouping activities to facilitate the achievement of the firm's goals. As we indicated, each method has its advantages and disadvantages. The selection of a particular departmentation strategy depends on the type of situation facing the firm. Because of the relative advantages of each type of departmentation, most complex organizations use several of these strategies in grouping activities. For example, at the senior vice-president level at IBM, the work is grouped according to product, as indicated in Fig. 7.5. The managers reporting directly to the vice-president are members of a particular operational or product grouping.

Another point to be considered is the use of different groupings with the functional area. Searle Optical managers have place and functional department heads reporting to them. Reporting to the vice president of marketing are the managers of the contact lens and regular lens departments, along with the managers of the advertising, planning and development, merchandising, and promotions departments. Thus, in this firm, a department manager is employing two bases (product and function) for grouping activities at the same organizational level. The senior vice president of marketing, James Rothe, states that the objective is not to build rigid structure, but to group activities that will best contribute to achieve the company's goals.

The practice of mixing departmentation is merely a reflection of the principle of division of work and of the enormous complexity of the organizing problem. Dividing the work is the initial step, but the problem of relating subordinates to supervisors and department to department remains. This involves coordination. The concepts basic to achieving coordination are unity of command, span of control, and delegation of authority.

It has often been said good people can make any organization effective. People who can work together and cooperate to get things done are valuable employees. Teamwork is especially relevant in sports; although coaches may spend hours practicing against "foreign" teams, the actual game situation is one of ambiguity for both offensive and defensive players. During practice sessions, however, coaches develop players who want to cooperate and work together most effectively. To do this, players need to know the part they are to play in any cooperative effort and how each relates to the others. Coordination is required to design and maintain these systems of roles.

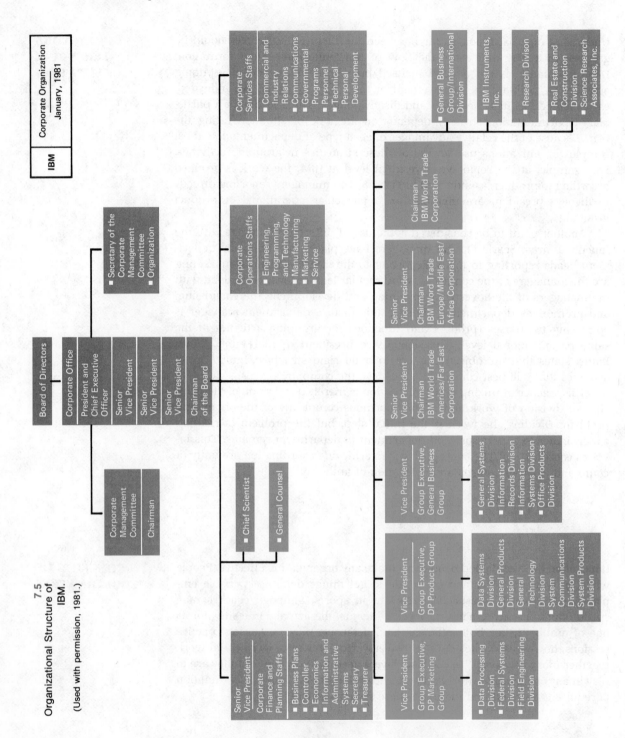

7.5
Organizational Structure of
IBM.

(Used with permission, 1981.)

According to traditional-management theorists, such as Taylor, Fayol, and Weber, one manager should be in charge of an area of responsibility. Moreover, a chain of command should be established so that all organization members know who they report to and who reports to them. Confusion over who gives orders and who implements them should be minimized. The **unity-of-command** principle forms the basis for most organizational hierarchy. It states that an individual have only one boss.

Unity of Command

The **scalar principle** refers to the chain of direct authority from manager to subordinate throughout the organization. The basic idea of this principle is that every employee should know his or her area of responsibility, and no one individual should report to more than one superior. If this principle is followed, subordinates know who delegates authority to them and to whom matters beyond their authority must be referred.

Scalar Principle

The basic scalar principle is indicated in Fig. 7.6, the structure of the police department for the City of Columbus, Ohio. The chief of police is responsible for the development of an efficient organization through which the primary objective of the Division of Police can be best achieved. Suppose a person in the Narcotics Bureau wants to discuss a case with someone in Internal Affairs. Adherence to the unity-of-command principle requires the former to follow the chain of command through the head of the Investigative Subdivision to the executive officer before talking with someone in the Internal Affairs Bureau. According to Fayol, communications between members of different departments should be approved by their respective superiors and the superiors should be kept informed of the outcome.[6] In this case, the narcotics person is responsible only to the head of the Investigative Subdivision and the person in the Internal Affairs Bureau is responsible only to the executive officer.

The unity of command grew out of the organization's needs for cooperation to achieve certain organizational goals. One way to ensure that this cooperative activity takes place with the least cost is for management to adopt a structure in which all employees know their superior. Obstacles to performance caused by confusion of assignments can be clarified by one's immediate supervisor.

Span of control deals with the number of subordinates who report directly to a superior. The problem of span of control is as old as organizations. There is the belief that a manager's mind is not capable of supervising too many people. This belief has been fostered by the fact that military organizations

Span of Control

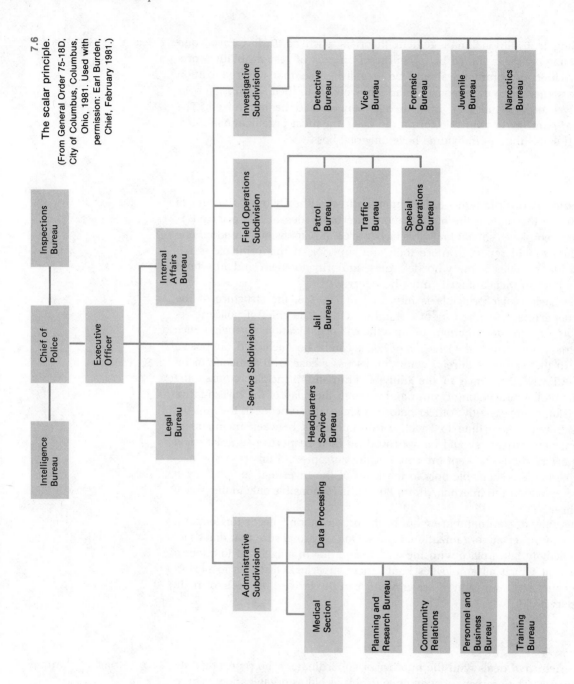

7.6

The scalar principle.
(From General Order 75-18D, City of Columbus, Columbus, Ohio, 1981. Used with permission: Earl Burden, Chief, February 1981.)

find narrow spans of control most effective in combat situations. Traditional-management practitioners specify that the number of subordinates reporting to any one manager should range between four and 12.

In actual experience, one finds a variety of practices. A survey of 100 large companies by the American Management Association found the number of executives reporting to the president varied from one to 24; only 26 presidents had six or fewer subordinates, and the median number was nine.[7] Comparable results have been found by other researchers.[8] One consistent result is that in large organizations (those with at least $1 billion sales), the span of control at the top tends to be no more than 12, with the span decreasing as company size decreases.

However, such findings are of limited usefulness. First, they typically measure the span of control only at or near the top level of the organization. Second, since many of the participating companies report varying spans of control, it is hard to generalize the findings. Perhaps more important is that simply reporting what companies do in practice is not the same as specifying what they ought to be doing. The fact that in 1975 the president of General Motors had two vice-presidents reporting to him and one of these had 13 managers reporting to him does not make that pattern "correct." By contrast, a regional vice-president of Sears, Roebuck receives reports from several hundred store managers. A further limitation is that some managers tend to regard the span of control as an end in itself. They measure the effectiveness of their organization in terms of clarity and completeness of a fixed number of employees reporting to any one supervisor. The creation of a fixed span is *not* completely desirable, as we shall see shortly.

Graicunas' formula

Several management scholars have attempted to measure the span-of-control principle to make its application more precise. In a paper published in 1933, V. A. Graicunas analyzed superior-subordinate relationships and developed a mathematical formula based on the geometric increase in complexities incurred as the number of subordinates reporting to a single supervisor increases.[9] Although the formula may not be applicable in every situation, it does serve as a guideline for managers because it focuses on three important issues in span of control: (1) the number of subordinates reporting directly to a given supervisor; (2) the relationship between the superior and each possible combination of subordinates, and (3) the cross-relationships that develop when one subordinate must deal with another.

From an analysis of these three issues, Graicunas developed the following formula to give the number of all possible types of superior-subordinate relationships requiring managerial attention. Where n represents the number of subordinates reporting to a manager and C represents the total possible contacts, the number of all kinds of relationships will be represented by $C = n(2^n/2 + n-1)$. The results of this formula are shown in Table 7.1. The data clearly show a geometric increase in the number of possible relationships occurs if the number of subordinates increases. For example, by adding a fifth subordinate, executives increase the possible relationships for which they are responsible by 127 percent (from 44 to 100). The data also indicate that the complexity of the manager's job resulting from the addition of one subordinate is potentially the greatest beyond spans of five.

The relationship between a manager and subordinate cannot be totally captured by this formula for several reasons. First, managers may do more than just manage; for example, a sales manager may also do some selling. Second, a critical dimension is how many people working with one another report to a manager. The vice-president at Sears, who has several hundred store managers reporting to him, can manage because each store is autonomous. There is no need for store managers to interact. All stores do the same kind of work and are appraised and measured by the same yardsticks. Third, what about the managerial ability of the superior? It is more likely that supervisors with exceptional managerial talent will be more successful in regu-

		7.1 ***Possible Relationships with a Variable Number of Subordinates.***
Number of Subordinates	**Number of Relationships**	
1	1	
2	6	
3	18	
4	44	
5	100	
6	222	
7	490	
8	1,080	
9	2,375	
10	5,210	
11	11,374	
12	24,708	
18	2,359,602	

From H. Koontz and C. O'Donnell, *Management: A System and Contingency Analysis of Managerial Functions*, 6th ed., New York: McGraw-Hill Book Company, 1976, p. 287. Used with permission of McGraw-Hill Book Company.

lating their time and frequency of contacts with subordinates and, therefore, use wider spans of control than executives with lesser talents. Fourth, if a subordinate has been a member of the organization for a long time, and has developed appropriate patterns of behavior, a superior might spend less time with him or her than with a newcomer experiencing organizational life for the first time.

There is no "right" number of subordinates a manager can supervise effectively. Rather, there are several general factors that affect a superior's span of control. The National Conference Board lists the following general factors to be taken into consideration in determining the optimum span for a given situation:

Contingency factors affecting span of control

1. the competence of the superior and subordinate;

2. the degree of interaction between departments being supervised;

3. the extent to which the supervisor must carry on nonmanagerial work;

4. the similarity or dissimilarity of activities being supervised;

5. the incidence of new problems in the supervisor's department;

6. the extent of standardized, objective rules and procedures within the organization;

7. the degree of physical dispersion of activities.[10]

CASE STUDY

Lockheed

One company that has attempted to use some of these variables for an answer to the span-of-control problems is Lockheed Aircraft Corporation. After a large-scale study, Lockheed found that six factors were important in determining span of control.[11] Although the study was aimed at the middle-management group in which the spans were narrow (only three to five), and although the underlying variables used at Lockheed were not precisely the same as those suggested by the National Conference Board, there were many similarities.

The variables Lockheed used for its analysis are shown in Table 7.2. These six variables (labeled "span factors" in the table) were then given a weighting score (indicated in parentheses), which was based on the analysis of the 150 middle managers and department directors studied at Lockheed. After the scores for a given manager's position had been determined, that person could compare the total span-factor weighting to determine his or her suggested span of control. For example, let's

Span Factor					
Similarity of functions	Identical	Essentially alike	Similar	Inherently different	Fundamentally distinct
	(1)	(2)	(3)	(4)	(5)
Geographic contiguity	All together	All in one building	Separate building, one plant location	Separate locations one geographic area	Dispersed geographic areas
	(1)	(2)	(3)	(4)	(5)
Complexity of functions	Simple repetitive	Routine	Some complexity	Complex, varied	Highly complex, varied
	(2)	(4)	(6)	(8)	(10)
Direction and control	Minimum supervision and training	Limited supervision	Moderate periodic supervision	Frequent continuing supervision	Constant close supervision
	(3)	(6)	(9)	(12)	(15)
Coordination	Minimum relation with others	Relationships limited to defined courses	Moderate relationships easily controlled	Considerable close relationship	Extensive mutual non-recurring relationships
	(2)	(4)	(6)	(8)	(10)
Planning	Minimum scope and complexity	Limited scope and complexity	Moderate scope and complexity	Considerable effort required, guided only by broad policies	Extensive effort required, areas and policies not charted
	(2)	(4)	(6)	(8)	(10)

From H. Koontz and C. O'Donnell, *Management: A Systems and Contingency Analysis of Managerial Functions,* 6th ed., New York: McGraw-Hill Book Company, 1976, p. 295. Used with permission of McGraw-Hill Book Company.

assume that a first-line foreman supervised subordinates performing identical tasks in close physical proximity; the task itself was simple and repetitive, required little subordinate training and minimum contact with others, and had little planning. In this case, the foreman would receive a score of 11. On the opposite end of the continuum would be a manager who was supervising employees who were performing fundamentally distinct functions, who were geographically dispersed, who were performing highly complex and varied tasks that required close and constant supervision in coordination with others, and whose tasks required extensive planning. This manager would receive a score of 55. The higher the score, the smaller the suggested span of control.

Despite these rather crude methods, Lockheed was able to eliminate one level of supervision and widen the span of middle management, with a consequent reduction of over $70,000 in supervisory costs. Although the index was used successfully by Lockheed, the company's management is quick to point out that these factors and their corresponding weights should not be used blindly. The Lockheed method should not be applied in a mechanical way. In practice, considerable managerial judgment is needed in determining the extent to which each factor is present in a manager's job, whether other factors should enter into the picture, and whether the suggested standard is appropriate in a given situation.

The Lockheed model is intended to be used only as a general guide which, when supplemented with judgment based on experience, may assist the manager in making more effective span-of-control decisions. Most managers seldom have the opportunity to design their control system. Span-of-control decisions develop according to historical relationships, personnel development plans, union contracts, and budget availability, among other things.

Behavioral issues

There has been a considerable amount of span-of-control research by behavioral scientists interested in the operation of small groups. Group size is the major behavioral variable affecting span-of-control relationships.[12] Several relevant conclusions emerge from this body of research:

1. Group cohesiveness (attraction of one individual to a group) is best with approximately five members. A small group does not provide sufficient interaction for cohesiveness, and a larger group tends to break down into subgroups or cliques.

2. Small groups tend to generate higher member satisfaction than do larger ones, largely because of the opportunity for participation by those members who want it.

3. As groups become larger, the demands on the leader become more exacting and complex and require the leader to become more directive. This leadership style is needed because of the difficulties of coordinating the efforts of the larger group.

In summary, some confusion has arisen from specific statements about the ideal maximum number of subordinates which should report to any one supervisor. There is, of course, no one such number. Rather, the maximum number of subordinates a manager can manage effectively is a function of several contingency factors, as well as several behavioral consequences. Although there is probably a limit, that number will vary in accordance with the contingency factors and the importance attributed to them by the manager and the organization.

AUTHORITY STRUCTURE

The authority structure of the firm is the underlying thread that makes the division of work and its coordination possible. The authority structure is the means by which activities can be placed in a manager's job and the coordination of the organization's activities carried out. ***Authority*** is the right to make decisions. Authority is the cement of the organization's structure.

Authority

Authority provides the direction and control of the flow of decisions from the top of the organization downward through the unity of command. It is the power needed to carry out one's obligations. Authority includes, therefore, the power to make decisions with respect to the activities of subordinates. For example, if A tells B to perform a task, B may not perform it. But if B does, there are two possible reasons. First, A may have persuaded B by providing certain information that has led B to perform the task. Second, B may have accepted A's decision without really giving it any thought, feeling that it was in A's power to make the decision. Management theorists maintain that authority always comes from top management and is legitimized by the person in that role.

Chester Barnard, President of New Jersey Bell Telephone Company from 1927 to 1948, maintained that authority flows in the opposite direction, from the bottom up.[13] This view is known as the acceptance theory of authority. Barnard realized that not every decision made by one's immediate supervisor could be consciously analyzed, judged, and either accepted or rejected. Rather, most decisions or orders fall within a subordinate's "zone of indifference." If a decision falls within that zone, the subordinate will comply without question; if it falls outside the zone, the person will question whether to accept or reject it. The width of the indifference zone depends on the degree to which rewards exceed the burdens and sacrifices. A manager's asking a secretary to take some dictation probably falls within the secretary's zone, because it is a part of the job description. The manager's asking the secretary to dinner, however, probably falls outside that zone, and the secretary may refuse to comply. If we merge the traditional definition of authority with that of Barnard, we can define authority as a superior's right to command the subordinate's acceptance of a superior's right to command.

Responsibility may be thought of as an owed obligation to perform an assigned activity. It is acquired when an individual accepts an assignment of certain objectives, activities, and duties. The manager has duties to carry out and is responsible for the actions of his or her subordinates. Mark Rigg, Personnel Manager at Southland Corporation (owners of Seven-Eleven Stores and Chief Auto Parts), delegates authority to John Castle to conduct training programs for new employees. Castle is responsible for conducting these sessions and achieving the agreed-upon results. Responsibility demands that Castle take his job seriously and that Rigg provide him with the tools (e.g., training rooms, manuals, visual aids, store managers' time) to accomplish the objectives.

Responsibility

Accountability is the process of establishing an obligation to perform the work and make decisions within certain limits. The manager can hold subordinates answerable for making decisions that are part of their job. At some point in the work process there is a need to check to ensure that the job is performed properly and decisions are made the way they should be. Since the manager cannot check everything a subordinate does, the manager solves the problem by establishing limits within which the work must be done and by holding people answerable to perform within these limits. Accountability requires each member of the organization to report on his or her discharge of responsibilities and to be judged fairly on the basis of their record of accomplishment. In the secretary-manager example, the secretary is accountable to the manager for dictation. Thus, accountability, unlike authority and responsibility, always flows from the bottom up. It is an explicit contract to perform certain task-related activities in return for some reward, usually money.

Accountability

Barriers to Delegation

Managers often fail to delegate because of psychological and organizational barriers. Psychological hurdles arise primarily because the manager is afraid subordinates will not do the job properly, and, as a result, the manager's performance suffers. "I can do it better myself;" "My subordinates are not capable;" "It takes too much time to explain what I want done," are reasons why managers do not delegate. These reasons are justified if subordinates are untrained or poorly motivated. However, the manager's responsibility is to take positive action to overcome these deficiencies.

Managers may be reluctant to delegate because they expect subordinates to work and make decisions precisely as the boss would if he or she had the time and energy to do everything. When this attitude exists, the underlying problem might really be that managers fear subordinates may do the work too well and, hence, outshine them.

Organizational barriers may block delegation. The first barrier is the failure to define responsibility and authority. If a manager does not know what to do, it is unlikely that he or she will be able to delegate decision-making to others. If a manager delegates under these conditions, it not only affects the manager but demoralizes subordinates because they feel that they are just "spinning their wheels." Second, when the manager needs to check on the work being done, there is a need to hold individuals accountable. To delegate effectively, managers should assume the total obligation for the work of subordinates. If there is not complete accountability so errors can be pinpointed, subordinates can "pass the buck."

Overcoming Barriers to Delegation

The most basic principle to effective delegation is the willingness by managers to give their subordinates real freedom to accomplish their delegated tasks. Managers have to accept the fact that there are usually several ways of handling a problem and that their own way is not necessarily the one their subordinates would choose. In fact, subordinates may well make errors in carrying out their tasks. They have to be allowed to develop their own solutions to problems and to learn from their mistakes. This is very difficult for many managers to accept. Unless managers accept this idea, they cannot delegate effectively. They will be so busy with minor tasks or with checking on subordinates that their own important tasks will remain undone. Managers must keep in mind that the great advantages of delegation justify giving subordinates freedom of action, even at the risk of allowing mistakes to occur.

The barriers to effective delegation can also be overcome through improved communication and understanding between managers and subordinates. Managers who make it a point to learn the strengths, weaknesses, and preferences of their subordinates can more realistically decide which tasks can be delegated to whom. They will then have greater confidence in their delegation. Subordinates who are encouraged by their managers to use their abilities and who feel that their managers will "back them up" will in turn become more eager to accept responsibility.

Aside from these general guidelines, there are several specific techniques for helping managers delegate effectively. Louis Allen has listed six useful principles of delegation:[14]

1. *Establish objectives and standards. Subordinates should participate in developing the goals they are expected to meet. They should also agree to the standards that will measure their performance. This will free people to work out their own methods and make it unnecessary for the manager to maintain close personal supervision of everything that is done.*

2. *Define responsibility and authority. Subordinates should clearly understand the work and authority delegated to them and should recognize and accept their accountability for results.*

3. *Motivate subordinates. The challenge of the work itself will not always encourage subordinates to accept and perform delegated tasks. Managers can motivate subordinates by involving them in decision-making, by keeping them informed and by helping them to improve their skills and abilities.*

4. *Require completed work. Subordinates should be required to carry work through to completion. The manager's job is to provide guidance, help, and information.*

5. *Provide training. Delegation can be only as effective as the ability of people to perform the work and make the decisions required. This calls for continuing appraisal of delegated responsibilities and training programs aimed at building on strengths and overcoming deficiencies.*

6. *Establish adequate controls. Timely, accurate reports should be provided so that subordinates can compare their own performance to agreed-on standards and correct their own deficiencies. A reliable control system frees managers to concentrate on the work only they can perform.* *

Decentralization

The question is not what kind of authority should be concentrated or dispersed throughout the organization but how much? Authority is a fundamental aspect of delegation. There is neither absolute centralization nor absolute

---

* From Louis A. Allen, *The Professional Manager's Guide*, pp. 120–122. Copyright © 1981 by Louis A. Allen Associates, Inc., Palo Alto, CA.

decentralization. No one manager makes all decisions; total delegation would eliminate the need for managers. In other words, there is a continuum of centralization and decentralization. An organization may be relatively centralized in some functions and relatively decentralized in others.

Authority is delegated when a superior gives decision-making powers to a subordinate. Clearly, supervisors should not delegate more authority than they have nor should they delegate all of their authority, in effect passing the buck to subordinates. The process of delegation involves determining results expected, assigning tasks and the authority to accomplish them, and the responsibility for the task's accomplishments. In practice, these processes are impossible to split.

Decentralization refers to both a high degree of delegated authority and a basic management philosophy. It requires a careful selection of which decisions to delegate and which to retain for top management, selection and training of personnel to make decisions, and the formulation of adequate control mechanisms. At General Electric, for instance, only top corporate management can make the decision to abandon a business or go into a new one. At Sears, the Chicago headquarters decides what kinds of goods — hard wares, appliances, fashion goods, and so forth — each store must carry. Similarly, Tandy headquarters in Fort Worth specifies levels of inventory and sales targets for all Radio Shack stores.

General Motors is partially decentralized; its divisions are Chevrolet, Oldsmobile, Cadillac, Pontiac, Buick, Allison, and Frigidaire. Corporate strategy, formulated by top-management committees, provides underlying guidelines for decisions made by division-level executives. Each operating division has the authority to purchase, manufacture, and distribute its products. Similarly, each division is evaluated by two objectives: (1) base pricing, which measures the productive efficiency and rate of return on capital invested in each of the divisions; and (2) share-of-market standing, which indicates how well the division is competing in the marketplace as a seller.

GM is really quite centralized in other areas, such as finance, styling and personnel. As was indicated in Fig. 7.3, the location of the finance committee reflects the critical importance of money. A general manager of Oldsmobile can decide to offer a diesel engine to customers but cannot implement this decision until funds are approved by the finance committee. Styling is quite centralized because of GM's traditional product line that looks similar to a young person's career ladder; as income increases, the individual can upgrade purchases of GM cars from the Chevrolet to the Cadillac. Labor contract negotiations are also centralized because of the power of the United Automobile Workers. General Motors must ensure standard policies and adherence to the contract at all locations. Thus, GM is a mixture of centralization and decentralization with financial, personnel, and styling decisions made by top-level executive committees. It is the job of these committees to coordinate the various product-line managers.

Many other major corporations, such as First National City Bank, Chase Manhattan, IBM, and General Electric have implemented the idea of decentralization very successfully. Others, such as General Dynamics, Bonanza Sirloin Pit, and Philips have suffered major financial setbacks while attempting to implement this strategy. There are no universal benefits to be derived from decentralization, although several factors appear to be important.

Because managers operating in a decentralized structure have to make decisions, they are being *prepared for promotion* into positions requiring greater authority and responsibility. Decentralization encourages the professional development of managers. That is, during this apprenticeship period, managers must adapt and prove themselves to the company. They are being compared with others, and this may lead to a *healthy achievement-oriented* atmosphere within the firm. General Electric's statement of company goals notes that decentralization fosters the development of all of an individual's *human resources.*[15] The development of generalists rather than specialists is encouraged, thereby facilitating succession into positions as general managers.

However, not all companies have gained from a decentralized design. For example, prior to 1957, General Dynamics had decentralized authority, although the company president made almost all of the decisions through continual direct communication with the operating divisions. When the president died in 1957, the new president was unable to coordinate the diverse interests of the 11 divisions effectively and direct them toward a common corporate goal. Formal communications were poorly developed, since the previous president had used a system of frequent visits to each division. From 1960 to 1962, the Convair Division of General Dynamics lost over $435 million on the Convair 880/990 commercial jet, yet the new president communicated with the head of this division fewer than 10 times.[16] Lack of information about the operations of each division culminated ultimately in the loss of any semblance of control. When Convair's costs began to get out of hand, critical production delays developed, and key sales were lost, General Dynamics's management was unable to cope with the crisis. Even the board of directors was not informed when the vice-president of the corporation personally negotiated a sale of aircraft to American Airlines which, if finalized, would have produced a substantial loss for the firm.

It should be clear from General Dynamic's experience that not all companies have benefited from the decentralization of decision-making. Although the style of the individual manager often affects the extent to which authority is delegated, other factors also enter in.

Contingencies affecting decentralization

Costliness of the Decision   This is perhaps the most important factor in determining the extent of delegation in an organization. As a general rule, the more costly the decision to be made, the more probable it is that the decision will be made by top management. The cost of a decision may be in dollars or in such intangibles as the company's reputation, competitive position, or employee morale.

In many firms, top management may feel it cannot delegate authority for the expenditure of capital funds. In General Motors Corporation, the financial aspects of company operations are centralized under an executive vice-president (see Fig. 7.3) who reports to the chairman of the board of directors rather than to the president.

Uniformity of Policy   Managers who value consistency invariably favor centralization of authority. The management may wish to assure customers they will all be treated alike with respect to quality, price, credit, delivery, and service. Uniform policies have definite advantages in the areas of cost accounting, production, and financial records because they enable management to compare the relative efficiencies of various departments. The administration of a union-management labor agreement is helped by a uniform policy with respect to wages, promotions, vacations, fringe benefits, grievances, and other matters.

History of the Firm   Whether authority will be decentralized depends on the firm's past history. Marshall Field and Company and International Harvester Company have shown a marked tendency to keep authority centralized. Similarly, when Henry Ford, Sr., the founder of the Ford Motor Company, ran the organization, it was highly centralized. Ford took pride in having no organizational titles in top management except those of president and general manager; he insisted, to the extent possible, on making all decisions in the company himself. Other companies, such as Sears, Roebuck & Company, have a history that fosters decentralization.

Availability of Managers   Underlying decentralization of authority is the assumption that competent and well-trained managers are available to make decisions. Too often there is a shortage of good managers. To have decentralization, many corporations ensure the adequate supply of trained managers by permitting managers to make mistakes that involve little costs. In this manner, the organization is developing managerial potential, because it feels the best training is actual experience.

Control Mechanisms   Even the most avid proponents of decentralization, such as General Motors, duPont, and Sears, believe controls are needed to determine whether performance is conforming to plans. To decentralize should not be to lose control, as happened in General Dynamics. One cannot expect good managerial performance without some way of knowing whether it will be used properly.

Environmental Influences   The contingency factors affecting the extent of decentralization dealt with so far have been internal to the organization. External factors such as governmental controls, national unions, federal and state regulatory agencies, and tax policies are also important factors affecting the degree of decentralization within a firm. Governmental policy in the employment of minorities, for example, makes it hard to totally decentralize authority in hiring decision(s). If the federal government limits the number of hours worked and the minimum wages to be paid, the local manager cannot freely establish wages and hours outside of these guidelines.

The impact of national unions on long-term contracts has a centralizing influence on many organizations. So long as individual departmental managers can negotiate the terms of the labor contract, authority to negotiate may be delegated by top management to these managers. But where national unions bargain with the entire company — such as General Motors, B. F. Goodrich, the National Football League, and many other international firms — a company can no longer chance decentralization of certain decision-making prerogatives to local management.

LINE AND STAFF RELATIONSHIPS

Traditional theorists suggest that an organization with both line and staff functions offers the best potential for growth. In the typical manufacturing organization, for example, the *line* person is concerned with the achievement of the organization's objective through delegation of authority, work assignments, and supervision of others. The *staff* person, on the other hand, indirectly influences the work of others through the use of suggestions, recommendations, and advice.

This distinction between line and staff is usually easy to establish in a manufacturing organization. Line units denote a *command* relationship; staff units, an *advisory* relationship. In a nonbusiness organization, such as a hospital or university, this distinction between line and staff is less clear. In a hospital, the physicians (technical staff) treat the patients, and the administrators concern themselves with hospital maintenance. Similarly, in a university, the faculty (professional staff) works toward the fulfillment of the basic objectives of the school through teaching and research, and the administrators (deans, vice-president, etc.) are involved in the supportive and auxiliary functions.

7.7
Line and staff relationships

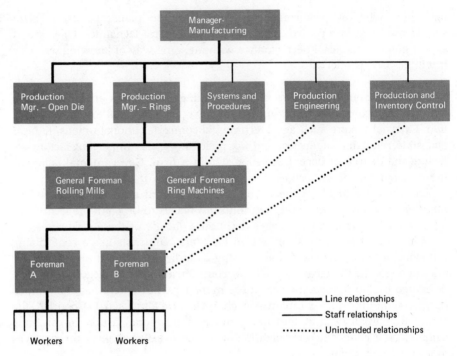

According to traditional theory and practice, staff departments are supposed to *assist line departments* in work that requires *technical expertise* and detailed attention. Staff people become experts in a given field, and line managers rely on them for specialized advice. Figure. 7.7, which shows the production department of Standard Steel Company, illustrates this condition.

In Standard Steel's manufacturing division, the staff performs three types of specialized assistance: systems and procedures, production engineering, and production and inventory control. Staff specialists also prepare and process data which line managers need for making decisions. For example, the production and inventory-control department customarily collects data on the cost of making a late delivery to an important customer, the number of jobs completed in each shop per day, and the level of inventory that should be stockpiled per product for anticipated demands. These experts on data analysis work closely with the systems and procedures personnel. When these experts have studied their problem(s), they submit their recommendations to the manager of manufacturing, who accepts the appropriate recommendations for implementation by line managers.

When staff functions are separate from the line organization, as in Fig. 7.7, a decision must be made as to what authority the staff personnel should be given. Observation of staff departments in action suggests there are at least four types of authority relationships: staff advice, compulsory staff advice, concurring, and command authority. Figure 7.8 portrays this authority continuum for staff units.

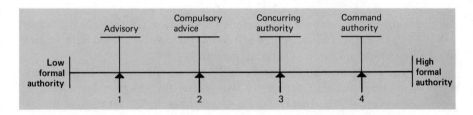

Many staff activities are *purely advisory* in nature. The manager is *free to seek* (or not seek) the advice of staff specialists. The manager who is looking for a new operations researcher may seek information from the personnel department as to the average starting salary for such personnel, the universities most likely to have qualified young candidates, and the like. However, it is the *prerogative* of the department manager to accept or reject the comments and information given by the personnel department.

In the case of *compulsory* staff advice, the manager must at least listen to the appropriate staff agency, but need not follow its recommendations. Although such a procedure does not limit the manager's decision-making discretion, it ensures that the manager has *made use of the specialized talents* of the appropriate staff agency.

Concurring staff authority requires that the *line and staff managers agree* on the particular course of action to be followed. This procedure expands the staff manager's authority and restricts the line manager's decision-making discretion to areas in which there is mutual agreement on a particular course of action. Thus, the manager of the production department and the head of the personnel office must agree that certain criteria are valid, certain universities should be visited, and the like. Decisions involving the recruitment of foremen are made jointly. When agreement cannot be reached, the issue is moved to the level of the organization where one individual has authority over both the line and the staff units.

The strongest form of staff authority occurs when the line grants *limited command authority* to a staff unit, permitting it to give orders and expecting that other organizational units will comply. If the personnel department has the authority to screen prospective candidates and reject those who do not meet quality standards, the personnel department is exercising *command authority* in the area of hiring. In many organizations, personnel and industrial-relations departments exercise command authority over the use of psychological testing, hiring policies and procedures, employee counseling, and related employee activities and benefits.

Line and Staff Conflicts

Authority problems between line and staff units have created much friction and conflict in organizations. There are many reasons for these conflicts, but we shall examine only some of the major ones.

One factor aggravating line-staff conflict is that of *personal characteristics.* A group of line and staff managers was asked to rank the desirability of personality traits on the basis of their importance to the success of the respondents' management positions.[17] Traits included characteristics such as forcefulness, imagination, independence, cooperation, adaptability, and caution. The results indicated that *staff* managers felt they had to be more *cooperative, adaptable,* and *cautious* (to succeed in their jobs) than did line managers.

A comparison between line and staff personnel in three industrial plants led another researcher to conclude that staff people were generally younger, better educated, more concerned with dress and appearance, had different recreational interests, and came from different backgrounds than did the line people.[18] *Line* people are generally oriented toward *advancement with the company*; *staff* people toward *advancement in their profession.* The former see their future in terms of loyalty to the organization; the latter, to their profession. This difference in commitment and loyalty to the organization can lead to a conflict in interests. Thus, for example, scientists may be interested in making a contribution to their field with the development of a new product, whereas their manager is interested in getting the product into consumers' hands and quickly recovering the costs for research and development.

A second source of conflict is the fact that staff units are usually located higher in the organization and are often called on by top management to make reports and analyses of operating divisions. Thus, they acquire *informal command authority*, much to the dismay of line personnel. These staff efforts are often perceived by line managers as attempts to control and check on the line units. For example, consider the unintended relationship, using Fig. 7.7. The dashed line represents informal functional authority acquired by each staff person from the line officer. In our case, let's assume that the production engineer notices that Foreman B's section has been incurring unusually high costs. In a discussion with Foreman B, the staff person notices that the foreman shows a general lack of respect for the engineer's capabilities and work.

After the general foreman of rolling mills and the manager of manufacturing receive the staff person's report, they ask the specialist to explain why Foreman B's engineering costs are out of line. Relating the uneventful meeting with Foreman B, the production engineer complains of an inability to influence the foreman.

The two managers realize that these costs must be kept under control, and they arrange a meeting with the foreman to explain why costs must be kept down and that the production engineer has spent a great deal of time and effort on developing procedures to cut costs. After the meeting, the production engineer has a very pleasant conversation with Foreman B, who now seems very receptive to the staff person's ideas. Realizing that both the manufacturing and rolling mill managers relied on the production engineer as an authority on engineering costs, the foreman no longer viewed the specialist as a "staff" person, but as an individual with *authority in this area.* Eventually, the acceptance of staff recommendations and suggestions by lower management, as representative views of top management, tends to create an authority link that is quite different from the prescribed formal arrangements. This is often more representative of the real working relationships of the group. The consequences, as indicated by the dashed lines in Fig. 7.7, are unintended but real.

Of course, not all conflict between line and staff managers is inherently bad or adversely affects the performance of a line unit. In many cases, these differences have some merit and can lead to better decisions. In the situation involving the foreman and the production engineer, the former's lack of attention to costs prevented the unit from operating at peak efficiency, and the production engineer's overriding concern with only the cost aspect was probably too narrow a focus on the problem. In this situation, the compromise solution that was ultimately worked out incorporated the thinking of both the production engineer and the foreman. What is important to the organization is that the disruptive effects of conflict be minimized and that a constructive resolution of conflicting viewpoints be effected. Intraorganizational conflict and methods to reduce disruptive conflict will be discussed further in Chapter 17.

**Location of Staff
Units**

The location of staff specialists in an organization's structure is usually determined by the differences between the general and specialist staffs. If the services of a staff department are used extensively throughout an organization, the unit may need to be located relatively high up in the organization, as shown for General Motors in Fig. 7.3. A functional general staff is usually found at the top of most large corporations. In the case of General Motors, offices that handle corporate legal, public-relations, marketing, finance, and manufacturing problems constitute the general staff. These staff offices are usually headed by vice-presidents who are in policy-making positions rather than in charge of operating units. For example, in General Motors, the vice-president in charge of industrial relations is given responsibility for personnel and industrial-relations policies for all divisions. This staff unit handles selection of the psychological tests to be used in screening prospective employees and the development of brochures for use by division personnel managers outlining the company's benefits and promotion policies.

If a staff group is assigned to provide needed services to a specific line function, the unit should be located near that function. At Standard Steel, for example, the production and inventory-control staff people report to the firm's manufacturing manager because a major portion of their work is provided to manufacturing, as indicated in Fig. 7.7. Staff specialists perform supportive functions (some of which would have to be performed by a line manager if staff specialists were not present) in a specific area and usually report to the line officer of that division.

SUMMARY A basic problem facing all managers is how to organize tasks and personnel to achieve the organization's goal(s) most effectively. The basic process of grouping activities is departmentation. There are four strategies for grouping activities — function, place, product, and customer — and each has specific advantages and disadvantages. Each of the bases of departmentation raises the problem of how the manager can coordinate the activities of the various groups. The basic concepts of coordination are the scalar principle and span of control.

The scalar principle refers to the chain of direct authority relationships from superior to subordinate throughout the organization. In nearly every organization there is a problem of determining how many individuals should report to one manager. The span-of-control principle addresses this problem. A number of contingency factors affect how wide a manager's span of control should be to maintain an effective department.

The authority structure of an organization is the means by which the organization maintains its viability. *Authority* refers to the manager's power to make decisions and the subordinate's acceptance of this power. *Accountability* flows from the bottom of the organization upward and refers to the subordinate's acceptance of a given task to perform. *Responsibility* is an owed obligation and should go hand in hand with authority. Whether authority should be concentrated or dispersed throughout the organization depends on the degree of centralization or decentralization. However, though decentralization is closely related to delegation of authority, it also reflects a basic underlying philosophy of the organization and its management.

Most large organizations employ staff groups to provide specialized assistance to line management. The power granted to staff groups by line management may vary from primarily advisory to actually making decisions in specified areas. In many large organizations, both general and special staff departments have been created to make recommendations and decisions with respect to the solution of organizational problems. Authority and personal discrepancies between line and staff officers have been at the root of some conflicts within organizations.

KEYWORDS

accountability
authority
decentralization
departmentation
by customer
by function
by place
by product

line
responsibility
scalar principle
span of control
staff
unity of command

DISCUSSION QUESTIONS

1. Why is departmentation of activities needed?

2. What is customer departmentation?

3. What is functional departmentation?

4. What is place departmentation?

5. What is product departmentation?

6. What is the principle of unit of command?

7. What is the principle of span of control? List some of the important contingencies affecting the span of control.

8. Why do some managers hesitate to delegate?

9. How do accountability, authority, and responsibility differ?

10. How may an organization decentralize its authority structure?

11. Why has there been conflict between line and staff for so long and in so many companies? What are the roots of this conflict?

12. Identify several positions in an educational, military, or business organization and classify them as either line or staff. What were some of the problems that you encountered in performing this task?

13. What would you recommend Burt do to reorganize the company?

Management Incidents and Cases

PEACHTREE HOSPITAL

The administrator and the personnel director of a large hospital were discussing problems of the hospital's organizational structure. It has been their practice to meet at least bimonthly to review the operations of the hospital and the staffing situation. The hospital had been open for less than one year, and the staff had spent the better part of its time recruiting and training employees. The administrator believed that sufficient time had elapsed to "shake down" the hospital staff and that organizational problems encountered would be "exceptions" to policies on the books. The administrator, however, was presently concerned with the high turnover (over 45 percent for nurses and LPs), absenteeism, uncleanliness of the wards, and loss of medical supplies.

The personnel director argued these were still "start-up" problems and would be solved within another month or so. The administrator, who believed that the organization's charts, job descriptions, and policy manuals clearly covered all areas, couldn't understand the problem. Furthermore, all of the hospital's personnel had been trained by the hospital, and many had had several years experience with other hospitals before coming into this new hospital.

The personnel director agreed with many of the points raised by the administrator, but added that formal organization charts and job descriptions did not ensure that employees would behave correctly. However, the personnel director did agree to conduct a survey within the hospital to determine the extent to which employees understood the organization.

The questionnaire was completed by nearly all 1200 of the hospital's administrators, doctors, nurses, maintenance workers, and others. The questionnaire included more than 150 items dealing with a variety of issues concerning the organization's structure. The results were tabulated, and a summary was prepared for the administrator. Some of the important findings were:

1. Twenty-five percent of the orderlies and maintenance workers felt that there was uncertainty concerning the goals of their jobs.

2. Thirty percent of the orderlies and maintenance workers felt that they often had difficulty in obtaining job-related information from their supervisors.

3. Thirty percent of all workers could not name their immediate supervisor.

4. Thirty-five percent of the administrative staff felt that they were not given authority commensurate with their responsibility.

5. Twenty percent of the nurses did not know their decision-making rights.

6. Forty percent of all workers did not know whether they were performing line or staff functions in the hospitals.

The hospital administrator was shocked to read these statements.

1. What would be your response to the administrator if you were the personnel director?

2. What are some authority and responsibility problems in the Peachtree Hospital?

3. What seems to be the major problem area?

4. How would the administrator know that the structure of the hospital was the most efficient?

In December 1979, the Tack Company franchised eight large chains, totaling over 750 stores, in order to reach a previously neglected market. This was in addition to more than 14,000 existing independent dealers already selling electrical appliances. Although the general sales manager, Ms. Smith, knew this would create more work for the 200 salespersons, she also knew it would help the division's profit picture. It was decided that Mr. Kelley (Ms. Smith's old boss) would head the department. Although Mr. Kelley was nearing retirement and rarely agreed with Ms. Smith's policies, it was felt that through her management and organizational ability she would be able to quickly turn the department into a profitable venture.

Within six months, many of the independent dealers began to complain and threatened to cancel their franchises with Tack. Because the chain stores were buying quantity, they were severely undercutting the independent dealers' prices. Because of this situation, Ms. Smith sent to all Tack zone managers and personnel letters which in effect stated that the independent dealers are important to the company.

Although there was no indication of a previous problem, in December 1980 the chain stores began to complain that Tack's salespersons were ignoring them. Mr. Kelley authorized an investigation, and within three weeks

---

* Adapted and updated from J. Murray and T. Von der Embse, *Organizational Behavior*, Columbus, Ohio: Merill, 1973, p. 184.

he had the results. The results showed that all stores had been contacted when taking on Tack products, but that only 20 percent of the stores had had at least one subsequent contact up to the time of the study. Mr. Kelley knew that unless this situation improved, the chain stores would switch to other suppliers. Therefore he sought answers as to why the contact was so poor for the chain stores.

Questions

1. How was the company organized? To whom were the salespersons responsible?

2. What was the relationship between Ms. Smith and Mr. Kelley?

3. What would you do to correct the problem?

THE DYNAMIC CORPORATION

The Dynamic Corporation is a national manufacturing firm producing and selling toys and games. Prior to 1972 the company specialized in adult toys, but in 1973 the toy market for children became so lucrative the Dynamic Corporation decided to compete in that line too. Adult games have no single, correct strategy and therefore require a great deal of thought on the part of the player. In true adult games, such as checkers, bridge, chess, there is no one right way to win; everything depends on what one's opponent does and on one's own skill.

After an intensive study of the children's toy market, Dynamic Corporation decided to market children's toy dolls. The doll industry's volume is estimated at $450 million annually, and the large producers, such as Mattel, spend well over $1 million in research and development.

In 1979, because of growing sales, the management of Dynamic Corporation was considering a reorganization. At the time, the firm was organized along functional lines (see Fig. 7.1). However, Trudy Smith, the president of the company, thought it might be wiser to change to product departmentation. Some of the marketing people thought so too. The production department, however, felt there was more to be gained from a functional departmentation. The finance and accounting department people seemed indifferent.

The president's reorganization plan was to set up three product divisions: baby toys, young girls' toys, and adult games. The baby toys and adult divisions accounted for over 60 percent of the firm's sales, but the young girls' division was growing rapidly. According to the marketing research department, sales for the girls' division would soon catch up.

1. Draw the proposed reorganization chart.

2. What are the advantages of product departmentation over functional departmentation?

3. What recommendations would you make to the president? Explain your reasons as much as possible.

REFERENCES

1. P. Drucker, *Management: Tasks, Responsibilities and Practices.* New York: Harper & Row, 1974, pp. 529–557.

2. J. Child, *Organization: A Guide to Problems and Practice.* London: Harper & Row, 1977, pp. 72–94.

3. J. Price, "The Impact of Departmentalization on Interoccupational Cooperation." *Human Organization* **27,** 1968, 362–367.

4. J. Daniels, E. Ogram, and L. Radebaugh, *International Business: Environments and Operation.* Reading, MA: Addison-Wesley, 1979.

5. *Time Magazine*, February 5, 1979. Special edition of Gulf & Western Industries, Inc., 1978 Annual Report.

6. H. Fayol, *General and Industrial Management,* trans. C. Storrs. London: Pitman, 1963, p. 34.

7. *Business Week*, August 19, 1951, pp. 102–103.

8. H. Mintzberg, *The Structuring of Organizations.* Englewood Cliffs, NJ: Prentice-Hall, 1979, pp. 134–147.

9. A. Graicunus, "Relationship in Organization." In L. Gulick and L. Urwick (eds.) *Papers on the Science of Administration.* New York: Institute of Public Administration, 1937, pp. 183–187.

10. J. Stieglitz, "Optimizing the Span of Control." *Management Record* **24,** 1962, 25–29. Also see D. Van Fleet, and A. Bedeian. "A History of the Span of Management." *Academy of Management Review* **2,** 1977, 356–372.

11. D. Barkdull, "Span of Control: A Method of Evaluation." *Michigan Business Review* **15,** 1963, pp. 25–32. Also see: D. Van Fleet, "A Partial Test of the Van Fleet – Bedeian Span of Management Control." Unpublished manuscript, Texas A & M University, College Station, TX, September 1979.

12. R. House and J. Miner. "Merging Management and Behavioral Theory: The Interaction Between Span of Control and Group Size." *Administrative Science Quarterly* **14,**

1969, 451–466. Also see: L. Cummings and C. Berger. "Organization Structure: How Does It Influence Attitudes and Performance?" *Organizational Dynamics*, 1976 (Autumn), 34–49.

13. C. Barnard, *The Functions of the Executive*. Cambridge, MA: President & Fellows of Harvard University, 1938.

14. L. Allen, *Professional Manager's Guide*, 5th ed. Palo Alto, CA: Louis Allen Associates, 1981, 120–122.

15. R. Cordiner, *The New Frontiers for Professional Managers*. New York: McGraw-Hill, 1956, pp. 55–57. Also see L. Jennergren, "Decentralization in Organizations." In *Handbook of Organizational Design*. Wm. Starbuck and P. Nystrom (eds.). Fairlawn, NJ: Oxford University Press 1981, pp. 39–59.

16. "General Dynamics: Winning in the Aerospace Game." *Business Week*, May 3, 1976, 86ff.

17. V. Nossiter, "A New Approach Toward Resolving the Line and Staff Dilemma." *Academy of Management Review* **4**, 1979, 103–107.

18. For an excellent review, see: A. Filley, R. House, and S. Kerr. "Professionals in Organizations and Line-Staff Relationships." in *Managerial Process and Organizational Behavior*, 2nd ed. Glenview, IL: Scott, Foresman, 1976, pp. 380–409; and P. Browne, and R. Golembiewski. "The Line-Staff Concept Revisited: An Empirical Study of Organizational Images." *Academy of Management Journal* **17**, 1974, 406–417.

Chapter 8

ORGANIZATIONAL DESIGN: MODERN APPROACHES

After reading this chapter, you should be able to:

LEARNING OBJECTIVES

1. Discuss the key factors affecting the design of an organization.

2. Discuss the differences between the general and task environments.

3. Identify the mechanistic and organic approaches to organization design.

4. Explain why there are no universal designs for all organizations.

5. List under what conditions the matrix and bureaucratic forms are appropriate.

6. Discuss the advantages and disadvantages of matrix management.

7. Describe the role of the organization president in different environments.

PREVIEW CASE

Fox-Bat   When Gene Alton started Harris Communications in 1965, its three founders stated the firm's basic goal as one of "inventing and manufacturing sophisticated telecommunication equipment." Over the next 10 years the company prospered, thanks to the high degree of technical expertise possessed by the owners and the staff of engineers they hired. In 1975, however, the three men decided that they had had enough. They wished to retire and spend the rest of their years pursuing leisure activities. They were approached by Fox-Bat, a large multinational conglomerate, and sold the company for $500 million. This was Fox-Bat's first venture into the telecommunications field; its divisions include candy, fishing equipment, electrical motors, sportswear, and plastic toys. Nevertheless, the board of directors liked the profit picture and felt that Harris would make an excellent addition to their product line.

Soon after the takeover, the personnel at Harris were told that there would be no radical changes; it was to be "business as usual." The only change that Fox-Bat intended to institute was that of reorganizing the structure. The new owners wanted to install a functional organization, create small spans of control, and make sure that the "principles of good management were not violated." When asked about the reasons for this change, one of the Fox-Bat board members said, "We feel that the firm is too disorganized. We want to create more formal lines of communication and authority-responsibility relationships. This way everyone will know what he is supposed to be doing and to whom he should report. At the present, we don't have any idea of what's happening.''

Within one year after the reorganization, however, the financial statements from Harris indicated that something was wrong. Instead of high profitability, the newly acquired division was reporting its first loss in five years. The president of Fox-Bat was unable to explain why. One of the board members stated, ''We tried to straighten out the firm's chaotic structure by introducing some good management principles into it. But instead of becoming more profitable, they're losing money. Perhaps we need more structure than we initially thought. All of our other divisions are organized along functional lines and follow the principles of good management. In any event, something has to be done.''

Organization design is a central problem for managers. What is the ''best'' structure for the organization? What are the criteria for selecting the ''best'' structure? What signals indicate that the organization's existing structure may not be appropriate to its tasks and its environment? In the case of Fox-Bat, the choice of a new organization structure did not improve the performance of Harris Communications. Why?

What do Robert Hall Clothes, W.T. Grant Company, World Football League, Penn Central Railroad and the all-volunteer U. S. Army all have in common? All were unsuccessful. With the exception of the Army, all are out of business.

At the other extreme are the Miller Brewing Company, K-Mart, McDonald's, and Seven-Up. All have been quite successful.

This chapter analyzes the environments in which organizations operate. It explores how managers can operate successfully using a variety of practices, technologies, and organizational forms.

Environments in which an organization operates help determine the tasks undertaken. Tasks have important implications for an organization's design and on its choice of personnel. For example, the Jet Propulsion Laboratory (JPL), at the California Institute of Technology, operates a high-technology, science-based industry. It gives special attention to organizing research and development activities that encourage inventiveness among personnel while controlling expenditures. The JPL employs a wide variety of occupational specialists whose actions must be coordinated adequately to continue the non-manned space probe of Jupiter.

Similarly, the conglomerate International Telephone and Telegraph (ITT), which has been operating in an uncertain political climate in countries such as Chile, felt it necessary to build a system of political intelligence to provide ITT an ability to anticipate and adapt to changing environmental conditions. ITT operates its hotel chain (Sheraton), however, under quite different environmental conditions and does not use the same type of personnel, marketing systems, and other managerial support systems as the telephone division. This means that within one company there exist variations in structure, personnel, and technology designed to meet different business situations.

As we indicated in Chapter 2, one of the primary differences between the Traditional and Systems approaches to the study of organizations is in the underlying assumptions about the external environment. The *traditional approach* emphasizes things that are controllable by the organization through use of rules, regulations, job designs, recruitment practices, and structures. The environment in which the organization is operating received less attention in favor of making the internal operations of the organization as efficient as possible. The *systems approach* assumes that the organization and its environment are in an active relationship with each other. Just as individuals learn to adapt to their environment, so too must organizations. The structure of the organization and its departments must be keyed to the environment in which they operate. Each department provides some function needed for survival of the organization. Organizations survive because they adapt to the environment in which they function.

In Chapter 7 we discussed some of the basic principles in management. These principles are still applied today in most effective organizations. Modern managers, however, need to become familiar with the internal and external conditions facing their organizations before deciding on how to apply any of the basic management principles (unity of command, scalar principle, span of control, etc.). Effective organizational design results not from the use of universal management principles, but from matching appropriate principles with the particular set of conditions facing the organization. Under certain business conditions, rules and regulations may lead to high performance; under other conditions, they may not.

DEFINING THE ENVIRONMENT

In the broadest sense, the environment is everything external to the organization's boundaries. It may be more useful, however, to think of the environment as (1) the general environment, which affects all organizations in a given society, and (2) the specific task environment, which affects the individual organization more directly.[1]

The *general environment* is the same for all organizations in a given society. Many of the general environmental forces that influence organizations were discussed in Chapters 3 and 4. Some of these forces are cultural, technological, educational, political, sociological, and economic. Frequently, managers take these conditions as given, with little recognition of how they affect the success of an organization. These conditions are the general characteristics under which all organizations operate in a society.

An organization may not be influenced directly by all of the conditions in its environment, nor can it respond to all of them. The *task environment* is defined as those specific forces that can affect the success of the firm.[2] The task environment is made up of groups beyond the organization's own boundaries that provide immediate inputs, exert pressures on decisions, or buy the organization's products. The sudden shift of American consumers away from gas-guzzling cars to more economical cars in 1980 caused a major slump in car sales and caused automobile manufacturers, especially Chrysler and Ford, to lay off thousands of workers. The automobile industry's task environment changed because fuel became scarce. Many of us waited hours in gasoline lines in the summer of 1979. California, Texas, and New Jersey, among others, adopted the odd-even system as a way of allocating the dwindling supply of gasoline. The fuel conditions, however, did not directly affect a host of other industries (printing, chemical, leather, or bicycles, for example). The economic recession during 1979–1980 was the general environment for all firms, including automobile manufacturers.

The distinction between the general and task environments is not always clear-cut. Forces in the general environment are continually breaking through to the task environment of the organization. For example, until the middle or late 1960s, universities had been able to maintain barriers to the general environment. During the Vietnam War, and especially after the Kent State shootings in May 1970, conditions in the general environment — such as international conflicts, gay rights, political activities, minority-rights movements, and women's lib — became relevant forces in the universities' task environment.

Conditions in the general environment may also bring other institutions into the task environment of the organization. When equal opportunity legislation was passed in 1964, for instance, many firms had to change hiring procedures, as well as the criteria used for promotion. Federal controls on the quality of air caused shifts in types of fuel used in the design of American and foreign-made automobiles.

Relevant conditions   The relationship between the general and task environments is illustrated in Fig. 8.1. The figure also shows three levels of management — top, middle, and first-line — discussed in Chapter 1. The organization's task environment can be thought of as a subset of the general environment. Only the relevant conditions in the task environment affect the organization's performance. The five factors composing the relevant task environment are general enough to encompass all types of organizations — voluntary, service, business, governmental, educational, religious, custodial, and military. The two factors we will discuss — market and technological factors — are most useful in analyzing problems of designing organizations.[3]

Market Factors   Organizations produce some sort of product, service, or value for customers. These clients use the products — televisions, cars, hamburgers, books, pens — for many different things. People also use many services — welfare and the Better Busines Bureau. Organizations like the Bet-

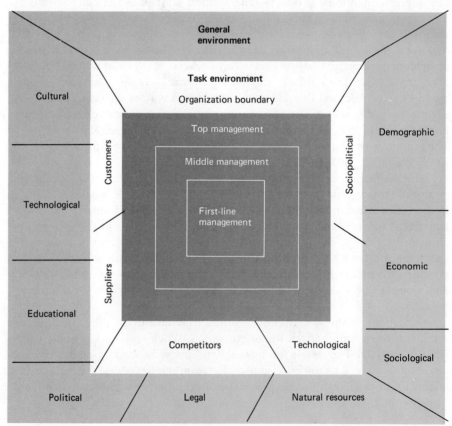

8.1
Relationship of general
and task environments to
the organization.

ter Business Bureau and Planned Parenthood provide information. Hospitals provide a variety of services.

Markets may vary in several dimensions — time, size, shape, and cost. Some markets exist for only a very short time but recur periodically. For example, the demand for fireworks is very high around the Fourth of July, then drops off sharply until the following July. Other markets vary by cost, shape, and size. Sales of pocket calculators rose from $4 million in 1971 to an estimated $1.8 billion in 1980. When the Sharp pocket calculator was introduced in 1971, the price was $395. In 1981, Sharp was selling a more complex instrument for $10.95. The market for transistorized calculators has expanded rapidly, whereas the market for slide rules has declined.

Fast-shifting consumer preferences have shortened the life cycle for many products. Approximately 55 percent of the products sold today did not exist 10 years ago, and of the products sold then, about 40 percent have been removed from the shelf. In the pharmaceutical and recording industries, a product is often obsolete within six months. In 1977, Polaroid introduced instant home movies. Using the same logic that had made its still camera a huge success, Polaroid spent millions on advertising and technology. Initially, consumers rushed to buy this new product and sales looked good. By September of 1979, however, Polaroid announced that sales were lagging because of technical problems. The company had lost over $68 million during the two years the product was on the market. Polaroid stopped marketing this product by the end of September 1979.

In a large organization, the various departments have different task environments. Some of Westinghouse's departments operate in fairly stable task environments (such as broadcasting), others, in more changing ones (such as power systems and defense). To be effective, Westinghouse must structure each department differently to reach its goals. It is important to realize that departments within an organization may differ. The structure of each department reflects its unique problems and opportunities. When discussing different types of organizational designs, keep in mind that one organization can have multiple bases for grouping activities into departments, each attempting to adapt to its own task environment.

Technological Factors   The technological segment of the task environment has two parts. The first is the availability of the *mechanical means* for production of goods and services. This often means the replacement of human effort through automated production lines, computer systems, monitoring equipment, and other hardware. How this hardware is brought into the firm and set up is an important issue facing managers on the production line. Technical advances within the organization cannot be carried any further than the technology available on the market or created by the organization through its own research and development efforts.

But the economic or social costs of some technological advances may be too high for the organization. Large department stores, such as J. C. Penney; Sears, Roebuck; May Company; and Montgomery Ward have data-processing centers for charge accounts. The local travel agency might still bill customers by a hand-posting method.

The second aspect of technology refers to the *accumulated knowledge* about the means to produce the goods or services. In this sense, technology is the skill and brains of individuals. It is the application of science to real-world problems. Accountants may use the computer in performing their auditing job, but they also use knowledge of accounting procedures in accomplishing the job. In most production companies, there are three basic technologies:

1. Mass production of a large number of very similar items with substantial number of interchangeable parts. Assembly lines turning out Oldsmobiles, telephone receivers, and electric light bulbs fall into this category.

2. A job shop includes the design and production of a unique product, singly or in small numbers. Rather than an assembly line, this production system requires the workers to build from the ground up. Examples of this technology would include IBM computers, Boeing 747s, or any custom-made product.

3. Continuous process technologies turn out a similar product from automated equipment operating around the clock. Mobil, Texaco, Exxon, Con Edison, and Bordens produce products using continuous process technologies. This technology is very specific and inflexible. Mobil may vary the proportion of home heating oil to gasoline it produces, but Mobil cannot convert its refineries to the manufacture of helicopters or aspirin.

Characteristics of the task environment We have defined the relevant task environment of an organization as having both market and technological factors. Although other aspects of the task environment undoubtedly could affect the design of an organization, most research has concentrated on these two dimensions of an organizations's task environment.

The central theme of today's approach to management is that the degree of change and market segmentation in the task environment influences an organization's structure, bases of departmentation, coordination mechanisms, and control systems. A firm that produces a stable product in a market with little technological innovation and relatively few competitors has a different set of problems from that of a firm providing a product or service in a market that is growing, changing, and competitive. The first environment is stable, the second, changing or uncertain. As we indicated in Chapter 3, the firm's environment may be thought of as a continuum ranging from stability to instability. These two states of the environment have substantial implications for the internal structure of the organization, the type of individual likely to be effective in the organization, and the type of management practices used in the organization.[4] In general, firms operate in both environments. Some departments have undergone little change, others a lot. For example, at Xerox, the production and marketing departments have undergone changes in order to respond to new technological advances and competitors, but the finance department has experienced little change. At Xerox, these departments have different structures and coordination mechanisms.

The Stable Environment   The *stable environment* is characterized by:

1. products and services that have not changed much in recent years;
2. lack of technological innovations;
3. a stable set of competitors and customers, with few new competitors;
4. stable political, economic, and social conditions; and
5. consistent government policies toward regulation and taxation.

Changes in a stable environment are relatively small. When they do occur, they have a minimal impact on the internal operations of the organization. Top management can keep track of what is going on and make virtually all necessary policy decisions alone. Companies in the brewing, insurance, candle-making, coal-mining, glass container, and food-staples (e.g., flour and gelatin) industries operate in relatively stable environments. Although there may be slight changes in the product (e.g., the introduction of low-calorie beer in the brewing industry), these changes can be incorporated easily into the existing technology of the firm.

Changes in a stable-environment product are likely to be in size (e.g., amount of beer produced, number of life-insurance policies or loaves of bread sold). Such changes probably have little impact on the structure of the organization. The product itself is unlikely to change significantly, and there will be little need to change the production processes. Production managers are not faced with changes in production processes. Firms in highly stable environments are likely to develop extensive distribution systems and invest heavily in capital equipment. These firms adapt to changes in demand by changing the size of the work force, not by changing the product or the method of production. For example, in the brewing industry, the continuous-process production system requires high capital investment and an extensive distribution system (e.g., beer distributors, trucks, warehouses). If there is a shift in demand, changes in the production system would emerge rather slowly, because the final product is still beer. If beer sales dropped off, Anheuser-Busch, Schlitz, or Coors, for example, would reduce the number of employees rather than seek new products (e.g., making wine or "hard" liquor). Change in the production equipment would be too costly.

A stable environment provides a high level of predictability. Firms operating in this environment are able to use common business indicators for planning and sales efforts. The U.S. Department of Commerce prepares annual output projections for various industries based on changes occurring in the industry over the last 10 years. Firms operating in stable environments can use these indices for forecasting market changes and sales trends. For example, the soft drink industry has nearly 49 million customers who are between the ages of 13 and 24. Each of these people drinks an average of 823 cans (or the equivalent) of soda per year, while the average for all age groups in the United States is 547 cans. According to the Bureau of the Census, the number of people in the 13–24 age bracket will decrease by four million from 1981 to 1984. This means that the market for soft drinks will shrink by 3.3 billion cans during that period. The Pepsi-Cola Company, which has a 21.7 percent share of the market, has bought other companies — Wilson's sporting goods, Frito-Lay, Pizza Hut — in order to maintain its profit picture.

The Changing Environment   The *changing environment* is characterized by:

1. products and services changing moderately or continually;

2. major technological innovations which may make the old technology obsolete;

3. an ever-changing set of actions by competitors and customers;

4. unpredictable and changing governmental actions, reflecting political interaction between the public and various groups for consumer protection, pollution control, and civil rights; and

5. rapid changes in the values of a large number of individuals.

Firms in this type of environment are likely to feel an ongoing need to adapt their structures to the environment. In this environment, customers, prices, demands, etc., are changing. Products based on consumer preferences must be changed to meet new preferences and fads. Organizations in the electronics, fashion, pharmaceutical, and watch industries operate in changing environments.

When the technology is also changing, new ideas and concepts must be generated quickly. These new ideas can affect a product or the way in which it is manufactured. In the electronics industry, breakthroughs in integrated circuits and miniaturization have affected the nature of the products. The introduction of electronic digital watches has had a tremendous impact on the market. For centuries, Swiss-made watches dominated the industry. The Swiss firms were independent and stressed the craftsmanship that went into each time piece. When technology changed from hand-wound to electronic and digital watches, the Swiss were unable to meet the competition of the new innovations. As a result, the entire Swiss industry suffered declining sales and revenue.

In the United States, the high cost of labor, intense competition, and lack of governmental protection created a different set of environmental conditions for the watch industry. Only two firms — Timex and Bulova — were able to survive changes in their task environments; they innovated successfully to meet the demands of the new technology. According to Ardith Rivel, a vice-president at the Benrus Corporation, electronic digital watches that had been selling for $125 to $135 a few years ago sold for less than $30 in 1976.[5] Texas Instruments currently sells a watch for less than $10.00. Watches with light-emitting diodes and liquid-crystal displays have changed the nature of the entire industry. As the technology changed, more watchmakers gradually began producing electronic digital watches, and prices dropped rapidly.

The home electronic market is another example of a changing industry. Until recently, the home computer has been only for the hobbyist. In 1980, one could buy a computer at Radio Shack for something less than $500 or one at Montgomery Ward's for around $400. These computers will keep financial records, things-to-do-lists, appointments, and phone numbers; they can turn off lights and even compose Christmas cards. Computerniks have already formed some 700 informal clubs, and electronic stores are opening like the fast food outlets did in the mid-70s. Mattel, Clicko, and others are producing electronic football, basketball, soccer, and baseball games. Milton Bradley created "Simon," the hottest selling electronic toy during the 1978 Christmas season. TV games are available in most department stores.

Organizations face different task environments. The underlying assumption of the modern approach is that organizations will adapt to these environments by designing their structures to fit the demands of the environment. Some organizations will not adapt their structure(s) and will instead try to change the nature of the environment.[6] As indicated in Chapter 3, some strategies used by organizations to respond to changes in the environment are bargaining, lobbying, coalition formation (e.g., OPEC nations), representation, and socialization. Where a stable technology exists, as in the safety razor, fountain-pen, or leather industries, firms may spend large amounts of time and advertising to avoid a technological breakthrough that will alter the industry radically. For example, when the electric razor was introduced in 1938, both the American Safety Razor Corporation and Gilette Safety Razor Company were one-product companies. They both engaged in large-scale marketing campaigns to prevent the electric razor from dominating the shaving market. It was not until 1956–58 that sales of electric razors exceeded those of

Environment-Organization Link

razor blades. Since 1958, razor blades have regained and maintained their sales lead.

Some firms have managed to retain organizational structures in spite of changes in the environment. Most organizations, however, adapt their structure to demands of the environment. These environments have both stable and changing characteristics. Marketing and technological factors may be highly stable or change frequently. Firms in a stable market and technological environment probably will perform routine operations, be fairly formalized, have centralized decision-making, and/or rely heavily on rules and regulations. Such an environment does not require a complicated organizational structure and/or decision-making rules. But to deal successfully with a changing environment puts a premium on a decentralized organizational structure and on managers keeping informed about new business developments. A flexible communication system is needed. This system may bypass the formal hierarchy when it is necessary to bring specialists together and create a structure that can give emphasis to new products and services when opportunities are detected. People who can accept ambiguity (uncertainty) as they change tasks and positions are needed most in a changing environment. They must cooperate with people of differing backgrounds and from different functional areas.

CONTINGENCY APPROACHES TO ORGANIZATIONAL DESIGN

Organizational structures will differ according to the conditions of their task environments. That is, the structure of the departments within the organization will differ, depending on whether the market and/or technology are stable or changing. Table 8.1 provides an overall framework for developing the contingency approach to the design of organizations. Stability and complexity are the two key factors. *Stability* refers to the amount of change over time in the dimensions in the organization's task environment. That is, are the number of customers, supplies, manufacturing methods, and price structures stable or changing? In the video cassette industry there have been numerous changes in the technology (laser beam, tape, or disc) and potential numbers of customers. This task environment would be classified as changing. The production of flour, on the other hand, has not changed much and its uses are fairly limited. Examples of industries in task environments which might be labeled stable include firms in the primary metal industry, printing and publishing, rubber, baking, stone, clay and glass products, leather products, and lumber. Firms in the electrical equipment industry, chemicals and allied products, petroleum industry, plastics, apparel, textile products, and computer industries would be examples of firms operating in changing task environments. *Complexity*, on the other hand, refers to the degree to which the task environment is segmented — numerous buyers, customers, and sellers, or few

Complexity	Stability	
	Stable	Changing
Simple	I	II
Complex	III	IV

Adapted from J. Thompson, *Organizations in Action.* Copyright ©, 1967, McGraw-Hill. Used with permission of the McGraw-Hill Book Company, p. 72.

buyers, customers, and sellers. A complex task environment has many buyers and different types of customers and sellers; a simple task environment has few buyers and limited types of customers and suppliers. The resulting four quadrants present different kinds of problems to the organization and therefore require different organizational structures.

Simple and Stable Task Environment (I)

A stable and simple task environment is defined as one in which technological changes are few, the markets are fairly well defined, and there is stability in both suppliers and customers. The bureaucratic form of organization structure is probably most appropriate when the market and technology are stable and simple. As indicated in Chapter 2, bureaucracy is characterized by a high degree of centralized control by top management and a fairly rigid hierarchy. Lines of authority and responsibility are clear, jobs are well defined through the use of detailed position descriptions, and each manager has clearly specified goals. Promotion through the organization is based on expertise and seniority. Individuals who do get promoted will probably have the same viewpoint as those who promoted them. Thus, members of the management team have a high degree of similarity in point of view, attitude, and background. Most likely there will be a small proportion of managers to workers.

Information needed by the president and vice-presidents from the task environment is gathered from technical reports published by the government and other sources, such as trade magazines, trade meetings, and general business news sources. This information is then sent to lower-level managers, who are not actively involved in the decision-making process. It is the job of the president to maintain the status quo by making all the decisions.

Bureaucratic organizations have been criticized for failing to adapt and cope with the environment. If the environment is stable and simple, however, the hierarchical form of organization is precisely the kind of structure needed to cope effectively with the task environment. To have a different organizational form under these conditions would likely lower the success of the organization.

In a study of 20 industrial firms in the United Kingdom, Burns and Stalker found that firms operating in stable and simple task environments (e.g., rayon mills) were more successful when they adopted a "mechanistic" system of management.[7] The dimensions of the **mechanistic management system** are as follows:

1. Organizational problems and tasks are broken down according to specialized functions.

2. Coordination occurs through the formal hierarchy.

3. The job duties and responsibilities assigned to each position are defined precisely.

4. The structure of control, authority, and communication is hierarchical.

5. Interaction between members of the firm follows the chain of command.

6. Greater importance and prestige are attached to internal rules and regulations than to general knowledge, expertise, and skill.

7. The behavior of all workers and managers tends to be governed by rules and regulations.

The production tasks performed are routine and repetitive. That is, a standard way of performing the job is established and routinized through the use of time-and-motion studies or other principles of scientific management. Tasks are repetitive; all members are usually assigned only a few tasks which are performed over and over, day after day. The limited skill required by the task can lead to the workers' increasing demand for employment stability. It is easy to replace workers, since probably a large pool of unskilled labor is available to perform the task. Production workers have very limited control over what they do and how they produce the work.

Firms with such production tasks are capital intensive rather than labor intensive. Managers must know how to design and maintain a production system so it can achieve maximum productivity with the equipment. Bureaucratic organizations in the private sector often require a high volume to break even, and even minor fluctuations in productivity can adversely affect the economies of the system. When the International Association of Machinists and Aerospace Workers (IAM) walked off the job on March 31, 1979, United Airlines found themselves in what turned out to be an eight-week standstill. While negotiations were in effect, 350 transports were left sitting at airports, management was put on a 50 percent wage rate for a full-day's work, ticket agents were laid off with many being rehired by other airlines, and all major airports and carriers reported being crowded with freight cargo piling up in warehouses.

It was fortunate for United that they were financially well off and could withstand the approximate $1.5 million a day loss incurred due to the strike. A similar airline could not have done so, since the mutual aid pacts were cancelled in 1978. The time was used by maintenance management to work on the aircraft, which they said are now in better shape than before, and although United suffered losses for the year and lost ground in many of their once "established flight paths," they expected to regain their market share through a discount fares campaign.[8]

Channels of distribution are fairly well defined and standardized. A successful distribution system might require 10 years or more to set up. New distribution channels will be opened only if the current methods become highly inefficient. It is likely that the organization will have a great deal of influence over the distribution system.

CASE STUDY

McDonald's

An analysis of McDonald's highlights organizations facing a stable, simple environment. The typical franchise organization, such as McDonald's, Kentucky Fried Chicken, The Pancake House, or Dunkin' Donuts, operates in a simple market environment. Competitors have similar promotional strategies and production technology. Technology tends to remain relatively constant, and the potential market (fast service) is defined as the same for all firms.

Ray A. Kroc, Senior Chairman and founder of McDonald's Corporation. Courtesy of McDonald's Corporation

Ray Kroc, founder of McDonald's, opened his first restaurant in the Chicago area in April 1955.[9] By 1981, with more than 6200 restaurants and annual sales of over $6 billion, McDonald's had become the largest food-service organization in the world. McDonald's first menu focused on the hamburger, shake and french fries. It has been expanded to include several sandwiches — the Big Mac®, the Quarter Pounder®, and Filet-O-Fish® — and several kinds of desserts. A breakfast menu was introduced in 1976 and was an instant money maker. What are some reasons for McDonald's success?

First, McDonald's franchisees and managers must attend an intensive 10-day training program at Hamburger University, McDonald's international management training center in Elk Grove Village, Illinois. Their curriculum includes not only work experience in a McDonald's restaurant, but also an intensive classroom program. Subjects, which are taught by H.U. professors, range from day-to-day management of a McDonald's restaurant to courses in business management, accounting, marketing, personnel management, and community relations.

Second, the coordination mechanisms developed by McDonald's include not only a detailed organizational structure but also continual service (in terms of operations, public relations, advertising). To ensure that the franchisees conform to McDonald's rules and regulations, the restaurants are visited regularly by field consultants who are assigned to specific areas. McDonald's operations manual is a 385-page book covering the most minute facet of operating an outlet.

Third, because each member of the McDonald's organization has a specified role, it is not difficult to get integrated programs of action. Extensive collaboration among headquarters departments and organizational offices leads to similarity in design and control processes among the restaurants. For example, the design department at the parent organization works closely with the site and location department on the regional level to ensure that each restaurant meets the standards set by the organization and also blends with the general atmosphere and appearance of the community.

Fourth, the promotional strategy involves Ronald McDonald, who despite having become an international hero and celebrity, remains the same fun-loving clown that Kroc introduced to the world in 1963. A company survey indicated that 96 percent of all American children can identify Ronald McDonald, second in recognition only to Santa Claus. As Fred Turner, McDonald's Chief Executive Officer since 1973, says: "In an age when so many Americans are on the move, one of our main assets is our consistency and uniformity. It's very important that a man who's used to eating at a McDonald's in Hempstead, L.I., knows he can get the same food and service when he walks into one in Albuquerque or Omaha."

Summary   Firms operating in a simple and stable environment:

    1. have a relatively fixed or stable market share;

2. try to maximize production efficiency;

3. attempt to maintain competence in the product or service line currently offered;

4. have "mechanistic," or bureaucratic structure;

5. have a mass-production technology, which permits few exceptions, requires a heavy capital investment, and provides employees with routine jobs;

6. assign the role of top management to create distribution channels to reach customers, maintain the status quo of the organization's design, and/or make small product changes as needed.

The mechanistic organization has been found to be effective because it can adapt and cope with demands of its task environment. Given a stable and simple task environment, the bureaucratic organization is likely to be effective.[10] The stability of the environment means that organizations need to maintain set relationships with the environment if they are to remain effective.

Firms operating in this task environment are faced with the problem of changes in customers' attitudes, habits, and tastes, but not their number. A simple and changing environment is defined as one in which the firm is still dealing with a relatively constant group of buyers, etc., but the services and products these individuals want keep changing. Since the significant changes are likely to take place in marketing, the top managers of the organization need to stay in close contact with the customers' changing desires. In general, product changes will reflect style or design changes more than they do radical product changes. For example, Schlitz's introduction of "light" beer reflects a change in the style of brewing beer rather than in the product line.

The major task of the top managers is to monitor the environment for changes and then make decisions as to how the organization should adapt to them. Appropriate changes in the product should improve the organization's distinctive competence in the industry and hopefully stimulate demand. Decisions by corporate presidents and their staffs have a long-term impact on the firm. Once built, production facilities are relatively inflexible and can be changed only at major expense; the total investment is likely to be large and development of a market is long-range. The major task of the president and the staff is to maintain and create new product markets that can be produced.

A hierarchical form of organization is likely to be effective and should probably resemble the "mechanistic" form. However, individuals performing the marketing and other functions dealing with customers are likely to have more decision-making power because they must monitor the changes and

Simple and Changing Task Environment (II)

relay them to the appropriate members of the organization. If the market isn't present, one must be created to gain economies of scale. In 1890, for example, Standard Oil Company gave free kerosene lamps to the Chinese peasants to create a market for kerosene. In this case, Standard Oil created a new product and then sold it to a stable group of customers.

The problems facing organizations in quadrant II lead to programmed production tasks performed within a stable technology. A continuous-process type of production technology usually is found in this quadrant. For example, the end products of an oil refinery are determined by the process it uses. Changes in the process can change the octane rating of gasoline or change leaded gas to unleaded. The refinery makes these process changes in order to meet the changing wants and demands of customers, other businesses, and governmental regulations. All continuous-process production companies, including chemicals, milk processors, paint manufacturers, and plate-glass plants, concentrate on a few products, but segment the market enough to capture the changes in the customers' tastes. Pittsburgh Paints, for example, offers its customers 200 different shades of colors. Each of these paints appeals to a stable set of consumer tastes.

Continuous process production requires very high capital investment and a high volume to break even. The typical plant in the chemical or plate-glass industry can operate profitably only at or near peak capacity. It has a great diversity of product mix and requires high skill on the part of schedulers, maintenance, and other managers, but low skill on the workers' part.

CASE STUDY

Miller Brewing Company

Courtesy of Miller Brewing Company

In 1855, Frederick Miller purchased an idle brewery on the outskirts of Milwaukee and produced 300 barrels of beer a year. Additions to brewery size, capacity and sales outlets, together with product quality, created a demand for Miller's beer that was instrumental in increasing production to 500,000 barrels a year by the 1920s. After Prohibition, Miller Brewery began an intensive modernization program, and by 1968 was producing 3.8 million barrels a year. Philip Morris purchased the brewery in 1969.

Philip Morris brought its marketing techniques and advertising know-how to Miller. These were the techniques used to make Marlboro the top-selling cigarette in the nation. A corporate objective was to reposition Miller within the beer industry by stressing quality in all areas — taste, freshness, marketing, people, and finance. Because Philip Morris was new to the beer business, it could implement creative marketing strategies that were ignored by Anheuser-Busch, Schlitz, Pabst, Coors, and Shaefer.

The initial step was to determine who beer consumers were and what they wanted. Philip Morris discovered that consumers could be divided into special groups. Miller High Life was the "Champagne of Beers" and appealed to the "upper-class" who would drink one or two beers at a time. Budweiser and Schlitz were attracting the same number of consumers, but each consumer averaged almost a six-pack a day. To appeal to "suds downers," Philip Morris gave Miller a new slogan "If you've got the time, we've got the beer." Miller spent from 10 to 30 million dollars annually using that theme as an appeal to the masculine image. This approach put Miller High Life in the top three of beer sales.

In June 1972, Miller acquired a brewery that produced a reduced-calorie beer, Lite. While other breweries had little success in marketing this type of beer, Miller found that the challenge was to produce a taste that would allow Lite to compete against Coors. After a year of trying, the goal was achieved. The campaign slogan, "Lite beer from Miller — everything you always wanted in a beer and less," was delivered by former athletes. In 1979, Lite sales reached about 10 million barrels. Miller had again found a market segment that the larger breweries said did not exist and proceeded to supply that segment.

In April 1974, Miller entered into an agreement with Lowenbrau Brewery of Munich allowing Miller to import Lowenbrau into the United States. In late 1977, Miller adopted a new strategy to challenge Anheuser-Busch's Michelob, a superpremium beer and the market leader. The theme, "Tonight let it be Lowenbrau," was introduced to the nation and appears to be another success.

Philip Morris has changed Miller from the number seven spot with a 4.2 share of the market to second, with over 20 percent of the market and producing over 25 million barrels of beer a year. Miller achieved these successes not by cutting prices, but by having advertising that reached three different markets not previously recognized by other breweries.[11]

Summary Firms operating in a simple and changing task environment:

1. have a relatively fixed market share, and adjustments are made or created to gain production efficiency;

2. try to improve the economies of scale;

3. have as their major marketing strategy the improvements of their distinctive competence by making minor modifications in the product itself:

4. use a mechanistic form of organization, but less so than firms in Quadrant I;

5. use a continuous process technology, which allows for few exceptions, programmed descriptions for production workers, and heavy capital investment;

6. assign the president the job of searching for information in the market place concerning the changing styles, habits, or attitudes of the firm's customers.

Complex and Stable Task Environment (III)

A complex and stable environment is defined as one in which the task environment is relatively constant, in terms of customers and suppliers, but there are a great number of suppliers and competitors who are trying to differentiate their products in terms of taste and styling options. Conglomerates, such as Dart Industries, SCM, AMF, Walter Kidde, Indiana Head, and Gulf Western, typically operate in this type of task environment. The job of top management is to stay in close contact with a continually changing consumer or client group by monitoring changes in the market. To reach new customers, changes are generally made in the product's style or design.

A hierarchical, or mechanistic, type of authority structure is likely to prevail throughout the organization. Control systems to monitor the changes in and adapt to the environment will be developed in such a way as to be keyed by decisions made in the marketing department. In conglomerates, the structure is highly differentiated. Each firm within the conglomerate is assigned specific responsibilities, product lines, and targets for profitability. For example, each division of Textron, Inc. (Homelite Saws, Bell Helicopter, Talon Zipper Company) is a profit center responsible for its own sales, marketing research, and manufacturing. A top Textron executive stated that his firm wants to give the management of acquired companies independence. Because of the independence of Textron divisions, the only coordination needed is in the financial area. This coordination is achieved through Textron's annual budgeting process.[12] General Motors also operates in a complex and stable task environment. GM is organized along product lines — e.g., Pontiac, Frigidaire, Delco, Oldsmobile, Chevrolet — and is able to respond effectively to changes in each of the product's market segment. Each of GM's product divisions is a profit center responsible for its own sales and manufacturing processes. The divisions' activities are coordinated through financial and administrative committees. The financial committee provides guidelines for capital expenditures, methods of accounting to be used by each product manager, rate of return on investment, and other financial matters; the administration committee is concerned with long-range planning activities, production and sales policies, purchase commitments, and the like. Day-to-day operating decisions are handled at the product-manager level; long-term decisions requiring coordination among the various product lines are handled by top management committees.

Since the type of task environment confronting firms operating in this quadrant is relatively stable, most manufacturing is by mass production, assembling parts in standardized ways. The large number of Japanese Buddhist temples built between A.D. 700 and 1600 look quite different, yet each temple was put together with essentially standardized parts (e.g., beams, roofing, intervals between the various levels of a pagoda, and so on). The individually distinctive features, e.g., doors or iron grilles or the ornamentation of the tiles on the roof's edge, were added at the very end. Japanese temples, built of wood, burned again and again. But they always could be rebuilt exactly from drawings showing only the exterior appearance.

General Motors often points out there are so many options in its cars — colors, body styles, seat fabrics, accessories, and so on — that the consumer can actually choose from millions of different final-product combinations. More important is the fact that all GM passenger cars use the same frames, the same bodies, and very substantially, the same engines, braking systems, lighting systems, and the like. Yet the cars look different, appeal to buyers in different income brackets, and represent a great variety of combinations of basic standardized parts because each customer wants something different. Henry Ford, who in 1928 said, "The customer can have a car in any color as long as it's black," treated the market as simple. Customers did not like this uniformity and began to buy automobiles from manufacturers who gave them various color combinations. Similarly, American Motors is at a very real disadvantage in the automobile market because it has to turn out a variety of cars — at least in looks and styling — without General Motors' volume.[13]

Insurance companies also fall into this quadrant. The services offered vary because the clientele's needs for insurance (fire, health, marine, life, burglary, and so on) vary widely. However, insurance companies process clients in standardized ways that resemble mass production. The input and output for insurance companies are standardized. The input is a standard form, and the output is the payment of a check. Only the amount of the check varies, and this amount, of course, is determined in advance by the policy.

Mass-production technologies are usually labor-intensive. They require a high volume to break even. Top management needs managers who are highly skilled in the maintenance and design of the production system, but management needs individuals who use little judgment on the assembly line. For example, the typical insurance company has numerous highly qualified actuaries who design life insurance programs. Insurance companies also employ thousands of low-skilled clerks to handle the paperwork of processing clients' claims, payments, and adjustments.

CASE STUDY

Fuller Brush Company

In 1906, Albert Fuller started making brushes in his basement. By 1911, he had more than 100 salespeople selling brushes throughout the United States.[14] The salespeople carried brushes in suitcases from door-to-door. Fuller told the salespeople, "Know the product well. Persuade the homemaker to hold the item and observe it in use. It will sell itself." While the company was the point of many jokes, sales reached $12 million in 1920.

All brushes were mass produced by workers on incentives. Salespeople had to pay for brushes before delivery. Fuller reasoned that all employees had to produce. The turnover was high, seven out of 10 salesmen lasted less than three months. When Albert died, his son continued to operate the company as a door-to-door operation, but expanded the product line into vitamins, cosmetics, and toiletries in an effort to produce higher profit margins and more repeat sales. These products added diversity to Fuller's traditional product line, but the salespeople were calling on a stable set of customers.

After World War II, changes in the market took place. The suburbs were expanding rapidly and high-rise apartments dominated the housing market in cities. Sears, W. T. Grant, and Kresge were expanding rapidly into the suburban areas, offering a wide variety of products. This greatly added to the complexity of Fuller's task environments. Fuller introduced a catalog that was sent to prospective customers one week before the salesperson's call in an attempt to inform the customer of Fuller's product line. Not only did the catalog contain product listings, it included short stories of interest to homemakers.

In 1959, sales were $109 million, but by 1978, sales had declined to $60 million. Why? Costs had climbed, and salespeople found it difficult to reach homemakers because of : (1) laws prohibiting door-to-door selling, and (2) the increased number of women working. Fuller's distribution channels became expensive and inefficient compared to the national discount chain stores (e.g., K-Mart, Woolco, Grant). Shipments from the factory to salespeople were sporadic. Recruiting, which always was a problem, was a bigger problem because people were seeking a more prestigious line of work.

By 1968, Fuller was acquired by Consolidated Foods. This conglomerate has such well-known divisions as Sara Lee, Shasta Beverages, Popsicle, Gant Shirtmakers, and Electrolux Vacuum Cleaners. Consolidated's management decided to move heavily into cosmetics and toiletries in an effort to compete with Avon. However, Avon had a loyal and effective sales organization that gave Avon high repeat sales. Fuller's product mix didn't take any business away from Avon, and in 1974, Consolidated fired the executive who had been instrumental in tackling Avon.

In 1975, Fuller underwent drastic cost-cutting practices. Over a period of time, management had opened too many plants and product lines in anticipation that Fuller was destined to become a big corporation. Plants were closed and various layers of management eliminated. Changes were also made in merchandising. Prices were updated, slow-moving items eliminated, and new products, such as smoke detectors and fire extinguishers, added. Cost centers were established for each product.

Summary

Firms operating in the complex and stable quadrant:

1. have a relatively fixed share of the market;

2. try to improve economics by planned change;

3. aim to improve the distinctive competence of each product produced in order to segment the market into easily identifiable customers;

4. use a mechanistic form of organization, with profit centers created for each product;

5. use mass-production technology;

6. assign the president the job of gathering data from a number of sources and integrating all products.

Complex and Changing Task Environment (IV)

Complex and changing environments are defined as those in which there are continual changes in products or services, major technological innovations, and rapid changes in the values and behaviors of customers, suppliers, and others. Many managers today believe that they face this type of environment. Successfully dealing with these changes puts a premium on managerial creativity and marketing know-how. The type of organizational structure successful under these conditions is different from that found in the other environments. Perhaps most of all, the complex changing environment requires people who can accept ambiguity as they change tasks and positions on various teams where they must cooperate with people of differing backgrounds and perspectives.

In their study of 20 industrial firms, Burns and Stalker also found that firms facing changing task environments needed a different management system from those facing a stable environment. They labeled this system "organic." An **organic management system** has the following dimensions:

1. Organizational goals are continually assessed.

2. Authority is based on expertise rather than position.

3. Communication is consultative in nature rather than command-giving.

Organizational Property	Task Environments				8.2 Organizational Differences Between Task Environments
	Simple/ Stable	Complex/ Stable	Simple/ Changing	Complex/ Changing	
Hierarchy of Authority	Centralization			Decentralization	
Basis of Authority	Position in hierarchy			Expert power	
Division of Labor	High			Low	
Amount of Rules and Regulations	High			Low	
Formal Communication Flows	Rigid, formal			Flexible, informal	
Objectives	Short range			Long range	
Management System	Mechanistic			Organic	

Mechanistic	Factor	Organic
Low	Tolerance for ambiguity	High
Low	Integrative complexity	High
Toward position power	Attitudes toward authority	Toward autonomy
Low	Individualism	High
Low	Outside reference groups	High
Low	Professional values	High

Adapted from S. Tosi and S. Carroll, *Management Contingencies, Structure and Process*, Chicago: St. Clair Press, 1976, p. 467.

4. Team leadership involves frequent meetings to improve cooperation between teams.

5. Authority structure is decentralized.

6. There are few hierarchical levels.

Table 8.2 shows the relative degree of differences between "mechanistic" and "organic" management systems and how they relate to differences in the task environments facing the firm. Firms operating in simple and stable environments are likely to adopt "mechanistic" management systems, where firms in complex and changing business situations are more likely to adopt "organic" management systems. Although a particular organization may not have all these characteristics, these seem to be the most obvious. Let's examine the differences between the personnel and structure of these management systems.

Researchers have concluded that different kinds of management systems will attract and retain individuals with different value orientations.[15] Table 8.3 summarizes some of the differences among individuals in mechanistic and organic management systems.

Tolerance for ambiguity refers to the individual's ability to function effectively in uncertain situations. A person with high tolerance can make decisions under conditions of unclear job definition, unclear lines of authority and responsibility, and high degrees of uncertainty about the criteria for effective

Personnel differences

performance. A person with a low tolerance for ambiguity has a need for the structure and definition of activities usually found in mechanistic management systems. The stability of the task environment fosters adherence to rules and regulations in order to achieve maximum efficiency. Middle and first-line managers are evaluated on how well they follow orders from the top.

Integrative complexity is an individual's capacity to deal with a variety of information, understand it, and integrate it in order to solve problems. Managers in charge of research laboratories have a greater need for this skill than do the managers in charge of production-line workers. The production-line manager is concerned more about scrap, production efficiency, downtime, and other technical problems than about marketing, accounting, finance, and other organizational problems. On the other hand, the manager of an R&D laboratory should be concerned with all functions as they affect a project; as the task environment changes, so do the problems of these basic business areas.

It has been found that individuals working in organic management systems have higher educational levels than those in mechanistic systems. In general, those with higher education levels are less tolerant of directive leader behavior. Managers in changing task environments tend to have a greater preference for autonomy than do managers in more stable task environments. On the other hand, managers in mechanistic organizations prefer the strong authority relationships provided by the organization's hierarchy and its rules and regulations.

Managers and professionals with an inside-the-organization orientation are sometimes referred to as **locals,** whereas those who identify with outside reference groups are called **cosmopolitans.** Cosmopolitans adhere to what they perceive to be the values of their profession and are less committed and loyal to the organization's values and norms than are locals.[16] Professionals and scientists tend to be cosmopolitans because of their expertise and problem-solving abilities. They are typically employed in organizations in changing task environments (e.g. Texas Instruments, Honeywell, 3M, or Rand Corporation). Professionals are concerned less with money, promotions, and the value of the scientific approach, and more with the intrinsic nature of the job (e.g., feelings of achievement, challenge). These different perspectives and value orientations can create hostility and dissatisfaction in organizations employing a large number of professionals and line managers.

Organization structures

There are alternative forms of structure that firms facing a complex/changing environment may use. At one time or another, almost every organization forms *project teams* to handle special problems. The project team can be watched closely because incentives and penalties frequently are built into the tightly drawn cost schedule and performance requirements. Oftentimes projects are at the very frontiers of the company's technology. Project leaders become "mini-general managers" because they acquire and assemble relevant resources; they plan, organize, and control the activities of the project. The Boeing Company created many project teams when it built the United States' version of the SST. Most projects, however, are not large enough to contain their own resources and those of numerous subcontractors. Standard Steel President John Fogarty created a five-member project team to look into the desirability of buying a foreign steel mill. Each team member was able to provide a unique contribution to the project as it moved through different decision stages. For example, the financial person focused on the capital requirements needed to undertake this acquisition, the marketing person focused on marketing channels and import-export problems, the industrial relations person looked into staffing and union policies. At the same time, Fogarty was able to maintain overall control. Because of the temporary nature of the project — completing a task within cost, being on time, and performance requirements — the objective of the project manager is to go out of business.

Product management is oriented in an almost opposite direction. It takes a product or brand and makes it as successful as possible for as long a period of time as possible. Brand managers are used commonly in the soap, food, toiletry, and chemical industries. At J. C. Heinz, General Foods, or Procter & Gamble, the brand manager's role is to create and implement product strategies, monitor the results, and take corrective action. Cutting across functions, this manager concentrates more on the technical aspects of the product than on marketing considerations. At Texas Instruments, the "Product/Customer Center" manager spends more time with engineering and laboratory technicians than with advertising and marketing personnel.

Matrix management   The Establishment of effective means for dealing with problems of uncertainty and the management of diverse specialists can also be handled by a matrix. A **matrix** is an organization that represents a compromise between functional and product departmentation and employs a multiple authority structure.[17] In the matrix organization, individuals from various departments are assigned to one or more project teams to work together for the duration of the assignment. Hughes Aircraft Company, for example, is organized into five product lines — space and communications, industrial electronics, Hughes international, a research center, and research laboratories. When Hughes Aircraft is awarded a contract, the work is performed by the divisions that have the needed specialists. Thus if the contract is awarded to the Systems Division, the manager of that division determines the extent to which other divisions may be used in completing the contract. The impact of a newly awarded contract requires that a large number of people in various divisions work together closely to complete the contract. The continuous influx of new contracts, with subsequent allocation of products or tasks to all divisions, places continual burdens on a product or functional organization.

	Favors			8.4
	Functional	*Matrix*	*Product*	*Characteristics of Different Organization Structures*
Uncertainty	low	high	high	
Technology	standard	complicated	new	
Complexity	low	medium	high	
Time Criticality	low	medium	high	
Differentiation	low	high	medium	
Customer	diverse	several	one	

Adapted and abridged from R. Youker, "Organization Alternatives for Project Management," *Project Management Quarterly*, March 1977, p. 21.

Hughes' handling of contracts not only necessitates changes in the numbers and orientations of people but also in the mix of managerial, professional, and technical personnel required to complete any given project. The pressures from new technological advances and short lead times have made it necessary to establish some type of organizational structure to coordinate all of the various activities associated with a particular project.

Matrix management really represents a compromise between functional and project departmentation. In the functional organization, each department has its own specialists (e.g., accounting, marketing, personnel, production); in the product organization, all of the different specialists needed to produce a given product are in the same unit. Functional organization obviously makes it more difficult to achieve coordination of the different specialists, whereas product organization usually does not allow specialists sufficient access with one another and can lead to too many specialists of a certain type working at less than their capacity on a particular product.

A useful way to think about the differences among functional, product, and matrix organization forms is presented in Table 8.4. This table indicates that organizational designs may range from the purely functional to the purely product organization. In the functional organization, heads of the various functions make all decisions that affect their departments. Their authority is based on their position in the organization's hierarchy, policies, rules, regulations, and job descriptions. At Frito-Lay, turnover of people packaging chips was over 90 percent. Ben Dowell, Manager of Management Development, created a task force to examine the problem critically and report recommendations to the entire department. On the other hand, a product organization places the decision-making responsibilities on each product manager. These managers make decisions in a semiautonomous manner with respect to the other product managers. The matrix form uses advantages of both the product and functional forms.

Essential Characteristics of Matrix Organization   A recent article summarizes the five essential characteristics of matrix organizations.[18] We will briefly list these and then present a case study to enrich them.

1. Some managers report to two bosses rather than to a single boss.

2. Firms tend to adopt matrix forms when it is absolutely essential that they be responsive to two sectors: markets and changing technologies.

3. Matrix organization is more than matrix structure. It must be reinforced by matrix systems, such as dual control and performance evaluation systems, a manager whose leadership style operates informally rather than by the book, and a management system that fosters open discussion of problems.

4. Most matrix organizations assign dual command responsibilities to functional departments (marketing, finance, accounting) and to product departments.

5. Every matrix organization contains three unique and critical roles: the top manager who heads up and balances the dual chain of command; the matrix bosses who share subordinates; and the two-boss employees who report to two different bosses.

CASE STUDY

American Sterilizer Company

Since 1894, American Sterilizer Company has consistently seen its mission as one of providing quality products and services in the health-care industry.[19] AMSCO is a designer, manufacturer, and distributor of a broad range of equipment, instruments, and related supplies used primarily in hospitals. It also designs and installs automated material processing and distribution systems for hospitals and sells its products to educational, industrial, and food service markets. As we indicated in Chapter 7, AMSCO is organized by function (see Fig. 8.2). Recent changes in the marketplace had caused the vice-president of hospital products and systems marketing to evaluate the entire organization's structure critically. Some of the factors affecting a reorganization decision included:

1. the need to retrain the entire sales force;

2. the increasing intervention of the federal government in terms of legislation;

3. the increasing costs of new product development;

4. the increasing costs of new product liability coverage.

8.2
Structure of American
Sterilizer Company, Erie,
Pennsylvania.
(From *Marketeer*,
November/December 1978, p.
3.)

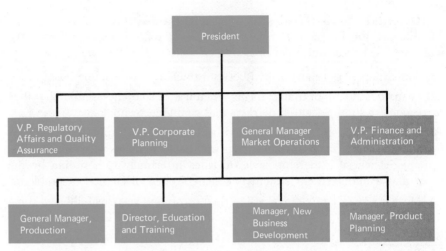

The decision to choose a matrix form centered on the marketing department's need to be more responsive to the customer needs and to changes in technology. The manager of the marketing department also recognized that human resources and financial controls needed to be better used to increase the quality of customer service. According to Frank Plasha, vice-president of employee and public relations, a manager has to have the ability to call on all human resources, in whatever functional department they might be, to complete a project.

The matrix structure of American Sterilizer has two major teams: product and market. The product manager looks at what the company can supply profitably and is responsible for product integrity. This means ensuring that AMSCO's products have all the features and benefits, including service and warranty, that will make them acceptable to the market. The products include: steam sterilizers, chemical sterilizers, washing and water machines, transportation systems, lighting equipment, tables, and allied equipment. The marketing manager is aware of what the customers want and provides feedback to management, such as: What do customers want that is different? What could be changed about a piece of equipment that will make it better? According to the President of AMSCO, the principal difference between the product and market managers is their point of view. The market manager looks at what the market demands, while the product manager looks at what the company can supply at a profit. Accordingly, AMSCO has identified seven market areas: surgical, processing and transportation, patient care, industrial, international, dealer-distribution, and national accounts.

Figure 8.3 can help clarify these relationships. At AMSCO, the two arms represent the functional and product managers. In this case, the left arm is the list of functional groups, or what might be thought of as the resource or input side of the organization. The right arm lists the various markets AMSCO serves. This is the output side of the organization. Depending on how many people from a functional group are needed and how extensive the product line is, several management levels can be developed within practical limits of control. At the foot of the figure is the matrix manager. This manager is responsible for the performance of a given team. At AMSCO, this manager is given agreed-on financial resources and performance goals by superiors on the output side and human resources and equipment from the resource (functional) managers. The matrix manager at AMSCO must handle high volumes of information, weigh alternatives, make commitments on behalf of the organization as a whole, and be prepared to be judged by the results.

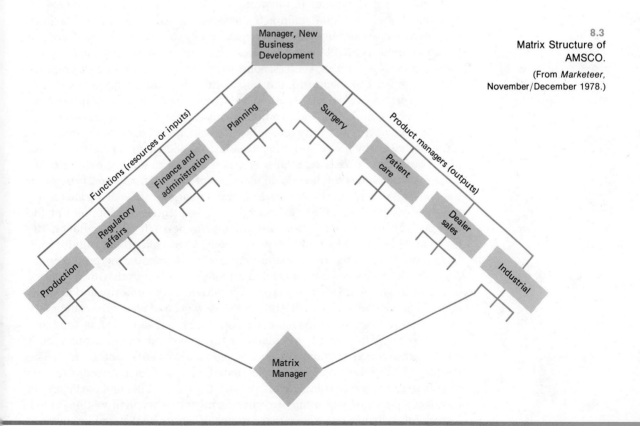

8.3
Matrix Structure of
AMSCO.

(From *Marketeer,*
November/December 1978.)

The matrix manager staffs a project with members from the functional areas. The assignment patterns may vary as follows: (1) full time for the duration of the project; (2) full time for one phase of the project; (3) part-time assignment; and (4) contract services from the functional department. In the last assignment pattern, the functional specialist never becomes part of the project team; rather, the project manager arranges for certain services from the functional department. In engineering, for example, the project may not be able to use certain specialized personnel or equipment all of the time; a solid-state physicist may be needed only occasionally, and the project may need an expensive environmental test laboratory or prototype shop only part-time.

The technology used in each stage of the project is likely to change. The basic work is performed in related stages. The building of a traditional, single-family house is one of the oldest examples of project management; the four stages are: (1) preparing the foundation; (2) erecting the frame and roof; (3) installing plumbing and wiring; and (4) finishing the interior. Each stage of the building process requires different workers and different technologies. It is the job of the contractor to integrate the skills of the various craftsmen to erect the home. Each craftsman is a specialist trained in technical functions, e.g., electricity, plumbing, carpentry, plastering, carpeting, etc. Similarly, in the space industry, NASA's great success was due to the integration of activities of its far-flung offices, centers, contractors, and subcontractors. Computer systems helped, but the most important element was the energy and commitment of various project managers, who traveled among the various contractors discussing problems and promoting concern for the entire mission.

The manager's authority and influence flow in different directions from those described by Fayol and other classical management theorists. A manager's authority flows horizontally, across the superior-subordinate relationships existing within the functional activities of an organization. Throughout the life span of a given project, personnel with varying skills at various levels must contribute their efforts to allow for the sequential development of the project. For each new project awarded the firm, new lateral information/decision-making networks must be worked out. These may differ significantly from those used in the functional organization. In essence, the project manager has no clear-cut communication channels but is faced with a web of communications that frequently crosses vertical lines of authority and involves outside subcontractors as well. Authority is *de facto* and stems from the manager's charge from top management to get the project done within time and cost constraints. In practice, the manager must rely heavily on alliances built with peers through negotiations, knowledge, and resolution of conflict. The building of these relationships supplements the lack of formal authority over all resources needed to complete the project. Success will depend partly on the manager's personality to influence other members rather than just his or her formal authority in the organization. Authority cannot be dictated in advance.

The changing nature of project work and the dynamics of matrix organizations, in which many competing managers vie for the firm's scarce resources (e.g., personnel, capital, machinery), make ambiguity a way of life.

Another example of a matrix structure can be found at TRW Systems. The company develops and manufactures earth satellites, landing modules, etc. An internal TRW document describes this structure as follows:*

> TRW Systems is in the business of application of advanced technology. The company's organization has been expressly planned for effective performance of the projects that comprise our business and for flexibility for future shifts in this business.
>
> The hardware work that we do is awarded by our customers in bid packages that usually involve a number of technical fields and integration of hardware from these into a single end item. We have several hundred of these projects in operation at a time. They range in people assigned from three or four to several hundred. Most of the projects are small — only a few fall in the "large hardware projects" category we are mainly concerned with here.
>
> From the standpoint of personnel and physical resources, it is most efficient to organize by specialized groups or technologies. To stay competitive these groups must be large enough to obtain and fully utilize expensive special equipment and highly specialized personnel. If each project had its own staff and equipment, duplication would result, resource utilization would be low, and the cost high. It might also be difficult to retain the highest caliber of technical specialists. Our customers get lowest cost and top performance by organization and specialty.
>
> For these reasons, the company has been organized into units of individual technical and staff specialties. Each customer's needs call for a different combination of these capabilities.
>
> A way of matching these customers' needs to the TRW organization elements that can meet them is necessary. The [matrix] system performs this function.
>
> In the [matrix] system, a project office is set up for each customer program. The project office reports to a company manager of appropriate rank in the organization with cognizance in the technical area of the project. The overall . . . organization is similar for each project. The [matrix] manager has overall management responsibility for all project activities and directs the activities through the project office and substructure described in the following.

---

* From H. Rush, *Behavioral Sciences: Concepts and Management Application*, pp. 158–159. Copyright © 1969 by The National Industrial Conference Board. Used with permission.

The . . . office is the central location for all project-wide activities such as project schedule, cost and performance control; system planning, system engineering, and system integration; and contract and major subcontract management. Assistant project managers are appointed for these activities as warranted by project scope.

The total project effort is divided into subprojects, according to the technical specialty involved, thus matching the TRW Systems' basic organization structure. Each subproject has a subproject manager who takes project direction from an assistant project manager. The subproject manager is responsible for performance in his specialty area to the supervisor of the organizational element that will perform the subproject work. The subproject manager is the bridge between the project office and the organizational element. The members of the next subordinate level of management in that organization take project direction from him. The work is further subdivided and performed within their organization.

The document also describes how people interact in a matrix structure.

In an organization like TRW, when getting a job done cuts across departmental boundaries, contact with a large number of other people is a way of life. . . . Because of the necessity for interaction of a technical and personal nature, the team approach is viewed as the most manageable system. Since the teams comprise a heterogeneous group of technical specialties and individuals, conflict is understandable enough.

As one executive expressed it, ". . . groups and individuals in TRW derive the necessary discipline from the job itself and the preciseness of the technological and support specialties required to get that job done effectively. We focus on the problem and organize ourselves to solve that particular problem."

Because people are encouraged to do things "a different way," and because the company has designed a system in which a man's responsibility emerges from the job to be done, he must obtain the cooperation of others over whom he has little traditional, direct authority. . . . "Making the matrix organization really work can be difficult and frustrating; we attempt to reduce the difficulties by encouraging openness and cooperation," comments a training specialist. If openness exists, a man can devote his time and energies to the real job of making an effective organization, instead of politicking and empire building which dissipate energy and drain off effort that ought to be used constructively on the job.[20]

Pros and Cons   Matrix organizations have disadvantages like any other organization form. Matrix organization is relatively new and companies that have adopted it, like General Electric, Citibank, Diamond Instrument, E. F. Hutton, have been learning by trial and error. There are several common problems.[21]

First, there are *power struggles* between product groups. In the functional form of organization, the hierarchy is well defined. Rules and regulations detail actions considered acceptable. In a matrix structure, ambiguity and shared authority are built into the design. Authority and responsibility overlap between product and functional managers. This permits some managers to use the ambiguity to their own advantage — that is, securing the most and best resources (financial and human), not sharing information with other groups to protect one's "turf," and setting objectives that will show a profit in the short-run but not in the long-run. Second, a matrix organization can get into trouble because of *group behavior*. We have seen one matrix organization that had a bad case of "groupitis." Each product of a multiproduct steel company had a product manager and a product team drawn from the various functional areas. One of the product groups believed all decisions had to be made in group meetings. Some individuals seemed to enjoy a steady diet of group meetings, but others felt that their time, especially on Saturday mornings, was being wasted and preferred having the best informed people of the team make decisions. The manufacturing people were especially critical of meetings that called them away from their shops.

The third common problem is that senior management either has not understood the concept or has not been able to implement the concept by delegating the proper amount of *authority and responsibility*. For example, at American Sterilizer, only the product and marketing managers found the idea useful. Other managers did not reorganize their divisions. Even at Dow Corning, a $3 billion corporation with over 50,000 employees, only 1000 managers are actually involved in the matrix. The important point for top management is to delegate authority and responsibility where it is needed.

Fourth, the emphasis in flexibility rather than permanency of job assignments affects the *attitudes of employees* who work within a matrix structure. Insecurity about future employment after the project's completion, career retardation, and personal development are concerns of employees. Therefore, they may feel less loyal to the organization and are more likely to report frustration on the job than are employees in a more conventional, functional type of organization. As the project begins to phase out, members attempt to latch onto new projects for fear of being laid off. In some instances, the organization cannot absorb these employees into other projects, either because of the stage of the project or because of the lack of contract awards. This fear of possible unemployment causes special problems in project organizations.

Although matrix management has been confined mostly to the aerospace and construction industries, it may find increasing application in many other

8.5
Summary of Organizational Design Relationships

	Simple/Stable	Simple/Changing	Complex/Stable	Complex/Changing
1. Market share	Relatively fixed and predictable	Need for identification and minor adjustment; relatively fixed and stable	Changing	Varied and unpredictable
2. Firm's objective	Maximization of current product line	Improve economies of operation to maximize product line	Maintain ability to adjust to varied needs of customers	Develop effective problem-solving methods to cope with uncertain task environment
3. Market strategy	Maintain competence in product line	Improve distinctive competence by creating demand for product(s)	Contingency planning; search for advanced information	Adapt to changes in the market and technology
4. Organization form	Mechanistic	Fairly mechanistic	Mixture between organic and mechanistic profit centers	Organic
5. Dominant technology	Mass production or assembly line; programmed tasks, heavy capital investment; few product exceptions; low skill requirement for workers	Continuous process; few exceptions in inputs, but varied final products; low skill requirement for workers, high skill requirement for managers and designers of system	Mass production, few exceptions, and capital intensive	Craft or job shop; major exceptions; no dominant technology
6. Role of chief executive officer	Little active search in the task environment; maintain status quo; create effective distribution channels to get product(s) to customer at minimal cost	Commitment to a conservative search process in the task environment; create demand for product(s) through advertising media	Adaptive planner and searching for information in the task environment	Secure orders for the firm; active search for information in the task environment

areas where there is increasing demand for advanced technology and sequential development of related subsystems. Matrix management in other sectors, such as transportation systems, urban renewal, and pollution control, may provide important innovations in the structure of industries operating in these sectors.

SUMMARY

Structure should be derived not from abstract principles but from the organization's markets, technology, and task environment. Standardization and stability are desirable in mechanistic management systems operating in stable task environments. On the other hand, when the task environment is unpredictable, innovative organizations, such as the matrix form, are needed to provide more flexibility in the organization's response to the environment. Although the relationships are not inevitable or certain, the usual association of structure, technology, task environment, and management systems is illustrated in Table 8.5.

Consistency in management is not necessarily a virtue. Not all parts of a large organization need be similarly structured. Manufacturing consumer products, for example, is much different from designing nuclear power systems and defense systems, although all of these activities are taking place at Westinghouse. Each department of the organization is responding to its own task environment. Since manufacturing an automobile is different from designing a missile defense system, these two units in GM should not be similarly structured, nor should they attract and retain the same type of personnel. The emerging organizational principles offered by the contingency approach are designed to promote the responsiveness of the organization to the demands of its task environment.

KEYWORDS

changing environment   *mechanistic system*
cosmopolitans   *organic system*
locals   *stable environment*
matrix   *task environment*

DISCUSSION
QUESTIONS

1. What is a stable environment? What structure tends to characterize organizations in such an environment?

2. What is a changing environment? What structure tends to characterize organizations in such an environment?

3. What is a "mechanistic" organization?

4. What is an "organic" organization?

5. Provide some examples of firms operating in the different quadrants in Table 8.1.

6. What is the relationship between an organization's technology and its structure?

7. How is matrix management accomplished?

8. Discuss the role of the chief executive officer in stable/simple and changing/complex environments.

Management Incidents and Cases

ROOSEVELT HOSPITAL

Roosevelt Hospital is a large, privately endowed hospital in Louisville, Kentucky. The hospital cares for patients who pay for services as well as patients who do not have funds. The latter were referred to as "charity" patients; now, hospital personnel usually refer to them as "limited-resource" patients. Money for such patients is provided by the city of Louisville, by the state and federal governments, and by endowment funds. Recently, the city of Louisville requested all hospitals receiving such funds to provide statistics on cost per patient per day for such items as room and board, pharmaceuticals, and doctors' fees. Because the hospital director knows that the city will channel funds to hospitals that do not show excessive costs, he has instituted certain control reports. For example, he must be notified when the total cost of drugs for one patient exceeds $1000.

Two months ago Dr. Gillam, a staff physician decided to try a drug experimentally for a limited-resource patient who had chronic arthritis. The drug, Milozene, was reported in medical journals as "a tentative help for severe arthritic conditions. It has passed all federal tests for safety, but we have not established that it actually results in patient improvement. That will not be known until clinical experiments have occurred over two to three more years."

The cost of Milozene is $150 per ounce. Gillam estimated that 30 ounces of this drug would be needed for extended treatment. When the $4500 requisition reached Dr. Jackson, the hospital pharmacologist, the latter called Dr. Gillam to inquire why it was being purchased. Dr. Gillam explained and the pharmacologist ordered and paid for the requisitioned drug.

Dr. Prichard, the hospital director, asked Dr. Gillam, Mr. Travis, the financial director, and Dr. Jackson to come to his office for a general discussion of hospital costs, and said he had noticed a large number of high-cost requisitions made by Dr. Gillam.

Dr. Prichard: Jane, of course I'm not questioning your judgment on treating patients. I just thought we'd understand better our cost situation if we took the Milozene requisition as a case in point. As you know, we're under pressure to lower costs, and under city pressure in terms of further support.

Dr. Gillam: Well, I did have the patient's interest in mind. I've used most of what is known in the way of medications. The patient responded somewhat. I know Milozene is an 'iffy' proposition, and that it may or may not help. In addition, I knew for sure I could include this in medical research. It is valuable research either way — if Milozene is found not to be an effective drug, that's as important to know as that it is effective. What I'm saying is that there's a payoff for our $4500, regardless of what the results are for the patient. We won't know for another year.

Dr. Prichard: But don't you remember the decision of our board two years ago about the place of research in the hospital? It was agreed that we are primarily a healthcare hospital, and not a research hospital. We leave that to the universities and the university hospitals. I'm surprised that you didn't consider that, and that Dr. Jackson didn't bring it up when he saw the requisition.

Dr. Gillam: In view of the possible benefit to the patient, I view it as health care.

Dr. Jackson: Well, Jane gave me those reasons at the time we talked. I ordered the Milozene not on my own judgment, but hers. It really isn't my job to treat patients. I'm here to check the specifications of items wanted by the staff and to make sure that we get those exact specifications from manufacturers.

Mr. Travis: As members of the board of trustees, Dr. Prichard and I have been troubled deeply about such costs. Both city and federal agencies have intimated strongly that charity and poverty funds may be channeled to Louisville General Hospital rather than to us unless we can show we produce maximum care for the community for dollars invested. As of now our costs exceed General by $13 per day per patient. We're $4 higher in doctors' fees, $2 higher in rooms and meals, and $7 higher in drugs. Frankly, I believe Dr. Gillam made this decision on the basis of research, and it was the wrong decision.

Dr. Gillam: I said I had the patient's health in mind. If Dr. Prichard will give us some policy to follow, I'm more than glad to go along with it. I simply don't want to worry about decisions like this.

Dr. Prichard: Of course we don't want to intrude on the prerogatives of the individual doctor.

Mr. Travis: But don't you think we might work out some guidelines or procedures whereby the doctor gets a ruling on such matters from somebody higher up? Or maybe we could simply have someone check with the doctors to help them clarify their own courses of action.

Dr. Prichard: I don't see how we could ever operate other than on the individual doctor's judgment. Maybe everyone should just bear in mind that we want good patient care and wise use of our precious dollars.

Dr. Jackson: Well, I'd be glad to follow any procedure you may work out.

Dr. Prichard: I thank you all for coming in. And I'm sure it was worth our time. Let's just think about what's been said, and from time to time talk among ourselves when these things come up.

The meeting broke up with the usual good-natured comments about one another's family, the current political situation, and like matters. Each then returned to work. Later, Dr. Gillam commented: "Prichard is a gentleman and we all like him. Actually, he does conduct the most ineffective meetings in his office. If I'd thought about it carefully, I wouldn't have ordered the Milozene. But I simply cannot be a good doctor and researcher and be an economist-financier too. I'm not interested in those things, know nothing about them, and cannot worry during the day about such decisions. I'm bothered about the state of affairs in Louisville. I blame Roosevelt's rather bad reputation in part on Prichard. Some of us are also troubled because all of the best young doctors seem to be going to Louisville General. One of them told me he looks at Roosevelt as a good hospital, but one that is a little tired and messy to work in."

1. How is the environment of Roosevelt Hospital affecting its goals?

2. How are the various technical functions of the hospital influenced by these goals?

3. How are the motivations of people affected by the technology (goals plus tasks)?

4. What structural problems exist in the hospital? How does this affect staff coordination?

DOLPHIN POOL AND RECREATION SUPPLY SERVICE

Dolphin Pool and Recreation Supply Service is a 23-year-old specialized company engaged in manufacturing and selling recreational supplies in the southwest part of the United States. During its history, it has failed to show a profit only during the years 1956 – 1957. It began by producing croquet, archery, and badminton sets, and, in recent years, has diversified into closely allied lines, including swimming pools. Its largest sellers at the present time are bicycles and shoe-type roller skates.

During the fiscal year just concluded, Dolphin showed an operating loss of over $500,000 on sales of just over $26 million. The cash on hand has decreased but not markedly. The current cash account is about $1 million. The weekly payroll is $150,000. The stockholders and board members, as well as management and labor, are deeply concerned about the operating loss. Most people in the organization feel that immediate remedial action is required.

The company president not only feels this pressure but he also has a commitment to getting the company on the upward track again. He knows that the situation cannot continue as it is now, and he has called on the various departmental vice-presidents to meet with managers as a prelude to a meeting with him later at which some definite decisions about the future of the company will be reached.

He and the executive vice-president, who serves as vice-president of finance and who works closely with the president on overall company affairs, have been given as much latitude as they need by the board of directors.

They can deal with the various problems and formulate any new policies they wish.

The following memo was sent to all vice-presidents:

TO: All Vice-Presidents
FROM: Mr. J. Yaney, President, Mr. R. Bobbitt, Executive Vice-President
SUBJECT: Profit situation

As you are all undoubtedly aware, company profits took a substantial turn for the worse during the past year. This is a matter of serious concern and Mr. Yaney and I would like, therefore, to meet with all of you to discuss this problem. It would be helpful if before the meeting, each of you would:

1. Meet with your department heads and prepare an assessment of the strengths and weaknesses you see within your respective departments, i.e., areas where fat could be eliminated, sources of inefficiency, hidden assets we are not using, and so on.

2. Give some thought to the company as a whole and what we might be able to do to improve our position.

Each of the functional vice-presidents prepared a brief report in response to the memo. These are outlined below:

Marketing Department Situation

1. This is a sophisticated market research group that has developed skills at staying ahead of the competition by developing new markets.

2. The competition has cut into sales through lower prices on merchandise that was first introduced to the market by Dolphin.

3. The Dolphin advertising department has not been able to decide where future advertising dollars would be best spent.

Sales Department Situation

1. Sales department includes 50 field representatives, almost evenly divided between people who formerly sold other items (appliances, clothing, and the like) and people who taught recreation before joining Dolphin.

2. Sales to department stores have decreased as more former recreational personnel have joined the sales force.

3. Sales to schools and institutions have increased as former recreational personnel have joined the company.

Production Department Situation

1. During the past fiscal year, production was up 20 percent over the preceding year.

2. Labor costs, however, rose by 24 percent during the year, largely due to increased overtime and time lost through mechanical failure.

3. The rate of rejection of finished products increased by 14 percent from retailers and 19 percent from sales personnel.

Personnel Department Situation

1. Through the efforts of its personnel department, Dolphin has developed the reputation of being an excellent place to work.

2. Competition from other organizations and a slight increase in turnover have put added strain on the department in its efforts to recruit top quality people.

3. The department recently has begun to experiment with some new management development programs; not enough time has passed to evaluate the results.

Research Department Situation

1. During the past two years the research department has developed more patents than any company in the recreational field.

2. Only three of a total of 56 patents have reached the production stage.

3. Only one of these three items has been put on sale, with sales results so far inconclusive and unexciting.

Questions

1. What type of task environments is Dolphin facing? Are these the same for all of its products?

2. What type of structure is best for Dolphin?

3. Do you see any reasons for conflict between the departments?

4. What should the president's role be?

REFERENCES

1. J. Bourgeois, "Strategy and Environment: A Conceptual Integration." *Academy of Management Review* **5,** 1980, 25–40.

2. J. Pfeffer and G. Salancik, *The External Control of Organizations.* New York: Harper & Row, 1978.

3. For reviews of the technology/structure literature, see: J. Kimberly and M. Evanisko, "Organizational Technology, Structure and Size." In S. Kerr (ed.). *Organizational Behavior.* Columbus, OH: Grid Publishing Company, 1979, pp. 263–288. J. Ford and J. Slocum, "Size, Technology, Environment and Structure of Organizations." *Academy of Management Review* **2,** 1977, 561–575. R. Dewar and J. Hage, "Size, Technology, Complexity and Structural Differentiation: Toward A Theoretical Synthesis." *Administrative Science Quarterly* **23,** 1978, 111–136.

4. See: P. Lawrence and J. Lorsch, *Organization and Environment: Managing Differentiation and Integration.* Boston, Mass.: Graduate School of Business Administration, Harvard University, 1967. R. Duncan, "What is the Right Organization Structure?" *Organizational Dynamics,* 1979 (Winter), 59–79.

5. *Wall Street Journal,* April 16, 1975.

6. See Chapter 3 for a complete discussion of these tactics. Also: J. Pfeffer and H. Leblebici, "Executive Recruitment and the Development of Interfirm Organizations." *Administrative Science Quarterly* **18,** 1973, 446–461. J. Pfeffer, "Cooperation and the Composition of Electric Utility Boards of Directors." *Pacific Sociological Review* **17,** 1974, 333–363. D. Katz and R. Kahn, *The Social Psychology of Organizations* 2nd ed. New York: John Wiley & Sons, 1978.

7. T. Burns and G. Stalker, *The Management of Innovation.* London: Tavistock, 1961, pp. 120–122.

8. *Columbus Dispatch,* May 3, 1976.

9. J. Clark, *Businesses Today: Successes and Failures.* New York: Random House, 1979, pp. 7–13.

10. R. Miles and C. Snow, *Organizational Strategy, Structure and Process.* New York: McGraw-Hill, 1978.

11. J. Clark, *Businesses Today: Successes and Failures.* New York: Random House, 1979, pp. 32–43.

12. R. Pitts, "Toward a Contingency Theory of Multibusiness Organization Design." *Academy of Management Review* **5,** 1980, 203–211.

13. P. Drucker, *Management: Tasks, Responsibilities and Practices.* New York: Harper & Row, 1974.

14. J. Clark, *Businesses Today: Successes and Failures.* New York: Random House, 1979, pp. 88–94.

15. J. Lorsch and J. Morse, *Organizations and Their Members: A Contingency Approach.* New York: Harper & Row, 1974. J. Slocum and D. Hellriegel, "Organizational Design: Which Way to Go?" *Business Horizons* **22,** 1979, 65–76.

16. C. Halaby, "Bureaucratic Promotion Criteria." *Administrative Science Quarterly* **23,** 1978, 466–484.

17. For an excellent review of matrix management, see: S. Davis and P. Lawrence, *Matrix.* Reading, MA: Addison-Wesley, 1977.

18. P. Lawrence, H. Kolodny, and S. Davis, "The Human Side of the Matrix." *Organizational Dynamics*, 1977 (Summer), 47.

19. *AMSCO Marketeer* (November/December), 1978, 17.

20. H. Rush, *Behavioral Sciences: Concepts and Management Application.* New York: National Industrial Conference Board, 1969, pp. 158–159.

21. S. Davis and P. Lawrence, "The Matrix Diamond." *Wharton Magazine* **2,** 1978, 19–27.

Part IV presents the other two of the four basic management processes — decision-making and control — discussed in this book. The management processes of planning, organization design, decision-making, and control have no clear-cut boundaries in carrying out managerial responsibilities. For example, all planning activities involve decision-making, but not all decision-making is planning. Also, the best laid plans may go off course unless a good control process ensures that those plans are used and corrective actions are taken when they are needed. Part IV addresses ideas, models, and issues that directly affect the day-to-day performance of managers at all levels of the organization. The preceding part on planning and organization design focused more on helping middle- and top-level managers attend to their responsibilities effectively.

Chapter 9, "Decision-Making Concepts and Contingencies," develops a framework for the decision-making process. Three types of rationality are discussed: rationality of the decision; the five basic steps in a rational decision process; and rationality of the decision-maker. The central role of goals in the decision-making process is reviewed along with the states of nature under which decisions are made: certainty; risk; and uncertainty. All of these concepts concerning the rational view of decision-making are pulled together in an integrative model. Two major contingency variables are used to extend and build on the rational perspective to decision-making: "beliefs about causation" and "preferences about possible goals." They are used to create a model that identifies four distinct types of decision-making situations that managers may encounter. The recommended strategies for these decision situations are outlined.

Part IV

Chapter 10, "Decision-Making Models and Techniques," fleshes out the framework developed in Chapter 9. This chapter presents models and techniques for making better decisions. It broadly outlines four general normative decision models commonly used in dealing with a wide variety of decision problems focusing on economics variables. These models include the cause-and-effect diagram, the break-win model, the payoff-matrix model, and the decision-tree model. The chapter concludes with two techniques — the Osborn technique and the Nominal Group technique — often prescribed for stimulating creativity in the decision-making process.

Chapter 11, "Decision-Making in Operations Management," considers some of the key decision issues and aids in the production system of organizations. Operations management is defined as the use and interaction of inputs (resources) that are transformed through a production process into desired outputs (goods or services). The beginning of the chapter describes the basic elements of operations management: inputs; transformations; and outputs. Most of the chapter discusses some of the key decision-making areas in operations management and the general decision models in each area. Some of the key decision areas in operations management include forecasting, scheduling, inventory, and quality control. For example, three aids for making forecasting decisions of particular importance to operations management are presented. These include the moving-averages model, exponential-smoothing model, and regression-analysis model.

Chapter 12, "Control Concepts and Strategies," presents the fourth and last major management process that influences organizational effectiveness. Of course, the management of organizational behavior, which is developed in Part V, also has an important influence on organizational effectiveness. "Control" refers to the process by which a person, group, or organization consciously influences what another person, group, or organization will do. Two basic types of control — preventive and corrective — are reviewed, along with a description of how political influences affect the control process. We discuss the traditional corrective model of control and how managers can use it to "keep their units in line." We examine the impact on the control process of two key contingency variables — type of power and type of technology. The last part of the chapter focuses on six control strategies: human-input control strategy; reward-punishment control strategy; formal-structure control strategy; policies-and-rules control strategy; budget-control strategy; and machine-control strategy.

Chapter 9

DECISION-MAKING CONCEPTS AND CONTINGENCIES

After reading this chapter, you should be able to:

1. Describe rationality and irrationality.

2. Recognize different decision situations in terms of certainty, risk, and uncertainty.

3. Identify and apply the means-goal staircase.

4. Use two decision models in making individual or organizational decisions.

5. Classify decision situations on the basis of two contingency variables — beliefs about causation and preferences about goals.

6. Describe when to use the decision strategies of standard routines, negotiations, judgment, and inspiration.

PREVIEW CASE

**What's the
Problem?***

Let's listen to the dialogue of three experienced managers as they deal with some company prolems. Art, the General Manager, has called in Dick, the Production Manager, and Jack, the Distribution Manager. Art starts off by telling them, "There's a very serious problem here." After he gives them figures on the decline in profits on some of the company's products, the following conversation occurs.

Jack (Distribution Manager):   I can elaborate on that. The model C, of course, is bringing in the big profits, and that is one area where our industry situation is very critical. As I see it, a key production problem is that we're down to less than one-third day's inventory as of this morning. Our real problem is what

* Adapted from C. Kepner and B. Tregoe, *The Rational Manager: A Systematic Approach to Problem Solving and Decision Making,* pp. 7–11. Princeton: Kepner-Tregoe, Inc., 1976.

we're going to do about stepping up production to give us a chance to build up a little bit of inventory.

Dick (Production Manager): Jack says we're having complaints from the distributors, and we have a problem of low inventory. I think this relates to our recent change in production methods. We had some rejected units, had some sent back, and I think. . .

Art (General Manager): One bad problem you have in production, Dick, is quality control. I wrote a memo on this after we heard from industrial relations that Al Hawser, chief of quality control, has an ulcer condition. He's got a young assistant, who's new on the job, holding down the fort. I think you should check and make certain all quality control procedures are being followed very rigorously. We need to make sure he's not letting something slip out of here that is not up to standard.

This conversation tells us a great deal about the decision-making processes of the speakers. First, the word "problem" is used to mean different things, even to the same manager. For example, Jack (Distribution Manager) uses it to mean something that is out of line ("less than one-third day's inventory"), something that may be causing this trouble ("problem of production"), and for action that should be taken ("stepping up production"). Second, Jack, Dick and Art tend to jump to conclusions about the causes of the problems. For example, Dick (Production Manager) suggests that two problems, "low inventory" and "complaints from the distributors," are caused by the introduction of new production methods. In contrast, Art (General Manager) suggests that the complaints are caused by poor quality control procedures. Third, even when they center on a given problem area, such as customer complaints, these managers jump around in their decision-making process. They discuss details (units returned, quality control report), speculate about causes (low inventory, new production methods, low quality control), and recommend alternatives (stepping up production, checking on quality control procedures). While we could continue with the dialogue in this incident, it should be enough to note that their confusion, which they did not recognize, just got worse.[1] This chapter and the next two should be particularly useful in helping you to make decisions and avoid the type of confusion Jack, Dick, and Art created for themselves.

PRECONDITIONS FOR DECISION-MAKING

As suggested in Fig. 9.1, four preconditions must exist for meaningful decision-making to occur. There must be: (1) a *gap* between the present situation and a desired goal; (2) an *awareness* of this gap; (3) *motivation* to reduce the gap; and (4) *resources* that will permit something to be done about the gap. Meaningful decision-making is likely to take place only if the answer to the following four questions is *yes*.[2]

9.1
Preconditions for decision-making

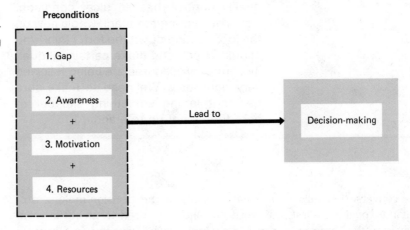

1. Gap
+
2. Awareness
+
3. Motivation
+
4. Resources

Lead to

Decision-making

1. *Is there a gap or difference between the present situation and some desired goal?* At first this gap may be in the form of some vague sense of dissatisfaction with the present. Let's assume you have been out of college four years and have received pay raises averaging eight percent per year. Considering your job responsibilities and your relative performance, you feel a sense of dissatisfaction.

2. *Is the decision-maker aware of the gap?* Over time, you realize that you should be earning about 20 percent more than you are. This feeling increased when you contacted a professional employment agency about another job.

3. *Is the decision-maker motivated to decrease the gap?* After discussing your dissatisfaction with your manager, you learn that the company is in such a weak financial position that pay raises for the coming year will be very low. The maximum raise will be eight percent. Your manager explains that many others in the organization are in the same situation as you. You decide to return to an employment agency to look at job alternatives. The discussions at the employment agency indicate that the only jobs available at the salary you feel you should have would require that you relocate 600 or so miles from home. This creates a lot of stress, since all of your friends and family are located in the city where you work. Because you want very much to maintain close personal and family ties, you never explore the other jobs. Thus, the decision-making process is ended without full exploration of alternatives.

4. *Does the decision-maker have the resources (ability, money, etc.) to decrease the gap?* Since you decided not to relocate, you think about opening up a McDonald's outlet. Unless you could raise $300,000 or more, there'd be no point in thinking about this possibility further.

Again, if the previous four questions cannot be answered with a "yes," the full process necessary for meaningful decision-making cannot take place.

RATIONALITY

Rationality is the condition of being rational, i.e., of being able to reason soundly and logically. How often have you told, or felt like telling, others that a decision they made was irrational? That's a common emotional response, but we need to consider rationality and irrationality in a more systematic manner. Much of the thinking on decision-making concerns the rationality of the decision, the decision process, and the decision-maker.

Rationality of the Decision

A rational decision maximizes goal achievement within the limitations of the environment in which it is made. This definition assumes that the goal is known, but it does not evaluate the rationality of that goal. Our position is that rationality must consider not only goals (what we want to achieve), but also *means* (how we are going to achieve them). An example is the turmoil in Congress over the discovery of bribes offered by some American corporations to foreign politicians and individuals. To some American executives, the bribes may have represented a decision that was needed to attain a goal of securing orders. From their view, to offer bribes may have looked like a rational decision. However, if other values and goals are applied – e.g., fair play and honesty – the decision to offer bribes may appear to have been irrational. Conflict over goals may cause the party on one side of the conflict to regard the person on the other side as irrational. When individuals are torn between conflicting goals, they often feel tension, anxiety, and stress. If personal goal conflicts become severe enough, individuals may make what others perceive as irrational decisions and may even be considered mentally ill.

**Rationality of the
Decision Process**

The concept of rationality often emphasizes the *process* used in arriving at decisions.

Five basic steps

As suggested in Fig. 9.2, a *rational decision-making process* includes at least five basic types. The steps are explained as follows:[3]

1. Explore the nature of the problem. Identify, define, and diagnose the problem and the goal.

2. Generate alternative solutions. Search out various means to reduce the problem and achieve the goal.

3. Evaluate and choose among alternative solutions. Gather information about the alternatives, evaluate or weigh the relative merits of each alternative, and select one of the alternatives.

4. Implement the chosen alternative. Take the actions needed to carry out the chosen solution.

5. Control the chosen alternative. Maintain it (keep it going), monitor it (know what's happening), and review it (assess actual effectiveness). This step will be explored in depth in the chapter on control.

The person who follows these five steps presumably would aproach the requirements of a rational decision-making process.

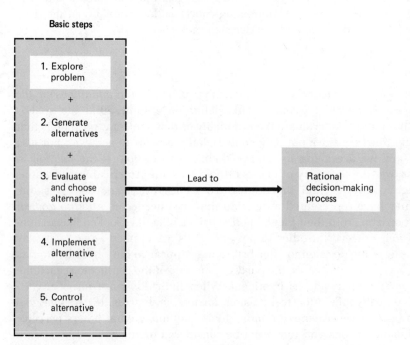

9.2
Five basic steps in rational
decision-making process

The degree of rationality in the decision process is shown by a study of how graduating seniors from the business school of a university went about the decision to interview certain firms.[4.] The students seemed to fall equally into three groups. The "maximizers" felt that the organizations differed significantly in salary, career opportunities, advancement potential, and working conditions. The only way they could actually collect and analyze company information was to take as many interviews and get as many job offers as possible. They would then "rationally" choose the best offer on the basis of what they were looking for. By contrast, "minimizers" tried to reduce the number of interviews by getting one offer and taking it. They tended to believe that all firms were about the same and did not feel that a choice of employment opportunities was important. Finally, the "validators," in between the other two groups, tried to get their favorite offer (determined very subjectively) and then get just one more interview to see if their favorite was really a good one. It appears that the maximizers were the most "rational" and the minimizers the least "rational." The maximizers followed the steps in the rational decision-making process more closely than did the minimizers.

**Rationality of the
Decision-Maker**

It is easy, but incorrect, to suggest that individual rationality or irrationality depends on the extent to which the right decision process is used. A decision-maker who defies laws of reason and logic is usually considered irrational by other groups or individuals. It is easier to make judgments of irrationality about "means" than about "goals." For example, a residential builder contractor interested in minimizing construction costs probably would consider it irrational to have carpenters use only hand hammers when faster and low-cost power hammers are available.

The significance of individual *values* and *goals* in assessing rationality or irrationality cannot be overstated. For example, individuals opposed to draft registration may view it as an irrational decision that will increase the chance of the United States engaging in another major war. On the other hand, proponents of registration may claim that it is a rational step, that it improves the country's ability to respond to threats to its security and serves as a deterrent to would-be enemies. Thus, many decisions cannot be viewed on a rationality-irrationality continuum. Differences in values and goals can cause one person to view a decision as rational while another calls the same decision irrational.

Bounded rationality

Bounded rationality is the tendency of managers to: (1) set less than optimal goals (satisfice); (2) engage in a limited search of alternatives; and (3) have inadequate information and control of the factors influencing the outcomes of their decisions.[5] The concept of bounded rationality provides a general *description* of the day-to-day decision processes used by many managers.

Bounded rationality is a useful concept because: (1) it emphasizes the limitations of the decision-maker's rationality and (2) partially explains the differences in decisions arrived at by individuals, even when they appear to have the same information. Let's consider the elements of bounded rationality further: satisficing; limited search; and inadequate information and control.

Satisficing

Satisficing means that an individual does not set an optimum goal in a decision problem, but instead establishes a very limited range of goals that would be acceptable. For example, one goal of a business might be to maximize profits. Profits often are expressed as desired goals, such as a 15 percent rate of return on investment or a 10 percent increase in profits over the previous year. These goals may not represent maximizing behavior. Those college students whose goal was to take as few interviews as possible to get a job were satisficing.

The concepts of satisficing and bounded rationality were first introduced by Herbert Simon in the mid-1950s. These concepts were significant factors in the decision by the Swedish Academy of Sciences to award him the 1978 Nobel prize in economics for his "pioneering research into the decision-making process within economic organizations." In an interview almost 25 years after introducing the concept of satisficing, Simon described it in these words for a management audience:*

> *Satisficing is intended to be used in contrast to the classical economist's idea that in making decisions in business or anywhere in real life, you somehow pick, or somebody gives you, a set of alternatives from which you select the best one — maximize. The satisficing idea is that first of all, you don't have the alternatives, you've got to go out and scratch for them — and that you have mighty shaky ways of evaluating them when you do find them. So you look for alternatives until you get one from which, in terms of your experience and in terms of what you have reason to expect, you will get a reasonable result.*

> *But satisficing doesn't necessarily mean that managers have to be satisfied with what alternative pops up first in their minds or in their computers and*

---

* From John M. Roach, "Simon Says: Decision Making is a 'Satisficing' Experience," *Management Review*, January 1979 (New York: AMACOM, a division of American Management Associations, 1979), pp. 8–9.

let it go at that. The level of satisficing can be raised — by personal determination, setting higher individual or organizational standards, and by use of an increasing range of sophisticated management science and computer-based decision-making and problem-solving techniques.

As time goes on, you obtain more information about what's feasible and what you can aim at. Not only do you get more information, but in many, if not most, companies there are procedures for setting targets, including procedures for trying to raise individuals' aspiration (goal) levels. This is a major responsibility of top management.[6]

Bounded rationality assumes that the individual or organization makes a very *limited search of the possible alternatives* which might be used to obtain the desired goal. The individual considers alternatives only until one is found that appears to provide adequate means for obtaining the desired goal. For example, in choosing the best job, college graduates cannot evaluate every possible job in the world for which they might be qualified. They might die of old age before obtaining all the information needed for a decision.

Limited search

Even maximizing behavior recognizes that identifying and assessing alternatives costs time, energy, and money. The key difference with bounded rationality is that managers stop considering alternatives as soon as they hit on one that seems acceptable for reaching their goal.

Bounded rationality holds that some factors outside the managers' control will influence the actual results of their decisions. Management might make a decision to purchase a number of automatic stamping machines to make disc brakes for automobiles. With the reduced cost of labor, the machines could pay for themselves within two years. But management did not anticipate the resistance to the machines by the union members and the decline in automobile sales. As a result, the automatic machines are not used effectively and the payback period is six years rather than two.

Inadequate control and information

In summary, bounded rationality suggests that decision-makers frequently have incomplete information about their decision problems. This supports the idea that rationality typically is tied to a limited frame of reference, whether it be that of an individual, a group, or an organization.[7]

The importance and role of goals to managers were extensively developed in the chapters on planning. Thus, our discussion of goals and decision-making is a limited one. Within organizations, middle and higher managers are especially responsible for the development of organizational goals. A manager's

GOALS AND DECISION-MAKING

authority to set goals will vary widely. It depends on the manager's level in the organization, the degree to which goal-setting has been decentralized, and how much personal influence that manager has with his or her superiors and others.

Nature and Importance of Goals

Goals are results to be attained. Goals also may be termed objectives, ends, missions, purposes, standards, deadlines, targets, and quotas. Regardless of the label, goals specify a state of affairs that some members think desirable for their organization. The goals chosen do not always prove to be effective for the organization's long-run survival and growth. Henry Ford's goal of producing only black Model-T Fords was ultimately detrimental to the company's success. One of A&P's goals was to promote only from within, but since the company did not have an active management-development program and did not adequately expand in suburban markets, it lost its leadership in the food retailing industry.

Even using relatively rational decision processes for its *means*, it is possible for an organization to establish what some might regard as irrational *goals*. W.T. Grant's goal of selling only softwares at low prices led to high profits before 1960. Unfortunately, Grant's realized too late that its customers wanted other merchandise and services.

As discussed in the chapter on strategic planning, types and levels of organizational goals represent a continuous decision problem facing all managers. A firm's general goals of survival, growth, and profitability often remain stable. But its subgoals, such as types of goods and services provided, usually show significant shifts over time. An example of a change in subgoals is Kresge's (K-Mart) change of goods and services in the mid-1960s to capture a new type of customer, the discount shopper.

Means-Goal Staircase

The general goals presented in organizational charters, public pronouncements by executives, and annual reports may not be much help in understanding the behavior and decisions made by managers. These statements are purposely general and ignore the many specific goals that organization members pursue.

The **means-goal staircase** refers to systematically linking the goals of lower-level units or individuals with those of higher level units or individuals. For example, Larry Wilson, President of Henry C. Beck Construction Company, stated a goal of reducing construction costs by 7 percent. To reach this goal, each of his managers was asked to reduce the number of job-related accidents by 10 percent. A 10 percent reduction in job-related accidents was believed to be a means of achieving the goal of 7 percent reduction in construction costs.

The means-goal staircase can be illustrated through an analysis of a large electric utility employing about 5000 people. The means-goal staircase is presented for only some of the utility's marketing units. Figure 9.3 shows several marketing goals of an electric utility in a means-goal staircase. That is, a goal at one level becomes a "means" for the level above, which has a new, higher goal of its own.

Taken from the company's manual, the goals in Fig. 9.3 have been abridged and the numbers are not actual. As you read *down* the means-goal staircase, the goals become narrower in scope and more specific. Dozens of means-goal staircases exist for the entire organization. In the marketing division alone, means-goal staircases would have to be pre-

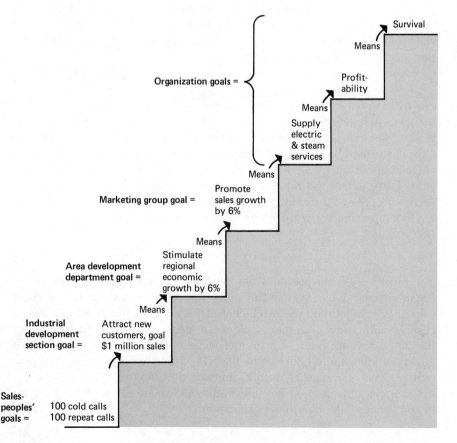

9.3
Means-goal staircase for
several marketing units of
an electric utility

Organization goals =
Survival
Means
Profit-
ability
Means
Supply
electric
& steam
services
Means

Marketing group goal =
Promote
sales growth
by 6%
Means

Area development
department goal =
Stimulate
regional
economic
growth by 6%
Means

Industrial
development
section goal =
Attract new
customers, goal
$1 million sales
Means

Sales-
peoples'
goals =
100 cold calls
100 repeat calls

sented for: (1) the Community-Development Section of the Area-Development Department, (2) Commercial Sales Department, (3) Eastern Sales Department, (4) Industrial Sales Department, and (5) the Marketing Services Department.

The means-goal staircase suggests that organizational decision-making is an orderly, conflict-free process as long as everyone keeps to their goals. In this condition, goals are *not* likely to be important to the decision-making process. However, goals are important when two or more managers or others have conflicting goals or need to develop new goals.[8] For example, management might have a goal of keeping pay increases to 9 percent when the union's goal is to get 12 percent.

Though they are not present in every decision-making situation concerning goals, there are four potential problems in the use of the means-goal staircase: (1) nonacceptance of goals, (2) conflicts in goals, (3) suboptimization, and (4) ambiguous situations.

Nonacceptance of goals

The means-goal staircase implies that the individuals will accept and support the goals assigned to them. However, individuals have many roles, e.g., employee, parent, spouse, church member. In each of these roles, individuals have particular goals. If conflict occurs between the goals in these roles, individuals cannot satisfy all of them simultaneously. When President Carter decided to try to free the American hostages in Iran by military force in 1980, Secretary of State Vance resigned his position over a conflict in goals. In almost any organization, some members will disagree with some of the organization's goals.[9]

Conflicts in goals

The means-goal staircase does not illustrate the inevitable conflicts between organizational departments. The marketing department's goal of increased sales may conflict with the production department's goal to achieve minimal cost-per-unit. The marketing people might decide the way to increase sales is through different products or greater variety of the same product. Given the goal to produce the product at the lowest possible cost, the production people may prefer to standardize outputs and schedule long production runs.

Chapter 17 is devoted to conflict and will explore this and the other types of conflicts usually found in organizations.

Suboptimization occurs when the maximization of one goal reduces the overall level of goal attainment for the whole individual or organization. This occurs when goals are interrelated, not when they are independent of one another. Suboptimization occurs only when the maximization of one goal reduces the level of achievement of other goals.

Students, for example, may decide to study as many hours as needed to earn all As. The goal requires a commitment to long hours of study. Although these students seek to optimize this goal, they may become more miserable each term because this behavior has produced undesirable effects on other personal goals. The decision to study long hours may prevent them from attaining goals of satisfactory interpersonal relationships, recreational activities, or involvement in campus political activities. Under the assumptions made, we can conclude that these students have suboptimized in terms of their total set of goals.

Suboptimization is likely in organizations with much division of labor and many different departments. Each department in the public utility example has goals that serve as means for attaining higher-level goals. If the manager's performance is evaluated only in terms of the attainment of the goals for his or her work department, decisions will be made with only that department in mind. The area-development manager could maximize departmental interests if the people in the industrial sales department would spend more time getting information about companies that are thinking about expanding or relocating. Excessive attention to such activities might interfere with the industrial salespeople's primary goal of increasing energy conservation by present customers.

Suboptimization usually can be avoided or reduced through strong leadership from each higher level, various management-development programs, and appropriate reward systems. These devices encourage managers to broaden their perspective beyond the narrowly defined goals of their departments.

An ambiguous decision situation includes one or more of the following characteristics: (1) The problem is defining what the problem is; (2) goals are unclear, shifting, and/or conflicting; (3) the decision situation is not understood because it is novel and complex; and (4) the environment of the decision situation is uncertain and changing rapidly.[10] Thus, an ***ambiguous decision situation*** has a high degree of uncertainty over the nature of the problem, the goals to be pursued, and the environment surrounding the decision situation. The energy crisis is an example of an ambiguous decision situation confronting U.S. business, government, and the public since 1973. It took the federal government until 1980 to formulate a plan to *begin* to cope with this decision situation.

A study of the perceptions of upper-level business managers identified the types of decision situations those managers considered to be both significant and ambiguous. A few of the decision areas identified by these managers include:

1. Strategic planning and forecasting.
2. Changing government regulation.
3. Organization designs to take advantage of new opportunities.
4. Effects of political attitudes and public pressures.
5. Lack of motivation and high performance among employees.
6. Effects of changing technology.[11]

Ambiguous decision situations are not solved by well-defined decision processes, such as the five steps in the rational decision-making process presented earlier in the chapter. Some ways of dealing with ambiguous decision situations are introduced later in this chapter.

STATES OF NATURE

States of nature are those conditions the decision-makers cannot control, but which can influence the results of their decisions.[12] Examples may be the rate of unemployment, level of inflation, new competitors, technological developments, and the state of international relations. Of course, organizations and their managers often try to influence and predict the states of nature facing them. Ford Motors lobbied the federal government in 1980 to limit the number of imported autos. The firm was attempting to influence its environment with respect to competing autos and the relative demand for its cars.

The probability that a particular state of nature will occur can vary considerably. The degree of uncertainty about the future greatly influences decisions and the decision-making process. Decisions are made under three sets of future conditions (states of nature): certainty, risk, and uncertainty. As shown

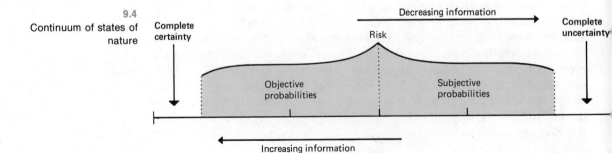

9.4
Continuum of states of nature

in Fig. 9.4, these states of nature can vary from certainty through risk to uncertainty.

Certainty exists in the decision situation when the individual is fully informed about the nature of the problem, the possible alternatives, and the results of those alternatives. Once a manager has identified the alternatives and their results, the decision is relatively easy. The manager simply chooses the one with the best results, or "payoff." All other things equal, we would expect a purchasing manager (for example) to purchase a standard grade of paper from the supplier who offers the lowest price.

In actual practice, the decision process is not quite so simple. There usually are many possible alternatives, and it would be extremely time-consuming and expensive to calculate all of them. The manager who decides not to investigate all possible alternatives can never be certain that the best alternative was chosen.

For top- and middle-level managers, decision-making under certainty probably is infrequent. There are some decision issues, especially those made by supervisors in manufacturing organizations, that approach certainty. For example, a manager may decide to have some employees who are doing routine tasks work overtime. The cost of the overtime can be determined with near certainty; the manager can expect with near certainty that at least a certain number of additional units will be produced, and so the cost of the extra units can be figured with near certainty before the overtime is ordered. In general, decision-making under certainty occurs with the more routine and repetitive decision situations facing first-line managers.

Risk occurs in the decision situation in which the individual can define the nature of the problem, the possible alternatives, and the probability of each alternative leading to the desired results. The risk condition assumes that there is enough information to predict the probability of different states of nature. *Probability* refers to the percentage of times a specific result (outcome) would occur if a particular decision was made a large number of times.[13] It is a fairly safe bet that, with enough tosses of a coin, heads will show up 50 percent of the time.

The amount of information about the states of nature can vary widely, and the interpretation of this information by managers under conditions of risk can vary even more. This is suggested by the considerable range of the continuum in Fig. 9.4. Figure 9.4 also indicates two types of probabilities — objective and subjective.

Objective probability

Objective probability refers to the decision situation in which the individual can determine, with relative certainty, the likelihood that each state of nature will occur. Although the manager cannot be certain *which* state of nature will occur, he or she can tell, by examining past records, which one is most likely to occur. Life insurance companies cannot determine when each of their policy holders is likely to die. However, they can establish objective probabilities of how many of their policy holders, in various age categries, will die in a particular year. These objective probabilities are based on the expectation that past experience will be repeated in the future.

Subjective probability

Subjective probability refers to the decision situation in which the individual can determine the likelihood of each possible state of nature on the basis of his or her own judgments and beliefs. The probabilities assigned may vary from manager to manager. The assignment of subjective probabilities can depend on the manager's intuition, previous experience with similar decision situations, expert opinions, personality traits (such as risk-taking vs. risk-avoidance), and other factors.

The use of subjective probabilities might be illustrated by a theater owner who is thinking about changing the price of popcorn. What effect would a 10 percent price increase have on the average amount of popcorn sold per theater customer? The decision-maker might believe that there is a 30 percent chance that sales would drop off by 5 percent, and a 10 percent chance that sales would drop by 10 percent.

Uncertainty

Uncertainty occurs in the decision situation in which the individual cannot even assign subjective probabilities to each of the possible states of nature. It is assumed the individual has no information, insight, or intuitive judgment to use as a basis for assigning probabilities to each state of nature. As explained in our earlier discussion of ambiguous situations, the level of uncertainty could be so extreme that it is not even possible to define the nature of the problem, or the goals, or the alternatives. In the more extreme case it may not even be possible to tell what the different states of nature are, let alone tell what their probability of occurrence will be. Dealing with uncertainty is central to the jobs of top-level executives and various professional groups in organizations, such as research and development engineers, market researchers, and planning staffs.[14]

The decision by the French and British governments to collaborate on constructing a supersonic passenger plane was a major decision made under conditions of uncertainty. When the plan for constructing the Concorde was announced in 1962, the estimated development cost was $150 million. By 1976 the cost had spiraled to more than $2 billion. It has been decided the first group of 16 Concordes will be the last. The Concorde costs about twice as much as a Boeing 747 and burns about three times as much fuel per passenger mile. It is five to 17 times as polluting, depending on the specific pollutant. Moreover, the noise levels and possible harm to the ozone layer are severe problems.[15] In short, many of the present-day concerns about the Concorde were not thought of as relevant problems in 1962 or were not expected to be problems.

Individual Differences

An individual's values, perceptions, and interpretations of states of nature affect how he or she will define problems and assess alternatives. Here we want to mention one type of individual difference important to managerial decision-making — the tendency to accept or reject risk and uncertainty. Individual differences with respect to risk-taking might be summarized as follows.

1. Risk-avoiders do everything possible to play it safe.

2. Risk-takers are willing to take chances and may aggressively seek out chancy situations which offer the possibility of significant payoffs.[16]

3. Risk-takers tend to view the acceptance of risks, including uncertainty, and the opportunity to obtain rewards as positively related to each other.

4. Risk-avoiders tend to prefer decisions where the potential loss is known to those decisions whose risks could lead to greater rewards or losses.[17]

In sum, a **risk-taker** is willing to take chances and may aggressively seek out chancy situations which offer the possibility of significant payoffs.

Self-appraisal of risk-taking

A brief self-appraisal questionnaire for assessing your risk-taking preference is shown in Fig. 9.5. You might want to take a minute and respond to these items by recording your responses from 1 through 9.

Total your responses by adding the number circled on the scale for each of the items. The higher the total score, the greater your general preference for risk-taking. Of course, your conscious perceptions on this questionnaire may

9.5

Self-appraisal of
risk-taking

Adapted from B. Bass, J.
Vaughn, and E. Schein,
Exercise Self-Appraisal.
Scottsdale, N.Y.: Transnational
Programs, 1975.

Risk-taking under uncertainty

1. Extremely
cautious   1 : 2 : 3 : 4 : 5 : 6 : 7 : 8 : 9   Extremely
adventuresome

Willingness to trust others

2. Completely
suspicious   1 : 2 : 3 : 4 : 5 : 6 : 7 : 8 : 9   Completely
trusting

Speed of decision

3. Defer
judgment
as long as
possible   1 : 2 : 3 : 4 : 5 : 6 : 7 : 8 : 9   Decide as
quickly as
possible

Impulsiveness

4. Think before
I speak   1 : 2 : 3 : 4 : 5 : 6 : 7 : 8 : 9   Speak before
I think

be biased and so would not truly show how you feel about risk-taking. This self-appraisal questionnaire was administered to 327 American managers as part of a larger study. You might like to compare your responses to the average scores obtained from these managers, as follows:

Item 1 = 5.4   Item 2 = 5.3   Item 3 = 5.9   Item 4 = 4.8

In sum, individuals may differ in their perceptions and decisions under conditions of subjective probability and uncertainty.

CASE STUDY

Edward Hennessy of Allied Chemical

Edward Hennessy provides one of the more dramatic illustrations of the impact of a risk-taking executive on a corporation. *The Wall Street Journal* sums up Hennessy's impact on Allied Chemical this way:*

> *When a stodgy, old company brings in a new chief executive from outside, he is expected to shake things up.*
>
> *But few managers can match the record of Edward L. Hennessy, Jr., who left United Technologies Corp. to become president and chief executive of Allied Chemical Corp. May 1, 1979, and chairman seven months later.*
>
> *Within six months, he brought Allied into the electronics business with the $588 million acquisition of Eltra Corp., reshuffled top management, and brusquely streamlined the corporate structure from*

---

* From Georgette Jasen, "Shake-up Artist: Allied Chemical Has Rapid-Fire Reactions Under Chief Hennessy." April 23, 1980. Reprinted by permission of *The Wall Street Journal,* © Dow Jones & Company, Inc., 1980. All rights reserved.

*eight divisions to four operating companies — chemicals, fibers and
plastics, oil and gas, and Eltra.*

*He disrupted things further by axing some 700 employees. At the
time of the layoffs, Hennessy hired a bodyguard for a week.*

*By the end of the year, he had sold off huge chunks of Allied and
settled some nagging litigation. He did more in five months than the
company had done in five years, says John P. Henry, a chemical-
industry analyst with E.F. Hutton & Co. Harold Buirkle, Allied's senior
vice-president for planning and finance, says, "He set our company
on a new and exciting course."*[19]

The basic concepts of rationality, goals, and states of nature will be useful
in understanding and applying the two models presented in the rest of this
chapter, as well as the specific decision models and techniques that are developed in the next two chapters.

In the rest of this chapter, a number of the themes and concepts developed in the first part of it will be pulled together and extended through the
presentation of two models. The first model, called the *dynamic process of
managerial decision-making*, provides a *prescriptive* framework of the major
factors surrounding decision situations and the step-by-step procedures for
dealing rationally with them. The second model, called the *contingency organizational decision model*, is more *descriptive* of and *specific* about the types of
decision situations facing managers and the basic decision strategies managers may need to use in each situation.

**THE DYNAMIC
PROCESS OF
MANAGERIAL
DECISION-MAKING**

Decision-making is not a fixed technique, and the fact that a decision has been
made does not mean that no further decisions will be necessary. Managerial
decision-making is a dynamic, ongoing process, and no matter how similar
they may sometimes appear, each decision is different from every other decision. Regardless of their differences, though, all managerial decisions have
elements in common; each is made against a background of certain surrounding factors and each involves certain basic steps.

Surrounding Factors

As shown in Fig. 9.6, four major factors influence and surround the managers'
general decision-making processes. Of course, additional factors, such as the
time available for decision-making or agreement or disagreement about goals,
could have been included as well.

9.6
The dynamic process of
managerial
decision-making

The "inner core" of this figure
is adapted from E. F. Harrison,
*The Managerial Decision
Making Process*, 2nd ed.
Copyright © 1981 by Houghton
Mifflin Company, p. 25.

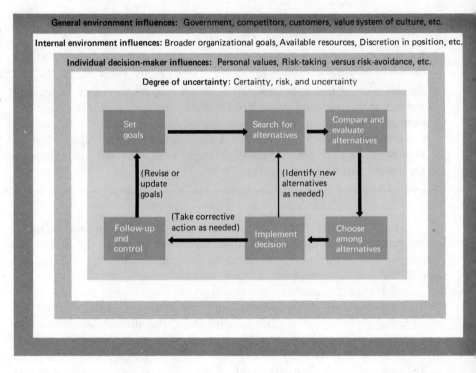

The first major factor consists of *general environmental influences*, such as government, competitors, customers, and societal values. For example, the affirmative action requirements enforced by government agencies have pressured many managements to set goals for the employment of women and minorities. Firms are expected to advertise available positions in minority-oriented publications, interview at women's colleges, and the like.

The second major factor is *internal environmental influences*. These influences include the broader organizational goals and the resources available for dealing with the decision situation. The amount of decision-making authority in the position and the pressures exerted by superiors, peers, or subordinates are also considered.

The third major factor is simply the *nature of the individual decision-maker*. The goals established, the alternatives identified, and the alternative chosen could be influenced by the manager's personal values and tendency toward risk-taking or risk-avoidance.

The fourth major factor surrounding the general decision-making process is the *degree of uncertainty* in the decision situation. The relative importance of the four major factors will vary with the type of decision situation.

The decision-making process, as shown in Fig. 9.6, begins with the establish-ment of goals and moves through a series of steps to follow-up and control.[20] These six basic steps are virtually the same as the five basic steps in the rational decision-making process outlined in Fig. 9.2.

The first step in this dynamic process is to set the goals to be achieved. The goals spell out the results desired — what is to be achieved by when. For example, a goal may be to reduce turnover to an annual rate of five percent within six months.

Set goals

In an uncertain decision situation, the establishment of goals could be the major decision problem, requiring a consideration of alternative goals, com-parison and evaluation of alternative goals, choice of goals, etc. You might have an overall goal of pursuing a career in business, but the specific business career to pursue may be uncertain right now. Should you set a goal of becom-ing an accountant, wholesale sales representative, or one of several hundred other identifiable careers in business? Regardless of your answer, it is neces-sary to consider alternative career goals.

Alternatives must be sought which might help achieve the desired goal. This might mean seeking information both inside and outside the organization, engaging in creative thinking, and analyzing what caused the decision situa-tion and what action should be taken. If there do not appear to be any mean-ingful alternatives for reaching the goal, it may be necessary to change the goal.

*Search for
alternatives*

Once the alternatives have been identified, they must be compared and evalu-ated. This element in managerial decision-making zeros in on the expected results, including the relative costs of each of the alternatives. Several of the specific techniques for making comparisons and evaluations in this "step" are presented in the next chapter.

*Compare and
evaluate
alternatives*

Depending on the results expected, the alternatives may fall into one of four categories, as follows:[21]

1. A *good alternative* is likely to lead to desirable results for the manager. It is expected to cost less than it will gain.

2. A *bland alternative* is unlikely to produce either positive or negative results for the manager. The federal government's public relations efforts of appeal-ing to "good citizenship" to cut energy consumption was a bland alternative. It was only *after* the prices of gasoline and electricity were allowed to rise, on the basis of supply and demand, that we found significant individual decisions to conserve energy.

3. A *mixed alternative* is likely to have both positive and negative results. For example, a manager may insist that subordinates deal with a problem in a particular way because it is technically the best solution. This may create resentment in the subordinates and cause their efforts to implement the solution to be half-hearted. This reduces the potential payoff from the technically superior decision. The use of time and motion study has, at times, been a mixed alternative. This technique may suggest more efficient steps to produce items, but it has also led to worker resentment and slowdowns.

4. A *poor alternative* is one that leads to negative results. Chrysler's decision to keep building their larger cars after the 1973 oil embargo proved disastrous to the organization. Without a loan guarantee program from the federal government of $1.5 billion, Chrysler would have been forced into bankruptcy in 1980.

Choose among alternatives   Decision-making is popularly associated with choice. But choice is really only one small step in the managerial decision-making process. Many managers complain that when recent college graduates are given a project they tend to present and discuss only one alternative. Without an explicit comparison and evaluation of alternatives, a manager must accept or reject the choice being presented. The rationality and limitations of a preferred choice become easier to understand and appreciate if all of the steps of the dynamic decision-making process are presented to the manager.

Choosing among alternatives might appear to be straightforward. Unfortunately, choosing among alternatives may be difficult when the decision problem is complex, ambiguous, and involves high degrees of risk or uncertainty. Several of these difficulties are summarized as follows:[22]

1. Two or more alternatives might appear *equally attractive*. This could justify further evaluation of the remaining desirable alternatives. Or the decision-maker could choose by flipping a coin.

2. If no single alternative is likely to meet the desired goal, it may be desirable to *implement two or three* of the alternatives identified. The goal of reducing turnover, for example, might be dealt with through a combination of alternatives; including changes in selection practices, compensation systems, working conditions, and managerial leadership practices.

3. The decision-maker may be *confused* and *overwhelmed* in the choice step because there are too many attractive alternatives. This might require lumping similar alternatives into groups and taking a second, more intense, look to compare and evaluate them.

4. There may be *no alternative* (singly or in combination) that will accomplish the desired goal. This may require a further search for alternatives or a revision in the desired goal to make it less demanding.

Implement decision

In one sense, the action step of decision-making begins with the implementation of the chosen alternative(s). A "good" decision is not necessarily a successful one. As suggested earlier, a technically outstanding decision may be offset by inadequate acceptance, especially by those who must implement it. If the decision cannot be implemented, an effort should be made to identify new alternatives. We will have more to say on this in later chapters.

Follow-up and control

Implementing the decision will not automatically lead to the desired goal. And if implementation starts to go off course, the manager must use various strategies to get it back on course.

Since many of the major factors surrounding the decision process are changing, the follow-up and control phase also may indicate a need to revise the goals. The feedback from this step could indicate that the entire managerial decision-making process should be started over.

The following case study of Pearle Vision Centers captures a variety of the major factors and steps in the dynamic process of managerial decision-making outlined in Fig. 9.6.

CASE STUDY

Pearle Vision Centers[23]

As part of an aggressive growth strategy for 1981, the Searle Optical Group, which operates Pearle Vision Centers, secured $600,000 incremental advertising dollars to supplement its existing 1981 advertising budget of $12,000,000. Since a complete schedule for the 1981 media plan had already been developed, the additional dollars could be used in any number of ways. Most of the executives, including the Senior Vice-President of Marketing,

James Rothe, Senior Vice President of Marketing, Searle Optical

felt that the television medium was most effective for Pearle Vision Center advertising. Given that media decision, the immediate problem was to identify alternative ways of spending the $600,000. The general goals were to increase awareness, improve image, and increase traffic and sales at the more than 700 Pearle Vision Centers throughout the country. The basic options identified with the assistance of the ad agency included: (1) buying an additional three weeks of network TV to supplement the planned 26 weeks targeted at reaching 7.8 million households; (2) increasing the advertising levels in the top 25 TV markets (New York City, Dallas, Los Angeles, San Francisco, etc.) for a month; (3) buying 14 weeks of ads on a spot schedule; or (4) sponsoring one of the early morning shows — *Today* (NBC), *Good Morning America* (ABC), or *Morning* (CBS).

The decision to purchase the sponsorship of one of the early morning weekday shows was made by James Rothe, Senior Vice-President of Marketing. He felt that this option provided the best awareness, exposure, and format for Pearle's advertising. In addition, he felt that the existing network and spot schedules were adequate. Thus, he was seeking alternative exposure options. In 1980, the *Good Morning America* show had slightly higher total Nielson ratings than the *Today* show, and substantially more than *Morning*. The ratings of *Good Morning America* indicated that it was viewed by a somewhat more affluent and well-educated audience. Also, more of the business travelers watched the show than the others. These data led James Rothe to select the *Good Morning America* show for the $600,000 in additional advertising of Pearle's optical products. Negotiations with ABC's executives enabled Pearle Vision Center to secure over 30 weeks of coverage on the *Good Morning America* show at the rate of two 30-second commercials per week. Additional merchandising assistance for their eyewear was also obtained from David Hartman. An announcement of the *Good Morning America* advertising was sent to each Pearle Vision Center to inform them of the additional promotional support their stores would have for 1981.

Additional Managerial Implications

The dynamic process of managerial decision-making outlined in Fig. 9.6 probably is most useful for decision problems that are moderately nonroutine, somewhat complex, and new. These decision problems usually involve states of nature under risk and possibly uncertainty. Routine, recurring, and less complex decision problems may not require a consideration of all of the steps and factors set forth in Fig. 9.6. If, for example, a particular type of decision problem tends to recur often, there would be no need to repeatedly search for alternatives. Most likely, a routine policy would be established to handle this decision problem.

The contingency organizational decision model is a second major model for understanding the process of managerial decision-making. This model extends and builds in three ways upon the model of the dynamic process of managerial decision-making just presented.

1. The model presents two important *contingency variables* that confront organizations and their managers in decision situations.

2. The model suggests an appropriate decision-making *strategy* for each of four types of decision situations.

3. The model identifies the type of organizational structure that may be effective for dealing with each of the four decision situations.

The contingency organizational decision model is closely related to the contingency model of organization design developed in Chapter 8. Both models are concerned with the degree of uncertainty and complexity in decision situations. The contingency organization decision model considers many general types of decision situations, whereas the organization design model is limited to decision situations involving the formal design and structure of organizations.

The contingency organizational decision model is based on the interaction of two basic contingency variables: beliefs about causation and preferences about possible goals.

Beliefs about causation refers to the amount of agreement or disagreement between two or more managers on the means that should be used to reach their goals. This contingency variable, as shown in Fig. 9.7, can be thought of as a continuum, ranging from complete agreement to complete disagreement between the managers on the cause-and-effect relationships in the decision problem.

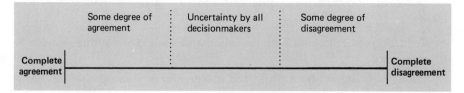

It is possible that none of the decision-makers will hold any beliefs about causation. This possibility is suggested by the middle area of the continuum in Fig. 9.7.

Disagreement over beliefs about causation were found in the Pearle Vision Centers case. Jim Rothe thought the additional advertising dollars should go into buying additional TV time to increase sales. In contrast, some of the other managers at Pearle claimed that sales could be improved by using the additional $600,000 in advertising for other promotional approaches, such as sponsoring marathon races, golf matches, or car races.

Preferences About Possible Goals

Preferences about possible goals refers to the degree of agreement or disagreement between two or more managers as to the goals that should be pursued. This contingency variable also can be thought of as a continuum, as shown in Fig. 9.8, ranging from complete agreement to complete disagreement over goals. The conflicts between the United States and Russian governments in various decision situations are often a result of basic disagreement about goals.

9.8
Continuum of preferences about possible goals

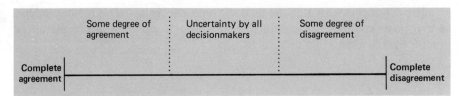

Framework of Model

The framework of the contingency organizational decision model is created by combining the two contingency variables (i.e. beliefs about causation and preferences about possible goals), as in Fig. 9.9. This figure shows four major types of decision situations and the decision-making strategy recommended for each. The major decision situations and strategies for managers are as follows.

Cell 1: Agreement about both causation and goals. The routine strategy is recommended.

Cell 2: Agreement about goals, but disagreement about causation. Judgment strategy is recommended.

Cell 3: Agreement about causation, but disagreement about goals. Negotiation (bargaining) strategy is recommended.

Cell 4: Disagreement about both causation and goals. Inspiration (intuition and creativity) strategy is recommended.

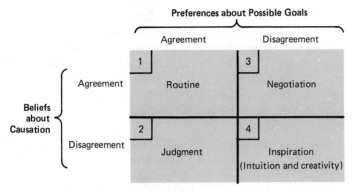

9.9
Contingency organizational
decision model

(Adapted and modified from J.
Thompson, "Decision Making,
the Firm, and the Market." In
W. Cooper et al. (eds.) *New
Perspectives in Organizational
Research.* New York: Wiley,
1964.)

Managers need to be sensitive to these different situations. They should not try to force a decision strategy into a situation for which it is not suited. Let's explore the nature and use of these decision strategies.

Routine strategy

The **routine strategy** is the use of well-established procedures or computational techniques that can be followed systematically to arrive at a decision. Decision-making with this strategy is a relatively mechanical and technical process. It is usually an appropriate strategy for repetitive and structured decision situations, for example: opening a charge account in a department store, processing savings deposits or payroll checks, and making a shake at Burger King.

A manager faced with decision situations in which the routine strategy usually is appropriate can use a bureaucratic structure and mechanistic system of management. For example, the teller's department of a bank will make heavy use of routine computational techniques to determine whether a teller is "in" or "out" of balance at the end of the day, whereas the bank's new-ventures department will need to make extensive use of the judgment strategy.

Judgment strategy

The **judgment strategy** uses personal beliefs and experience to choose among alternatives and decide how the selected alternative should be implemented. Managers use the judgement strategy when it appears that the available alternatives will not be effective. The managers have the same goal preferences, but disagree *or* are uncertain about cause-and-effect relationships. They may have many of the same "facts" related to the decision situation, but interpret them differently.

In business situations, the judgment strategy stems from (for example) the following questions: What combination of salary, fringe benefits, and working conditions will have the maximum impact on stimulating employee productivity? Will advertising in the newspaper, radio or TV have the greatest effect on company sales? What combination of workers and machines will result in the lowest cost per unit, yet maintain high quality? What is the best combination of stocks to hold to obtain maximum growth in the value of the firm's investments?

The organizational structures used to implement the judgment strategy include boards of directors, executive committees, project organizations, interdepartmental committees, special task forces, teams, superior-subordinate meetings, and the like.[25] The judgment strategy may involve majority voting. Presumably, all participants have an equal voice (one person-one vote) in the final decision with majority voting.

Negotiation strategy

The **negotiation strategy** uses bargaining and compromise to make adjustments in the goals of the decision-makers so they can reach agreement. If one goal can be satisfied only at the expense of another goal, the decision-by-negotiation strategy may be required. In this situation, the parties may view and interpret the facts in a similar manner, but disagree on the desirability of the goals served by the available alternatives.

Examples of decision situations requiring the negotiation strategy include: (1) the price charged to a major customer for the services or goods provided by a firm; (2) the amount of pollutants permitted in automobile emissions, as judged by the Environmental Protection Agency and the automobile manufacturers, respectively; and (3) the amount of service wanted by an industrial sales manager from the marketing research department vs. the ability and willingness of the marketing research manager to provide it.

Some of the same structural arrangements (i.e., boards of directors and task forces) are used for both the judgmental and negotiation strategies. The structural arrangements could also differ. For instance, the judgment strategy requires the widest possible participation. In the case of a trade union, this could involve voting by all its members. On the other hand, the negotiation strategy generally requires that decisions be made by representatives from the concerned groups. The collective bargaining process between United Rubber workers and tire firms involves only a handful of representatives from the union and each company. Of course, the judgment strategy is applied when the union members vote either to accept or reject the package their representatives have arrived at through the negotiation strategy. Other examples of groups who use the negotiation strategy include trial juries, the United States Congress, and the United Nations Security Council.

The **inspiration strategy** uses imitation, intuition, feelings or creativity. This strategy may be the least common of the four but it is often an essential strategy where there is confusion because: (1) the managers cannot agree on problem causes and goal preferences; or (2) the managers are *uncertain* about both causation and goals.

There are two common tactics employed when the problem is *disagreement* about both causation and goals. First, the managers may try to *imitate* their more successful competitors. Several years ago, Burger King began to copy McDonald's general promotional strategy, especially through television. Second, the key managers or owners may bring in well-known executives or prestigious consultants who tell them what their goal preferences should be and how to attain them. Allied Chemical's employment of Edward Hennessy, Jr., described earlier in this chapter, appears to be an example of this tactic.

A variety of decision processes may be used when both causation and goals are uncertain. We will briefly discuss two of these: intuition and creativity.

Intuition *Intuition* uses hunches, images, insights, or thoughts that often spontaneously surface to conscious awareness. The role of intuition in managerial decision-making has been discussed in various ways by managers. Let's listen to a few of their comments about intuition:[26]

"Intuition helps you read between the lines," says John Fetzer, owner of the Detroit Tigers and chairman of Fetzer Broadcasting Co. "Or walk through an office, and intuition tells you if things are going well."

"In a business that depends entirely on people and not machinery," says Robert Bernstein, chairman of Random House, "only intuition can protect you against the most dangerous individual of all — the articulate incompetent. That's what frightens me about business schools. They train their students to sound wonderful. But it's necessary to find out if there's 'judgment' behind the language."

Confronted in 1960 with what his lawyer called a bad deal — $2.7 million for the McDonald name — Ray Kroc says: "I closed my office door, cussed up and down, threw things out of the window, called by lawyer back, and said, 'Take it!' I felt in my funny bone it was a sure thing." Last year, system-wide sales of Kroc's hamburger chain exceeded $4.5 billion.

Creativity Intuition may or may not be a result of creativity. Moreover, creativity is a more involved process than intuition. In brief, **creativity** is defined as applied imagination. The four basic phases in the creative process include:

1. *Preparation* (saturating oneself in the problem).

2. *Incubation* (interruption of conscious effort to solve the problem).

3. *Illumination* (the floating up to consciousness of an essential element of the solution).

4. *Elaboration* (the process of confirming, expanding, tightening, reformulating, and revising the new idea so that it meshes with what is known and what is needed).[27]

Creativity helps managers and others to uncover or develop opportunities and provide novel solutions to decision problems. Several of the approaches for stimulating individual and group creativity in decision-making are presented in the next chapter.

Political Processes and Decision Strategies

The judgmental, negotiation, and inspirational strategies are all part of, and a consequence of, political processes within organizations. In Chapter 2 we presented some of the political strategies for dealing with groups *external* to the organization. At the middle and higher levels of management, many of these same strategies may be used in dealing with other individuals and groups within the organization.

Negotiations are frequently used to resolve differences among organizational members. Bargaining and compromise are key elements in most negotiations. Members within an organization may form a *coalition* to represent their common interests in a particular decision situation. For example, all of the workers may get together and sign a petition to protest a new overtime policy. Individuals or groups within the organization may *lobby* managers who have the power to make judgmental decisions. Sales managers may lobby higher management to allocate more of the marketing budget to the hiring of more salespersons. Within the organization, *cooptation* may be used by higher management in establishing "junior-executive boards" of younger managers. These boards may serve as advisory groups to higher management.

SUMMARY

The contingency organizational decision model attempts to capture the complexity and diversity of organizational decision-making and to be consistent with some of the political processes within organizations. The model is both descriptive and normative. It is descriptive in recognizing the various types of decision situations facing managers. It is normative in suggesting the strategies to use in different decision situations. Changes in the decision situation of the manager typically require like changes in the decision strategy used.

The model of the dynamic process of managerial decision-making is a more general and *prescriptive* framework. It identified the major factors surrounding most decision situations. These surrounding factors need to be evaluated in working through the step-by-step procedures for rationally dealing with decision situations. These procedures include setting goals, searching for alternatives, comparing and evaluating alternatives, choosing among alternatives, implementing the decision (chosen alternative), and following up on and controlling the implemented course of action.

The basic concepts and issues influencing these and all other decision models were developed. These basic concepts and issues include the necessary preconditions for decision-making, the role of rationality, the pervasive impact of goals on the decision-making process, and the effects of different states-of-nature (certainty, risk, or uncertainty).

As you will recall from Chapter 1, there are four managerial decisional roles: entrepreneur, disturbance handler, resource allocator, and negotiator. This chapter should especially contribute to your skills in performing the decisional roles of resource allocator and negotiator. Decision-making cuts across every possible managerial function, activity, and area of responsibility. Whether the manager is designing the structure of an organization or creating a new pay plan, resources must be allocated and important decisions usually require at least some negotiation. A manager's "batting average" in making the right decisions will be improved through the understanding and use of the concepts, processes, and models presented in this and other chapters.

Our concern in the next chapter is to provide more detailed decision-making aids and models that add "flesh and meat" to the decision-making skeleton developed in this chapter.

**DISCUSSION
QUESTIONS**

1. What is the difference between the rationality of the decision itself and the rationality of the decision-making process? Try to identify a personal example of a situation in which the decision seemed rational, but the decision-making process did not.

2. Why can an organization sometimes expect individuals, who are limited by the concept of bounded rationality, to make reasonably "rational" decisions?

3. Develop a means-goal framework for yourself. Begin with the taking of this course as the lowest subgoal (means).

4. Define suboptimization. Give an example from either your work or your college experience. Is there any way by which your example could be corrected?

5. What is meant by decision-making under the states of nature of uncertainty, risk, or certainty? Give a personal example of different decision problems you encountered that seemed to have been made under these three conditions.

6. How can the nature of the decision-maker influence the decision-making process? Give one example of how your nature seems to influence your decision-making.

7. Use the inner core of the dynamic decision-making process presented in Fig. 9.6 to identify one desired goal and work your way through the first four steps in this process. You should identify at least four alternatives in the "search-for-alternatives" step.

Management Incidents and Cases

**JARMAN'S
DECISION
PROCESSES***

When Chairman Franklin M. Jarman wrested control of Genesco Inc. from his father to become chief executive officer four years ago, one of his primary goals was to impose a system of financial controls over the $1 billion retailing apparel conglomerate. The 45-year-old Jarman did exactly that. His controls probably helped to save the company when it lost $52 million in 1973. But they were also chiefly responsible for his downfall last week.

Controls were an obsession with Jarman. According to insiders, he centralized management to the point of frustrating the company's executives and causing red tape and delay. Operations were virtually paralyzed by paperwork. One glaring example: Genesco's most recent annual report states that the company would spend $8 million this year [1977] to open 63 stores and renovate 124 others. Yet six months into the fiscal year, insiders report that little has been done because Jarman required more and more analysis for each project, postponing decisions.

Such delays and indecisions can be particularly harmful in a company like Genesco, whose business is mostly in the fast-moving fields of apparel and retailing. Among its major product lines are Johnston & Murphy and Jarman Shoes, and its retail outlets include Bonwit Teller and S.H. Kress. "It was a classic case of the boss being in the way, and he had to go," explains one Genesco insider, who was among the more than two dozen executives participating in the palace revolt last week when Jarman was stripped of his authority.

The Undoing

Two of Genesco's inside directors, vice-Chairmen Ralph H. Bowles and Larry B. Shelton, had become alarmed by Genesco's inertia in October. At the same time, many top managers complained to them that Jarman's management had been demoralizing. When Jarman seemed to be preparing to oust two key operating executives, Bowles and Shelton went to an outside director to explain how the company's fortunes were deteriorating. He, in turn, contacted other outside directors. Meantime, Bowles, Shelton, and several managers compiled for the directors a dossier of Jarman's managerial shortcomings.

Things all came together between Christmas and New Year's when Jarman was on vacation at Montego Bay. Bowles, Shelton, several managers, and four outside directors met in Washington. They called a special meeting of the board for the Monday after New Year's. With more than two dozen rank-and-file executives ready to quit if Jarman was not ousted — waiting in the cafeteria next door on the second floor of the Genesco building in Nashville — the board did the next best thing. It took away Jarman's titles of president and chief executive officer and gave them to William M. Blackie, 72, a retired executive vice-president and former director, and told Jarman that he must take his orders from Blackie.

Jarman declined to be interviewed by *Business Week* for this article. But sources close to him and the company say that he was treated shabbily by the Genesco board and executives — many of whom owed their jobs to him. These sources say Jarman was the victim of a conspiracy, which they say started after word got out that he was looking for a new president with marketing experience, a job for which he had hired the New York search firm of Knight & Zabriskie. According to this scenario, Bowles, 46, and Shelton, 42, feared that if a new president were brought in they would lose standing. Jarman came back from vacation and just before the board meeting issued a statement saying that it would be "inappropriate and contrary to the interests of the stockholders of Genesco to make any radical change in the company's management. . . With the approval of members of the board of directors, (Jarman has) been seeking to hire a new president." Bowles and Shelton maintain that they were not among those members, and that all they knew was that Jarman was looking for a senior marketing executive.

The Performance

In any case, Genesco's performance under Jarman was erratic. Although he pared many losing operations and improved the balance sheet, Genesco lost money in two of his four years as CEO. For example, last year earnings rebounded to $15.9 million, or about $1 a share, after a loss of $14.4 million the year before, but in the first quarter of this fiscal year ended Oct. 31, earnings were off 61 percent, and Jarman had projected similarly disappointing results for the important second quarter, which includes Christmas.

Insiders are convinced there was a correlation between Genesco's earnings and the overcentralized and inflexible management style they say Jarman favored. Many criticisms of Jarman's management were chronicled by Genesco executives and by Bowles and Shelton in the form of internal memoranda. The memoranda were put in dossiers several inches thick and given to each director. The board took its action last week largely on the basis of this material.

One Genesco director thinks that this approach was amateurish and unnecessary, although he voted to oust Jarman. He says the material in the dossier consisted principally of "record memoranda — written to the files of conversations with Jarman — that were very self-serving." The memoranda, he adds, contained many inconsistencies, such as that Jarman was too involved in detail or that he was not involved enough.

An insider who has read the material says that there are inconsistencies because Jarman was an inconsistent manager. He cites the example of a new shoe store under consideration. Jarman demanded a 75-page report on the $44,000 store dealing with such trifling details as whether it should have a water cooler and hot running water. On the other hand, this executive says that if a division executive had an overwhelming personality he could push through decisions with "no checks, no balances, not even pro forma financial statement" — as was recently done with a proposal for a new Bonwit Teller store.

As a matter of course, insiders say, Jarman got bogged down in minutiae. He delegated little real authority to his managers, even the two vice-chairmen.

"Better run it by Frank," was the company watchword for the most routine, everyday matters. He spent a great deal of time insisting that reports be bound properly in notebooks. Another criticism is that Jarman isolated himself and avoided contact with company executives. Typically, he dealt only with the four other members of the management committee, of which he was chairman and which included Bowles, Shelton, and two operating executives. Jarman, an engineer educated at the Massachusetts Institute of Technology, had come up through the financial side of Genesco and, as a director notes, "has never been good at handling people."

One executive says that ever since Jarman had become CEO, top people in the company had been trying to get him to visit the company's many plants and offices. This executive says Jarman did it just once. Moreover, Jarman cancelled the customary annual management breakfast meetings that brought all the top executives together with the chairman. Because of Jarman's isolation from other Genesco managers, the revolt against him could be carried out smoothly.

Jarman's style was to work from computer printouts, checking them for aberrations. He reportedly used to say that managing a corporation was like flying an airplane — his avocation. " 'You watched the dials to see if the plane deviated off course, and when it did you nudged it back with the controls,' Jarman explained," the insider says. At Genesco the computer printouts were the dials and Bowles and Shelton were the controls.

Sometimes, however, Jarman did not believe what the printouts said. He hired consultants to verify things, such as a division's overhead charges, or the quality and pricing of its products. The footwear division, which has been consistently profitable, got his treatment several times.

Still, a Surprise

Jarman's ouster, nevertheless, took many observers by surprise. To begin with, the board had recently granted him a $105,000 raise to $285,000 a year, even though Genesco pays no common stock dividend. (The board cut Jarman to $180,000 annually last week.)

Equally surprising was the fact that Genesco's board has been structured to Jarman's specifications in recent years. Over a four-year period, it was reduced from 18 to 10 members, and many of the father's supporters were replaced by the son's choices — such as Bowles, Shelton, and Wilson — with whom Frank Jarman served on several corporate and civic boards.

To insiders, however, things were different. First, after news broke of Jarman's 58 percent raise, Genesco employees signed petitions to protest. Moreover, there was overwhelming sentiment in middle management that Jarman had to go if Genesco was to survive. "You could count Jarman's supporters on the fingers of one hand," one executive said.

Last week the board started searching for an outsider to fill the presidency. Whoever lands the Genesco job will have a challenge not only to produce consistent earnings but also to gain the support of the managers, the vice-chairman, and the board of directors. "It's a slippery perch," says one corporate recruiter.

Questions **1.** Evaluate the apparent decision processes of both Jarman and the board of directors by using the model of the dynamic process of managerial decision making (Fig. 9.6).

2. What seemed to be the goal(s) of Jarman, the board of directors, and the other executives?

3. Was Jarman rational? Explain.

4. How does this case illustrate the contingency organizational decision model (Fig. 9.9)?

PRESIDENTIAL
DECISION MAKING*

"The biggest poker pot I ever raked in, I won with a pair of nines." The company's president paused for effect before his waiting executive group. "The point I'm trying to make is this: A sense of relative values and timing — waiting it out and hanging in there when the big chips are flying and the signals are confusing — is the key in our business, just as it is in poker. Lately, we've had to call some stiff bets — extreme interest rate fluctuations, an unprecedented sales drop, and a big inventory buildup. Our stock hasn't come back like it should have, either.

"Well, what do we do?" he asked. "Do we fold and wait for the next hand? Cut the dividend? Close down the new research center? Spin off your

*Taken from B. Bridgewater, D. Clifford, and T. Hardy, "The Competition Game Has Changed," *Business Horizons* **18**, 1975, 5-20. Reprinted by permission.

business, Al?" (This with a glare at the manager of the troubled WHIZ division, a high-technology growth business entered in the late 1960s that had consistently beaten its sales targets — and consistently lost money.)

"That might look like plain common sense under the circumstances," the president continued. "But I think we'd be damn shortsighted to take those kinds of steps. I'm convinced that we still hold winning cards. Know what's going to happen when the economy finally absorbs this last oil price increase completely, the Fed wakes up, and consumers start feeling the tax cut? Well, I'll tell you. By the end of the year, inflation's going to taper off to five percent or less, interest rates will settle back to normal, and our customers will start spending again. Now when that happens, do we want to be caught short of capacity?

"Of course we don't. If we're agreed on that, let's refigure the equity issue we planned for the fourth quarter, take another cut at the capital budget, tighten up where we can, and hold on to our cards for the next round." And so, rejecting the alternative of major strategic or structural change, the president and his executive group turned to a searching discussion of cost-reduction possibilities.

The president's metaphor is that business competition is a poker game. High stakes, a shrewd sense of his competitor's strengths, weaknesses, and likely next moves, and thoughtful management of his own resources — the common themes were there.

Questions

1. What assumptions did the president make about the states-of-nature contingency? Do you agree or disagree? Why?

2. Does the concept of bounded rationality seem to fit the president? Explain.

3. Identify the means-goal staircase implicity being used by the president.

REFERENCES

1. C. Kepner, and B. Tregoe, *The Rational Manager: A Systematic Approach to Problem Solving and Decision Making.* Princeton: Kepner-Tregoe, Inc., 1976, pp. 7–11.

2. K. MacCrimman, and R. Taylor, "Decision Making and Problem Solving," in *Handbook of Industrial and Organizational Psychology.* M. Dunnette (ed.), Chicago: Rand McNally, 1976, pp. 1397–1453.

3. G. Huber *Managerial Decision Making.* Glenview: Scott Foresman, 1980, p. 13.

4. W. Glueck, "Decision Making: Organization Choice." *Personnel Psychology* **27,** 1974, 104–110.

5. H. Simon, *Administrative Behavior: A Study of Decision Making Processes in Administrative Organizations*, 3rd ed. New York: Free Press, 1976, pp. 38–41, 240–244.

6. J. Roach, "Decision Making Is a Satisficing Experience." *Management Review*, **68,** 1979, 8–17.

7. R. Ackoff, *The Art of Problem Solving*. New York: John Wiley, 1978.

8. C. Perrow, *Complex Organizations: A Critical Essay*, 2nd ed. Glenview, IL: Scott, Foresman, 1979, pp. 153–160.

9. M. Keeley, "Organizational Analogy: A Comparison of Organismic and Social Contract Models." *Administrative Science Quarterly*, **25,** 1980, 337–362.

10. H. Mitzberg, D. Raisinghani, and A. Thearet, "The Structure of Unstructured Decision Processes." *Administrative Science Quarterly* **21,** 1976, 246–276.

11. M. Lyles, and I. Mitroff, "Organizational Problem Formulation: An Empirical Study." *Administrative Science Quarterly* **1,** 1980, 102–119.

12. A. Oxenfeldt, *Cost-Benefit Analysis for Executive Decision Making*. New York: AMACOM, 1979, p. 39.

13. E. Huse, *The Modern Manager*. St. Paul: West Publishing, 1979, 116.

14. R. Mack, *Planning on Uncertainty*. New York: Wiley-Interscience, 1971, p. 1.

15. R. Taylor, "The Concorde Going Nowhere Fast." *MBA*, 1976, 55–56.

16. S. Adler, "Risk-Taking Management." *Business Horizons* **23,** 1980, 11–14.

17. E. Harrison, *The Managerial Decision Making Process*, 2nd ed. Boston: Houghton Mifflin, 1981, pp. 196–202.

18. B. Bass and P. Burger, *Assessment of Managers: An International Comparison*, New York: Free Press, 1979, p. 82.

19. G. Jasen, Allied Chemical Has Rapid-Fire Reactions Under Chief Hennessey. *The Wall Street Journal* **65,** 1980, 1 and 26.

20. E. Harrison, *op. cit.*, pp. 22–45.

21. J. March and H. Simon, *Organizations*. New York: Wiley, 1958, p. 114.

22. M. Homes, *Executive Decision Making*. Homewood, IL: Richard D. Irwin, 1962, pp. 90–92.

23. J. Rothe (Senior Vice-President of Marketing, Searle Optical Group), January, 1981.

24. J. Thompson and A. Tuden, "Strategies, Structures and Processes of Organizational Decision," in J. Thompson et al., 3rd ed., *Comparative Studies in Administration*. Pittsburgh: University of Pittsburgh Press, 1959.

25. R. Miles, *Macro Organizational Behavior.* Santa Monica: Goodyear Publishing, 1980, pp. 248–277.

26. R. Rowan, "Those Business Hunches Are More Than Blind Faith." *Fortune* **99,** 1979, 111–114; R. Benhardt, "Managerial Intuition." *MBA* **13,** 1979, 13–19.

27. A. Oxenfeldt, D. Miller, and R. Dickinson, *A Basic Approach to Executive Decision Making.* New York: AMACOM, 1978, p. 157.

Chapter 10

DECISION-MAKING MODELS AND TECHNIQUES

After reading this chapter, you should be able to:

1. Describe the uses and limitations of normative decision models and techniques.

2. Apply the following normative decision models and techniques: cause-and-effect diagram, break-even model, payoff-matrix model, and decision-tree model.

3. Use two techniques for stimulating creativity in decision-making, including the Osborn technique and the nominal group technique.

4. Make better managerial decisions through the use of the models and techniques presented in this chapter.

PREVIEW CASE

Blackened-Filament Problem*

These events took place in a large, well-managed plant making plastic filament for textiles. The plant had six large machines that extruded viscose raw material through tiny nozzles into acid hardening baths where the viscose streams became plastic strands. As each filament moved through the acid bath it was supported by lead pulleys and ferrules. Each machine had an exhaust fan removing fumes from the enclosed acid environment through roof vents. There was a large air-intake duct at the rear of the building.

Each machine had 480 nozzles, and each of the 480 gossamer strands of filament produced was at one point in the process spun into a revolving hard rubber bucket. Centrifugal force of the spinning bucket threw each strand against the side of its bucket and thus built up layers of filament from the outside in toward the center. Every eight hours the case of filament strands in each bucket had to be emptied. The process

---

* From C. Kepner and B. Tregoe, *The Rational Manager: A Systematic Approach to Problem Solving and Decision Making*, pp. 24–38. Princeton: Kepner-Tregoe, Inc., 1976.

was timed so that the six doffers, the men who tended the buckets, could each empty a bucket on a machine every minute or 480 in an eight-hour shift. This tightly scheduled operation ran like clockwork 24 hours a day. A relief doffer was on call should there be any trouble.

Trouble came early one morning. One of the doffers on the midnight shift emptied bucket No. 232 on the work and noticed something strange. The last filament that had come off the machine was dirty black instead of translucent. He didn't stop to wonder about it, however, and went on to empty the next bucket a minute later. Again, there was even more blackened plastic in the core of the filament cake, and again he went on to handle the next bucket. Later it was found the blackening was caused by carbon being deposited on the filament. Possible carbon sources were identified as: a locomotive moving through the company yard; a coal burning boilerhouse; and carbon cars stockpiled in the yard.[1]

The prospect of a blackened-filament problem looms over every manager's head. This example raises two broad questions: (1) How have managers approached blackened-filament problems? (2) How could or should managers approach a problem such as this? The first question is concerned with *describing* how managers actually deal with such problems. The second question focuses on *prescribing* how managers ought to deal with such problems. This chapter is concerned with answering the second question. It presents normative models for improving the decision-making process of managers.

The Cause-and-Effect Diagram is one normative model for approaching the blackened-filament problem. Before explaining this model, however, we will first discuss the general uses and limitations of normative decision models.

Normative decision models are the various step-by-step procedures that prescribe how managers should make decisions to reach their goals.[2] The inner core of the dynamic process of managerial decision-making presented in Fig. 9.6 is a *general* example of a normative decision model. The inner core of this model prescribes the following steps to the decision-making process: set goals; search for alternatives; compare and evaluate alternatives; choose among alternatives; implement decision; and follow up and control. Each of the normative decision models presented in this and the next chapter consider

**NORMATIVE
DECISION MODELS**

some of these steps as they apply to specific types of decision problems. The many types of quantitative models and techniques for aiding decision processes illustrate normative decision models. The variety and potential complexity of these quantitative methods is so great that entire courses and curriculums have been constructed to teach students to understand and apply them. Our purpose simply is to introduce you to several of the common normative decision models.

Assumptions and Limitations

Normative decision models generally make the following assumptions:

1. The goals are known and agreed on.

2. The nature of the problem can be defined and agreed on.

3. Some information about the decision problem can be provided.

4. The state of nature in the decision problem could range from certainty to uncertainty.[3]

Normative decision models are of limited value when these assumptions cannot be met. Many of the thorniest and important problems facing managers involve the definition of goals and/or the need to reach agreement over goals. Moreover, under conditions of high uncertainty, it often is difficult to identify alternatives or reach any agreement on the effects of the various alternatives. Normative models have been of limited use in helping the manager cope with the many human problems that exist within organizations.

Benefits and Obstacles

While normative decision models may not provide hard answers to management problems, they can be very beneficial in aiding the *process* of decision-making and clarifying the risks or uncertainties facing managers. Through improving the process of decision-making, managers may derive the following *potential benefits* from normative models.

1. A manager's informal thinking is more likely to focus on the crucial elements of a decision problem.

2. Hidden assumptions and their logical implications are more likely to be brought out into the open and made clear. This is because normative decision models require the specific identification of assumptions and the assessment of different alternatives.

3. The reasoning underlying a recommendation may be communicated more effectively. If all assumptions, alternatives, probabilities, and the like are laid out in the open, the reasons for the final recommendation should be easier to follow.

4. A manager's judgment can be improved and the area in which judgment has to be exercised might be reduced.[4] This is because there usually is a greater emphasis on defining the true nature of the problem, collecting relevant information, and quantifying where possible.

Normative decision models are especially useful when decision problems focus on economic variables and when the goals are known and agreed on. But even with these types of decision problems, there are many *obstacles* to wider use of normative decision models. These obstacles were highlighted in a survey of management scientists working for organizations and specializing in the application of normative models. As shown in Table 10.1, the responses to this survey were classified into 10 categories of obstacles and problems.

This survey and others suggest that relatively few managers recognize the possibilities of such models and know how to use them successfully. In time, the educational process should reduce this obstacle. Some managers also *fear* that using normative decision models may reduce their personal power or uncover weaknesses in their own decision-making.

Obstacles and Problems	Percent Respondents N=112	*10.1 Obstacles and Problems in the Use of Normative Decision Models**
1. Selling models or methods to management	35%	
2. Neither top nor middle management have the educational background to appreciate models or methods	34	
3. Lack of good clean data	32	
4. Never time to analyze a real problem using a sophisticated approach	23	
5. Lack of understanding by those who need to use the results	22	
6. Too hard to define problems	19	
7. Sufficient payoff from using unsophisticated methods	16	
8. Shortage of personnel	12	
9. Poor reputation of management scientists as problem-solvers	11	
10. Individuals feel threatened by management scientists and their methods	10	

* Adapted from H. Watson and P. Morett, "A Survey of Management Science Implementation Problems." *Interfaces* **9**, 1979, 125.

Specialists and line managers differ in their perception of the use of normative models. Unlike the management scientists whose responses are summarized in Table 10.1, line managers emphasize the following obstacles to the use of normative decision models: (1) cost of developing and using these models; (2) expense of employing specialists in the use of such models; (3) difficulty of supplying required data;[5] and (4) the economic difficulties of dealing with important problems using these models and techniques.[6]

Changes will have to take place among management scientists and line managers to increase the use of normative decision models in organizations. Line managers must become better educated in these models and techniques, especially with regard to how managerial performance can be improved. Management scientists need to understand management's needs and learn to communicate better.[7] As Francis Bradshaw, former president of the Society for the Advancement of Management, has said, "Most managers would rather live with a problem they can't solve than use a solution they don't understand."[8]

With this introduction, we can present the broad outlines of four general normative decision models commonly used in dealing with decision problems that focus on economic variables: the cause-and-effect diagram; the break-even model; the payoff-matrix model; and the decision-tree model. The last section of the chapter will present two techniques often prescribed for stimulating *creativity* in the decision-making process.

CAUSE-AND-EFFECT DIAGRAM

The cause-and-effect diagram is one of several possible models for dealing with the blackened-filament problem presented at the beginning of this chapter. Before applying this technique to the blackened-filament problem, we will outline the nature and uses of the cause-and-effect diagram.

One of the most basic and flexible normative decision models, the **cause-and-effect diagram** is a graphic method for identifying both the factors that influence a problem or goals and the effects of those factors. It is most useful in the stages of problem formation, identification of possible causes, and the design of alternative solutions.

Basic Variables and Relationships[9]

A cause-and-effect diagram consists of interlocking arrows leading into and out of a problem or goal symbol. The basic framework of this model is shown in Fig. 10.1. The *main arrows* to the left of the problem-or-goal symbol (shown as a hexagon) represent the *principal* causes; those to the right represent the *main effects*. The cause-and-effect diagram is expanded, as needed, by adding smaller arrows directed toward the main arrows or by creating new main arrows. The smaller arrows represent subfactors to the main causes or main effects. The cause-and-effect diagram can easily be expanded or altered without changing nonrelated portions. This is done simply by adding or dropping factors, indicated by the arrows. Thus, the diagram can expand or contract as the manager gains insight into the decision problem or goal.

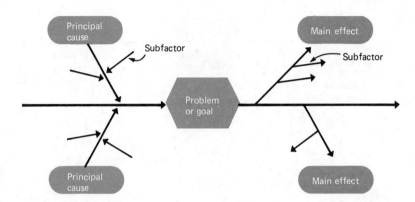

10.1
Basic cause-and-effect
diagram

A more concrete understanding of this model is obtained by applying it to the blackened-filament problem. Reread the problem at the beginning of the chapter; it will help you understand this application.

CASE STUDY

Blackened-Filament Problem

A suggested cause-and-effect diagram for the blackened-filament problem is shown in Fig. 10.2. The principal causes are indicated by the major arrows to left of the problem. The two principal causes identified in Fig. 10.2 are environment and production process. The diagram grew as the managers identified factors they believed influenced or controlled the principal causes. For example, carbon influences the environment, but can come from various sources. The main effects resulting from the principal causes are shown to the right of the problem box. Figure 10.2 shows filament quality and quantity as the two main effects. The basic effects, shown by small arrows from the main-effects arrows, are the result of the main effects. The basic effects of quality (a main effect) are rejects and filament clarity.[10]

The principal strengths of the cause-and-effect diagram are that: (1) It is easy to understand and use. (2) It encourages the expenditure of time in

10.2

**Cause and Effect Diagram
for Blackened-Filament
Problem**

From J. Anderson and M.
Janson, "Methods of
Managerial Problem Cause
Analysis," *Interfaces* **9**, 1979,
123.

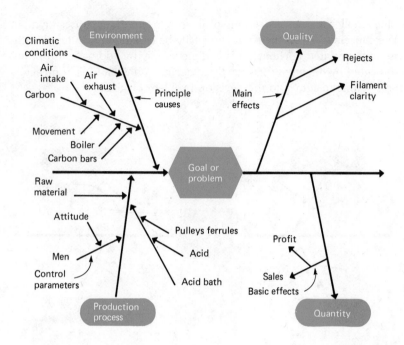

identifying possible causes. (3) It discourages simplistic thinking which assumes there is one cause or effect for every problem. Thus, this model forces managers to think about the possible causes and effects of a problem, rather than just reacting to symptoms.

BREAK-EVEN MODEL

The break-even model may prove useful for decisions on projecting profits, controlling expenses, and determining prices. The **break-even model** shows the basic relationships between units produced (output), dollars of sales revenue, and the levels of costs and profits for an entire firm or a product line. The model can be developed from historical data or from estimates. A break-even model based on historical data might be used to make year-by-year comparisons of a product line. It also can be used to determine what shifts seem to be taking place between units produced and costs per unit. A break-even model based on data estimates may be helpful as a starting point in the analysis of investment decisions.

The major variables in the break-even model include the following:

1. *Fixed costs* — those that remain constant regardless of the number of units produced. Within a limited time span (such as one year) and output levels, the following types of costs might remain fixed; insurance premiums, real estate taxes, administrative and supervisory costs, and mortgage payments on the physical plant.

2. *Variable costs* — costs that tend to vary with changes in the number of units produced. They do not necessarily vary proportionally for each additional unit of output. Variable costs might include direct labor, raw material, packaging, and transportation.

3. *Total costs* — the sum of the fixed and variable costs associated with different levels of production.

4. *Total revenue* — the total dollars received from sales for different numbers of units sold.

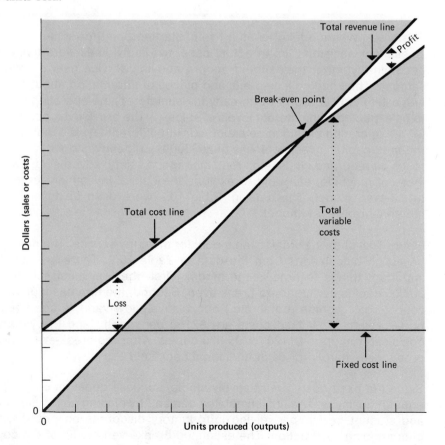

10.3
The break-even model.

5. *Profits* — the excess of total dollar sales over total dollar costs associated with certain levels of production.

6. *Loss* — the excess of total dollar costs over the total dollar sales associated with certain levels of production.

7. *Break-even point* — the point at which total costs equal total sales. It may be expressed in terms of total dollar revenues or total units produced.

Figure 10.3 presents one type of break-even model in chart form. It shows one set of possible relationships between the seven variables just defined. The vertical axis represents the dollar range of sales and/or costs. The horizontal axis represents ranges in units produced (outputs). The relationships between these variables are plotted to show losses, profits, the break-even point, and variable costs for various production levels.

CASE STUDY

Investment in Copy Service Firm

The break-even model often is a useful starting point for some types of investment decisions. In an actual case, two individuals were trying to determine whether they should open a copying service near a college campus. They had collected bits and pieces of information about actual and estimated costs and were ready to estimate: (1) the operating losses to be expected with different levels of sales; (2) the break-even point; and (3) the operating profits to be expected with different levels of sales. The required capital investment was only $3000, so the investors decided to focus on recurring costs (e.g., rent, manager's salary, advertising, paper, lease of machine, etc.) and to exclude the capital investment from the break-even model. The data in Table 10.2 were used to develop the monthly break-even model.

Figure 10.4 shows a break-even model for the copy service. The model is based on calculations from the data in Table 10.2. There are several important things to note in the model. First, the firm must sell about 60,000 copies per month to break even. Second, the firm has high fixed costs (e.g., machine rental, etc.) but relatively low variable costs (e.g., paper, toner). The fixed costs are $2150 per month, and the variable costs can run up to $1120 for 95,000 copies. After the break-even point, profits rise sharply for each additional copy sold.

Since the fixed costs are relatively stable, success depends on getting enough business. The firm stimulated demand by placing ads in the local and student newspaper, giving introductory discounts on prices, and guaranteeing satisfaction. The estimated break-even model of the copy

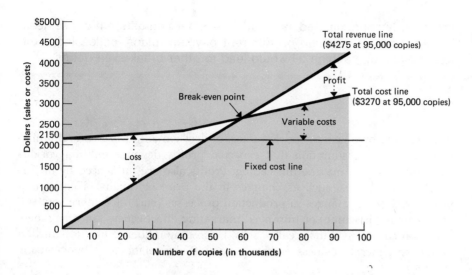

10.4
Monthly break-even model
for a copy service firm.

10.2
Data for Monthly
Break-Even Model

Fixed Costs		Monthly Basis
Rent (includes heat and electricity)	=	$ 200
Manager's salary and fringe benefits	=	590
Part-time help: (20 hrs per mo × $3.00 per hr)	=	60
Advertising	=	100
Lease of copying machine	=	1200
Total fixed costs	=	$2150

Constant Variable Costs		Per Copy
Paper (4 mills)	=	$0.004
Toner (ink) and developing fluid	=	0.002
Total	=	$0.006

Other Variable Costs		Per Copy
Part-time help (needed after 40,000 copies have been produced per month)	=	$0.01

Revenue		
Estimated revenue per copy (actual prices range from 5¢ to 2¢ per copy, depending on the number of copies of a single sheet)	=	$0.045

firm closely approximated its actual one. Charging different prices, leasing the copying machine on different payment plans, or leasing a different make of machine all would lead to other break-even points.

Limitations to Break-Even Model

Although the break-even model is a useful decision aid, it has several limitations. First, the assumption that expected profits depends only on various levels of units sold may be misleading. Profits also are influenced by impersonal market forces, such as changes in the price or quality of competing products. Second, changes in production processes (such as a more sophisticated copying machine) or improved marketing effectiveness (such as a new television commercial that really "sells") also may influence profits. Third, a decline in general business activity may shift the relationship between the variables.

These limitations can be partially overcome by developing several break-even models, each constructed on different assumptions and estimates. A manager still may need to consider additional factors or more complex relationships than those brought out in the break-even model. Some of these will be discussed in the following sections on the payoff matrix and decision tree.

PAYOFF-MATRIX MODEL

A third model for analyzing decision problems is the payoff matrix, a useful technique for helping evaluate alternatives.[11] The payoff matrix assumes that the decision-maker is able to both identify desired goals and specify alternatives (strategies). The payoff-matrix model can be applied to many decision problems. It can help answer such questions as whether to make a long-distance phone call person-to-person or station-to-station; whether to increase or decrease the price of a product; or whether or not to make a particular investment.

Basic Variables and Relationships

The *payoff-matrix model* is a two-dimensional list of figures or symbols arranged in rows and columns that identifies the possible states of nature, probabilities, and outcomes (payoffs) associated with each strategy (alternative). A payoff matrix is shown in Table 10.3.

The basic variables in the payoff-matrix model are defined as:

1. Strategies (S) — the alternative decisions that might be made or followed. They are shown in Table 10.3 as $S_1, S_2, S_3 \ldots, S_n$. In the previous example, the different prices for copies might represent the alternative strategies.

Strategies (Alternatives)	Possible States of Nature				
	N_1	N_2	N_3	...	N_m
	Probability that each state of nature will occur				
	P_1	P_2	P_3	...	P_m
S_1	O_{11}	O_{12}	O_{13}	...	O_{1m}
S_2	O_{21}	O_{22}	O_{23}	...	O_{2m}
S_3	O_{31}	O_{32}	O_{33}	...	O_{3m}
.	.	.	.		.
.	.	.	.		.
.	.	.	.		.
S_n	O_{n1}	O_{n2}	O_{n3}	...	O_{nm}

2. States of nature (N) — the future sets of conditions that could prevail in the environment and relevant to the decision problem. They are shown as N_1, N_2, N_3..., N_m in Table 10.3. As related to the previous example, they could refer to different levels of expected market demand for copies.

3. Probability (P) — the likelihood that each state of nature will occur. The sum of the probabilities must equal 1.0. It is always assumed that one of the alternative states of nature will occur. A matrix with four states of nature could have probabilities of 0.1, 0.2, 0.2, and 0.5 (equals 1.0). The payoff matrix in Table 10.3 assumes that the decision is to be made under conditions of risk. States of nature also could involve certainty or uncertainty. If certainty were the condition, the payoff matrix would show only one state of nature. If uncertainty were the case, the payoff matrix would not show any probabilities with the possible states of nature. The probabilities are shown in the model as $P_1, P_2, P_3 \ldots P_m$.

4. Outcome (O) — the "payoff" that can be expected for each possible combination of strategy and state of nature. An outcome could be a profit or loss. For example, O_{11} in Table 10.3 shows the outcome, or payoff, *if* the first state of nature (N_1) occurs and *if* the first strategy (S_1) is chosen. Each such outcome is labeled a *conditional value*.

In making a choice from the available strategies under conditions of certainty, only a part of the typical payoff matrix is needed because the future is known. Table 10.4 shows a payoff matrix under certainty. A manager would simply need to identify the strategy that provides the most favorable outcome

Certainty Condition

Strategies	State of Nature (N_1)	Payoff		10.4 Payoff Matrix Under Certainty
S_1	O_{11}	=	$1000 profit	
S_2	O_{21}	=	$ 900 profit	
S_3	O_{31}	=	$2000 profit	

(payoff). In Table 10.4, three hypothetical strategies are possible. Each yields a different total profit. Since strategy S_3 yields the highest profit, it should be selected.

Risk Condition The payoff matrix is most useful under conditions of risk — either objective or subjective probabilities. To work toward a decision when the matrix consists of two or more states of nature, one must calculate the expected values for each strategy. An ***expected value*** is the weighted average outcome for each strategy. The expected value for each strategy is the sum of all conditional values after each has been multiplied by its probability of occurrence. For example, the expected values for the payoff matrix in Table 10.3 can be presented as follows (where EV = expected value).

$$EV_1 = P_1 O_{11} + P_2 O_{12} + P_3 O_{13} \ldots P_m O_{1m}$$
$$EV_2 = P_1 O_{21} + P_2 O_{22} + P_3 O_{23} \ldots P_m O_{2m}$$
$$EV_3 = P_1 O_{31} + P_2 O_{32} + P_3 O_{33} \ldots P_m O_{3m}$$

$$\cdot \qquad \cdot \qquad \cdot \qquad \cdot \qquad \cdot$$
$$\cdot \qquad \cdot \qquad \cdot \qquad \cdot \qquad \cdot$$

$$EV_n = P_1 O_{n1} + P_2 O_{n2} + P_3 O_{n3} \ldots P_m O_{nm}.$$

CASE STUDY

Stadium Expansion Decision Let us assume that the president of a university is trying to decide how many seats to add to the football stadium. The information available and assumptions are as follows:

1. Most of the games during the past two years have been sold out.

2. If more seats had been available, additional tickets could have been sold.

3. The president and administrative staff believe the football team should be good, if not excellent, during the next three years because of the many first-team sophomores and juniors and the excellent crop of freshmen.

4. A modular seating system has been decided on because of its low cost, excellent quality, and ease of installation. The modular system under consideration comes in units of 4000 seats.

5. Moderate increases (four percent per year) are anticipated in the student population of 30,000 and the local town population of 100,000. The town is located 30 miles from a major metropolitan area.

The president has decided to consider four strategies and has developed subjective probabilities for four levels of demand for additional seats (states of nature). It has been determined the cost of each module of 4000 new seats will be $15 per seat per year during the period chosen to pay for the construction costs. The maximum potential revenue per season will total $40 per seat.

The conditional value for the first year can be determined for each strategy and state-of-nature combination by using the following equation:

$$CV = (R \times Q_D) - (C \times Q_C),$$

where CV = conditional value, R = revenue per seat, Q_D = quantity of seats demanded, C = total costs per seat, and Q_C = quantity of seats constructed. Thus, if 4000 seats are demanded (Q_D) and 4000 seats are constructed (Q_C), the equation can be applied as follows:

$$CV = (\$40 \times 4000) - (\$15 \times 4000)$$
$$CV = \$160,000 - \$60,000$$
$$CV = \$100,000 \text{ (profit)}$$

On the other hand, if 16,000 seats are constructed (Q_C) and only 4000 seats are demanded (Q_D), there will be a loss of $80,000. For this situation, the equation is applied as follows:

$$CV = (\$40 \times 4,000) - (\$15 \times 16,000)$$
$$CV = \$160,000 - \$240,000$$
$$CV = \$80,000 \text{ (loss)}.$$

Conditional values show what would happen *if* each demand and seat expansion combination occurs. See the conditional values given in Table 10.5. Note that there is *no* consideration of the probabilities as-

Calculating Conditional Values

Seats Constructed (Strategies)	Demand for Seats				10.5 Conditional Values for Stadium-Expansion Decision (in $ Thousands)
	(States of Nature)				
	4,000	8,000	12,000	16,000	
4,000	$100	$100	$100	$100	
8,000	40	200	200	200	
12,000	−20	140	300	300	
16,000	−80	80	240	400	

sociated with the states of nature (different possible demands). The calculations also are based on the fact that effective demand for each strategy cannot exceed the number of seats constructed.

Calculating Expected Values

Table 10.6 shows four levels of demand for seats and the corresponding subjective probabilities assigned by the president. The president believes there is a 50 percent probability that 4000 seats will be demanded, but only a five percent probability that 16,000 seats will be demanded.

From the information contained in Tables 10.5 and 10.6, we can develop the expected-value matrix by multiplying each conditional value by the probability of occurrence assigned to each state of nature. For example, the *expected value* for constructing 4000 stadium seats and having a demand of 4000 seats is determined as follows:

$$EV = CV_{4000} \times P_{4000}$$
$$EV = \$100,000 \times 0.50$$
$$EV = \$50,000$$

Seats Demanded	Probability of Demand	10.6 Possible Demand for Stadium Seats
4,000	0.50	
8,000	0.30	
12,000	0.15	
16,000	0.05	
	1.00	

Strategies (Seats Constructed)	Seats Demanded				Total Expected Value	10.7 Expected Values for Stadium-Expansion Decision (in $ Thousands)
	4,000	8,000	12,000	16,000		
	Probability of Demand					
	0.50	0.30	0.15	0.05		
4,000	$50	$30	$15	$ 5	$100	
8,000	20	60	30	10	120	
12,000	−10	42	45	15	92	
16,000	−40	24	36	20	40	

The expected value for each of the other combinations is shown in Table 10.7. The expected value for constructing 8000 seats is $120,000. Given the information and assumptions in this problem, the optimum solution would be to construct 8000 seats.

The **decision-tree** model identifies the relationships between future decision strategies, possible states of nature, and present decision strategies. It can be very effective in probing judgments when more than one individual is involved in making the decision — a common situation where group decision-making is used.

DECISION-TREE MODEL

If a sequence of decisions must be considered to analyze the initial decision problem, the decision-tree model may be more useful than the payoff-matrix model. The decision tree is useful when a decision problem can be broken into a sequence of logically ordered smaller problems. The solutions to the smaller problems can then be combined to provide a solution to the larger problem.

It is appropriate for complex problems with significant financial implications. These may include problems in marketing, investment in research, pricing, plant expansion, and new ventures or acquisitions. In short, the decision tree is an effective tool for assessing choices, risks, objectives, and monetary gains.[12]

There may be many calculations and branches on a decision tree, but the critical elements in its construction are the assumptions and probabilities from which the payoffs are developed. The basic variables in the development of a decision tree are:[13]

Basic Variables and Relationships

1. The *skeleton* of the decision tree which pictorially represents the possible *courses of action* (alternatives), the *outcome* from each course of action, and the relevant *states of nature* (variables over which the decision-maker has no control).

2. The *probabilities* of the various outcomes.

3. The payoffs (or costs) associated with the outcomes.

4. The *expected values* associated with the payoffs or costs.

The skeleton of the tree is made up of *nodes* (usually represented by circles, squares, and rectangles) and *lines* that indicate connections between the nodes. The nodes may represent: (1) a course of action to be taken, (2) an outcome from an action that is taken, or even (3) the probability of the various states of nature. Each of the outcomes is linked to a subsequent action. Through this process, every reasonable alternative course of action is considered and followed to its conclusion.

CASE STUDY

Oil-Drilling Decision

Berhold and Coffman[14] have developed an excellent case study of the decision-tree model. It demonstrates the impact of *individual differences* in payoffs and the probabilities of obtaining the payoffs, Let's assume that there is a decision-making group consisting of three individuals: Mr. Smith, Mr. Jones, and Ms. Williams. They are involved in a joint venture in speculative oil drilling. The three decision-makers must choose between two drilling sites because they can't afford to exploit more than one site at a time. They have read the geological reports and each has prepared a decision tree summarizing his or her thinking on the problem.

Figure 10.5 shows simple decision trees for Smith, Jones, and Williams. The figure shows that there are three possible outcomes if a well is drilled at a particular site: a gusher, a producer, or a dry well. In reality, there are many gradations between a gusher and a dry hole, but we want to keep the application simple. A careful review of Fig. 10.5 shows considerable variation in the three people's thinking about the sites. For example, Smith thinks that there is a 20 percent chance of having a gusher at Site 1. If a gusher occurs (conditional value), he thinks the payoff will be substantial — a whopping $1.4 million. Williams also thinks there is a 20 percent chance of a gusher at Site 1, but she is not nearly as optimistic as Smith over the conditional payoff from a gusher. Williams thinks the maximum returns from a gusher at Site 1 is $800,000.

The decision-tree model, like the payoff matrix, requires that conditional payoffs be adjusted by their probability of occurrence. The expected

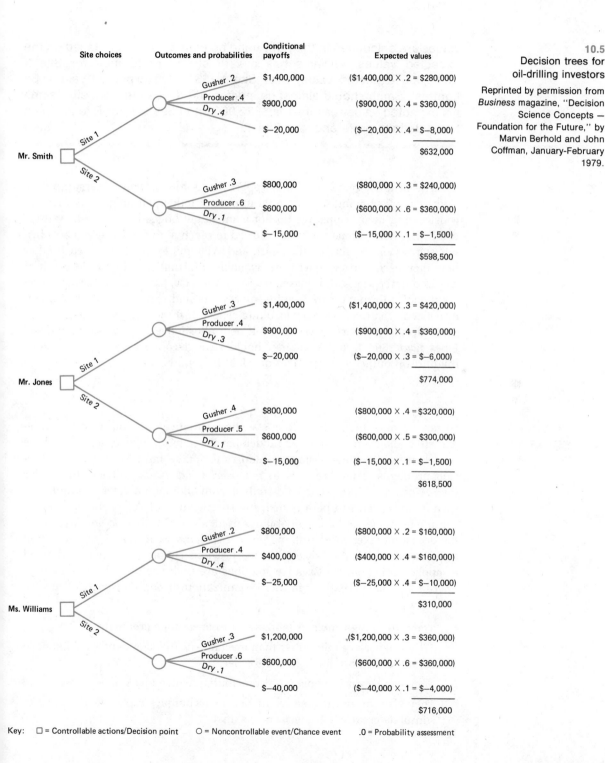

10.5
Decision trees for oil-drilling investors

Reprinted by permission from *Business* magazine, "Decision Science Concepts — Foundation for the Future," by Marvin Berhold and John Coffman, January-February 1979.

Site choices | Outcomes and probabilities | Conditional payoffs | Expected values

Mr. Smith

Site 1
- Gusher .2 — $1,400,000 — ($1,400,000 × .2 = $280,000)
- Producer .4 — $900,000 — ($900,000 × .4 = $360,000)
- Dry .4 — $−20,000 — ($−20,000 × .4 = $−8,000)

$632,000

Site 2
- Gusher .3 — $800,000 — ($800,000 × .3 = $240,000)
- Producer .6 — $600,000 — ($600,000 × .6 = $360,000)
- Dry .1 — $−15,000 — ($−15,000 × .1 = $−1,500)

$598,500

Mr. Jones

Site 1
- Gusher .3 — $1,400,000 — ($1,400,000 × .3 = $420,000)
- Producer .4 — $900,000 — ($900,000 × .4 = $360,000)
- Dry .3 — $−20,000 — ($−20,000 × .3 = $−6,000)

$774,000

Site 2
- Gusher .4 — $800,000 — ($800,000 × .4 = $320,000)
- Producer .5 — $600,000 — ($600,000 × .5 = $300,000)
- Dry .1 — $−15,000 — ($−15,000 × .1 = $−1,500)

$618,500

Ms. Williams

Site 1
- Gusher .2 — $800,000 — ($800,000 × .2 = $160,000)
- Producer .4 — $400,000 — ($400,000 × .4 = $160,000)
- Dry .4 — $−25,000 — ($−25,000 × .4 = $−10,000)

$310,000

Site 2
- Gusher .3 — $1,200,000 — ($1,200,000 × .3 = $360,000)
- Producer .6 — $600,000 — ($600,000 × .6 = $360,000)
- Dry .1 — $−40,000 — ($−40,000 × .1 = $−4,000)

$716,000

Key: □ = Controllable actions/Decision point   ○ = Noncontrollable event/Chance event   .0 = Probability assessment values are calculated in the right-hand column of Fig. 10.5. Based on the expected values, Williams has a very strong preference for Site 2 ($716,000 expected value) over Site 1 ($310,000 expected value). By contrast, Smith should almost be indifferent between the two sites since his expected value for Site 1 is $632,000 and $598,500 for Site 2. Jones has a definite preference for Site 1.

The primary purpose of this application is to help you understand decision trees by showing the potential impact of individual judgments made in constructing them. Thus, we do not want to get bogged down in how these conflicting perceptions could be resolved to reach a group decision. One obvious step would be for Smith, Jones, and Williams to clarify with each other how they used and evaluated the available information. This could result in changed perceptions and revised decision trees. Or, they might want to collect additional information by funding more tests and experiments. They might hire a geologist to provide a consulting report. If these steps fail, the investors could decide to "part ways" or seek new alternative sites. Since Smith and Jones favor Site 1 and Williams should strongly oppose this site, Williams might drop out so another investor could be found.

STIMULATING CREATIVITY IN DECISION-MAKING

So far we have highlighted four specific normative decision models: cause-and-effect diagram; break-even model; payoff matrix; and decision tree. These models prescribe step-by-step procedures for analyzing certain types of decision problems. They are aids to *managerial judgments*, not substitutes for them. Normative models depend on the formulation of managerial judgments, such as the goal(s) to be attained, the specification of the problems, the assumptions made, and the probabilities used. Moreover, they *do not directly* aid the decision-maker in identifying goals, problems, or alternatives. This often requires creativity. As indicated in the previous chapter, creativity is defined as applied imagination. Creative solutions are both useful and novel. Managers can stimulate creativity in their organization through a variety of means. For example:

- They can design their organizations to encourage creativity.
- They can use organic rather than mechanistic management systems, since creativity is more likely in the former.
- They can reward people who contribute creative ideas and proposals.
- They also can use normative models or techniques especially designed to stimulate creativity in decision-making.

Here we can highlight only two of the normative models for stimulating creativity: the Osborn technique and the nominal group technique. These techniques are most often prescribed as models for stimulating group creativity. Consideration will be given to group decision-making in the chapter on the group process (Chapter 16).

The **Osborn technique** is designed to encourage unconventional, intuitive, and freewheeling thinking. It suggests a set of unconventional questions for considering an issue through the use of brainstorming.[15]

Osborn Technique

These unconventional questions are designed to generate possibilities that might not normally be recognized. The questions considered through brainstorming could include the following.

*Unconventional
questions*

How can this issue, idea, or thing be put to other use?

How can it be adapted?

How can it be modified?

How can it be reduced?

How can it be substituted for something else, or can something else be substituted for part of it?

How could its elements be rearranged?

How could it be reversed?

How could it be combined with other things?

Obviously, this list of questions cannot be asked for any and all issues, ideas, or things. The specific questions used to guide and stimulate unconventional thinking would need to fit the situation.

In a group session, questions such as those identified above would be explored through brainstorming. **Brainstorming** is a method designed to encourage and support the free flow of ideas while suspending all critical judgments. There are four basic rules in the brainstorming phase of the Osborn technique.

*Brainstorming
phase*

1. Criticism is ruled out.

2. Freewheeling is welcomed: "The wilder the idea, the better."

3. Quantity is desired: The greater the number of ideas, the greater the likelihood of good results.

Basic Leadership Role

1. Make a brief statement of the four basic rules.

2. State the time duration for the brainstorming session.

3. Read the problem and/or related question to be discussed and ask, "What are your ideas?"

4. When an idea is given, you should summarize it, using the same words as the speaker to the extent possible, so that it can be recorded by an individual or an audio tape machine. Follow your summary with the single word "next."

5. There is little else you should say. Whenever the leader participates as a brainstormer, the productivity of the group is usually reduced.

Handling Problems

1. When someone talks too long, wait until he or she takes a breath (everyone must stop to inhale sometime). Break into the monologue, summarize what was said for the recorder, point to another participant and say "next." Caution the next contributor to keep his or her statement brief.

2. When someone becomes judgmental or starts to argue, stop him or her; say, for example, "That will cost you one coffee or coke for each member of the group." One such fine usually takes care of the argumentation problem.

3. When the discussion stops, relax and let the silence continue. Say absolutely nothing. No group of five or 10 persons can look at each other for more than three minutes without feeling compelled to say something. This pause should be broken by the group and *not* the leader. It is natural and to be expected that in the average 50-minute brainstorming session periods of silence will develop after somewhere between 20 and 40 minutes. This period of silence is called the "mental pause" because it is a change in thinking. All the usual ideas are exhausted; the participants are now forced to rely on their creativity to produce new concepts.

4. When someone states a problem rather than a solution, repeat the problem; raise your hand with your five fingers extended, and say, "Let's have five solutions to the problem." You may get only one or you may get ten, but you're back in the business of constructive thinking.

Adapted and taken from C. Gregory, *The Management of Intelligence: Scientific Problem Solving and Creativity.* New York: McGraw-Hill, 1967, pp. 196–197. Used with permission.

4. Building and "hitchhiking" on other peoples' ideas is encouraged.

These rules are intended to keep judgment apart from creative imagination. The two are incompatible and deal with different steps of the decision-making process.

The ideal number of individuals in a brainstorming session is between five and 10. The brainstorming phase should normally run not less than 20 minutes or over one hour. Of course, the brainstorming phase could consist of several idea-generation sessions. For example, a different session could be used for each of the questions identified previously. Key guidelines for conducting the brainstorming phase are outlined in Table 10.8.

After the oral brainstorming phase, it is usually advisable to ask the participants to identify from one to five of the most important ideas generated. This could be in terms of the overall brainstorming process or in terms of each of the questions considered. These ideas might be jotted on a piece of paper by each participant and evaluated on a five-point scale, such as "extremely important idea" (5 points) through "possibly important idea" (1 point). The results of this evaluation should indicate what actions or ideas should be investigated further. *Judgmental phase*

The Osborn technique has been used by many firms such as General Motors, IBM, and United States Steel. It has also been used by nonbusiness organizations including the Air Force, Army, and United States Civil Service.[16]

The **nominal group technique** is a structured group meeting designed to stimulate creative decision-making where the participants lack agreement or where there is incomplete knowledge about the nature of the problem. It is readily used where individuals, often with widely varying backgrounds, must pool their talents to invent or discover a satisfactory course of action. The nominal group technique is *not* for meetings dealing with routine matters (such as announcements or giving instructions), to improve coordination, or to engage in bargaining. **Nominal Group Technique**

The process and procedures for stimulating creativity through the nominal group techniques include the following:[17] *Process and procedures*

1. A group of five to nine individuals. Fewer than five individuals may stimulate conformity and avoidance of differing ideas. More than nine may tend to reduce the sense of involvement and responsibility to make contributions.

2. Members silently express their ideas in writing as to the nature of the problem or alternative solutions to the problem, if it has already been identified. The members may work alone in separate rooms or around a table in full view of each other.

3. At the end of some time period (10 to 15 minutes), the members share their ideas. This sharing is very structured in that each member presents, in round-robin fashion, only one idea at a time.

4. In full view of all members, a recorder writes a short, paraphrased version of each idea on a flip chart or board. This continues until all ideas, possibly 15 to 25, have been expressed. Ideas are not matched to people.

5. Each idea is then openly discussed by asking for clarification or stating support or nonsupport of it.

6. Each member privately and in writing rank-orders the ideas by preference. The group decision or recommendation would be the mathematically polled outcomes of the member rankings of each idea.

Expected effects The nominal group technique forces decision-makers to spend more time diagnosing the nature of the problem, generating ideas and new insights about the problem, and developing alternative outcomes. This often is achieved because the nominal group technique reduces the pressures for *conformity*, the enemy of creativity. The required procedures and process of this model serve to:[18]

1. Encourage the generation and expression of minority ideas or opinions. Creative ideas and insights often begin by seeming rather "odd," "strange," or "deviant" to the majority.

2. Support the expression of conflicting and incompatible ideas. This is achieved by putting ideas in writing and recording one idea from each person at a time and not permitting criticism in this phase.

3. Enable all individuals to participate equally in sharing ideas and contributing to the group products. Within organizations, subordinates may be inhibited and go along with opinions expressed by high-status participants, even if all parties claim that everyone is to feel free to participate fully.

4. Motivate involvement, since all participants have many opportunities to influence the direction of the group decision outcome.

*Managerial
Implications* The Osborn and nominal group techniques assume that most individuals and groups have the potential for greater creativity in decision-making. For a variety of reasons, however, this creativity becomes blocked. Both models are

designed to help *reduce* these blockages and to prescribe step-by-step procedures for *stimulating* creative insights and ideas. There is no guarantee of creative outcomes from the use of these models. Rather, we can say that the appropriate and sincere use of these two models or others will normally increase creativity in managerial decision-making.[19]

SUMMARY

This chapter provides some models you can use in decision-making roles. These models increase the likelihood of your making better decisions.

The cause-and-effect diagram, break-even model, payoff-matrix, and decision tree may be thought of as techniques for helping you become more "rational" in the decision-making process. Each of these models considers one or more of the elements and steps in the rational decision-making process. These elements and steps include: (1) exploring the nature of the problem and setting goals; (2) generating alternative solutions; (3) evaluating alternatives; (4) choosing among alternatives; (5) implementing the alternative; and (6) follow-up and control of the chosen alternative. The first four normative decision models presented in the chapter are primarily concerned with steps 2, 3, and 4, and they explicitly identify the relationships between these three steps. By contrast, the two normative models designed to stimulate creativity (Osborn technique and nominal group technique) zero in primarily on steps 1 and 2 in the rational decision-making process.

This chapter has focused on developing your skills in performing the decisional roles required of the entrepreneur and the resources-allocating manager. The decisional models and techniques should improve your ability to rationally assess new projects or proposals and to allocate resources (money, equipment, personnel, etc.) so as to obtain the best payoffs. In addition, the techniques for stimulating creativity should assist you in thinking and acting more like an entrepreneur.

All six models presented in this chapter prescribe ways for dealing with various types of decision problems found in virtually any department of an organization, such as accounting, finance, marketing, personnel, and production. The next chapter will focus on key issues and decision-making primarily relevant to the production/operations function of organizations.

KEYWORDS

break-even model	*conditional value*
break-even point	*creativity*
brainstorming	*decision tree*
cause-and-effect diagram	*expected value*
certainty	*fixed costs*

nodes
nominal group technique
normative decision models
Osborn technique
payoff-matrix model
probability
profits

risk
states of nature
strategies
outcome
uncertainty
variable costs

DISCUSSION QUESTIONS

1. What are the similarities and differences between the Osborn technique and nominal group technique?

2. What might a cause-and-effect diagram look like for someone who has failed the first major exam in a course?

3. When can a decision tree be used more effectively than the payoff-matrix model?

4. When can a payoff matrix be used more effectively than a break-even model?

5. Why are normative models not used more frequently by managers?

6. Why should you, as a future manager, be interested in models of decision-making?

7. How might differences in individual perceptions influence the use of the decision-tree model?

Management Incidents and Cases

PITTSBURGH STEEL WORKS

As manager of the Allegheny plant of Pittsburgh Steel Works, you have been approached by a representative of Ace Drug Company. He has offered to immunize your employees against the possibility of contracting a new strain of the American flu at a cost of $5 per employee. The flu has reached epidemic proportions on the West Coast. According to the Department of Public Health, there is a 10 percent chance that this flu will reach epidemic proportions in the East, a 10 percent chance that it will reach semi-epidemic proportions, and an 80 percent chance that it will strike one person in 1000. You estimate that if an epidemic occurs, half your employees will contract the flu. If a semi-epidemic occurs, 25 percent will be stricken. You have 2000 employees, and since the flu lasts three days, you estimate that each employee stricken will miss three days work (considering weekends do not count). The average employee-day lost costs $30.

1. Should you have your employees vaccinated?
2. Develop a payoff matrix to aid you in making this judgment.

Jim Smythe, director of personnel for the Djohn Company, was assigned the task of reconstructing a compensation program for five upper-middle-level managers of the company. The Djohn Company manufactures electronic circuit breakers for Pratt & Whitney jet engines. Jim knew that the available budget for these five men was $240,000. Jim also gathered the following data on each of the five managers:

Manager 1: purchasing; has a staff of 20; recently experienced personal financial difficulties; has 10 years seniority with the company, age 55.

Manager 2: manufacturing; has a department of 1000; holds MBA degree and is a "man on the move"; has several offers from other companies; one year's seniority; age 35.

Manager 3: finance; has staff of 50; has CPA degree; 25 years seniority; outstanding company record; age 65.

Manager 4: marketing; has a department of 200, mostly salesmen (industrial); 15 years seniority; excellent service record; has a BS in marketing; age 42.

Manager 5: research and development; has a staff of 20 professional employees; R&D is vital to this company, since it has an expanding technological environment; has a Ph.D. in engineering; has six months seniority; age 50.

1. What decision models outlined in this chapter appear to be relevant to this situation from the personnel director's point of view?
2. What ones appear relevant from the manager's point of view? (Assume that the managers are aware of the salary reconstruction assignment.)

The president and staff of Emperor Products Corporation, a medium-sized electronics-component manufacturers, are trying to decide whether to increase the current output of one of Emperor's products by installing an additional semi-automatic machine or by putting its employees on overtime.

Part One After much discussion, they agree that there is a 0.60 subjective probability that sales will increase 20 percent and a 0.40 subjective probability that sales would drop by as much as five percent. After developing figures on the dollar consequences for the next year only, they reached the following conclusions:

1. Strategies: overtime versus one new unit of equipment;

2. States of nature: sales rise (0.60 probability) versus sales drop (0.40 probability);

3. Net cash flow: the net-cash-flow implications of the alternative strategies are shown below:

| | Cash Flow | |
Strategies	New equipment	Overtime
a) 20% sales rise	+ $460,000	+ $440,000
b) 5% sales drop	+ $340,000	+ $380,000

A simple decision tree is constructed to take into account the probabilities of the two events. Their decision tree suggests that the expected payout will be $416,000 for the overtime alternative and $412,000 for the new equipment alternative. At this point, the "best" decision appears to be the overtime alternative.

Reconstruct this decision tree and show the calculations that serve as the basis for this initial decision.

Part Two The executives decided to further evaluate their apparently "best" alternative (strategy) by extending the decision-tree model another year. After extensive discussion, they concluded that the longer-term prospects for the product in question are excellent. Accordingly, they worked out the following probabilities:

■ If sales drop 5 percent the first year, there is a 0.80 subjective probability they will increase 20 percent in the second year and a 0.20 probability sales will increase by only 10 percent.

■ If sales rise by 20 percent in the first year, they expected a 0.50 probability that second-year sales will increase 20 percent and a 0.50 probability that sales will increase by 10 percent.

On the basis of this additional information, develop a two-year decision model. Which alternative now appears to be the best?

REFERENCES

1. C. Kepner and B. Tregoe, *The Rational Manager: A Systematic Approach to Problem Solving and Decision Making.* Princeton: Kepner-Tregoe, Inc., 1976, pp. 24–38.

2. S. Kassauf, *Normative Decision Making.* Englewood Cliffs, NJ: Prentice-Hall, 1970, p. 3.

3. P. Nutt, "Models for Decision Making In Organizations and Some Contextual Variables Which Stipulate Optimal Use." *Academy of Management Review* **2,** 1976, 69–80.

4. P. Moore, "Technique Versus Judgment In Decision Making." *Organizational Dynamics* **2,** 1973, 69–80.

5. T. Green, W. Newsom, and S. A. Jones, "Survey of the Application of Quantitative Techniques to Production/Operations Management in Large Organizations." *Academy of Management Journal* **20,** 1977, 669–676.

6. T. Levitt, "A Heretical View of Management 'Science'." *Fortune* **98,** 1978, 50–52.

7. H. Watson and P. Morett, "A Survey of Management Science Implementation Problems." *Interfaces* **9,** 5, 1979, 124–128.

8. T. Green and F. Schilagi, "Organizational Reluctance to Employ Decision Science Methods." Paper presented at the Southwest AIDS meetings, 1972.

9. M. Inoue and J. Riggs, "Describe Your System With Cause and Effect Diagrams." *Industrial Engineering* **3,** 1971, 26–31.

10. J. Anderson and M. Janson, "Methods for Managerial Problem Cause Analysis." *Interfaces* **9,** 5, 1979, 121–128.

11. R. Schlaifer, *Analysis of Decisions Under Uncertainty.* New York: McGraw-Hill, 1969.

12. A. Oxenfeldt, D. Miller, and R. Dickinson, *A Basic Approach to Executive Decision Making.* New York: AMACOM, 1978.

13. C. Churchman, L. Auerbach, and S. Sadan, *Thinking For Decisions: Deductive, Quantitative Methods.* Palo Alto: Science Research Associates, 1975.

14. This application is drawn from M. Berhold and J. Coffman, "Decision Science Concepts — Foundations for the Future." *Business* **29,** 1979, 9–16.

15. A. Osborn, *Applied Imagination.* New York: Charles Scribner's Sons, 1953.

16. C. Gregory, *The Management of Intelligence: Scientific Problem Solving and Creativity.* New York: McGraw-Hill, 1967.

17. A. Delbecq, A. Van de Ven, and D. Gustafson, *Group Techniques for Program Planning.* Glenview, IL: Scott, Foresman, 1975.

18. *Ibid.,* pp. 24–25.

19. L. Hoffman (ed.), *The Group Problem Solving Process: Studies of a Valence Model.* New York: Praeger, 1979.

Chapter 11

DECISION-MAKING IN OPERATIONS MANAGEMENT

After reading this chapter, you should be able to:

1. Describe operations management as a system.

2. Identify the three basic types of technology common to operations management.

3. Indicate the changing role and use of robots in certain transformation processes.

4. Describe four of the key decision-making areas in operations management: forecasting; scheduling; inventory management; and quality control.

5. Compare the moving-averages model, exponential-smoothing model, and regression-analysis model for purposes of forecasting.

6. Use the fixed-order-quantity model and the fixed-order-period model to assist in making inventory decisions.

This chapter was contributed by Kenneth Ramsing, University of Oregon.

7. Identify the concepts and issues involved in quality-control decisions.

401

PREVIEW CASE

Producing a Textbook[1]

The many steps and resources involved in producing this book can serve as a case of operations management in action.

Before a textbook can actually go into production, we were signed to write a book by an acquisitions editor. After the actual writing process, the manuscript is reviewed by other faculty members and analyzed to determine production costs. Market research and a variety of other issues are involved before the manuscript enters the production process.

Janis Jackson Hill, Business Editor

The operations management decision-making steps in our book production included the following:*

1. Janis Jackson Hill, a business editor at Addison-Wesley, notified the appropriate departments that the manuscript was ready for production. There is normally a meeting with key individuals from marketing, finance, etc. to decide how many copies of the book should be produced in the first printing. This decision requires a forecast of the sales likely during the first 12 months and an estimate of the number of complimentary copies to be sent to faculty members. This group also agrees on a specific date that the book should be available for distribution. This is the production planning stage. A detailed schedule is normally developed by the production manager in cooperation with the other affected individuals.

2. Through subordinates, the production manager — who in essence is the operations manager-supervisor of production from manuscript to bound books — selects, supervises, and coordinates the work of the various related publication specialists: production editor, book designer, artist, photographer or photo research, technical illustrator, compositor (often called typesetter).

3. Our production editor, Herb Merritt, was the first to work on the manuscript. This is a quality-control measure. Spelling, punctuation, syntax, organization, and style were checked, after which we reviewed the suggestions and changes. This is the beginning of the actual physical production of the book.

4. The production editor also coded the manuscript for the typesetter according to the specifications drawn up by the book designer, Marie McAdam.

5. The compositor set the manuscript into type. We and the production editor reviewed the typeset material. This first appeared in a form called *galley* proofs. These are long sheets of paper that usually do not contain any tables or art work, nor is the type broken up into pages.

6. After the galleys were proofread (quality control) and the compositor made the corrections indicated, the type was broken up into pages. The compositor inserted the tables and art work and added credit lines and captions where necessary. This second set of proofs is called *page proofs*. We saw the pages arranged as they would appear in the book, proofread them, and noted any corrections that must be made by the compositor.

---

* Adapted from E. Huse, *The Modern Manager*. St. Paul: West Publishing Co., 1979, pp. 549–551.

7. After the compositor completed page proof corrections, the camera-ready pages were sent to the production editor for a final review.

8. The production assistant wrote a set of manufacturing specifications (production control) to guide the printer. The printer printed the book pages, trimmed them, assembled them, and bound them in covers (which may have been manufactured elsewhere). The book copies were then ready for shipment from the warehouse and the manufacturing process was completed.

These decision-making steps and activities serve as a concrete case of operations management in action. *Operations management is the use and interaction of inputs (resources) that are transformed through a production process into desired outputs (goods or services).* Examples of inputs in the production of textbooks include production editor, printing press, paper, compositor, book-binding machine, typed manuscript, and the like. The transformation through a production process — from manuscript to bound book — involves all the steps outlined above. In this case, the output is the copies of the book. Operations management can best be thought of as one of the systems within an organization.

**OPERATIONS
MANAGEMENT AS A
SYSTEM**

From a systems point of view, operations management is concerned with transforming inputs into outputs. The specifics of operations management systems can vary widely within the same organization or between organizations. For example, the operations management system used to produce toasters at General Electric is substantially different from the one they use to create electric motors. The operations management system used to create unleaded gasoline at Exxon refineries is much different from that used to create our book. As a general system, however, operations management has certain basic common elements, whether the product is toasters, electric motors, unleaded gasoline, or textbooks.

Figure 11.1 provides a view of operation management as a system within a company. Many environmental factors will influence operations management. For example, in Chapter 4 you read about the Japanese emphasis on collectivism and how this leads to extensive group decision-making by all employees. This is an example of how values influence the nature of the transformation process. Strategic planning is also an "environmental" factor. Strategic planning managers determine the types of goods and services that will be marketed by the firm. They have a tremendous effect on the types of inputs and transformation processes necessary to create the desired goods and services.

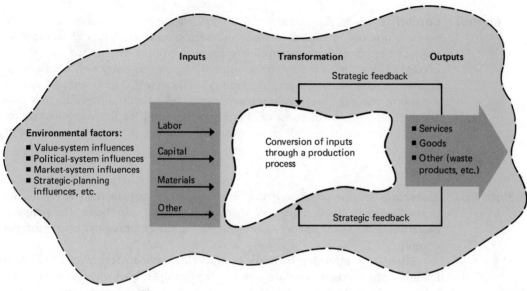

Inputs   Transformation   Outputs

Strategic feedback

Environmental factors:
- Value-system influences
- Political-system influences
- Market-system influences
- Strategic-planning influences, etc.

Labor

Capital

Materials

Other

Conversion of inputs through a production process

- Services
- Goods
- Other (waste products, etc.)

Strategic feedback

11.1
Operations management
as a system

   With this recognition of the crucial importance of environmental influences, we can move to the issues that are usually of more direct concern to operations managers: inputs, transformation processes, and outputs.

Three basic inputs are of central concern to operations management: labor, capital, and materials.

Inputs

Labor refers to the human resources (employees) in the organization. Operations management is typically most concerned with employees directly involved with the production process. At Gulf Oil, they are the manufacturing, production, and engineering managers as well as production workers. At the Mayo Clinic, they are the surgical nurses, floor nurses, and the like. As our society continues to move toward complex service industries, labor is becoming more important. Take, for example, a hospital. Currently, hospitals are the third largest industry in the United States. Since automation and technological breakthroughs are rapidly increasing in hospitals, the skill level of nurses and doctors needed to operate highly technical equipment has increased dramatically.

Labor

Capital   *Capital* refers to the money, machinery, equipment, buildings, and other assets of the organization. In some industries, such as steel and automobile manufacturing, massive expenditures for new equipment and machinery are needed during the next 10 years to improve the productivity and competitiveness of these industries. Computer and related electronic innovations (such as the use of robots) have revolutionized some well-established production processes. Tremendous amounts of capital are required for the computerization of many firms, whether for data entry and analysis or for process control of machines and facilities.

Materials   *Materials* are the physical items directly used or transformed to create the desired outputs. In the preview case on producing our book, the primary materials include ink, paper, glue (for the binding), and cardboard (for the covers).

There is a tendency to think of materials only in terms of production facilities which create tangible goods — for example, books, toasters, automobiles, and beer. Materials are also used in most service organizations. Major insurance firms use tons of paper daily as a part of their material inputs. Farmers use fertilizers, seeds, insecticides, etc. as material inputs to obtain better crop production.

Transformation   Labor, capital, and materials are the three main inputs to the transformation process. *Transformation* refers to conversion of inputs, through a production process, to create the desired outputs. The transformation process is more extensive in some industries than others. For example, the aluminum industry converts a whitish powder, bauxite, into aluminum pigs or ingots with the use of electric furnaces. The input does not look like or feel like the output. On the other hand, the input of trees to the sawmill has many similarities to the output — finished lumber. In service organizations e.g., insurance companies, it is even more difficult to "see" the similarities of the inputs (requests for payments of claims) and outputs (checks.). Yet there is a conversion process going on.

Much of the current national attention to productivity is actually concerned with finding the means to improve the efficiency of transformation processes. *Productivity* refers to the ratio of outputs (goods and services) created through the transformation process to the inputs (labor, capital, and materials) consumed.[2] Let's assume that the direct production costs for 10,000 copies of our book is $110,000 on January 1, 1982. The publisher orders new and more efficient computer-controlled printing and binding equipment. This equipment, while representing new capital inputs, substantially reduces the labor inputs required to print and bind the textbook, and the second printing of 10,000 copies of this textbook on January 1, 1983 costs $100,000. After adjusting for inflation and taking the additional capital costs into consideration, we could say that productivity improved by over 9 percent. We have also assumed that the sales price did not change after adjustments for inflation.

There are many ways to describe transformation processes. One way is in terms of the types of technology employed: unit or small batch production; mass production; or continuous process.[3] These three types of technology were discussed in Chapter 8 in terms of their importance to organizational design.

Unit or small batch production technology refers to the custom manufacturing of individual items. Examples include quality furniture, nuclear power plants, skyscrapers, custom homes, false teeth, a crown for a tooth, and this book. This type of technology usually has very skilled labor (craftsmen and professionals) directly involved in the transformation process. For example, high quality furniture manufacturers need skilled craftsmen to convert raw materials into tables, cabinets, chairs, etc.

Mass production technology refers to the manufacture of large volumes of identical or similar goods. Examples of items produced with this technology include automobiles, televisions, electronic calculators, and refrigerators. Some unskilled or semiskilled labor is often directly involved in this transformation process. Assembly-line paced work, as in the assembly of automobiles, is frequently used in mass production technology.

Continuous process technology refers to the ongoing flow of activities for transforming inputs into outputs, with virtually all physical activities being performed by machines. Examples of items produced with this technology include gasoline, chemicals, soft drinks, and milk. A high proportion of skilled labor is *indirectly* involved in the transformation process. These workers do not actually handle the raw materials, but monitor its progress via dials and meters. Computers are used to control other machines, such as the speed of the generators in an electric power plant.

The processes and techniques of control used with each of these types of technology are considered in the next chapter. The point here is that transformation processes can differ dramatically. These differences create unique problems of organizing, planning, decision-making, and controlling.

Transformation processes, especially those using the mass production technology, are beginning to face revolutionary changes as a result of the introduction of robots. According to the Robot Institute of America (an industry trade group), a *robot* is a reprogrammable, multifunctional manipulator designed to move material, parts, tools, or specialized devices through variable

Three types of technology

Robots: the next revolution[4]

programmed motions for the performance of a variety of tasks. The key words in this definition are "reprogrammable" and "multifunctional." At Coca-Cola plants, automatic machines (like bottle-cappers) are used to massproduce their soft drinks. These machines can perform only one task at a time. New work procedures require new machinery or extensive retooling. The industrial robots now being installed have control and memory systems, often in the form of microcomputers. Robots can be programmed to carry out a number of jobs. When necessary, they can be reprogrammed to carry out more or new tasks.

A robot's basic function is to do jobs that have been done by humans. To do a human's work, it needs a guiding brain (the computer) and an arm with claws for fingers. The computer is simply plugged into an electric outlet; cables run from the computer along the robot's arm and transmit instructions in the form of electric impulses to the claw. For heavy work, robots use hydraulic pressure. To become "smarter," robots are learning to "see" and "touch," and report to their computer brains what their new senses tell them. "Seeing" involves deciphering what appears before a TV camera. "Touching" may involve measuring the size, shape, temperature, or softness of the object grasped by the claw.

Julius Mirabel, an executive at General Electric, says he has looked at 20 vision systems and found none of them to be economical (as of 1981). Mirabel feels that "touch" is going to be very important, because all the robots need to know is that something is happening or is not happening. This one piece of information can be analyzed quickly.

Robots at Ford plant in Wixom, Mich. Photo by David Franklin. Reprinted by permission of TIME magazine.

Bernard Chern, program director for computer engineering at the National Science Foundation predicts enormous changes in production technology over the next 20 years. He claims that "advanced robots are going to perform tasks characterized by intelligence and decision-making: movement; manipulation; sensing and communication, both man-to-machine and robot-to-robot." Chern observes that the industrial revolution stemmed from the transfer of physical skills from man to machine. "The second industrial revolution, now in its infancy," he contends, "involves the transfer of intelligence from man to machine."

To date, most robot applications have relieved employees of tasks that are hazardous, dirty, or monotonous. Some examples include loading stamping presses, spraying paint in confined areas, and making the same spot welds on cars, day in and day out. More sophisticated applications are in the making. Westinghouse is working with the National Science Foundation to demonstrate the feasibility of an automated batch-assembly line. This line will turn out 450 versions of eight different fractional-horsepower motors at the rate of 1 million units a year. Aided by "seeing" robots, the operation would need only one third the workers of a traditional facility. American applications of robots are mushrooming because of industry's need to improve productivity and remain competitive, especially with the Japanese.

CASE STUDY

Japan's Use of Robots

In 1981, Japan operated most of the robots in the world (about 10,000) as compared to the 3000 in the United States. They are also outproducing this country in robots by at least five to one. You may recall from Chapter 3 that Japan has the national goal of becoming the world's leader in electronics, including the production of state-of-the-art robots.

The Japanese have adopted robot technology as no other country. Japan's government Ministry of International Trade and Industry is coordinating an intense drive to develop an unmanned manufacturing facility by 1985. Julius Mirabel, the GE executive cited earlier, recalls going to Japan in 1976 to compare production techniques. He found robots everywhere, including one cluster that had reduced the work force in a vacuum-cleaner plant from several hundred men to eight. "Unless we start doing something to increase U.S. productivity, the United States will be out of business as a country," says Mirabel, who returned from Japan to find that GE was using only ten robots in 1976. In 1980, GE had 111 robots but planned to add 47 more robots in 1981 at a cost of over $5 million. The eight plants in G.E.'s major appliance group may have a robot work force of over 1000 by 1990. GE and other major

U.S. manufacturers have felt the competition from the Japanese. They have made a major commitment to the use of robots to improve productivity in assembly and other routine tasks.

One of the reasons cited for Japan's ability to move so rapidly to robots is that major Japanese corporations follow the Nenko system. You may recall from Chapter 3 that the Nenko system emphasizes life-long employment, group loyalty, and group decision-making. Robots have not threatened the job security of Japanese workers. Job security could become an issue in the United States with the widespread introduction of robots. To date, General Electric has made sure no employees displaced by robots have been laid off. These employees have been retrained and transferred to other jobs. The total number of employees has been reduced through attrition, i.e., retirements and quits.

Outputs   Outputs are the last major component of operations management. **Outputs** are the goods, services, wastes, or other possible outcomes created by the transformation process. Outputs not only include the goods or services being created — steel, autos, toasters, calculators, insurance policies, or claims — but also wastes (air and water pollution) or impaired health (coal miner's lung disease).

As suggested in Fig. 11.1, strategic feedback loops are important to operations management. **Strategic feedback loops** provide vital information to the transformation system regarding characteristics of its outputs. Automobiles coming off the assembly line are tested to make sure that they run and the equipment works. As you might expect, the entire operations management makes extensive use of feedback. We will discuss the feedback concept in greater detail in the following chapter on control.

Overview   To this point we have focused on developing the basic parts and processes that make up operations management. The remainder of the chapter will deal in greater detail with the core of operations management — the transformation part. We do this by sampling a few of the key decision-making areas in operations management and the general decision models often used in each area. The key decision areas include forecasting, scheduling, inventory, and quality control. Each of these areas is only briefly touched on. An entire curriculum would be required to develop all of the conceptual and technical skills needed for managerial positions in operations management. From a strategic point of view, some of the key decision areas in operations management might include: (1) assessing and improving the overall effectiveness of the operations management system; (2) problems and issues concerning the interface of operations management with other parts of the organization — such as marketing, finance, personnel, and research and development — and (3) constantly monitoring and evaluating new technologies and procedures that may improve efficiency.

Forecasting is the process of predicting future events through the systematic analysis of relevant data. It is an important step in many planning tasks. We will focus on forecasting decisions that estimate the future demand for present goods or services. These forecasts are needed so that operations managers can form some notion of the quantity of particular goods or services their operation must provide — or may require — within a given time period.

There are three basic types of demand forecasts: trend, cyclical, and seasonal. These are illustrated in Fig. 11.2, where the vertical axis represents different levels in the market demand for the good or service and the horizontal axis

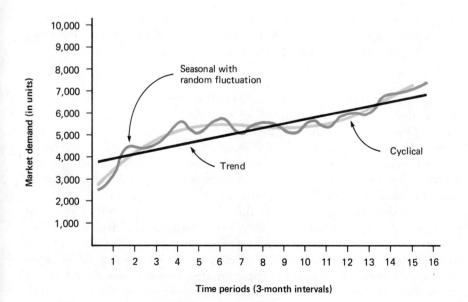

represents a period of time. The time periods can be expressed in weeks, months, quarters, or years.

A ***trend forecast*** is a forecast of long-term changes in market demand. The goal is to determine whether the market demand for a good or service over a period of, say, four or more years is likely to increase, decrease, or remain at a constant level.

Over a somewhat shorter period, such as eighteen months to four years, we may develop a cyclical forecast. A ***cyclical forecast*** is a forecast of changes in market demand that result primarily from changes in general economic conditions (recession, growth, stability). These changes are frequently associated with the general business cycle. In 1981, the housing industry built fewer homes than in any year since the early 1960s. Major reasons for this decline were the high interest rates and the high inflation rate.

A ***seasonal forecast*** is a forecast of changes in market demand that are primarily a result of the month of the year. The patterns in a seasonal forecast are usually repeated year after year. Swim suit sales jump sharply during the spring of each year in anticipation of the coming summer months.

Around each basic type of forecast are variations in market demand called randomness. ***Random demand*** refers to changes in market demand that have no pattern and cannot be forecasted. The amount of random demand in any forecast depends on the degree of uncertainty in the marketplace.

Types of Decision Models

There are many types of decision models used to develop trend, cyclical, or seasonal forecasts. Three of the more common ones are the moving-averages model, exponential smoothing model, and regressional-analysis model.

Moving-averages model

When there is too much random variation, it is sometimes difficult to have a good understanding of the demand for a good or service. To reduce the impact of randomness, the moving-averages model is often used. The ***moving-averages model*** is a method for smoothing or reducing the effects of random variations in market demand data. This is a decision model for eliminating a specific random occurrence. A moving average is the mean value of demand based on a key time period.

The moving-averages decision model can be most easily understood through a case application by a swimwear manufacturer. Vista Swim Wear has been concerned with the planning of its production labor force for the forthcoming quarter. Vista regularly collects data on the demand for its swim products. Each swim suit requires approximately the same amount of labor to make. The number of swim suits sold each month during the past year is shown in Table 11.1.

Month	Demand (# of Suits)	Three-Month Moving Average	Five-Month Moving Average	11.1 Demand for Vista Swim Suits
July	86,800			
August	62,000			
September	53,000			
October	51,000	67,267		
November	39,000	55,333		
December	46,000	47,667	58,360	
January	42,000	45,333	50,200	
February	56,000		46,200	
March	63,000		46,800	
April	89,000			
May	96,500			
June	121,000			

Using the data from the second column of Table 11.1, moving averages based on three-month time periods are presented. For example, the moving average for swim-suit sales for October is calculated as follows:

$$\frac{86,800 \text{ (July sales)} + 62,000 \text{ (August sales)} + 53,000 \text{ (September sales)}}{3}$$
$$= 67,267 \text{ swim suits.}$$

As you move from month to month with this decision model, the oldest sales period is dropped and the next one is added. The fourth column in Table 11.1 shows moving averages based on a five-month time period. Five data points are added and then divided by five to determine the moving average for a particular month. We have calculated moving averages for four periods with the three-month period and the five-month period. What would be the moving averages for the remaining periods?

Exponential smoothing model

The moving-average model gives the same weight to each time period. It may be desirable to give more weight to data from the recent time periods and less weight to the more distant past. This can be achieved with the exponential smoothing model. The **exponential smoothing model** estimates moving averages by adjusting them through a weighted difference of the actual demand and the past forecast. This is shown in the following form:

Forecast for current period
   = Past forecast + weighted difference (actual demand − past forecast)

The weighted difference shows the relative emphasis placed on the data from the most current time period. The weighted difference may vary from zero to one. A large value, such as 0.8, gives heavy weight to the most current time period. A smaller value, such as 0.2, gives much less importance to the current time period.

Let's assume that Vista Swim Wear Company has been using the simple forecasting procedure whereby the last year's preceding average monthly sales have been used as the forecast for each succeeding month this year. Using actual swim suits sales in the preceding April period (89,000), the past forecast for April (let's assume it was 66,275 suits), and a smoothing coefficient of 0.6 to weight the recent demand most heavily, the forecast for May would be:

$$\text{Forecast for May} = 66{,}275 + 0.6\,(89{,}000 - 66{,}275) = 79{,}910$$

Regression-analysis model

A more sophisticated approach to forecasting market demand is provided by the regression-analysis model. The **regression-analysis model** uses knowledge of one variable (the independent variable) to estimate the second variable (dependent variable). To explain this model, let's again return to the Vista Swim Wear Company.

To stabilize its work force, Vista has ventured into other products related to their production technology. About a year ago, the company invested in equipment to make socks. The market for this product is relatively stable. Sales seem to be very responsive to increases in advertising expenditures. Vista management has been keeping close records of advertising expenses and sales of socks since they began marketing this new line. Now they are interested in determining the possible relationship between advertising expenditures and sock sales. Vista management wants to make some decisions about the apparent value of advertising and have some estimate of the resulting sales. By using the regressions-analysis model, they have found the following relationship between advertising and sock sales:

$$Y = \$16{,}000 + 7.5X,$$

where:

Y = Dollar sales of socks
X = Each thousand dollars of advertising expenditures
$\$16{,}000$ = Intercept between advertising and sock sales

This equation is developed from the data shown in Fig. 11.3. The linear regression line in Fig. 11.3, relating advertising expenditures to sock sales, intercepts at $16,000. An increase of $7500 in sock sales for each thousand dollars of advertising expenditure is illustrated.

11.3
Regression model of
advertising expenditures to
sock sales

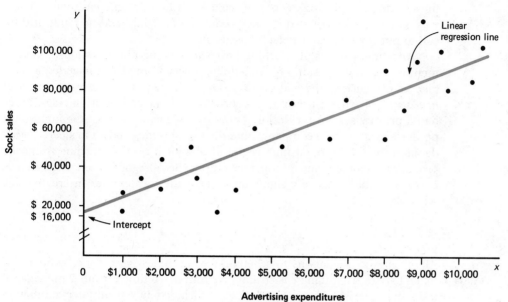

This regression-analysis model permits us to estimate sales for a given advertising expenditure up to $100,000 in sales. Estimating beyond this amount is not recommended because we do not know the relationship of advertising to sales beyond $100,000. So in this example, if Vista invests $6000 in advertising expenses, the regression-analysis model will get anticipated sales of $61,000, i.e., $16,000 + (7.5 × 6,000) = $61,000.

Once the operations managers have a fairly good fix on market demand, they can get into the specifics of scheduling what tasks are to be performed, by whom, and by what date.

SCHEDULING DECISIONS

Scheduling is the establishment of detailed timetables for transforming inputs, determining the exact times when particular inputs must be available, and estimating when specific quantities of outputs will be completed. There is almost an infinite variety of scheduling decision models. They range from those created and stored in the mind of the manager to those developed and maintained in elaborate computer models. Let's start with a scheduling decision model developed and maintained by Larry, a production scheduler.

Larry's Model

Larry is responsible for scheduling over 88 different products on 12 machines. These machines run 24 hours a day, seven days per week. Top management was not quite sure how he scheduled the machines. They knew, however, that the scheduling tasks took two or three days of Larry's time each week. Larry was asked how he decided on the production schedule, but he found it difficult to put the decision model he used into words.[5]

After many hours of watching Larry and asking him questions, management began to understand his scheduling decision model. It included a complex set of heuristics he had developed over many years. You may recall that *heuristics* are "rules of thumb," or intuitively developed decision rules. Larry had a priority system for deciding among categories such as: the number of products ordered by a company; quantity of a specific product in stock; overall demand for the product; time required to switch over a machine from one product to another; and production output. Because of his long experience, Larry was able to place weights on each of these categories in creating his schedules.

**Computer
Simulation Models**

All of Larry's calculations to schedule the machines were done by hand. To make Larry's scheduling easier and give him more time for other managerial tasks, his heuristic decision rules were included in a computer simulation model. This model simulated the operation of the machines, people, operating constraints, and customer orders for his department. Perhaps this entire project's greatest value to the company was that it showed management how Larry scheduled the products on the machines.

Not all scheduling involves so complex a decision model as Larry's. For example, in a shoe repair shop, the cobbler may work on customers' shoes on a basis of "first come, first served" (FCFS); that is, the first customers to bring in shoes will be the first to be served.

The cobbler may also elect to use the scheduling rule of *shortest operating time* (SOT). The SOT rule means that the repairs will be scheduled so that those jobs taking the least time will be processed first. Those taking the longest estimated time will be scheduled last.

It may seem as if the shortest-operating-time rule for scheduling is much less efficient than the first-come, first-served approach. Actually, the SOT rule typically gives a lower average time for jobs than the FCFS rule.

There are many other scheduling decision models. These are based on such things as the amount of available time before a due date, number of processing steps remaining, longest operating time, and so on. There are many combinations of scheduling rules for creating different decision models. For example, many computer systems that batch incoming jobs will use the SOT. However, when a job that is expected to take quite a while has been waiting for a fairly long time, its priority will increase. It will be moved forward in the line of waiting jobs. This is a form of dynamic scheduling. After waiting for a certain period of time, this long job will be processed even though jobs with shorter operating times may be on hand.

Scheduling is quite complex in many companies. Larry had his own decision model for scheduling machines and people, but there are many possible decision rules and models for performing scheduling tasks. And it does little good to have an ideal scheduling decision model if the necessary parts, supplies, materials, or finished goods are not on hand when needed.

Inventory refers to the amount of inputs or outputs kept on hand. Inventories are raw materials, work-in-process, supplies, and finished goods not yet shipped. Organizational resources must be spent to maintain inventories. Thus, it is important to control inventory levels.

Inventories serve many purposes, but we will consider five of the more important ones: (1) to maintain independent operations; (2) to allow flexibility in the production schedule; (3) to provide a safeguard against the problems that can arise when input materials have different delivery times; (4) to meet variations in product demand; and (5) to take advantage of economic purchase-order size. Let's look at each one of these purposes to see their impact on operations management.

1. To provide some independence of one work station from another, a supply of needed materials is kept available. This form of inventory uncouples the various work stations; if the operators at one station are delayed or slow, they will not delay all the following work stations. This inventory usually takes the form of in-process-inventory. **In-process inventory** is those goods which are partially completed and will have additional labor and materials added to obtain a finished good.

2. Inventories allow flexibility in the production schedule. An inventory of finished goods lessens the pressure on the transformation process to get goods out by a particular date. This inventory provides for longer lead times. **Lead time** is the amount of time between the placement of an order and the actual receipt of that order by the purchaser. Longer lead time permits smoother work flows and the production of economical order sizes.

3. Inventories provide a safeguard against the problems that may be caused by variations in the delivery dates of raw materials. The operations manager cannot always count on an order for raw materials to arrive at a specific date.

There are many reasons for possible delays: labor problems, transportation holdups, and late shipments. If there is no raw-material inventory, even slight delays could shut down an entire operation.

4. Inventories help meet variations in market demand for the firm's outputs. In the section on forecasting, we mentioned that there is random variation in demand. It is seldom feasible to produce the number of items to exactly match market demand. A common practice is to maintain a safety or buffer inventory. This inventory will absorb the variations in demand caused by unanticipated conditions of the market place. Of course, inventories may also be increased to meet changes in seasonal demand, such as in swim suits.

5. Inventories enable management to take advantage of economic purchase-order size. It costs money to order materials, to carry the materials in inventory, and to change the transformation process to produce the goods. These costs all become important in determining the most economic size of the order.

Inventories may serve other purposes in addition to the five listed. For example: stabilizing employment; beating inflation; reducing the risk of possible future shortages; and eliminating the need for possible future overtime.

Four Inventory Costs   *Inventory costs* are the expenses associated with maintaining an inventory. There are four basic types of costs in maintaining an inventory: (1) ordering costs; (2) carrying costs; (3) shortage costs; and (4) set-up costs. These costs should be considered when making decisions about inventory size. Obviously, there are other costs and trade-offs that need to be considered; such as using inventories to hedge against inflation or maintaining large inventories to reduce the need for future overtime. But let's briefly consider each of these four specific costs:

1. *Ordering costs* are the managerial and clerical expenses of actually preparing the purchase order. These costs are not generally very large.

2. *Carrying costs* are the expenses of holding goods in inventory. These costs include such items as obsolescence, insurance, storage facilities, depreciation, taxes, breakage, pilferage, and the cost of capital.

3. *Shortage costs* are those which occur when a customer orders a good, but there is none in inventory. The customer must either wait until the inventory is replenished or cancel the order. It is difficult to determine the costs of a customer who has canceled an order and decides to go elsewhere for future orders.

4. *Set-up costs* are the expenses of changing over to make a different product. They include the time required to get new raw materials, change the equipment set-up, change the routing, and clear out in-process inventories of other items. They also include additional administrative time, employee training, idle time, and overtime. These costs may be difficult to pinpoint, but should be evaluated in determining the quantity of a particular good created in a single productive run.

The specific inventory purposes and costs are part of the decision-making process in determining desirable inventory levels and the ideal size of orders to replace inventories. "How much do I order?" is a practical decision problem that every manager responsible for inventory levels must face. The order size for inventory replacement generally follows one of two basic inventory decision models: fixed-order quantity model or fixed-order period model.

The *fixed-order-quantity model* is a method for determining the standard number of items to be ordered when the inventory reaches a predetermined level. The amount of the order is always the same, but the timing of the order varies. Figure 11.4 identifies typical cost tradeoffs in determining ideal inventory levels. These costs must be assessed to develop the fixed-order-quantity model. The vertical axis in Fig. 11.4 shows the average annual costs associated

Fixed-Order Quantity Model

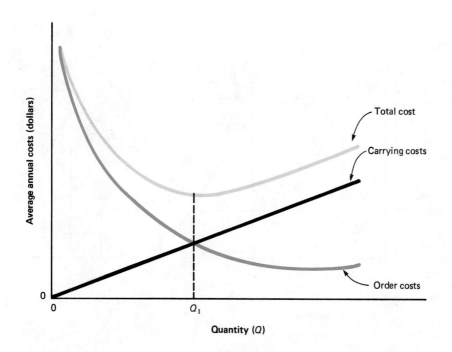

11.4
Two cost tradeoffs for determining inventory levels

with different reorder quantities and different carrying costs. The total-cost line is simply the sum of reorder costs and carrying costs at each possible quantity level. The different quantity levels are shown on the horizontal axis. Figure 11.4 suggests that as the quantity ordered increases, the ordering cost per unit decreases. However, as the inventory level increases, the carrying cost of the inventory also increases. This is because more money is tied up in the inventory, including more space to house it. The maximum inventory level is simply the quantity which provides the lowest total inventory costs. This is shown as Q_1 in Fig. 11.4. This point also influences the optimal reorder quantity. Figure 11.4 is used to help you visualize these relationships, but it is not very precise. The equation representing the fixed-order-quantity model is as follows:

$$FOQ = \sqrt{\frac{2DO}{C}},$$

where:

FOQ = fixed order quantity
D = average annual demand
O = ordering costs
C = carrying costs

**11.5
Fixed-order-quantity model**

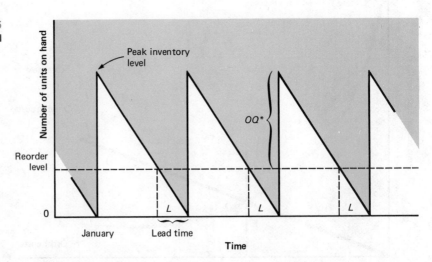

*OQ = Order quantity

Figure 11.5 provides a schematic form of the basic fixed-order-quantity model. In this figure, Q_1 represents the fixed order quantity. Inventory will have to be reordered when it reaches the reorder level designated by the dashed horizontal line in Fig. 11.5. This level of inventory assumes sufficient time for the order to be received when the inventory is exhausted. The delay in receiving the order is known as the lead time. Because unexpected factors could affect the lead time, management might want to maintain a "safety stock" of inventory. In this case, the reorder level in Fig. 11.5 would be made somewhat higher.

The **fixed-order-period model** is a method for determining the number of items to be ordered at fixed time intervals up to a predetermined maximum level. The timing of the order is always the same, but the amount of the order varies. Most supermarkets use this model. This model is "triggered" by specific times — such as each Friday, first of the month, or quarter of the year — rather than by a particular level of inventory.

The equation representing the fixed order period model is:

$$T = \sqrt{\frac{2O}{DC}},$$

Fixed-Order-Period
Model

where:

T = the optimal time period between replenishing inventory
O = ordering costs
D = average annual demand
C = carrying costs

Figure 11.6 shows the fixed-order-period model in schematic form. There continues to be a maximum inventory level. For example, a local soft drink distributor wants to maintain a maximum inventory of 1000 cases of Pepsi Cola. On the reorder date, the inventory of Pepsi is only 400 cases. An order would be placed for 600 cases. If the next reorder date found an inventory level of 700 cases, a reorder for only 300 cases would be placed.

Now that we have our inventory decisions under control, have developed detailed production schedules, and have a pretty good idea of the market demand for our product, we can focus on the decisions that will ensure the desired quality of our product. Of course, the inventory discussion has been based on very simple assumptions, such as that the consumption of inventories is uniform and steady during and between each time period.

**11.6
Fixed-order-period model**

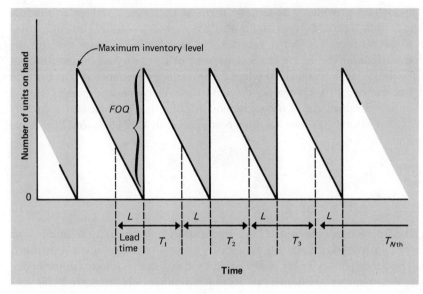

Note: $T_1 = T_2 = T_3 = T_{Nth}$

**QUALITY CONTROL
DECISIONS**

Quality control is concerned with assuring that outputs meet certain predetermined standards.

Quality means different things to different firms. Some organizations create a product or service with little quality. Others consider quality to be extremely important. This is often a reflection of the firm's strategy. Maytag, the manufacturer of clothes washers and other appliances, boasts of keeping their repairmen "the loneliest men in town" by maintaining extremely high quality. Their president, Sterling O. Swanger, has maintained quality as an important principle in the firm. He has held the line on quality in an era of widespread temptation to do otherwise. Unlike some appliance manufacturers, Maytag is producing a more reliable machine than ever. In the mid-1950s, the company's late president, Fred Maytag II, laid down a standard of ten years of trouble-free operations for the company's products. At that time, the company's average automatic washer was three years short of the target. Today, objective quality control tests show that a new Maytag washing machine should run 14 years without serious trouble.[6] This commitment to quality has its cost. Maytags are probably the most "expensive" appliances to purchase on the market. Of course, the Maytag salesperson would argue that it is the least expensive over the long haul.

Quality control procedures usually only sample the goods and services produced. On the basis of these samples, opinions are formed about the quality of the entire quantity of the goods or services produced. Sampling is one means of creating a feedback loop, as suggested in Fig. 11.1, from the goods and services created back to the transformation process. When the sampled goods do not meet the desired standards, this information is given to the key managers in charge of the operations management system. They will try to determine the reasons for the below-standard quality and take corrective actions in the transformation process. Of course, the problem could also exist in the receipt of below-par inputs. This requires corrective action with suppliers or possibly the securing of new supply sources.

Decision-making to ensure quality control generally zeros in on four areas: measurement; inputs; work-in-process; and outputs.

Measurement is the means used to assess the amount or degree of specific characteristics. For example, a person's weight is measured on a scale in pounds and ounces. Measurement is fundamental to quality control. The more accurate the measurement, the easier it is to compare the desired results (standards) against the actual results (outputs).

Quality control generally measures either by variable or by attribute. *Measuring by variable* refers to the assessment of characteristics for which there are specific standards. This can be illustrated by specified physical characteristics such as length, diameter, height, weight, and temperature. *Measuring by attribute* refers to the assessment of characteristics that must fall within specified upper and lower limits. It is usually easier to measure by attribute than by variable. Measuring by attribute provides acceptable quality so long as the goods or services fall within the upper or lower limits. Door manufacturers generally ship their doors so long as they are plus or minus one-quarter inch of the predetermined size. Of course, strategic decisions in setting quality limits are not usually this simple. In the recent case of the Flexible Bus, the trade-offs between strength needed in the bus frame and the light weight needed to improve fuel consumption was misjudged. Several cities purchased this proclaimed "new generation" bus and experienced numerous problems with it, including cracked frames.

Measurement

Quality control generally begins with the inputs — especially raw materials and parts — used in the transformation process. Automobile assembly plants could not function if the parts and other raw materials did not fall within upper and lower limits of predetermined standards. Assembly plants have inspectors who evaluate each new batch of inputs (usually through a sampling process) to make sure that they fall within the upper and lower limits. The

Inputs

combination of the recent public outcry against shoddy quality in some American autos and fierce foreign competition have caused American automobile manufacturers to both toughen and more vigorously enforce expected standards of raw materials and parts.

Work-in-Process

Quality-control inspections and assessments are also used between the various stages within the transformation process. Work-in-process inspections can result in reworking or rejecting the good before any more work is done on it.

The adoption of quality control circles, as discussed in Chapter 4, is one of the newer approaches for improving work-in-process quality control. A take-off on this approach was announced by Chrysler and the United Auto Workers in 1980. They developed the first agreement in the American auto industry that gives assembly line workers a role in controlling the quality of cars they make. Workers at two of the assembly lines producing Chrysler's K cars have the right to demand that defects be corrected as they occur in each stage of the assembly process. Workers are promised no reprisals for calling attention to shoddy quality. Marc Stepp, a United Auto Workers vice president, commented:

> *If a foreman tells a worker to 'forget it' — as has sometimes happened in the past — we will expect that worker to make a report, and if plant supervision doesn't blow the whistle on that foreman, the union will, and we will go straight to the top of the corporation.*[7]

Obviously, high quality is needed in the K cars if they are to compete successfully, especially with the Japanese imports. The union and workers obviously have a vested interest in helping the Chrysler K cars succeed in the marketplace. As of this writing, it will be interesting to observe if this and other Chrysler efforts are adequate to avoid bankruptcy.

Finished Goods or Services

The most recognizable form of quality control is the assessment made after a good is completed or the service has been provided. In the case of a good, quality-control assessments take place before the item is shipped to customers. Of course, goods returned by customers due to shoddy workmanship or other problems are also part of the overall quality-control process. American automobile manufacturers are now more prone to return parts or materials to suppliers if they find them lacking in some respect. In the case of services, a major quality-control checkpoint is after the service has been provided. For example, barbers and hairdressers usually involve their customers in this process by handing them a mirror and asking if everything is satisfactory. The satisfactory provision of a service is often more difficult to measure than the satisfactory manufacture of a product.

The ability to measure the level of product quality does not tell us what that level of quality should be. Desired quality levels are strongly influenced by company strategy, as in the case of Maytag, and by competition, as in the case of Chrysler's K car.

The importance of management strategy and attitudes toward quality-control decisions cannot be overstated. Stephen Moss, a consultant with the Arthur D. Little consulting firm, has worked with corporations in both Japan and America, and made the following observation:

> *The U.S. manager sets an acceptable level of quality and then sticks to it. The Japanese are constantly upgrading their goals. The American assumes a certain rate of failure is inevitable, while the Japanese shoots for perfection and sometimes gets close.*[8]

Fortunately, the marketplace seems to be operating and U.S. industry is actively gearing up to meet the new standards of quality set by the Japanese. For example, in March 1980, Hewlett-Packard announced the results of tests it ran on purchased semiconductors. The failure rate of U.S.-made chips was six times that of the Japanese. This public announcement seemed to have a good effect on the U.S. semiconductor industry. When Hewlett-Packard ran similar tests about six months later, the U.S. firms had cut their failure rate to three to one.

SUMMARY

Quality-control decisions are influenced by available means and costs of measurement. Quality-control decision models usually focus on inputs, work-in-process, and outputs. Outputs are the finished goods or services provided in the marketplace. The quality-control discussion was in the form of general guidelines and issues rather than specific techniques.

The inventory decision models were much more specific than the quality-control guidelines. The specific purposes and costs of inventories are major factors in determining inventory levels and the size of orders. Aids for guiding you included the fixed-order-quantity model and the fixed-order-period model.

A general rather than operating knowledge of scheduling decisions was presented. Scheduling decision models can range from those created and stored in the mind of a manager to those maintained in computers. Various decision rules for setting priorities and sequencing orders are common to all scheduling decision models. They include the shortest-operating-time (SOT) decision rule; first come, first served (FCFS) decision rule; and the dynamic-scheduling decision models.

Forecasting decisions affect the quantities produced by the operations management system within particular time periods. The basic types of market forecasts frequently used in operations management are trend, cyclical, and seasonal. Seasonal forecasts are probably the most sensitive to random fluctuations. Three forecasting models were described: moving-averages model; exponential smoothing model; and the regression-analysis model.

Operations management as a system — including inputs, transformation, and outputs — was developed to provide an understanding of the scope and focus to this area of management. By presenting the setting of operations management and several of the areas in which decisions must be made (forecasting, scheduling, inventories, and quality control), we hope to develop your ability to perform the decision roles of *monitor* and *resource allocator*. The monitor role focuses on scanning the environment. The section on forecasting decision models zeros in on the skills needed for effective monitoring of the environment. The resource-allocator decision role makes choices for the effective use and allocation of resources. The discussions on scheduling, inventories, and quality control are vitally concerned with the allocation and use of resources within the operations management system.

As suggested in our comments on feedback loops and quality control, the managerial and organizational controls bear upon operations management as well as on all management processes. Accordingly, the next chapter addresses control issues and processes in organizations.

KEYWORDS

capital
continuous process technology
cyclical forecast
exponential smoothing model
fixed-order-period model
fixed-order-quantity model
in-process inventory
inventory
inventory costs
labor
lead time
mass production technology
materials
measurement
measuring by attribute

measuring by variable
moving-averages model
operations management
outputs
productivity
quality control
random demand
regression-analysis model
robot
scheduling
seasonal forecast
strategic feedback loops
transformation
trend forecast
unit or small batch technology

1. Give two examples from a service industry and manufacturing industry of each of the following: (a) inputs, (b) transformation process, (c) outputs, (d) feedback loops.

2. What major applications do you think will be made of robots over the next 10 years?

3. What types of problems should management anticipate with the introduction of robots?

4. Can the simple forecast that "tomorrow will be the same as today" be applied *reasonably* successfully to the weather, gasoline prices, and foreign relations? Explain.

5. How might Exxon use trend, cyclical, and seasonal forecasts for its unleaded gasoline?

6. Using the data from Table 11.1, calculate a two-month and a six-month moving average for Vista swim wear during November and December.

7. Can you think of other scheduling rules besides FCFS and SOT? When might they work best?

8. What scheduling rules are used by your computer center in processing student requests for courses? Are they effective from your point of view? From the computer center's point of view?

9. Jackson Hole Manufacturing has an annual demand for its product of 6300 units, while ordering costs are $19.00 and holding costs are $3.00 per unit. What is the economic order quantity? What happens when demand increases to 7500 units per year?; to 3850 units per year?

10. What happens if the data from question 9 are used in a fixed-order-period model?

11. It is claimed by some that American industry is losing its competitive edge because the quality of foreign-made products selling at the same price is superior. Do you agree? Why? Can you cite specific personal experiences for your feelings?

Management Incidents and Cases

Ski Products Incorporated is a high growth division of Dramun Forests. This recreational products division was established several years ago by Mr. Dramun. He and his advisors concluded there would be a strong market for recreational products.

* Adapted from R.A. Dunn and K.D. Ramsing, *Management Science: A Practical Approach to Decision Making.* New York: MacMillan, 1981. Used with permission.

Loran Forsythe had been hired six years ago by Ski Products division when he graduated from college. He joined the company because he envisioned himself doing a lot of skiing, thus fulfilling a first love. Loran had been on the school's ski team and was also a "hot-dog" skier. Although Loran's job did not provide for skiing, he had been successful with the company. His hard work and pleasing personality resulted in a series of promotions to his present position as manager of the cross-country ski product line. He had only been in the position a short time, but he was aware of the need for better inventory control methods. He set as a high-priority objective the establishment of an effective inventory control system. He asked the company's analyst, Mary Williams, to meet with him to discuss some of the inventory problems as he saw them. Before the meeting, his administrative assistant, John Bell, developed a list of each part used in the manufacture of skis. Bell ranked each item by its dollar usage. As he stated, this was quantity used per year times its cost. Bill also gathered demand data and costs of some critical parts. At their meeting, Loran said, "Mary, I have several items that I want you to look at in terms of how much I should order and when. I've gotten together some data for you. Let me tell you about each of the items independently. I think it will make more sense."

Loran explained to Williams that he was very concerned about the inventory policies for the cross-country skis and the bindings installed on them. He pointed out that they manufactured the skis but purchased the snap binding outright. As he explained, the company had been installing a ski binding costing $4.85 per unit on about 3000 of the 4500 skis they made. The bindings normally arrived eleven working days after the order was placed. Depending on the quantity ordered, the bindings arrived either by common carrier or by a delivery service. Loran estimated the cost of storing the bindings at about 75¢ per binding per year. There is little obsolescence in bindings because model changes are known far in advance. However, the inventory holding costs included insurance, storage area facilities, and the cost of capital invested in the bindings.

Loran Forsythe estimated that it cost $7.50 per order when dealing with outside suppliers. This included clerical time in writing and sending the orders. Loran also mentioned that the company currently supplying the bindings had offered a new quantity discount scheme. The discount was based on the amount of each order. For each order of 500 or more pairs, the cost was $4.33 per pair. For quantities of less that 500 pairs but at least 200 pairs, the cost was $4.85 per pair (what was currently being paid). For any order of less than 200 pairs, the cost would be $5.00 per pair.

Loran said, "Mary, I am concerned about the cost of not staying precisely with the optimal order quantities. What I need is some indication of the optimal order size."

He went on to explain there were two other areas where he wanted to assess their inventory practices: ski inventories and thermal resin inventories and purchases.

Another inventory problem Loran discussed with Mary involved the manufacture of the skis themselves. The company normally worked 260 days per year in the production of the 4500 pairs of skis that they anticipated selling. The average production rate was 25 pairs per day. Thus, they could meet this current demand in only 180 days. The remaining time was devoted to making other recreational items with similar manufacturing requirements.

Each time a batch of skis was to be manufactured, the cost of setup and breakdown was estimated at $145. Because of scheduling other products, a minimum lead time (the period from order to completion) of five working days was necessary to begin making skis. It cost the company $4.80 per pair per year to store the skis in rented warehouse space. The cost of interest on invested capital amounted to 12 percent alone. The storage and insurance costs were low compared to the alternative cost of capital. While carrying costs of $4.80 for each pair of skis seemed high, Loran felt it was reasonable and was actually lower than most other companies, but he was not sure. The projected selling price for each pair of skis was $58 f.o.b. for the company. Direct costs were estimated at $36. Loran pointed out if they produced more skis than demanded by the stores, he had an outlet to sell the overage at $25 each.

Finally, the company bought a thermal resin for the manufacturing of their cross country skis in 100 kilogram drums. Normally, they reordered each 20 working days, based on the supply at that time. The cost of the resin was $4.48 per kilogram. Each pair of skis required an average of 1.043 Kg of resin. The resin is not difficult to store and storage probably costs only about 20 percent of the total resin cost per year.

Questions

Assume that you are Mary Williams and Loran Forsythe ends his comments to you with the following questions. How would you respond to each?

1. How might we determine the number of bindings to keep in inventory and the best quantity to order?

2. How might we go about determining the number of pairs of finished skis to keep in inventory? How should this inventory decision be related to our sales forecasts?

3. How might we determine the amount of thermal resin to purchase and keep in inventory?

REFERENCES

1. E. Huse, *The Modern Manager.* St. Paul: West Publishing Co., 1979, pp. 549–551.

2. E. Adams and R. Ebert, *Production and Operations Management: Concepts, Models, and Behavior.* Prentice Hall, Inc. Englewood Cliffs, NJ, 1978, p. 737.

3. J. Woodward (ed.), *Industrial Organization: Behavior and Control.* New York: Oxford University Press, 1970.

4. The information for this section is drawn and modified from: "Robots Join the Labor Force." *Business Week,* June 9, 1980, 62–76: "The Robot Revolution." *Time,* December 8, 1980, 72–83; G. Bylinsky, "Those Smart Young Robots on the Production Line." *Fortune* **100,** 2, 1979, 90–96.

5. K. Ramsing and D. Dilts, "The Transformation of Opinions, Beliefs, and Heuristic Rules into a Scheduling Simulation Model," in R. Huseman, (ed.) *Academy of Management Proceedings, 1979.* Atlanta, Ga: Academy of Management, 1979, pp. 162–164.

6. E. Faltemayer, "Lonely Maytag Repairmen." *Fortune* **100,** 9, 1979, 190–195.

7. M. Feinsilber, "Chrysler Gives Workers Voice in Controlling Quality of K Cars." *Houston Chronicle,* June 28, 1980, Section 1, 21.

8. J. Main, "The Battle for Quality Begins," *Fortune* **102,** 13, 1980, 28–33.

Chapter 12

CONTROL CONCEPTS AND STRATEGIES

After reading this chapter, you should be able to:

1. List the uses of controls within organizations.

2. Use the corrective model of control.

3. Describe how two key contingency factors — type of power and type of technology — will influence the controls used in a department or organization.

4. Describe how political influences impact on control practices within society as a whole and organizations in particular.

5. Identify and discuss six of the control strategies used by managers — human input, reward-punishment, formal structure, policies and rules, budgets, and machine.

6. Describe how control processes are likely to differ in mechanistic versus organic systems.

431

PREVIEW CASE

Lois — Profile of a Developing Manager*

About five years ago I was asked to a party at a neighbor's house to celebrate Lois' promotion to an assistant manager's position at the insurance company where she worked. I was impressed and congratulated her on her appointment. She shrugged it off with the comment that insurance companies have as many assistant managers as a hound dog has fleas, but admitted she was pleased with the recognition. A short time afterwards she moved out of the neighborhood and I lost touch with

---

* Adapted from A. Carlisle, "The Golfer." *California Management Review* **22**, 1, 1979, 42–52.

her for about five years. Then I ran into her at a cocktail party and asked if she was with the same company. She said she was, but in a different capacity — she had just been promoted to executive vice-president. Remembering the comment on her last promotion, I asked her if insurance companies have as many executive vice-presidents as the proverbial hound has fleas. Lois' response was that she was one of the two line officers reporting directly to the president. Not bad for a woman in her early forties I thought. "Can you identify any decision you made during your managerial career that you feel particularly affected your success, and at what point you made it?" I asked. "That's a tough question," she replied, but she gave me an answer. As well as I can remember, it went like this:

"Broadly speaking, there are two main routes to the top of a casualty company like ours: marketing and underwriting. When I started work I chose the underwriting side. I did the job so well that I was promoted to supervising underwriter. Three years ago I was transferred back to the head office and given additional responsibilities. I supervised a greater number of underwriters, but still did some of the technical work myself. The job was pretty much the same qualitatively, but its scope had increased quantitatively. Soon I started to think about the chaotic nature of my workday. It struck me that I was spending too much time telling people how to do their jobs rather than emphasizing what had to be done. Perhaps because of my fascination with the process of underwriting I was concentrating on method rather than output. I made an effort to stop doing this. I cut down on it drastically and spent more time negotiating and reaching agreement between my subordinates and myself as to what I expected from them in terms of production. I explained what organizational resources, including my time to a very limited extent, were available to help them with problems they encountered. In addition, I designed a control system which promptly and accurately reported to both them and me the quality and quantity of their output. This was critical, for to be effective such a system must be precise, timely, and trusted by them as well as me. That was no small order, but I felt the time spent designing such a control mechanism would pay off handsomely for my subordinates, myself, and of course for the organization.

"At this stage of my managerial career it was becoming increasingly clear to me that my job was largely one of getting commitment to the attainment of organizational objectives and monitoring the output of my subordinates. To get real commitment, not just verbal agreement, to these goals from my subordinates required that time be available to explore differences in opinion and perception. It's easy for a superior to confuse agreement reluctantly given under implicit pressure and with unstated reservations by a docile and somewhat intimidated subordinate with *real* commitment between two mature people negotiating, to the extent possible, as equals. Believe me, this takes skill as well as time on the part of the superior. For me to have this kind of time required development of some means whereby virtually all the problems encountered by the underwriters would be solved at that level and not passed up to me. This task I accomplished by refusing to answer questions on process problems, by referring the asker to one of several subordinates whom I had designated as official problem-solvers and, in the case of particularly difficult situations, requesting an ex-post-facto report on how it was handled. This approach, coupled with my control mechanism, enabled me to assess accurately the capabilities of several of my most promotable subordinates. I really had this system working well when I was transferred out to the field again, this time as an assistant branch manager. That's when I made the decision never to underwrite again, for that was no longer what I was paid to do. My new assignment was not to perform technical tasks, rather it was to design and manage a system to insure that responsibilities for underwriting, and those for marketing, accounting, personnel, were being carried out as effectively as possible.

"I realized I had to stop doing my subordinates' work for them, no matter how intriguing it might be, and concentrate instead on my own broader and different responsibilities. This I did successfully and had the time I needed to negotiate outputs with my subordinates, and the time to plan, to reflect on the developments within and outside of the company and to develop a variety of control approaches to deal with them before they reached critical stages."[1]

This account of how Lois went from assistant manager to executive vice president ties together a number of themes in our chapters on management processes: — planning; organization design; decision-making; and control. The links in these management processes and their general importance to organizations are suggested in Fig. 12.1. The boundaries from planning to organization design to control do overlap. While decision-making has been presented as a separate management process, it also needs to be recognized that the planning, organization design, and control processes operate within and through managerial decision-making. Thus, they are considered within decision-making in Fig. 12.1.

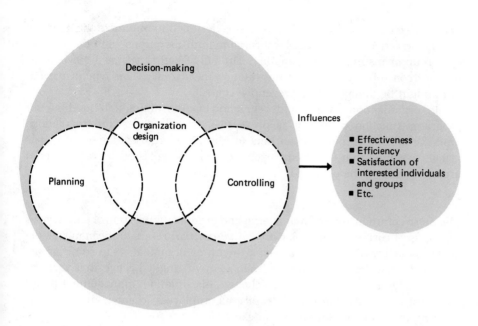

Lois clearly recognized each of these management processes as a link in a chain — with the chain being only as strong as the weakest link. In particular, she came to understand the need to control her own time and activities. Lois also recognized the need to use various control approaches to prevent problems as well as to take corrective action on problems before they reached crisis levels.

This chapter focuses on contingencies influencing organizational control and the control strategies used by managers to help the organization reach its goals. We will not discuss how government, unions, customers, or other groups exert "control" over the organization and its managers.

INTRODUCTION TO CONTROL

Basic Types of Control

In its broadest sense, **control** is the process by which a person, group, or organization consciously determines or influences what another person, group, or organization will do.[2] Within organizations and society in general, reaction to the word "control" is very negative, often being interpreted to imply restraining, coercing, delimiting, directing, enforcing, watching, manipulating, and inhibiting. This is partially due to the strong belief in such cultural values as individualism and democracy, which appear to be inconsistent with the notion of control. Individualsim is based on self-control and some external controls.

Preventive control

Preventive control refers to mechanisms designed to minimize the need for taking corrective action. Some laws serve to limit the imposition of control by one group or institution over another. The Bill of Rights acts as a mechanism to limit (control) the actions of the state on its citizenry. This type of mechanism might be thought of as preventive control.

In organizations, rules and regulations and training-and-development programs function primarily as preventive controls. Rules and regulations limit the actions employees can take to reach the organization's goals. It is usually assumed that if the employees comply, the goals of the organization are more likely to be achieved.

Corrective control

The more common view of managerial and organizational control emphasizes a process of corrective control. **Corrective control** refers to mechanisms designed to return the individual, department, or organization to some predetermined condition. For example, management might believe that theft by some employees has increased. To change this situation, management might now post a security guard and require all employees to enter and leave the building from a common entry and exit area.

Managerial control needs to be both preventive and corrective. Distinctions between the two types may be found within a single managerial practice. The performance-appraisal practices used in companies may prevent shoddy workmanship, tardiness, etc. by promising rewards for compliance. They may also attempt to correct for deviations by providing punishments or withholding rewards. In the preview case, Lois effectively made use of both preventive and corrective controls. You might reread the preview case and try to identify each of her actions that represented preventive or corrective controls.

Political Influences and Control

The issues of societal and organizational controls seemed to underlie much of the conflict and unrest that erupted on the campuses and in the street during the late 1960s and early 1970s. Although the physical conflicts over questions of control have now declined, we should not conclude that the questions have all been satisfactorily answered. Rather, the approaches for dealing with the issues of control have shifted. Instead of attacking organizations and institutions from the outside by riots, boycotts, and the like, people are more likely to work within those institutions to bring about the desired changes by legitimate, nondestructive means.

One of the main purposes of the political system of a society is to resolve issues of control: *who* has the authority to do *what* to *whom*. The means for resolving those issues can vary widely, depending on the political, cultural, and economic systems of the society. At one extreme, some societies use coercive practices, such as jailing or executing those who challenge the existing controls. At the other extreme, some societies deal with challenges to the existing control structure by participative practices, such as open debate, sharing or eliminating control, and increased rewards.

Current issues involving questions of control and the practices used by institutions or individuals in our political system can be found in the daily newspaper (i.e., state vs. federal control, civil rights for minorities, equal rights for women, government control of business, the executive branch vs. congressional control over foreign affairs, and so on). As suggested in Table 12.1, similar challenges to control practices have been taking place within organizations.

12.1
Fundamental Questions
of Organizational
Control

■ Who is to control?

■ What types of controls are appropriate or acceptable?

■ How much control is needed?

■ When do increases in control become ineffective for both the employee and the organization?

■ What contingencies influence the amount and types of controls within organizations?

Formal controls are put to many uses in organizations. For example: **Uses of Controls**

1. Controls are used to *standardize performance*. This is accomplished by supervisory inspections, written procedures, or production schedules.

2. Controls are used to *protect an organization's assets* from theft, waste, or misuse. Record-keeping requirements, auditing procedures, and division of responsibilities all control access to assets.

3. Controls are used to *standardize the quality* of products or services offered by an organization. This is done through employee training, inspections, statistical quality control, and incentive systems.

4. Controls are used to *limit the amount of authority* that can be exercised by managers. These limits are seen in job descriptions, policy directives, rules, and accounting requirements.

5. Controls are used to *measure and direct employee performance.* Among such controls are merit-rating systems, direct supervisory observation, and reports on output or scrap loss per employee.[3]

Formal controls have many other uses besides those listed. Such controls are needed to ensure profitability and survival, and they are spread throughout every aspect of organizations. But there are still many unresolved questions, such as: How much control should the organization exercise? What is the appropriate basis for an organization's control system (reward-centered or punishment-centered)? What types of control strategies are acceptable. Issues of organizational and societal control are intimately related to questions of values. In the People's Republic of China, for example, the intensive socialization of the people, along with the unique Chinese cultural heritage, have caused most of that country's citizens to agree on the right of the government to control many aspects of individual behavior.

Economics of Controls

Controls are a means

Formal controls should be recognized as *means* to help the organization achieve its desired results. The costs of formal control systems must be compared with their benefits just as are other organizational processes. Analysis of the economics of control systems, strategies, and practices involves three basic questions:

1. What are the costs vs. benefits of various amounts of formal controls?

2. What are the cost-benefit relationships of alternative strategies for controlling the same activity?

3. At what point or for what activities should controls be used?

The economic *benefit* of a formal control system is the difference between its costs and the improvement in performance it creates. For example, when the quality of output is unsatisfactory, is it more economical to: lower the span of control (that is, have more superiors more closely supervising fewer subordinates); give workers more pay as the quality of their work increases; substitute machines for humans; or relocate controls to detect errors earlier?

Cost-benefit model of control

A cost-benefit model of the economics of a formal control system is shown in Fig. 12.2. This model suggests that the manager and the organization have a problem of *trade-offs* in deciding what emphasis to place on formal controls. The *horizontal axis*, which indicates the intensity of the formal controls, varies from low to high. The *vertical axis* indicates the dollar costs or benefits of a control practice. For purposes of illustration, the *costs-of-control* curve is shown as a direct function of the amount of formal control. There could be,

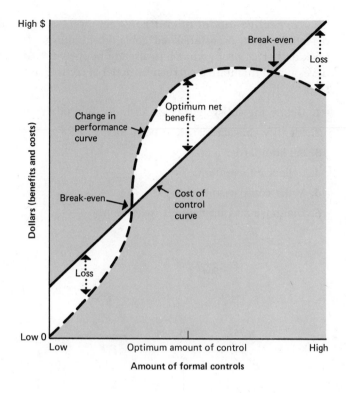

however, a proportionate relationship between increases in the number of rules and the costs of enforcing them.

We're assuming that it's possible to plot the changes in benefits for each degree of formal control. With a small amount of control, the control structure is so weak that the costs exceed its benefits. As the amounts of formal control increase, so does managerial effectiveness — up to a point. Beyond that point, continued increases in formal controls could decrease efficiency and lower performance. For example, management might acquire net benefits by reducing the span of control from 20 to 15 employees. But to further reduce the span of control from 15 to 8 employees would mean paying more supervisors, and the cost could outweigh the benefits to management. It could also create hostility among the workers, who might very well feel oversupervised and under too much pressure. This could lead to worker indifference, greater absenteeism, and higher turnover. The end result is likely to be that the increased formal controls greatly reduce performance.

Although management is not able to arrive at the *optimum amount* of control, as shown in Fig. 12.2, it can probably come pretty close to it.[4] Note that the two break-even points shown in Fig. 12.2 show the increasing and decreasing effectiveness of additional amounts of formal control.

**CORRECTIVE
MODEL OF
CONTROL**

The ***corrective model of control*** is the process of detecting and correcting deviations from preestablished goals or standards.[5] It relies heavily on feedback and reaction to what has already happened.[6] As shown in Fig. 12.3, to develop and maintain a corrective model of control requires six interconnected steps:

1. Define the subsystem (e.g., an individual or department).

2. Identify characteristics to be measured.

3. Set standards.

4. Collect information.

5. Make comparisons.

6. Diagnose and implement correction.

12.3
Corrective model of
control

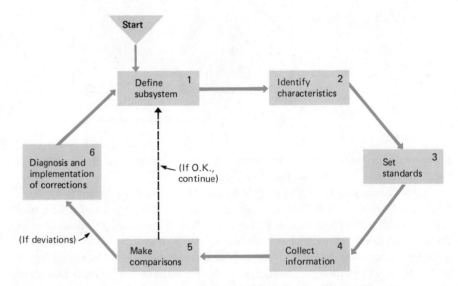

**1. Define the
Subsystem**

A formal control process might be created and maintained for a single employee, a department, or a whole organization. The controls could focus on specific inputs, production processes, or outputs. Controls on *inputs* often limit how much the raw materials used in the production process can vary from company standards. This reduces uncertainty about the quality and quantity of inputs into the production process. For example, at the Joseph P. Schlitz breweries, elaborate controls (including human inspections and laboratory testing) are used to make sure that the water and grains used in the production of beer meet predetermined standards.

The *production* process (operations system) consists of a web of controls: length of time for cooking the brew, temperature in the vats, sampling of the brew, laboratory testing of the brew in each stage of the production process, inspection of the beer prior to final packing, etc. Controls on the *output* of goods and services will range from levels of inventories to monitoring consumer attitudes toward the company's goods and services.

2. Identify
Characteristics

The *types* of information that can and should be obtained about the subsystem must be identified. Establishment of a formal corrective-control process requires early assessment of such questions as: What characteristics can be measured? How do the economic costs of obtaining information on each characteristic compare with the expected benefits? Does variation in the characteristic affect the performance objectives of the subsystem?

These questions suggest that managers should usually be selective in the characteristics measured. The "principle of selectivity," also known as Pareto's law, is often a useful guideline in the establishment of controls. The *principle of selectivity states that in any series of elements to be controlled, a small number of elements always accounts for a large number of effects.*[7] The control aspect of a Management-by-Objectives (MBO) system is based on this principle. The direct control of objectives makes possible the control of the few, but vital, elements that can account for major variations in performance. In brewing beer, for example, three of the critical characteristics are water, temperature, and length of brewing time. These three factors, among others, influence the beer quality.

3. Set Standards

Management should set standards for each characteristic measured. **Standards** are the criteria for evaluating the activities undertaken by the subsystem.

Since standards are often interrelated, there has to be considerable coordination between organizational departments. For example, a consulting firm whose goal is to provide only the highest-quality services must have strict standards for screening its personnel. These selection standards might include a minimum of a master's degree, three years of applicable experience, and the like.

Management is increasingly developing control systems based on performance standards. For example, American Airlines has established several types of standards for judging the quality of performance for each of its airport ticket offices.[8] The specific quantitative levels for each of these types of standards are summarized in Table 12.2.

12.2
Selected Standards for
American Airlines
Ticket Offices

■ *Waiting time:* At least 85 percent of the customers arriving at an airport ticket counter shall be waited on within five minutes.

■ *Baggage mishandlings:* Baggage mishandlings by airport ticket sales personnel, skycaps, and ticket-lift agents shall not exceed 1 per 100 checked and rechecked bags.

■ *Customer impact:* At least 90 percent of airport customer contacts shall be rated acceptable.

■ *Posted flight-arrival times:* At least 95 percent of the flight-arrival times posted in the "will arrive" columns on the arrival board shall be accurate to within 15 minutes of the time posted.

---

4. Collect Information   The collection of information is a means of obtaining measurements on each of the designated characteristics. Information can be collected by people or by mechanical means (as with a counting device). Information may also be collected by the individual or group whose performance is to be controlled. In some cases, this can result in a loss of meaningful control.

CASE STUDY

Union Planters National Bank   A few years ago the new president of Union Planters National Bank of Memphis, Tennessee, found considerable corruption among eight executives and even some clerks. Three of the former employees were sent to jail and several others were indicted. The president claims that executives were getting payoffs in exchange for making shaky multimillion dollar loans. Other employees were found to be simply embezzling money. Why did this happen? According to the new president, the lack of formal controls combined with low pay scales encouraged dishonesty. To solve these problems, he gave a hefty across-the-board pay increase to the bank employees and installed a new control system to prevent shaky loans and detect corruption quickly.[9]

Problems of distortion   Often employees are motivated to distort or conceal data that can be used as a basis for punishing, demoting, or criticizing themselves. For example, if American Airlines relied on its airport ticket counter employees for the data used to measure performance standards, we might expect some motivation to conceal or distort the data. This might become especially troublesome if the data were then used as a basis for punishing the employees.

Top managers create special departments to act as information collectors by auditing certain activities of other departments. A personnel department collects data to see that standards regarding pay raises are being met or that affirmative action guidelines are being followed. Similarly, a controller's department collects and analyzes information to see that expenditures of funds are completed according to certain standards.

**5. Make
Comparisons**

To *make comparisons* managers must see whether there is a difference between what *is being done* and what *should be done*. This means that they must compare their information with the organization's standards. (These standards might be contained in written rules, or computer programs, or be on tap in the managers' memory.) A purely comparative activity might occur when a graduate assistant of a professor:

1. obtains the output of student scores on a multiple-choice test from the college's computer center;

2. compares these scores with the professor's standards;

3. determines the extent to which the students' scores (performances) differ from the standards; and

4. gives these analyses to the professor for the evaluation of grades because the results are not consistent with the established standards.

If there appears to be no difference between what is happening and what should be happening, the department or individual normally continues to function without any change.

**6. Diagnosis and
Implementation of
Corrections**

This means assessing the types, amounts, and causes of the *deviations*, then choosing and applying a course of action that would eliminate those deviations.

Let's return to the American Airlines example and assume that mishandling of baggage has gotten above the acceptable standard. The reason for the increase would have to be diagnosed. Depending on the apparent causes of the deviations, management might consider such corrective mechanisms as further employee training, dismissal or demotion of certain employees, creation of incentive schemes, changed procedures, etc. These mechanisms would be used to correct the baggage-handling problem.

Implications　The fact that a characteristic *can* be controlled does not necessarily mean that it *should* be controlled. The corrective model of control just described emphasizes the "Principle of selectivity." This model suggests a framework by which managers can concentrate on the control of deviations or exceptions. This makes overmanaging less likely and encourages a more efficient use of a manager's scarce time. Within an organization, at any level, the specific nature of corrective and preventive controls is likely to be influenced by two key contingency variables: type of power and type of technology.

TYPE OF POWER AS A CONTINGENCY INFLUENCING THE CONTROL PROCESS　Different control practices are closely linked to different kinds and combinations of power used within the organization. As a general definition, **power** is the ability to limit choices. There are five types of power: reward, coercive, legitimate, referent, and expert[10] and an organization may use them in many different combinations. In Chapter 14 these types of power are also discussed in relation to leadership. Table 12.3 briefly defines each of these types of power.

12.3
Basic Types of Power in Relation to Control

- *Reward Power:* ability to control others by allocating benefits they value.
- *Coercive Power:* ability to control others by administering punishments.
- *Legitimate Power:* ability to control others on the basis of the formal authority in one's position.
- *Referent Power:* ability to control others on the basis of their identification with the individual.
- *Expert Power:* ability to control others on the basis of the knowledge and skills possessed by the individual.

Reward Power　**Reward power** is the ability to provide varying amounts and types of benefits to others. Superiors often grant different pay increases for different levels of performance by subordinates. Managements have often resisted the formation of unions in their organizations because collective bargaining tends to reduce their discretion to reward employees according to different levels of performance. Within business organizations, this is probably the most important type of power used to achieve "control" over people. It is usually considered desirable to base rewards on performance measures. This is because it should increase the motivation to perform well.[11] Management by objectives is one system that attempts to link rewards directly to performance.

Coercive power is the ability to administer punishments to others. In the political system, obvious forms of coercive power include physical punishments (e.g., inflicting pain, deformity, or death), and the forceful control over basic human needs (e.g., prisons). Coercive power in business organizations is commonly expressed through dismissals or threats of dismissal, demotions, and social pressure.

Coercive Power

Social pressure is a subtle form of coercive power. A superior may cut off communications with a subordinate until the latter "shapes up." Or the superior may monitor the subordinate's performance. This is what occurred when a senior salesman, who had been with a certain firm for 25 years, decided not to give his "fair share" to the firm's United Way drive. The company had a schedule indicating each employee's "fair share." This was used to justify the company's claim that it was socially responsible. The flow of communication from upper management to the salesman was direct and intense. The salesman wasn't threatened with dismissal or demotion, but appeals for cooperation on a moral basis created more and more pressure on him. First, his immediate supervisor appealed to him on two occasions. No change! Then there were two sessions with the department manager. The salesman still did not pledge, but he weakened! Finally, a 30-minute session with the vice-president of marketing did it. The salesman made out a new pledge in the "recommended" amount.

*Use of social
pressure*

The employees in this department came to interpret the firm's recommendation as a requirement. The salesman seemed to react to the social pressure he had received as a form of psychological punishment. In this situation, as in most others, it is highly probable that other types of power were also operating.

Control systems based on coercive power tend to create job dissatisfaction, apathy, or aggressive behavior in those being coerced. Thus a paradox is created. Management often claims that coercive power is necessary to get employees to cooperate in helping the organization to attain its goals. But if employees feel excessively coerced, they may become uncooperative. They may actually be motivated to withdraw from their work, to become passive and

*Problems with
coercive power*

indifferent, creating an even more difficult control problem. To reduce their frustrations, they may also militantly strike back.

The massive unionization in the late 1930s was partly a reaction to the coercive power used by some business organizations. In the public sector, some segments of the population view court-ordered busing as an exercise of coercive power by the courts and other government agencies.

Legitimate Power

Legitimate power is the right of a person or group to influence the actions of others. Faculty members have a legitimate right to assign students grades on the basis of academic performance.

Employees who believe in the institutions of private property and the basic framework of a free-enterprise system may feel that for a superior to control their behavior to obtain profits is quite appropriate. In contrast, employees who believe in public ownership and control of the means of production may interpret managerial controls over their work as a form of exploitation. In this case, the superior would be seen as having little legitimate power. This makes the superior's control of such individuals much more difficult.

Referent Power

Referent power refers to the desire of one individual or group to identify with or be like another person or group. It is often expressed by copying the actions, style, and beliefs of that individual or group. A manager who defines getting ahead as obtaining successively higher positions in an organization is prone to control through referent power. This individual, placed under an effective manager, may rapidly develop many of the same skills and philosophy of his or her superior. This occurs because of the strong psychological identification with the superior and the need for recognition from that person. In such cases, referent power may be functional for both the individual and the organization.

Expert Power

Expert power refers to a person's level of knowledge and skills. A person gains expert power through special experience, training, reputation, or demonstrated ability. Professional programs in colleges and universities (e.g., business, engineering, and law) develop expert power in their students. Many positions in business organizations rely on various types of expertise, e.g., engineers, accountants, statisticians, market researchers, skilled tradesmen, and professional managers.

The degree to which different combinations of power help create effective control systems can vary between organizations as well as between departments of a single organization.[12]

Figure 12.4 shows a hypothetical graph with the relative emphasis on each type of power in organic and mechanistic management systems. Organic systems are usually effective in unstable, complex, and changing task environments. As you may recall from Chapter 9, **organic systems** exist in organizations that are usually decentralized, rely on employee participation in the decision-making process, and continuously monitor and adapt to changes in the task environment. Mechanistic systems, by contrast, tend to be effective when the tasks are routine and the environment is stable. **Mechanistic systems** exist in organizations that are usually centralized, rely very little on employee participation, and emphasize the development and use of rules and regulations.

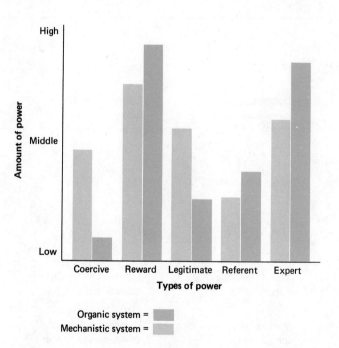

12.4
Types of power in
mechanistic vs. organic
systems

Figure 12.4 also suggests that there is likely to be more emphasis on coercive power in a mechanistic system than in an organic one. Formal authority is the basis for intergrating and controlling tasks in a mechanistic system. On the other hand, the organic system relies on mutual trust and problem-solving to obtain integration and control of activities. Expert power, as possessed by engineers and other professionals, is likely to be given more emphasis in the organic system. This emphasizes the importance of special abilities, self-control, and the contributions of professional expertise to solving the firm's problems. In contrast, the mechanistic system seems to place higher values on the loyalty and obedience of employees to the organization and on legitimate power.

12.4
*Control Techniques in
Mechanistic Versus
Organic Systems*

Control Techniques	Type of System	
	Mechanistic system	*Organic system*
■ Use of top-down orders and controls	High	Low to moderate
■ Use of detailed rules and regulations	High	Low to moderate
■ Use of job descriptions	Detailed, emphasizes activities	General, emphasizes objectives to be achieved
■ Use of participants' self-control	Low	High
■ Use of suggestions, persuasion, advice, and information-sharing	Low to moderate	High
■ Use of shared goals and participation in decision-making	Low to moderate	High
■ Use of performance appraisals	Top-down, little participation	Interactions between superiors and subordinates
■ Use of budgets	Very detailed, top-down, little flexibility	Somewhat detailed, developed with interaction between levels, more flexible
■ Use of training and socialization	Limited	Extensive
■ Use of rewards	Emphasis on monetary rewards	Emphasis on monetary and nonmonetary rewards

Based on the differences in the use of different combinations of types of power, Table 12.4 highlights the control techniques likely to be emphasized in mechanistic vs. organic systems. All of these control techniques are found in organizations and departments — to some degree. The key difference is in their *relative* emphasis and application in mechanistic vs. organic systems.[13]

TYPE OF
TECHNOLOGY AS
AN INFLUENCE ON
THE CONTROL
PROCESS

Technology and
Types of Controls

The types of controls found in the operations (production) system of an organization are influenced by the type of technology used: unit; mass production; or continuous process.[14] As explained in the previous chapter, *unit-production technology* is the custom manufacturing of individual items. The control system is likely to emphasize the employee's self-control, managerial surveillance, and control through detailed plans. There is likely to be only a slight use of mechanical controls.

Mass-production technology is the manufacture of large volumes of identical or similar goods. The control system shifts toward impersonal rules and regulations and mechanical controls, e.g., assembly-line-paced work.

Continuous-process technology is characterized by an ongoing flow of activities for transforming inputs into outputs. Most of the physical activities are performed by machines. The workers do not handle the material itself, but monitor it via dials. This type of technology relies heavily on mechanical controls. Machines are likely to control other machines. These controls are based primarily on the corrective model of control presented earlier.

The manufacturing plant of the Sara Lee Company at Deerfield, Illinois, has a continuous-process technology and provides one example of mechanical control. The company's computer system is used to mix, bake, package, freeze, and store 12 different kinds of cakes. It can even start goods on their way to the store. "Their computers direct operations at about 15,000 points in the plant, issue 180,000 instructions every three seconds, monitor some 300 variables in the cake-baking process, and scan 200 incoming messages per second."[15]

The patterns of controls with each type of technology are shown in Table 12.5. The means for controlling production of goods in an organization can vary from personal (self) controls to impersonal (mechanical) controls. Personal control may be possible because of the individual's extensive training and socialization. Craftsmen (such as tool and die makers, computer programmers, and electricians) and professionals may be classified at this end of the continuum of control. These types of controls are strongly emphasized in unit-production technology. At the other extreme of the continuum, there is a

12.5
Technology and
Patterns of Controls

	Type of Technology		
Continuum of control	Unit	Mass production	Continuous process
Self	High	Low	Low
Managerial surveillance	Medium	High	Low
Rules and regulations	Low	High	High
Mechanical process	Low	Medium	High

Adapted from E. Burack, "A Commentary and Critique of Four Organizational Behavioral Models." In A. Negandi and J. P. Schwitter (eds), *Organization Behavior Models*, Kent, Ohio: Bureau of Economic and Business Research, Kent State University, 1970, pp. 11–14.

strong emphasis on the use of machines, such as computers, to control the operations (production) processes. These controls are likely to be found in continuous-process technologies. Of course, there are a variety of control strategies between these extremes, e.g., surveillance by managers and reliance on rules and regulations.

In sum, unit technology emphasizes personal control; continuous-process technology is characterized primarily by impersonal control. Mass-production technology is a blending of personal and impersonal control. Within the operations system managers need to use controls that are consistent with the type of technology being used.[16]

There is no ideal control system. This is consistent with the contingency approach. Rather, the "ideal" control system will depend on such contingency factors as: the technology used to produce the goods and services; the values of the participants; the types of power in the organization, and the degree of uncertainty and change in the organization. We have zeroed in on two of these contingency variables here — type of power and type of technology.

COMMON CONTROL STRATEGIES USED BY MANAGERS

In this part, we review six strategies of control used by managers: human-input control; reward-punishment system; formal structure; policies and rules; budgets; and machine controls. As suggested in Fig. 12.5, these strategies are not mutually exclusive. In fact, in an effective control system they are closely linked to each other. To control many activities usually requires that two (or more) of these strategies be used at the same time. In other words, a combination of strategies allows greater control than if each strategy was used separately.

Our discussion emphasizes the strategies for controlling an organization's employees and managers. There are two reasons for this emphasis. First, for most organizations, human resources are the greatest cost factor. Second, controlling human resources (labor) can be an effective means of controlling the other resources used to create the organization's outputs.

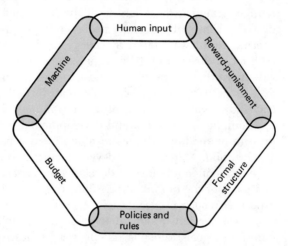

12.5
The chain of control
strategies used by
managers

**Human-Input
Control Strategy**

Effectiveness in organizations improves when managers control the instability, variability, and spontaneity of individuals. Personnel selection techniques screen employees for each position in the organization. Training and socialization programs change the skills and attitudes of employees. These are two means for controlling unwanted behaviors and attitudes. If the organization is to prosper, selection and training or socialization controls are needed.

Selection

Selection controls are used in hiring people and promoting or transferring employees within the organization. In a scarce labor market, few candidates are available. The organization may find it necessary to lower its standards or use fewer controls. To offset the reduced quality of the work force, management might increase the amount of training.

How controls are used in the selection process depends partly on how much decision-making power the manager using them is supposed to exercise. Two interrelated aspects of discretion and power are important. First, how much can the manager's decision harm or help the organization? Second, how much formal power does the manager have to use and allocate the organization's resources? For example, compared to the controls used in selecting marketing executives who develop sales strategies, control budgets, and supervise others, controls used in selecting file clerks are minimal.

*Training and
socialization*

Training and socialization is the organization's conscious attempt to change the skills, knowledge, attitudes, values, or motivations of individuals. In most types of training, the interests of the individual and their organizations are probably compatible.[17] Many professional programs (such as business, engineering, and law) offered by colleges and universities serve the interests of both the students and their organizations. These professional programs provide more than a specific set of skills and technical knowledge. Students are exposed to various social controls, both formal and informal, that can influence individual attitudes, motivations, and values.

Company orientation and developmental programs are usually designed to form or modify attitudes to make them consistent with the needs of the organization. Management development, in contrast to technical and skill training, is often intended to develop a sense of commitment to the philosophy and goals of the organization.[18] Blue-collar employees are likely to have little exposure to such programs.

The effort an organization puts into socializing individual values, attitudes, and goals depends on the results desired – which may range from relative indifference to intensive indoctrination. This is suggested by Fig. 12.6. Chaos and instability might result if managers had highly incompatible goals, values, and attitudes. At the other extreme is the absolute conformity of the "organization man" stereotype. Intensive conditioning may lead to a static organization, one that is unable to adapt and change.

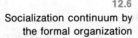

12.6
Socialization continuum by
the formal organization

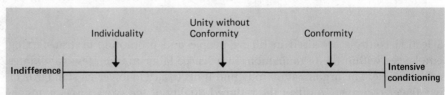

The ideal strategy might be to employ deliberate conditioning to create *unity without conformity.*[19] Management by Objectives (MBO) programs may provide the means of achieving unity without conformity. The open discussion of objectives, whether written or unwritten, is encouraged. Then an effort is made to reach agreement on which objectives should be pursued. Finally, the individuals are given some discretion for working toward the objectives in a manner of their own choosing.

Rewards and punishments through formal performance appraisals are another control strategy used to direct individuals' behavior. As suggested earlier, the form and effectiveness of such systems varies greatly. Here we present a broad framework showing the range of reward-and-punishment combinations from an extremely mechanistic organization to an extremely organic system.

Reward-Punishment Control Strategy

In a *mechanistic* system there are attempts to control employees by emphasizing *extrinsic* rewards for desired performance. Extrinsic rewards are wages, pension plans, some types of status symbols (size of office, access to information, etc.), and job security. At times, the typical mechanistic system may rely on certain forms of punishment, such as demotions or dismissal. Many business organizations, farmers' cooperatives, some peacetime military organizations, and labor unions make use of this pattern of rewards and punishments.

Mechanistic vs. organic systems

In *organic* management systems, by contrast, there is an attempt to control employee behavior through *intrinsic rewards* (satisfying work), self-control (personal sense of responsibility for one's work), interpersonal control (through advice and suggestions by those with the expertise), and a reasonable degree of extrinsic rewards. Organizations approaching this control pattern include research and development organizations (especially for managers and skilled personnel), colleges and universities (especially for faculty and administrators), and voluntary and professional associations. You might also refer back to Table 12.4 for a review of the control processes and techniques in mechanistic vs. organic systems.

Punishment is not likely to be a dominant control mechanism in most organizations.[20] It is simply not a very effective method of controlling behavior. Individuals and organizations occasionally use punishment for the following types of reasons.[21]

Use of punishment

1. It may suppress undesired behavior when all other means for modifying it have failed.

2. It may be an effective deterrent even when it has little actual deterrent effect on those being punished (it may reinforce conformity to prevailing standards by other group members).

3. The taking away of rewards may become psychologically indistinguishable from punishment (e.g., failure to receive a regular increase in salary may be considered a penalty).

4. The desire of individuals to "get even" for harm done to them may cause them to seek to punish others. Thus, revenge or retribution may itself become a source of reward.

**Formal-Structure
Control Strategy**

*Patterns of
authority*

Formal organizational structures are attempts by top management to control the pattern of authority.[22] Organizations typically have formal, written job descriptions that describe the responsibilities of each position. In mechanistic management systems, job descriptions will be very specific. In organic management systems, job descriptions are likely to be broader and may consist of only the major responsibilities of the individual in the position. In either case, job descriptions set limits on the formal authority of the individual.

*Flows of
communication*

Formal structures also establish control by prescribing flows of communication. The collection, evaluation, and transmission of information can vitally influence organizational and individual performance. If there is too much information, those receiving it may feel swamped. On the other hand, inadequate amounts of information (or the wrong information) can result in poor decisions and performance.

Formal communication systems frequently follow the organizational hierarchy. Formal structures can specify lateral and diagonal communication and coordination flows as well. This is apparent in the project form of organization and in some support or auditing units. For example, the personnel department may be required to exercise varying degrees of control over certain activities, such as affirmative action. If the personnel department has a high degree of control over affirmative action, it has functional authority over this particular activity.

Individuals may disagree on the amount and appropriateness of formal control to be exercised by a department. These disagreements can cause interdepartmental misunderstandings, political processes, and conflicts — and may decrease the effectiveness of the whole organization.[23]

Another structural variable affecting the control system is the span of control (the number of people reporting to a superior). Changing a manager's span of control partially controls how he or she controls. All else being equal, it may be possible to increase the control over the activities of each lower level by *narrowing* the span of control. A *wider* span of control might prevent managers from supervising subordinates too closely, creating too much subordinate dependence, and becoming too involved with subordinates on a social and emotional basis.

Policies and rules are also major strategies for exercising control over many organizational activities and functions. They define how much discretion a position or department has and indicate required actions.

A *policy* is a guide for carrying out action. A policy is general rather than specific, and expresses a condition or relation. Thus, a promotion policy might be worded: "Promotions will be based on merit."

A *rule* specifies a course of action that must be followed. It is established to create uniformity of action and may or may not be prohibitive. An example of a rule is: "Courses may be dropped by the student up through the third week of classes without a grade being assigned."

Flexibility is the most basic difference between policies and rules. Policies tend to be made by top-level managers. Rule-making occurs at all management levels.[24] Policy-making at General Motors, for example, is the responsibility of the Executive and Finance committees. These committees consist entirely of the company's directors. Subcommittees of the Executive and Finance committees include representation from major divisions and departments of the entire organization. They frequently develop rules to implement the firm's general policies.

Rules may have both desirable and undesirable consequences for the formal organization. The following list summarizes the major consequences of rules:

1. Rules *reflect formal authority.* They help structure relationships and ensure action consistent with the organization's purposes. For example, rules may define the relative authority of the personnel department and other managers in the organization with respect to the hiring of employees.

2. Rules may *reinforce apathy* by defining the minimum acceptable standards for subordinates. For example, a rule may specify that employees who do not average 300 units of output per week will be subject to a disciplinary layoff. This type of rule may well create negative attitudes toward management and simply motivate employees to produce 300 units and no more.

3. Rules may inadvertently result in a *"means-end reversal"* for the organization. A rule may become a goal (an end) rather than a means to an end. For example, a rule may state that the organization will stop serving its clientele at 5:00 P.M. When one of the authors was standing in line at a library on a Saturday afternoon, the clock struck 5:00 P.M. Even though several people protested, the clerk cited the rule and refused to check out any more books.

4. Rules can have a *domino effect* (rules beget rules) as management attempts to deal with hostile worker groups. For example, rules may specify the number of vacation days employees receive based on number of years worked. Conflict might arise between management and workers over how this vacation time should be taken — all at once or spread out. If specific requests cannot be worked out cooperatively and with some give and take on both sides, an elaborate network of formal rules may be developed to specify how vacation time can be taken.

**Budget Control
Strategy**

Budgets define and link proposed expenditures with desired future objectives.[25] Budgets are usually expressed in terms of dollars. Production budgets may be expressed in units (hours of labor per unit, machine downtime per thousand hours of running time, etc.).

**Corrective and
preventive control
aspects**

The control aspect of budgets may be either corrective or preventive. In the *corrective* model, considerable effort may be spent on identifying *deviations* from the budget. Deviations serve as a basis for subsequent managerial action. This action is to identify the causes for the deviations or decide whether the budget itself should be changed.[26]

The power of a budget, especially as a *preventive* control mechanism, depends on whether all parties view it as an informal contract that they have agreed to. One study investigated this and other issues by mailing a comprehensive questionnaire to lower-level supervisors to obtain their views about how the company budget was used.[27] They were asked: "Do you feel that frequently budgets or standards are a club held over the head of the supervisor to force better performance?" Twenty percent of the 204 respondents replied yes and 68 percent answered no.

Those who must live by budgets usually find their budgets acceptable. Others, however, regard budgets quite negatively. Budgets may also be viewed with fear and hostility,[28] usually when an organization enforces its budgeting system with punishment and the threat of punishment.

Acceptability of budgets

As a means of control, machines have developed through several major stages. First, they extended the capability of workers, enlarging individuals' physical control over certain activities. Second, workers and machines responded to information from each other, creating a mutual control system. Third, a new threshold was reached with automation. Machines control other machines, as in the case of robots. Now machines perform the managerial control function and participate with managers in the control process. For example, computers in oil refineries are used to monitor and make automatic adjustments in the operations process. These adjustments are based on data collected from numerous stages of the refinery process.

Machine Control Strategy

Stages of development

As discussed in the previous chapter, there has been a steady shift toward machine controls in the operations system. The shift was initially from human to machine control of nonhuman resources (e.g., using automatic sensors instead of visual inspection in the production of steel). With the advent of advanced mass-production technology, machines supplemented rules and regulations for controlling production workers. Now, in continuous-process operations, machines control machines with no direct application of human energy, skill, intelligence, or control.

Shift to machine controls in operations systems

The impact of automatic machine control on management has been reported in a number of studies. One researcher found that the introduction of an advanced automated system in one large factory reduced the number of middle-management jobs by 34 percent.[29] **Automation** refers to processes that are primarily self-regulating and are able to operate independently in a wide range of conditions. Automation usually involves joining machines that perform work with other machines (especially some type of computer) that perform a control function.[30] There are several instances of advanced machine control in the automobile industry. Chevrolet installed in its brake plant at Saginaw, Michigan, an automated system that controls four cranes, records inventory, directs five miles of conveyors, and diagnoses tool problems for the maintenance staff. Chrysler's computer-controlled system in its Syracuse, New

Impact of automation

York, plant expands or contracts a boring tool to adjust for the temperature and wear condition of the tool. The system feeds the exact diameters of finished pistons to the machines bearing the cylinder blocks so they can adjust their bits.[31]

ORGANIZATIONAL
POLITICS: THE
CONFOUNDING
FACTOR

Organizational politics is the use of power by individuals or interest groups to increase or protect: (1) their control over resources and (2) their authority to set and control the objectives being sought with those resources.[32] Organizational politics are most obvious when individuals or interest groups disagree about objectives (goals) and/or the best means for achieving them. These situations were described in the discussion of the contingency organizational decision model (Fig. 9.9) in Chapter 9.

Table 12.6 identifies types of organizational situations that commonly involve issues of control and that are influenced by organizational politics.[33] Major changes are associated with very high levels of organizational politics. This is probably because reorganization efforts create the greatest amount of uncertainty and concern relating to the amount of power, resources, tasks, and responsibilities for every person and interest group affected by the changes.

For our purposes, an **interest group** is two or more individuals who perceive themselves as having common objectives that can be best achieved

Types of Situations	Degree of Concern with Issues of Control	12.6 Types of Internal Organizational Situations Commonly Influenced by Organizational Politics
■ Reorganization changes	Very high	
■ Interdepartmental relations	Very high	
■ Budget allocation and use	High	
■ Key personnel changes	High	
■ Setting goals and objectives	Moderate to high	
■ Establishing performance standards and reward systems	Moderate to high	
■ Policy and rule changes	Moderate to high	

through united action.[34] The reasons for forming interest groups vary tremendously in organizations. For example, a proposed major reorganization in a firm might cause the marketing department, production department, finance department, personnel department, etc., to evaluate the proposed changes in terms of how each department will be affected. If the finance department, let's say, expects to be negatively affected by the change, they are likely to oppose it on the grounds that it will hurt overall organizational effectiveness. This might put the department in a position to bargain with higher management over the proposed change. In most cases, the bargaining involves issues of control.[35] For example, a proposal to centralize decision-making authority is really a proposal to decrease the control that a department has over the use and allocation of resources.

In Chapter 3, we noted that bargaining is a central political strategy used by management in dealing with groups *external* to the organization. For some types of control issues that are *internal* to organizations (see Table 12.6), organizational politics uses a variety of bargaining tactics and approaches. The political tactics used by individuals are developed in the leadership chapter (Chapter 14). Organizational politics are generally associated with conflict. Thus, the chapter on conflict (Chapter 17) examines interpersonal and intergroup conflict.

In sum, organizational politics is a confounding factor that influences certain issues in organizations. The political processes often involve bargaining over the relative control of resources, determination of objectives, and the like.

SUMMARY

The formal control process serves to *prevent* and *correct* unwanted deviations from goals and standards. The control process is used by management in a variety of ways to achieve goals. Contrary to some popular ideas, however, more controls do not necessarily lead to a more effective organization. First, controls cost money and may not pay for themselves through increased effectiveness. Second, controls, unless carefully designed, can lead to negative reactions by those who must abide by them.

As we saw in the preview case, Lois learned over time how to effectively use various controls in combination with the other essential management processes. This chapter should help Lois and you to more effectively perform the managerial roles of *disturbance-handler*, *monitor*, and *leader*. A few examples will illustrate these ties. The feedback model of control should be helpful in performing the disturbance-handler role. The discussions of types of power as a contingency variable as well as the reward-punishment control strategy should provide you with knowledge useful in performing the leader role. Finally, the monitor role should benefit from the discussions of formal structure and budgets as control strategies.

The corrective model of control probably represents the most common view of the formal control process. The basic "steps" in this process are used to correct deviations from defined standards through feedback. Two of the key contingencies likely to directly influence the control strategies used are the types of power found within the organization and the type of technology employed.

The chapter has provided a description and explanation of six strategies of control used by managers: (1) the control of personnel through selection and training/socialization; (2) the use of reward-punishment systems; (3) the formal structure, which helps establish control through position descriptions, specification of communication flows, the creation of special units to audit various activities of other units, and the span of control; (4) the development of policies and rules, which are used to guide behavior and decision-making; (5) the use of budgets; and (6) the application of machine controls. These strategies are interrelated. Managers usually employ *combinations* of them to achieve the control desired.

KEYWORDS

automation
budgets
coercive power
control
corrective control
corrective model of control
expert power
interest group
legitimate power
mechanistic system

organic system
organizational politics
policy
power
preventive control
principle of selectivity
referent power
reward power
rule
standards

DISCUSSION QUESTIONS

1. Control has been defined as a superior dominating the work life of his or her subordinates. Discuss this statement in the light of your new knowledge of the control process.

2. How might the control process used on your instructor differ from that used on a sales clerk at the local McDonald's?

3. How might the control process in a marketing research department differ from that in a production department that had the task of bagging potato chips?

4. Drawing on your own work experience, develop an example of the application of the corrective model of control. Try to identify each of the "steps" in the corrective model of control as shown in Fig. 12.2.

5. In what ways are control processes likely to differ between mechanistic and organic management systems?

6. Evaluate this statement: "The more the control processes become like those in the organic management system, the more likely they are to be effective."

7. How does type of power act as a contingency factor influencing the use of control processes and strategies?

8. Why are formal controls important to management?

9. Evaluate this statement: "The fewer the controls in an organization, the greater the likelihood that it will be effective."

Management Incidents and Cases

Jim Richards was the purchasing manager in a highly centralized company, the Rigid Corporation. Feeling a sense of hopelessness in this situation, he quit and has just taken a similar job with the Hart Manufacturing Company, which was reorganized two years ago. A planning and control department was created, and Richards was told that a policy of decentralization of authority has been adopted. Richards' predecessor has just been transferred and is not available to instruct him about his new job. Joe Urban, who has served on a continuing basis as a consultant and advisor to the company, was asked to orient Richards. The orientation went much as follows:

CONTROL AND FREEDOM FOR A PURCHASING MANAGER*

Urban   From what you tell me, you will probably find that the methods of management at the Hart Manufacturing Company are almost

---

* Adapted from Raymond Villers, "Control and Freedom in a Decentralized Company," *Harvard Business Review* (March-April): 89–96. Copyright © 1954 by the President and Fellows of Harvard College. All rights reserved.

exactly the opposite of those you have been used to at the Rigid Corporation. You will find that no one here will check on how you are doing your job.

Ralph, whom you met this morning, is the head of the planning and control department. He will tell you what materials are needed for production and when. Every six months he will give you a general purchasing program and you will place the orders. You get the specifications from the engineering department. You select the suppliers yourself. You decide yourself about what prices you want to pay.

You will find that for most materials used, we have standard prices. The variance between the price you pay and the standards are carefully followed up by Ralph's department and reported both to you and to your vice-president, who keeps in touch with the market and will step in if he feels that the prices you are paying are too high. Incidentally, if you find a way of getting lower prices, he will step in too — to congratulate you.

But, in any case, he will step in *after* you, under your own responsibility, have placed the purchase order, not before — unless you turn to him for advice, which you may do at any time. In some exceptional cases, he may take the initiative, but you will find this a very rare occurrence.

For planning purposes, the weeks of the year are designated by consecutive numbers. Every week you will receive a release schedule which will tell you what materials, on order but not yet delivered, are needed for production during each of the following eight weeks. As you know, we are short of materials. This release schedule is therefore a very important matter. Check it carefully when you receive it. If you do not call Ralph within a few days after you have received it, you are considered as having accepted it.

It then becomes your responsibility to supply the materials on time. Any delay will disrupt production. The cost of the disruption will be evaluated by the planning and control department and will be charged against your department.

Richards You know how suppliers are. They may say yes and yet they don't deliver. They may just say perhaps. What do you want me to tell Ralph, when I receive his release schedule, in a situation where I am 50-50 sure?

Urban   Your position is fully appreciated. But you must realize that in the whole organization, you are *the one* who is in the best position to evaluate the situation. Now, someone has to take responsibility. As you know, a plant cannot have a "perhaps" production schedule or "perhaps" tools on hand or a "perhaps" machine setup. It has to be yes or no. Sometimes we will be disappointed. Everyone agrees that it can happen that you will say yes, and yet the material will not be there on time. But that doesn't lessen your responsibility.

The real issue is how often it will occur and what the damage will be. At the end of the year, two accounts will tell the whole story. The price-variance account will show how active you have been in getting good prices. The time-lost account will show how reliable your deliveries to the production department have been.

In addition, of course, we expect that your materials will be up to specifications — and that you will not systematically protect yourself by refusing to accept Ralph's release schedules.

Richards   What do I do if I think that I cannot get the material in time?

Urban   You call Ralph and tell him so. Nine times out of ten, even more often than that, you will settle the matter between yourselves by changing the production schedule. Your release schedules are issued weekly for an eight-week period. As a rule, this gives you at least four weeks' advance notice, inasmuch as we avoid changing the coming four weeks unless it is absolutely necessary. Now, if you and Ralph cannot see eye to eye, the matter will have to be referred to the executive committee, but you will find that Ralph is pretty good at solving problems.

By the way, let me make this clear to you. Ralph is no more your boss than you are his. If the foreman of the tool room needs to purchase anything, you know that he is not permitted to go and buy it outside. He must send you a requisition. Now, this does not make you his boss. You are the head of a service department, available to service him. Ralph is the head of another service department. The release schedule he sends you is a service he renders to you and to the whole organization. It is important for you to understand the spirit in which his department functions.

You will find that the control you are submitted to is very detailed, but it is objective. You receive an assignment. You may accept it or reject it. But if you accept, you must perform. There is no excuse for a failure — no argument either. If you fail, the damage is evaluated. We all make mistakes. The important point is to avoid making too many mistakes and also to understand fully that this extensive control is the necessary balance to the great freedom of action you are being given.

No one will ask you what time you arrive in your office, why you did not show up last Thursday, or whether you have neglected to write to this or that supplier. You are your own boss as far as your function is concerned.

Questions   **1.** What do you think of the control processes and techniques used on the purchasing manager? Explain.

2. What advantages and problems would you anticipate with these control processes and techniques?

3. How would you diagnose the control processes and techniques used with respect to the two contingency factors discussed in this chapter, including type of power and type of technology.

SUPERVISORY CONTROLS You are the manager of an accounting department for a major industrial firm. Last year you hired a recent college graduate with no supervisory experience to be supervisor of one of your most troublesome sections. In the past, this section has been inefficient, costly, and in general poorly organized. You gave your new supervisor a free hand to reorganize the ten-person section.

Some months later this section was described by a manager as "the most efficient, well-run, disciplined section in the whole firm." However, several employees in this section have recently asked for transfers, and two senior-level employees have retired prematurely. In informal conversations, they have revealed that they cannot perform their duties as they wish.

1. What control concepts and techniques might account for these changes?

2. What "human factors" might need to be considered from "here on out" to make sure performance of the section remains at a high level?

REFERENCES

1. A. Carlisle, "The Golfer." *California Management Review* **22,** 1, 1979, 42–52.

2. G. Giglioni and A. Bedeian, "A Conspectus of Management Control Theory: 1900–1972." *Academy of Management Journal* **17,** 1974, 292–305.

3. W. Jerome, III, *Executive Control: The Catalyst.* New York: John Wiley, 1961.

4. J. Emery, *Organizational Planning and Control Systems: Theory and Technology.* New York: Macmillan, 1969.

5. E. Lawler, III, and J. Rhode, *Information and Control in Organizations.* Pacific Palisades, CA: Goodyear, 1976.

6. G. Hofstede, "The Poverty of Management Control Philosophy." *Academy of Management Review* **3,** *1978, 450–461.*

7. R. Boyce, *Integrated Management Controls.* London: Longman's, Green, 1967.

8. M. Miller, *Objectives and Standards: An Approach to Planning and Control.* New York: American Management Association, 1956, 77–78.

9. "How a Memphis Bank Stopped Its Crime Wave." *Business Week.* October 25, 1975, 63, 68.

10. J. French, Jr., and B. Raven, "The Bases of Social Power," in D. Cartwright and A. Zander (eds.). *Group Dynamics: Research and Theory.* New York: Harper and Row, 1969, pp. 607–623.

11. R. Aldag and A. Brief, *Task Design and Employee Motivation.* Glenview: Scott, Foresman, 1979.

12. W. Ouchi, "A Conceptual Framework for the Design of Organizational Control Mechanisms." *Management Science* **25,** 1979, 833–848; S. Kerr and J. Slocum, "Controlling the Performance of People in Organizations," in W. Starbuck and P. Nystrom (eds.), *Handbook of Organizations*, Vol. II, Oxford Univeristy Press, 1981.

13. P. Connor, *Organizations: Theory and Design.* Chicago: Science Research Associates, 1980.

14. J. Woodward (ed.), *Industrial Organization: Behavior and Control.* New York: Oxford University Press, 1970.

15. G. Bell (ed.), *Organizations and Human Behavior.* Englewood Cliffs, NJ: Prentice-Hall, 1967, p. 9.

16. W. Ouchi, "The Transmission of Control Through the Organizational Hierarchy." *Academy of Management Journal* **21,** 1978, 173–192.

17. E. Flamholtz, "Organizational Control Systems as a Management Tool." *California Management Review* **22,** 2, 1979, 50–59.

18. W. Scott, "Executive Development as an Instrument of Higher Control." *Academy of Management Journal* **6,** 1963, 191–203.

19. F. Kast and J. Rosenzweig, *Organization and Management: A Systems and Contingency Approach* (3rd ed.). New York: McGraw-Hill, 1979, pp. 451–454.

20. A. Grimes, "Authority, Power, Influence and Social Control: A Theoretical Synthesis." *Academy of Management Review* **3,** 1978, 724–735.

21. P. Blau, *Exchange and Power In Social Life.* New York: John Wiley, 1964, pp. 225–226.

22. H. Mintzberg, "Structure In 5's: A Synthesis of the Research on Organization Design." *Management Science* **26,** 1980, 322–341.

23. I. MacMillian, *Strategy Formulation:* Political Concepts. St. Paul, MN: West Publishing Co., 1978.

24. L. Sayles, "The Many Dimensions of Control." *Organizational Dynamics* **1,** 1972, 21–31.

25. A. Wildavsky, *Budgeting: A Comparative Theory of Budgetary Processes.* Boston: Little, Brown and Co., 1975.

26. A. Stedry, *Budget Control and Cost Behavior.* Englewood Cliffs, NJ: Prentice-Hall, 1965, pp. 46–50.

27. B. Sord and G. Welsch, *Managerial Planning and Control.* Austin: University of Texas, Bureau of Business Research, 1964, pp. 93–99.

28. C. Argyris, *The Impact of Budgets on People.* New York: Controllership Foundation, 1952

29. T. Whisler and C. Myers, *The Impact of Computers on Management.* Cambridge: M.I.T. Press, 1967.

30. A. Toffler, *The Third Wave.* New York: William Marrow and Co., 1980.

31. "The Smart Machine Revolution." *Business Week,* July 5, 1976, 38–44.

32. A. Cobb and N. Marguiles, "Organization Development: A Political Perspective." *Academy of Management Review* **6,** 1981, 49–59.

33. D. Madison, R. Allen, L. Porter, P. Renwick, and B. Mayes, "Organizational Politics: An Exploration of Managers' Perceptions." *Human Relations* **33,** 1980, 79–100.

34. S. Bacharach and E. Lawler, *Power and Politics in Organizations: The Social Psychology of Conflict, Coalitions and Bargaining.* San Francisco: Jossey-Bass, 1980.

35. J. Perry and H. Angle, "The Politics of Organizational Boundary Roles in Collective Bargaining." *Academy of Management Review* **4,** 1979, 487–496.

Part V focuses on the people variables that managers must consider in order that employees may be attracted to the organization and remain productive once they join. Major topics included in this part include motivation, leadership, communication, groups, and conflict management.

Chapter 13, "Motivation," focuses on what causes employees to behave as they do. The ways by which managers can ensure that employees are striving to meet the organization's goals are discussed. Three approaches to motivation are presented: individual, job, and organizational. The individual's wants and needs are described in terms of Maslow's hierarchy of needs. How the characteristics of the job affect the motivation of workers is discussed in the section on job enrichment. Job-enrichment strategies are described that permit the employee to gain satisfaction and achieve greater productivity. Finally, the Porter-Lawler model of motivation is presented to integrate both individual and job approaches.

Chapter 14, "Leadership," defines leadership as an influence process. The bases for influence are presented. Two specific approaches are described: traditional and contingency. The traditional approaches direct our attention to the traits of effective leaders. Contingency approaches emphasize the fact that effective leadership depends on the characteristics of the leader, the follower, and the situation. The ability of the manager to accurately diagnose the situation and then choose the appropriate style of leadership is discussed in detail.

Part V

Chapter 15, "Communication in Organizations," stresses that communication is the major way managers influence subordinates. Verbal, nonverbal, and written communication processes are discussed. Also discussed are the skills the sender and receiver need for effective communication. Special attention is directed at the importance of perception. Barriers to effective communication are addressed, as are means of overcoming these barriers.

Chapter 16, "Managing Effective Groups," focuses on the properties of groups in organizations. Most of a manager's time is spent in group meetings. Being an effective manager requires that you understand why people join groups and how groups can affect the individual's behavior. Characteristics of effective and ineffective groups are discussed. Guidelines are presented that permit you to decide when groups are likely to be more effective than individuals working alone.

Chapter 17, "Conflict Process," deals with how the effective manager can reduce conflict in ways that stimulate high productivity. The chapter examines conflict within the individual that results from either too many conflicting demands on the person or from unclear job expectations. Given that conflict must be managed, different styles of managing it are presented. Various techniques are presented that managers can use to understand and reduce the harmful effects of conflict.

Chapter 13

MOTIVATION

After reading this chapter, you should be able to:

1. Describe and compare three factors affecting the motivational process.

2. Describe a basic motivation process.

3. Describe how individual needs and desires affect motivation to perform.

4. Identify job characteristics that effect employee satisfactions and performances.

5. Analyze the job charateristics in a given situation, using Herzberg's two-factor theory and Hackman-Oldham's job-enrichment model.

6. Describe the organizational characteristics that effect individual motivation.

7. Analyze the organizational characteristics in a given situation, using the Porter-Lawler model of expectancy theory.

PREVIEW CASE

Airlines Reservation Office*

Barbara Myers has a routine job. She works for a large airline where she takes calls for reservations from 8:00 each morning until 4:30 each afternoon. By the end of the week, she has answered more than 1000 calls.

How does she feel about her job? She loves it. Barbara has been with the airline since her husband died nine years ago. Her day begins at 7:30 A.M. when she leaves her home in Arlington, Texas. After a short ride to the Dallas-Fort Worth Airport, she gets ready to answer calls. She puts on her headset and looks at the flight schedules.

Barbara's goal is to answer the phone before it rings three times. If all lines are busy, an automatic switching device answers the phone and the caller hears a recording. The reservation agents try to avoid customers being put on hold because top management believes customers get annoyed and sales are lost. Barbara's productivity rate is far above the minimum set by the company. After ten years on this job, she can carry on lively conversations with her co-workers and still answer the phones.

* Adapted from: D. Nadler, J. R. Hackman, and E. Lawler, III, *Managing Organizational Behavior.* Boston: Little, Brown, 1979, p. 26. Copyright © 1979 by David A. Nadler, J. Richard Hackman, and Edward E. Lawler, III. Reprinted by permission of Little, Brown and Company.

Barbara earns about $15,500 a year. She has made her job her life. "I would not recommend it to someone with a good education or who wants to move ahead," she says, "but for someone like me, it's great. You learn to take all calls in stride. I have made up my mind that I'll do this until I retire and I do not get bored."

Barbara cannot imagine any other way of spending a day. To her, going to the airport is as natural as eating and sleeping. It is, she says, "like anything else — you gotta eat, sleep, and work." Indeed, to her the airport is almost like home. "I was here in the ice storm, when most others stayed home," she said.

Barbara is proud of her good record and is resentful of younger workers who are not willing to devote as much to the job as she. "They want this job because they can fly to resort places with the company discount. I like this place, but it requires effort to be good."

One of the women that Barbara is resentful of is Susan Markham. Susan works on the same shift as Barbara. Most of Susan's time is spent answering calls like Barbara's. Susan is 20 years old and graduated from a local high school two years ago. Susan failed to find an office job after graduation and took "what was available at the time."

Although she used to try hard, Susan has never mastered her job. Her performance is constantly below standards. She seems to lack an appealing telephone voice and the finger dexterity and hand speed required to do her job.

How does Susan feel about her job? "I dread coming to work. The pay is too low, and the boredom is driving me crazy. Most of the other employees are older and have little interest in traveling and meeting men. Did you ever hear of TGIF (Thank God It's Friday)? I cannot wait until my shift is over. My biggest fear is that I am trapped in this job, and I will never be able to get an office job."

Susan may not find an office job, but there is a good chance that she'll be leaving before she finds one. Her supervisor, Janet Near, has just about given up on her. According to Janet, "Susan is a nice girl, but she just does not fit in here. She does not seem to be able to learn the job and she is more interested in her social life than in the work. I just cannot tolerate this any longer. I am afraid that I am going to have to let her go."

While driving down the North Central Expressway to her office, Janet wondered what happened to Susan. Janet was confused. Janet believed in the tradition of hard work. Her philosophy of encouraging others to achieve high performance and doing what they wanted were major reasons why she thought the airline was so successful. In trying to analyze Susan's behavior, Janet arrived at several possible conclusions about Susan: (1) She was lazy and tired. (2) Personal problems, such as a family illness, boyfriend difficulties, or alcoholism were affecting her performance. (3) She was involved in a basic personality clash with the others and could not work with them. (4) She was poorly placed in her present position. (5) She just wasn't motivated any more. Janet analyzed each of these possibilities and concluded that Susan's motivation was the real problem.[1]

Clearly, the reactions of Susan and Barbara to their jobs are quite different. They differ in how they feel about their jobs, what they want from their jobs, and the needs each is attempting to satisfy on the job. This chapter is concerned with how managers can motivate subordinates so that performance and satisfactions are increased. To some extent, a manager's ability to motivate others will determine the manager's effectiveness.

THE IMPORTANCE OF MOTIVATION

Motivation, that which causes, channels, and sustains people's behavior, has always been an important but puzzling subject for managers. It is puzzling because many motives cannot be seen; they are inferred from behavior. In the airline example, what motivated Barbara? Susan? In many respects a manager's job is to channel the employees' motives toward organizational goals. There are many theories and ideas about how to motivate. John Teets, president of Greyhound Food Management — a chain of restaurants that replaced many of the company's bus-station restaurants — told a group of businessmen, "You do not motivate by fear, or people will go down the street and work."[2] Managers should not forget that people are their most important asset. The ways managers motivate can have a dramatic effect on company profits. At Greyhound, Teets urges his managers to motivate employees with incentive programs, plaques, and pats on the back.

Before beginning a discussion of various theories of motivation, we should note that managers have begun to devote a lot of time and energy to addressing three behavioral requirements of a firm.[3] These are:

1. People must be attracted not only to join the organization but also to remain in it.

2. People must perform the task for which they were hired.

3. People must go beyond routine performance and engage in creative and innovative behavior at work.

In other words, for an organization to be effective, it must come to grips with the motivational problems of stimulating the individual to join the organization, to produce on the job, and to be innovative on the job.

First, to induce people to join the firm and remain in it, companies provide pension plans, group life and medical insurance policies, stock options, vacations, and other programs. IBM, for example, operates three $1-a-year country clubs for workers and their familes. IBM rebates tuition for those who go back to school, and it runs a vast network of schools and training centers where employees can learn everything from computer programming to international finance.

Second, to ensure that employees perform the tasks for which they were hired, applicants are screened carefully to determine whether they have the skills for the job. Once hired, employee performance is evaluated by a performance appraisal system. This system indicates strengths, weaknesses, and skills needed for the next job. At Holiday Inn, if a motel manager does not have the needed technical, administrative, or human relations skills to be promoted, it is the responsibility of both the employee and the supervisor to help the employee learn that skill. These skills may be gained through educational programs or different kinds of on-the-job experiences.

Third, many companies are faced with problems requiring creative and innovative behavior from employees because of increased foreign competition

13.1
Quality circle at
Westinghouse
Business Week, June 30,
1980, p. 100.

and inflation. Westinghouse Electric Corporation's Public Systems Company formed more than 150 "quality circles" to find more innovative ways to do things.[4] We indicated in Chapter 4 that these circles were developed by Japanese managers. A *quality circle* consists of workers and supervisors (see Fig. 13.1) who meet on a regular basis to discuss product-quality improvement. The purpose of these circles is to find better ways of producing quality goods, not to serve as a sounding board for worker complaints. According to some members of Westinghouse's program, quality circles improve the worker-supervisor relationship by opening lines of communication. For Westinghouse, changes made by the circles resulted in more than $1 million savings in two years.

FACTORS AFFECTING THE MOTIVATIONAL PROCESS

So far we have explained that there appear to be three reasons why motivation is receiving greater attention by managers. How can managers gain an overview of factors affecting the motivation process? Porter and Miles have identified three factors affecting motivation in organizations: individual characteristics, job characteristics, and organizational characteristics[5] (see Table 13.1). These variables are merely introduced here; they will be discussed in greater detail later in the chapter.

13.1
Variables Affecting the Motivational Process in Organizational Settings

Individual Characteristics	Job Characteristics	Organizational Characteristics
1. Interest	**1.** Degree of Skill Utilization	**1.** Immediate Work Setting ■ peers ■ supervisor
2. Attitudes (examples) ■ toward self ■ toward job ■ toward aspects of the work situation	**2.** Degree of Autonomy	**2.** Organizational Practices ■ reward systems ■ rules and regulations ■ politics
3. Needs (examples) ■ security ■ social ■ achievement	**3.** Amount of Direct Feedback on Performance	
	4. Degree of Variety in Tasks **5.** Task Significance	

Adapted from L. Porter, and R. Miles, "Motivation and Management." In J. McGuire, (ed.) *Contemporary Management: Issues and Viewpoints,* © 1974, pp. 547. Reprinted by permission of Prentice-Hall, Inc., Englewood Cliffs.

Individual charateristics are the interests, values, attitudes, and needs workers bring to the job. We saw in Chapter 4 that individuals in foreign countries have motivations that are different from those found in the United States. And in the present chapter we saw that Susan's motivation to join the company was money, while Barbara was motivated by friendly co-workers and her job. Each posed problems for Janet, who was attempting to increase the office's productivity. For example, to motivate Susan to perform better, Janet might rely on monetary incentives, while Barbara might respond to being given more responsibility and taking charge when Janet is absent.

Individual
Characteristics

Job characteristics are the characteristics of the worker's task. The variety of work, responsibility for completing the entire job, and the knowledge of results are all important job characteristics that can affect worker motivation and job satisfaction. In the airline reservation case, Susan and Barbara were doing the same tasks, but each viewed the job differently. The jobs were the same in the degree of skill required, amount of freedom available to make decisions, opportunity to talk with customers, and opportunity to work with others. But the two reacted to the job in different ways.

Job Characteristics

Organizational characteristics refer to dimensions of the organization. Is the organization structured clearly or poorly? Do managers reward or ignore high performance? Are promotions based on performance or on political connections? Do managers set themselves apart from the workers and view them as robots? How did Barbara see her job? Susan? For example, Susan viewed her job as temporary, a way of marking time until something better came along. Barbara saw her job as a career, an important part of her life.

Organizational
Characteristics

These three sets of characteristics interact to influence motivation to perform. In the next section we will discuss a motivation theory that focuses on the characteristics of individuals.

The motivational process begins with needs as illustrated in Fig. 13.2. The basic blocks in the model are: (1) needs, desires, or expectations; (2) behaviors; (3) goals; and (4) feedback.[6] People possess, in varying strengths, a multitude of needs, desires, and expectations. For example, some managers may have a high need for power, a strong desire to be well-liked, and an expectation that working long hours will make them powerful and well-liked. Needs, desires, and expectations create tensions managers find uncomfortable. To relieve these tensions, a person behaves in a certain way. The goal of the

MOTIVATION:
INDIVIDUAL
CHARACTERISTICS

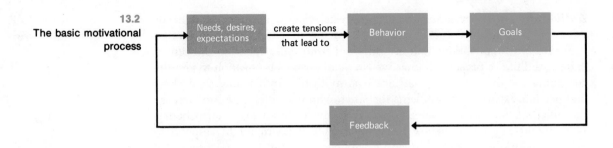

behavior is to reduce tension. This behavior provides feedback to the person concerning the level of tension. For example, Frank Borman, president of Eastern Airlines, has a strong desire to succeed (need for achievement). He has turned the airline around by talking directly to employees (behavior) in hopes of obtaining high profits (goal) for Eastern's stockholders.[7]

At first glance, this approach to motivation seems simple. It suggests that managers can determine subordinates' needs by observing their actions — and predict subordinates' actions by becoming aware of their needs. Actually, motivation is far more complicated. There are four reasons for this.

First, needs differ widely among individuals. Many ambitious managers, highly motivated to achieve power and status, have found it hard to understand that not all the people working under them are influenced by the same values and drives. Such managers find that trying to motivate these people is a frustrating and discouraging experience. Differences among subordinates greatly complicate a manager's motivational task.

Second, people translate their needs into behavior in different ways. One person with a strong security need may play it safe, and avoid responsibility for fear of failing and being fired. Another, with the same need, may seek responsibility — for fear of being fired for low performance.

Third, people's actions are not always consistent — nor are the needs that motivate them. On one day a subordinate will exceed our highest expectations on a difficult assignment. Another time, he or she will perform poorly.

Finally, people react in different ways when they fail to fulfill their needs. Some people with high security need who fail to attain their goals (say, as top-level executives) may become frustrated and give up. Others may be motivated to redouble their efforts (such as by attending executive programs and/or seeking additional duties).

The more familiar we become with those around us (and with ourselves), the more predictable become the processes by which needs are translated into behaviors. However, each step in the process is complex enough, and has alternatives enough, to make our predictions wrong a fair number of times.

The most widely used theory for the study of motivation in organizations is Maslow's hierarchy of needs.[8] Maslow, a psychologist, proposed that people have a complex set of needs. These are arranged in a hierarchy of importance. There are four basic assumptions in the hierarchy:

Maslow's Hierarchy of Needs

1. A satisfied need is not a motivator. When a need is satisfied, another need emerges to take its place, so people are always striving to satisfy some need.

2. The need network for most people is very complex, with a number of needs affecting the behavior of each person at any one time.

3. Lower-level needs must be satisfied, in general, before higher-level needs are activated sufficiently to drive behavior.

4. There are many more ways to satisfy higher-level needs than there are for lower-level needs.

Maslow's theory outlines five need categories: physiological, security, affiliation, esteem, and self-actualization. They are arranged in hierarchical order in Fig. 13.3.

**13.3
Hierarchy of needs**

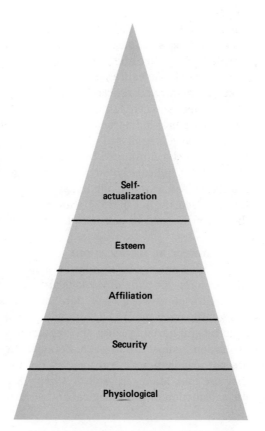

Physiological needs   Food, water, air, and shelter are all ***physiological needs.*** They are at the lowest level in the hierarchy. People satisfy these needs before turning to the higher-order needs. A very hungry person is primarily motivated to obtain food. There are many people who are deprived of the basic physiological needs, especially in Third World countries.

    Managerial Implications   If employees are motivated by physiological needs, their main concern is not with the work itself. Any job that fills their needs is acceptable. Managers who use this need system to motivate subordinates assume that people work primarily for money; to achieve comfort, avoid fatigue, and the like. They will try to motivate employees by offering wage increases, better working conditions, more leisure time, longer coffee breaks, and better fringe benefits. In organizations, there are usually some employees whose physiological needs are not met. When the physiological needs are satisfied, managers turn their attention to security needs.

Security needs   The need for safety, stability, and the absence of pain, threat, or illness are all ***security needs.*** Just as with physiological needs, when security needs are not satisfied, people become preoccupied with satisfying them. For many workers, security needs are expressed in the desire for a safe, stable job with medical, unemployment, and retirement benefits. In the mid-1960s, many contractual agreements between labor and management focused on job security for workers. Several industries, most notably airlines, newspapers, railroads, and shipping, have negotiated extensive provisions for workers whose jobs have been or may be eliminated by technology. The Occupational Safety and Health Act of 1970 indicated that the federal government is trying to reduce the number of safety and health hazards in industry. The Employment Retirement Income Security Act of 1974 was passed to assure workers that the monies they have invested in pension plans will be there on retirement.

    Managerial Implications   Persons motivated primarily by security needs value their jobs mainly as a defense against the loss of basic need satisfactions. As with physiological needs, security needs involve issues not centered around work itself. Any job that affords safety, security, and long-range protection against layoffs will be valued. Managers may focus on this need by emphasizing rules and regulations, job security, fringe benefits, and protection against automation. Subordinates who have strong security needs are not usually innovative; they try not to rock the boat and generally do as they are told. Managers with a Theory X philosophy are likely to emphasize the satisfaction of physiological and security needs.

Friendship, love, and belonging are all **affiliation needs.** When physiological and security needs are satisfied, affiliation needs serve as a source of motivation. This level in the hierarchy represents a clear-cut step above the first two physical needs. When affiliation needs are not met, this may affect the mental health of the employee and may result in frequent absenteeism, poor productivity, low job satisfaction, emotional breakdowns, and high stress levels.

Affiliation needs

Managerial Implications   When affiliation needs are the primary source of motivation, people value their work as an opportunity to find and establish warm, harmonious, interpersonal relationships. Jobs that afford opportunities for social interaction among co-workers are likely to be valued. Managers who see that their subordinates are striving to satisfy this need system are likely to act in a particularly supportive and permissive way. They emphasize being accepted by co-workers and taking part in extracurricular activities, such as organized sports programs and company picnics. Managers will encourage a high level of employee satisfaction and loyalty. This may reduce job peformance, however, since the employees may put more effort into their social relationships than into their work.

Esteem needs include both personal feelings of achievement or self-worth and recognition or respect from others. In satisfying affiliation needs, people want others to accept them for what they are. In satisfying esteem needs, people want to be seen as competent and able. They are concerned about the opportunities for achievement, prestige, status, and promotion that others will provide as recognition of their competence and capabilities. To excel at something, to master some problem or skills, and to be independent may satisfy needs for self-esteem. Respect, prestige, increased responsibility, promotion, recognition, and appreciation by others are external indicators of one's status that also can fulfill the need for esteem. The fulfillment of esteem needs leads to feelings of worth, adequacy, and self-confidence. The inability to fulfill these needs may lead to discouragement.

Esteem needs

Managerial Implications   Managers who focus on esteem needs to motivate employees tend to emphasize public reward and recognition for services. Emphasis on the difficulty of the work and the skills required for success characterize managers' contacts with employees. Lapel pins, articles in the company paper, published performance lists, and the like may be used as a means of promoting pride in one's work. To the extent that this need system is dominant, managers may promote both high satisfaction and performance rates through exciting and challenging work.

Self-actualization needs

Self-fulfillment, or the realization of one's potential, is the goal of ***self-actualization needs.*** A person who has attained self-actualization experiences acceptance of self and others, increased problem-solving ability, increased spontaneity, and a desire for privacy. To become everything one is capable of becoming requires that a person partly fulfill other needs at some time. Self-actualizers, however, may be so intent on fulfilling this highest need that they may consciously or unconsciously neglect the fulfillment of lower-level needs.

Managerial Implications   When self-actualization needs are dominant, people channel their most creative and constructive skills into their work. Managers who focus primarily on these needs recognize that every job has areas that allow innovation; that managers are not the only people who may be creative. Managers who emphasize self-actualization are likely to use techniques for making work more meaningful. They may involve employees in decision-making, restructuring of jobs, or special assignments that use their unique skills. Managers with a Theory Y philosophy are likely to emphasize the satisfaction of self-actualization needs.

Summary of the need hierarchy

Maslow's theory of needs assumes that people are motivated to satisfy the needs that are important in their lives. The strength of any particular need depends on its position in the need hierarchy and the extent to which it and all lower-level needs have been satisfied. The theory predicts a dynamic, step-by-step, causal process of motivation in which behavior is governed by a continuously changing set of "important" needs. Maslow did not claim that the hierarchy is fixed rigidly in order for all people. This is especially true for the middle-level needs (affiliation and esteem), where the order may vary from person to person. Maslow indicates clearly, however, that the physiological needs are the most basic, and the self-actualization needs are the least fulfilled.

Research supports the view that unless basic needs are satisfied, people will not be concerned with higher needs. There is, however, very little evidence to support the view that the hierarchy exists as shown in Fig. 13.3 for any but the basic needs.[9] For example, studies do not indicate that social needs must be satisfied prior to self-actualization. There are those who pay little attention to social needs so long as they are free to do what they do best, whether that be playing chess or lifting weights. Based on the research, then, it seems best to assume a two-step hierarchy with physiological and security needs at the lower level and the remaining three needs at the upper level. Unless the lower needs are satisfied, the others will not affect behavior. It also means that when the lower needs of a person are threatened, they will become most important. The existence of a two-step hierarchy means that if basic needs are satisfied, no need is likely to be the "best" or "only" need motivating the person. In fact, there is evidence to show that more than one need may be important simultaneously. For example, look at the needs motivating Barbara Myers. In her case, the social as well as basic needs are being satisfied by her job at the airline. There also is evidence to indicate that people differ widely in which needs will be important once the basic needs are satisfied. As a result, managers must continually adjust their ideas about what is motivating their subordinates.[10] Again, look at the airline reservation case. What needs motivate Susan Markham?

Job characteristics are the second variable influencing motivation of people in organizations. Behavioral scientists have attempted to discover how a particular job motivates an individual to perform. The appeal of scientific management to a manager was the promise that it would lead to increased organizational efficiency.* Jobs designed according to the principles of scientific management tend to be highly specialized and standardized. Under such a system, mistakes are unlikely because each worker is doing one — and only one — part of the job the best possible way. This should lead to high quality, because every worker can easily become an expert in a particular job. In addition, a supervisor need only to glance at a worker to know whether he or she is performing effectively. Assuming that a worker is at his or her station and doing a simple repetitive task, production should proceed according to management's plan.

The benefits of simple and highly specialized jobs seem clear to managers. Since training workers costs little, they can be replaced without a great deal of expense. This increases management's control over the workers, since the threat of being fired can be very real to workers whose productivity is not up to standard. A solid case can be made for the economic advantage of having simple, repetitive, and relatively routine jobs.[11]

Despite those economic advantages though, problems occur. Many employees dislike such jobs intensely and find them terribly boring and nonmotivating. In many cases, employees find that their needs for self-actualization, affiliation, and recognition are not met by this type of job. One of the first behavioral scientists to contribute to our understanding of the relationship between job characteristics and motivation was Frederick Herzberg.

MOTIVATION: JOB CHARACTERISTICS

Herzberg and his associates examined the relationship between job satisfaction and productivity among a group of accountants and engineers.[12] Through

Herzberg's Two-Factor Theory

---

* See Chapter Two for a discussion of scientific management.

the use of semistructured interviews, they accumulated data on various factors that affected the workers' feelings toward their jobs. The research was built around two questions to managers: "Can you describe, in detail, when you felt exceptionally good about your job?" and "Can you describe, in detail, when you felt exceptionally bad about your job?" In analyzing the answers, the researchers found that employees named different job experiences related to good and bad feelings about the job. If responsibility led to good feelings about the job, lack of responsibility was seldom given as a cause of bad feelings. In fact, there appeared to be two separate and distinct kinds of experiences. If lack of job security, for example, caused dissatisfaction, it did not follow that high job security caused satisfaction. Since this theory presents two separate kinds of factors — one set that satisfies and another that dissatisfies — it has been labeled the **two-factor theory.**

Motivator and hygiene factors

Herzberg's research led him to the following conclusions:

1. There are some factors associated with positive feelings about the job. He called these motivators. **Motivators** include the work itself, recognition, responsibility, and advancement and growth. If these five factors are present, they build a high level of motivation and spur the individual to superior performance.

2. Some job factors cause job dissatisfaction when they are not present. Herzberg called these hygienes. **Hygienes** include company policies, supervision, working conditions, co-workers, salary, and job security. When these are present, they do not lead to high performance and job satisfaction, but are needed to maintain a reasonable level of satisfaction.

There is a major difference between motivators and hygienes. The motivators are *job centered* and related to the nature of the job itself. Is the job exciting, challenging, rewarding? Conversely, hygienes are associated with the *context* in which the work is performed. Is the cafeteria air-conditioned? Does the firm have free parking spaces? These are "context" factors. Herzberg suggests that just because the cafeteria is air-conditioned and employees can park free does not necessarily mean that they will be more highly motivated to perform than if the cafeteria were not air-conditioned and they had to pay to park.

Table 13.2 lists some motivators and hygiene factors. For example, Susan Markham is dissatisfied with her working conditions (hygienes). That is, she took the job because it was the only one available at the time, dislikes the work itself, and has few friends at work who share common interests. On the other hand, Barbara Myers enjoys the challenge of her work (motivators) and the friends she has made at the airport. Go back to the preview case and pick out the motivators and hygiene factors.

		13.2 Examples of Motivators and Hygienes
Motivators	**Hygienes**	
■ Achievement	■ Company policy and administration	
■ Recognition	■ Supervision	
■ Work itself	■ Working conditions	
■ Responsibility	■ Co-workers	
■ Advancement and growth	■ Salary, status, and job security	
Sources of Job Satisfaction	Sources of Job Dissatisfaction	

Assessment of Herzberg

Herzberg's method for collecting data has been criticized, as have the job characteristics that comprise the hygiene and motivator dimensions. For example, when Herzberg asked people to describe what were the most "satisfying" and "dissatisfying" elements of their job, most took credit for satisfactions and blamed others for their dissatisfactions. A number of studies have indicated that the two-factor theory is an oversimplification of the relationship between satisfaction and motivation. In many instances, *hygiene* factors, such as salary, working conditions, and the supervisors' leadership style, have led to job satisfaction, and a negative state of *motivator* factors (lack of recognition, advancement, and achievement) could lead to job dissatisfaction. Furthermore, the factors may vary among individuals or as the person's career plans change.

Herzberg's theory has received considerable attention from managers and researchers. First, it is simple to understand and has a great deal of face validity. Managers find it easy to identify hygiene and motivator factors. Second, his recommendations for improving performance are straightforward. If a person is to become a superior performer, management must adequately provide the hygiene factors so that the worker can concentrate on the task itself. Third, many job-enrichment programs have been inspired by his work.

Hackman-Oldham's Job-Enrichment Model

The job-enrichment approach has focused on extending the work of Herzberg. Researchers have focused on understanding how the changing of specific job elements can affect motivation and satisfactions. While there are a number of different approaches,[13] they all look at those elements that enrich the job by enabling the worker to use it to meet more higher-order needs. One of the most popular models tested extensively is the job-enrichment model developed by J. Richard Hackman and Greg Oldham.[14]

Three psychological states

As shown in Fig. 13.4, the **Hackman-Oldham job-enrichment model** is based on the view that three key psychological states are critical to increase motivations and satisfactions on the job. The first state is **experienced meaningfulness** — the degree to which work is viewed as important, valuable, and worthwhile. If the person believes that he or she is performing a trivial task, such as counting rubber bands being packed in a box, then motivation to perform is not likely to be very high. This would be the case even when the person has the sole responsibility for doing the task and receives feedback on how well or poorly he or she is doing it. The second state is **experienced responsibility** — the extent to which the person feels personally responsible and accountable for the work being performed. If people view their work as dependent on rules and regulations, they have less reason to feel personally responsible for their actions. The opposite situation exists when people are accountable for their behavior without following rules and regulations. The third state is **knowledge of results** — the extent to which workers receive feedback on how well or poorly they are performing their jobs. If people's work is so arranged that they cannot see the results of their own efforts and know whether they performed poorly or well, they are not likely to have any feeling about how well or poorly they performed.

The more these three states are experienced, the more workers feel motivated to accomplish their tasks. Thus, as people work effectively they will experience something *meaningful* for which they are *responsible*, and know that it is *done effectively*. To the extent that workers view these elements as desirable, they will be motivated to perform highly.

13.4

Psychological states affecting motivation

J. R. Hackman and G. Oldham, *Work Redesign.* Reading, MA: Addison-Wesley, 1980, p. 73. Reprinted by permission.

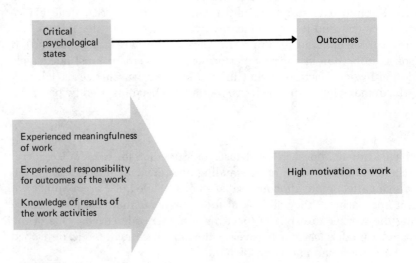

If any of the three psychological states is low, motivation is low. One of the authors likes to play golf. Golf provides the golfer with immediate knowledge of results: the player hits the ball and sees where it goes. The total score on each hole indicates how well the player is playing against a standard (par). Personal responsibility for performance is high, although many times golfers make excuses for their poor performance. Experienced meaningfulness can also be high as the wagers accumulate and a missed putt can be costly. So in golf, all three psychological states are present and motivation among regular players usually is high. Indeed, golfers exhibit motivated behavior rarely seen at work: getting up before dawn (for an early tee time), playing in rain and snow, feeling despair or happiness (depending on how the round went), and even violence (such as destroying equipment when the results are poor).

Hackman and Oldham identified five job characteristics leading to these psychological states. Table 13.3 provides a list of these. As shown in Fig. 13.5, the first three job characteristics — *skill variety*, *task identity*, and *task significance* — all lead to increased feelings of meaningfulness. When individuals do things that result in a whole piece of work with a visible outcome, and when that work has a significant effect on the work of others, work is more meaningful. At the John Deere tractor plant in Dubuque, Iowa, where the average blue-collar worker earns more than $21,000 a year, Pat Dillion, president of the local union says:[15]

Job characteristics

> *Guys used to have pride in their work. Not any more. Sure, some of the younger guys still worry about scratches on the hood. But there's too much repetition.... Monotony, boredom, and regimentation are all most guys have to look for at work.*

These Deere workers have lost any meaningfulness in their work because of the repetition and monotony of the assembly line. To pass time at work, some think about their families, others watch the clock, and still others engage in mind games. Parking lot attendants and traffic cops occasionally admit to playing license-plate poker in their heads. A former newspaper carrier designed a game to keep himself motivated. He'd keep score on how many porches he hit with papers. He even created teams for the days of the week and created a series to determine which day won. A bus driver with Trailways kept score on how many cars passed him versus how many cars he passed on a given trip. The more cars he passed, the better he felt.

Skill variety, task identity, and task significance contribute to the overall meaningfulness of work. If a given job is high in all three characteristics, such as teaching college students or managing a sports team, an individual is very likely to experience meaningful work. Because there are three different task characteristics that contribute to meaningfulness, a person can experience meaningful work even if one or two characteristics are quite low. The worker who set the type for this book, whose task surely is below average in skill variety, could find meaning in the work if it were sufficiently high in significance and task identity.

Autonomy fosters increased feelings of personal responsibility. When a job provides substantial autonomy, performance will be viewed as highly dependent on personal efforts and decisions, rather than on immediate supervisors. As autonomy increases, people tend to feel more personally responsible for success and failures on the job. They are more willing to accept personal accountability for their decisions.

The results of one's work are affected by the amount of *feedback* received. Feedback should be obtained from the task itself — such as when a golfer shoots par, or when a sales representative closes a deal with a customer — rather than from a supervisor.

13.3
Key Job Characteristics
for Job Enrichment

Skill variety	The degree to which the job requires a variety of different activities in carrying out the work. It involves the use of a number of skills and talents.
Task identity	The degree to which the job requires completing the whole job, an identifiable piece of work. That is, doing a job with a visible outcome from beginning to end.
Task significance	The degree to which the job has a substantial impact on the lives or work of others in the company.
Autonomy	The degree to which the job provides substantial freedom, independence, and discretion to the individual in scheduling work and determining the procedures to be used in carrying out the task(s).
Feedback	The degree to which carrying out the work activities required by the job results in the individual's obtaining direct and clear information about the effectiveness of his or her performance.

Adapted from J. R. Hackman and G. Oldham. *Work Redesign.* Reading, MA: Addison-Wesley, 1980, pp. 78–80. Reprinted by permission.

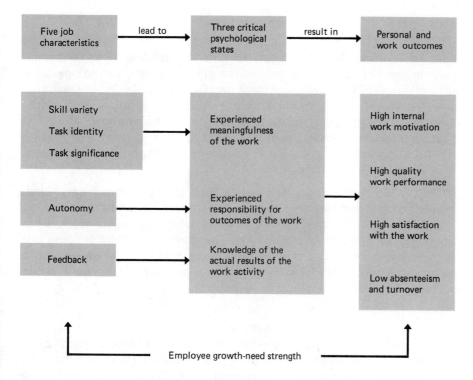

13.5
Hackman-Oldham's
job-enrichment model

Adapted from J. R. Hackman
and G. Oldham, *Work
Redesign*. Reading, MA:
Addison-Wesley, 1980, p. 83.
Reprinted by permission.

*Growth-need
strength*

Hackman and Oldham's model has one additional feature. Different people respond to the same job in different ways because they come to it with different desires and needs. As indicated in our discussion of Maslow, some want only to satisfy their lower-order or affiliation needs on the job, but not their higher-order or achievement desires. Therefore, what may be a good job for one may be a bad job for another. The model demonstrates this by showing that the relationship among job characteristics and a person's work outcome is moderated by the strength of that person's need for growth. ***Growth-need strength*** refers to the individual's desire for personal accomplishments and learning on the job. Where people have high needs for growth, creativity, and challenge, they are more likely to respond positively to jobs that provide more meaningfulness, responsibility, and knowledge of results. Where people's growth needs are low, an enriched job may increase tension and job dissatisfaction.

Let's look at how one company used the concepts of job enrichment to improve productivity.

CASE STUDY

Sherwin-Williams Paint Company

Sherwin-Williams instituted a job-enrichment program in its Richmond Virginia plant in 1980.[16] The goal of the plant manager was to operate a safe, clean, profitable, efficient plant producing the highest quality automobile refinishing paint in the world. The company thought that productivity could be greatly improved by enriching the workers' jobs. The manager said he believed people wanted to work in open and trusting ways and participate in business decisions as responsible employees.

To implement these ideas, employees were grouped into teams. Each member of the team was trained to perform all jobs assigned to the team. The teams have the autonomy to decide where members work, what work they do, and how to train others. For example, instead of doing just housekeeping chores, a worker does several different tasks related to the group's job. These tasks might include operating equipment, doing maintenance work, keeping quality control records, or restocking supplies.

The group is responsible for the results of its work. Raises are given to individual employees and are based on performance. Peers and the team leader evaluate each person's performance against standards set by the group and management. This occurs only after that person has mastered a set of skills. This establishes responsibility for performance and gives the employee feedback on how well he or she is doing.

Employees are hired from applicants the company feels would enjoy working on challenging and significant tasks. They are encouraged to feel responsibility for the entire production process. They also are expected to acquire a working knowledge of customers' needs and the uses of Sherwin-Williams products. The technology requires careful production and quality control. Roughly $5 of the cost of producing a gallon of paint goes for raw materials. Since a typical batch is 4000 gallons, the cost of a single spoiled batch could come to $20,000 — a good reason to have employees trained as skilled operators.

The plant itself is designed to foster job enrichment. It has an open work space that encourages workers to identify with the entire task and to share responsibility for all phases of production. This open space allows interaction between workers for both social and problem-solving chats.

Overall, the plant has been very successful. Absenteeism at the Richmond plant is 63 percent lower than at other Sherwin-Williams plants. There is very little turnover, and productivity is 30 percent higher than at the other plants. Cost per gallon of paint is 45 percent lower. The plant manager says that 75 percent of this reduction can be traced directly to the employees' superior performance.

*Managerial
implications*

During the past 10 years, job-enrichment programs have met with mixed success. Several reasons for this may readily be seen.[17] First, most managers are skeptical about workers' ability to perform highly enriched jobs and maintain the same level of productivity. Through the application of scientific management principles, managers have economic "proof" that these industrial engineering principles work. Now behavioral scientists are challenging these principles. Second, it is very difficult to assess "bottom line" results of job-enrichment programs. Managers ask, "What is the cost of a poor quality decision? Of redundant inspections? Of absenteeism, turnover, or sabotage?" Unless measurements are able to answer these questions, it is nearly impossible to determine whether job enrichment pays for organizations as anticipated. Third, union leaders and many workers are not interested in enriching their jobs. The worst possible circumstance for a manager is to enrich a job for an employee who wants only to satisfy physiological and safety needs at work. Clearly the job would be too much for that worker. Turnover, absenteeism, and shoddy workmanship might result. On the other hand, if the worker is capable of doing the work required in a complex and challenging job and has a strong desire for on-the-job personal growth, a job-enrichment program well fits the needs of the individual and organization. Fourth, according to Hackman and Oldham, productivity can be improved only by dealing with either or both of these two problems:

1. Employees show low productivity because they are "turned off" by routine tasks.

2. There are redundant inspections which result in inefficient use of time.

If such problems are present, job enrichment probably will improve employee attitudes and increase the quantity and quality of work.

Table 13.4 summarizes the managerial and motivational assumptions of job-enrichment programs. While these assumptions give some basis for choice, the manager still has questions: Are motivation and satisfaction problems? Are the job characteristics indeed low? What aspects of the job are causing problems? Many performance problems are not caused by job design.

		13.4 Summary of Job-Enrichment Points
Problem diagnosis	Jobs are extremely monotonous, segmented, and routine. Apathy, absenteeism, and turnover are excessive.	
Motivational assumptions	Intrinsic rewards from job content (e.g., challenge and autonomy) are the keys to long-run motivations, because people want to satisfy higher-level needs on the job.	
Job-type applicability	Lower-level jobs which are typically routine and repetitive.	
Time frame for distribution of rewards	Workers receive intrinsic satisfaction on completion of a challenging job.	
Motivational implications (Positive)	Jobs are more interesting and challenging; thus people are motivated to improve quality and to lower absenteeism and turnover.	
Negative	Employees may feel they have more to say about their jobs than they really do or management intended. Some employees may not want challenging jobs but simply a chance to earn money in order to satisfy their needs off the job.	

Adapted from R. Beatty and C. Schneier, "A Case for Positive Reinforcement," *Business Horizons* **18** (1975), 59. Copyright © 1975, by the Foundation for the School of Business at Indiana University. Reprinted by permission.

Perhaps the individual doesn't have the needed skills and abilities; or the company has a poorly designed pay system; or the supervisor is ineffective; or the equipment is old. In these cases, a job-enrichment program may not increase the workers' performance and satisfaction. Thus, the manager must diagnose the work situation to determine whether problems exist, and, if they do, whether they are related to the characteristics of the job.

MOTIVATION: INDIVIDUAL, JOB, AND ORGANIZATIONAL CHARACTERISTICS

The first two approaches to motivation (individual and job characteristics) focused on parts of the motivational processes illustrated in Table 13.1. Maslow reasoned that an individual is motivated to satisfy needs and, depending on that individual's need state, certain types of behavior are more likely than others. Herzberg called our attention to job characteristics and how these can affect motivation. In this last section, we will look at how individual needs and job and organization characteristics all together can affect motivation.

Needs can be satisfied only by proper behavior. In many situations, people must choose among sets of behaviors. You might ask yourself: "Do I watch the football game on TV or study?" "Should I call home for money or try to make it last?" "Should I get married?" "Should I take the job at General Motors or IBM?" The most widely accepted approach to explaining how people make these decisions is called *expectancy theory.*[18] ***Expectancy theory*** says that people choose behaviors that they see leading to outcomes (such as pay, recognition from the boss, challenging assignments) that satisfy their needs. Expectancy theory analyzes and predicts what courses of action a person will take when he or she must make a choice. Expectancy theory states that the individual will make a rational decision. Needs and past experiences influence the rational decision process. This can lead to decisions which others would not consider rational.

Expectancy Theory

According to David Nadler, J. Richard Hackman, and Edward Lawler, expectancy theory is based on three assumptions:[19]

1. *Behavior is determined by some combination of forces in the individual and work situation.* Maslow stated that people have different needs. How these needs will be fulfilled is influenced by the work situation. For example, the airlines reservation situation met Barbara's needs but not Susan's. Susan's behavior on the job was inferior to Barbara's.

2. *Individuals make conscious decisions about their own behavior in organizations.* People make decisions about whether or not to join the organization, come to work or call in sick, put in overtime, etc.

3. *Individuals make decisions among alternative behaviors based on the expectation that a given behavior will lead to some desired outcome.* In essence, people tend to behave in ways that they believe will lead to rewards, and avoid behaving in ways that they believe will lead to undesirable consequences (e.g., demotion, lay-off).

Figure 13.6 presents the expectancy theory graphically. It shows that as people think about performing at some level, they consider several factors. First, *the probability that if they put forth effort in task-related activities, they will be able to attain the desired performance level.* This is called ***expectancy.*** For example, if you attend class, study, and take notes, what is the probability that you will achieve the grade you desire in this class? If you believe that these activities will not lead to your desired performance level, your expectancy would be zero. Therefore, you should not study, attend class, or take notes. Second, if the desired level of performance is achieved, *what is the probability* *that this performance level will lead to outcomes you desire?* This is called **instrumentality.** For example, if you achieve an A in this course, will that lead to things which you desire, such as an improved grade-point average, opportunity for graduate school, or a chance of securing a better job? Given this model, the motivational force to behave in a certain way is greatest when a person believes that: (1) a high level of performance is possible (expectancy); and (2) performance can lead to desirable outcomes (instrumentality).

**13.6
Basic expectancy
approach to motivation**

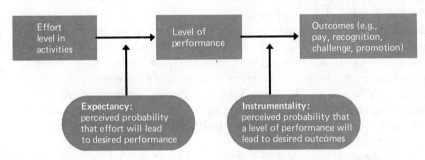

Applying this model to the performance of Barbara Myers and Susan Markham, we can see why Susan has a low motivation to perform at the airline reservation office. To begin with, she does not believe that high performance can lead to anything she wants (instrumentality). The pay is low, work is boring, and she does not have any common interests with co-workers. Furthermore, she does not believe that she can perform at high levels (expectancy) because she lacks the skills and abilities (finger dexterity) to achieve a high performance level. The situation for Barbara Myers is just the opposite. She believes she has the skills and abilities to do the job well and values the benefits the job brings her (e.g., friendly co-workers, pay, interesting work). Therefore, in this case, people in the same organization developed very different expectations about what kinds of behavior will lead to promotions, pay increases, and job security.

**The Porter-Lawler
Model**

A belief widely held among managers is that a happy worker is a productive worker. According to this belief, job satisfaction determines performance. This belief has a great deal of intuitive appeal because it reflects the notion that "all good things go together." Most managers view high satisfaction and performance as desirable, and so feel that they ought to be related to one another.

Lyman Porter and Edward Lawler have extended the basic expectancy theory model to see whether this belief is true.[20] The **_Porter-Lawler model_** states that satisfaction is the result of performance rather than a cause; that is, performance causes satisfaction. Different levels of performance lead to different rewards that, in turn, produce different levels of job satisfaction.

Figure 13.7 shows the complete Porter-Lawler expectancy model. This model draws together individual, job, and organizational characteristics to explain the motivational process.

13.7
Porter-Lawler expectancy
model

From L. W. Porter and E. E.
Lawler III, *Managerial Attitudes
and Performance*, p. 165.
Copyright © 1968 by Richard
D. Irwin, Inc. Reprinted with
permission of Richard D. Irwin.

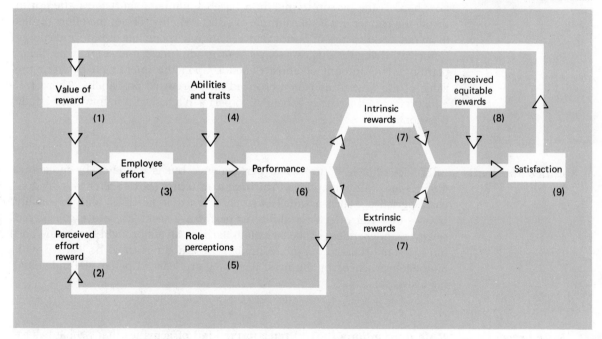

The *value of reward* (box 1 in Fig. 13.7) is the various benefits a person might hope to obtain from the job — the friendship of co-workers, promotion, merit salary increases, a feeling of acomplishment. For Barbara Myers, the friendship of co-workers might be highly desired. For Susan Markham, a valued reward might be money. The value of reward reflects the individual's state of need satisfaction. A hungry person (physiological need) would value food more than a person who had just eaten dinner.

The value of reward

Perceived effort-reward   The ***perceived effort–reward*** (box 2) refers to a person's expectations that given amounts of reward depend upon effort. Suppose a manager desires a transfer from the Northeast to the Sunbelt. The manager might feel that her chances of obtaining a transfer have very little to do with her level of performance. Virtually no transfers are being made, and when they are made, she believes, they depend on things other than performance (luck, "pull," the state of the economy). Under these conditions, the manager would perceive a low effort–reward possibility.

Effort   Effort (box 3) means the amount of energy exerted in any situation. That is, how hard is the person trying? In a baseball game, a shortstop's attempt to throw the runner out is an example of effort. Whether or not the effort results in an out is a measure of performance. You may spend lots of time and energy (effort) studying for this course, yet your grade (performance) may be disappointing. The amount of effort depends upon the interaction between the value of the reward and the perceived effort–reward probability. Therefore, effort refers to the energy expended to perform a task, not to how successfully it is done.

Abilities and traits   Effort does not lead directly to performance but is mediated by individual abilities and role perceptions. ***Abilities and traits*** (box 4) refer to individual characteristics — such as intellectual capacity, manual skills, and personality traits — that can affect the ability to perform a task. These are considered relatively independent of the situation. Barbara Myers brought her typing and interpersonal skills to the job. Although these abilities could be learned with on-the-job practice, for the most part they are learned before the individual begins work.

Role perceptions   ***Role perceptions*** (box 5) refer to the kind of activities that people believe they should perform if they want to perform a job successfully. At the Standard Steel Corporation, many middle-level managers believe that the best way to perform well on their job (in order to get a promotion and raise) is to become highly knowledgeable in their field, such as metallurgy, finance, melting, marketing, or accounting. If a manager can demonstrate proficiency, efforts to improve should pay off. However, if top management at Standard Steel considers broad administrative capabilities a prime requirement for advancement, then a manager who puts effort into developing technical skills might actually be hampering promotion. Role perceptions deal with the way people define their jobs and the types of efforts that they believe are essential to effective performance.

Performance

The value of the rewards and the perceived effort–reward relationship lead to performance (box 6). ***Performance*** refers to the level of the individual's work achievement. Performance comes after effort has been exerted. Performance depends not just on the amount of effort exerted, but also on ability and the way people perceive their roles. In other words, even though employees exert a great amount of effort, if they have little ability and/or have inaccurately assessed what it takes to succeed in the organization, their resulting performance might be low.

Rewards

Rewards refer to outcomes desired by the individual. Figure 13.7 identifies two basic types of rewards: extrinsic and intrinsic (both box 7). ***Extrinsic rewards*** are given by the organization and include such job-related rewards as supervision, working conditions, salary, status, job security, and fringe benefits. Extrinsic rewards are what Herzberg called hygiene factors. ***Intrinsic rewards*** are administered by the individual and include such things as achievement, self-recognition for a job well done, work itself, responsibility, and personal growth. Intrinsic rewards are what Herzberg called motivators. In the Porter-Lawler model, both intrinsic and extrinsic rewards are desirable. For most managers, intrinsic rewards are much more likely to produce higher job satisfaction than are extrinsic rewards.[21]

Intrinsic rewards can be increased by the organization through job enrichment. If a job provides sufficient variety, feedback, autonomy, and challenge so that employees feel they have performed well, they can reward themselves. If the design of the job does not involve these characteristics, then there will be little relationship between good performance and intrinsic rewards. Thus, the relationship between performance and intrinsic rewards depends on the makeup of the job.

*Perceived equitable
rewards*

Perceived equitable rewards (box 8) refers to the amount of reward people feel they should receive as the result of a given level of performance. In most jobs, people have an implicit notion about the rewards they ought to get for the type of work they do. These might include a salary bonus, personal secretary, private office, reserved parking place, car, country-club privileges, challenging job assignments, recognition, office windows, and carpeting. Such notions are based on how the employee sees the requirements of the job, the demands the job makes on him or her, and the contributions he or she makes to the company. In essence, these reflect a fair level of rewards that the individual feels should be granted for high performance in a particular job.

Satisfaction

Satisfaction (box 9) is an attitude. ***Satisfaction*** is determined by the difference between what people receive and what they feel they should have received.[22] The bigger the difference, the greater the dissatisfation. The degree of dissatisfaction or satisfaction is influenced strongly by what others receive. That is, people seem to compare what they are getting from the company with what others get from it. If people believe that the comparison shows them to be unfairly treated, then they are dissatisfied. At State Farm Insurance Company, all salaried employees receive a cost-of-living adjustment regardless of performance. That is, the clerk with the highest performance in the company receives the same cost-of-living increase as the lowest-performing clerk. High-performing employees are generally dissatisfied with this arrangement because the *actual* rewards are below what they feel would be fair *on the basis of performance.* A similar problem faces most public school teachers. Raises usually are given across the board on the basis of time in the system and number of credits taken beyond a baccalaureate degree, rather than on performance in the classroom.

Satisfaction is important for several reasons.[23] First, managers believe that satisfaction has a major effect on job performance. However, research shows that the relationship is not so much "satisfaction leads to performance," as it is *"performance leads to satisfaction."* Second, satisfaction has been related to turnover, absenteeism, tardiness, and commitment. The more satisfied the employee, the less likely he or she is to be absent or late or to leave the company for another job. This seems to be because satisfaction influences people's expectations about what will please them in their work environment. Satisfied employees see more positive things about going to work. Therefore, they are more likely to be on time and committed to the organization (as in the case of Barbara Myers).

Managerial implications

Employee satisfaction and performance are the result of complex processes yet to be agreed on by researchers. It is fairly well established, however, that the equity or inequity of rewards can produce differences in job satisfaction. For the manager who wants to enhance the job satisfaction of subordinates, the appropriateness of the reward is important. There must be a relationship between the reward and what the individual needs or wants. A manager must recognize, however, that there are often significant differences among individuals in what they consider rewarding. A 7- or 8-percent salary increase may satisfy one person but have little or no positive effect on another. Furthermore, a person might find a certain reward sizable in one situation and too little in another. Generally speaking, extrinsic rewards have their greatest value when the individual is most strongly motivated to satisfy what Maslow referred to as lower-level needs — physiological needs, security needs — and those higher-level needs linked to status. Pay, just for example, may be valued because of a belief that it is a determinant of social position. It is a means for acquiring status symbols.

Intrinsic rewards are more likely to be valued by employees after lower-level needs have been satisfied. Most managers realize that an employee must be adequately satisfied with extrinsic rewards before intrinsic rewards can be used effectively. For many employees the manager needs to provide meaningful work assignments. That is, work with which the subordinate can identify and become personally involved. Challenging yet attainable goals can be established. In some cases it may be advantageous to create conditions that improve the employee's chances for success. For subordinates known to be motivated by higher-level needs, the manager may consider such things as delegation of authority or extension of the scope and depth of their jobs. In summary, managers should match the rewards they can give, both intrinsic an extrinsic, with what the subordinate shows a desire for. Varying the magnitude and timing of the rewards helps establish clearly in the subordinate's mind the desired relationship between effort and performance.

While granting different rewards (extrinsic or intrinsic) may cause various levels of satisfaction or dissatisfaction, the relationship between *performance* and rewards often is not so simple.[24] Other influences on performance may have a greater impact. The work environment, previous job experience, the leadership style of the manager, type of technology, and group processes may affect this process. Where the norm of the work group is to restrict performance, for example, the subordinate will restrict performance to the extent that he or she wants group acceptance. Chapter 16 will explore further how a group can affect a worker's performance levels.

SUMMARY

Motivation is an extemely important subject for managers. Managers must be able to motivate employees to achieve organizational and personal goals. In Chapter 1 we indicated that managers play three roles: interpersonal, informational, and decisional. The manager whose goal is to increase a subordinate's performance might have to play all three roles. The manager will have to make *decisions* regarding the amount and kinds of rewards given to high and low performing subordinates. A subordinate may keep performing poorly regardless of the rewards unless the manager is able to communicate what is desired. Communications are a part of the *informational role*. The manager, in addition to providing appropriate rewards and communicating adequately to subordinates, must have the ability to understand what the individual needs from the job. These needs are uncovered through the *interpersonal role*.

We identified three characteristics that play an important role in understanding the motivational process: individual, job, and organizational practices. Maslow is a theorist who contributed to our understanding of how individual needs affect motivations. Maslow stated that individuals are motivated to fulfill five needs: physiological, security, affiliation, esteem, and self-actualization. A satisfied need can no longer motivate the individual. We said that the satisfaction of each need is generally associated with certain managerial behaviors.

Herzberg contributed to our understanding of how the characteristics of one's job can affect motivation to perform and job satisfaction. He developed two classes of job characteristics — motivators and hygienes — that lead to different personal outcomes. He recommended that to increase an employee's motivation to perform, managers should enrich a worker's job. We examined the Hackman and Oldham job-enrichment model. This model emphasized certain job characteristics that could lead to three psychological states: meaningfulness, responsibility, and knowledge of results. These states can affect job satisfaction, absenteeism, and performance. The case study of the Sherwin-Williams Paint Company illustrated how these concepts were put to use in an organization.

The expectancy theory approach, including Porter and Lawler's model, seemed to pull together individual, job, and organizational factors to show how they interact to affect the motivational process. The expectancy model of motivation sees motivation, performance, and satisfaction as dependent on the outcomes the individual expects from the job. It indicates that perceptions of one's work situation lead to beliefs about what performance is possible and what outcomes will follow performance. If the individual believes effort will not affect performance and that rewards (pay, promotions, status symbols, etc.) are not linked to performance, he or she will choose not to perform.

KEYWORDS

abilities and traits
affiliation needs
autonomy
critical psychological states
esteem needs
expectancy
expectancy theory
experienced meaningfulness
experienced responsibility
extrinsic rewards
feedback
growth-need strength
Hackman-Oldham
job-enrichment model
hygienes
individual characteristics
instrumentality

intrinsic rewards
job characteristics
job enrichment
knowledge of results
motivation
motivators
needs
organizational characteristics
perceived effort–reward
perceived equitable rewards
performance
physiological needs
Porter-Lawler model
quality circle
rewards
role perceptions
satisfaction

security needs
self-actualization needs
skill variety
task identity

task significance
two-factor theory
work outcomes

DISCUSSION
QUESTIONS

1. Why has the subject of motivation assumed greater importance for today's managers than for managers of the past?

2. What factors affect an individual's motivation on the job?

3. Describe a basic model of motivation.

4. How is Maslow's hierarchy of needs related to employees' behavior?

5. What is Herzberg's approach to motivation?

6. How do job characteristics affect an individual's motivation to work?

7. What are some limitations of trying to enrich a person's job?

8. How do Herzberg's motivator and hygiene factors relate to Maslow's need hierarchy?

9. According to the Porter and Lawler model, how do people select a performance level to achieve?

10. Discuss the relationship between job satisfaction and job performance.

Management Incidents and Cases

MINER FOOD
STORE

In 1980, the management of the Miner Food Company realized that demand for food products was increasing in their area. Expansion of existing facilities and a wider diversity of products was necessary if this demand was to be met and the market position of the firm maintained. As a result the company began to expand, and constructed warehouses and retail store facilities.

One of the retail outlets affected by this expansion plan was located in the medium-sized town of Plano, Texas. Having served the community for more than 27 years, it was still the kind of store where clerks waited on each individual customer. The location was above average in sales potential and customers were on friendly terms with the employees of the store.

In addition to the store manager, there were three clerks working in the grocery department, one clerk in the produce department, and three butchers. All the employees were very friendly with one another and they often stopped to chat or joke with each other. Mr. McGill, the store manager, was a very efficient and cordial person. He insisted on certain work standards, but seldom interfered with his subordinates. All the employees, including Mr. McGill, had been working for the company for at least ten years. Consequently, it was understood and evident that each man knew his particular job.

The congenial relations which existed among the employees may be exemplified further. Certain informal expectations existed. Rothe, Wooton, and Barrett — the grocery clerks — were equally capable workers. When they had nothing to do, they often helped the meat department fill orders, or they unloaded deliveries. Churchill, the produce clerk, generally had enough to keep him busy, and when he couldn't handle all the work, Barrett gave him a hand. Besides helping each other with their jobs, the employees had various other arrangements. Vacations were mutually scheduled so that no more than one employee was absent at a time; a fund had been established to help any employee who suffered loss from sickness; all belonged to the same club, and five played on the same bowling team.

This was the situation in 1980 when the division manager came to the Plano store to acquaint Mr. McGill with the plan for expansion. He stated that, because of the increase in sales in the area, the company directors had decided to open a new supermarket in Plano to replace the old store. Mr. McGill was told that the new store would be ready within eight months and that all employees, except himself, would become part of the staff of the new store. Mr. McGill was to report to the main office in Dallas as part of the division staff. The employees received the news optimistically, realizing the advantages of the new store and feeling that their experience and seniority would provide them with opportunity for better jobs.

Eight months later, the new store was completed, and the seven employees of the old store reported to the supermarket for their assignments. Rothe, Wooton, and Barrett were assigned as grocery clerks, with no pay raise; Reynolds, the meat manager in the old store, was made assistant meat manager in the new store at $12 per week more; the two other butchers from the old store were given meat-cutting jobs with no raise; Churchill, the produce clerk, was transferred to the dairy department with no raise.

During the next few months the old employees found that routines in the new supermarket were quite different from the old. Within a short time they found that work assignments were received from the various department managers at the beginning of each day, and there was little time for fraternizing. In addition, they found that the new store manager, Mr. Holmes, had little to do with employees directly. Once when Rothe asked for a day off, he was told by Mr. Holmes to "request such privileges through the proper channels."

The butchers from the old store had even greater problems. Reynolds, the assistant meat manager, had 23 years of experience with the company but reported to a meat manager with only nine years of experience. The latter, a Mr. John Myers, placed most of the work load on Reynolds and gave him great freedom in running the department. However, when supervisors were present, Myers became very bossy and took most of the credit for the meat department's good showing. Of course, Reynolds resented this.

Even worse, the other two butchers found that they now had to cater to a group of women who packaged the meat as it was cut, and distributed it to self-service freezer boxes. Often the women blamed the butcher for any shortage in supply, even if he had nothing to do with the situation. The women used abusive language. Sometimes they shouted at the butchers when a customer was in the freezer, talking with one of the butchers who used to serve her at the old store.

As time passed, tremendous pressure was put on all employees because the ratio of sales to labor was declining. Contact between employees was almost nonexistent. When Rothe, Wooton, and Barrett learned that two better jobs in the store had been filled by new employees, they all quit. Within two months after this, Reynolds asked for a transfer, and the other two butchers quit.

1. What are the problems in this case?

2. What changed from the old to the new store?

3. Using the Porter and Lawler model, can you explain the behavior of Rothe, Wooton, and Barrett?

4. What is the relationship between job satisfaction and job performance for Churchill?

Jane Taylor has been involved with the administrative functions of the American National Insurance Company for almost 20 years.* About three months ago, Jane was appointed group manager of the Policyholder Service and Accounting Departments at the home office. Before she actually assumed

---

* This case and the analysis are adapted (with permission) from Alber, Antone F., An Exploratory Study of the Benefits and Costs of Job Enrichment, Ph.D. dissertation, The Pennsylvania State University, 1977. Figures are reproduced directly, and major portions of the text are quoted directly.

the job, Jane was able to get away for a three-week management development program at the State University College of Business. One of the topics covered in the program was the concept of job enrichment, or job redesign. Jane had read about job enrichment in several of her trade journals, but the program was her first opportunity to think about the concept in some detail. In addition, several of the program participants had had some experience (both positive and negative) with job redesign projects.

Jane was intrigued with the idea. She knew how boring routine administrative tasks could become, and she knew from previous supervisory work that turnover of clerical personnel was a real problem. In addition, her conversations with the Administrative Vice President and Joe Bellows, the Personnel Manager, led her to believe that some trials with redesigning the work would be supported and favorably regarded.

Group Policyholder Service Department

The principal activities undertaken in this department are the sorting and opening of incoming mail and then matching to accounting files; reviewing of Group Insurance Bills from policy holders; and coding required changes to policies (e.g., new employees and terminations). These activities are carried out by approximately 28 people; 53 percent of whom were over age 35, 82 percent female, 89 percent high school graduates, and 53 percent with less than two years experience in their current job.

Organizationally, the department is headed by a manager. The employees are grouped into the four functional categories of clerical support, senior technician, change coder, and special clerk. The general work flow and a more specific list of the tasks carried out within each functional category are shown in Fig. 13.8.

The Group Policyholder Service Department shares the same physical working area as the Accounting Department. The people within Policyholder Service who work in the different functional categories are in very close proximity to one another, frequently just one desk away. The files for the department are located at one corner of the work area and the supervisors had offices along one side (see Fig. 13.9).

In the last few months, Jane has observed that the functional breakdown and the accompanying physical arrangement of people and files leads to a number of problems. Since work is assigned or selected on a random basis, there is no personal accountability for it. Files are at one corner of the work area where they can be retrieved by the clerical group and distributed to a senior technician who randomly distributes them to be processed. After a file is coded, it is placed in a holding area for processing by the Accounting Department. Here, assignment of work is also done on a random basis. It was difficult to respond to phone calls or written requests for information promptly, because it is frequently difficult to find a file. In fact, several people are kept busy doing nothing but looking for files.

The typical employee performs a job which consisted of two tasks on approximately an 11-minute cycle. All work is cross-checked. The training for the job is minimal and there are a number of individuals performing the same set of tasks on files randomly issued. A clerk occasionally corresponds with a policyholder, but all correspondence goes out with the manager's signature on it. The manager thus receives all phone calls and correspondence from policyholders.

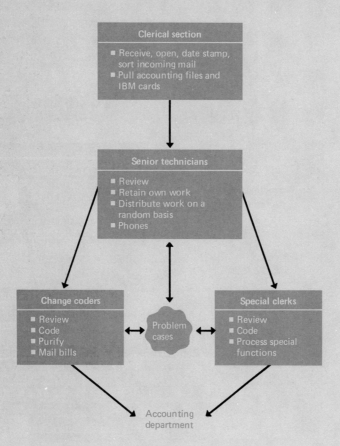

13.8
Policyholder Service Department work flow and tasks.

Because of the random distribution of work, individual performance is difficult to measure. There are spot checks on some completed work by someone other than the doer, but it is difficult or impossible to determine the specific individual who was responsible. Consequently, it is not possible to provide specific information to individuals at regular intervals about their work performance.

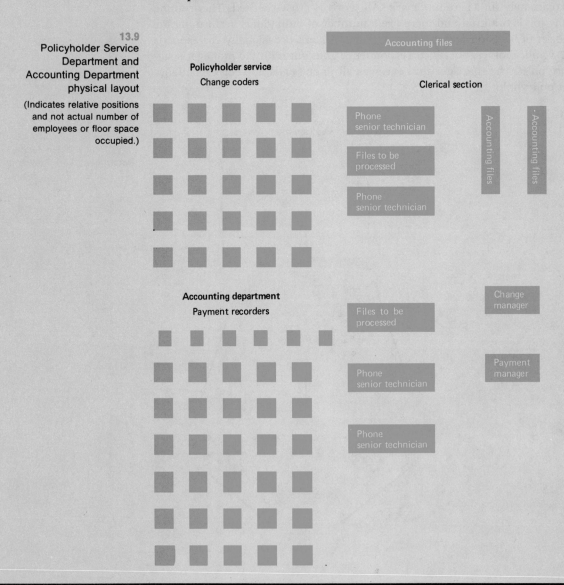

13.9
Policyholder Service
Department and
Accounting Department
physical layout
(Indicates relative positions
and not actual number of
employees or floor space
occupied.)

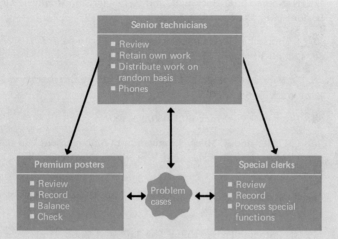

Accounting Department

The Accounting Department processes the files, bills, and checks received from the Group Policyholder Service. Premiums are posted on IBM cards and worksheets. Necessary adjustments are made to accounts and the checks, cards, and worksheets are balanced. Approximately 28 people are employed at any one time performing these tasks. Seventy-seven percent of the work force are under 35 years of age. Everyone is at least a high school graduate and 54 percent had less than two years experience in the job they were performing.

The department has both a manager and a supervisor. The employees are divided into senior technicians, premium posters, and special clerks. The general work flow and tasks carried out in each of these functional areas is shown in Fig. 13.10. As shown in Fig. 13.9, the Accounting Department shares its work and files with Policyholders Service.

Work is selected on a random basis. Clerks go to a bookcase file and choose the cases they wish to do. Occasionally, correspondence with a policyholder is necessary, and is signed by the manager.

Questions

1. What are the problems in this case facing Jane Taylor?

2. List the hygiene and motivator factors.

3. What assumptions are you making about the employees' needs?

4. Using the Hackman-Oldham job enrichment model, what job characteristics would you change and why?

REFERENCES

1. D. Nadler, J. R. Hackman, and E. Lawler, III, *Managing Organizational Behavior.* Boston: Little Brown, 1979, p. 26.

2. J. Simnacher, Executive Surveys Food Fortunes. *Dallas Morning News.* September 30, 1980, B-10.

3. D. Katz and R. Kahn, *The Social Psychology of Organizations*, 2nd ed. New York: John Wiley & Sons, 1978.

4. *Business Week*, June 30, 1980, 99–100.

5. L. Porter and R. Miles, "Motivation in Management." In J. McGuire (ed.) *Contemporary Management: Issues and Viewpoints.* Engelwood Cliffs, NJ: Prentice-Hall, 1974, 545–570.

6. R. Steers and L. Porter, *Motivation and Work Behavior.* New York: John Wiley & Sons, 1979.

7. M. Putney, "Flying High: The Life and Good Times of Frank Borman." *Dallas Times Herald*, Sunday Supplement, January 27, 1980, 8–10.

8. A. Maslow, "A Theory of Human Motivation." *Psychological Review* **80,** 1943, 370–396; *Motivation and Personality* (rev. ed.). New York: Harper & Row, 1970.

9. For reviews of the literature, see: M. Wahba and L. Bridwell, Maslow Reconsidered: "A Review of Research on the Need Hierarchy Theory." *Organizational Behavior and Human Performance* **15,** 1976, 212–240; and J. Miner, *Theories of Organizational Behavior.* Hinsdale, IL: Dryden Press, 1980, pp. 18–43.

10. J. Rauschenberger, N. Schmidt, and J. Hunter, "A test of the Need Hierarchy Concept by a Markov Model of Change in Need Strength." *Administrative Science Quarterly* **25,** 1980, 654–670.

11. A. Van de Ven and D. Ferry, *Measuring and Assessing Organizations.* New York: John Wiley-Interscience Publications, 1980, pp. 203–240.

12. F. Herzberg, B. Mausner, and B. Snyderman, *The Motivation to Work.* New York: John Wiley & Sons, 1959.

13. For an excellent overview of this literature, see: R. Aldag and A. Brief, *Task Design and Employee Motivation.* Glenview, IL: Scott Foresman, 1979. J. Champoux, "A Three-Sample Test of Some Extensions of the Job Characteristics Model of Work Motivation." *Academy of Management Journal* **23,** 1980, 466–478; and H. Arnold and R. House, "Methodological and Substantive Extensions to the Job Characteristics Model of Motivation." *Organizational Behavior and Human Performance* **25,** 1980, 161–183.

14. J. R. Hackman and G. Oldham, *Work Redesign.* Reading, MA: Addison-Wesley, 1980; and G. Oldham and J. R. Hackman. "Work Design in the Organizational Context." In *Research in Organizational Behavior*, Vol. 2, 1980, B. Staw and L. Cummings (eds.), Greenwich, CT: JAI Press 1980, pp. 247–278.

15. B. Nossiter, "In Tidy Dubuque, Money and Malaise." *Washington Post*, April 22,

1979, A4. For similar comments, see: P. Harper, "Reworking the Work Ethic." *Dallas Times Herald*, April 27, 1980, G1.

16. A. Poza and M. Markus, "Success Story: The Team Approach to Work Restructuring." *Organizational Dynamics*, 1980 (Winter) 3–25. For an experiment in a coal mine, see M. Blumberg, "Job Switching in Autonomous Work Groups: An Exploratory Study in a Pennsylvania Coal Mine." *Academy of Management Journal* **23,** 1980, 287–306.

17. R. Dunham, "The Design of Jobs." In *Introduction to Orgnizational Behavior: Text & Readings.* L. Cummings and R. Dunham (eds.). Homewood, IL: Richard D. Irwin, 1980, pp. 387–404; and J. Slocum and H. Sims, A Typology for Integrating Technology, Organization and Job Design. *Human Relations* **33,** 1980, 193–212.

18. V. Vroom, *Work and Motivation.* New York: John Wiley & Sons, 1964.

19. D. Nadler, J. R. Hackman, and E. Lawler, *Managing Organizational Behavior.* Boston, MA: Little Brown, 1979, p. 32.

20. L. Porter and E. Lawler, *Managerial Attitudes and Performance.* Homewood, IL: Richard D. Irwin, 1968; L. Cummings, "Organizational Behavior." *Annual Review of Psychology* **33,** 1982.

21. G. Gorn and R. Kanungo, "Job Involvement and Motivation: Are Intrinsically Motivated Managers More Job Involved?" *Organizational Behavior and Human Performance* **26,** 1980, 265–277.

22. J. Sheridan and J. Slocum, "The Direction of the Causal Relationship Between Job Satisfaction and Work Performance." *Organizational Behavior and Human Performance* **14,** 1975, 159–172. Also see M. Stahl and A. Harrell, "Modeling Effort Decisions with Behavioral Decision Theory: Toward an Individual Differences Model of Expectancy Theory." *Organizational Behavior and Human Performance* **27,** 1981, 303–325.

23. R. Rice, J. Near, and R. Hunt, "The Job-Satisfaction-Life Satisfaction Relationship: A Review of Empirical Research." *Basic and Applied Social Psychology*, 1981; A. Abdel-Halim, "Effects of Higher Order Need Strength on the Job Performance–Job Satisfaction Relationship." *Personnel Psychology* **33,** 1980, 335–347; and C. Cook, Guidelines for Managing Motivation. *Business Horizons* **23,** 2, 1980, 61–69.

24. S. Kerr, On the Folly of Rewarding A, While Hoping for B. *Academy of Management Journal* **18,** 1975, 769–783. S. Kerr, "Some Characteristics and Consequences of Organizational Reward Systems." In *Research in Organizational Behavior*, Vol. 3, B. Staw, and L. Cummings (eds.). Greenwich, CT: JAI Press, 1981.

Chapter 14

THE LEADERSHIP PROCESS

When you have finished reading this chapter, you should be able to:

1. Identify the elements in the leadership process.

2. List the reasons why people want to become leaders.

3. Describe how people get power in organizations and how power affects their leadership abilities.

4. Describe three major approaches to the study of leadership.

5. List the situational factors that affect the leadership process.

6. Identify the three contingency approaches to leadership and the major points in each approach.

PREVIEW CASE

Colgate-Palmolive Company*

In 1979, the board of directors of the Colgate-Palmolive Company replaced David Foster with Keith Crane as its Chief Executive Officer (CEO). The major reason for this move was the board's belief that Foster's leadership style was no longer effective.

The 58-year-old Foster had ruled Colgate with an iron hand since taking over as CEO in 1971. When he took over, Procter and Gamble was outselling Colgate domestically by three to one. Foster transformed Colgate from a stodgy soap and detergent marketer with annual sales of $1.3 billion into a conglomerate doing more than $3.1 billion in 1979. Foster developed a program of diversifying into business not directly competitive with Procter Gamble — such as Bancroft (a tennis racket manufacturer), Ram Golf equipment; and the Dinah Shore Circle Golf Championship. By late 1977, profits began to drop and the value of Col-

---

* From H. D. Menzies, "Changing of the Guard at Colgate." *Fortune*, September 24, 1979, 92. By permission of FORTUNE magazine.

gate's stock declined sharply on the New York Stock Exchange. The board reasoned that Foster's one-man show and autocratic style of leadership was the major cause of Colgate's poor financial performance. Foster stated, "I am not a delegator. It's not my style." Promising executives sought opportunities elsewhere. Foster's acquisitions had turned Colgate into a complex organization and, because he did not delegate authority to others and train them to make decisions, the effectiveness of Colgate suffered.

Crane, on the other hand, delegates authority and believes subordinates should be involved in providing needed information to make decisions. He has been known to rise at two or three in the morning and put in a couple of hours of work on a subordinate's request before going back to bed. As a result, his subordinates are committed to the decision and feel they can take their problems to him. Crane pushes subordinates hard but gives them the authority to make important decisions. He believes a strong management team is essential for the continued growth of Colgate.[1]

Looking at the Colgate experience, why was Foster successful for eight years and then unsuccessful? In choosing Crane as Foster's replacement, Colgate's board of directors chose a person whose leadership style was vastly different from Foster's. Why? This chapter attempts to answer these and other questions related to the leadership process.

IMPORTANCE OF LEADERSHIP

Leadership involves influencing a person or group toward the accomplishment of certain goals.[2] It involves the behavior of a leader and followers in a specific situation. From the large numbers of leadership training programs and the persisting number of organizational decisions that depend on a manager's leadership abilities, it is clear that leadership is important. Since ancient times, writers of various beliefs and philosophies have sought to advise managers how to lead their organizations to greater effectiveness. Particularly influential in the past were such writers as Confucius, Plato, Aristotle, contributors to the Bible, and Machiavelli. They told leaders to be wise, bold, good, willing to compromise, unscrupulous, and well-advised.

Their advice found an eager audience. Many managers think that communication, motivation, and leadership are cure-alls that will solve the problems of their organizations. As a result, many writers found a ready and eager market for their cook-book answers that have generated a number of fads in leadership. The results have been costly. Strategies — such as "be democratic," or "rule with an iron hand" — which have succeeded under one set of circumstances have been applied without much thought to other situations for which they were not well suited. Managers and administrators have plenty of incentives to search for better ways to exercise their leadership talents. Top corporate administrators receive high salaries for their ability to increase organizational effectiveness.

Managers are those persons in charge of the organization or one of its departments. They are given formal authority over a department, which leads to two basic managerial purposes. First of all, managers must ensure that the organization produces its goods and services efficiently. Managers must design the organization's basic operations to be stable; they must maintain that stability; and yet they must make it adaptable to its changing environment. To accomplish this, managers must create a unified whole rather than direct each department separately. One analogy is of a symphony orchestra's conductor, through whose efforts, vision, and leadership instrumental parts become the living whole of a musical performance. But the conductor is only an interpreter of the composer's score; the manager is both composer and conductor. Managers must ensure that the organization serves the ends of those persons who control it. They must interpret the desires of the stockholders (e.g., 10 percent annual growth, be a socially responsible citizen, maintain high profits) and combine these to produce results.

In Chapter One we indicated that most managers play three roles: interpersonal, informational, and decisional. Leadership is most clearly seen in the *interpersonal role*. Every manager must motivate and encourage his or her employees, somehow reconciling their individual needs with the goals of the organization. In virtually every contact the manager has with subordinates, subordinates wonder: "Does she approve?" "How would he like the report to turn out?" "Is the company more interested in saving a buck in the short run or gaining a bigger market share in the future?" Charming an important customer or preparing a performance appraisal for a subordinate are parts of the interpersonal role that managers play. Similarly, company presidents who work through the details of a bank loan, negotiate a big contract, or preside at a dinner in honor of long-service employees do so because they are the leaders. They are expected to handle these activities because of their status and their inspirational, legal, and ceremonial role in the organization.

To help you understand the leadership process, this chapter has been organized into three major sections. First, we discuss the nature of the leadership process and the sources of power leaders have at their command to influence subordinates. Second, we present two traditional approaches used to understand the leadership process. The third section discusses three contingency approaches to leadership.

Whenever two or more persons get together, who is the leader? Is the leader the person with whom others identify and whom they wish to imitate? Or the person who is most popular in the group? Or the person who exercises influences over the group's decision and behavior? In order to answer these questions, we must difine the "leader" and the leadership process.

NATURE OF
LEADERSHIP

What is Leadership?

Leadership has been defined as an influence process. Leaders are persons others want to follow. Leaders are the ones who command the trust and loyalty of followers — the great persons who capture the imagination and admiration of those with whom they deal. For example, young golfers who admire Jack Nicklaus, Tom Watson, Carol Mann, or Nancy Lopez might try to copy their swings or dress patterns or use clubs named after these golfing professionals. When teaching children about our country's history, teachers in public schools usually point to great people such as George Washington or Abraham Lincoln, and they often refer to these figures as "born leaders."

Most of the world's work, however, is done by "ordinary" people who work in hospitals, insurance agencies, universities, steel mills, and government offices. Among other things, people in these organizations plan, organize, communicate, and accept the responsibility to reach organizational goals. For example, Ms. Smith works for a large university and has been elected chairperson of the local United Way drive. An important part of this job is to prepare the budget, talk, write letters, make phone calls, and perform many other duties that do not directly involve the supervision of others. She is a *leader* in the sense that she *is able to communicate ideas to others in such a way as to influence their behavior to reach some goals.* She is being asked to get others to act in a way that will lead to achievement of the goals of the United Way.

Even though leadership is something a person does, it should not be confused with an individual's activity level. Aggressiveness and the constant direction of others do not necessarily indicate leadership. At times a good leader may hesitate before making a judgment, or stay in the background so others may talk.

Leadership emphasizes the relationship between two or more persons.[3] The dynamics of leadership include the leader, the follower, and the specific situation. Figure 14.1 illustrates this point. Leadership cannot be studied in a vacuum; it must be studied in group settings. Effective leadership occurs only if the leader influences the activities of followers. Usually, one cannot really threaten or force people to behave in specific ways. Leadership is the result of an exchange between followers and a leader, and it must carry satisfaction for both parties. In accepting a leader's ways of doing things, followers voluntarily give up some of their freedom to make decisions. In effect, they permit the leader to make decisions that affect them in specific situations. In return for permitting themselves to be influenced by another person, followers want to receive certain economic and psychic rewards from the leader. For example, the coach of a sports team demonstrates coaching abilities by leading the team to a championship. The players follow the coach's advice on the field and suspend their own judgment because of the coach's ability to bring psychic and economic rewards to them. Examples of psychic rewards might include a sense of achievement from winning, media focus on the team, or the fulfillment of players' personal goals. Economic rewards might include a bonus for winning a championship, opportunities to make commercial endorsements, and so on.

14.1

Basic factors in the leadership process

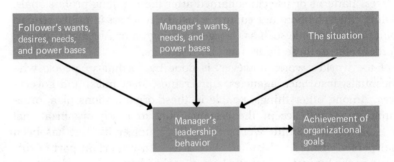

Motivation to Lead

Why do people want to be leaders?[4] First, it is important to realize that very few people are forced to assume leadership positions against their will. Those who don't *want* to become leaders usually don't. Employees often decline promotions to supervisory and managerial positions. These people simply are not motivated to become leaders in these particular situations.

Though some people avoid leadership roles, many others view them as having great deal to offer, and seek them out. If top managers hope to attract the best people to perform leadership functions, they should know what attracts those people to leadership jobs.

There is little doubt that leadership positions can provide important rewards. Economic rewards are among these. For example, in 1980, Harding Lawrence, President of Braniff Airlines, had a salary over $450,000; John Brookout, President of Shell Oil, has a salary over $540,000, and John Thompson, President of Southland (owners of Seven-Eleven and Chief Auto Parts), earned more than $400,000. Are these men worth these salaries? During Lawrence's 15-year tenure at Braniff, Braniff's revenues have gone from $100 million in 1964 to nearly $1 billion in 1980. The company has expanded its operations into running hotels, vocational training, security and other airport services, and private-plane servicing. Few would argue that during Lawrence's presidency, Braniff has become one of the nation's fastest-growing airlines.

Leadership, however, is often sought when there are no economic rewards. For example, the team captain, union steward, church leader, and PTA president are not paid for their positions, but people who willingly occupy these positions usually exercise leadership. Why? Because leaders can satisfy their needs for self-actualization.

Followers make it possible for leaders to satisfy some of these needs. Knowing that one can affect one's own destiny and the destiny of others, or being recognized as the best in a given field can be important personal rewards for the leader. This is the price followers pay for the leadership of others. The leader receives rewards from the group, just as group members receive rewards from the leader. Therefore, to remain in a leadership position, the leader must help group members gain satisfactions otherwise beyond their reach. In return, the group satisfies the leader's needs for power and prominence while helping reach organizational goals.

Sources of Power

A leader has certain power or resources to provide or withhold from the group to help it reach its goal(s). To influence anyone, you must appeal to one or more of their needs. These needs were discussed in the chapter on motivation. If you are holding a gun to my head and look as though you might fire it, chances are I will do what you ask. History demonstrates, however, that there are many situations in which people refuse to obey even when faced with severe punishment. The implication for the leader is clear: Effective leadership depends as much upon the follower accepting direction as on the leader giving it. Whether the leader can successfully influence others depends on the answers to these implicit questions from the followers:

1. What is the probability that I can achieve the objectives expected of me?

2. If I meet the objectives, what is the probability that the leader will reward me or withhold punishment?

3. What is the probability that the reward will satisfy my needs?

4. Does the leader have the power to make things happen?

Because power and influence are central to the manager's job, let's turn our attention to the reasons why a subordinate will follow a leader — the bases of the leader's power. One of the most useful frameworks for understanding these bases of power was developed by French and Raven.[5] These authors have identified five different sources of power: (1) legitimacy, (2) control over rewards, (3) coercion, (4) referent or personal liking, and (5) expertise.

1. Legitimate power is based on one's position in the hierarchy. It is a manager's formal authority. The corporation president has greater legitimate power than has the vice-president of manufacturing to speak on issues of corporate policy. By the same token, the vice-president of manufacturing has more legitimate power than the first-line supervisor to decide on issues of capital expenditures, work flow, inventory levels, and the like.

2. Reward power is the ability of a supervisor to give out rewards valued by subordinates. Subordinates comply with their supervisors' requests in the belief that their behavior will be rewarded. Reward power, then, depends on the leader's ability to reward those subordinates (with either intrinsic or extrinsic rewards) for their compliance. The supervisor may be able to reward them through favorable job assignments, vacation schedules, lunch breaks, and pay increases. At Peat, Marwick, and Mitchell, an accounting firm, supervisors distinguish between the good and poor CPA's by giving the poor CPA's "bag" jobs — those having clients with which it is usually very difficult to work. By giving some accountants bag jobs, the company is saying that their work is unacceptable to the firm and that they should start looking for another job.

3. Coercive power is based on fear and punishment. If subordinates change their behavior because of fear of punishment from a superior, they are responding to coercion. Punishments might be in the form of official reprimands, poor work assignments, or a strict enforcement of all work rules. A manager who says, "I want these shipped by June fifteenth or heads will roll," is using coercion.

The behavior resulting from the use of coercion is highly unpredictable. Coercion may stop undesired behavior, but it does not necessarily produce desired behavior. The worker who is reprimanded for shoddy work, for example, may simply stop performing the task at all. Some workers may seek to avoid being reprimanded by falsifying performance reports rather than by changing the quality of their performance.

4. Referent power is based on the followers' identification with the leader. This identification may be based on personal admiration and usually includes followers' desire to be "like" the leader. In other words, referent power usually is associated with people who possess admirable personal characteristics, charisma, or good reputations. Some famous people who appear to have had great referent power include Abraham Lincoln, John F. Kennedy, Martin Luther King, and Franklin Delano Roosevelt.

5. Expert power stems from a belief that the leader has some talent or special knowledge subordinates do not. Street gangs usually assign expert power to those who can fight the best; academicians, to those colleagues who write journal articles and books. Expert power is narrow in scope, since a person's expertise generally is limited to specific task areas. For example, a star tennis player with high expert power on the courts may not possess such power in a chemistry class.

Power ultimately comes from the subordinates' willingness to follow the directions of a leader and the leader's ability to satisfy subordinates' needs.[6] Access to resources and information and the ability to act quickly make it possible for the manager to accomplish more and to pass on rewards and information to subordinates. For this reason, people tend to refer to some managers as having "Clout." **Clout** is a person's pull or political influence in an organization. Some common examples of managerial clout are listed in Table 14.1.[7] Looking at these, one gets the impression that a manager's power does not come from a style or skill so much as from the manager's location in the formal and informal systems of the organization. Subordinates cooperate with a manager largely because they feel that the manager has the power to "make things happen."

Where does power come from?

If a manager's power is related to perceived connections within the system, what are the factors that generate power or powerlessness? Some of these are listed in Table 14.2. Power is most easily gained when a manager has a job that is designed and located to allow *discretion* (nonroutine), *recognition* (visibility and notice), and *relevance* (being central to major problems pressing the organization). Power comes to the manager who has relatively close contact with *sponsors* (higher-level managers who give approval, prestige, and backing). *Peer networks* (circles of friends who provide information

**14.1
A Manager with
"Clout" Gets:**

- A good job for a talented subordinate
- Approval for expenditures beyond the budget
- Above-average salary increases for subordinates
- Items on the agenda at meetings
- Access to top people in company
- Early information about decisions and policy shifts

Factors	Generates power when factors are:	Generates powerlessness when factors are:
Rules inherent in the job	few	many
Predecessors in the job	few	many
Established routines	few	many
Task variety	high	low
Rewards for unusual performance/ innovation	many	few
Flexibility around use of people	high	low
Approvals needed for nonroutine decisions	few	many
Physical location	central	distant
Publicity about job activities	high	low
Relation of tasks to current problem areas	central	peripheral
Interpersonal contact in the job	high	low
Contact with senior officials	high	low
Participation in programs, conferences, meetings	high	low
Participation in problem-solving task forces	high	low
Advancement prospects of subordinates	high	low

14.2
Organizational Factors that Contribute to Power or Powerlessness

faster than the formal communication system) also provide power. *Subordinates* (who can be developed to relieve managers from some of their work and who can go to bat for the manager's plan) are another source of power.

Managerial implications   When managers are in powerful situations, it is easier for them to accomplish more. They are likely to be motivated themselves and to have motivated and committed subordinates. Their activities are likely to be on target and turn out successfully. They can interpret policies to meet the needs of a situation. Because powerful managers have connections and are oriented to get results, they tend to delegate more.

Those managers who have power know how to play "games" to obtain and control information and make it practically incomprehensible for others. The advent of the computer has made "games" easier to play for managers who want power. Once a company invests millions of dollars in a computer system, people in the company feel obliged to pay some attention to the information the computer produces. In a large steel company, the vice-president of finance was successful in compiling data on such complex forms that only he and his subordinates could explain the results. Whatever the question, the computer was likely to provide several responses, none of them in the form that nonfinancial people could understand. This vice-president had all the information needed to keep his position in the organization very powerful.

Managers who are relatively powerless tend to live in another world. Since they lack money, personnel resources, materials, and are not part of the "in-group," things do not happen easily for them. They tend to use coercive power to make things happen. When managers overuse coercive power, problems arise with morale and the flow of information. In a large nationwide insurance company, supervisors in district offices complain, "Our employees' attitudes are negative. They turn people against the company. They put down top management. They build themselves up by always complaining about head-quarters, but they prevent their staff from getting information quickly."

TRADITIONAL APPROACHES TO THE STUDY OF LEADERSHIP

In Alfred Sloan's book *My Years with General Motors*, the former chief operating officer of General Motors asks whether or not managerial leadership is a property of the individual or a term describing relationships among members of a group.[8] For years, many have tried to answer this complex question by turning to all sorts of gimmicks. The analysis of handwriting (graphology), the study of skull shapes (phrenology), and the investigation of the position of the stars and other celestial bodies (astrology) have been used. To appreciate the complexity and diversity of the leadership problem, we shall review several approaches to the study of leadership.[9] In this part, we review the trait and behavioral approaches.

Trait Approach

For centuries, philosophers and scientists have argued the "great man" theory. Was the destiny of the world shaped by individuals such as Alexander the Great, Queen Elizabeth I, and Winston Churchill? Was there something in their personalities that enabled them to have a singificant impact on history? Or do such people become leaders because they just happen to have been in the right place at the right time? Your own personal biases will influence how you answered these questions. Under the proper circumstances, there could be an individual whose personality and leadership style fit the situation and who also happened to be in the right place at the right time.

The controversy surrounding the "great man" theory has called attention to the "trait" approach to leadership. Much of the early study on leadership was directed at identifying the characteristics of leaders. The ***trait*** approach assumes that certain physical, social, personality, and personal traits are inherent within leaders. These traits can be used to distinguish leaders from nonleaders. The traits commonly identified with leaders included the following:

1. *Physical traits:* Over 6 feet tall, weigh over 175 lbs, physical attractiveness, vitality, physical stamina, muscular body shape.

2. *Social traits:* Empathy, tact, patience, employee-oriented, status, emotional maturity.

3. *Personality traits:* Dominance, aggressiveness, extroversion, self-esteem, integrity, confidence.

4. *Personal traits:* Verbal skills, judgment, intellectual capacity, achievement-oriented, capacity to work hard, responsible.

There is considerable common-sense support for the notion that successful leaders have interest patterns, abilities, and perhaps also some personality traits, that differ from those of less successful managers. However, most researchers have come to regard the "trait" approach as not very useful to our understanding of the leadership process. Researchers have failed to identify leadership traits that can be used consistently as standards for designating individuals as either leaders or nonleaders.[10] This does not imply that individual traits have nothing to do with leadership, only that their significance must be evaluated in relation to other things.

The major criticisms of the trait approach focus on physical and personality traits. Physical traits have not been found to have a consistent relationship with successful leadership. In the military or police, for example, members must meet certain minimal standards of height and weight in order to perform their tasks effectively. Although these attributes may be helpful in the physical performance of jobs, height and weight do not relate to being a successful leader. Likewise, while some personality traits have been found related to leadership, the results have not been consistent. For example, some of the personality traits found to relate to a salesperson's success (in terms of sales volume) include gregariousness, risk-taking, impulsiveness, exhibitionism, and egocentrism. On the other hand, successful coaches of team sports — such as football, basketball, hockey, and soccer — have personalities that include self-assertion, self-assurance, a strong need for power, and a low need for security. But there are successful coaches who have a different personality profile.

Despite its limitations, the trait approach should not be discarded too hastily. It has made some contributions toward clarifying the nature of leadership. Most universities, for example, are run by educators who hold doctoral degrees and have educational experience; hospitals require the chiefs of their medical staffs to have medical degrees; and supreme court justices have legal backgrounds. These can be considered "personal traits." Many practicing managers will argue that people with certain personal traits are still more likely to become leaders than others. Such personal traits may include: an ability to verbalize feelings and concepts, above average intelligence (but not genius), sympathy for group members, some insight into group situations, a high technical skill, and flexibility in formulating new concepts and ideas. Although none of these personal traits is absolutely necessary, they all help the individual perform in his or her leadership role.

The one personal trait that those who assume leadership roles *must* have is the *motivation to be a leader*.[11] In general, the stronger a person's motivation to be a leader, the more likely that person is to achieve a leadership position. Of course, the reasons for that motivation could be many: e.g., an urge to dominate others, devotion to the group and to the group's goals, a high-level aspiration for either self or group, a need for prestige and esteem, and economic rewards.

All of the personal traits mentioned may have an influence on the group's *choice* of a leader. However, the *success* of a leader often depends more on situational factors than on personal traits. People may become leaders simply because they are in the right place at the right time. They may have specific knowledge or abilities directly fitting the requirements of a leadership role. They may have the greatest seniority among group members. They may be the correct age. They may have access to important information and be able to control the flow of this information to other group members.

To summarize, the idea that leadership can be determined by personal traits has proved to be too simple. The dream of a method by which leadership could be measured and the person with the largest amount of it selected as the leader has not yet been fulfilled.

**Behavioral
Approach**

While it seems that no set of traits distinguishes leaders from nonleaders or effective leaders from less effective leaders, it is still possible that some methods or styles of leadership are more effective than others. Instead of looking at the traits of effective leaders, perhaps we should be searching for behavioral indicators of effective leadership. Effective and ineffective leaders may be distinguished by their behaviors.

Interest in the behaviors of leaders emerged during the 1930s and is now evident in two major research programs begun in the late 1940s. These were carried out at Ohio State University and the University of Michigan. During the 1930s, researchers conducted a study with small children to determine the effect of three types of leadership styles on their performance.[12] Researchers labeled the leadership styles as autocratic, democratic, and laissez-faire (literally, "let it be").

The **autocratic leader** led by command, and the commands were generally obeyed to avoid punishments. This leader was task-centered and tended to give criticism when productivity slowed. The **democratic leader** permitted the group to discuss and make decisions. They encouraged members to work with whomever they chose, and were supportive of the children's work. The **laissez-faire leader** allowed the group total freedom and exerted a minimal amount of personal influence.

The findings indicated that although the quantity of work produced was greater in the autocratic groups, the quality of the work in the democratic groups was superior. When the autocratic leader left the production area, the children almost completely stopped working (a sign of job dissatisfaction). By contrast, the performance of those under the democratic leader decreased only slightly in the leader's absence. In general, the laissez-faire approach — complete permissiveness and indifference — was not effective in stimulating performance. It did not produce either higher quality or more quantity than the other two approaches. In fact, there was less work done under laissez-faire leadership, and the work was of poorer quality than that of either the democratic or autocratic group.

From this early leadership study of children, researchers at Ohio State have identified three styles of leadership: supportive, participative, and instrumental.[13]

Supportive style   **Supportive leadership** considers the needs of subordinates and is concerned with their well-being, status, and comfort. Supporting leaders seek to create a friendly and pleasant working climate for employees. They assume that subordinates want to do their best, and their job is to make it easier for subordinates to achieve their own goals. Supportive leaders seek to gain acceptance by treating subordinates with respect and dignity. They tend to downplay their formal position in the company and the use of coercive power. Researchers at Ohio State have identified some typical behaviors of supportive leaders:

1. They express appreciation when subordinates do a good job.

2. They do not demand more than subordinates can do.

3. They help subordinates with their personal problems.

4. They are friendly and can be approached easily.

5. They see that subordinates are rewarded for jobs well done.

Believers in the supportive leadership style claim that it is effective because it is more readily accepted by subordinates than are impersonal or autocratic styles. They contend that supportive leader behavior generates goodwill among the subordinates and leads to feelings of high job satisfaction. These attitudes will lead to close cooperation between the leaders and their subordinates, increase the motivation of subordinates to work, and create a productive work group.

In groups where leaders are rated high in supportiveness, subordinate satisfaction usually is high and turnover and grievance rates are low. Supportive leader behavior frequently has been found to have a positive effect on departmental and individual productivity.

Not all the research shows that supportive leader behavior results in higher job satisfaction and task performance. The major contingency was the task. If employees were working on interesting tasks and/or had considerable freedom from their supervisor, supportive leadership was not strongly related to their satisfactions or performance. Thus, it appears that the task is a *contingency* influencing the relationship between supportive leader behavior and the job satisfactions and performance of subordinates.

Participative leadership is characterized by the sharing of information, power, and influence between superiors and subordinates. The manager who uses this style treats subordinates as equals and allows them to influence decisions. This style ensures that all subordinates for whom a decision is important will have an opportunity to influence that decision. To accomplish this, participative leaders do the following:

Participative style

1. They share information with subordinates.

2. They seek out opinions, facts, and feelings from concerned parties.

3. They minimize blame.

4. They encourage alternatives.

5. They delay evaluation of alternatives until all have been presented.

Participative leaders try to make sure that all subordinates are involved in the decision-making process. They do not give up their roles by becoming members of the group. They encourage suggestions, independent thinking, and creativity by subordinates.

Participation should improve decision-making because the subordinates can use their expertise and knowledge on problems. Participative leadership is an effective means for obtaining relevant subordinate expertise and thereby improving the quality of the decision. Other researchers have stated that participation:

1. Clarifies the means of accomplishing goals.
2. Enables subordinates to select goals they value.
3. Increases the employees' control over what happens on the job.
4. Increases individuals' ego-involvement in the decision.

Considerable research has been done to determine the effects of participative leader behavior on subordinate satisfaction, performance, acceptance of decisions made by supervisors, and the quality of group decisions. Later in this chapter we will present a model that shows when a participative style of leadership works best. For now, let's look at how two *contingency* variables affect a leader's ability to use a participatory style — the *task* and the *personality characteristices* of the individual employee.

If the task itself does not permit the individual to take part in the decision-making process or become ego-involved with it, the participative style has little impact on performance. Simple, machine-paced tasks (such as those of an axle assembler on an automobile assembly line or an individual counting the bolts on a Vega's door) do not lend themselves to this style. There is little opportunity for participation in these tasks because they are controlled by a mechanically paced line. In fact, employees performing such tasks might see participation as a farce or sham.

Subordinates who have a high need for independence and who respect non-authoritarian behavior are likely to find the participation process satisfying and rewarding regardless of the task. Participation has its most positive effects on productivity and satisfaction when subordinates are predisposed toward participative leadership.

The success of a participative leader depends in large part on the intelligence of his or her subordinates and the amount of knowledge they have. Subordinates with high intelligence contribute more to the participative decision-making process than do those of low intelligence. Further, when subordinates have knowledge relevant to the decisions and supervisors do not have such knowledge, the participative style is likely to be more effective than when the opposite conditions prevail.

In summary, for participative leadership to be effective, subordinates must have favorable attitudes toward participation, the task must be complex or nonroutine, and there must be a high quality of subordinate acceptance or involvement. Participative leader behavior, much like supportive behavior, can have positive effects on job satisfaction and performance, but it is based on contingency factors — the task and personality of subordinates.

Instrumental leadership is characterized by managers who plan, organize, control, and coordinate the activities of subordinates to reach departmental or group goals. Some typical behaviors of instrumental leaders that have been identified by researchers at Ohio State include the following:

Instrumental style

1. They assign members to particular tasks.

2. They establish standards of job performance.

3. They inform subordinates of the job requirements.

4. They schedule work to be done.

5. They encourage the use of uniform procedures.

Like the results found in the previous sections on supportive and participative leader behavior, the evidence is mixed. Instrumental leader behavior is most likely effective when any of the following conditions are present:

1. There is great pressure for output due to demands imposed by sources other than the leaders.

2. The task is satisfying to subordinates.

3. The subordinates' attitudes, expectations, or personalities predispose them toward being told what to do and how to do it.

4. Subordinates' tasks are nonroutine.

5. The number of people working for the same leader is high (span of control greater than 12).

These obviously suggest that there are several critical conditions a leader must consider before using this style of leadership.[14] The real strength of the instrumental leader lies in his or her ability to control available resources and to use them in the most effective way for accomplishing the group's task.

The answer to this question is: PROBABLY NOT. For example, an instrumental leader skilled at motivating employees to produce more might be very successful in a highly competitive market. Mary Kay cosmetics needs leaders who have the you-all warmth of a Southern belle and the mind of a computer. In this company, a successful leader is well-organized, and can demonstrate the full line of cosmetics to her subordinates. At Mostek, an electronics company manufacturing specialized high-quality components, such leadership behaviors would be less useful. Under these conditions, the manager's success would depend on using a supportive or participatory style to maintain product quality and service.

Is There a
Universally Effective
Behavioral
Leadership Style?

Robert Tannenbaum and Warren Schmidt have suggested that a manager should consider three sets of forces before choosing a leadership behavior.[15]

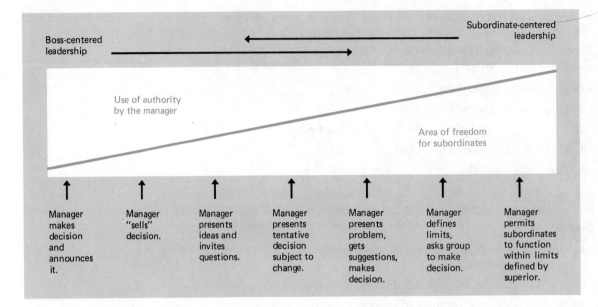

Boss-centered leadership ← → Subordinate-centered leadership

Use of authority by the manager

Area of freedom for subordinates

| Manager makes decision and announces it. | Manager "sells" decision. | Manager presents ideas and invites questions. | Manager presents tentative decision subject to change. | Manager presents problem, gets suggestions, makes decision. | Manager defines limits, asks group to make decision. | Manager permits subordinates to function within limits defined by superior. |

14.2
Continuum of leadership behavior

1. Forces in the manager.

2. Forces in the subordinates.

3. Forces in the situation.

The relationships between these forces are suggested in Fig. 14.2. How a manager leads will be influenced primarily by his or her background, knowledge, values, and experience (*forces in the manager*). For example, a manager who strongly values individual freedom may allow subordinates a great deal of independence in carrying out their job tasks. A manager who believes that the needs of the individual must come second to the needs of the organization may take a much more directive role in subordinates' activities.

Forces in the subordinates must also be considered before managers can choose an appropriate leadership style. According to Tannenbaum and Schmidt, a manager can allow greater participation and freedom under the following conditions:

1. When subordinates crave independence and freedom of action.

2. When subordinates want to have decision-making responsibility.

3. When subordinates identify with the organization's goals.

4. When subordinates are knowledgeable and experienced enough to deal with the problem efficiently.

5. When subordinates' experience with previous bosses leads them to expect participative management.

Where these conditions are missing, managers may have to lean more toward the authoritarian style. They can, however, vary their behavior once their subordinates gain self-confidence in working with them.

Finally, in choosing an appropriate leadership style, a manager must reckon with various *situational forces*. These forces might include such things as the organization's climate, the work group's norms, the nature of the group's work tasks, the pressures of time, and even environmental factors, which may affect organization members' attitudes toward authority.

Most managers seem to move toward a leadership style that will conform to the type of behavior favored by their own superiors. If their superior emphasizes human relations skills, the manager will be likely to choose an employee-centered style. If the decisive, take-charge style seems favored, the manager will tend to be task rather than employee oriented.

The specific work group also will affect the choice of style. A group that works well together may respond better to a free and open atmosphere than to close supervision. The same holds true for a group confident of its ability to solve problems as a unit. But if a work group is too large or spread over too wide an area, a participative management style may be difficult to use.

The nature of the problem and the pressures of time also influence the choice of managerial styles. For example, a complex problem requiring highly specialized skills and knowledge that only the manager possesses may require direct instructions and close supervision. Similarly, in situations where quick decisions are essential (as in emergencies), even democratic managers may revert to an authoritarian leadership style.

The leadership style a manager uses is not so important as its appropriateness for the manager, his or her subordinates, and the work situation. The most effective leaders are not authoritative or democratic but *flexible*. They are able to select a style that is comfortable for them and appropriate for the situation. Let's look at how David McLaughlin, president of Toro Company, adapted his leadership style to fit the situation.

CASE STUDY

McLaughlin's Leadership at the Toro Company*

Since 1973, David McLaughlin has been chairman and chief executive officer of the Toro Company, a manufacturer and marketer of outdoor maintenance equipment.[16] When McLaughlin joined Toro in 1970 as its 39 year-old president, the firm was known for its lawnmowers. Sales were around $57 million annually. During the next decade, under McLaughlin's leadership, Toro's image and marketing changed dramatically. In 1980, sales topped $375 million. McLaughlin assigned subordi-

---

* From "The Toro Team Has a Winning Game Plan." *Nation's Business* 67, 8 (August 1979), 34.

nates to develop new products other than lawnmowers, such as snow-throwers and automatic irrigation systems. He structured Toro into four new divisions: International, Consumer, Irrigation, and Institutional Products (example of instrumental style). In addition, McLaughlin attracted young managers to the company and established bonus systems to encourage initiative and product development.

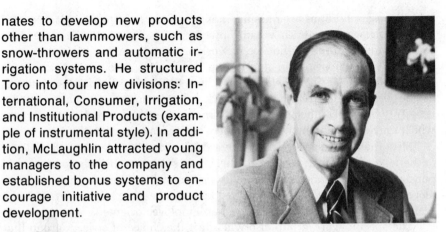

David T. McLaughlin, Chairman and Chief Executive Officer, The Toro Company. Photo courtesy of The Toro Company.

Toro seems to reflect the low-key but intense leadership style of McLaughlin. He calls it a "hands-on approach," and is a stickler for details. McLaughlin says, "I really get into some operating areas in greater detail than most people probably would. When broad decisions have to be made, I want to be able to put as much knowledge behind them as I can."

McLaughlin likes to be at his office no later than 7:30 A.M. He drives himself to work, saying that a chauffeur "isn't my style; too showy." Ten or eleven hours later he departs for home, bringing with him about one and a half hours of more work. He regards time as his biggest problem. Airline flights provide him with the opportunity to work. Early morning hours — sometimes 5:30 — are ideal for accomplishing special projects (another example of instrumental style).

Toro has grown in large part because McLaughlin delegates authority to subordinates, gives them responsibility, backs them, and lets them develop a concept (an example of participative style). As far as McLaughlin's relationship with his employees goes, he says it is respectful but not as fulfilling as he would like. He is not an autocratic leader but provides a strong sense of direction (instrumental style). When he feels strongly about something, he expresses his views. He says that people are not hesitant to disagree with him if they think differently. "There are many issues that I don't win." He realizes that it is unhealthy, especially in management, to take too strong a position on issues.

McLaughlin played football in college. He says that this is when he sharpened his competitive instinct, learned to accept defeats, and began to understand that "because you must rely on other people, you had better associate yourself with the strongest team possible" (an example of a supportive style). In fact, he recognized that his own management style needed *balancing* by someone who was more democratic. He hired Jack Cantu as president for just this reason. Jack had come up through the ranks and was viewed by other Toro employees as one who could help younger managers improve their decision-making abilities.

What can we learn from McLaughlin's experience? First, few people can use one style of leadership in all situations. At Toro, different situations required that McLaughlin use different leadership styles. Second, when McLaughlin recognized that his leadership style was not going to be effective in all situations, he hired Cantu. Cantu's leadership style was complementary to McLaughlin's and as a team, they will be able to extend Toro's success in the 1980s.

CONTINGENCY APPROACHES

We have shown how situational forces are important to understanding the process of leadership. It is still not possible to say with certainty just what kinds of leader traits or behaviors are characteristic of effective leaders. The leadership problem is apparently more complex. We now begin to look at a number of characteristics that make up the various contingency approaches to leadership. Contingency approaches suggest how managers should behave to lead most effectively. In this part, we will not review all the contingency models of leadership that have been developed. We will, however, review three of the more recent and well-known models:[17] Fiedler's model, House's Path-Goal model, and Vroom-Yetton's model.

Fiedler's Contingency Model

The first contingency model of leadership effectiveness was developed by Fiedler and his associates. This model, a departure from the trait and behavioral models of leadership, specifies that a group's performance depends on: (1) the motivation system of the leader; and (2) the degree to which the leader has control in a particular situation. The effectiveness of a leadership style depends on how it relates to the situation.[18]

Leadership style

A person's leadership style is measured on a scale that asks that person to "indicate the degree to which a person described favorably or unfavorably his *Least Preferred Co-worker* (LPC)" — That is, the employee with whom the leader could work least well. The high LPC person, one who describes his or her least preferred co-worker in a more favorable light, is motivated to seek strong emotional ties with co-workers. Fiedler calls this person a **relationship-motivated leader.** A relationship-motivated leader will regard such emotional ties with subordinates as an important part of being an effective leader.

A leader who describes his or her least preferred co-worker in an unfavorable manner is what Fiedler has come to call a low LPC leader. This person tends to be managing, task-controlling, and less concerned with the human-relations aspect of the job. To Fiedler, this is a **task-motivated leader**. This leader wants to get the job done. How subordinates feel about his or her leadership style is not that important.

Situational variables   Fiedler has identified three elements in the work situation that help determine which leadership style will be effective: leader-member relations, task structure, and the leader's position power.

Leader-Member Relations   *Leader-member relations* refers to the leader's feeling of being accepted by the group. This is the most important influence on a leader's effectiveness. If the manager gets along well with the rest of the group, and if the group respects the leader for his or her expertise and ability to get things for the group, then the leader may not have to rely on formal authority. On the other hand, if the leader is disliked or not trusted, cannot deliver rewards for members, and/or appears to lack "clout" with upper management, he or she may have to rely on orders to get his or her own subordinates to accomplish their tasks.

Task Structure   *Task structure* is the extent to which the task is simple and routine or is complex and can be done in numerous ways. A routine task is likely to have clearly defined performance goals (such as make a hamburger in 20 seconds) and detailed instructions on how to perform the task. Managers in such situations have a great deal of authority because there are clear guidelines by which to measure worker performance (the hamburger is made or it isn't). The manager can back up instructions by referring to the rulebook.

When the task is nonroutine and complex, the leader may have no more knowledge than the subordinates. Managers who are social workers, detectives, marketing researchers, controllers, and the like, perform jobs for which there are many ways to achieve the goal(s). That is, there are no clear guidelines on how best to proceed. Under these conditions, group members can easily disagree with or question the leader's instructions.

Leader Position Power   *Leader position power* is the extent to which the leader has legitimate, coercive, and reward power to influence subordinates. As we indicated earlier, some positions in business organizations carry a great deal of formal power and authority. In most voluntary organizations, the leader has little position power over volunteer workers. High position power simplifies a leader's ability to influence subordinates, while low position power makes the leader's task more difficult. The types and sources of power for a manager were illustrated in Tables 14.1 and 14.2.

The three aspects of the situation most important in determining the leader's influence and control are: (1) whether the work group accepts or rejects the leader (leader-member relations); (2) whether the task is relatively routine and simple or nonroutine and complex (task structure); and (3) whether the leader has high or low position power (position power). A group may be classified first by its leader-member relations, then by its task structure, and finally by its leader's position power. The higher each of these is (i.e., the more pleasant the leader-member relations, the more structured the task, and the greater the leader's position power), the more favorable the situation for the leader.

Matching the situation to the leader

Figure 14.3 shows Fiedler's contingency model of leadership. The three basic contingency variables are shown on the horizontal axis. The eight numbered blocks represent combinations of the three variables. These are arranged in order of leader favorableness, from most to least favorable. The model assumes that a leader will have the most control and influence in groups that fall into block 1. Here the leader is accepted and has high position power, and subordinates perform relatively structured tasks. A leader will have somewhat less control and influence in block 2, where the leader is accepted and has little position power, and the task is structured. In block 8, the leader's control and influence are very limited. Here the leader is not accepted by the group and has little position power, and the group performs an unstructured task.

Telephone offices, craft shops, meat departments, and grocery departments are typical of blocks 1 and 5. Team games (e.g., hockey, football, basketball) and surveying parties are typical of blocks 2 and 6. General foremen, ROTC groups, research chemists, military planning groups are representative of blocks 3 and 7. Racially divided groups, disaster groups, church groups, and mental health groups seem to illustrate blocks 4 and 8. The critical question is: What kind of leadership style is most effective in each of the different group situations?

Figure 14.3 shows the average results of the many studies conducted by Fiedler and his associates. The horizontal axis indicates the favorableness of the situation for the leader. Remember that the most favorable situation is on

Effectiveness of different leadership styles

14.3

Basic contingency model

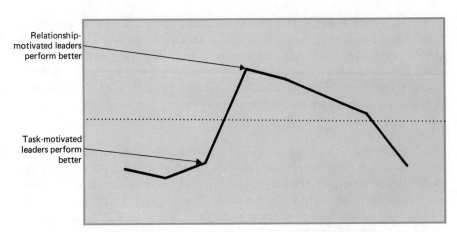

Leader-member relations	Good	Good	Good	Good	Poor	Poor	Poor	Poor
Task structure	Structured		Unstructured		Structured		Unstructured	
Leader position power	Strong	Weak	Strong	Weak	Strong	Weak	Strong	Weak
	(1)	(2)	(3)	(4)	(5)	(6)	(7)	(8)

the far left and ranges to least favorable on the far right. The vertical axis indicates the leader's style. The solid line on the graph above the midline indicates a positive relationship between a leader's style and group performance. That is, relationship-motivated leaders performed better than task-motivated leaders. The solid line below the midline indicates that task-motivated leaders performed better than relationship-motivated leaders. The solid line represents the best predictions between a leader's LPC score and work-group effectiveness.

Task-motivated leaders perform most effectively in the very favorable situations (blocks 1, 2, and 3) and in the least favorable situation (block 8). In favorable situations, there is good group atmosphere, the leader's position power is high, and the task is structured. In the most unfavorable situations (block 8), the task is unstructured, the leader lacks group support, and has low position power. The only hope for achieving the primary goal of the group appears to be through the use of task-motivated leadership.

Figure 14.3 indicates situations in which a relationship-motivated leader is most likely to perform better. Relationship-motivated leaders obtain best group efficiency under conditions of moderate or intermediate favorableness (blocks 4, 5, 6, and 7). Blocks 4 and 5 describe situations in which (1) the task is structured but the leader is disliked and must demonstrate care for the emotions of subordinates, or (2) the leader is liked but the group has an unstructured task and the leader must depend on the willingness and creativity of the group's members to accomplish the goals.

In summary, the performance level of a relationship-motivated leader is as follows:

Block: 1   2   3   4   5   6   7   8
Performance: Low $\rightarrow$ Low $\rightarrow$ Low-medium $\rightarrow$ High $\rightarrow$ High $\rightarrow$ High $\rightarrow$ Low-medium $\rightarrow$ Low

For the task motivated leader, this process is reversed:

Block: 1   2   3   4   5   6   7   8
Performance: High $\rightarrow$ High $\rightarrow$ High-medium $\rightarrow$ Low $\rightarrow$ Low $\rightarrow$ Low $\rightarrow$ Low-medium $\rightarrow$ High

Managerial implications

There are several important implications of this model. First, both relationship-motivated and task-motivated leaders perform well under some situations but not others. An outstanding salesperson who gets promoted to district manager may fail because his or her leadership style does not match the demands of the situation. Fiedler's contingency model suggests that the person's failure in the new position reflects a change in the situation for the leader. For example, the structure of the task has probably become more complex and nonroutine. The person's task-motivated leadership style no longer fits the situation. The new situation may call for a relationship-motivated style.

Second, it is not totally accurate to speak of a "good" or "poor" leader. Rather, one must think of a leader who performs well in one situation but not in another. Third, the performance of a leader depends on his or her motivational system and three key elements in the situation. Top management might change a leader's effectiveness by attempting to change the leader's style or by modifying the favorableness of the situation. To us, the real challenge for management is to recognize that effective leadership is influenced by the three variables described by Fiedler: leader-member relations, task structure, and leader's position power.

Research has failed to either verify or refute Fiedler's model.[19] Nevertheless, the model illustrates how a manager's leadership style can be highly effective in one situation and not effective in others. Fiedler's model was the first attempt to develop a contingency model of leadership.

House's Path-Goal Model

Puzzled by the contradictory findings in the leadership area, House developed the path-goal model of leadership based on expectancy theory of motivation (see Chapter 13).[20] As with all contingency leadership models, the path-goal model of leadership does *not* indicate the "one best way" to lead. It suggests that a leader must select the style most appropriate to the particular situation and the needs of his or her subordinates. House's model uses two styles of leadership: supportive and instrumental. These were discussed on pages 524 and 527 but we will redefine them briefly for you.

Leadership style

Supportive leadership is demonstrated by a friendly and approachable leader who shows concern for the status, well-being, and needs of subordinates. A supportive leader does little things to make the work more pleasant, treats members as equals, and is friendly and approachable. Instrumental leadership is demonstrated by letting subordinates know what is expected of them, giving specific guidance as to what should be done and how it should be done, scheduling work to be done, and maintaining definite standards of performance. An instrumental leader tells subordinates what to do to accomplish the task most easily and with a minimum of effort.

One of the functions of a leader is to increase the personal satisfactions of subordinates. The leader does this by clarifying what has to be done, reducing the roadblocks, and increasing opportunities for subordinates to obtain personal satisfactions. To the extent that the leader does these things, subordinates' motivation will increase. Subordinates should be satisfied with their jobs if their performance leads to things they value highly (e.g., promotions, salary increases). The function of the leader is to help subordinates reach their highly valued, job-related goals. The specific style of leader behavior should be determined by two contingency variables — characteristics of the subordinates and the task structure.

Characteristics of subordinates

The model states that a leader's style will be acceptable to subordinates to the extent that they see it as an immediate source of satisfaction or as necessary for future satisfaction. For example, if subordinates have high needs for self-esteem and affiliation, a supportive leadership style may satisfy these needs. On the other hand, subordinates with high need for autonomy, responsibility, and self-actualization are more likely to be motivated by leaders whose style is instrumental rather than supportive.

Task structure

The second major contingency variable in House's model is task structure. When the ways to perform the task are routine and simple, subordinates will regard any further clarification by the leader as unnecessarily close supervision. The close supervision of instrumental leadership may increase performance by preventing "goofing off," but it also can decrease job satisfaction. Workers are likely to view it as redundant, excessive, and directed at keeping them working on unsatisfying tasks. Given a routine and simple task, a supportive leader is likely to have more satisfied employees. This style is likely to increase the worker's satisfaction with the supervisor and company policies.

On the other hand, when the tasks are nonroutine and complex, an instrumental leadership style is appropriate. It helps subordinates to perform the task. A manager of an industrial relations team who explains to a general foreman how to process a grievance for arbitration is trying to help the general foreman present the company's case as well as possible to the labor arbitrator.

Figure 14.4 illustrates the dynamics of House's path-goal leadership model. The model indicates that different leadership styles are effective under dif-

Managerial implications

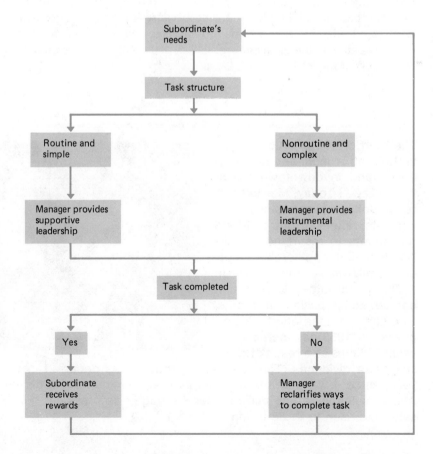

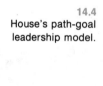
14.4
House's path-goal leadership model.

ferent conditions. A supportive leader will offer a wide range of rewards to subordinates — not only pay and promotion, but encouragement, pats on the back, and respect. In addition, a supportive leader is likely to tailor rewards to the needs and desires of individual subordinates. Supportive leadership will be most effective when the task is relatively routine and simple. An instrumental leader, on the other hand, will offer a narrower set of rewards based on the individual's performance — e.g., salary increases, bonuses, promotions. The subordinates of an instrumental leader will know exactly the productivity or performance level they will have to reach to gain these rewards. According to the model, this style of leadership is most effective when the subordinates are performing nonroutine and complex tasks.

Because the path-goal theory of leadership is fairly new, research evidence is still inconclusive. Some early findings indicate that workers on routine and simple jobs have reported higher job satisfactions when their leader uses a supportive rather than an instrumental leadership style. Workers performing nonroutine and complex tasks are more productive when the leader uses an instrumental style, but they do not necessarily report higher job satisfactions.[21] This approach is still highly promising because it attempts to explain *why* a particular leadership style will be more effective in one situation than in another. Looking at the leadership practices of J. W. Marriott should highlight the path-goal model.

CASE STUDY

J. W. Marriott's Leadership at Marriott Corporation

J.W. Marriott, Jr., President and Chief Executive Officer, Marriott Corporation.

The Marriott Corporation began in 1928 as a mom-and-pop root beer stand in downtown Washington D.C.[22] Today, Marriott is a billion-dollar-a-year business with interests ranging from fast-food restaurants to resort hotels, airline food catering, cruise ships, and family amusement parks. In 1978, Marriott Corporation earned $54.3 million in profits. One share of Marriott stock purchased in 1953 has increased in value 30 times as a result of stock splits and dividends. The spectacular growth has occurred in the 15 years since J. W. Marriott, Jr. took over as president from his father. Annual sales were $85 million when he began as president. By 1980, sales had risen to $1.55 billion.

The young Marriott logs more than 100,000 air miles a year visiting each of the 46 company-owned or -managed hotels and 17 franchised inns. He calls at many of the 60 flight kitchens that provide food service to airlines scattered throughout the world. He finds time to eat at Marriott's Big Boy coffee shops and Roy Rogers restaurants. He also is able to inspect personally many of Marriott's other businesses as well.

Marriott says, "This is a business of many details." There are few details that escape him. He delegates authority to his managers to run the restaurants (routine and simple tasks), but he gets deeply involved with the hotels and airline kitchens (nonroutine and complex tasks). He has a staff meeting every two weeks. These give Marriott a chance to find out what others are doing, allows the staff people to find out what he is doing, and gives him an opportunity to provide subordinates with feedback. Open communication is an important aspect of his leadership style.

Marriott travels in the field because he believes that he could not obtain the knowledge, information, and input needed to make right decisions if he stayed at his desk. He tries to provide a climate where "people can work together in harmony" (an example of supportive leadership). He believes people at *all* levels should be making decisions, and they should not be afraid to try new things or to make mistakes. He says that the key elements he expects from Marriott people are hard work and a dedication to excellence.

Because of the problems in the hotel and airline kitchen businesses, Marriott spends a lot of time on details, clarifying what he wants done, and not enough time on broader issues (instrumental leadership). He tries to delegate more detail, but he admits "I am still involved in an awful lot that I shouldn't be." He feels that since he has been in the business longer than anyone that reports to him, he is more experienced at knowing what to do and what not to do.

Vroom-Yetton Model

Vroom and Yetton have developed a contingency model of leadership that focuses on the degree of participation leaders should use in reaching a decision.[23] Earlier in this chapter we indicated that a participatory leadership style can be effective *if* certain conditions exist. The **Vroom-Yetton model** attempts to clarify the conditions.

Leadership styles   Vroom and Yetton have identified five styles of leadership, ranging from highly autocratic to highly participative. The highly autocratic style is used when the manager has all the information needed to make a decision and simply announces it to the group. The group may accept the decision by virtue of the position the leader occupies (legitimate power), because the leader is an acknowledged expert (expert power) or because the leader is strongly admired by the group (referent power). In such conditions, it is not at all difficult for the leader to "sell" his or her decision to subordinates. The participative style is used when it is needed to attain the group's acceptance and information. It is the best means for permitting individuals to express their views. Vroom and Yetton's five styles are shown in Fig. 14.5.

14.5

Five Leadership Styles

Leadership styles	Degree of subordinate participation encouraged by managers
	Low (Autocratic)
■ You solve the problem or make the decision yourself using information available to you at that time.	1
■ You obtain the necessary information from your subordinate(s), then decide on the solution to the problem yourself. You may or may not tell your subordinates what the problem is in getting the information from them. The role played by your subordinates in making the decision is clearly one of providing the necessary information to you, rather than generating or evaluating alternative solutions.	2
■ You share the problem with relevant subordinates individually, getting their ideas and suggestions without bringing them together as a group. Then you make the decision that may or may not reflect your subordinates' influence.	3
■ You share the problem with your subordinates as a group, collectively obtaining their ideas and suggestions. Then you make the decision that may or may not reflect your subordinates' influence.	4
■ You share a problem with your subordinates as a group. Together you generate and evaluate alternatives and attempt to reach agreement (consensus) on a solution. Your role is much like that of chairman. You do not try to influence the group to adopt "your" solution, and you are willing to accept and implement any solution that has the support of the entire group.	5
	High (Participative)

The authors suggest that there are eight questions managers can ask themselves to diagnose the situation. It has been found that managers can diagnose a situation quickly and accurately by answering these questions:

A. If the decision were accepted, would it make a difference which course of action was adopted?

B. Is there a quality requirement such that one decision is likely to be better than others?

C. Do I have sufficient information to make a high-quality decision?

D. Is the problem structured?

E. Is acceptance of the decision by subordinates critical to effective implementation of the decision?

F. If I were to make the decision by myself, is it reasonably certain that it would be accepted by my subordinates?

G. Do subordinates share the organizational goals to be attained in solving this problem?

H. Is conflict among subordinates likely between preferred solutions?

The answers to these questions help the manager diagnose the situation. Once the manager has diagnosed the situation, then he or she must choose a leadership style.[24] This assumes that a manager can change his or her leadership style depending on the situation.

Diagnosis of situational factors

The various combinations of situation and leadership style are shown in Fig. 14.6. This approach indicates that there is more than one leadership style that can be used. The eight situational factors are presented across the top of the figure. The numbers on the decision tree within the figure refer to each of the five leadership styles illustrated in Fig. 14.5. Style 1 is autocratic and style 5 is the most participative. To use this model, start at the top and work toward the bottom. Ask yourself the question that appears to the left of each box you come to. When a circle is reached, the number in the circle indicates the style of leadership that is most effective. Let's look at a concrete example.

Mark Rigg, Vice-President for Human Resources at Southland Corporation (owners of Seven-Eleven, Chief Auto Parts Stores and Oak Farm Dairies) is faced with a problem of high turnover of store clerks — about 300 percent a year. He investigated the problem and found that employee satisfaction is low because of a recent company policy regarding pay. In this situation, group acceptance will be important in devising a solution to this problem. The Vroom-Yetton model indicates that Rigg can meet with individual clerks (leadership style 3 or 4), or meet with the entire group at once (leadership style 5). Rigg would choose leadership style 3 or 4 if he believed that there is

Situational and leadership style combinations

14.6
Leadership choices in various situations. The model shows the preferred leadership style for each situation. The preferred style for each situation is indicated by the circled numbers.

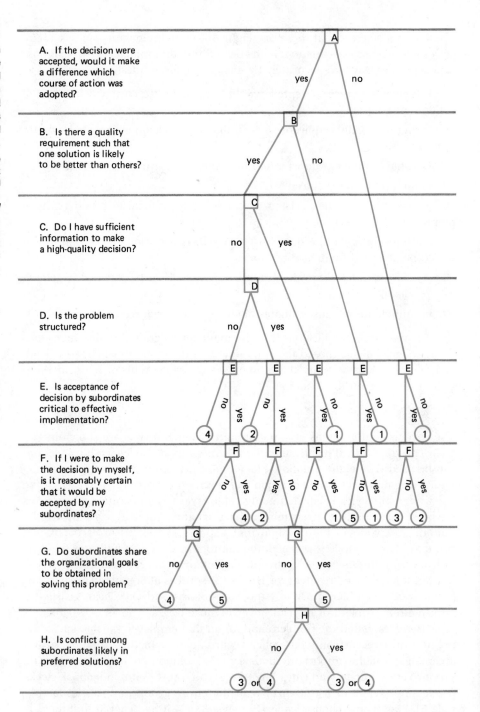

A. If the decision were accepted, would it make a difference which course of action was adopted?

B. Is there a quality requirement such that one solution is likely to be better than others?

C. Do I have sufficient information to make a high-quality decision?

D. Is the problem structured?

E. Is acceptance of decision by subordinates critical to effective implementation?

F. If I were to make the decision by myself, is it reasonably certain that it would be accepted by my subordinates?

G. Do subordinates share the organizational goals to be obtained in solving this problem?

H. Is conflict among subordinates likely in preferred solutions?

likely to be a conflict among the clerks concerning the preferred solutions (situation H). Mark will choose leadership style 5 if he believes that all clerks share his concern to solve this problem (situation G). In this case, Rigg probably should choose leadership style 5. Meeting with the entire group of clerks at once would clearly be the least time-consuming way to approach this problem.

Managerial implications

To use the Vroom-Yetton model, a manager needs to answer the eight questions listed on page 541. The selection of a particular leadership style will depend on whether or not the manager *diagnosed* the situation correctly and if one or more subordinates will be affected by the leader's decision. To the extent that participation is desired, appropriate, and permitted by time, the leader can choose a leadership style that is more participative. Participative leadership style often increases subordinates' commitment and avoids the problem of asking them to carry out a plan when they have had no input to it. Under these conditions, they are likely to feel powerless and less concerned about the outcome of the decision. The model has been used to help managers diagnose their own leadership styles and pinpoint areas where leadership styles might be modified to fit different situations.[25]

CASE STUDY

General Foreman on the Alaska Pipeline

Each of five general foremen has charge of a 20-man crew who lay sections of the oil pipeline in Alaska. They have to estimate their expected rate of progress in order to schedule material deliveries to their next field site.

They have been living in Alaska for the past five years and know the nature of the terrain. People at headquarters have the historical data needed for them to compute the rate of travel over that type of terrain. Given these two variables, it is a simple matter to calculate the earliest and latest times at which materials and support facilities will be needed at the next site. It is important that the estimates be reasonably accurate. Underestimates result in idle foremen and workers, and an overestimate ties up materials for a period of time before they are used.

Progress has been good, and the five foremen and other members of the gangs stand to receive substantial bonuses if the project is completed ahead of schedule.

According to the Vroom-Yetton model, which style of leadership should they choose? What are the characteristics of their situation? We believe the situation is described in row F in Fig. 14.6. They should choose leadership style 1. Do you agree or disagree? Why?

You might be wondering how we arrived at our leadership style. Looking at Fig. 14.6, we believe that it will make a difference which decision was accepted because of the bonuses, etc. that are tied to the decision. If we answer *yes* to question A, we proceed to question B. We also believe that the most appropriate decision to use can be calculated on the basis of facts and figures that can be supplied from headquarters. Therefore, our answer to question B is *yes*. Once we have received the data from headquarters, we believe that the general foremen will have sufficient information to make a high quality decision. The answer to question C is *yes*. The acceptance of the decision by the gangs is critical to reaching our goals. Therefore, the answer to question E is *yes*. Since the decision is of critical importance to all members of the gangs and involves the calculation of data that most members of the gangs have little knowledge of, our answer to question F is *yes*. Therefore, the most appropriate leadership style is 1: autocratic.

Similarities and Differences in the Contingency Approaches

Even for the most experienced managers, deciding on the most appropriate style of leadership or reconciling the differences between approaches is not an easy task. We will describe a situation and then present an analysis illustrating how each one of the three contingency approaches would advise you.

Tom Barry is a professor of marketing at Southern Methodist University. Tom teaches a course in advertising management and divides the class up into student advertising agencies. Each agency is responsible for developing a detailed marketing and advertising campaign for local financial and retailing clients as well as for national clients such as Dr. Pepper, *Sports Illustrated*, *The Wall Street Journal*, and the like. There are from four to six persons in each agency with different responsibilities in marketing research, strategy, media, creative, and account services. At the end of each semester, managers from the various client organizations attend class to listen to the competitive agency pitches for their respective organizations. Each client has three agencies working on the account. The managers critically judge the agency presentations and then award the account to one of the three competitors. The presentation heavily influences the grade for this class. You are the Account Executive for one of the student groups preparing a campaign for Sugar Free Dr. Pepper. What style of leadership should you use?

According to *Fiedler*, the style of leadership depends on the degree to which you have control and influence over the group and your particular leadership style. Let's look at the basic elements in his theory. First, the task is relatively unstructured. You and your group might ask: "How should we do this? What's important? Does anybody's father work for Dr. Pepper? Who's the competition? Are we going to use movies, slides, or just what in front of the executives?" Second, you and your fellow students will probably develop good leader-member relations. Undoubtedly you were chosen because others in the group perceived you as trustworthy and as an easy person to work with. Third, your formal power to influence the members of the group to work on their assignments rather than watch TV or go out for a beer is weak. That is, you have no formal power to tell others what to do. Given these conditions, what style of leadership is Fiedler likely to recommend? A relationship-motivated leader is likely to work best. Look at Fig. 14.3. What block are you operating in? (Ans: 4).

According to *House*, a leader's major function is to increase the personal satisfactions of followers. This is done by clarifying the nature of the task, increasing the opportunities of subordinates to obtain satisfactions from the work itself, and assisting members in completing the task. Let's apply these to your problem. First, the task is unstructured. Many of the reasons for this were indicated earlier. Second, the group needs to complete the task well so that it will achieve a good grade in the class. Given these situations, what would House recommend? An instrumental leadership style. Following the outline in Fig. 14.4, you should choose this style because it will enable you to give specific directions on what's supposed to be done when, where, by whom, and at what level of performance. If you can provide answers to these questions, you will clarify to your group how they should proceed in order to reach their goal, getting an A in the presentation.

According to *Vroom and Yetton*, your diagnosis of the situation will enable you to choose a leadership style. The diagnostic questions are indicated below with your probable answer.

A. If the decision were accepted, would it make a difference which course of action was adopted? Ans: *Yes*

B. Is there a quality requirement such that one decision is likely to be better than others? Ans: *Yes*

C. Do I have sufficient information to make a high quality decision myself? Ans: *No*

D. Is the problem structured? Ans: *No*

E. Is acceptance of the decision by others in the group critical to the effective presentation of our advertising campaign? Ans: *Yes*

F. If I were to make the decision by myself, is it reasonably certain that it would be accepted by others in the group? Ans: *No*

G. Do others in the group share the same goal of trying to get an A? Ans: *Yes*

H. Is the disagreement between members of the group over the most preferred solution? Ans: *Yes*

Now that you have diagnosed the situation, which style of leadership should you choose? Turn to Fig. 14.6. According to the logic presented, you should choose a highly participative style of leadership (5). You should not try to get the group to adopt your solution but should try to get the group to rally around the best solution that has the support of the entire group.

Why do these three contingency theorists recommend different solutions? Vroom and Yetton believe that a *leader can choose* a style depending on the situation. The style chosen by the leader is based on two factors: the quality of the decision and the effective implementation of that decision by the group. Fiedler believes that a leader's style is dependent on the motivational system of the leader and is *relatively fixed.* If you are a task-oriented leader, your group's performance would be low because your style does not fit the situation. Therefore, Fiedler would recommend that you either change the situation to fit your style, or not exercise leadership. House's model depends on the structure of the task. Once the leader diagnoses the situation as simple/routine or complex/nonroutine, then he or she should be able to see that either a supportive or an instrumental leader will be most effective.

Clearly, we are a long way from being able to offer you advice on the one best way to lead. It should be apparent that there is considerable controversy between knowledgeable people in the field over which style of leadership is best. Each approach offers its own logic. Which do you think is best?

SUMMARY Leadership is an important subject for managers because of the interpersonal roles leaders play in their organizations. We defined leadership as *an influence process.* Followers let themselves be influenced by a person as long as that person is able to satisfy their needs. The bases of a leader's influence stem from the sources of power from which the leader has to draw. We discussed the five bases of power — reward, coercive, legitimate, referent, and expert. How leaders acquire power in organizations was briefly reviewed.

Three approaches to the study of leadership were identified: trait, behavioral, and contingency. The *trait* approach assumed that individuals who have certain personality, physical, social, and personal traits will be leaders. We indicated, however, that few studies have been able to consistently distinguish leaders from nonleaders or effective from ineffective leaders on the basis of traits alone.

The *behavioral* approach focused on the styles leaders use to influence their subordinates. Studies of leadership styles have isolated three basic styles: instrumental, supportive, and participative. The *instrumental* leader is one who plans, organizes, and controls the activities of subordinates. The *supportive* leader seeks to gain acceptance by treating subordinates with respect, helping them with their personal problems, and seeing that they are rewarded for jobs well done. The *participative* leader shares information with subordinates and allows them equal participation in the decision-making process. Under the right circumstances, each style of leadership can be effective.

The difficulty in trying to relate traits or styles to performance led researchers to try and determine how situational variables will cause one leadership style to be more effective than others. Tannenbaum and Schmidt, for example, indicated that a manager's choice of a leadership style will be influenced by the various needs of the manager, subordinates, and the situation. The *contingency* researchers used combinations of these three factors to predict which leadership style will be most effective in a given situation.

Fiedler's model suggests that leader-member relations, task structure, and the leader's power position are the most important situational variables. It predicts which style of leadership (relationship or task motivated) will be the most effective in the eight possible situations. Fiedler suggests that when leader-member relations are good, the task is structured and the leader has high position power, then a task motivated style in leadership is most effective. In conditions where the leader-member relations are poor, the task is unstructured and the leader has low position power, a relationship-motivated leader performs best.

House's *Path-Goal model* suggests that the most important function of a leader is an ability to give rewards to subordinates for successful performance. The leadership style a manager uses will affect the types of rewards the manager offers and what specific activities subordinates must do in order to gain these rewards. The style of leadership (supportive or instrumental) most effective depends on the structure of the task and the needs of the subordinates.

The *Vroom-Yetton model* focuses on the degree of participation a leader should use in a situation. After diagnosing the situation, the leader should choose the style of leadership most appropriate to the situation. In evaluating the situation, the leader evaluates the reactions of subordinates, especially if their acceptance of a decision is necessary for the leader's style to be effective.

autocratic leader	*democratic leader*	**KEYWORDS**
clout	*expert power*	
coercive power	*Fiedler's model*	

instrumental leadership	*position power*
laissez-faire leader	*referent power*
leader-member relations	*relationship-motivated leader*
leader position power	*reward power*
leadership	*supportive leadership*
least-preferred co-worker (LPC)	*task-motivated leader*
legitimate power	*task structure*
participative leadership	*trait*
path-goal model	*Vroom-Yetton model*

**DISCUSSION
QUESTIONS**

1. Define leadership. What are the important elements in your definition?

2. "All managers are leaders." Is this statement true or false? Why?

3. Why do some managers have "clout"? How do they get it?

4. What are the sources for a leader's power?

5. Leaders are born, not made. Comment.

6. What is the difference between the trait and behavioral approaches?

7. What are the three basic styles of the behavioral approach? How do these differ from each other?

8. What basic assumptions underlie Fiedler's model? How did Fiedler differentiate leadership styles?

9. Under what conditions do relationship-motivated leaders work best? Under what conditions do task-motivated leaders work best?

10. On what model of motivation is the path-goal model based? What variables, according to this theory, help to determine the most effective leadership style?

11. What are the major characteristics of the Vroom-Yetton model? What are the five leadership styles of this model? How would you match each style to the appropriate situation facing the leader?

Management Incidents and Cases

**BUDGET MOTORS,
INC.***

Plant Y was the largest and oldest of six assembly plants of Econocar division, a subsidiary of Budget Motors, Inc. It had close to 10,000 employees and

---

* This case was written by Professor Sami Kassem, University of Toledo, Toledo, Ohio.

was managed by Mr. Wickstrom. During the last few years, it fell behind all the others in performance. Not unexpectedly, headquarter management (HQM) started showing some uneasiness as there were signs that things would not improve in the foreseeable future. In its attempt to straighten things out, it has exerted steady pressure and issued specific directions for local plant management to follow.

Wickstrom was a respected and competent manager. He was not new to the responsibility of running a large plant. After all, he came up the hard way through the ranks, and was well known for his ambition, technical competence, human-relations skills, and hard work. Moreover, he was a no-nonsense manager, well liked by his subordinates. Under his leadership, plant Y had performed adequately until the energy and environmental crises teamed up to hit the auto industry really hard in the early 1970s. At that time, in all six plants, there was a hysteria to fill the demand for little compacts that are economically cheap to run and environmentally safe to use. The speed of the lines was stepped up, three-shift operations were begun, workers (mostly immigrants) were hired, and a large number of managers had to be placed in new jobs.

Although all the plants of the Econocars division had their share of the stress and strain inherent in the sudden changeover from bigger to smaller cars, the managers of these plants adapted themselves differently to this new development in the market situation. Instead of comparing Wickstrom's adaptive behavior with that of his counterparts in other plants, we would rather concentrate on contrasting his own style with that of Mr. Rhenman, his successor in the same plant. Following are some examples that illustrate how Wickstrom tried to cope with this crisis atmosphere:

1. One day, while doing his regular plant tour, he personally ordered the foreman of a given section to change the sequence of assembling the instrument panels. He thought this change would speed up the operation. When his production manager, Mr. Aberg, found out about the new system, he got upset because it disturbed the schedule. He went to see Wickstrom in his office and to make a new suggestion about the sequencing — one that coordinated Wickstrom's plan with his own. Much to Aberg's surprise, Wickstrom reacted in a rude manner and told Aberg that things would remain the way he had ordered.

2. When Wickstrom read the weekly performance record of the body assembly line, he flew into a terrific temper and called in the foreman of this line, Jorgen, to his office and threatened to fire him if the production was not speeded up. This tactic shook up Jorgen who instantly thought of the incident two weeks before when his colleague, Ulf, had indeed been fired. He tried to justify the slowness of production by complaining that he was operating against overwhelming handicaps: antiquated and rundown equipment, inexperienced workforce, and uninteresting and noninvolving job structure. Unfortunately, nobody cared to listen to him.

3. One day the supply of electric power for the plant was reduced and the next day it was shut off completely. This was due to a breakdown in the power station outside the plant. It was not Wickstrom's policy to run the plant by committee meetings, but faced with this crisis at hand, he summoned a meeting of the production managers and the foremen. It was clear the electric company would need at least a week to repair its network. The upshot of the meeting was a decision to shut down production and to seek union's support for a half pay for the workers in exchange for two days of the paid holidays. Upon submitting the minutes of this meeting to the HQM, his decisions were vetoed immediately. The HQM argued that since economical compacts sell almost as fast as they can be rolled off lines, production should not stop and that a mobile auxiliary power unit be brought in, no matter what its cost would be. This proved to be a very expensive proposition and it also meant a lot of trouble for workers and managers alike. For no sooner than Wickstrom called in his second meeting to inform his top aides as to the feedback he received from the HQM, than some of his managers angrily protested this high-handed interference in their "domestic affairs." Here again, they said, is one more example of the H.Q. boys telling us how to run our show. Other plant managers, equally concerned, blamed their boss, Wickstrom, for his inability to stand by his guns, fight his case back with the HQM and challenge its excessive domination like other plant managers do. They felt they were put at the order-receiving side by the HQM which had no real feeling for what was going on in the plant. Some plant managers further complained that carrying out daily instructions from HQM had become Wickstrom's chief preoccupation. Managers in such staff services as accounting, quality control, material control, and personnel also complained that they themselves were receiving too many specific orders from HQM. Like their line counterparts, they generally resented this controlling behavior on the part of the HQM. They complained that they were no longer allowed to run their own departments or stations, or to manage within their sphere of competence. This in turn, left them no choice but to withdraw legitimate authority from their immediate subordinates and interfere in the handling of the subordinates' affairs, thereby compounding the problem throughout the hierarchy.

In responding to the voices from below, HQM argued that the trouble with plant Y lay in Wickstrom's lack of control rather than in bad equipment, boring jobs, and inexperienced personnel.

With the intensification of the energy crisis caused by the sudden outbreak of the Mideast War of October 1973, the demand for little cars far outstripped the available supply. Being dissatisfied with plant Y's performance, HQM decided to replace Wickstrom with Rhenman. The latter accepted the job on condition that he should have "carte blanche" in running his own show for a reasonable period of time. This he got from HQM, which also assured him that there would be no interference and that he was free to proceed in any manner he saw fit.

At the outset, Rhenman indicated that although HQM thought that deadwood should be removed from the staff, he disagreed and would give everyone ample opportunity to prove their worth. (It developed, in fact, that only a handful of people in an organization of 10,000 were dismissed during his regime.) He asked for money from HQM to modernize the plant, starting first with the cafeteria and washrooms used by blue-collar workers. Rhenman also went to the cafeteria during lunch hours, mingled with workers, foremen, and the lower-level managers. He not only listened to their complaints, but also secured their cooperation and suggestions. He encouraged groups to meet regularly to solve common problems and, more important, to engage his long-range planning and consultation to prevent daily crises. His foremen often met informally, thereby increasing lateral communication. He structured an ongoing problem-solving dialogue between his staff and line personnel. Through this dialogue, staff personnel had learned how irrelevant or self-defensive their services had been in the line. He inspired confidence and loyalty and erased the fear-and-crisis syndrome that had prevailed. He did not change the formal organization structure of the plant. He expected his managers to set goals for their units and be responsible for their achievements. He delegated to them the requisite authority, and left them alone to perform their jobs.

Now, after about six months in his job, plant Y has started heading towards a rebound. Its performance record shows marked improvements. Rhenman was promoted to a top executive job at the H.Q. Interestingly enough, plant Y is performing well without him. On the other hand, Wickstrom was given an early retirement.

Questions

1. Compare and contrast the leadership style of Wickstrom and Rhenman.

2. Who is to blame for Wickstrom's failure? Why did he lose his magic touch?

3. What caused plant Y to become an outstanding success?

4. Does it really make sense to talk about choosing your own leadership style?

AL WAYLAND Al Wayland, the founder, owner, and president of SS Electronics, was an avid student of modern business practices. He had recently completed a management seminar and had been especially impressed by a lecture entitled, "Your Leadership Style: Is It the Best?" For Wayland, the theme of the lecture was that only results count. To increase a person's results, managers should let workers participate in decisions that affect their work. Morale will improve and so will productivity. After the class Al asked the instructor, Professor Richard Hansen, if the concept applied to all workers. In a rather offhand manner, Professor Hansen said that it probably could.

Several weeks later, Wayland called all his employees together and informed them that each employee would be given certain objectives to attain. Normally, they would not be required to work any particular number of hours so long as they attained the required results. There were certain exceptions to this policy; such employees as the receptionist and the warehouseman were required to be present whenever the firm was open.

Together with his office manager, Al worked out the objectives for each of the 10 employees to which the policy applied. A week after his announcement, the new system was started. As far as Wayland could determine everything was generally going well. Sales and profits were slightly higher than in previous periods.

Wayland felt there was one problem area. Jane Rothe, who had been in charge of answering certain inquiries, was arriving for work at 10 o'clock and leaving at 2 o'clock. Since no one else worked for so short a period, Al decided to discuss the matter with Miss Rothe. One day as she was leaving the building, he called her into the office and asked her how things were going.

"Is there any problem, Mr. Wayland? Have I forgotten to answer any letters?"

"No, nothing like that, but I think that the rest of the office resents the hours you keep."

"But, Mr. Wayland, we agreed that my objective was to have every inquiry answered within 24 hours. And I have always done that."

"Yes, I know. But we had been receiving an average of 40 inquiries each work day. It takes an average of 12 minutes to answer each. If you are really doing your work, you should be spending eight hours on your job."

"Oh, that was before you adopted your new leadership style of encouraging us to find ways to improve our own efficiency. I had been analyzing the correspondence for months. All but five percent of the letters can be answered by some combination of 50 paragraphs. I put those 50 paragraphs on tape for the new computer-controlled typewriter. Now I can have 95 percent of the letters answered in five minutes each. Since we get the mail at 10 o'clock, I can have all the programmed letters ready by 11. By one o'clock I have answered the hard ones, and by one-thirty the automatically prepared letters are ready for me to sign. Why should I stay?"

Questions

1. What should Al do now?

2. In your opinion, why did this situation arise?

MUSTANG TRAVEL INTERNATIONAL

In September, Mustang Travel International opened two branches of their agency in the area surrounding Dallas. Although the president, Debbie Churchill, knew this would create some problems, she also knew it would generate more sales and help the firm's profit picture. It was decided that Bob German would head the North Dallas office and Beverly Spear would head up the Irving office. Both had been among the highest producing travel agents for years. Churchill thought both had the leadership abilities to quickly turn these offices into profitable ventures.

Within six months, many of the old customers began to complain and threatened to take their business elsewhere. Churchill asked German and Spear to come into the home office for a chat. Both indicated that they were not sufficiently staffed with qualified agents to handle the increased flow of travel requests. When they called the home office for assistance, the travel agents were not willing to help them because "it was not their client." After German and Spear left, Churchill called in her agents and asked them about the claims made.

The agents said that although they had no problems with German and Spear when they were in the office as travel agents, once they were promoted, problems arose. The agents said German wanted total control over his customers and had been unable to recruit top-notch salespeople because of his autocratic style of leadership. On the other hand, Spear spent so much time with the "big" customers, travel problems arose frequently and she didn't have time to handle them. When a problem came up, she said, "Call the home office. They'll straighten it out." Churchill thanked her salespeople for being open and honest and wondered what to do about the problem.

Questions

1. Why are Bob and Bev having leadership problems in their new jobs?

2. If you were Debbie, what would you do? Why?

REFERENCES

1. H. D. Menzies, "Changing of the Guard at Colgate." *Fortune*, September 24, 1979, 92.

2. R. Stogdill, *Handbook of Leadership: A Survey of Theory and Research.* New York: The Free Press, 1974, p. 9.

3. R. House and J. Baetz, "Leadership: Some Empirical Generalizations and New Research Directions." In *Research in Organizational Behavior.* Barry Staw (ed.). Greenwich, CT: JAI Press, 1979, pp. 341–424.

4. D. Katz and R. Kahn, *The Social Psychology of Organizations*, 2nd ed. New York: John Wiley & Sons, 1978, pp. 525–576.

5. J. French and B. Raven, "The Bases of Social Power." In *Studies in Social Power.* D. Cartwright (ed.). Ann Arbor, MI: Institute for Social Research, 1959, pp. 150–167.

6. S. M. Bacharach and E. Lawler, *Power and Politics in Organizations.* San Francisco, CA: Jossey-Bass, 1980, pp. 10–44; and L. Roos and R. Hall, "Influence Diagrams and Organizational Power." *Administrative Science Quarterly* **25,** 1980, 57–71.

7. R. Kanter, "Power and Failure in Management Circuits." *Harvard Business Review* 1979, **57,** 4, 1979 65–75. Also see G. Salancik and J. Pfeffer, "Who Gets Power–And How They Hold on to It: A Strategic-Contingency Model of Power." *Organizational Dynamics*, 1977 (Winter), 3–25; M. Korda, *Power.* New York: Random House, 1975.

8. A. Sloan, *My Years with General Motors.* New York: Macfadden, 1965.

9. For excellent reviews of this literature and the entire field, see R. Stogdill, *Handbook of Leadership: A Survey of Theory & Research.* New York: Free Press, 1974; and M. Evans, "Leadership." In *Organizational Behavior.* S. Kerr (ed.). Columbus, OH: Grid Publishing Company, 1979, pp. 207–240.

10. R. Stogdill, "Personal Factors Associated with Leadership." *Journal of Psychology* **25,** 1948, 35–71.

11. E. Ghiselli, *Explorations in Managerial Talent.* Pacific Palisades, CA.: Wordsworth Publishing Company. 1971.

12. R. White and R. Lippett, "Leader Behavior and Member Reaction in Three 'Social Climates'." In *Group Dynamics: Research and Theory*, 3rd ed. D. Cartwright and A. Zander, (eds.). Harper & Row, 1967, pp. 318–336.

13. Support for statements in this section can be found in C. Schriesheim and S. Kerr, "Theories and Measures of Leadership: A Critical Appraisal of Current and Future Directions." In *Leadership: The Cutting Edge.* J. Hunt and L. Larson, (eds.). Carbondale, IL: Southern Illinois University Press, 1977, pp. 9–45, 51–56.

14. S. Kerr, C. Schriesheim, C. Murphy, and R. Stogdill, "Toward a Contingency Theory of Leadership Based upon the Consideration and Initiating Structure Literature." *Organizational Behavior and Human Performance* **12,** 1974, 62–82.

15. R. Tannenbaum and W. Schmidt, "How to Choose a Leadership Pattern." *Harvard Business Review* **36,** (May-June), 1958, 95–106.

16. "The Toro Team Has a Winning Game Plan." *Nation's Business* **67,** August 1979, 8, 34.

17. For an excellent summary of these models, see J. Miner, *Theories of Organizational Behavior.* Hinsdale, IL: The Dryden Press, 1980, pp. 290–370.

18. F. Fiedler, *A Theory of Leadership Effectiveness.* New York: McGraw-Hill, 1967. Also see F. Fiedler and M. Chemers, *Leadership and Effective Management.* New York: Scott Foresman, 1974.

19. D. Hosking and C. Schriesheim, "Review Essay." *Administrative Science Quarterly* **23,** 1978, 496–505; and C. Schriesheim and S. Kerr, "Theories and Measures of Leadership: A Critical Appraisal of Current and Future Directions." In *Leadership: The Cutting Edge.* J. Hunt and L. Larson (eds.). Carbondale, IL: Southern Illinois University Press, 1977, pp. 9–45, 51–56. See also R. Rice, "Leader LPC and Follower Satisfaction: A Review." *Organizational Behavior and Human Performance* **28,** 1981, 1–25.

20. R. House, "A Path-Goal Theory of Leader Effectiveness." *Administrative Science Quarterly* **16,** 1971, 321–338.

21. J. Schriesheim and C. Schriesheim, "A Test of the Path-Goal Theory of Leadership and Some Suggested Directions for Future Research." *Personnel Psychology* **33,** 1980, 349–370.

22. "The Marriott Company." *Nation's Business,* October 1979, 51–56.

23. V. Vroom and P. Yetton, *Leadership and Decision Making.* Pittsburgh, PA: University of Pittsburgh Press, 1973.

24. V. Vroom and A. Jago, "On the Validity of the Vroom-Yetton Model." *Journal of Applied Psychology* **63,** 1978, 151–162; and A. Jago and V. Vroom, "An Evaluation of Two Alternatives to the Vroom-Yetton Normative Model." *Academy of Management Journal* **23,** 1980, 347–355.25.

25. V. Vroom, "Can Leaders Learn to Lead?" *Organizational Dynamics* **4,** 3, 1976, 17–28.

Chapter 15

COMMUNICATION IN ORGANIZATIONS

After reading this chapter, you should be able to:

1. Explain the nature and purpose of communication.

2. Identify the six elements in the communication process.

3. Name the three types of nonverbal behavior in the communication process.

4. List different methods organizations use to communicate with employees.

5. Identify the ways for improving feedback in organizations.

6. List the barriers to effective communication.

7. Apply the guidelines for effective communication.

LEARNING OBJECTIVES

PREVIEW CASE

**Peachtree
Rent-A-Car***

Shelley Farrell, Vice-President of Marketing for Peachtree Rent-A-Car, announced some plans to her assistant, Bob Bessar: "Finally, Bob, I think we're in a position to hit the big boys at the airports. Our price is just too low for us not to be able to tackle Avis, Budget Car, Hertz, and National. Sometimes even I wonder how we can make a profit on the car."

"Let me tell you more about my plans. What we have to do is tie in our car reservations with airline and motel reservations. The big four are all tied into the airlines. I think we can do that also. A person renting a car from us usually stays in a moderately priced motel and is on a tight budget. I have to see what our line of credit is with the bank, but I really think we can pull this off."

Bob replied: "Shelley, don't you think that you had better check our rental reports? According to these figures, our rentals have dropped by 35% in the last four months in the Dallas area and 45 in the Atlanta area. I think the market is saturated by car rental agencies and I am not so sure that the airlines want to make a deal with us. Have you seen the latest losses in the airline industry?"

"Bob," said Shelley, "I know the airline industry's down, but our rentals have been steadily increasing. Look at the past three years! We have made nice profits; our cars are among the newest in the market. Ac-

---

* Adapted from A. DuBrin, *Fundamentals of Organizational Behavior*, 2nd ed. New York: Pergamon Press, 1978, pp. 341–342.

cording to personnel's latest survey, employee morale is great. We're constantly in touch with our employees and send them all sorts of forms, etc. that advise them how to increase profits from the fleet.''

"I have an idea," said Bob. "Let's call Roger in our Boston office and see if he notices any problems.''

Over the phone, Roger said, "You have got to be kidding. We have tremendous problems here ranging from a lack of communications with your office to trying to keep track of the cars we rent. The computer system is down most of the time and there are only three of us in this office. Presently, we have cars in ten states. Customers are constantly complaining about the conditions of the cars. Before you make this commitment, I think that you and Bob should get into the field and find out what's going on for yourself.''

After Shelley and Bob discussed Roger's comments, they agreed to fly to Atlanta and rent one of their own cars without telling anyone of their plans. When they arrived in Atlanta, they went to the Peachtree Rent-A-Car booth and no one was there. After fifteen minutes, Mick showed up and asked if he could help them. They said that they would like to rent a car and drive to Savannah. Mick said: "Quite frankly, I would not rent from us. Savannah is over 100 miles from here and our cars aren't in the best condition. In fact, the only one that I can let you have has over 40,000 miles. However, if you want it, it's yours for a real bargain rate.''

Shelley and Bob looked at each other in amazement. Here was one of their own employees telling customers not to rent a car. Bob asked Mick, "Why is that?''

"No offense meant, sir," said Mick, "but the people in the home office just do not understand our problems. Why just in the last week, I heard that the marketing gal thought that it would be a good idea to expand and tie into the motel business. She's crazy. Do you know why I wasn't here when you arrived? The reservations clerk is parking cars. Our maintenance employee is so overworked that I was trying to lend him a hand. The person who washes and cleans the cars is a deadbeat and will not take orders from anyone. He says if you don't like it, fire me. However, I cannot do that because the people in the home office will think that I cannot manage my people and what cars we rent would stay dirty. The people in the home office seem to be more concerned with new marketing gimmicks than with helping us out. We fill out reports, but never hear anything except 'Rent Cars'.''[1]

Why do communications breakdowns take place so often? The above example, which by no means is unusual, is an example of poor communications. In this chapter, we will look at the reasons why such failures occur. Shelley did not want to hear that there were problems because she wanted to expand the business. To Mick, the memos from the home office communicated more pressure to rent cars and not mention problems. As a result, the individuals involved in this case were not receiving the communication needed to make a wise decision.

INTRODUCTION TO COMMUNICATION

Importance of Communication

Communication is the process by which information is exchanged by two or more people.[2] Effective communication is important for two reasons. First, as indicated in chapter one, *communication is the process* by which the functions of management (planning, organizing, decision-making, controlling, motivating, and leading) are carried out. The proper information must be communicated to managers so that they make good decisions. In the case of Peachtree Rent-A-Car, an ineffective communication system failed to provide Shelley with the proper information to enable her to make a decision. Eventually, a new organization structure was designed to clearly communicate job assignments. A new control system was installed, preventing cars with over 15,000 miles from staying in the fleet. Managers were required to write job descriptions for their subordinates. Measurable goals were set (e.g., no customer should wait more than three minutes for service; phone calls should be answered before ten rings, etc.). In short, managers do not manage in isolation: they carry out their management function by communicating with others.

Second, a large portion of a *manager's time* is spent communicating with others. Managers rarely spend time thinking alone at their desks. A manager's day is typically devoted to face-to-face communication with superiors, peers, and subordinates. When not communicating directly with others, managers may be writing memos, letters, or reports, or talking on the phone.[3]

Henry Mintzberg, whose work we discussed in Chapter 1, has described the manager's job in terms of three classes of roles.[4] Communication plays a vital part in each of these types:

1. In the *interpersonal roles*, managers act as figureheads and leaders of their organization. Mintzberg indicates that managers spend about 45 percent of their contact time with peers, about 45 percent with people outside their company, and only about 10 percent with superiors.

2. In their *informational roles*, managers seek information from peers, subordinates, and other personal contacts about anything that may affect their job and responsibilities. They give out interesting or important information in return. In addition, they provide suppliers, peers, and groups outside the organization with information about their organization.

3. In their *decisional roles*, managers implement new projects, handle disturbances, and allocate resources to their departments. Some of the managers' decisions will be reached in private, but they will be based on information communicated to them. The managers, in turn, will have to communicate these decisions to others.

Managers have a strong personal preference for oral communication. Oral communication is timely and current; it often informs the manager about immediate problems or opportunities. Written communication is often not current. Because managers tend to live by the "grapevine," they need to receive and send information quickly. Managers may spend up to 80 percent of their time communicating.

> *A plumber from New York developed what he thought was an excellent method for cleaning drains. He wrote the Bureau of Standards to tell them that he was using hydrochloric acid and to ask them if it was harmless. The bureau replied, "The efficacy of hydrochloric acid is indisputable, but the chlorine residue is incompatible with metallic permanence."*
>
> *The plumber wrote back, thanking the bureau for agreeing with him. Alarmed by his response, the bureau wrote another letter, saying, "We cannot assume responsibility for the production of toxic and noxious residues with hydrochloric acid, and suggest that you use an alternative procedure." The plumber wrote again, explaining how happy he was to learn that Washington still agreed with him.*
>
> *At this stage, the bureau put the problem in simple terms: "Don't use hydrochloric acid. It eats the hell out of the pipes." Finally, the plumber understood.* * [5]

The plumber and the Bureau of Standards both thought they were communicating with each other. In fact, communications were not effective until the message from the Bureau was sent in a form the plumber could understand. The goal of any manager should be to convey information — instructions, policies, rules, etc. — that the receivers can use.

Communication between people involves many factors.[6] Major variables in the communication process include:

A MODEL OF THE COMMUNICATION PROCESS

1. Sender/encoder

2. Message

3. Channel

---

4. Receiver (s)/decoder(s)

5. Feedback

6. Perception

The way in which these variables interact is illustrated in Fig. 15.1, a model of the communication process. Communication is the essence of managerial decision-making. It is central to the control and survival of the firm and important to being a successful manager. This model is intended to increase your awareness of the variables a manager needs to consider for a communication to be successful.

15.1

A communication model

From *Business Communication: Strategies and Skills*. R.C. Huseman, J.M. Lahiff, and J.D. Hatfield. Copyright © 1981 by the Dryden Press, A Division of Holt, Rinehart & Winston, Publishers. Reprinted by permission of Holt, Rinehart & Winston.

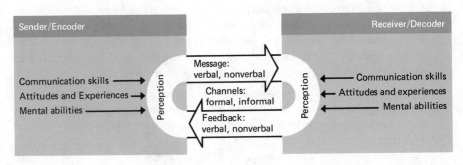

Sender/Encoder　The **sender** is the source of information in the communication process. In the Peachtree Rent-A-Car case, Shelley was the sender. It was her plan to expand the services provided by the company. In the plumber's case, the plumber was the sender. In both cases, the sender must first picture the receiver and then choose communication symbols and skills that will enable the receiver to understand the message.

Encoding is the process of translating thoughts or feelings into messages.[7] Imagine that you want to write a company about possible summer job openings. You have certain ideas you want to communicate in that letter. For example, you will want to offer reasons why you chose that company. You will probably need to provide some background information about your qualifications for the job and how the job will help your career. When you put these ideas on paper, you are encoding.

(It's probably pretty obvious that the sender/encoder isn't going to get much in the way of response unless there is somewhere a receiver/decoder. Those last two terms are discussed at some length in a later section of this chapter. So that we may use them here, however, definitions are in order now.

The *receiver* is the person who gets the sender's message. *Decoding* is the process of translating messages into thoughts or feelings. For example, when you read a letter you have received, you are decoding.)

There are five principles for increasing the accuracy of the encoding process:

1. Make the message relevant for the receivers. If receivers are to understand the message, they must be able to relate the information they are receiving to what they already know. Therefore, the message should be presented in a form that says to the receivers: "This is important and significant to you." This can be done by using symbols or gestures that the receiver understands.

2. Reduce the messages to the simplest possible terms. The sender should use as few symbols or gestures as possible to communicate thoughts and feelings to the receivers. The simpler the message, the more likely it is to be understood. Return to the plumber and Bureau problem. Did the Bureau keep this in mind when communicating with the plumber? Obviously not.

3. Organize the message into a series of stages. A well-organized message increases the receiver's understanding. It is probably best to develop one thought or feeling at a time so that the receiver is not overloaded. A message can be packaged into a series of stages, with one stage completed before the next is introduced. Let's go back to your letter asking for a summer job. How did you organize your letter?

4. Repeat the key points of the message. The principle of repetition is important. Repetition is particularly important in oral communication, where words may not be clearly heard or fully understood the first time. The sender needs to use enough repetition to ensure clear understanding of thoughts and feelings.

5. Focus on the essential aspects of the message. Communication goals and key points should be sharply focused. This will avoid losing the message in details and making it unclear. In oral communication the impact of significant points can be heightened by a different tone of voice, pauses, or hand gestures. In written communication it can be done by underlining or otherwise emphasizing key sentences and phrases. You may have noticed that every keyword in this book has been set in boldface italic type.

The *message* part of the communication process contains the verbal and nonverbal symbols that represent the information we want to send to receivers.[8] It is important to remember that a message is like a coin: it has two sides. There is the message as seen by the sender/encoder and the message as seen by the receiver/decoder. The two are not necessarily the same. The se-

Message

lection and interpretation of messages may differ dramatically because of the differences between the sender and the receiver or because the sender is sending two different messages at once. If you sent your resume off to a company asking for a summer job, was it typed or hand-written? Was it neat or sloppy? Did it describe your educational background or not? If you sent it handwritten containing misspelled words, the message that this sends to the receiver is that it is not important and you are not a neat person. There are three types of messages managers use: nonverbal, verbal, and written. The use of nonverbal communication has become extremely important and we will give greater emphasis to this type of message than to the others.

Nonverbal communication

Nonverbal communication can be defined as all those messages that are not encoded with words.[9] You're sitting in class, second row, first chair. The lecture is not the greatest; in fact, it's one of those days when you really wish you'd forgotten to set the alarm clock. For something to do, you glance around the room ... and in the second row, last chair, there's a very attractive student of the opposite sex staring at you.

You look away.

The other looks away quickly.

You glance back.

The other glances back.

You smile faintly.

The other smiles faintly.

You incline your head toward the professor and roll your eyes.

The other smiles wider and nods once.

You glance toward the door.

The other looks at you, then at the clock, then at the door.

Without saying a word, you've set up a meeting place, a time, and an opening conversation with another student. This is nonverbal communication. Nonverbal communication is so prevalent that it is important for you to understand how you communicate messages. While there are many forms of nonverbal communication, we shall discuss three types: how we communicate with space, how we communicate through dress, and how we communicate with our bodies.

Communicating With Space   How close or far we stand in relation to the person we're communicating with, where we sit in the room, or how we arrange our office has a real impact on communication. Status or power is often communicated through spatial arrangements.[10] The size of the office, whether one has a personal secretary, where one sits when a group is meeting (the higher-status person generally sits at the end of the table), and whether the manager requires subordinates to come to his or her office for discussions — all communicate messages.

According to John Dean, counsel to former President Nixon, space in the White House conveyed status and power.[11]

Everyone jockeyed for a position close to the President's ear, and even an unseasoned observer could sense minute changes in status. Success and failure could be seen in the size, decor, and location of offices. Anyone who moved to a smaller office, was on the way down. If a carpenter or wallpaper hanger was busy in someone's office, this was a sure sign that he was on the rise.... We learned to read office changes as an index of the internal bureaucratic power struggles.... The actual costs (of these changes) had less to do with it than the need of its occupant to see tangible evidence of their prestige.

Richard Huseman, John Lahiff, and John Hatfield, in a study of communication,[12] noted that the higher up people are in the organization, the more and better space they are given. In most universities, deans have more attractive offices than do assistant professors. They have more windows, better carpeting, larger offices, and better furnishings. Look at the offices in Fig. 15.2. Which one belongs to the superior? Subordinate?

Communicating with Dress   Many of you have heard the saying, "Clothes make the person." John Molloy, a dress consultant with major corporations, believes that the way a person dresses communicates something to others. In his book, *Dress for Success*,[13] he asked a series of questions of more than 100 top company executives. Let's read some of his results:

1. He showed executives five pictures of men each wearing expensive, tailored, but high-fashion clothing. He asked the executives if this was proper dress for a junior business executive. Ninety-two said *no*; eight said *yes*.

2. He showed them five additional pictures of the same people neatly dressed in conservative clothing and asked if they were dressed properly for a young executive. All said *yes*.

3. He showed them five additional pictures of the same people obviously dressed in lower-middle class attire and asked if these people were dressed properly for a young executive. Forty-six said *yes*, fifty-four said *no*.

4. He then asked the executives if they thought that the people dressed in the middle-class suit would succeed better in corporate life than those dressed in the lower middle-class suit. Eighty-eight said *yes*, twelve said *no*.

15.2
Office space

In short, there can be little doubt that appearance can communicate messages in the business world.

Communicating with Our Bodies   The body and its movements can communicate. The face and eyes are the most expressive means of body communication. The ability to interpret facial meaning is an important part of communication. Look at the facial expressions in Fig. 15.3. To test your ability

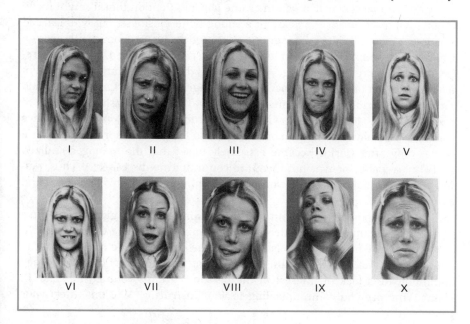

15.3

From Dale Leathers,
*Nonverbal Communications
Systems.* Copyright 1976 by
Allyn, & Bacon, Boston.
Reprinted with permission.

Facial Meaning Sensitivity Test, Part 1	Class of Facial Meaning	Number of Expression
	Disgust	_____
	Happiness	_____
	Interest	_____
	Sadness	_____
	Bewilderment	_____
	Contempt	_____
	Surprise	_____
	Anger	_____
	Determination	_____
	Fear	_____

The correct answers for Part I of the FMST are disgust = I; happiness = III; interest = VIII; sadness = X; bewilderment = II; contempt = IX; surprise = VII; anger = VI; determination = IV; and fear = V.

to perceive facial expression, study the ten photos in Fig. 15.3, then place the numbers in the appropriate blanks.

Eye contact is one of the most direct and powerful nonverbal ways people communicate. In the United States, social rules suggest that in most situations, eye contact is appropriate for a short period of time. Prolonged eye contact can be interpreted as a threatening symbol or a sign of romantic interest.

There are unspoken norms of eye contact. For blacks or Chicanos, looking away does not necessarily mean the same lack of attention that it might mean among whites. Consider the case of a young white businessman who learned this lesson when he was managing a group of people predominantly from a Chicano community. The businessman kept reprimanding Carlos for a repeated error in record keeping. As he tried to discuss the matter, Carlos kept averting eye contact. The manager became angry and said, "Look at me when I'm talking to you." To this manager, the lack of eye contact showed a lack of respect. For the stock boy (following his own cultural norms), maintaining eye contact would have been a sign of disrespect to the person reprimanding him. It was only after Carlos became extremely upset that the manager realized that Carlos' behavior was not meant to communicate disrespect.[14] Thus, patterns of nonverbal communication can be highly variable between groups and cultures.

A person's posture also communicates meaning. Posture gives us clues to a person's self-confidence or interest in the topic. If you are interested in a subject, you are more likely to lean toward the person you're communicating with, showing an interest in him or her. Sitting back, on the other hand, may communicate a lack of interest in the person.[15] What's your posture like in class? What are you communicating to your instructor? Will this affect your grade?

Verbal (oral) communication

Oral communication is the form of communication most frequently used by managers. As illustrated in Chapter 1, this is how managers spend most of their time. Oral communication can be of two types: face-to-face and by telephone. Face-to-face communication can involve more nonverbal communication methods than telephone communication. This is why many managers prefer it to telephone communication. To get your meaning across on the telephone, you must choose your words and tone of voice carefully.

All of us have listened to lectures from teachers, ministers, and our parents. Why are some people good oral communicators and others not? While the qualities for effective oral communication can vary greatly depending on the communication and the situation, researchers have identified some of the most common characteristics of effective oral communicators. Some of these characteristics are:[16]

1. Self-confidence

2. Knowledge

3. Articulation

4. Pleasing voice quality

5. Sincerity

6. Reasoning

7. Sympathy

8. Open-mindedness

9. Honesty

10. Personal appearance

11. Concern for listener

12. Humor

13. Character

14. Tact

15. Friendliness

From this list, it appears that the sender must (1) encode the message in words (and nonverbal cues) that will convey it effectively to the receiver; (2) convey the message in a well organized manner, and (3) try to eliminate "noise" factors in the situation.

The alternative to verbal and nonverbal communication is written communication. Managers prefer verbal communication because it's quicker and it's a two-way street. However, many forms of written communication are used in business, such as reports, memoranda, letters, newsletters, and the like. The following are some guidelines for good written communications:[17]

Written communications

1. The written message must be drafted with the receiver's needs clearly in mind.

2. The facts of the message must be thought through *ahead of time.*

3. The message should be as brief as possible. Eliminate all unnecessary words and ideas. Important messages should be prepared in draft first, then corrected.

4. If the message is long, place a summary of the report on the first page. This summary should make the main points clear, with page references for details on each item.

5. The message should be carefully organized. State your most important point first, then the next most important point, and so on. This way if the receiver reads only the first few points, the main message will get across.

6. Make the subject clear by giving the message a title.

7. Use simple words. Make the message more readable by using short, clear sentences.

Selecting the best method of communication
In conveying thoughts and feelings the manager must choose between oral and written communications. While nonverbal communication is important, it is very limited, and for the most part it is not used consciously. Table 15.1 lists

15.1
Methods of Communication Within Organizations

Method	Advantages	Disadvantages
Telephone	Speed Permits questions and answers Convenient Two-way	No record of conversation Message might be misunderstood
Face to Face	Visual; personal contact Can "show" and "explain" Can set the mood Two-way	Timing may be inconvenient Requires spontaneous thinking May not be easy to terminate One person may feel subject to pressure by power or status Conversation may be heard by unintended receivers
Meetings	Visuals can be used — charts graphs, films, etc. Involves several minds at once	Time consuming Timing may be inconvenient Can deteriorate into one-way communication
Memorandum	Brief Provides a record Can prethink the message	No control over receiver One-way
Formal Report	Complete; comprehensive Material organized at writer's leisure Can be disseminated widely	May require considerable time in reading Language may not be understandable Expense One-way

Adapted and summarized from A. Uris, *The Executive Deskbook*. New York: Van Nostrand Reinhold Company, 1970, pp. 27–28.

the methods available for communicating in organizations. Each of these methods has its advantages and disadvantages. Also, they are not mutually exclusive.

The **channel** is the style of transmission. A manager might think: "Should I communicate with the receiver face-to-face or on paper?" The choice of an oral or written channel depends on: (1) the importance of the message; (2) whether a written record of the communication is needed, and (3) whether immediate feedback from the receiver is needed. We want to emphasize that most managers use both oral and written channels to communicate with others and that no channel is "best" in all conditions. Do you remember when the hostages were released from Iran? What type of channel was used? In this instance, the American people wanted immediate feedback on their release and what happened. The media used oral communication to provide us with feedback.

Channel

We can think of channels that are formal and informal. **Formal** channels follow the hierarchical structure of the organization. **Informal** channels are not found in formal structure. These channels arise from employees talking, have no official sanction, and frequently contain a high proportion of misinformation. There are three kinds of formal channels used by managers: downward, upward, and horizontal.

Downward channels are used by management for sending orders, directives, goals, policies, memorandums, etc. to employees at lower levels in the organization. There are five reasons why managers use downward communication:[18]

Downward channels

1. Job instructions — communication pertaining to performance of a certain task.

2. Job rationale — communication relating a certain task to others in the organization.

3. Procedures and policies — communication about organization policies, rules, regulations, and benefits provided by the company.

4. Feedback — communication about the individual's job performance.

5. Indoctrination — communication designed to tell the employees about certain events that the company thinks are important for employees to participate in — charitable organizations, blood drive, and the like.

Downward communication is probably the most frequently used channel in organizations. It may also be the most misused, since some managers place little emphasis on upward communication. The basic problem with downward communication is that it's usually a one-way street: it does not provide for feedback from those who receive it. Too many managers fail to see the value of encouraging employees to fully discuss the policies and plans of the company. They do not provide a clear channel for transmitting information through the company.

Upward channels **Upward channels** send information from subordinate to supervisor to provide feedback for management. They are the major means that employees have for communicating to higher levels in the organization. Most of you complete a faculty evaluation survey at the end of the course. This survey asks you to rate the course, book, and instructor. This would be an example of an upward communication channel.

Managers should encourage upward communication because it provides feedback on how well employees understand the downward communication. It can encourage employees to submit valuable ideas. For upward communication to be effective, it must be allowed to occur freely, not just at the whim of the manager. Upward communication can provide an emotional release and, at the same time, give the employee a sense of personal worth because management listens.

The manager should be aware, however, that certain failures may occur in upward communication.[19] First, few employees want their boss to learn anything negative about them, so they usually screen out of their communication anything that's not positive. Most employees try to impress their superior by indicating their contributions to the company. Some try to make themselves look better by pointing out how others in the department have not contributed. Second, an employee's personal anxieties, aspirations, and system of beliefs and values almost invariably color what he or she says. How many of you would tell the faculty member instructing this course that it is terrible? Few would because of the fear that the faculty member would hold this against you when determining your grade in the class. Finally, the employee may be competing for the manager's job and thus willing to sit by and let the manager stumble into problems. In Chapter 12, we illustrated some of the political maneuvering that goes on in organizations.

Horizontal channels **Horizontal channels** flow across lines of communication. They might be classified as formal or informal depending on whether they follow the formal organization structure. Horizontal channels are frequently used between people on the same level. Messages usually relate to task coordination, information sharing, and conflict resolution. Horizontal channels have become increasingly important for organizations that have adopted matrix structures because decisions need to be made quickly without following the "chain of command."

Although we have emphasized formal channels of communication, we should not underestimate the importance of informal channels. We know less about these, but the "grapevine" is one source of information for managers. The grapevine is fast, highly selective and discriminating, operates across formal lines of authority, and supplements the formal channels.[20]

The grapevine has some good and bad characteristics. It is desirable because it gives management insights into employee attitudes, provides a safety valve for employee emotions, and helps spread useful information. It is undesirable because it spreads false rumors, cannot be controlled by management, and has no permanent members. Do you recall how the grapevine worked during the release of the Americans held hostage by Iran? Was it helpful?

As we said a bit earlier in this chapter, the **receiver** is the person who gets the sender's message. For the message to be clearly communicated, the receiver must decode the message. **Decoding** is the process by which receivers interpret messages and translate them into meaningful thoughts or feelings for themselves. This process is affected by the receiver's past experiences, intelligence, personality characteristics, and expectations about the sender. The plumber could not decode the message from the Bureau of Standards. The Bureau used language the plumber could not understand because of his level of formal education. There are two major processes that affect the receiver: listening and feedback. We will briefly discuss listening and more fully develop the concept of feedback.

One of the major processes that affect the receiver is listening. Some experts state that managers spend more than 75 percent of their time in some type of communication. Of that time, about 50 percent is spent listening. Most people can recall only about 50 percent of what someone tells them immediately after they have heard it. Two months later, they can recall only 25 percent.[21] How can we become better listeners? We have listed some guidelines for effective listening:

1. Stop talking.

2. Establish rapport with the sender; put the sender at ease.

3. Indicate a willingness to listen. Look interested.

4. Cut out distractions. Have the secretary hold telephone calls and try to eliminate distracting noises.

5. When you are not sure of the message, try to restate it or go over what you believe to be the major points already discussed.

6. Allow others to finish their message. Wait your turn to ask questions.

There are many more guidelines that we could list. Receivers should provide feedback to the sender to make sure that the message is actually being received and understood.

Feedback

Feedback is the receiver's response to the sender's message. Effective communication must be two-way. Feedback is the best way to determine that a message has been received and how well it has been understood. Unfortunately, managers sometimes fail to recognize that they must have reliable feedback if they want effective communication. Managers should not assume that everything they say or write will be understood exactly as intended. All other things equal, the manager who does not allow feedback will be less effective than the manager who receives feedback.[22]

Effects of feedback

The effects of feedback have been researched by many people. We have been able to identify four consequences of feedback. *First*, the actions of the sender affect the reactions of the receiver. The reactions of the receiver affect the subsequent actions of the sender. Carol Sellers sent a message to Joyce Crawford indicating that the Procter and Gamble account was assigned to her (Joyce) and a market survey was needed within three months for a new shampoo. After three months, Carol had not received the survey. This feedback told Carol that she needed to clarify her original message. *Second*, reactions of the receiver serve as feedback and tell the sender how well the objectives are being accomplished. In Carol's case, the objectives were not accomplished by Joyce. Carol must discuss the reasons with Joyce. *Third*, a sender who receives feedback that is rewarding will continue to produce the same kind of message; if the feedback is not rewarding, the message will eventually change. Because Carol did not receive the survey on time, the feedback was not rewarding for her. After discussing the reasons with Joyce, Carol determined that Joyce needed more detailed instructions on how to conduct a market survey. *Fourth*, the receiver exerts control over the sender by the kind of feedback he or she gives to the sender. Joyce's lack of performance was a message to Carol that further messages must be in greater detail and that biweekly meetings were needed.

Let's consider some guidelines recommen..ea   ~ter and Gamble, Exxon, and others in their training programs to improve .~ec   .k.[23] These guidelines are summarized in Table 15.2.

Improving feedback

1. Feedback should be *intended to help* the receiver. One way to test this is to ask yourself: "Do I really feel that what I'm about to say is likely to be helpful to the receiver?" If the receiver can not relate the information to what he or she already knows, the feedback is not likely to be helpful.

2. Feedback should be *descriptive rather than evaluative*. If you describe a situation and tell the sender the effect it had on you, the feedback is more likely to lead to desired changes. "You interrupted me just when I was trying to tell you my problem" is descriptive, and is more effective feedback than "You're a self-centered egotist who won't listen to anyone's ideas," which is certainly evaluative.

3. Feedback should be *specific rather than general*. Include all the information the receiver needs in order to understand the message. The manager who says "Do section seven over again," is giving general rather than specific information. The manager might say "In section seven, pages three and four need job descriptions for the clerk's position."

4. Feedback should be given when the receiver appears *ready to hear it. It is well timed*. The reception of feedback is affected by the situation in which it occurs. Is the setting an office, someone's home, or during half-time at a football game? Giving feedback to a person during half-time is altogether different from giving the same person feedback in the office.

5. Lastly, feedback *should not overwhelm the receiver*. This guideline is related to how much feedback individuals can receive at one time. Oral communication requires the receiver to depend heavily on memory. In the listening section, we indicated that most people forget 50 percent of what they hear. Oral feedback is less effective than written feedback for handling large amounts of information. Effective communicators know that it is rare for an

---

15.2
Characteristics of Good Feedback

- It is intended to help.
- It is specific rather than general.
- It is well timed.
- It is descriptive rather than evaluative.
- It does not overwhelm the receiver.

employee to absorb more than three things at one time. The average person tends to tune in and out of conversations. Therefore, they often fail to grasp what the speaker is saying if the message is long and complex.

Perception

Perception is the selection and organization of a message into meaningful experience.[24] Figure 15.1 indicates that perception influences both the sender and receiver in the communication process. Perception determines behavior, and is itself affected by many factors. We will highlight the important role perception plays in the communication process.

Our perceptions are influenced by objects seen, the ways in which we organize these objects, and the meanings we attach to them. Individual perceptual awareness varies. Some people who have entered a room only once can describe it in detail, whereas others barely remember anything. Your mental ability to discern differences is important. How we interpret what we perceive is also affected by our *past experiences.* A clenched fist raised in the air by a football player can be interpreted as an angry threat against the opposition or as an expression of team solidarity. Our world is constantly changing. The final class bell fills you with joy if you have completed your work and are about to start the weekend; it fills you with panic if you still have three more answers to complete on your management examination.

In all likelihood, the sender and receiver will bring different attitudes, past experiences, and mental abilities to the communication process. Let's look at a true incident:[25]

> *The president of a major firm was considering promoting one of the upper-level managers to a top position in the firm. The prospective candidate was invited to the president's home for dinner. At the end of the main course, pie was served. The candidate made the mistake of putting the tines (prongs) of the fork straight into the pie instead of using the side of the fork. The president rejected the candidate because of the individual's lack of sophistication. The president told the Personnel Department that anyone so naive in his approach to such a simple matter as eating pie could not be trusted to make corporation-wide decisions.*

The president rejected the candidate because of his belief that a person who ate pie in what the president considered an awkward manner would make poor decisions. To the candidate, how he ate the pie was of no consequence; to the president it was crucial. The perceptual world of the president was quite different from the perceptual world of the candidate.

Perception is a major cause of communication breakdowns. One reason is that we are not careful to record what we perceive. Read aloud the following sentence.

Finished files are the result of years of scientific study combined with the experience of many years of experts.

How many times does the letter "f" appear? Many people count three; there are seven. Can you identify them? Read aloud the sentences in the two triangles pictured below. Did you notice that "the" appeared twice in the first triangle and "a" twice in the second? If not, it is because your past experience with these sayings controlled your ability to perceive and, in this case, to read accurately what was written.

In brief, our ability to encode and decode is based on our ability to accurately perceive the situation. People often perceive the same object in different ways. The type of message they send, the channel of communication they use, and their ability to respond all depend on their perceptions.

"They never listen anyway." "How did I know that management really meant it?" "I thought that the test was tomorrow."

One of the first steps to communicating more successfully is learning what barriers stand in the way. These barriers hinder the sending and receiving of messages by distorting or sometimes even completely blocking intended meanings. There are almost as many barriers as there are writers to list them,[26] but we have briefly summarized them in Table 15.3. For the sake of convenience, we have divided these into organizational and individual barriers, although there obviously will be some overlapping.

Whenever one person has a higher position than another, there are potential communication problems. The more levels in the organization, and the further away the receiver is from the sender, the harder it is for the message to effectively communicate what is intended. Likewise, with knowledge becoming more and more specialized, it is not difficult to see how a person at a certain level in one field might find it difficult to communicate successfully with a person at the same level in a completely unrelated field.

BARRIERS TO EFFECTIVE COMMUNICATION

Organizational Barriers

Organizational level

Organizational

- ■ Structure of the organization.
- ■ Specialization of task functions by members.
- ■ Different goals.
- ■ Status relationships among members.

Individual

- ■ Conflicting assumptions.
- ■ Semantics.
- ■ Emotions.
- ■ Communication skills.

Figure 15.4 illustrates the amount of information that is correctly understood as messages are passed down the hierarchy. Assuming that top management represents 100 percent understanding, by the time the message travels through another five levels, only 20 percent of the original message will be understood.

Different goals   In growing dynamic organizations, problems arise because managers do not understand the general goals of top management. Every department develops its own ideas on how to solve problems and reach goals. Attempts to work with other departments, except in times of crisis, are often avoided. Each department exhibits "tunnel vision" and cannot see the long-range needs of the organization. For a large construction company erecting business or residential buildings, the goal of the construction crew is to get the tenant into the building as fast as possible. To accomplish this goal, once the architect's plan has been drawn, the fewer changes the better. The goal of the owner is also to get tenants into the building as soon as possible. Unfortunately, sometimes the goal of an architect is to build a "monument." The incompatibility of these goals can lead to delays and cause each group to view the other as the "enemy."

Status is the position of an organization member in relation to other members. Some typical signs of status in organizations include titles, work schedules, office size, office furnishings, carpeting, and parking space. These and other symbols are used to clearly show different levels of importance. Status

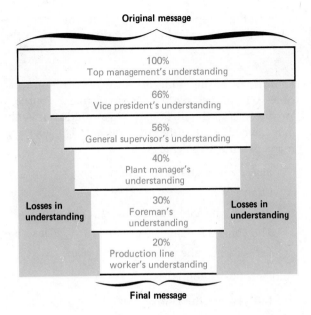

15.4
Levels of Understanding as
Information is Transmitted
Down the Organization

Adapted from E. Scannell,
*Communication for
Leadership: New York:
McGraw-Hill Book Company,
1970, p. 5. Reproduced with
permission.*

can hinder the flow of communication. In the section of this chapter on non-verbal communication, we discussed these symbols and how they influence communication.

Individual Barriers

It is very important that the manager be able to give clear and effective messages. Words, phrases, and references that may be clear to some employees may be puzzling and obscure to others. The problem is often due to conflicting assumptions, semantics, emotions, and lack of effective communication skills.

**Conflicting
Assumptions**

When individuals send messages, senders assume that the receivers will interpret the messages as the senders intended. But a key word or phrase may mean one thing to the sender and something else to the receiver. For example, a sales representative of a large organization phoned in a special order and asked that it be shipped "as soon as possible." Five days later, the sales rep got a call from the upset customer wanting to know when the order would be delivered. On checking with the shipping department, the rep found that the order was being shipped that day "I thought I told you to ship it as soon as possible," shouted the rep. "That's just what we're doing," yelled the person in the shipping department. To the salesperson, "as soon as possible" meant *now.* To the shipping department, that often received that kind of order from reps, it meant something totally different.

Semantics

Semantics is the study of the way words are used and the meaning they convey. Improper word usage is a major source of communication failure. Most words in the dictionary have multiple meanings. Some common words may have up to 18 different meanings. One example of a common word with many meanings is "charge":

> Please put a charge on the battery.
>
> Charge it.
>
> You are charged with running a red light.
>
> The charge for this service is $25.00. Please pay now.
>
> Let's charge ahead on this new plan.

Another illustration is "run:"

> Did you see the run by Dorsett?
>
> Run to the store and get a six-pack.
>
> Who will run for President in 1988?
>
> You have the run of the place.

When two individuals attribute different meanings to the same words and do not realize it, a barrier exists. Faculty members who say to their class, "This is an easy test," can mislead the students if the students do not know the faculty member's definition of an "easy" test.

Emotions

Emotions *refer to feelings.* All communication has an emotional part. When we recall past experiences, we recall not only the event, but the feelings that accompanied it. The sender's feelings at the time the messages are sent influence both the sender and receiver. Do you recall the excitement of Al Michaels, the announcer for ABC during the winter 1980 Olympic games, when he was describing the U.S. hockey victory over the Russians and then Czechoslovakia? Do you recall the emotions shown by the hostages when they were freed after 444 days of captivity in Iran? Emotions are part of the communication process.

Communication skills

Individuals vary in their ability to communicate. Some differences in communication skills are attributable to education and training, while others stem from more basic personality characteristics. For instance, articulate, persuasive, and confident people communicate more effectively than others who are less articulate. Some people are better listeners than others by virtue of education, training, personality characteristics, or physical characteristics (e.g., level of hearing ability). Anxious people sometimes are too preoccupied with their personal problems to pay an appropriate amount of attention to messages from other people. People under considerable organizational stress may also show some decrease in listening capability.

Effectiveness of communication is also influenced by the *timing* of messages. Managers who relay important instructions to employees on the Friday afternoon before a holiday show poor timing. By that time, most people will be shifting their attention away from work and toward vacation. In contrast, the department manager who asks for new funds after the company has achieved its financial objectives for the year shows good timing. Under these circumstances, the department manager's superior is more likely to listen to the request.

To be effective communicators, managers must understand not merely the concepts presented in Fig. 15.1, but also the ways they can improve their communication skills. While these were presented throughout the chapter, we will pull the important guidelines together in this section.

The American Management Association has compiled a list of eight guidelines managers can use to improve their communications.[27] These are highlighted in Table 15.4 and explained below.

1. Clarify your ideas before communicating. The more you analyze the problem before communicating, the clearer it becomes in your mind. Some managers fail to communicate effectively because of inadequate planning. Good

**GUIDELINES FOR
EFFECTIVE
COMMUNICATION**

15.4
*Guidelines for Effective
Communication*

- Clarify your ideas before communicating.
- Examine the true purpose of the communication.
- Consider the setting in which the communication will take place.
- Consult with others, when appropriate, in planning communications.
- Be mindful of the nonverbal messages you send.
- Take the opportunity to convey something of help to the receiver.
- Follow up the communication.
- Be sure your actions support your communication.

planning considers the goals and attitudes of those who will receive the communication.

2. *Examine the true purpose of the communication.* Before you communicate, ask yourself what you really want to accomplish with your message. Do you want to obtain information, make a decision, persuade someone to take action? Do not try to accomplish too many purposes with each communication.

3. *Consider the setting in which the communication will take place.* Meanings and intent are conveyed by more than words alone. Attempting to communicate with a person in another room presents more difficulties than does speaking face-to-face.

4. *Consult with others, when appropriate, in planning communications.* It is often desirable to seek the participation of those who will be affected by the communication. These people can often lend a viewpoint on the problem that you might not have. Remember Peachtree Rent-a-Car? The visit to Atlanta proved invaluable to Bob and Shelley.

5. *Be mindful of the nonverbal messages you send.* Your tone of voice, facial expression, eye contact, dress, and physical surroundings all influence the communication process. These factors are frequently overlooked. Receivers judge communications on the basis of the sender's words *and* nonverbal messages.

6. *Take the opportunity to convey something of help to the receiver.* Consideration of the other person's interests and needs frequently points up opportunities for senders. Individuals can make their communication clearer by placing themselves in the other person's shoes. Effective communicators really try to see the message from the listener's point of view.

7. *Follow up the communication.* Your best efforts at communication can be wasted unless you succeed in changing the other person's behavior or feelings. In the "Feedback" section of this chapter we reviewed the five ways you can test whether or not your communication has been effective.

8. *Be sure your actions support your communication.* In the final analysis, the more effective communication is not in what you say, but in what you do. Actions speak louder than words.

SUMMARY For a number of reasons, the role of communication has greatly increased over the past few years. First, the tremendous growth in the sheer number of organizations makes managing a more difficult task and requires improved communication. The U.S. postal service handled over 91 billion pieces of mail in 1977, an increase in over seven billion pieces since 1970. Ninety-six percent of American homes have telephones, and about the same percentage have television sets. As workers become more specialized, they become more dependent on others to get their jobs completed. As workers become more competent to perform a narrow set of tasks, communication needed across tasks is decreased and the use of jargon is increased. Third, better communication is usually associated with job satisfaction. Workers are more likely to be satisfied with their jobs if they are satisfied with the amount of information they receive on the job. People who are left out are not as satisfied as those who are "in the know."

To understand the important role of communication in organizations, we defined communication as a process by which information is exchanged between two or more persons. Communication is important because managers spend up to 80 percent of their time communicating. Effective communication is important to achieve the objectives of the organization.

We described the six basic elements in the communication process. The *sender/encoder* is the person with a need to communicate with another person. The burden is on the sender to accurately send the information to the receiver. The sender must choose symbols that represent the information that the receiver should receive. We discussed three types of *messages:* nonverbal, oral, and written. Nonverbal communication involves the use of your voice (volume, speed, pitch, etc.), gestures, and body to convey the information. Most people are unaware of how they communicate nonverbally. Oral or verbal communication was described next. We indicated that most managers prefer to communicate face-to-face because they can pick up nonverbal messages in the process. The section on written communication consisted of a brief discussion of effective writing. We listed the advantages and disadvantages of the most commonly used messages by managers.

The *channel* is the style of communication. First, the downward channel (chain of command) and its potential advantages and problems were discussed. Highly bureaucratic organizations frequently rely on this type of channel to communicate with employees. The upward channel provides the subordinate with an opportunity to provide feedback to upper management. We indicated how difficult it is to establish effective upward communication because employees usually do not like to have their superiors find out about things that show them in a bad light. Finally, we described the informal or grapevine. Managers make decisions based on hunches or gossip.

The *receiver's* ability to get the message depends on listening and feedback. Both of these processes are affected by the receiver's past experience with the sender, intelligence, personality, and expectations about the content of the message.

Feedback is vital if effective communication is to occur. We indicated various ways you can improve your ability to give feedback.

How the sender and receiver *perceive* the communication is also important. Behavior is a function of perceptions. Your ability to accurately perceive the communication is affected by your past experiences.

In the section on barriers to effective communication we briefly discussed some of the major organizational and individual barriers. By now, you should have learned that managers spend many hours communicating and that not all messages are received. This section indicated some of the reasons why messages are not always understood by receivers.

KEYWORDS

channel
communication
decoding
downward channels
emotions
encoding
feedback
formal channels
horizontal channels

informal channels
message
nonverbal communication
perception
receiver
semantics
sender
upward channels

DISCUSSION
QUESTIONS

1. Define communication and give an example.

2. Give one example of how the three roles played by a manager (interpersonal, informational, and decisional) are influenced by communication.

3. Why is the encoding process important? What role does this play in the communication process?

4. Visit a faculty member's office. What nonverbal communication does this office communicate to you?

5. How does the grapevine work? Why is it so important for managers? How does it differ from formal communication?

6. What are some methods that managers use to communicate with others? List the advantages and disadvantages of each method.

7. What are the guidelines for improving feedback? Who bears the primary responsibility for good feedback?

8. Give an example in which you misperceived something. What happened?

9. What types of communication barriers can you identify in the Peachtree Rent-A-Car case?

10. Using the American Management Association's guidelines for efficient communication, how would you improve the communication process in Peachtree Rent-A-Car?

Management Incidents and Cases

Dovies International is a large production company that operates three divisions: Dovies Records, Dovies Production and Dovies Advertising. Dovies Records produces and distributes several lines of pop music and country and western stereo tapes and records. Dovies Production independently produces and markets television game shows and several variety programs that have been purchased by over 100 local television stations in the United States. Dovies Advertising is a new business venture for the company. The objective of this division is to develop promotional programs for large corporations.

Jim Dovies, the president, began this business in 1975 after spending fifteen years as a vice-president for a national marketing company. He has been responsible for the growth and profitability of the company. Each of the divisions is headed by a vice-president who reports to Mr. Dovies. Mr. Dovies has decentralized much of the decision-making authority to these vice-presidents.

Recently, Mr. Dovies became aware of the fact that the advertising division was running into some problems. He had received this information from two highly valued clients while playing golf at the country club. These clients claimed that their promotional programs were running three weeks behind the schedule originally agreed on by Ron Evans, the vice-president for Dovies Advertising.

When Jim returned to the office Monday morning, he called his executive assistant, Janet Hardy, and said, "Janet, I think that we have some problems with Ron's operation. Apparently they have fallen behind schedule on two important programs. You know that I believe each division should run its own business, but perhaps I've fallen out of touch with the division heads. What do you think about setting up a weekly luncheon meeting at the club where I could sit down with the three people and iron out problems?" "It sounds fine to me," said Janet. "Do you want me to arrange it?" Jim nodded his head.

Jim's office sent out the following memo that afternoon to the three vice-presidents.

MEMORANDUM

To: Vice-Presidents, Dovies International
FROM: Janet Hardy
RE: President's Luncheon

President Dovies directed that I establish a weekly luncheon to be attended by each of you and Mr. Dovies. The topic of discussion will be problems each of you is having in your divisions. The first of these is scheduled for next Monday, July 10th in the executive dining room at Canyon Creek Country Club at 12 noon. Please try to attend.

The luncheon meeting was a disaster. Each of the vice-presidents sat down and didn't say a word about the business. The conversation drifted from golf handicaps to plans for the weekend trip to Las Vegas. Mr. Dovies tried to steer the conversation away from social things to business. He asked Ron to discuss any problems that he was having with the advertising programs.

"I really do not have any," said Ron. "You know, the usual routine. We are a little behind on two clients. I understand that they have already talked to you about the problems. Believe me, Jim, their expectations are unrealistic. We agreed to have these programs ready, but the changes have been causing my people to work overtime."

At this point the vice-president from records said that he was concerned about the conversation. He thought that the luncheon was going to be a friendly chat and not a grill session. He said that if Dovies did not like the way he ran his operation, he would be happy to resign.

Jim was dumbfounded by all of this. He was surprised at their reactions and tried to reemphasize the fact that these lunches were intended only as a friendly means for sharing ideas and solutions to problems. After three more lunches, which followed the same pattern, Janet Hardy suggested that Jim drop the idea. He agreed.

Questions

1. What do you think started the reactions of the VP's to the memo?

2. Do you think that the source of the memo had anything to do with the problem? What about the place of the meeting?

3. Can you suggest an alternative way of communicating the information without having this meeting?

EVERETT PAPER MILLS* Everett Paper Mills was a division of a large forest-products company. Ed Barrett, the new production superintendent, had recently moved to Everett Paper from a small independent mill where he had been the manager. The

---

* Adapted from J. Wofford, E. Gerloff, and R. Cummins, *Organizational Communication: The Keystone to Managerial Effectiveness.* New York: McGraw-Hill Book Company, 1977, pp. 226–228.

three line managers reporting to Ed had all had 20 or more years' experience with Everett paper in the same mill. They had seen it go from a productive mill to one that was badly troubled with problem workers and poor performance.

In talking with one of the supervisors, Ed learned that a good many of them were upset over the fact that they had to report any machine breakdown to the production manager or one of his assistants within 15 minutes of the breakdown. They felt that this did not give the workers the opportunity to repair the machine themselves. Once the breakdown was "on report," it was forwarded to the production superintendent's office. The assistants told Ed that the word was that once a worker got five reports, he was taken off the machine and given a lower paying job.

1. What should Ed do?
2. What other problems (unidentified by Ed) might be present?
3. What additional steps might the supervisors take?

One of the major problems that Ed faced was that only about 40 percent of the jobs listed for scheduled maintenance shutdowns were ever performed. During an informal conversation with Neal Churchill, Everett's personnel director, Ed learned that the maintenance department was operating at about 30 percent efficiency. Neal also said that the maintenance workers had recently staged a slowdown in order to force the company to increase their wages. Neal also told Ed that it had been a common practice for maintenance workers to quit about an hour early in order to wash up.

The head of the maintenance department had worked his way up through the ranks. He started with Everett immediately after he graduated from high school and had been with the company 25 years. His reason for the "inefficiency" was that there were not many qualified maintenance people in the area and the personnel department sent him individuals who were not qualified to perform maintenance on the mills. He did not have time to train each newly hired worker, but assigned this responsibility to other workers, usually those who had been around for awhile.

1. How might Ed approach the maintenance head?
2. Who else should Ed talk to?

Part C Two months after Ed had joined Everett, the company held its annual picnic at a local park. Most of the employees and their families were there. Ed saw Neal at the picnic and handed him a beer. The following conversation then took place:

Neal: Hey, Ed, got a minute?

Ed: Sure. What's up?

Neal: Well, I was talking with one of your foremen that I know pretty well. You know, an off-the-record chat about the company.

Ed: Yeah?

Neal: He told me that the company's management style is the mushroom style: keep 'em in the dark and feed 'em a lot of manure. He said that nobody knew you were hired until you showed up at the plant. We heard that the guard didn't even know who you were.

Ed: Yeah, I guess that's so.

Neal: This foreman said that he has been doing his job for ten years and has never received any performance appraisal. His raises are just added into his check. No one has pointed out his strong and weak points.

Ed: Yeah, I guess that's so. But, I'm not totally sure. You know that I've been here only a few months myself.

Neal: Yeah I know that, but listen to this. Tom Kerr, the new head of industrial engineering, has not talked to or even been introduced to anybody in the paper-machine area and Tom has been on the job for three months.

Ed: Neal, how widespread do you think this feeling is about the mushroom style of management?

Neal: I don't know, Ed, but I think that you ought to find out if you want this place to produce.

Questions 1. What steps can Ed take?

2. What does this conversation tell you about the company? What organizational barriers may exist in this company?

3. What role has the informal communication channel played in this case?

1. A. DuBrin, *Fundamentals of Organizational Behavior*, 2nd. ed. New York: Pergamon Press, 1978, pp. 341–342.

2. P. Lewis, *Organizational Communications: The Essence of Effective Management.* Columbus, OH: Grid Publishing Company, 1975, p. 5.

3. R. Huseman, J. Lahiff, and J. Hatfield, *Business Communication: Strategies and Skills.* Hinsdale, IL: Dryden Press, 1981.

4. H. Mintzberg, *The Nature of Managerial Work.* New York: Harper & Row, 1973, pp. 58–93.

5. E. Huse, *The Modern Manager.* St. Paul, MN: West Publishing Company, 1979, p. 246.

6. Huseman et al., p. 25.

7. J. Wofford, E. Gerloff, and R. Cummins, *Organizational Communication: The Keystone to Managerial Effectiveness.* New York: McGraw-Hill, 1977, pp. 25–26.

8. Huseman et al., p. 26.

9. Huseman et al., p. 73. Also see M. Knapp, *Nonverbal Communication in Human Interaction*, 2nd ed. New York: Holt, Rinehart & Winston, 1978, and D. Leathers, *Nonverbal Communications Systems.* Boston: Allyn & Bacon, 1976.

10. E. Hall, *The Hidden Dimension.* New York: Doubleday, 1966.

11. J. Dean, III, *Blind Ambition.* New York: Simon and Schuster, 1976, pp. 29–30.

12. Huseman et al., pp. 81–82.

13. J. Molloy, *Dress for Success.* New York: Peter Wyden, 1975.

14. M. McCaskey, "The Hidden Messages Managers Send." *Harvard Business Review* **57,** 6, 1979, 146–147.

15. R. Harrison, *Beyond Words: An Introduction to Nonverbal Communication.* Englewood Cliffs, NJ: Prentice-Hall, 1974, pp. 132–133.

16. Huseman et al., p. 261.

17. These have been taken from: A. Burack, *The Writer's Handbook.* Boston: The Writer. 1972; J. Lindauer, *Communicating in Business.* New York: Macmillan, 1974; R. Lesikar, *Business Communication.* Homewood, IL: Richard D. Irwin, 1972.

18. D. Katz and R. Kahn, *The Social Psychology of Organizations*, 2nd ed. New York: John Wiley & Sons, 1978, p. 440.

19. C. O'Reilly and L. Pondy, "Organizational Communication." In S. Kerr (ed.). *Organizational Behavior.* Columbus, OH: Grid Publishing Company, 1979, pp. 135–136.

20. K. Davis, "Business Communication and the Grapevine." *Harvard Business Review* **31,** 1, 1953, 43–49.

21. Huseman et al., p. 261.

22. L. Strong, "Do You Know How to Listen?" In *Effective Communications on the Job.* J. Dooher and L. Marquis, (eds.). New York: American Management Association, 1956, p. 28.

23. J. Anderson, "Giving and Receiving Feedback." *Managers and Their Careers: Cases and Readings.* J. Lorsch and L. Barnes (eds.). Homewood, IL: Richard D. Irwin, 1972, pp. 260–267.

24. D. Hellriegel and J. Slocum, *Organizational Behavior*, rev. ed. St. Paul, MN: West Publishing Company, 1979, p. 142.

25. Condensed from R. Powell, *Race, Religion, and the Promotion of the American Executive.* Columbus, OH: Faculty of Administrative Studies, Ohio State University, 1979, No. AA-3.

26. For other barriers, see L. Porter and K. Roberts, "Communications in Organizations." In *Handbook of Industrial and Organizational Psychology.* R. Dubin (ed.). Chicago: Rand McNally, 1976, pp. 1548–1585; C. O'Reilly "Individuals and Information Overload in Organizations: Is More Necessarily Better?" *Academy of Management Journal* **23,** 1980, 685–696; T. Bonoma and G. Zaltman, *Psychology for Management.* Boston: Kent Publishing Company, 1981.

27. These are summarized from *Ten Commandments of Good Communications.* New York: American Management Association, 1955.

Chapter 16

MANAGING GROUPS

After reading this chapter, you should be able to:

1. Explain the importance of formal and informal groups to the process of management.

2. Use a basic group process model to analyze how groups operate and can be made more effective.

3. Assess the sentiments of work groups and the impact of sentiments on effectiveness.

4. Determine when to use groups for decision-making purposes.

5. Apply a contingency approach to group decision-making.

PREVIEW CASE

**Group
Decision-
Making at
Exxon***

The room is half the size of a tennis court, lined in walnut and thickly carpeted. The table is long and tapered, pieced from six massive sections of Indian laurel.

The eight men who sit in the swivel chairs around it are a blur of blue, gray, and tan suits. They are here to make what for them is a routine decision involving the expenditure of several hundred million dollars. They run the Exxon Corporation, the biggest industrial concern in the world.

Clifton C. Garvin, Jr., chairman and chief executive officer, has entered the boardroom from one of the far corners through a private door from his executive suite. Howard C. Kauffmann, president and No. 2 at Exxon, has a mirror-image set of offices on the other side of the boardroom. As always, the two chieftains have taken the center seats on the long sides of the boardroom table, facing each other and flanked by the six senior vice-presidents, who have entered through two doors at the other end of

---

* *Houston Chronicle*, August 22, 1980. Adapted by permission.

the room. These lead through anterooms to the main corridor beyond; even there, the sounds of the street 51 floors below rarely penetrate.

In theory, the ultimate power of a corporation lies with its board of directors. In the case of Exxon, the board consists of these eight men who are employees and the 10 men and one woman who are outside directors. The board meets once a month to review the company's activities. But it is the eight men around this table, members of what is known as the management committee, who really rule Exxon.

The committee gathers, on the average, three mornings a week. Other than a few aides, only committee members usually attend, though on this day a writer representing *The New York Times* magazine sits on the sidelines, one of the few strangers ever to witness a formal meeting of Exxon's top management.

The committee secretary, a polished young man on Garvin's right, presses one of the buttons on a control panel in the drawer in front of his seat. It signals an attendant at a console outside that six men who have been waiting there may now enter. They file in and take assigned seats at the ends of the long table.

For the next 60 minutes, these six employees of the Exxon Chemical Company will explain why they think the corporation should invest in a major new petrochemical plant. They will show a score of technical slides to illustrate why they want to build the plant, what they think are the best, worst, and most probable returns that can be expected from such an investment — and how political factors might affect those returns.[1]

Group meetings for the purpose of making decisions, sharing information, or coordination are quite common at all levels of management, not just at the highest levels as in the Exxon case. The Exxon story suggests the importance of managerial groups to the organizational decision-making process. At Exxon, we learned of only three of the thousands of groups of managers and employees that meet to dicuss everything from menus in the employees' cafeterias to the proposed funding of a new petrochemical plant. You will recall that this proposal was presented by the six-member top-management group of Exxon Chemical to the eight-member executive committee of Exxon Corporation. The third decision-making group mentioned at Exxon is the board of directors. The board consists of the eight members of the executive committee plus 11 outside directors.

The importance of group meetings for managers is suggested by the amount of time managers spend in them. For example, William Smithberg, the president of Quaker Oats, figures group meetings take up 50 percent of his time. Frank Considine, the president of National Can Corp., puts his figure at 60 precent.[2] The time spent by first-level managers in group meetings will vary between 25 to 60 precent.

While group meetings consume a great deal of time, a survey of high-level managers from nine nations, including the United States, ranked group meetings as the fourth-biggest time waster. The worst time waster was telephone interruptions, second was drop-in visitors, and third was ineffective delegation.[3] No one expects the use of groups to decline in organizations. Thus, this chapter is intended to improve your understanding of groups and develop your skills for using them effectively. This will serve to minimize the perception of groups as time wasters.

THE NATURE OF GROUPS

Definition of a Group

First, some background. Consider the major ways groups differ from organizations. A group is usually gathered within a physical space that permits the members to hear and see one another. Each member usually can communicate verbally with every other member. Finally, a group does not have the many hierarchial levels found in an organization.[4]

These characteristics are necessary, but they are not all the conditions needed for the existence of a group. For example, if five strangers start playing basketball together just to pass a few spare minutes, they probably do not constitute a group. Individuals must be aware of one another and consider themselves to be members of a group. Thus, a **group** is three or more individuals who come into personal, meaningful, and purposeful contact on a relatively continuing basis. If five individuals play basketball together on a continuing basis, share a common goal of winning games, communicate freely among themselves, and the like, they are a group.

Most of us belong to six or so groups.[5] At work, we might be members of two or three groups. A formal work group is likely to consist of our immediate superior and fellow workers. We also could belong to some informal social group at work. An informal social group might be five or six workers who sit together every day during breaks to eat and play cards or who are members of the same bowling league.

Characterstics of Effective Groups

Much of this chapter focuses on making groups more effective. First, we need to know how to recognize effective or ineffective groups. In brief, an effective group has the following characteristics:

- It knows why it exists.
- It has guidelines or procedures for making decisions.
- It has achieved communication among its members.
- Members have learned to receive and give help to one another.
- Members have learned to deal with conflict within the group.
- Members have learned to diagnose their processes and improve their own functioning.[6]

The degree to which a group is weak in one or more of these characteristics determines whether — and to what extent — it is ineffective.

There are many ways of classifying groups in organizations. We will simply distinguish between formal and informal groups.

Basic Types of Groups

A **formal group** is one whose goals and activities relate directly to the achievement of stated organizational goals. In this chapter's preview case, three formal groups at Exxon were identified: the eight-person executive committee, the nineteen-person board of directors, and the six-member management team of Exxon Chemical. Formal groups are part of the structure of the organization. Formal groups are departments, sections, task forces, project groups, committees, and boards of directors.

Formal groups

An **informal group** is one that develops out of the day-to-day activites, interactions, and sentiments of the members for the purpose of meeting their needs. A social group is one of the most common types of informal groups in or out of organizations.

Informal groups

The purposes of informal groups are not necessarily related to formal organizational goals. The formal organization, however, often has considerable influence on the development of informal groups — through the physical layout of work, the leadership practices of superiors, and the type of technology used. For example, moving some people from one building to another is likely to have an impact on the membership of informal groups. The distance between them may make it difficult to communicate on a face-to-face basis. Or, a new manager taking over a department might tell the members to "shape up or ship out." With this type of threat, an informal group may form to unite its members against the new manager.

Positive and Negative Views of Groups

Some managers see groups as providing a number of benefits to the organization. Groups might increase employee creativity and problem-solving, stimulate work, or decrease turnover and absenteeism.[7]

From management's viewpoint

Other managers believe that close-knit groups have undesirable effects on the organization. These managers often view groups as a potential source of anti-establishment power, as a means for holding back information when the group does not identify with organizational goals, or as a means of pressuring individuals to hold down production.

From the members' viewpoint

Groups can provide their members with several desirable benefits, e.g., security and protection. Some groups set production maximums for members, fearing that management might use the outstanding worker as a standard for output and that increased production might lead to some workers being laid off. An informal group can provide reinforcing feedback to other members. The all-too-common belief in the United States that higher productivity will work against the interests of workers is kept alive and enforced by some informal groups within organizations. You might recall our discussion in Chapter 5 of the Hawthorne Experiments conducted at a Western Electric plant. We noted that the informal groups at the Hawthorne plant had a significant influence on productivity. Group pressure, based in part on mutual antagonism toward the "bosses," resulted in informal control of productivity.

It is common to hear of the undesirable powers informal groups have over individual members. These powers usually fall into two categories. First, a group may be able to manipulate rewards and punishments and thus pressure members to conform to its standards of behavior. For example, a Detroit policeman quit his job rather than accept bribes when stopping people for traffic violations. After a bribe had been offered and refused three times, he would arrest the party for attempting to bribe an officer. He told the press that the harassment and pressure from fellow policemen was so intense that he had to quit the force. Second, a group may restrict a member's freedom and the ways by which the social needs of its members can be satisfied on the job. Informal groups have been known to ridicule some members or give them the silent treatment for not conforming to group standards of "acceptable" production. Such treatment may threaten the individual's physiological, security, and social needs.

Informal groups in organizations cannot always be classified as positive or negative. From a managerial point of view, It is probably better for management to try and minimize the undesirable effects of informal groups than to try eliminating them.

INDIVIDUALS IN FORMAL GROUPS

When joining a new work group, it is quite common for people to experience feelings of tension, anxiety, or frustration. Managers can help new members with these emotional problems by minimizing their problems of adjustment.

Managers can create a sense of belonging by introducing new members to fellow employees, inviting them out to lunch with fellow employees, and chatting with them frequently during the first month or so to assist and reassure them. As for the group's adjustment, a manager can give a group an opportunity to work out its own problems in adjusting to new members, rather than trying to impose solutions.

Once individuals have become full-fledged members of a group, they generally emphasize different roles. Figure 16.1 presents one framework for the different types of group role behavior. This framework was developed from a study of middle- and upper-level managers in problem-solving groups.[8] The vertical axis indicates the degree of social behaviors shown by the individual, from low to high. **Social behaviors** are such actions as joking, laughing, rewarding others, and agreeing with others. The horizontal axis shows the degree of task behaviors, also from low to high. **Task behaviors** are such actions as giving suggestions, providing information, analyzing problems, evaluating alternatives, and making decisions.

By cross-classifying the variables of social behaviors and task behaviors, we can identify four "pure" role types: social specialists; stars; technical specialists; and the underchosen. We emphasize that these are pure types from the four corners of the grid. As with any classification of human beings any individual — such as yourself — is more than likely to fit into two or more categories at once, and so could fall at any point on this grid. For example, we plotted two hypothetical work groups of seven members each on the grid. Based on these plottings, group A is likely to be ineffective and group B effective in performing work-related tasks.

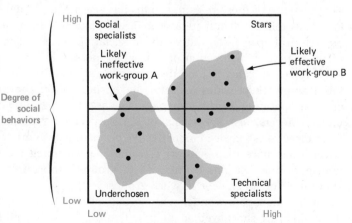

16.1
Roles of individuals in
groups
Adapted from D. Moment and
A. Zalenznik, *Role
Development and
Interpersonal Competence: An
Experimental Study of Role
Performance in
Problem-Solving Groups,*
Boston: Division of Research,
Graduate School of Business
Administration, Harvard
University, 1963, pp. 10–18.

Degree of task behaviors

Types of roles in groups   The four role types show little difference in their satisfaction with the way groups operate. However, they differ widely in other respects. Let's consider each of the pure roles a little further.

Social specialists show a great deal of feeling and support for others. They avoid criticizing, disagreeing with, or showing aggression toward other group members. They are interested in keeping the group operating as "one happy family."

Stars are active group members and exhibit a variety of behaviors. Stars let others know where they stand and show open, honest involvement without appearing too anxious. They address other members personally and do not emphasize only task or social behaviors. They show different behaviors for different situations. As a rule, stars are more likely to be satisfied with group decisions than are the other types.

Technical specialists show great concern with task-related problems and with using their expertise to solve them. They often avoid confronting social and emotional problems and display little interpersonal expression. As seen by others, they are not supportive or hostile to group members. When they do speak at meetings, they tend to elaborate on the task. Their limited desire for social contact is usually expressed through jokes that seem to meet personal rather than group needs.

Underchosen participants are uncommitted to the group and tend to show interest only in their personal needs. They are relatively serious, are the most aggressive and hostile of the four types, and are not the quietest. In group meetings, they talk more than the technical and social specialists but less than the stars. Their perceived lack of importance is due more to inefectiveness than to "invisibility"

Managerial implications   The existence of these roles in groups has several implications for managers. First, it is unlikely all individuals can or will play the same role.[9] Some prefer to be technical specialists, others to be social specialists. The role any group member plays is a function of his or her personality, communication style, level of need satisfaction, and the leadership style of the group leader. Second, this framework provides a useful diagnostic tool for the manager when a group is operating poorly. A manager can ask: Is the group overbalanced with underachievers, task specialists, or social specialists? Domination by any of these three roles may lead to ineffective performance. A group should be more effective as more members are capable of performing the star role. Third, managers may use this framework of group-member roles to gain insight about their own behavior in work groups.

If the managers wonder why no one ever questions their decisions and discussions are short lived, it could be that they're acting out the underchosen role.

Our discussion suggests a few of the basic issues and ways of thinking about individuals in groups. We now turn our attention more to the group as a whole — while keeping in mind that each member is an important foundation to group process.

One of the more useful means for describing and analyzing groups is the Homans Systems model, which George Homans presented in 1950.[10] It was modified and developed further in a book published in 1961.[11] Homans' concepts are few in number and as close as possible to common observations of group life.

BASIC GROUP PROCESS

The Homans Systems model is useful because it:

- Provides at least partial explanations of why people act as they do within groups.
- Provides managers with a means for diagnosing group processes within organizations.
- Considers contingency factors likely to affect the processes and outputs of groups.
- Suggests how groups are likely to change over time.

The model consists of two major parts — the internal and the external systems. Of course, these distinctions are relative, and the systems are quite interdependent.

Internal System

The ***internal system*** refers to the sentiments, activites, interactions, and norms that group members develop over time. These develop from the external system. The external system represents the "givens," conditions that existed before the internal system came into being. In the following case of a mythical professional football team, the external system is the coaching staff and the top-level managers. The case is intended to develop an initial understanding of the interface between the group's internal and external systems.

The Brawnsburgh Bashers football team might draft and keep 10 new players each year. Most of them are likely to form one or more new informal groups. Several also may become members of established informal groups. In this situation, the informal groups would not have developed if there was no formal organization — the Brawnsburgh Bashers.

The formal organization of the Bashers influences the informal groups, even their very survival. For example, if management decided to cut four of a six-member informal group, this would effectively "kill" that group. Once the internal system is established, however, it is likely to act on the external system as well. If the Bashers players felt that they were being treated unfairly by one of the coaches, they might join together and present their complaint to the head coach. A favorable response would be an example of the internal system (a group of unhappy players) affecting the external system (Bashers coaching staff).

Compared to that of the external system, the power of the internal system on individual member behavior can vary widely. For example, the Bashers' coaching staff, part of the external system, has the power to say who will make the team; the internal system does not. However, once the cuts are made and the team is in the regular season, the internal system plays a stronger role in day-to-day player behavior. The internal system influences who travels with whom, who plays cards together, who eats with whom, and other aspects of the team's operation.

As mentioned, the internal system consists of the group's activites, inter-actions, sentiments, and norms. Fig. 16.2 suggests these variables are inter-related; a change in one may result in a change in the others. A group should be considered as a system, not simply as a sum of member behaviors. It is how the members interact that substantially influences their effectiveness as a group.

16.2
Internal system of group

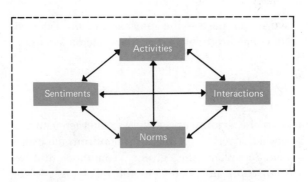

Activities   **Activities** are what individuals do to or with others or with inanimate objects (e.g., machines and tools). In the Homans Systems model, task behaviors — such as analyzing problems, evaluating alternatives, and making decisions — would be included as part of the activities variable.

Within business organizations, task activities take up most of a manager's time. The civil engineer is likely to be most concerned with the typography, soil conditions, and site preparation for the construction crew. Socially relevant activities, such as playing cards or pitching pennies, are likely to be of secondary interest.

Interactions are the starting actions and following reactions between two or more individuals. They are essentially patterns of communication among group members. This variable can be identified through such questions as:

■ With whom do the individuals talk?

■ How often do the members talk to one another?

■ How long do they talk?

■ Who starts the conversations?

Interactions occur in task behaviors and social behaviors. By defining job responsibilities and communication channels, the formal organization strongly affects the interaction patterns of work groups. Informal groups usually determine the interaction patterns of social behaviors.

Sentiments include day-to-day feelings (such as anger, happiness, sadness) as well as deeper feelings (such as trust, openness, and freedom). Sentiments can be thought of as the emotional climate of the group. The four sentiments most likely to influence the effectiveness and productivity of groups are: trust, openness, freedom, and felt interdependence. The more these sentiments are present, the more likely it is that the work group will be effective and productive.[12]

Assessing Group Sentiments   Table 16.1 provides a brief questionnaire for assessing the group sentiments of trust, openness, freedom, and interdependence. Take a couple of minutes and complete this questionnaire for a work or informal group in which you have been a member.

The scoring of the questionnaire in Table 16.1 should be done as follows (possible range is 0–15 points each):

■ *Trust:* Add point values circled for statements 1–5 =

■ *Openness:* Add point values circled for statements 6–10 =

■ *Freedom:* Add point values circled for statements 11–15 =

■ *Felt interdependence:* Add point value circled for statements 16–20 =

Add the above for grand total of sentiments (possible range of 0–60) =

The higher the scores, the more likely the group is to be effective and productive. A score of five or less on one of the dimensions may suggest that it is blocking group effectiveness and should be worked on by the manager. Likewise, a grand total of 20 or less suggests severe problems in group sentiments.

Interactions

Sentiments

Instructions: After each of the following statements, circle the number that corresponds to your degree of agreement or disagreement with that statement. The following scale is used: SD = strongly disagree; D = disagree; A = agree; SA = strongly agree.

Statements	SD	D	A	SA
Trust				
1. Members of this group trust each other very much	0	1	2	3
2. People are playing roles in this group and not being themselves	3	2	1	0
3. Some members are afraid of the group	3	2	1	0
4. The group treats each person in the group as an important member	0	1	2	3
5. Members seem to care very much for each other as individuals	0	1	2	3
Openness				
6. Members in this group are not really interested in what others have to say	3	2	1	0
7. Members of this group tell it like it is	0	1	2	3
8. Members often express different feelings and opinions outside of the group from those they express inside	3	2	1	0
9. Members of the group are afraid to be open and honest with the group	3	2	1	0
10. We don't keep secrets here	0	1	2	3
Freedom				
11. Members do what they ought to do in this group out of a personal sense of responsibility to the group	0	1	2	3
12. This group puts excessive pressure on each member to work toward group goals	3	2	1	0
13. When decisions are being made, members quickly express their thoughts	3	2	1	0
14. The group spends a lot of energy trying to get members to do things they don't really want to do	3	2	1	0
15. Members of this group are growing and changing all the time	0	1	2	3
Felt Interdependence				
16. Everyone in this group does his or her own thing with little thought for others ...	3	2	1	0
17. People in this group work together as members of a team	0	1	2	3
18. We need a lot of controls here to keep the group on track	3	2	1	0
19. There is little destructive competition in this group	0	1	2	3
20. You really need to have some power if you want to get anything done in this group ...	3	2	1	0

Adapted from J. R. Gibb, "TORI Group Self-Diagnosis Scale," in J. E. Jones and J. W. Pfeiffer (eds.) *The 1977 Annual Handbook for Group Facilitators*, San Diego, CA: University Associates, 1977; and from J. R. Gibb, *Trust: A New View of Personal and Organizational Development.* Los Angeles: Guild of Tutors Press, 1978. Used with permission.

Interpretations of Group Sentiments   What might high or low scores on each of these sentiments mean? The following are the possible meanings:

- High scores on *trust* might indicate these sentiments: "I trust the group. I see the group climate as trusting and as a good environment for me and other members." Low scores on trust might tell you; "I distrust the group. I see members as being impersonal and staying in roles. I see the group as a threatening and defensive environment for me and the other members."

- High scores on *openness* may suggest: "I see the group as open and spontaneous and the members as willing to share feelings with each other." Low scores on openness may suggest: "I see the group as fearful, cautious, and unwilling to show feelings and opinions, particularly if they are negative or nonsupportive."

- High scores on *freedom* seem to reveal these sentiments: "I see the group as allowing individual discretion and as a good environment for directing my energies toward desired goals." Low scores on freedom might be saying: "I see the group creating great pressures on members to conform, to do things they don't want to do, and to work toward group goals, regardless of the significance of those goals."

- Finally, high scores on *interdependence* may be saying: "I see the group as a smoothly functioning unit which works effectively and cooperatively." Low scores on interdependence might mean: "I see the group as unable to work well as a team, and missing significant ingredients necessary for effective functioning."

In sum, the sentiment-variable in the Homans Systems model has a critical influence on the group's effectiveness, as well as on the other internal system variables of norms, activities, and interaction. For example, negative sentiments by a work group toward higher management may result in a group norm to limit the productivity of individual members.

Norms

Norms are standards of behavior widely shared and enforced by members of the group. Norms develop out of the group's interactions. Norms set standards for members on what they ought to do or should not do under specific circumstances. Norms of work groups often define how much and how little work should be done by members, what to wear, where to eat, what kinds of jokes are acceptable, how you should feel toward the organization, and so on.

Criteria for Group Norms   Group norms exist when three criteria have been met.[13] First, *there must be standards of appropriate behavior* for group members. For example, members of a work group may share norms for the amount of work they should do on their shift, but these norms would not apply to a member's part-time job with another company. Second, *members must pretty generally agree on the norms.* This does not mean that all members of a group need to share the norms. But if most of the members have significantly different opinions about how much work is enough, the group does not have a productivity norm. Third, the members must *be aware that the group supports a particular norm through a system of reward and punishment* — reward for compliance and punishment for violations.

Power of Group The ability of a group to enforce its norms depends, in part, on the *importance* of the group's rewards and punishments and the *probability* that they will be used.[14] The factors of importance and probability have to be considered from the point of view of the members. Individuals who value the rewards and respect the punishments might still violate the norms if they believe they're not likely to be caught. This is especially true if they see other rewards from violating the norms. Take, for example, a salesperson whose work group punishes for bringing in orders above a certain norm. If the salesperson feel that there is little likelihood of being caught while earning additional income, then he or she might exceed the norm.

The importance of group rewards and punishments reflects the importance of the group to the individual. An individual who does not value the rewards or respect the punishments provided by the group may have little motivation to follow its norms. This is particularly true if the rewards and punishments are inconsistent with the individual's own standards. For example, a person who strongly identifies with management might be placed in a work group as part of a company's training program. If this work group is hostile toward management and has a number of norms to keep production down, that person may reject those norms. This individual's productivity could remain far above the norms, even though the group continues to try to punish the "violator" through harassment or the "silent" treatment.

Deviation from Norms A *deviant member* does not follow the standards of behavior established by the group. As implied in Fig. 16.3, Dick most frequently violates the group's norms and is barely regarded as a group member. In some instances, a group with a deviant member may bring that member into line by controlling the flow of materials or information that he or she needs. For example, one of the authors once had a summer job at a 17-acre distribution center for the Goodyear Tire and Rubber Co. His job was to unload automobile tires from railroad boxcars during the afternoon shift, which had three towmotor drivers and six unloaders working the rail dock. The towmotor drivers brought and removed the pallets on which the tires were stacked. During his first week, he was unloading three to four boxcars a day. Then word got out! Several workers told him to lower his output to about two boxcars a day, the group's norm. He didn't cut his output. By the middle

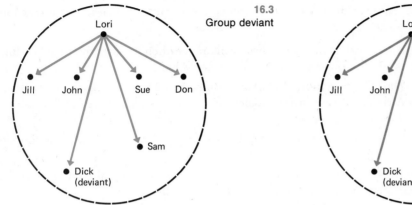

16.3
Group deviant

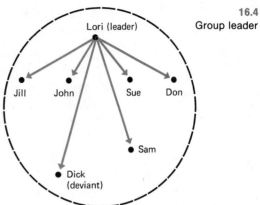

16.4
Group leader

of the second week, the towmotor drivers had reduced the flow of pallets to him and let loaded pallets stack up outside of the boxcar. The other workers were able to enforce their own norms without ever creating intense interpersonal conflicts or engaging in threats.

As suggested in Fig. 16.2, activities, sentiments, interactions, and norms can interrelate in a variety of ways. Several of these interrelationships are summed up as follows:

Interrelationships among internal system variables

■ The more frequently individuals interact with one another, the stronger their friendships are apt to be.

■ Individuals who like one another will express those sentiments in activities over and above the required activities of the external system.

■ Individuals who interact with one another frequently are more like one another in their activities than they are like other individuals with whom they interact less frequently.

Social Structure The pattern of sentiments, activities, and interactions is likely to differ among group members. These differences form the group's *social structure,* which is determined by such factors as the contribution of each member to the group's goals, how much each member accepts the norms of the group, and the personal characteristics of the members. In Fig. 16.4, it is implied that Lori is the group leader, Dick is the deviant, and four of the individuals are solid group members of equal status. An analysis of a group's social structure requires an evaluation of the group leader, the group's communication patterns, and the status (differential ranking) assigned to members. Some of the relationships among sentiments, activities, and interactions are suggested in the following statements:

- An individual of higher social rank more often initiates interaction with a person of lower social rank than vice versa.

- The higher an individual's social rank, the wider the range of interactions. A chef in a restaurant usually communicates with more employees than does a waiter or waitress.

- The sentiments of the group leader carry greater weight than do those of the followers.

- The higher the rank of an individual within a group, the more nearly his or her activities conform to the norms of the group.

The social structure and norms of some work groups have created problems for women and minorities. Sex-role stereotyping by work groups may not give women a fair opportunity to demonstrate their abilities. One of the more tragic examples of this is the case of a professional woman, Dr. A., newly promoted to chief of a community consultation unit for a mental health center. A researcher describes the problems of Dr. A. in establishing an equal status with other members of the top management group:

> *Throughout most of her tenure, Dr. A. was the only woman unit chief in the center; there were no women division heads, no women in central administration. Therefore, many meetings of center leadership were all-male groups, with the exception of Dr. A. and perhaps a female secretary to take minutes. Such meetings often opened with discussion of current male sports events — a "locker room" kind in which Dr. A. was out of place. Her femaleness was a covert group issue. In one meeting, the joking comment was made that since Dr. A. was seated in a chair occupied the day before by the male governor of the state perhaps she might be impregnated by his aura. On another occasion, when she commented that it was too warm in the room, she was asked jokingly if she was having hot flashes.*[15]

The males with whom Dr. A. worked with were all supposedly highly educated — holders of master's and doctoral degrees. It is obvious that sex-role stereotypes occur even among people who have reached the highest formal educational levels.

External System

The second part of Homans' model is the external system. The ***external system*** refers to the conditions that existed before the group was formed such as the members values, the type of technology used, and higher management leadership practices. These conditions would continue if the group should cease to function. For work groups, these factors include the interactions and activities required by technology, the physical setting, and the power of higher management. Compared to that of gangs or friendship groups, the external system of work groups is relatively explicit.

The potential power of management on the internal system of a group was highlighted in the example of the Brawnsburgh Bashers. Moreover, the important role of values in influencing individual and group behavior was developed in Chapters 2 and 3. Thus, we elaborate only on the potential impact of different technologies on work-group freedom.

Types of technology

The type of technology (i.e., unit or small-batch, mass-production, or continuous-process) influences the relative freedom of the group. As explained in earlier chapters, in *unit-production technology*, the firm is engaged in the custom manufacturing of individual items. Each product is built to the customer's specifications. Since the firm manufactures different items, standardization of procedures and work flows is difficult to establish. In *mass-production technology*, firms are engaged in producing a large volume of goods that are either identical or so similar that it is practical for management to build the technology and work flow around these particular items (e.g., automobile assembly). *Continuous-process technology* demands that activities be performed constantly. Thus, a chemical plant cannot shut down without incurring heavy start-up costs. The continuous-process technology is distinct in that the worker does not handle the material itself, except for occasional testing. Instead, the worker monitors the work flow and diagnoses how the process is progressing from automatic meters and charts. Workers need to cooperate in preventing breakdowns, but when one does occur, they need to move quickly as a team in getting the process started again.

Impact of technology

As suggested in Fig. 16.5, workers in a unit technology have a greater potential for the formation of highly autonomous groups than do those in mass-production technology. This is because the workers have a high degree of control over the pace of their work and how their tasks are performed. They often need to interact with others to get the job done.

With mass-production technology, groups are likely to have little freedom, and so they have less opportunity for developing their internal system. This is because workers must stay at their work stations and perform individual operations on materials continually passing by them on the line. The opportunities to interact with fellow workers on the line also may be made difficult by the high noise levels and distance between workers.

The degree of group freedom in a continuous-process technology (e.g., an oil refinery) is somewhat greater. With this technology, work-group members are highly interdependent and must communicate with one another on a con-

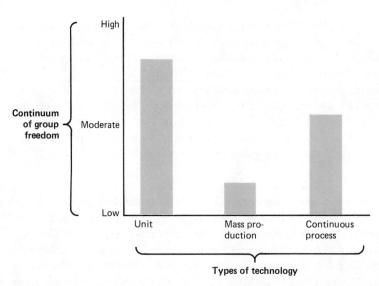

16.5
Impact of technology on
group freedom

The figure shows a bar graph. The vertical axis is labeled "Continuum of group freedom" with values from Low to Moderate to High. The horizontal axis shows "Types of technology" with three categories: Unit, Mass production, and Continuous process.

tinuing basis. Continuous-process technologies might permit giving the work group considerable control over the allocation of certain tasks, including self-selection of members (after initial requirements established by management have been met) and election of a leader by the group members. For management, *who* performs the tasks is not so important as encouraging workers to act as a team. It takes teamwork to keep the process going, prevent breakdowns, and restore production as soon as possible when a breakdown occurs.[16] Here, the group-leader's role might be limited to coordinating assigned tasks, leading discussions on subjects requiring group decisions, and serving as the group's spokesperson with management.[17]

Managerial Use of the Group-Process Model

The actions of a group can be understood and predicted only by analyzing both the internal and external systems. Homans' model pulls together a number of observations and findings about groups. For practicing managers, its main contribution is in providing a mental map for understanding and predicting the behavior of groups. The statements illustrating the relationships among sentiments, interactions, activities, and social structure should be useful in suggesting the patterns of behavior to be expected in groups. For example, a manager who issues an order inconsistent with a group norm (such as changing the dress code of employees) may well face a united group wanting to have the order changed. Or, if a manager tries to change or eliminate established communication patterns, the consequences may range from complaints to increased absenteeism and even turnover.

The manager provides more effective leadership by encouraging the establishment of group norms that support the formal goals of the department. Where there is high task interdependency and a great need for cooperation among group members, the effective manager increases the use of group rewards rather than emphasizing individual rewards. These rewards could be in the form of praise and recognition to the group as a whole or even a compensation system based on group production.

CASE STUDY

The Sanitation Department*

Homans' system model has been applied to a case study of the Sanitation Department on the night shift of a food-processing plant.[18] This case focuses on the changes in the internal system over 15 months, especially on the impact of the external system (i.e., management-initiated changes) on the internal system. This study is somewhat unique because it started very soon after the plant was opened and before informal groups had been formed.

External System

The factory, which employed about 600, was the newest and most modern of a large national food corporation. The plant was nonunion and the pay and fringe benefits were better than comparable union plants. The twelve-person group worked in the Sanitation Department. This department had a total of about 50–65 individuals and was divided into three work groups. The primary task of the department was to clean all equipment, floors, windows, and walls in the plant. The jobs were divided into two basic categories. The higher job category involved disassembling equipment for cleaning, washing parts, and reassembling them. The lower job category involved more washing tasks, including floors and windows. Eligibility for and assignment to the higher job category was based on seniority. The main difference between the two job categories was the amount of technical knowledge and skill required to disassemble and reassemble the equipment. The lower job category could be learned in one day; the higher job category in about two weeks.

Emergence of Internal System

The new hires in the group were relatively similar — white, native-born American males under 30 years of age. As they began to interact, the members became differentiated on an informal basis. Initially, these differences showed up in personality characteristics, background experiences, and nonwork social positions. Some of the members had military experience, others had traveled, one was known for his heavy drinking

---

* Adapted from D. Johnson, "Social Organization of an Industrial Work Group: Emergence and Adaptation to Environmental Change." Sociological Quarterly **15**, 1974, 109-126.

on weekends, and another for his self-proclaimed sexual exploits. In time, the relative skill and speed in job performance became the primary factors for placing individuals in the developing social structure of the group. Gradually, the speed with which one could perform his job became the dominant shared norm of the group. There was continuing effort to improve speed, and members would even race to get finished. Eventually, most members could finish their work 30 minutes to an hour before quitting time. In brief, speed in task performance became a major group norm and the most important factor in the informal ranking of members in the social structure.

Fast workers were given high group status; slow workers, low status. Quality of work also emerged as an important basis for informal ranking. A reward for the speedy and high-quality workers was the "free" time at the end of the shift, when workers would relax and engage in social activities. The supervisor did not object to this so long as all of the work was done properly and the members did not make it too obvious. At the end of the work shift there were rewards for those conforming to the group's norms and punishments for those who failed to conform. Those who finished early often teased or joked in a friendly way about those not yet finished. During this initial period, the internal system encouraged a fairly high commitment to the job and also provided for the social needs of the members. This period lasted about six months and was characterized by a somewhat laissez-faire leadership style by the supervisor. In general, the sentiments of the group toward management were characterized by a reasonable degree of trust, openness and freedom.

Changes in the External System

After this first period, several major changes in the external system disrupted the internal system and eventually led to a new internal system.

Supervisory style changes

The first change came in supervisory style. The change resulted from the finding of a time-and-motion study conducted on all jobs in the plant. During this study, workers continued enthusiastically to try to complete their work as fast as possible. As a result, top management pressured the immediate supervisor to become less permissive and more authoritarian. For example, at the end of the shift, the supervisor would assign miscellaneous special projects (e.g., wiping grease off electric motors, scrubbing water hoses, cleaning light fixtures, etc.) to those who finished their regular jobs early. This change dramatically disrupted the informal social life of the group. The extra work projects were viewed as menial busy-work and extremely distasteful. The workers soon realized that speedy work was punished rather than rewarded. Workers in the higher job category complained bitterly that their rank was no longer associated with the privilege of freedom from busy-work.

Following the change in leadership style, two technical changes were imposed by the external system. One change, developed by the Quality Control Department, permitted considerable work simplification in the performance of certain tasks. The second change involved the installation of new equipment which was to be cleaned by one person. Previously, two individuals were required to clean equipment. Since no time-and-motion studies had been done on cleaning this new equipment, the supervisor simply determined the time requirements by observing and questioning workers and then announced them to the group.

In response to this, the workers banded together and agreed to define the time requirements in the maximum terms they thought the supervisor would accept. The workers' consensus was that the cleaning of each piece of new equipment would take between one and two hours, depending on the condition of the machines. In practice, each machine could usually be cleaned within 30 minutes. Through this collective effort, the group was able to regain some of the freedom it possessed previously.

From these informal adaptations to the external system, there emerged a new primary norm and ranking system within the group. This new norm emphasized the need to pace the work so that it would be completed just before quitting time. The result of this new norm was that very fast and very slow workers were given low informal status. Either of these patterns of work was seen as attracting unfavorable attention from the supervisor. Most of those who had been fast workers adapted successfully by slowing their pace and retaining their high status.

The new, informal patterns could not provide nearly so well for the purely social and recreational needs of the group. Group horseplay was practically eliminated, and the lively and boisterous conversations involving the entire group took place less often. The decline in morale and satisfaction was apparent. The sentiments of the group toward management definitely had shifted toward low levels of trust, openness, and freedom.

Technical changes

New Internal System

Figure 16.6 shows an overview of the Homans Systems model. This figure suggests the impact of the external system on the internal system, which, in turn, affects member satisfaction and group productivity. The dynamics of

Summary of the
Group Process
Model

this process over time were developed in the discussion of the Sanitation Department's work group.

The case study of the Sanitation Department clearly illustrates several of the generalities about group life made by Homans:

- If individuals continue over time to be together in a common situation, they develop their activities, interactions, and sentiments beyond that which is required for sheer survival. This gives rise to an internal system and social structure.

- Freedom to develop the internal system in a task group is positively related to fulfillment of members' social needs, group morale, individual satisfaction, and commitment to the task.

- Changes in the external system of a group generate changes in its internal system. The external system refers to the activities, interactions, and sentiments imposed by higher management and required for the group's survival.

- There is a close relationship between a group's internal system and external factors; such as higher management, technology, and member values.

16.6
Group process model

One obvious implication of this case study for management practice is that individuals in industrial work groups may exert a greater effort to fulfill management's goals if they are allowed some degree of freedom consistent with formal job requirements. Conversely, if group freedom is reduced severely, members may well reduce their commitment to management's goals. The groups may continue to perform satisfactorily, but with minimal commitment to the formal goals of the organization.

So far in this chapter, we have suggested that the existence of groups within organizations is inevitable. The manager usually has some discretion over whether to use a group approach to decision-making rather than an individual approach. There are several basic factors and questions managers need to consider in the use of group decision-making:[19]

■ Does the nature of the task or problem facing the manager justify the use of group decision-making?

■ Will the potential benefits to group decision-making be realized?

■ Can the potential liabilities to group decision-making be avoided or minimized?

■ Will the situational factors in a decision-making group play a positive or negative role in influencing group outcomes?

■ What approach should be used by the manager in the decision-making group?

You may recall our discussion of the Vroom-Yetton leadership model at the end of Chapter 14. Several of these questions are the same as those identified by Vroom and Yetton for deciding the appropriate leadership style to use with group members. Thus, there is very close relationship between the Vroom-Yetton model and this presentation of the contingency approach to group decision-making. The remainder of the chapter will address each of these questions.

The first factor — and one of the most important — in determining whether an individual or group should be used is the nature of the task or problem facing the manager. Some form of group decision-making is desirable when one or more of the following conditions exists between members:

1. Various bits of information must be brought together to produce a solution, such as developing a business strategy or developing a new product.

2. Members have skills and knowledge that need to be pooled in dealing with complex tasks under conditions of risk and uncertainty, such as how to reduce labor costs by 8 percent during the coming year.

3. The members have different ideas about the best means for dealing with a problem or task (e.g., they disagree in their beliefs about causation).

4. The members have conflicting goals with respect to an issue (e.g., they disagree over preferences about goals).

Factors three and four were discussed in Chapter 7 under the contingency organizational decision model.

Nature of the Task or Problem

When the problems being considered by a group do not have one or more of these characteristics, we are likely to find managers regarding group meetings as a "waste of time."

Benefits The benefits of having some form of group decision-making may include greater knowledge, more approaches, increased acceptance, and better understanding.[20]

Greater knowledge A group's information and knowledge should be greater than that of any one member. If the group's members have varying sources of expertise related to their problem, each might be able to fill in the knowledge gaps of others. For example, when Chrysler decided to produce its K-cars, people from such fields as marketing (customer acceptance), engineering (design), production (production feasibility), accounting (cost considerations), personnel (labor requirements), legal (safety and patent consideration), were brought together in group meetings.

More approaches Individuals tend to develop "tunnel-vision" in their thinking and approach to problems. That is, they regard only their own part of each problem as important. Although all individuals in a group may have the same problem, their interaction and communication can stimulate the search for more alternatives. By challenging one another's thinking, members of a decision-making group may arrive at a decision which takes all viewpoints into account, i.e., a consensus or workable compromise.

Group decision-making, a common activity in organizations.
Photo courtesy of Kevin Higginbotham.

*Increased
acceptance*

By its very nature, group decision-making may lead to increased acceptance of the decision by members and so result in more effective implementation of the solution. A person who has a chance to influence the group's decision may have a greater commitment to the decision and assume responsibility for making it work. A high-quality solution handed down from on high may not be as effective as a low-quality solution arrived at more democratically. This conclusion is somewhat dependent, however, on the relative power of the group to resist or implement the solution. The individual who solves the problem may have the additional task of persuading others to accept and implement the solution.[21]

*Better
understanding*

A person who solves problems alone usually needs to communicate the solution to others. Organizational problems are often caused by the inadequate communication of decisions from managers to subordinates. But if those who must act on the decision have helped to make it, a failure in communication is not so likely. Because they looked at the problem and helped with the decision, they already know how and why the decision was made. Of course, this may be beneficial only so long as those who helped with the decision have some influence over how it is applied.

Liabilities

The potential assets to group decision-making are not guaranteed. Group decision-making can create liabilities for the manager in overconformity, domination by an individual, and goal displacement.

Overconformity

Because of social pressures for friendship and the avoidance of disagreement, groups can become instruments for maintaining conformity. Conformity is especially a problem when a solution should be based primarily on facts rather than on feelings or wishes. Thus, a group's acceptance of a decision is not necessarily related to the quality of the decision. If a group is advisory, the manager might serve as a check on the group's decision or might encourage the members to diagnose and analyze the group processes.

*Domination by an
individual*

Group effectiveness can be reduced if one individual dominates the interactions through too much communication, persuasion, or persistence (tiring the opposition). Having these abilities does not automatically make the one who has them a good problem-solver. This problem may be increased in groups whose leaders believe it is their duty to control the groups and provide the major input to decisions. Managers need to beware of their potential domination of groups. Even the best problem-solver may be unable to upgrade and influence the group's decisions if he or she is not permitted — or even encouraged — to contribute.

Goal displacement

One major goal of a decision-making group is to find an effective solution. To accomplish this, members need to consider alternatives. Some members may be enthusiastic about one alternative and attempt to win support for it rather than find an optimal solution. This type of goal displacement can lower the quality of the decision. It probably would be better to go back to the beginning, to generate alternatives and avoid evaluating them for the time being. If evaluation is clouded by lack of facts, or controversy over them, the group session can be disbanded until the facts can be clarified and supplemented. (Other suggestions are provided in the next chapter).

Situational Factors Within the Group

There are five situational factors, substantially under the control of the group leader, that can influence whether the group decision-making process leads to effective or ineffective outcomes. These situational factors include group size, role of the leader, disagreements, time requirements, and who changes.

Group size

Effects of Group Size As groups increase in size from two to 20 members, a number of changes occur in their structure and performance. A critical point of change seems to be at about seven members. In larger groups, it becomes increasingly difficult for the members to interact with all members at once. In general, *as group size increases:*

- The greater the demands on the leader and the more the leader is differentiated from the membership at large.
- The greater the group's tolerance of direction from the leader and the more centralized the proceedings.
- The more the ordinary members inhibit their participation, and the less exploratory and adventurous the group's discussion.
- The less friendly the group atmosphere, the more impersonal the actions, and the less satisfied are the members as a whole.
- The longer it takes to get to the nonroutine and judgmental decisions.
- The more subgroups (coalitions) form within the membership and the more formalized the rules and procedures of the group.[22]

Implications for Managers These findings suggest that managers can influence group performance by controlling group size. For intensive decision-making, the ideal group size is from about five to 12 members.[23] If the group has 20 or more members, the manager should break it into smaller groups. This will help members in the process of analyzing task-related information. The larger group can then be used to confirm the subgroups' recommendations.

A large-group manager needs to recognize the existence of several subgroups or cliques, each with its own informal leader. Although there are more potential resources available in large groups, these resources could have negative effects on overall group performance if each subgroup focuses on lobbying for its own solution.[24] In addition, it usually is necessary to use some type of formal procedure, e.g., Robert's Rules of Order, to keep the agenda moving in large decision-making groups. Voting is often used to reach agreement in large groups. Unfortunately, merely voting may not reveal the intensity of members' feelings, either positive or negative.

Large groups may be efficient when the primary purpose of the group is to communicate or reinforce new policies, procedures, plans, and the like. With an adequate opportunity for members' questions, the objective "to inform" can be satisfied.

In sum, the manager's behavior in small-group sessions will need to be substantially different from that in large-group sessions. With large groups, a more task-oriented style of leadership is necessary.

Group decision-making can be effective if the manager differentiates between his or her leadership role and membership role. Being the focal point does not require that the leader dominate the group.

Role of group leader

Leaders should not reject or promote ideas according to their personal needs. They must be receptive and accept contributions without evaluation. Good group leaders summarize information to facilitate integration, stimulate exploratory behavior, create awareness of members' problems, and detect when the group is ready to resolve differences and agree to a unified solution.[25] In terms of the Vroom-Yetton model discussed in Chapter 14, this behavior would represent the group G style of leadership. There is an extremely high level of member participation in decision-making with this style.

This type of role may be strange to many managers. It certainly is not consistent with the popular image of what it means to be a "leader."[26] This role is desirable for the manager when:

■ The manager sincerely wants the subordinates to participate as a group to resolve or provide suggestions on a problem.

■ The problem is related to the tasks performed by the subordinates.

■ The subordinates can provide meaningful inputs to the problem's solution.

■ The subordinates can influence success in implementing the proposed solution.

■ The goals of the group members basically are compatible with respect to the problem.

Disagreements   A skillful group leader will create an atmosphere for disagreement that stimulates innovative solutions. At the same time, the leader must minimize the risks of some members leaving the group with bitter feelings, especially if these members will need to implement the decision.

Disagreements can be managed if the leader permits differences within the group, delays the reaching of a decision, and separates idea generation from idea evaluation. This last technique makes it less likely that an alternative solution will be perceived as "belonging" to one individual rather than to the group.

Time requirements   The leader must strike a proper balance between permissiveness and control. Rushing through a group session prevents full discussion of the problems and leads to negative feelings. On the other hand, unless the leader keeps the discussion moving, members will become bored and arrive at poor solutions. Unfortunately, leaders tend to push for an early solution because of time constraints. This often ends the discussion before the full potential of the group has been achieved.

Who changes?   When there are disagreements in a group, some members have to change their minds for the group to reach a consensus. This can be either an asset or a liability. If members offering the best alternatives are persuaded to change, the outcome suffers. The leader plays an important part in protecting individuals with a minority view by discouraging others from expressing hostility toward them. The leader also can give persons with a minority view the chance to influence the majority position. This can be done by keeping the minority view before the group, encouraging communication about that view, and reducing misunderstanding.

Procedural Approaches   A group's decision-making procedures have a direct impact on its activities, interaction, and sentiments. If problems cannot be solved through standardized procedures or through appeal to facts, procedures encouraging more participation often lead to better decisions than do those involving less participation.[27] This is due partially to the error-correcting potential of group interaction. There are four major procedural approaches, including: decision by person with power, decision by minority, decision by majority, and consensus.

What is it? Here the manager obtains the views and feelings of others and then announces the solution. This approach is characteristic of a highly authoritarian and bureaucratic organization. The topic of many cartoons, this type of manager may even go so far as to begin the group session by announcing the proposed solution and then inviting alternative solutions or comments. Figure 16.7 suggests the interaction patterns in such a group.

Although managers eliminate the possibility of a solution they do not like, employees may very well feel less committed to implementing the decision than they otherwise would. This may be the case even if the manager believes the best decision has been made. The meaning of "best" can vary among individuals, and will depend in part on what they think will happen to them as a result of the proposed solution.

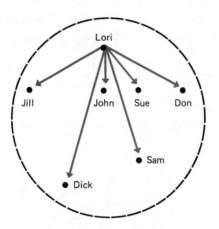

When is it likely to be effective? The decision-by-person-with-power approach is likely to be effective under the following conditions.

1. The group has simple goals, and the decision is relatively routine.

2. The group has a clear-cut division of labor.

3. There are strong external pressures toward unity (e.g., pending bankruptcy).

4. Group members see speedy action as necessary (crisis situation).

5. Group members expect the manager to make the decision.

6. The decision will be unpopular (e.g. layoff of group members).

7. The person with power has the information and ability to make a quality decision.

Decision by minority

What is it? This approach occurs when a small part of the group forms a coalition, either before or during the group session, to push continuously and force its solution. A ***group coalition*** is two or more individuals who band together to maintain or increase their outcomes (such as money, free time, etc.) relative to another person or group. In popular terms, the minority group's effort to push its position is often called "railroading," and may entail ridiculing, name-calling, and charging others with foot-dragging. The minority group is likely to prevent voting by fostering boredom, fatigue, or resignation in the rest of the group. Figure 16.8 suggests the interaction pattern when a minority of the members control the group's decision-making.

This approach may have several harmful effects. In the short run, it may mean that the majority will feel no personal commitment to the minority decision. In the long run, the other group members may be motivated to form their own coalitions. This often leads to a hostile atmosphere within the group, including low levels of trust and openness.

When is it likely to be effective? Under certain conditions, however, the decision-by-minority approach has some advantages. These are likely to occur when:

1. Some group members cannot meet to deal with the problem.

16.8
Decision by minority

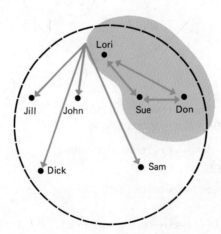

2. The group is under such time pressure that it must delegate responsibility to a subcommittee.

3. Only a few group members have the knowledge and resources needed for a decision.

4. Broad member commitment is not needed to implement the decision.

5. The problem is relatively routine and simple.

What is it?   In very large groups, face-to-face interaction may be impossible. Here, the decision-by-majority approach is often necessary and desirable. The approach is so popular that it is often used even in small-group problem-solving situations. Figure 16.9 suggests one possible pattern of interaction with the decision-making-by-majority procedure.

*Decision by
majority*

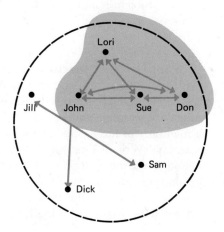

16.9
Decision by majority

Majority voting usually involves making a motion, debating it, and voting. Often, however, discussion is soon closed on issues that are highly complex and important for the group. There are several limitations to this process. First, the group spends relatively little time on the development of ideas and alternatives. Therefore, it moves too quickly to the evaluation stage. Second, the group members are motivated to divide too rapidly into separate coalitions of those for the motion, against it, or neutral toward it. The interaction tends to be dominated by the "for" and "against" coalitions, which leaves the neutrals with little influence in the discussion. Third, this approach reduces the middle ground for the introduction of new alternatives or compromises. Finally, the problem of commitment continues. A small group whose members are evenly divided still has to gain acceptance of the decision. Those with the minority view might be hostile or become indifferent toward implementing the decision. If the minority continues to have intense negative feelings, it is probably best to reconsider the problem.

When is it likely to be effective?   If the limitations of this approach can be minimized, decision-by-majority is likely to be a useful approach when:

1. Group members have somewhat conflicting goals.

2. The problem must be dealt with on the basis of judgment.

3. Several solutions are likely to be effective.

4. The members believe in the appropriateness of a "democratic" approach.

5. There is not enough time to reach a consensus.

6. The problem is not important enough to justify the time to reach a consensus.

Decision by consensus

What is it?   **Consensus** is agreement, usually after alternatives have been raised, discussed, and modified. Members respect one another's views, even when there are serious disagreements. Members recognize that all alternatives are tentative until the group is ready to make the final choice. Usually, all members of the group are highly committed to the choice. This does not mean that everyone totally agrees with it, but the opposed members are more likely to implement it because they feel they have been treated fairly. This approach uses the resources of all members and helps ensure the future decision-making ability of the group. Figure 16.10 suggests the possible interaction patterns with decision-making by consensus.

16.10
Decision by consensus

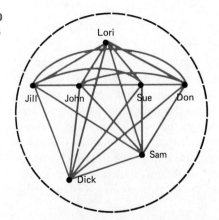

Decision by consensus usually takes longer than the other decision-making methods we have discussed. The manager must weigh the cost of this additional time against the benefits obtained from higher commitment and understanding of the decision. On some problems, this approach may be impractical because of the number of decisions that must be made, time pressures, and situations requiring quick responses. Since the consensus approach requires trust and a full exchange of information among members within as well as outside of their group sessions, it is more likely to be used in an organic management system than in a mechanistic one.

When is it likely to be effective? Decision by consensus is most likely to be effective when:

1. Innovative, creative, and high-quality decisions are needed.

2. The members agree on basic goals but not on the best means for reaching those goals.

3. The problem is important and complex, and all of the member's resources must be tapped to solve it.

4. Member commitment is crucial for the successful implementation of the solution.

5. It is desirable to increase the capacity for problem-solving throughout the group so that there will be less dependency on the presence of one or two members.

Although the consensus approach may be the ideal for decision-making groups, particular circumstances may require the use of the other approaches. This is especially true for the decision-by-the-person-with-power and/or expertise approach and the decision-by-majority approach.

SUMMARY

This chapter should improve your skills in performing the leader, liaison, and disseminator manager roles, among others.

Many of the decisions made by managers occur in group settings. Moreover, many of the problems and opportunities for managerial achievement occur within groups. Regardless of our personal preferences, all of us must contend with groups — if not as leaders, then certainly as members. The necessity of working with and through others in group settings at all levels of the organization is increasingly recognized by top managers.

"There is a definite trend these days toward fewer and fewer followers," says George S. Dively, honorary chairman of Harris Corp. and one of the business community's most respected elder statesmen. *"Everyone wants to be part of the action."*

Dively's perception is strongly seconded by Thomas MacAvoy, president of Corning Glass Works. "Younger people won't put up with being kept in the dark," MacAvoy observes. "You can't spring decisions on them and expect them to be happy." In MacAvoy's view, senior executives must expect to pay dearly for keeping today's young executives outside the decision-making process. "You have got to give young people a chance to participate," he warns. "If you decide you're not going to operate this way, you're not going to keep smart people."[28]

Thus, groups are inevitable in organizations. Their impact on organizations and their own members' behaviors can be wide-ranging. Groups can be a source of resistance and antagonism from the manager's point of view, or they can supplement the formal motivational and control system by reinforcing quality and quantity performance standards.

A number of guidelines have been presented to help managers work with and use groups more effectively. These guidelines can be used to identify: (1) the major factors that must be evaluated by the manager when interacting with groups; and (2) the probable consequences of using different approaches to group decision-making. Some of these factors are technology, formal leadership, group size, and group norms. Four approaches to group decision-making are: decision by the person with power; decision by a minority; decision by the majority; and decision by consensus.

KEYWORDS

activities	*norms*
consensus	*sentiments*
deviant member	*social behaviors*
external system	*social specialists*
formal group	*social structure*
group	*stars*
group coalition	*task behaviors*
informal group	*technical specialists*
interactions	*technology*
internal system	*underchosen*

DISCUSSION QUESTIONS

1. Identify one formal group and one informal group to which you belong. Use the characteristics of effective groups identified at the beginning of the chapter to evaluate the two groups. You might want to start by ranking your informal and formal groups as high, medium, or low on each of these characteristics.

2. On the basis of your personal experience, do you feel that the work groups to which you belonged had desirable or undesirabale effects on you and the organization? Explain.

3. How well did your last superior help you meet the emotional problems often experienced when entering a new group? What steps did he or she take or fail to take that can reduce emotional problems?

4. Why is it necessary for both task behaviors and social behaviors to occur in a group?

5. Joe described his work group as ". . . friendly, just great. All the guys get along together, and we bowl and play softball after work." However, production records show that Joe's group is one of the poorest in the plant. Why might this be?

6. Under what circumstances do you believe that the decision-by-majority approach would be effective? Under what circumstances would it be ineffective?

7. How might group size, sentiments, and norms be interrelated in affecting the behavior of group members?

8. What is meant by goal displacement in group decision-making? Give an example of this from your personal experience.

Management Incidents and Cases

Northwest Industries was a growing company that manufactured recreational vehicles. One of the factories was located in Salem, Oregon. The recreational vehicle market was strong in the western United States, and there was good demand for Northwest's products. The market reached its peak in mid-June and tapered off during the winter months. The factory tried to maintain a fairly constant production flow by building up inventories during the low winter months. During the summer months, a number of college students were hired to help boost production and bring inventory back to the desired level.

NORTHWEST INDUSTRIES*

* Reproduced by permission from *Organization and People; Readings, Cases and Exercises in Organizational Behavior*, by J. B. Ritchie and Paul Thompson. Copyright © 1979, 1980, West Publishing Company. All rights reserved.

Organization The Salem plant had a three-level management structure (see Fig. 16.11). Craig Hansen, age 52, was the general plant foreman. He had started working on the lines and had worked up to his position after 17 years. Hansen knew "everything about trailers and could perform any job involved in the construction of a trailer." He was in charge of schedules for each run of trailers that was sent through. He also decided which line the trailer would go on and how long it would take to construct it. Hansen was serious about the business and conferred with Northwest's home office several times each week.

Joe Mackay, age 35, was assistant plant foreman. His job was to help the foreman solve any problems he couldn't handle and to see that the plant complied with all safety rules and regulations. He also was responsible for raw materials inventory and ordering. The men viewed Joe as a walking bomb and therefore tried to stay out of his way. When he was called to help correct an error, Joe demanded to know who had made it and an explanation of how the workman could be so "dumb."

Eight foremen comprised the third management layer. During the winter, four of them worked in other areas of the plant and weren't involved in construction. Each foreman was assisted by a lead man who helped manage

16.11

Organizational chart for the Salem plant, Northwest Industries

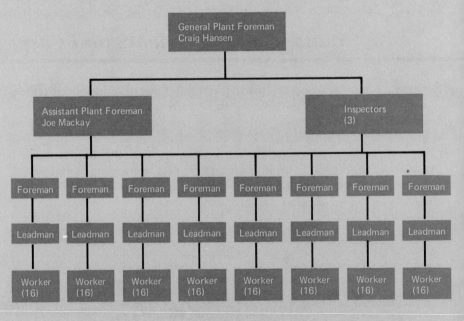

the 16-man production crew. Foremen had salaries of $1600 per month, while lead men received 20 cents extra per hour, or $6.00 per hour.

Ted Nelson, age 28, was one of the regular foremen. He didn't have much, good or bad, to say about the college kids. In fact, he didn't say much about anything. On Nelson's line, when a mistake was made, he would correct it himself and not say anything to the one who had made the mistake. If it happened again, Nelson would point out the mistake to the worker and then correct it himself while the worker went back to the job. Nelson also managed the time cards and handed out the paychecks.

Quality control in the plant was maintained by three inspectors who reported directly to Hansen. The inspector's position was considered prestigious, perhaps even more prestigious than foreman, even though both received the same salary. Inspectors had to be especially knowledgeable and trustworthy and able to find production mistakes quickly.

Upon completion of each trailer, the foreman would call one of the inspectors, who would examine the trailer and test all components. Any defects were noted on a "squawk sheet." These "squawks" then had to be fixed before the inspector would sign the release form. An average trailer generally has four or five minor squawks, which a good "squawker" could repair within 20 or 25 minutes. The idea was to have a good squawker, so people would not be pulled off the line and lose time fixing production errors.

Workers with some experience were hired at $4.40 per hour, and unskilled help started at $3.70 per hour. Provided the unskilled worker produced well, a raise would be given after two months on the job to $4.40 per hour. After four or five years, the workers usually earned $5.80 per hour.

The inspectors, the year-round workers, and the foremen were a very close-knit group. They enjoyed many activities together, such as parties, bowling, raft races, and, occasionally, light refreshments. Lunch and break times were looked forward to. All made a regular contribution to support the highly enjoyed numbers game, which accompanied each pay period, as well as to fund such things as birthday or sympathy cards.

Most of the employees at Northwest had completed high school and then started with the company. They worked hard and took pride in what they were making. Most planned to stay with Northwest all their lives. About 75 employees worked year-round, with 65 seasonal workers helping out in the summer months.

Northwest's usual procedure was to run four of the eight production lines during the winter. During the summer, enough new people were hired to staff all eight lines. Most of the stations on a line required two people to complete each job. Ample space existed between stations to permit a trailer to sit between work areas. This spacing procedure facilitated line moves and allowed for the time differences in performing each job.

The New Plan   This year, Hansen decided to eliminate some of the past problems. Six of the foremen had been complaining about the inefficiency of those college kids, who were reported to be slow, stubborn know-it-alls. They admitted the kids were hard to train, got bored easily, but for the most part did a good job.

Hansen decided to run four lines as normal, leaving most of the older, regular employees on those lines. The younger people who were already working for the company were distributed to two of the other lines, and as the college kids were hired, they were paired up with the younger but experienced workers for training. Hansen's strategy was that, as the college kids learned, they would be able to expand to the other two lines, and eventually all eight lines would be in full production.

The plan was adopted readily by the foremen. Four were assigned to the four lines with the regulars, and the other four were assigned in pairs to the two new lines, with one designated as the foreman and the other as assistant foreman.

The new plan seemed to be working well. Halfway through July, the plant was running at full production. The newer workers enjoyed working together, and a substantial rivalry had been created between them and the older workers. Hansen had seen to it the younger lines were given routine, long production runs to work. These runs generally consisted of 30 or 40 units that were exactly the same, and thus the training periods were minimized and errors were reduced. The older, more experienced lines were given the shorter runs to work.

At first the rivalry was in fun, but after a few weeks the older workers became resentful of remarks that were being made and felt those kids should have to work on some of the more difficult runs. The younger lines met production schedules easily, and some spare time was left for goofing around. It wasn't uncommon for someone from the younger lines to go to another line, under the guise of looking for some material, and then give the older workers a hard time. Some of the older workers resented this treatment and soon began to retaliate with sabotage. They would sneak over during breaks and hide tools, dent metal, install something crooked, or do other small things that would slow production in the lines with the younger workers.

To Hansen everything seemed to be going quite well, and he was proud of himself and his plan. Towards the end of July, however, he began hearing reports of the rivalry and sabotage. As most of the longer production runs had been completed, Hansen decided "those kids needed to quit playing around and get to work." He gave them some of the new runs, which were basically the same as before, except for a few changes in the interior walls and the wood roof.

Nelson was the foreman of one of the younger lines. He heard about the new run coming on his line and decided to go ahead of the first trailer to help each station with the forthcoming changes. He carefully explained each change to the workers as the lead trailer came into their station and then went on to the next. The kids seemed to be picking up the changes okay, so Nelson did not worry too much about the new run.

As the first trailer was pushed out, ready for inspection, Nelson called the inspector. A half hour later, the inspector emerged with two pages of squawks — 49 of them. Not seeing Nelson anywhere, the inspector called in Hansen and Mackay to point out the uncommonly high number of squawks. It took about five minutes for things to completely explode. Nelson walked on the scene just in time to hear Hansen yell to Mackay, "Get that line into gear in one week and get those squawks fixed or fire the whole bunch!"

Questions

1. What are the key groups in this case? How are they affecting each other?

2. Analyze this case through the use of the group process model. You might find Fig. 16.6 particularly helpful.

3. What decision procedural approach(es) seem to dominate in this case? Are they effective or ineffective? Explain.

4. What are your recommendations? Why?

HOW TO CONDUCT A GROUP MEETING

You have just completed a week-long supervisory training program put on by the personnel department of your organization. As part of this program, you received the following handout on how to conduct a group decision-making meeting:

Restating the problem: You should be a good clarifier and indentifier of subproblems during the meeting. Ask each member to write a statement of the problem. Record for all to see.

Metaphoric vacation: After working for a time on the problem, ask everyone to put it out of their minds. Draw on one of the written subproblems for a lead and create an artificial, instant vacation from the problem. "Can anyone think of a striking image in the world of weather?"

Toward the solution: Bring the vacation to close by asking the group to return to the subproblem which suggested the "metaphoric vacation." Continue toward solutions to the problem.

Rules for the supervisor:

1. Never compete with group members.

2. Listen to the group members.

3. Don't permit anyone to be put on the defensive.

4. Keep the energy level high.

5. Keep the members informed about where they are and what is expected of them.

6. Keep your eye on the expert; when he or she shows interest in an idea, give him or her some time.

7. Do not manipulate the group.

List of steps:

1. State the problem.

2. Discuss it with possible solutions.

3. Restate the problem as each participant understands it.

4. Select one of the restatements.

5. Take the group on a "vacation."

   a) Select one key element (a striking image, say).

   b) Pick out an area in which to concentrate (e.g., weather).

   c) Then ask for examples of the key element (e.g., striking images in weather).

6. Select an example (e.g., "thunderhead") and ask for further examination.

7. End the vacation and ask for possible solutions to the original problem.

8. Make a decision.

Questions

1. Which of the guidelines, rules, and steps are consistent with the materials in this chapter?

2. Which of these guidelines, rules, and steps are inconsistent with the material in this chapter?

3. What contingencies exist and how might they influence your decision whether to follow all of these guidelines, rules, and steps?

REFERENCES

1. A. Parisi, "The Exxon Dynasty: A Corporate Giant Beyond Comprehension." *Houston Chronicle*, August 22, 1980, Section 2, 6.

2. H. Meyer, "The Meeting-Goer's Lament." *Fortune* **100,** 8, 1979, 94–102.

3. H. Meyer, *op. cit.*, 95.

4. G. Miller, "Living Systems: The Group." *Behavioral Science* **16,** 1971, 302–398.

5. M. Mills, *The Sociology of Small Groups*, Englewood Cliffs, NJ: Prentice-Hall, 1967, p. 2.

6. L. Bradford and D. Mial, "When Is A Group?" *Educational Leadership* **21,** 1963, 147–151.

7. P. Bernstein, "Workplace Democratization: Its Internal Dynamics." *Organization and Administrative Sciences* **7,** 1976, 1–127.

8. D. Moment and A. Zaleznik, *Role Development and Interpersonal Competence: An Experimental Study of Role Performance in Problem-Solving Groups.* Boston: Division of Research, Graduate School of Business Administration, Harvard University, 1963, pp. 10–18.

9. R. Bales, *Interaction Process Analysis.* Cambridge, MA: Addison-Wesley, 1950.

10. G. Homans, *The Human Group.* New York: Harcourt, Brace, 1950.

11. G. Homans, *Social Behavior: Its Elementary Forms.* New York: Harcourt, Brace, 1961.

12. J. Gibb, TORI Theory and Practice. In J. Pfeffer and J. Jones (eds.). *The 1972 Annual Handbook for Group Facilitators.* La Jolla, CA: University Associates, 1972.

13. A. Athos and R. Coffey, *Behavior In Organizations: A Multidimensional View.* Englewood Cliffs, NJ: Prentice-Hall, 1975.

14. J. Davis, *Group Performance.* Reading, MA: Addison-Wesley, 1969.

15. M. Bayes and P. Newton, "Women in Authority: A Sociopsychological Analysis." *Journal of Applied Behavior Science* **14,** 1978, 7–20.

16. J. Hackman and G. Oldham, *Work Redesign.* Reading, MA: Addison-Wesley, 1980.

17. G. Susman, *Autonomy at Work: A Sociotechnical Analysis of Participative Management.* New York: Praeger, 1976.

18. D. Johnson, "Social Organization of an Industrial Work Group: Emergence and Adaptation to Environmental Change." *Sociological Quarterly* **15,** 1974, 109–126.

19. N. Maier, "Assets and Liabilities In Group Problem-Solving: The Need for an Integrative Function." *Psychology Review* **74,** 1967, 239–249.

20. S. Stumpf, D. Zand, and R. Freedman, "Designing Groups for Judgmental Decisions." *Academy of Management Review* **4,** 1979, 589–600.

21. S. Stumpf, R. Freedman, and D. Zand, "Judgmental Decisions: A Study of the Interactions Among Group Membership, Group Functioning, and The Decision Situation." *Academy of Management Journal* **22,** 1979, 765–782.

22. B. Berelson and G. Steiner, *Human Behavior: An Inventory of Scientific Findings.* New York: Harcourt, Brace, 1964, p. 358.

23. G. Manners, "Another Look at Group Size, Group Problem-Solving and Member Consensus." *Academy of Management Journal* **18,** 1975, 715–724.

24. J. Davis, *op. cit.*

25. N. Maier, *op. cit.*, 246.

26. F. Miner, "A Comparative Analysis of Three Diverse Group Decision Making Approaches." *Academy of Management Journal* **22,** 1979, 81–93.

27. T. Cummings, "Self-Regulating Work Groups: A Socio-Technical Systems Synthesis." *Academy of Management Review* **3,** 1978, 625–634; "Designing Effective Work Groups." In *Handbook of Organizational Design, Vol. 2, Remodeling Organizations and Their Environments.* W. Starbuck and P. Nystrom (eds.). New York: Oxford University Press, 1981, pp. 250–271.

28. H. Meyer, *op. cit.*, 96.

Chapter 17

CONFLICT PROCESS

After reading this chapter, you should be able to:

1. Evaluate the different points of view often taken toward conflict.

2. Diagnose different conflict situations through the use of a contingency conflict model.

3. Describe three different levels of conflict — role conflict, interpersonal conflict, and intergroup conflict.

4. List the causes, effects, and ways of managing each of the three levels of conflict.

5. Apply a contingency approach to the successful management of conflict.

633

PREVIEW CASE

Abboud of First Chicago*   After four and one-half controversial years as chairman and chief executive officer of First Chicago Corp., A. Robert Abboud was fired April 28, 1980. First Chicago is the parent of First National Bank of Chicago, the nation's ninth largest bank.

Ben W. Heineman, president of Northwest Industries and a director of First Chicago, said that, although the board respected Abboud's ability as a banker, it wanted someone "with greater people skills."[1]

It is reported that Abboud was famous for reserving an enormous amount of the decision-making authority to himself and, upon occasion,

---

for even taking over the powers of his managers. One day he went so far as to push aside a subordinate and take personal command of the bank's foreign-currency trading department. Says one former bank officer, "I was an $80,000-a-year flunky, and I didn't like it."[2] *The Wall Street Journal* provides the following account of the firing of Abboud and the conflicts at First Chicago.[3]

In the bank, "people were singing 'Ding-dong, the witch is gone,'" one employee says. And in a Chicago suburb, the wife of a senior bank executive told a friend, "It's steak and champagne at our house tonight."

Such glee wasn't surprising, for the 50-year old Abboud has been an unpopular, autocratic boss ever since being named chairman in 1975. His abrasive style permeated the bank-holding company, sending more than 200 officers fleeing and inhibiting others from admitting mistakes or even discussing problems openly.

But from conversations with directors, former and current executives, and outside observers, it also is clear First Chicago's problems did not start with Abboud's arrival and will not end with his departure when a successor is named. The successor will face a bank full of employees who have been more concerned with internal political goings-on than with the bank's own future, a loan department that is depleted and has lost much respect in the business world and a complex organization that many believe does not use its manpower efficiently.

It will take a long time to erase the internal squabbling that has preoccupied, and some say poisoned, the bank ever since 1972, when Chairman Gaylor Freeman announced that four officers were in the running for the top job. Abboud won the race in 1975, but two of the losers, and many of their supporters, left the bank. Meanwhile, many who remained harbored bitter feelings.

"Our tendency (since 1972) always has been to take sides and then take swipes at the other team," says a long-time bank employee, who, like many others, was willing to talk if he wasn't named. This middle-level employee says people in the bank "are identified by what side they are on. If they aren't with you, then just give them as many digs as possible."

An example, he says, came in January (1980), when top financial executive Edwin H. Yeo III resigned amid a rumor, since proved false, that his decisions were to blame for the company's 47 percent drop in profits in 1979's fourth quarter. In addition, there was talk that Mr. Yeo was the source of a newspaper story that outlined management changes.

"I don't remember where I heard it, and I had no idea if any of it was true," recalls an employee, who calls himself an Abboud loyalist. "But I passed it on anyway. Yeo was the enemy."

Whatever its basis, the friction within the bank is regarded by many observers as so severe that it has affected operations. As one senior vice-president puts it, "If people don't trust each other, don't even like each other, they can't work together."

To illustrate, this senior vice-president goes back a couple of years when most major banks were introducing business loans on which the interest was below the prime rate and was tied to money-market rates. "That takes cooperation between the guy who is buying money, the guy making loans and others. But we couldn't get it together." As a result, he adds, "First Chicago was the last bank of its size to offer it to its customers."

Many insiders contend Abboud's habit of playing executives against one another intensified the infighting and that the bank's top managers have been so immersed in the political squabbling they haven't understood the damage it does. Meanwhile, Abboud's tendency to criticize subordinates in public, some say, made employees reluctant to discuss the infighting or any other problems openly. "There has been a history of the messenger being shot for bringing bad news." says one vice-president who left the bank recently. "So people tend to not bring bad news."

On June 24, 1980, about two months after the firing of Abboud, First Chicago Corp. named Barry F. Sullivan, a 49-year-old executive vice-president of Chase Manhattan Bank, as its new chairman and chief executive officer. Observers say Sullivan meets the criteria the board sought in a new chairman: "firm, kind, and nice." Despite the warm, friendly image, "He can be intimidating, if he has to be," according to one close observer. And those who have worked with him say he's "thorough and meticulous," often asking several different subordinates their opinion on the same issue before making a decision.[4]

"He's willing to listen and he's receptive to ideas," agreed one underling, who added Sullivan is a "tough, hands-on, kind of guy."

We only highlighted the conflicts that have been reported at First Chicago between 1972 and 1980. This is one of the more recent, dramatic illustrations of several types of conflicts that can have strong negative results on both the employees and the organization. This case illustrates different types of conflict usually found in organizations. The case also demonstrates that Abboud's overemphasis on the "forcing" style was counterproductive. The contingency approach to the management of conflicts at First Chicago would have reduced the intensity of many of those conflicts and increased the probability of their successful management.

Conflict is the result of disagreement or opposition within one individual or between two or more individuals.[5] Conflicts within individuals refer to simultaneously opposing tendencies to accept *and* reject a given course of action — such as whether to get married or stay single, take a new job, or sign a business contract. Typical symptoms of conflicts *within* an individual are hesitation, vacillation, sleeplessness, and stress or anxiety.[6]

To many, the word "conflict" suggests negative situations — war, destruction, aggression, violence, and competition. For others, the word has positive connotations — excitement, intrigue, adventure, and challenge. Others respond to conflict with mixed feelings; this is probably the most realistic and useful point of view for a manager.

The classical school of management (see Chapter 4) typically viewed conflict as undesirable. This school felt that conflict could be reduced or eliminated through careful selection of people, training, detailed job descriptions, elaborate rules, and incentive systems. These prescriptions are still useful for reducing and preventing some undesirable conflicts. In our view, however, conflict management is *relative* rather than absolute. To us, organizational conflict is a certainty, and at times may be highly desirable. It is possible to prevent many conflicts but some need to be met and managed. Conflicts that often need to be managed such as those among co-workers, superiors and subordinates, departments, and the organization and external groups — e.g. major customers, unions, and government agencies.

VIEWPOINTS TOWARD CONFLICT

Negative View

An employee who experiences frequent and high levels of conflict may show withdrawal psychologically (apathy and indifference) and physically (tardiness, absenteeism, and turnover). In other cases, aggressive and hostile behavior may result, such as stealing or damaging property.

From a decision-making standpoint, intense conflicts often lead to biased perceptions and gross distortions of reality.[7] This can cause managers to make decisions that increase conflict rather than reduce or resolve it. From a control standpoint, managers might dislike conflict because they believe it interferes with productivity and efficiency. In sum, many managers believe that conflict disrupts organization routines and life and is, therefore, undesirable.

Positive View   From a decision-making standpoint, conflict may result in better choices. When there are different viewpoints, the positions offered must be developed. Conflict can stimulate managers to search for ways to reduce or solve their disagreements, and this process often leads to innovation and change. Conflict may provide individuals with opportunities for monetary and personal rewards. For example, status and esteem needs can be met by managers who successfully compete on performance objectives or achieve a promotion over other candidates.

From a control standpoint, conflict can indicate the need for adjustments in managerial processes (such as organizational structures, decision systems, planning processes, or goals) or in behavioral processes (such as motivation, communication, or leadership patterns). In addition, conflict provides managers with information about their operations and show where corrective actions might be needed. The positive viewpoint toward conflict is that it is a necessary condition for the attainment of individual and organizational goals.

Balanced View   More realistically, conflict has both positive *and* negative aspects. Therefore, it must be managed. Proper management of conflict often can minimize the negative effects and maximize the positive effects. This balanced view is at the heart of the contingency model of conflict and is the theme of this chapter.

CONTINGENCY MODEL OF CONFLICT   The contingency model of conflict helps managers diagnose the basic conflict situations they will face. The model suggests that different conflict-management approaches are appropriate for different types of conflict situations. This model is constructed from two contingency variables that serve to identify four basic conflict situations.[8]

The *distributive variable* refers to the degree to which one or more goals of the individuals or groups in conflict are perceived as incompatible. This variable is shown as the distributive continuum in Fig. 17.1 and varies from high to low. In a highly distributive relationship, one person's (or group's) gain is another's loss. For example, most team sports are played until one team wins and the other loses. The *integrative variable* refers to the degree to which one or more of the goals of the individuals or groups in conflict are perceived as compatible. This variable is shown as the integrative continuum in Fig. 17.1 and varies from low to high. In a highly integrative relationship, one person or group can gain only as another person or group gains. For example, double partners in tennis have a vested interest in each other playing well and improving. Cooperation and support between them increases the probability of their winning more matches.

By cross-classifying the distributive and integrative variables, we can construct a four-cell contingency model of conflict. This too is shown in Fig. 17.1.

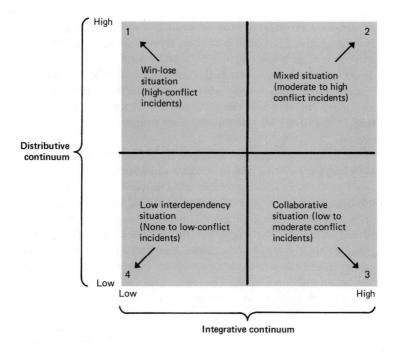

A few words about the entire model might be helpful before discussing each of the four basic types of conflict situations.

The total relationship between any two individuals or groups need not be restricted to one cell. While one of the cells may dominate, the individuals or groups may be placed in different cells for different issues. In a collective bargaining relationship, for example, management and the union may feel that the wage issue is a win-lose situation (cell 1). A gain by the union is a loss to management, and vice versa. On other issues, such as adjusting to technological changes, the union and management are in a mixed situation (cell 2). They need to cooperate in introducing technological changes so the firm can remain competitive and survive. This is necessary if the union members are to have jobs. Intense conflicts may still exist over who will gain the most benefits from the new technology. Thus, this conflict situation consists of both "high-distributive" and "high-integrative" relationships.

The conflict-management approach should depend on the particular situation. The description of the conflicts at First Chicago, presented at the beginning of this chapter, suggests that there was a strong tendency by the managers to view conflicts as win-lose situations. Thus, there was an overemphasis on the use of "forcing" and political tactics in dealing with conflicts.

The four major conflict situations presented in Fig. 17.1 are extreme positions on the grid. Real-life conflicts can occur at any point on the grid, including the borderline positions.

**Win-Lose Conflict
Situation**

A *win-lose conflict situation* occurs when there is a high-distributive and low-integrative relationship. This is shown in cell 1 of Fig. 17.1. One person's gain is another's loss. Typically, a win-lose situation occurs when there is a direct conflict in goals. Organizations normally try to minimize internal win-lose situations because of their negative effects on performance and employee attitudes. The win-lose conflicts at First Chicago were so intense that more than 200 middle and top managers resigned in a four and one-half year period.

Internal win-lose situations are closely associated with workplace politics. *Workplace politics* refers to the maneuvering that organization members do when they are seeking selfish goals that are opposed to the goals of others in the organization. A recent study found that certain organizational processes are more political than others.[9] These processes most often relate to success or failure at work, relationships with superiors, and intergroup relations. This study included a survey of 428 employees at all levels in a variety of firms. The survey asked them the extent to which political considerations influenced 11 organizational processes. The overall politicization of the 11 organization processes, from highest to lowest, was:

Rank	Process	Percent who Responded "Always" or "Frequently"
1	Interdepartmental coordination	68
2	Promotions and transfers	60
3	Delegation of authority	59
4	Facilities, equipment allocation	49
5	Performance appraisals	42
6	Budget allocation	38
7	Pay	33
8	Grievances and complaints	32
9	Personnel policies	28
10	Hiring	23
11	Disciplinary penalties	22

These findings are consistent with the conflict incidents reported for First Chicago. You may recall the comment by one long-time bank employee: "Our tendency (since 1972) has always been to take sides and then take swipes at the other team." This is only one of several examples of problems of interdepartmental coordination at First Chicago. Conflicts and politics over promotions were illustrated in 1972 when the chairman announced that four officers were in the running for the top job. Abboud "won the race" in 1975. Conflicts and politics over delegation of authority were shown by Abboud's taking personal command of the bank's foreign currency department. The bank officer of this department resigned and commented "I was an $80,000-a-year flunky, and I didn't like it." In sum, in win-lose situations, we can expect the frequency and intensity of conflict incidents and politics to be quite high.

A *mixed conflict situation* occurs when there is both a highly distributive and highly integrative relationship. This is shown as cell 2 in Fig. 17.1. Union-management relationships often are mixed situations. Distributive issues usually concern the relative allocation of rewards and the relative priority placed on goals.[10] For example, management focuses on the goal and priority of increased profits while the union's emphasis is on pay increases, fringe benefits, and the like.

The integrative part in a mixed situation often includes the following:

■ The individuals or groups decide jointly on the terms for relating to each other. For example, the management and union representatives may agree on when they will hold meetings, how their meetings will be conducted, and issues to be discussed at each meeting.

■ The individuals or groups recognize that they can obtain rewards from their mutual association and that losses will occur from a termination or deterioration in their relationship. A long drawn-out strike results in losses to both the firm and the union — the firm experiences deficits and lost profits while union members sacrifice their paychecks.

■ The individuals or groups believe that they will *increase* the rewards to each other from their association.[11] For example, a study of the cement industry suggesting union-management cooperation and mutual problem-solving led to gains in productivity of from six to eight percent.[12] Through higher productivity, it is possible to improve both employee benefits and profit levels.

Relationships in the mixed situation are more varied and seemingly inconsistent than those in the other three cells of Figure 17.1. The description of Sullivan, the successor to Abboud at First Chicago, suggests that he recognizes that different conflict situations, including the mixed situation, occur in organizations and must be managed on a contingent basis. You may recall that Sullivan was characterized in these apparently inconsistent terms: "firm, kind, and nice;" "He can be intimidating, if he has to be;" "He's willing to listen and he's receptive to ideas;" and "a tough, hands on, kind of guy."

Managers can tilt mixed-situation issues toward either the win-lose cell or the collaborative cell in Fig. 17.1. The direction of this tilt is influenced by the attitudes, communication patterns, and decision processes established between the managers and others. At First Chicago, Abboud tilted and redefined mixed situations more as win-lose situations. In contrast, the description of Sullivan, who replaced Abboud, suggests that he has a tendency to tilt mixed situations toward the collaborative cell.

Collaborative
Situation

A **collaborative situation** occurs when there is a high integrative and low distributive relationship. This is shown in cell 3 in Fig. 17.1. The actions of one individual or group have desirable effects on the other. Since the goals are compatible and often mutually reinforcing, goal attainment by one helps goal attainment by the other.

Conflicts will not be as intense or as long-lasting as in the win-lose or mixed situations. However, conflicts will still occur because of interpersonal difficulties, task interdependencies, and debates over the most effective *means* to reach the common goals. A husband and wife in conflict over how to spend their money because they do not have enough to meet all their needs is an example of a conflict over scarce resources in a small organization. The goal of the wife and husband is to alter the distribution of the resources within the family. Even after the conflict has been resolved, there still could be conflict over what to do. If they decide to buy a car, they might still disagree over what car to buy or how to pay for it.[13]

It's not too unusual for individuals or groups to make an *incorrect* diagnosis and view a collaborative situation as a win-lose or mixed situation.

Low-
Interdependency
Situation

A **low-interdependency situation** occurs when there is both a low-distributive and low-integrative relationship. This is shown as cell 4 in Fig. 17.1. Conflict is nonexistent or at a minimum in this situation. Individuals or groups simply have no reason to get together. The manager of the local Safeway supermarket seldom discusses local business problems with the manager of a Safeway in another state.

CASE STUDY

Elgin and Bowie Districts*

This case study is concerned with the relationship between the sales and production departments within two districts of the same organization.[14] The two districts are similar with respect to technology, economic and market conditions, structure of the departments, and basic tasks. Coordination between the two departments is primarily an *ad hoc* arrangement in each of the districts. The districts produce a wide variety of metal windows, doors, and sashes for industrial and building customers.

Task Interdependence

The primary areas of coordination between production and sales are acceptance of new orders, production scheduling, and quality control. These tasks are important because items are usually produced only on

---

* Adapted from J. Dutton and R. Walton, "Interdepartmental Conflict and Cooperation: Two Contrasting Studies." In *Managing Group and Intergroup Relations*, L. Lorsch and P. Lawrence (eds.). Homewood, IL: Richard D. Irwin and the Dorsey Press, 1972, pp. 285–304.

Dimensions	Elgin: win-lose situation	Bowie: collaborative situation
■ Goals and orientation to decision making	■ Each department emphasizes the requirements of its own particular task	■ Each department stresses common goals whenever possible and in other cases tries to balance goals.
■ Information handling	■ Each department: (1) minimizes the other's problems or tends to ignore them when recognized and (2) minimizes or distorts the information communicated.	■ Each department tries to: (1) understand the other's problems and give consideration to them and (2) provide the other with full, timely, and accurate information relevant to joint decisions.
■ Freedom of movement	■ Each department tries to gain maximum freedom of itself and to limit the freedom for the other through such tactics as: (1) going around formal procedures; (2) emphasizing rules; (3) trying to fix the future performance of the other department; (4) restricting interaction patterns; (5) using pressures tactics, such as hierarchical appeals; (6) blaming the other for past failures in performance.	■ Each department tries to increase its freedom to attain goals through the following actions: (1) accepting informal procedures which help task achievement; (2) down-plays the differences between production and sales; (3) not trying to fix the department's future performance; (4) encouraging open interaction patterns; (5) searching for solutions rather than using pressure tactics; (6) focusing on the diagnosis and correction of rules rather than placing blame.
■ Attitudes	■ Each department develops negative feelings toward the other. Desires to threaten, vent hostilities, and retaliate are common.	■ Each department adopts trusting and positive attitudes toward the other.

Adapted from J. Dutton and R. Walton, "Interdepartmental Conflict and Cooperation: Two Contrasting Studies." In *Managing Group and Intergroup Relations*, L. Lorsch and P. Lawrence (eds.). Homewood, IL: Richard D. Irwin and the Dorsey Press, 1972, pp. 285–304.

request from customers. The size of the orders can vary from several dozen to several thousand items. These factors create the potential for both collaboration and conflict between the production and sales departments.

Contrasting Relationships

Table 17.1 summarizes the contrasting relationships between the sales and production departments in the two districts. The Elgin district is characterized as a win-lose situation; the Bowie district, a collaborative situation.

Several factors help collaboration at Bowie and increase win-lose conflicts at Elgin. First, with better relations and help from the home office, Bowie is able to produce more items for inventory. This reduces the peak-load pressures on the production department that increase conflicts between sales and production. Second, Bowie's equipment and physical plant are better. Third, there is a greater status gap between sales and production managers at Elgin — in terms of age, education, and experience — than at Bowie. Finally, managerial styles at Elgin differ more than those at Bowie. For example, Elgin's sales manager has an aggressive personal style, and the production manager lacks human and conceptual skills. These differences may be important factors for explaining how their relationships develop either as collaborative or competitive.

Case Implication

One of the most important implications of this case is that individuals, through their actions and attitudes, can *move* toward a different situation. In this case, we started with the assumption that the relationship between sales and production is basically a mixed situation. Through their actions and attitudes, the individuals at Elgin move from a mixed to a win-lose situation and at Bowie from a mixed to a collaborative situation.

Uses of Model

The contingency model is a useful framework for *diagnosing* the nature of the conflict between two or more individuals or groups. The model suggests that different conflict-management approaches are appropriate for different conflict situations. For example, a win-lose conflict may be dealt with partially by some form of third-party intervention, such as the conflicting individuals' superior or an arbitrator. On the other hand, to reduce the development of negative attitudes and stereotypes, a mixed-conflict situation should be dealt with through improved problem-solving and confrontation approaches.

A **role** is a group of related activities carried out by an individual. Roles may occur within organizations (superior, subordinate, peer) or outside of organizations (husband or wife, father or mother, female or male). Roles do not exist independently of the people in them. Figure 17.2 reviews common activities in a student role.

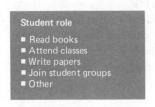

17.2
Student role activities

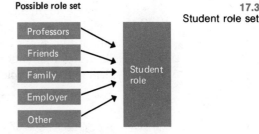

17.3
Student role set

A **role set** is the collection of roles directly related to the activities of an individual. A press foreman in a plant producing trim parts for automobiles has a role set consisting of 19 other roles: general foreman, superintendent, sheet-metal foreman, inspector, shipping-room foreman and 14 press operations.[16] The individuals in these roles influence and are influenced by the press foreman role.

Role Set

The members of a role set are influenced by the individual's performance and actions. They may be rewarded or punished because of that person's behaviors and may require certain actions from this person in order to perform their own tasks. For a quarterback to complete a pass, for example, the line must block and the receivers must be able to hold onto the ball. Since the members of the offensive team are influenced by the quarterback's performance and actions, they develop attitudes about what should and should not be done as part of the role. These "do's" and "don'ts," called *role expectations*, can vary from expectations about how a person should dress, to how much or how little should be produced. A professor telling students to read each chapter in the text at least three times is an example of a role expectation. Expectations are communicated by the members (**role senders**) of the role set to the individual (**focal person**) whose role is under consideration. A possible role set for a student is suggested in Fig. 17.3.

Besides providing information, role senders exert pressure on the focal person to carry out their expectations. These acts are called *role pressures*. A professor telling students they must have an average of 90 or higher for an A grade is an example of a role sender creating role pressure. Pressures are exerted through the use of one or more types of power, such as reward power. The nature and intensity of role conflicts are influenced by the type of power used by those in conflict and their relative power.[7] If two individuals can reward each other in meaningful ways, they will probably be strongly motivated to seek a win-win solution.

So far we have suggested that the role sender and the focal person are different individuals. Actually, though, one person can fill both roles. One's "inner voice" provides the do's and don'ts for each role a person fills. Thus, Jane Doe might have an idea of her ideal role as a student and an awareness of her actual role as a student. If there is a large gap between the two and she cannot figure out how to reduce it, there may be a role conflict. Figure 17.4 illustrates a situation where there is a gap and conflict between a student's ideal and actual roles.

17.4

Student's ideal vs. actual role

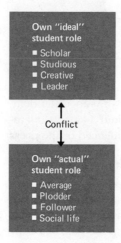

Model of Role Episode

A **role episode** includes: (1) attempts by one or more role senders to influence the behavior of a focal person and; (2) the responses of the focal person — which, in turn, influence the future expectations of the role sender(s). A simplified model of a role episode is provided in Figure 17.5. For example, the *expectations* of the manager are translated into pressures that are sent to a subordinate. The subordinate has both emotional and cognitive responses to these pressures.

The *emotional response* is the subordinate's feelings about the "pressures" — good, angry, frustrated, happy, etc. The *cognitive response* is the subordinate's visualization of what the manager wants done. On the basis of

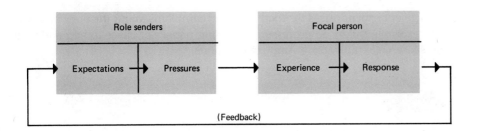

these feelings and thoughts the subordinate responds to the manager. The responses provide feedback to the manager; this feedback influences the manager's future expectations and the pressures he or she exerts on the subordinate. For example, a supervisor who responds with hostility to pressures from the production manager will be thought of and responded to differently than one who responds with submissive acceptance. If the supervisor shows signs of extreme tension and stress from the pressures, the production manager may "lay off" or consider reassigning the supervisor.

Nature of Role Conflict

Role conflict occurs when two or more incompatible pressures are placed on an individual. Responding to one set of pressures makes it difficult for a person to respond to some or all of the other sets of pressures. The intensity of the role conflict depends on the *strength* of the role pressures (i.e., power of the role senders) and the focal person's *desire* to respond. Pressure from two fellow workers to share information about a new product may be relatively easy to deal with. But pressure from two managers to immediately complete different projects may result in severe role conflict. In general, incompatible pressures lead to conflict and stress *within* the focal person and *with* one or more of the role senders.

There are four basic types of role conflict: intrasender role conflict, intersender role conflict, interrole conflict, and person-role conflict.

Intrasender Role Conflict

Intrasender role conflict occurs when the do's and don'ts from a single role sender are incompatible. A manager might tell a subordinate that a particular task is to be completed today and a short time later assign another task to be completed today. (Figure 17.6 suggests an intrasender role conflict situation for an employee.) This may make it difficult, if not impossible, to complete the first assignment. Another example occurs when one spouse pressures the other to cut expenditures for food and then complains about the poor meals. A final example might be professors assigning papers or cases to be handed in the same week they are giving examinations.

17.6
Intrasender role conflict

Intersender Role Conflict

Intersender role conflict occurs when pressures from one role sender are perceived as being incompatible with pressures from one or more other role senders. For example, intersender role conflicts are quite common for managers who must deal with multiple interest groups that place conflicting demands on the organization. A study of directors of 67 manpower agencies indicated that they experienced conflicting pressures from three powerful interest groups: their own staff, the local community leaders, and the state and regional administration from which their budget came. Support from all three of these groups was needed to offer an effective manpower program.[18] Figure 17.7 suggests an intersender role conflict situation for an employee.

17.7
Intersender role conflict

17.8
Interrole conflict

Interrole Conflict

Interrole conflict occurs when role pressures associated with membership in one group or organization are in conflict with those stemming from membership in other groups or organizations. Pressures requiring overtime or take-home work may conflict with pressure to give more attention to family matters. When this type of conflict becomes intense, individuals may simply withdraw from one of the roles. For example, a spouse might change jobs or get a divorce. Figure 17.8 suggests a case of interrole conflict between the individual's role as an employee and his or her role in a family.

Interrole conflicts are quite common for single or married women desiring a career.[19] Of course, the interrole conflicts for women with children can be especially difficult. Joann Lublin, a professional journalist who returned to work three months after giving birth to a son, describes her role conflicts and experiences in these terms.

> *Despite the knowledge that I'm not alone, I have gut-wrenching qualms about my decision. I'm happier working than I would have been at home. And I'm unhappier than I expected. I didn't realize juggling job and junior would be so difficult, so nerve-frazzling, so filled with guilt.*
>
> *The main hassle that we employed mothers face is the lack of social acceptance for our dual roles. Society still dictates that a working mother must be a lousy mother. The view is reflected by the needling comments from some of my male colleagues. "Where do you dump your kid every day?" asked one. Noticing my annoyance about a 20-minute wait for the bus home, another colleague cracked, "Well, Joann, you don't have to be here. You could be home rocking your baby in the rocking chair."*
>
> *My first week back was the worst. I blew everything out of proportion. The scorecard reads: two stomach upsets, one anxiety attack, one episode of hysteria and two fights with my husband. When I got home from work those initial evenings, I carried Daniel around the house for hours in a baby carrier — just to be comforted by his warmth and to remind him I was still his mother.*
>
> *The initial crises have passed, but little things continue to bother me.[20]*

Person-role conflict occurs when incompatibilities arise between the pressures of the focal person's role(s) and his or her own needs, attitudes, values, or abilities. The college student who, because of parental pressures, enrolls in a management major rather than in a preferred art program, may experience person-role conflict. Figure 17.9 suggests a case of person-role conflict between the individual's managerial role and his or her own personality.

Person-Role Conflict

17.9
Person-role conflict

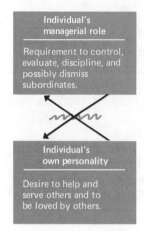

Individual's managerial role

Requirement to control, evaluate, discipline, and possibly dismiss subordinates.

Individual's own personality

Desire to help and serve others and to be loved by others.

CASE STUDY

M. Helen Anderson

The career-minded woman may experience person-role conflicts such as those seen in the story of M. Helen Anderson. She is described as an all-American girl who, at the age of 29, was a senior associate with McKinsey Company, a major consulting firm.

The conflicts and ironies of her success aren't lost on Anderson, who says she's just begun to learn that she can't be all things to all people. "I would love to be beautifully groomed, constantly throwing dinner parties, and be considered Miss Socialite. But at the same time I'd like to be a highly respected businesswoman. You can do both," she reasons, "but you can't be tops at both."

Like many ambitious single women, Anderson found that more and more conflicts are resolved in favor of her career. "I know it's all right that I don't look like a fashion model all the time," she says, although a hefty chunk of her salary still goes for clothing. As the nurturing of her career takes precedence, work hours grow longer and life a little lonelier.

"I'm trying not to let my work run my life. Nevertheless, it does get in the way." She's stopped dating men who wanted her to be "more on call. They'd demand that I show up at a dinner party two weeks hence, and when I said I couldn't promise they'd get furious," she recalls.

The basic problem, Anderson feels, is that these men wanted her to accept the more traditional female role adopted by most of the girls she grew up with in Hoopeston, Illinois (pop. 6000). "Some of these men could never understand why I work so hard. I feel I work hard because I have a lot to do. It offended me that they didn't think enough of me that they'd approve of my working."[21]

Role conflicts are often minor and the resulting tensions are probably essential for the development of competent and mature individuals. But intense role conflicts can have adverse effects for the individual and for the organization through undesirable turnover and reduced effectiveness. Individuals in intense role conflict situations over a period of time often experience high levels of job-related stress, tension, dissatisfaction, and low levels of confidence in superiors and their organizations.

Stress is the physiological and/or psychological response(s) an individual makes to potentially harmful external events or situations.[22] Physiological responses could include alcohol and drug abuse, absenteeism,[23] increased heart rate and blood pressure, dryness of the mouth, difficulty in breathing, hot and cold spells, indigestion, numbness and tingling in the limbs, impaired speech, and accident proneness.[24] Psychological responses could include anxiety, aggression, apathy, depression, nervousness, irritability and bad temper, moodiness, inability to make decisions and concentrate, hypersensitivity to criticism, mental blocks, and frequent forgetfulness.[25] Physiological and psychological responses are often found together in someone experiencing stress. It should not be assumed that these responses are always caused by stress, however; they could also occur for reasons totally unrelated to stress.

There are a variety of approaches and ways for assessing stress. Table 17.2 provides a brief stress-assessment instrument directly related to the types of role conflicts we have been discussing. We suggest you use Table 17.2 to record your reactions for a job you have now or had in the past. The questionnaire items in Table 17.2 are classified into four major factors: conflict and uncertainty, job pressures, job scope, and rapport with management. All of these factors have been found to create role conflicts which lead to work stress.

The scoring directions to the stress assessment instrument in Table 17.2 are as follows:

1. Add the three numbers you circled within each of the four areas and enter these totals here:

■ Conflict and uncertainty _____

Instructions: Listed below are various kinds of problems that may —
or may not — arise in your work. Indicate to what extent you find each of them to be a problem, concern, or
obstacle in carrying out your job duties and responsibilities.

Factors

Responses

This factor is a problem ...	Never	Sel-dom	Some-times	Usually	Always
Conflict and uncertainty:					
1. Not knowing just what the people you work with expect of you	1	2	3	4	5
2. Feeling you have to do things on the job that are against your better judgment	1	2	3	4	5
3. Thinking that you will not be able to satisfy the conflicting demands of various people over you	1	2	3	4	5
Job pressures:					
4. Feeling you have too heavy a workload; one you can't possibly finish during an ordinary day	1	2	3	4	5
5. Not having enough time to do the work properly	1	2	3	4	5
6. Having the requirements of the job affect your personal life	1	2	3	4	5
Job scope:					
7. Being unclear on just what the scope and responsibilities of your job are	1	2	3	4	5
8. Feeling you have too little authority to carry out the responsibil-ities assigned to you	1	2	3	4	5
9. Not being able to get the informa-tion you need to carry out your job	1	2	3	4	5
Rapport with management:					
10. Not knowing what your manager or supervisor thinks of you — how he or she evaluates your performance	1	2	3	4	5
11. Not being able to predict the re-actions of people above you	1	2	3	4	5
12. Having ideas considerably differ-ent from those of your managers	1	2	3	4	5

McLean, *Work Stress,* © 1979, Addison-Wesley Publishing Company, Inc., Chapter 9, pages 131–132,
"Stressors Checklist." Reprinted with permission.

- Job pressure   _____
- Job scope   _____
- Rapport with management   _____

2. Add the four scores for your overall total score   _____

    Scores in each of the four areas can range between three and 15. Scores of nine or more perhaps suggest that the area presents a problem deserving your attention. The overall total score can range from 12 and 60. Scores of 36 or more may suggest a more than desirable amount of overall stress. This could be a reason for low job satisfaction or a desire to quit the job.

There is no single pattern used by individuals or organizations to manage intense role conflicts. The personality of the focal person and the characteristics of interpersonal relationships with the role senders are important influences on what approaches are used to manage role conflicts.

Managing Role Conflicts

Individuals with high role conflict are likely to resort to defense mechanisms, such as projection and rationalization, to manage role conflicts. **_Projection_** is how people protect themselves from feelings of guilt by blaming others for their own faults. Subordinates who miss being promoted may blame their immediate superior. They might claim that the boss is always out to get them or that the boss never really liked them. **_Rationalization_** refers to creating a reason or excuse that the individual believes is less ego-deflating than the true reason. Employees with low output might believe this is caused by obsolete or poor machinery rather than their own lack of ability or motivation.

    From a managerial point of view, these personal tactics for managing intense role conflicts have negative effects on job performance, absenteeism, and turnover.[26] Avoidance behavior may be especially bad on the individual's performance. The manager is likely to increase pressure on the subordinate to produce. Individuals who use avoidance mechanisms to manage their role conflicts are defeating themselves in the long run.

    As suggested in Fig. 17.10, there tends to be a curvilinear relationship between level of role conflict and organizational effectiveness.[27] If there is no role conflict or very little role conflict throughout the organization, the members probably have accepted the status quo and are not challenging one another in a positive way. At the other extreme, role conflict can become so intense that the members are either fighting through win-lose power struggles or avoiding one another. Under this condition, there is little cooperation, sharing of information, or trust. A moderate to high amount of each of these factors is necessary for organizational effectiveness.

Personal tactics

17.10
Relationship between role
conflict and effectiveness

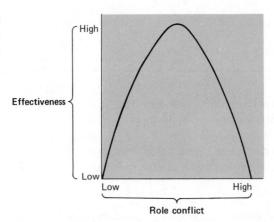

Organizational tactics

Management can use various tactics to keep role conflicts at tolerable levels. For example, structural changes in the organization can reduce interdependencies between jobs and departments. Manufacturing organizations often use expeditors to coordinate the desires of the marketing department (for quick customer service) with those of the production department (for a steady flow of work). At Standard Steel Corporation, expeditors are assigned to large sales orders to ensure that they are manufactured to specification and shipped to customers on time.

Some organizations provide counseling for those who need help in learning to tolerate and cope with role conflict. Also, more considerate leadership practices and opportunities for social gettogethers could improve the interpersonal relationships among organizational members. Several of the organizational tactics for managing role conflict are developed further in the following sections.

INTERPERSONAL CONFLICT

Interpersonal conflict focuses on patterns of communication between the focal person and the role senders and the attitudes and behaviors that they show toward each other. *Interpersonal conflict* can be broadly defined to include: (1) disagreements over policies, practices, or plans; and (2) emotional issues involving negative feelings, such as anger, distrust, fear, rejection, and resentment.[28] Though the two types of interpersonal conflict are often interrelated, each type may require different strategies for resolution. The resolution of planning, goal, and policy conflicts should emphasize problem-solving and compromise (bargaining). Resolution of emotional conflict should emphasize the necessity for all parties to modify their perceptions and increase their positive feelings toward each other. Both types of conflict might benefit from interventions by third parties. In union-management relations, the third party could be a mediator, arbitrator, or even a court judge; in family matters, a counselor or lawyer. Figure 17.11 suggests a case of interpersonal conflict between a subordinate and manager.

17.11
Interpersonal conflict

A basically collaborative relationship on substantive issues may be *interpreted* as being win-lose if emotional issues are allowed to create negative attitudes and perceptions between the parties. This is illustrated by the case of Fred and Irv, two owners of a small market-research company in the New York area. The partners suspected each other of shirking duties and were on the edge of breaking up at the time they sought the aid of Cresheim Company of Philadelphia, a management-consulting firm.

Effects of Win-Lose vs. Collaborative Relations

> *Fred, in particular, was rankled at Irv's failure to do more selling, even though Irv had been saddled with overseeing the firm's bookkeeping and most of the work being done for clients. Employees exploited the rift by playing one partner against the other to seek salary increases. The internal problems reached a crisis when profits tumbled, forcing Fred and Irv to cut their own $45,000 annual salaries by 25 percent.*
>
> *"Communications in these cases tend to get very bad," says James Barrett, one of the Cresheim men assigned to the case. Fred had never told Irv about his resentment; he just exploded in private talks with Barrett, the consultant recalls.*
>
> *The solution, worked out over a nine-month period, included assigning each partner precise duties — Fred to work mostly in sales, Irv to handle mostly inside work. Although the bill came to nearly $15,000, the partners agree that the counseling produced a big improvement, Mr. Barrett says.[29]*

In the collaborative relationship, one person's chances for goal attainment increase or decrease along with the other person's chances. In contrast, in a win-lose relationship, one person's chances for goal attainment increase as the other person's chances decrease. In the extreme win-lose situation, the individual will have difficulties in solving problems and may use tactics that result in ineffective performance for the entire organization.

When the Pennsylvania Railroad and the New York Central Railroad merged to create the Penn-Central, for example, the two are reported to have continually fought each other. Cooperation was at such a low level that the two groups could not integrate their computer-based information systems. This resulted in thousands of filled railroad cars being misrouted, late deliveries, and billing errors. Many customers sought other means for shipping their goods, which ultimately contributed to the bankruptcy of the Penn-Central.

Interpersonal Styles for Managing Conflict[30]

Interpersonal styles of managing conflicts may be used when managers are parties to the conflict or when they are coming in on a conflict situation, such as between two subordinates. There are five major interpersonal styles for managing conflict: avoidance, compromise, smoothing, forcing, and collaboration.

Avoidance style

The **avoidance style** is the tendency to withdraw from or remain neutral in conflict situations. The manager may be unavailable for a conference, defer answering a disturbing memo, or refuse to get involved in the conflict. The avoidance-prone manager may act merely as a communication link by transmitting messages between superiors and subordinates. When asked to take a position on controversial issues, the manager might say: "There has not been time to study the problem fully." or "I would need more facts before making a judgment;" or "Perhaps the best way is to proceed as you think best." The avoidance style is symbolized in Fig. 17.12.

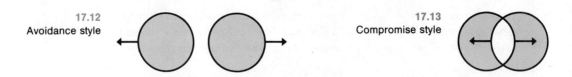

17.12
Avoidance style

17.13
Compromise style

When unresolved conflicts influence the tasks for which the manager is responsible, the avoidance style will have a negative impact on organizational effectiveness. However, the avoidance style is desirable when:

1. the issue is so minor or of passing importance that it's not worth the time or energy to confront the conflict;

2. one's power is so low relative to the other individual that there is little opportunity to effect a change (such as major, top-level organizational policies); or

3. others can more effectively resolve the conflict than the manager, e.g., the subordinates themselves.

The **compromise style** is the tendency to sacrifice one's own position by seeking a middle ground by splitting the differences in conflict situations. The compromise-prone manager often says: "I let other people have some of their positions, if they let me have some of mine," "I try to find a fair combination of gains and losses for both of us," or, "I try to find a position between their's and mine." The compromise style is symbolized in Fig. 17.13.

Compromise style

There are several problems with the *early use* of the compromise style. First, the manager is encouraging compromises on the expressed issues rather than the underlying ones. Early use of compromise results in less diagnosis and exploration of the nature of the real conflict. Oftentimes, the first issues raised are not the real ones, but are used merely as openers. For example, students telling professors their courses are really tough and challenging may be trying to negotiate a better grade in the course. Second, the tendency is to accept the initial positions presented, rather than to explore and search for additional alternatives acceptable to all. Third, compromise may be inappropriate to all or part of the conflict situation. There may be better ways of resolving the conflict than those suggested by either party. Much more problem-solving may be needed in the search for additional alternatives. Thus, the conflict issue might require both the confrontation and compromise styles.

Our primary concern is not that this style may be used, but that it may be used *too early* in the conflict situation, when another style may be more appropriate. If the parties to a conflict have relatively equal power and are in a win-lose or mixed situation, such as typical union-management relationship, compromise through the bargaining process will be useful.

The *compromise style is desirable when both parties recognize that:*

1. there is a possibility of reaching an agreement in which each party would be better off — or not worse off — than if no agreement is reached;

2. more than one agreement could be reached; and

3. some of their goals are conflicting or their interests opposed with regard to the different agreements that might be reached (distributive part of the relationship).

Compromise is a cornerstone to negotiation. **Negotiation** is a process in which two or more individuals or groups, who have both common goals and conflicting goals, put forth and discuss proposals concerning terms of a possible agreement. Of course, the overall process of negotiation could involve the use of five interpersonal styles for managing conflict. The dominant styles in effective negotiations are compromise and collaboration. The underlying role of compromise in the process of negotiation has been summed up this way.

Even with its proper limits, negotiation often falls short of the idea of bene-fiting both parties. Sometimes one wins and the other loses. A really bad bargain is when both lose. Many negotiations go on for weeks or months, only to be broken off. Such waste of time and effort is a risk inherent in the process.

Despite its limitations, abuses, and hazards, negotiation has become an in-dispensable process in free societies. More effective than any alternative anybody has thought of so far, it enables us to realize common interests while we compromise conflicting interests. Since these are among the basic objectives of rational people, negotiation has to be counted among the greatest of human inventions.[31]

Smoothing style

The **smoothing style** refers to the tendency to minimize or suppress the open recognition of real or perceived differences in conflict situations while emphasizing common interests. The smoothing-prone manager might state: "If it makes others happy, I try not to challenge their views," "I always try not to say something that might hurt the feelings of others when discussing problems," or, "Our friendship shouldn't be upset by this problem, so let's not worry too much about it, because things will work out." The smoothing style is symbolized in Fig. 17.14.

17.14
Smoothing style

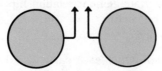

In the smoothing style, the manager acts as though the conflict will pass with time and appeals to the need for cooperation. This manager tries to reduce tensions by reassuring and providing support to the parties. Although there is some concern expressed about the emotional aspects of the conflict, there is little recognition of — or interest in working on — the goals, plans, and policies that are part of the conflict. The smoothing style simply encourages the individuals to cover up and avoid expression of their feelings. Therefore, and not surprisingly, it is generally ineffective.

However, *the smoothing style is effective on a short-term basis when:*

1. the parties are in a potentially explosive emotional conflict situation, and smoothing is used to defuse it;

2. keeping harmony and avoiding disruption are especially important; and

3. the conflicts are based primarily on personality characteristics of the individuals and can't be dealt with in the prevailing organizational climate.

The **forcing style** refers to the tendency to use coercive and reward power to dominate the other party by suppressing differences in conflict situations and requiring the adoption of ones own position. The successful use of the forcing style results in outcomes that are satisfactory to only one of the parties. The forcing-prone manager may use such phrases as: "If you don't like the ways things are run, get out," "If you can't learn to cooperate, I am sure others can be hired who will," or, "When people disagree with me, I try to cut them off to win my position." The forcing style is symbolized in Fig. 17.15.

Forcing style

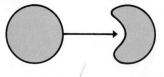

17.15
Forcing style

The forcing-prone manager assumes that conflicts involve win-lose situations. When dealing with conflicts between subordinates or between departments, the manager may threaten — or actually apply — punishments, e.g., demotion, dismissal, or a poor performance evaluation. When conflicts are between peers, one individual might try to get his or her own way by appealing to a common superior. In this manner a superior is used to force the decision on the opposing party. Our description of Abboud (the dismissed president of First Chicago) at the beginning of the chapter shows an example of a manager who appeared to overuse the forcing style. He was described as sending more than 200 officers fleeing and inhibiting others from admitting mistakes or even discussing problems openly. It is claimed that Abboud played his executives off against each other and criticized them in public.

Overreliance on forcing lessens the motivation of the individual whose interests have not been considered. Furthermore, relevant information and other possible alternatives are ignored.

There are some situations in which the forcing style is necessary, such as when:

1. there are extreme emergencies and quick action is necessary;

2. unpopular courses of action must be taken for long-term organizational effectiveness and survival (such as cost-cutting and dismissal of employees for unsatisfactory performance); and

3. others are trying to take advantage of someone, and the person needs to take quick action for self-protection.[32]

Collaborative style

The **collaborative style** requires the willingness to identify underlying causes of conflict, openly share information, and search out an alternative considered to be mutually beneficial. The collaboration-prone manager might say: "I will try to deal with all concerns — theirs and mine," "I will try to get all viewpoints and issues out in the open," or, "If we don't have much agreement at first, let us spend some time thinking about the causes of conflict and then thrash around for an alternative we agree is the best we can do." With the collaborative style, conflicts are recognized openly and evaluated by all those concerned. Sharing, examining, and assessing the reasons for the conflict leads to a more thorough development of alternatives. This process increases the probability of discovering an alternative that effectively resolves the conflict and is acceptable to all of the individuals. The collaborative style is symbolized in Fig. 17.16.

17.16
Collaborative style

Barriers to Use If collaboration is so effective, one might ask, why isn't it used more frequently? Some of the barriers to using the collaborative style are:

■ Time limits often inhibit direct confrontation of feelings and issues involved in a conflict.

■ Group norms (e.g., shared feelings that managers should not express negative feelings toward others).

■ Personal role concepts (e.g., a boss who feels able to engage in a conflict with a subordinate is nonetheless limited by her or his supervisory role).

The use of collaboration is influenced by the type of management system (mechanistic vs. organic) and the leadership style of one's superior. The supportive and participative manager uses the collaborative style more than the autocratic manager does. The collaborative style is more natural in the organic than in the mechanistic managerial system. If external factors, such as type of management system or leadership style, do not prevent the use of collaboration, is it simply a matter of "opening up" and "going at it"? The answer is yes, but only when the conflicts are limited to plans, policies and procedures. When extreme emotional issues enter in, collaboration can backfire and increase interpersonal conflicts.

Collaboration Guidelines The collaboration guidelines in managing interpersonal conflicts are as follows:

- Ask for and give feedback on the major point.

- Consider compromise *after* the analysis of the "real" problems and the generation of alternatives. Remember, the other's view of reality may be just as valid as yours, even though you may differ.

- Never assume you know what the other person is thinking until you have checked out the assumption in plain language.

- Never put labels (e.g., "coward," "neurotic, or "child") on the other person.

- Forget the past and stay with the here-and-now. What either of you did last year or last month or yesterday morning is not as important as what you are doing and feeling now.[33]

These guidelines are easy to state but difficult to practice in a spontaneous and natural manner. Effective collaboration requires more than opening up to others; it also demands opening up to oneself and gaining self-insight.

Conditions for Use *The collaborative style of conflict management is desirable when:*

1. the individuals have common goals (i.e., a basically integrative relationship) but are experiencing conflict over the *means* to achieve these goals;

2. a consensus should lead to the best overall solution to the conflict; and

3. there is a need to make high-quality decisions on the basis of the best expertise and information available.

The collaborative style has great potential for effectively managing conflicts, but those involved must be ready and willing to abide by the types of guidelines presented. Otherwise, the adoption of a collaborative style may lead to a deterioration in relationships and increase conflict. Although collaboration is regarded as the best overall style, each style is useful under specific situations.[34] Those who are in conflict may need the assistance of third parties — external consultants or internal specialists in organizational behavior — to assist them in developing skills and self-insights necessary for effective use of the collaborative style.

INTERGROUP CONFLICT

Intergroup conflict refers to differences and clashes between groups, departments, or divisions within an organization. It is symbolized by Fig. 17.17. Before exploring some of the causes, effects, and mechanisms for managing intergroup conflict, let's briefly consider the interrelationships between the three levels of conflict emphasized in this chapter.

17.17
Intergroup conflict

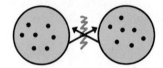

Interrelationships Among Levels of Conflict

There is no simple cause-and-effect or beginning-and-end relationship between role conflict, interpersonal conflict, and intergroup conflict. This is suggested in Fig. 17.18

We have gone from the simple to the complex in considering the levels of conflict. Intrasender role conflict (i.e., incompatible expectations of a manager toward a subordinate) on plans, policies, and goals could lead to broader interpersonal conflict involving emotional issues of distrust, secrecy, and the lack of communication. Interpersonal conflict (e.g., between managers) could be enlarged to influence the relations between all of the managers' subordinates. The managers might limit the exchange of necessary information between the groups of subordinates. Or, by expressing bitter and hostile attitudes toward the other department, they can influence the development of similar feelings within subordinates.

Intergroup conflicts could trigger role conflicts. For example, the sales department might have large orders from two customers who are both pressuring for early delivery and threatening to take future business elsewhere if

17.18
Interrelationships between three levels of conflict.

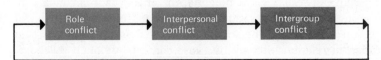

their demands are not met. As a result, members of the sales department pressure the production department to meet *both* delivery dates, but production finds it difficult, if not impossible, to meet both time schedules within the normal work week. This leads to intrasender role conflict for members of the production department The sales department responds that there is really no problem, since production can work overtime. However, intersender role conflict could become a problem if the production manager finds it difficult to meet the department's efficiency standards because of the relatively higher labor costs of overtime. Thus, the production supervisor is under pressure from the sales manager for overtime and from the production manager to keep per-unit labor costs within certain limits. One of the more obvious ways for managing this situation is to push the conflict up the line for resolution by a common superior.

The discussion of the interrelationships between the three levels of conflict is illustrative rather than exhaustive. Our aim is to caution that a fuller understanding of conflict situations can be gained by diagnosing them in terms of *all* three levels of conflict. The initial cause of a conflict can stimulate other levels of conflict. This, in turn, can increase the intensity of the initial cause of the conflict and compound the problem of resolving the total conflict situation.

Our discussion has suggested that role conflicts and interpersonal conflicts can cause intergroup conflict. Some of the other causes of intergroup conflicts are: (1) task interdependencies; (2) task dependencies; (3) inconsistent performance criteria and rewards; (4) intergroup differences; and (5) problems in sharing scarce common resources. Naturally, conflict between groups can stem from more than one of these causes. The potential interrelationships in the causes of intergroup conflicts is suggested in Fig. 17.19.

Causes of Intergroup Conflict

17.19
Causes of intergroup conflict

Task interdependency

Task interdependency is a major cause of work-related conflicts among groups, whether they be peers or superiors and subordinates. **Task interdependency** refers to the extent to which two groups or individuals rely on each other for service, information, and goods to accomplish their own tasks and goals. Although task interdependency should suggest a collaborative situation, the groups can encounter severe conflicts. An increase in demand may increase pressure on one or both groups to provide the necessary added services and/or to provide them more quickly. This overloading can increase tension and frustrations and lead to intergroup conflicts. It is not unusual to find this taking place between the computer-processing department and other departments during certain peak periods. The production, marketing, personnel, and finance departments may all demand and need programming assistance and computer runs at the same time.

Interdependent groups also may engage in conflicts because of ambiguities or uncertainties about the tasks each is to perform. The following is an example of ambiguity over the jurisdictions of the commercial department and plant department in a telephone company.

> *The commercial department receives recognition for sales orders that it handles. The plant department receives credit for additional or replacement orders made by its installers. If the customer takes a replacement (say, a princess phone rather than a slim-line phone), then the commercial department loses recognition for its sales; therefore, it is important to the commercial department that the plant department installation men carry the proper equipment on their trucks and follow installation orders. Even then, there is ambiguity about who can initiate substitute service ideas for the customer's consideration.*[35]

The most consistent source of conflict was confusion about which department had responsibility for particular tasks. The departments responded to the ambiguity by trying to avoid responsibility for tasks requiring time and personnel. Where it was advantageous to control the tasks, there was conflict because of mutual attempts to claim jurisdiction over common areas.

Task dependency

Task dependency refers to situations in which one group or individual must rely on another group or individual for services, information, or goods. The independent group has less incentive to cooperate than the dependent group. Thus, the dependent group generates pressure to gain the needed assistance. This leads to either cooperation or a negative response by the independent group. For example, the assembly departments at Mack Truck are dependent on the flow of parts (doors, engines, tires, etc.) from other departments. If the parts do not arrive on time, or if they vary from specification, the assembly department has difficulty in performing its tasks. An inventory of parts at each work station on the assembly line could serve to minimize this type of conflict. Because of the costs of storing parts, inventories are kept at a minimum. A major breakdown in a supplying department quickly affects the assembly department. The assembly department may then respond by putting heavy pressure on the supplying department to get parts.

In a study of line and staff conflicts, one researcher found that staff departments could justify their existence only by providing services to the line departments.[36] Since the staff departments could not require the use of their services, they had to promote their ideas and follow a policy of understanding the problems of the line departments. Line-staff conflicts are made worse by the reward system. Staff departments push for changes to prove their worth to top management. To line departments, the proposed changes may imply that their previous activity was below standard.

Inconsistent performance criteria and rewards refers to evaluating and rewarding interdependent groups or individuals on the basis of criteria that motivate them to concentrate on their self (or competing) goals rather than on common goals. The greater the interdependency of groups, and the more top management emphasizes their separate rather than combined performance, the more conflict there will be between them.

An example of the way performance criteria can stimulate conflict between departments was provided by the previously mentioned telephone company study.

> *The plant department maintains all equipment; failure in some pieces of equipment subtracts directly from its efficiency indices; failure in others reduces indices of the traffic department, which must often request the plant department to give priority to maintenance or repair work on equipment that is especially vital to the performance of the traffic department. If other maintenance work is also required, which is important to the efficiency and evaluation indices of the plant department, then there is a strong conflict of interest in this situation.*[37]

Intergroup differences are the extent to which groups perform different tasks and deal with different parts of the organization's environment. As a result of such differences, groups may vary in their goal orientation, time orientation, formal structure, and interpersonal orientation. These variations have been useful in understanding the intergroup conflicts between research, sales, and production departments.

*Inconsistent
performance
criteria and
rewards*

*Intergroup
differences*

Goal orientation could differ in terms of scientific knowledge (research department) vs. customer problems and market opportunities (marketing department) vs. costs of producing units (production department). *Time orientation* refers to how long it takes the department to know the results of its actions. The research department has a long time horizon (one year or more), the sales department a moderate time horizon (one month to six months), and the production department a short time horizon (one day to one month). The *formal structure* of departments refers to their relative strictness of rules, span of control, and frequency and specificity of supervisory control. The research department has the least formal structure, the production department the most formal structure, and the sales department something in between. *Interpersonal orientation* refers to the relative openness, sociability, and permissiveness in relationships within the department. The sales department is usually the most open and social interpersonally, the production department the least, and research in between.

Figure 17.20 summarizes the relative differences in these categories for the production, sales, and research departments of six organizations in the plastics industry.[38] The data suggest that the greater the differences between departments, the greater the difficulty of coordinating tasks between them. In turn, these differences may be causes of intergroup conflicts.

17.20
Interdepartment differences in six plastics firms

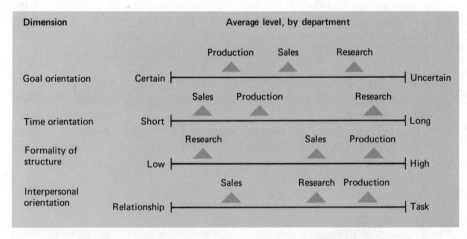

Sharing scarce common resources

Sharing scarce common resources refers to groups drawing from a common source services or goods which are not sufficient to meet all of their needs. Groups might compete for physical space, equipment, operating or capital funds, and centralized services (typing, printing, or computer time).

Summary

Intergroup conflict has a variety of causes: task interdependencies; task dependencies; inconsistent performance criteria and rewards; intergroup differences; and the need to share common resources. It is not possible to eliminate all these sources of intergroup conflict. Appropriate managerial actions and decisions can do much to reduce such conflicts and keep them at levels that do not cause poor performance.

Effects of Intergroup Conflict

An overview of the positive and negative effects of intergroup conflict is shown in Table 17.3. Extreme competition between two groups typically stimulates aggression or withdrawal, depending on the personalities of the group

17.3
Effects of Intergroup Conflict

Characteristics of Intergroup conflict	Positive Effects	Negative effects
■ Competition	Increases motivation Contributes to a system of checks and balances Increases number of new ideas to compete with established ones	Decreases motivation May deprive higher-level management of information
■ Concealment and distortion of information		Lowers quality of decisions
■ Appeals to superiors for decisions	Superior becomes more informed about operations and subordinates May lead to confrontation with superior as a third-party facilitator	Superior may become overloaded by referrals May lead to forcing with superior handing down edicts without full knowledge
■ Rigidity and formality in decision procedures	May increase stability in the system	May lower adaptability to change
■ Decreased rate of intergroup interaction	May decrease problem *if* a group or person is used to provide the necessary liaison	Hinders coordination and implementation of tasks
■ Low trust, suspicion, hostility	Increased cohesion within group contributing to cooperation within group	Psychological strain and turnover of personnel

Adapted from R. Walton and J. Dutton, The Management of Interdepartmental Conflict: A Model and Review. *Administrative Science Quarterly* **14**, 1969, 73–83.

members. To some managers, conflict is a major threat; for others, it stimulates energy and involvement. If either group has the ability to conceal and distort information needed by the other, less timely and poorer quality decisions will probably result.

If the groups cannot resolve even minor issues and continuously appeal to a common superior, the manager may soon be overloaded with their problems. This can have serious negative effects. The superior has to keep working on day-to-day instead of long-range problems. On the other hand, the common superior may want to become involved in important conflicts between the groups because it increases awareness about the operations and subordinates.

In sum, the characteristics of conflicting intergroup relationships may have positive or negative effects or, in some cases, both types of effects.

Managing Intergroup Conflict

Mechanisms used to manage role and interpersonal conflicts are also useful in managing intergroup conflicts. In particular, the most effective interpersonal styles for managing intergroup conflicts are collaboration and compromise.[39]

Conflict can also be reduced by changes in a company's reward system, better personnel selection, and more effective training programs. A reward system placing greater emphasis on collaboration will encourage that type of behavior. Group incentives based on plant-wide productivity encourage interdepartmental collaboration. Separate and different departmental incentives, especially when the departments are interdependent, can lead to undesirable competition between the groups. Task interdependencies, one of the principal sources of all conflict, can be reduced by such means as: (1) reducing dependence on common resources; (2) loosening up schedules, establishing inventories, or using contingency funds; and (3) simply reducing pressures for consensus.[40] Each of these techniques has its own set of costs. Managers must evaluate whether the benefits gained from decreased conflicts are greater than the costs of the techniques used to reduce them.

There are, of course, a variety of other mechanisms for managing intergroup conflicts — interventions by superiors, use of superordinate goals, separate integrating groups, and standardized practices. As might be expected, the greater the differences between groups and the more they need coordination, the greater the emphasis on a variety of conflict-management tactics.[41]

Interventions by superiors

In one successful container organization (manufacturer of beer cans and cardboard boxes), the knowledge needed to resolve intergroup conflicts was found to exist primarily at the top levels of the organization.[42] The environment of the container organization was stable. Management faced few uncertainties about technology, customers, legal regulations, and the like. The main competitive issues — delivery times and quality — required tight coordination between the sales and production departments. Only the top executives had the knowledge necessary to understand all the factors. These superiors kept the sales and production departments informed of critical problems, helped ease problems, and prevented poor decisions.

This case shows that groups with moderately different structures and orientations can have their conflicts resolved effectively through intervention by a common superior. In such situations, the use of more involved mechanisms may simply make coordination and conflict resolution more difficult.

Superordinate goals are the shared goals of groups that can be achieved only through cooperation. For example, in dealing with conflicts between marketing and production, a president might emphasize that the cooperation of *both* groups is needed if the firm is to earn profits, survive, and grow. These outcomes are superordinate goals for the production and marketing departments.

Superordinate goals

If groups are engaged in intense conflicts, it may be difficult to get them to perceive any superordinate goals *unless* a common threat appears on the scene. A common threat acts as a superordinate goal when the groups realize that they will lose something unless they cooperate. A common threat might be a new competitor making substantial inroads in the firm's market. For example, in the early 1970s IBM's introduction of its line of high-quality copiers was regarded as a major, long-term threat to Xerox, then dominating the copier market. Similarly, competing national political parties may present a united front if the country goes to war. Groups set aside some of their differences and conflicts in order to beat the enemy, a superordinate goal.

If accepted, superordinate goals will quickly reduce the level of emotional conflict between groups.[43] Unless other steps are taken, the use of superordinate goals alone will not resolve long-term disagreement. For example, once the war is won, the political parties will bring their old conflicts to the surface.

A separate integrating group may help to resolve conflicts and achieve coordination between two groups. Use of this third group would be necessary only when the conflicting groups are highly interdependent, require tight coordination, and are very different from each other in terms of goals, time horizon, and structure.

Separate integrating groups

In the study of six plastics-industry organizations mentioned previously, the two most successful organizations had integrating groups. The successful integrating groups had the following characteristics:[44]

- In terms of their goal, time, and interpersonal orientations and their degree of structure, the integrating personnel were midway between the members of the linked groups. This intermediate position enabled the integrating groups to communicate with all other groups and gave them a neutral posture.

- The integrating personnel had relatively high influence, based on their expertise and formal authority.

- The integrators felt that higher-level superiors evaluated and rewarded them on overall performance measures, which included the activities of the groups they were responsible for integrating. In contrast, the integrating managers in the poorly performing organizations thought that individual performance or performance of their subordinates was more important.

- The more effective organizations openly confronted differences between groups rather than smoothed or forced them.

These findings suggest that the creation of integrating groups requires careful judgment by high-level managers.

Standardized practices

There are a number of formal procedures and practices that can aid in the management of intergroup conflicts.

- Permanent teams or committees of representatives from the interdependent groups should meet on a regular basis. This reduces the tendency of parties to withdraw from conflicts in the short run and helps prevent conflicts from building up before they finally are confronted.[45] Higher-level managers might encourage direct contact of individuals between groups and levels. This may aid problem-solving and prevent the development of intense conflicts between groups or individuals.

- Procedures may be established for appealing to a common superior. One of the potential weaknesses of such procedures, however, is the possibility that the parties involved will perceive their conflict as a win-lose situation.

- Training sessions in interpersonal and intergroup dynamics and/or third-party interventions by behavioral scientists may be effective.[46]

Just as there is no single cause of intergroup conflict, there is no single mechanism for managing them. A manager can err by creating a too-elaborate conflict-resolution network, since it may spend too much time on minor conflicts. On the other hand, an elaborate conflict-resolution network may be desirable when there are major differences between the groups as well as high needs for coordination.

SUMMARY

This chapter should be helpful in improving your skills to perform a variety of managerial roles; especially the leader role, disturbance handler role, and negotiator role.

Focusing on internal organizational conflict, we only briefly noted the effect of the external environment. Conflict is neither good nor bad in and of itself. The contingency model is a starting point for diagnosing any level of conflict. The model presents three major types of conflict situations — win-lose, mixed, and collaborative. We considered the causes, effects, and tactics for managing role conflict, interpersonal conflict, and intergroup conflict. Role conflicts occur because of excess inconsistent pressure on the individual. There are four types of role conflict: intrasender, intersender, interrole, and person-role. High levels of role conflict can have negative effects, such as poor performance and job stress. Role conflicts often are dealt with through such personal tactics as avoidance, rationalization, and projection. They also can be dealt with more positively through collaboration and various organizational tactics.

The causes of interpersonal conflicts may range from disagreements over policies, practices, or plans to emotional issues. Among the interpersonal styles for managing conflicts are avoidance, compromise, smoothing, forcing, and collaboration.

At a more complex level, intergroup conflicts may be caused by task interdependencies, task dependencies, inconsistent performance criteria and rewards, differences between groups, and problems in sharing common resources. The ultimate effects of high levels of intergroup conflict include lower profits, poor service, and reduced long-term effectiveness. Some of the tactics for managing intergroup conflicts are interventions by superiors, superordinate goals, separate integrating groups, and standardized practices.

Since these conflict levels are quite interrelated, a manager should not rush to a conclusion about "the" cause of a particular conflict. A manager needs to first diagnose the conflict in terms of each of these levels and then develop a meaningful course of action for dealing with it.

KEYWORDS

avoidance style
collaborative situation
collaborative style
conflict
compromise style
distributive variable
focal person
forcing style
inconsistent performance criteria
and rewards
integrative variable
intergroup conflict
intergroup differences

interpersonal conflict
interrole conflict
intersender role conflict
intrasender role conflict
low-interdependency situation
mixed-conflict situation
negotiation
person-role conflict
projection
rationalization
role
role conflict
role episode

role senders
role set
smoothing style
stress
superordinate goals

task dependency
task interdependency
win-lose conflict situation
workplace politics

DISCUSSION QUESTIONS

1. Why is conflict inevitable in organizations?

2. Give an example of a "mixed-conflict" situation from your past, using the contingency model of conflict. Identify those elements that contributed to the distributive nature of the conflict.

3. Why is it important to diagnose a conflict situation prior to entry into it, if possible?

4. Drawing on your own experience, give an example of intergroup conflict. What were its causes?

5. Discuss the likely relationships between the relative power of individuals and intensity of their perceived role conflicts.

6. How does personality act as a contingency between role senders and focal persons in influencing the mechanisms for managing conflicts?

7. When can conflict help individuals, groups, and organizations be more effective?

8. When can conflict hurt the effectiveness of individuals, groups, and organizations?

9. Why is avoidance or withdrawal so commonly used as an interpersonal mechanism for managing conflicts?

Management Incidents and Cases

CONFLICT STYLE INCIDENTS*

Instructions: Your task is to rank the five alternative courses of action in each of the following four incidents. Rank the sections from the most desirable or appropriate way of dealing with the conflict situation to the least desirable. Rank the most desirable course of action "1," the next most desirable "2," and so on, with the least desirable or least appropriate action as "5." Enter

---

* A. Zoll, *Explorations in Managing*, 1974, © Addison-Wesley Publishing Company, Inc., Based on a format suggested by Allen A. Zoll, III. Reprinted with permission.

your rank for each item in the space next to each choice. Next, identify the conflict style being used with each of the possible courses of action, e.g., forcing, smoothing, avoidance, compromise, or collaboration.

Pete is lead operator of a production molding machine. Recently he has noticed that one of the men from another machine has been coming over to his machine and talking to one of his men (not on break time). The efficiency of Pete's operator seems to be falling off, and there have been some rejects due to his inattention. Pete thinks he detects some resentment among the rest of the crew. *If you were Pete, you would:*

_____ *a.* Talk to your man and tell him to limit his conversations during on-the-job time.

_____ *b.* Ask the foreman to tell the lead operator of the other machine to keep his operators in line.

_____ *c.* Confront both men the next time you see them together (as well as the other lead operator, if necessary), find out what they are up to, and tell them what you expect of your operators.

_____ *d.* Say nothing now; it would be silly to make something big out of something so insignificant.

_____ *e.* Try to put the rest of the crew at ease; it is important that they all work well together.

Sally is the senior quality-control (Q-C) inspector and has been appointed group leader of the Q-C people on her crew. On separate occasions, two of her people have come to her with different suggestions for reporting test results to the machine operators. Paul wants to send the test results to the foreman and then to the machine operator, since the foreman is the person ultimately responsible for production output. Jim thinks the results should go directly to the lead operator on the machine in question, since he is the one who must take corrective action as soon as possible. Both ideas seem good, and Sally can find no ironclad procedures in the department on how to route the reports. *If you were Sally, you would:*

_____ *a.* Decide who is right and ask the other person to go along with the decision (perhaps establish it as a written procedure).

_____ *b.* Wait and see; the best solution will become apparent.

_____ *c.* Tell both Paul and Jim not to get uptight about their disagreement; it is not that important.

_____ *d.* Get Paul and Jim together and examine both of their ideas closely.

_____ *e.* Send the report to the foreman, with a copy to the lead operator (even though it might mean a little more copy work for Q-C).

Incident Three   Ralph is a module leader; his module consists of four very complex and expensive machines and five crewmen. The work is exacting, and inattention or improper procedures could cause a costly mistake or serious injury. Ralph suspects that one of his men is taking drugs on the job or at least is showing up for work under the influence of drugs. Ralph feels he has some strong indications, but he knows he does not have a "case." *If you were Ralph, you would:*

_____ *a.* Confront the man outright, tell him what you suspect and why and that you are concerned for him and for the safety of the rest of the crew.

_____ *b.* Ask that the suspected offender keep his habit off the job; what he does on the job *is* part of your business.

_____ *c.* Not confront the individual right now; it might either "turn him off" or drive him underground.

_____ *d.* Give the man the "facts of life"; tell him it is illegal and unsafe and that if he gets caught, you will do everything you can to see that the man is fired.

_____ *e.* Keep a close eye on the man to see that he is not endangering others.

Incident Four   Gene is a foreman of a production crew. From time to time in the past, the product development section has tapped the production crews for operators to augment their own operator personnel to run test products on special machines. This has put very little strain on the production crews, since the demands have been small, temporary, and infrequent. Lately, however, there seems to have been an almost constant demand for four production operators. The rest of the production crew must fill in for these missing people, usually by working harder and taking shorter breaks. *If you were Gene, you would:*

_____ *a.* Let it go for now; the "crisis" will probably be over soon.

_____ *b.* Try to smooth things over with your own crew and with the development foreman; we all have jobs to do and cannot afford a conflict.

_____ *c.* Let development have two of the four operators they requested.

_____ *d.* Go to the development supervisor — or his or her foreman — and talk about how these demands for additional operators could best be met without placing production in a bind.

_____ *e.* Go to the supervisor of production (Gene's boss) and get him or her to "call off" the development people.

PANTHER INN*

In October 1972, Midland University became a member of the Small Business Institute, an experimental program under the auspices of the Small Business Administration. The objective of the institute was to provide university students who would give management assistance to small businesses. The student consultants thus had the opportunity to complement their academic experience through exposure to "real world" problems.

One of the 20 cases assigned to the students at Midland University was the Panther Inn (PI), a family restaurant and lounge located at the intersection of I-88 and State Route 127 near Bloomfield, Illinois. Located in the Panther Valley, PI has a scenic view of rolling farmland. PI is located in Midland County about 40 miles from Midland University.

PI was assigned to a team of three management students: Dave, Helen, and Jim. All three were a little older than the average student, having pursued other careers before continuing their education, and all three had prior small-business consulting experience. The institute's policy was for each team to work on two cases per quarter. In addition to Panther Inn, the team was consulting with Alpha Electronics, a small electronics repair shop. The team enjoyed an excellent working relationship with Alpha Electronics.

PI was founded by Harvey Adams, who had secured a loan of $300,000 from the SBA. The loan was 90 percent guaranteed by the SBA, with an

---

* This case was prepared by Professor T. F. Urban (Texas A&M University) and H. J. Brightman (Georgia State University). Copyright 1973 by Thomas F. Urban and Harvey J. Brightman. Used with permission.

interest rate of eight percent on the unpaid balance. Four months later, he secured a loan of $350,000 from the SBA. The first $300,000 of this loan was to cancel the original note; the remaining $50,000 was for additional financing. An additional $10,000 was borrowed from relatives in order to provide working capital. The restaurant and surrounding property had a current net worth of $70,000, but was expected to reach $1 million at completion.

Since Adams was involved in other business activities, he handed PI over to his son, Chuck, who became owner and manager. Chuck was 22 years old, married, a high school graduate, and had no prior business education or experience.

In their initial meeting, both Adams and Chuck enthusiastically welcomed the proposed counseling by the team. Chuck admitted he knew nothing about a restaurant business. He had originally just wanted to be the bartender for the lounge. Since the restaurant was entering the operational phase, Dave, Helen, and Jim outlined their approach to the problems of PI. Their initial conclusion was that special attention should be directed toward market research, inventory control, financial and accounting operations, and overall management of the restaurant and the lounge.

In touring the facility, the team noted that there were two distinct operations located at PI: restaurant on the main floor and lounge on the lower level. Seating capacity for the restaurant included two counters with 15 seats each and a table capacity of 175 customers. The party rooms were not operating at full capacity (approximately 200 persons). The lounge area was currently operating at its 100-person capacity, but when fully completed, two bars would be operating with a capacity of 200 customers.

Chuck stated there were 24 full-time and part-time employees. Because of the continual turnover and anticipated increases in personnel needs, Chuck had been spending a lot of time interviewing and filling positions.

After touring the restaurant facilities, the team began to discuss the specific needs, of PI. Chuck stated that although he didn't know much about business, he thought he should be making a profit because so many customers came in, but there didn't seem to be any money left over. He was too busy hiring people and tending bar "to look into money matters." Chuck wasn't sure where the customers were coming from, but many seemed to be tourists. He also wanted to know how to order the supplies needed for the restaurant. Sometimes they ran out of food; at other times the employees had to eat it in order to keep it from going to waste. Chuck concluded by stating, "I want to be a good manager, but how? I never have any time left over to take care of anything. Just tell me what to do, and I'll do it."

The team told Chuck they needed to develop a cost analysis of the restaurant and lounge, as well as a labor analysis of the current wage structure.

Since Chuck had no idea as to whether the restaurant and/or lounge was making a profit, he relied on his accountant to provide these figures. The team said they would need more data and figures to analyze the situation. Chuck said that they could get this from the accountant if he had it, adding that the accountant was an old family friend of his father and was a "nice guy." In addition, the team recommended a market research program in order to determine the extent of PI's potential market share. Finally, Chuck wanted an analysis of his parking lot layout and facilities. The first meeting closed on a friendly note as Chuck had to return to the lounge and tend bar. He promised to get all the records from the accountant and said, "You can do anything you want. I just don't know that much about business and you're the experts. I'm glad the SBA put you in to do the work for me."

Several weeks later, Dr. Urman, the team's faculty adviser, was grading papers when he was interrupted by Dave, Helen, and Jim. "We're quitting PI," said Jim. "He's not going to get any more cheap labor from us. He never does anything, and now he's taken off for Florida — a two-week vacation because he 'had to get away.'" "Yeah!" said Helen, "we drove all the way up there and he's in Florida. That's it! He never does anything we want him to."

"Hold on a second," said Dr. Urman, "we just can't drop a case because it's too tough. We have a contract with the SBA and that's one of our cases. Let's start at the beginning."

"Okay," said Jim. "The first time we went out, we told him what we were going to do and what we needed. He never did anything. He wants us to do everything. When we went back a few days later, he hadn't gotten the records from the accountant. In fact, the accountant hadn't even filed a tax return for PI. We told him to place a register at the door to have people sign it. We could get our market information from this as to where the customers come from — tourists, families. We drew up a plan for his parking lot. He wanted us to go out and paint the lines for parking spaces for him. Us — management students!"

"Yeah!" said Helen. "Look at our progress reports. We tell him to do something, and it's never done. The only way we get him to do anything is to do it ourselves. Look at that accounting mess! We finally drove out to his accountant's and got the books. That dumb bookkeeper! He even wears green eye shades! He still uses a single-entry system. We analyzed the books, and he didn't have any of the data we needed. We finally worked up a cost analysis by collecting the data ourselves. Then we found he made a $2300 error. He didn't post figures in the ledger and when he did post, he put the figures in the wrong places. We finally broke the figure down into separate listings for the lounge and restaurant. When we told Chuck to get rid of him, he said that he can't because the accountant is a friend of his father."

"I took care of his personnel problems," said Dave. "We prepared a wage analysis. Then I wrote the ads for the papers and went to the employment agencies myself. I made up an organization chart and job descriptions for each position. All Chuck wants to do is tend bar. He keeps saying, 'Do what you want to do. The SBA sent you in. You're the experts.' He just thinks that everything will work out. He doesn't have any experience and wants us to take care of everything. He doesn't want to be a manager!"

"I had to take care of his marketing," said Jim. "I wrote the ads and put them in the paper. He can't rely on tourists all year. We designed the billboard for him and he never put it up. We have to do everything for him. We advertise low prices and he raises everything on his menu by $1 to $2.50. He didn't need to do that without asking us. Then we advertise a family restaurant, and he still won't put in a kid's menu. We wanted him to give out balloons or panthers or something, and he still hasn't even looked into it. Chuck apologizes to us for not carrying through and he admits that he's lazy. All he wants to do is tend bar."

"If we can't quit this case, Dr. Urman, how can we get him to do the things we want him to? We've done more work on this than any of our other courses, and we don't have anything to show for it. He just wants us to do the busywork — and now he goes to Florida."

Questions

1. What types of conflicts are there in this case?

2. What are the causes of these conflicts?

3. What mechanisms for managing these conflicts might be used?

REFERENCES

1. L. Rout, "First Chicago Chairman Abboud Is Fired, Firm's No. 2 Officer, Kapnick, Resigns." *The Wall Street Journal* **65,** 84, 1980, 1.

2. H. Menzies, "The Ten Toughest Bosses." *Fortune* **101,** 8, 1980, 62–72.

3. L. Rout, "First Chicago With Or Without Abboud, Is A Place of Tension." *The Wall Street Journal* **65,** 94, 1980, 1, 20.

4. L. Rout and E. Foldessy, "First Chicago Taps Chase Bank's Sullivan as Successor To Abboud In Top Positions." *The Wall Street Journal* **65,** 124, 1980, 1.

5. S. Robbins, *Managing Organizational Conflict: A Nontraditional Approach.* Englewood Cliffs, NJ: Prentice-Hall, 1974, p. 23.

6. I. Janis and J. Mann, *Decision Making: A Psychological Analysis of Conflict, Choice, and Commitment.* New York: Free Press, 1977, p. 46.

7. M. Deutsch, *The Resolution of Conflict: Constructive and Destructive Processes.* New Haven: Yale University Press, 1973.

8. Adapted from R. Walton and R. McKersie, *A Behavioral Theory of Labor Negotiations: An Analysis of a Social Interaction System.* New York: McGraw-Hill, 1965. Also see R. Kilmann and K. Thomas, "Four Perspectives on Conflict Management: An Attributional Framework for Organizing Descriptive and Normative Theory." *Academy of Management* **3,** 1978, 59–68.

9. J. Gandy and V. Murray, "The Experience of Workplace Politics." *Academy of Management Journal* **23,** 1980, 237–251.

10. M. Kelley, "Organizational Analogy: A Comparison of Organismic and Social Contract Models." *Administrative Quarterly* **25,** 1980, 337–362.

11. R. Walton and R. McKersie, "Behavioral Dilemmas in Mixed-Motive Decision-Making." *Behavioral Science* **11,** 1966, 370–384.

12. K. Clark, "The Impact of Unionization on Productivity: A Case Study." *Industrial and Labor Relations Review* **33,** 19b 0, 451–469.

13. A. Roark and L. Wilkinson, "Approaches to Conflict Management." *Group and Organization Studies* **4,** 1979, 440–451.

14. J. Dutton and R. Walton, "Interdepartmental Conflict and Cooperation: Two Contrasting Studies." In *Managing Group and Intergroup Relations*, L. Lorsch and P. Lawrence (eds). Homewood, IL: Richard D. Irwin and the Dorsey Press, 1972, pp. 285–304.

15. Adapted from R. Kahn, D. Wolfe, R. Quinn, and J. Snoek, *Organizational Stress: Studies In Role Conflict and Ambiguity.* New York: John Wiley, 1964.

16. R. Merton, *Social Theory and Social Structure*, 2nd ed. Glenview: Free Press, 1957.

17. J. Nagel, *The Descriptive Analysis of Power.* New Haven: Yale University Press, 1975.

18. D. Whetten, "Coping with Incompatible Expectations: An Integrated View of Role Conflict." *Administrative Science Quarterly* **23,** 1978, 254–271.

19. K. Bartol, "The Sex Structuring of Organizations: A Search For Possible Causes." *Academy of Management Review* **3,** 1978, 805–815.

20. J. Lublin, "Juggling Job and Junior." *The Wall Street Journal* **65,** 57, 1980, 23.

21. D. Yaeger, "The Balancing Act: No Tea, No Sympathy." *MBA* **11,** 1977, 23–24, 39.

22. J. Ivancevich and M. Matteson, *Stress and Work: A Managerial Perspective.* Glenview, IL: Scott, Foresman, 1980.

23. L. Warshaw, *Managing Stress.* Reading, MA: Addison-Wesley, 1979.

24. T. Cox, *Stress.* Baltimore: University Park Press, 1978.

25. A. Zaleznik, M. Kets de Vries, and J. Howard, "Stress Reactions in Organizations: Syndromes, Causes, and Consequences." *Behavioral Science* **22,** 1977, 151–162.

26. A. McLean, *Work Stress.* Reading, MA: Addison-Wesley, 1979.

27. R. Miles, "A Comparison of the Relative Impacts of Role Perceptions of Ambiguity and Conflict by Role." *Academy of Management Journal* **19,** 1976, 25–35.

28. A. Filley, *Interpersonal Conflict Resolution.* Glenview, IL: Scott, Foresman, 1975.

29. B. Schorr, "Small Companies Act to Patch Things Up Rather Than Split Up." *The Wall Street Journal* **65,** 89, 1980, 19, 43.

30. Adapted from R. Blake and J. Mouton, *The New Managerial Grid.* Houston: Gulf Publishing, 1978.

31. M. Ways, "The Virtues, Dangers, and Limits of Negotiation." *Fortune* **99,** 1979, 86–90.

32. K. Thomas, "Conflict and Conflict Management." In M. Dunnette (ed.) *Handbook of Industrial and Organizational Psychology.* Chicago: Rand McNally, 1976, pp. 889–935.

33. R. Walton, *Interpersonal Peacemaking: Confrontation and Third-Party Consultation.* Reading, MA: Addison-Wesley, 1969, pp. 94–115.

34. H. Bernardin and K. Alvares, "The Managerial Grid as a Predictor of Conflict Resolution Method and Managerial Effectiveness." *Administrative Science Quarterly* **21,** 1976, 84–92.

35. R. Walton, J. Dutton, and T. Cafferty, "Organizational Context and Interdepartmental Conflict." *Administrative Science Quarterly* **14,** 1969, 527.

36. M. Dalton, *Men Who Manage.* New York: John Wiley, 1959.

37. Walton, Dutton, and Cafferty, *op. cit.,* 527.

38. P. Lawrence and J. Lorsch. *Organization and Environment.* Homewood, IL: Richard D. Irwin, 1967, 110–124.

39. J. Martin and L. Biasatti, "A Hierarchy of Important Elements in Union-Management Relations." *Journal of Management* **5,** 1979, 229–240.

40. L. Pondy, "Organizational Conflict: Concepts and Models." *Administrative Science Quarterly* **12,** 1967, 264–319.

41. J. Gandz, "Resolving Conflict: A Guide for the Industrial Relations Manager." *Personnel* **56,** 1979, 22–32.

42. P. Lawrence and J. Lorsch. *Organization and Management, op. cit.,* 110–124.

43. J. Hunger and L. Stern, "An Assessment of the Functionality of the Superordinate Goal in Reducing Conflict." *Academy of Management Journal* **19,** 1976, 591–605.

44. P. Lawrence and J. Lorsch. *Organization and Environment, op. cit.,* 54–83.

45. J. Perry and H. Angel, "The Politics of Organizational Boundary Roles in Collective Bargaining." *Academy of Management Review* **4,** 1979, 487–496.

46. M. Beer, *Organization Change and Development: A Systems View.* Santa Monica, CA: Goodyear, 1980.

Part VI discusses how managers can successfully manage change and what it will be like to manage in the future. Chapter 18, "Organizational Change," focuses on the two objectives for change: adapting the organization to its environment and changing the way employees behave. A model is presented that allows you to diagnose the various steps in managing change. When change occurs, it can affect people, structure, jobs, and technology. Because change involves doing something new, it is very often resisted. Ways are presented to overcome resistance to change. Chapter 19, "Challenges to Management in the 1980s," describes the significant challenges that you will face. Changes are taking place in the composition of the work force, the values of employees, and governmental-business relationships. As organizations grow, managers are faced with different problems. Some of these include new organizational structures, different styles of leadership, and different methods of planning and controlling the activities of the organization.

Part VI

Chapter 18

ORGANIZATIONAL CHANGE

When you have finished reading this chapter, you should be able to:

1. Discuss the key external and internal factors affecting organizational change.

2. Summarize the seven phases of the organizational change process.

3. Identify the sources of resistance to change and the ways this resistance can be overcome.

4 Describe the four major approaches to change and give an example of each.

5. Identify the conditions leading to success and the pitfalls to avoid in a change program.

PREVIEW CASE

Macungie Corporation

The manufacturing operations at the Phelps plant of the Macungie Corporation consist of fabricating and assembling trucks — over-the-road, fire engines, and panel trucks. Traditionally, the manufacturing systems have been designed and built around an assembly-line operation.

As general production manager of the Phelps plant, Mr. Schaadt, who has developed through the management ranks largely by following the basic principles of management, must give final approval to all system changes that will affect the operations of this plant. A new design for an engine of the over-the-road truck has been completed by product engineering. In turn, it has been released to manufacturing engineering for implementation into the assembly-line system.

The manufacturing engineering group recently studied the available research on the advantages of job enrichment and how it compares to the traditional method of an assembly line, in terms of providing the workers with more challenging tasks, relief from boredom, and greater responsibility for the product. Management realized that job satisfaction and motivation continued to be a problem on assembly-line work. A system that included job enrichment was developed to assemble the new components of the engine along with the traditional conveyor-paced system. After the systems had been in operation for six months, the results of each system were presented to Mr. Schaadt for his approval. The manufacturing engineering group recommended that he adopt the job-enrichment system because it relieved workers from performing dull, meaningless, and repetitive tasks. Mr. Schaadt, being aware of the perceived monotony and boredom of the assembly line, decided to accept the recommendation from the manufacturing engineering group.

As the production date arrived, the facilities were completed, and a number of operators moved from the assembly line process to a new job. They, in turn, were told to completely assemble the engine and stamp their work with a personalized identification stamp that Macungie had provided.

Output and quality during the first week were 10 percent below that expected, and during the next few weeks very little improvement was shown. In fact, the output was significantly below that of similar engine work on an adjacent conveyor-paced system.

Mr. Schaadt's boss was upset, since efficiency was low and excessive overtime was necessary to meet the heavy demands for trucks. Mr. Schaadt, realizing that he is responsible for production at the Phelps plant, is trying to determine what happened and what course of action to take.

What are the problems? What factors are influencing the change process? How should Mr. Schaadt have introduced the change in the plant? What should Mr. Schaadt do now? After you have finished reading this chapter, you should be able to answer these questions.

Organizations really are never static. As shown by the problems facing Mr. Schaadt, managers are in continual contact with groups making demands on them to change. These groups include competitors, suppliers, outside pressure groups, governments, employees, and customers. Shifts in consumer preferences, technical breakthroughs, and demands from diverse groups in society are examples of the forces that underlie organizational change. The pace of change will vary from organization to organization, but change is a part of our society. Many changes, of course, will be beyond the control of the organization; others can be created and guided by the organization. One author has stated:

Change has always been a part of the human condition. What is different now is the pace of change, and the prospect that it will come faster and faster, affecting every part of life, including personal values, morality, and religion, which seem almost remote from technology. . . . So swift is the acceleration, that trying to "make sense" of change will become our basic industry[1]

In his penetrating book, *Future Shock*, Alvin Toffler argues that humanity is now a part of an environment so unfamiliar and complex that it is threatening millions with "future shock."[2] **Future shock** occurs when the types of changes and their speed of introduction overpower the individual's ability to adapt. The problem comes not from a particular change one cannot handle but from the fact that since so many things are changing, new ways of dealing with the "temporary society" are needed. This temporary society is characterized by the temporary nature of housing, jobs, friendships, and neighborhoods. Things move so quickly there is no time for long-term stability, and values may become a part of a "throw-away" society. Some of the areas of change are noted in Fig. 18.1.

18.1
Dimensions of change during the past 100 years.

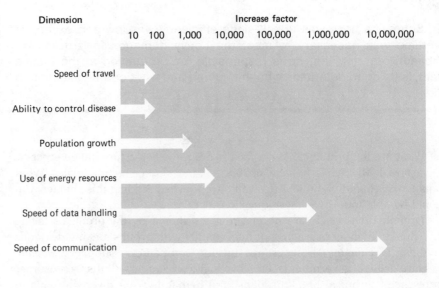

No one can escape change. Change is so rapid there is no time to adjust before more change takes place. The decade of the 1970s has been called the decade of the explosion -- in knowledge, technology, communications, and economics. The dramatic change among youth and minority groups and in morals and politics contribute to the challenge of the 1980s. For today's organization, the lesson is clear: Yesterday's corporate successes mean very little in a world of rapidly changing markets, products, values, and life-styles. In order to survive, organizations must devise means of continuous self-renewal. They must be able to recognize when it is necessary to change, and, above all, they must be able to change when it is required. Some companies have created specialized units whose primary purpose is organizational planning. These units spend a great deal of time developing and implementing new structural, technological, and motivational programs to improve the organization's ability to survive.

Executives today are bombarded on all sides by constantly changing information and work. No managerial functions appear to be immune from the knowledge explosion. Personnel, organizational development, and training managers are faced with many new employment, training, and safety acts. And of course there is an ever-increasing demand for industrial relations skills to cope with the fluctuating attitudes and aspirations of the workforce. Production, research and development, maintenance, and transportation people are faced with tremendous technological advances in the fields of communications and electronics. Financial managers have to cope with many new accounting procedures in addition to the many changes in taxation, company laws, and the ever-increasing fluctuation of the money markets.

It is an important part of the manager's job to achieve stability in the face of constant interruptions. Just as a symphony conductor must coax acceptable music from an orchestra whose members have personal problems, while stage hands are having trouble with the lights and the air conditioning system is changing the auditorium into a giant freezer, so must the manager bring order to the system.

To deal constructively with change and stability, there are two major responses managers can take: (1) They can react to changes as needed. This approach is called *fire-fighting.* Every time a problem appears, small changes are sought to deal with the particular problem or (2) they can develop a program of planned change. Using this approach, managers deal not only with present problems, but also with anticipated problems that are not yet facing the organization.

The first response — which is simpler and less expensive than the second — was appropriate when the pace of change was slower, the competition for raw materials and natural resources was not as severe, and when organizations were smaller and less complicated. Today, such a response is appropriate only for minor adjustments that are integral parts of the manager's day-to-day job. Here are two examples: Jerry Cooper, vice president of Human Resources for Henry C. Beck Company, designed a new performance appraisal form to take into consideration the rising cost of job-related injuries on construction sites; Jerry Nash, plant manager of a Xerox parts distribution service center, modified a sales form because the old form led to many errors. These are small changes and can be handled quickly by an effective manager. We will not deal specifically with these kinds of responses because, throughout the book, the description of daily problems facing managers has been highlighted.

The second response is found more often in today's organizations than in the past. Planned organizational change is the deliberate attempt to modify the functioning of the total organization or one of its major departments in order to increase effectiveness. Planned change usually is greater in scope and magnitude than "fire-fighting." It involves a greater commitment of time and resources; it requires more skills and knowledge for implementation to be successful; and it can lead to more problems if implementation is unsuccessful. Because of the scale and complexities involved in planned change strategies, we will be dealing with ways in which an entire organization, or a major portion of it, must prepare for and adapt to change. For example, in February 1980, General Motors announced a plan to replace aging and less efficient facilities in St. Louis and Pontiac with two car-assembly plants that will cost more than $1 billion. The change effort is part of a multibillion dollar plan to cut manufacturing costs and improve G. M.'s operating efficiency and its competitive position in the automobile industry.

OBJECTIVES OF ORGANIZATIONAL CHANGE

If asked why an organization was changing, a manager might respond: "To achieve higher performance, get a new product accepted in the marketplace, increase the productivity of employees, reduce turnover, increase the motivation of employees to work for the company's goals, and to be socially responsible." Organizational changes are aimed frequently at one or more of these general goals. Underlying these more obvious goals are two objectives: (1) changes in the organization's responses to its environment; and (2) changes in the behavior of its employees.

Responding to External Changes

Since the environment is composed of groups and organizations external to the company, the company must try to adapt to their demands with internal changes that allow it to be more effective. The forces external to the organization may change as a result of technological innovation, market changes, changes in legal requirements, and pressure from their own outside groups. This type of pattern is shown in Fig. 18.2.

Changing technology

In some industries, such as electronics, communications, and pharmacy, technological breakthroughs are a way of life. The competitive nature of the market determines how fast organizations adapt to new production processes.

The development of microcircuitry made it possible to reduce the cost and size of computers and pocket calculators. The development of optical scanners by National Cash Register to read cost, item type, and size data from food packages made it possible to use data processing and computers at supermarket checkout counters. The main reason store owners have switched to automated checkout is that it reduces human error. The average tired checker can make errors of 1.5 percent on a checkout.

The implications of such a move in the supermarket industry may be tremendous. The nature of the checker's job will change from actually checking out items to monitoring the groceries, meat, and produce as they pass over the electronic eye. The stock clerk's shelf check to determine the amount of items sold, at what price, and on what day will now be performed by an inventory manager who will have inventory levels determined almost instantaneously. Ordering of products can be more responsive to sudden shifts in customers' preferences. The computer printout will tell the manager the per-

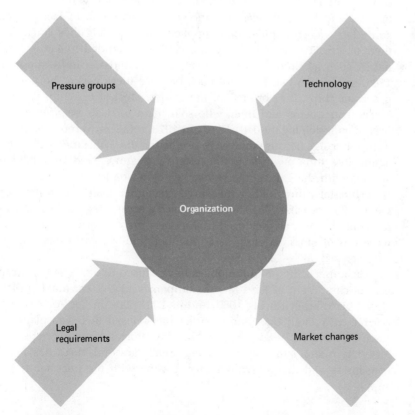

18.2
External forces to change

centage of sales in each department, when to reorder, how consumers responded to store coupons, and how many food stamps, manufacturers' coupons, and bottle refunds were cashed.

Such an innovation is having implications for the manufacturers of both cash registers and scanning equipment. They must now devise new marketing strategies to integrate these new systems into the existing structure of the supermarket and the data-processing capabilities of the computer firm. All of these advantages have costs associated with them. James Edelman, National Cash Register account manager, says that equipment for each checkout costs about $9500, and the computer is about $30,000. NCR claims that for high-volume stores, savings from clerk error alone should pay for the system within a short time.[3]

Changing markets   The nature of the market may change as consumers become aware of new ideas or methods. The increased use and knowledge of electronics had long been familiar to the business world, but by the late 1970s electronics was affecting even the toy industry. Consumers were demanding games that could beep, light up, and talk. The first four electronic games were introduced in 1977 and by 1980 sales had increased twelve-fold. In fact, the electronic game fad was so popular that suppliers were finding they couldn't meet all their orders. The initial four game choices expanded to 115, with familiar names such as Simon, Mattel's sports games, and Merlin heading the list. In 1980, production had been cut back because there was a shortage of microprocessor chips, the "brains" of the games. Most of the chips were made by Texas Instruments and Intel, who sold them to business-oriented industries first, then to the toy industry. Early in 1979, retailers weren't concerned about a chip shortage because they were predicting that consumer tastes would shift again, this time away from the electronic games; and by not being over-stocked with the games, the retailer wouldn't be left with a large inventory. Unfortunately, they hadn't measured consumer tastes accurately, and sales were still increasing. The shortage caused a scramble by consumers at Christmas time in 1979 as they tried to purchase their favorite games. Some stores were out of stock as early as September and weren't expecting any more shipments.[4]

Customer shifts in automobiles have caused drastic changes in the offerings of cars. Eight of Ford Motor Company's 13 U.S. car-making plants were closed periodically during 1980, and its LTD plant in Los Angeles was closed permanently. Both G.M. and Chrysler have closed their van plants in Lordstown and Detroit because of the high inventories of unsold vans on dealers' lots. The manufacture of gas-saving small cars and buses has increased as consumers and the government try to cope with the uncertainty of U.S. oil supplies.[5]

Enacting new laws or amending old ones often will have a major impact on an organization. In 1977 Congress amended the Clean Air Act, and gave the Environmental Protection Agency the power to require compliance with the Act. Some polluters ignored the Act, preferring to pay court costs rather than install expensive pollution-control devices. Organizations violating the law had a two-year grace period (which ended in 1979) during which they had to install controls. Those who didn't, faced a noncompliance penalty equal to the cost of installation. However, our society still has problems. For example, National Parks officials still aren't sure the pollution problem will be solved even with the restrictions new power facilities face. A new problem, acid rains, linked to the sulfur oxides released by coal-burning power plants, is threatening their parks and wildernesses now that the energy crisis has turned companies to using coal instead of oil.[6]

Changing legal requirements

In some cases, organizations have been forced to adapt their internal operations because of the pressures exerted by outside groups. The impact that environmentalists and feminists have had upon corporations is remembered easily. Many activists of the 1960s and 1970s are now trying to achieve their changes by working within the system to influence the policy-makers. With the Three-Mile-Island problem during the spring of 1979, the anti-nuclear energy group found the stepping-stone they needed to get more recognition and support. Jane Fonda and Tom Hayden made a 52-city tour during November 1979 during which they campaigned against nuclear power. They hoped to make solar power vs. nuclear power a major issue in the 1980 presidential election. Another anti-nuke group, MUSE (Musicians United for Safe Energy), held concerts to raise money for the movement. Fonda's movie, "The China Syndrome," helped crystallize the antinuclear feeling, and people began sporting T-shirts, bumper stickers, and hats showing their antinuclear opinions. Politicians felt the pressure, and, in California, Gov. Jerry Brown called for the shutdown of the Rancho Seco plant until it could be proven safe. Similar shutdowns occurred in Glen Rose, Texas, and Seabrook, New Hampshire. Blaming political and regulatory uncertainties, Cleveland Electric Illuminating, Toledo Edison, Ohio Edison, and Duquesne Light cancelled joint plans to build four nuclear power plants worth $7.3 billion.[7]

Outside pressure groups

The second goal of organizational change is to change the employee's behavior. The need for this goal becomes evident if one recognizes that the external forces facing the company cannot be dealt with unless many of its employees change their behavior. Organizations do not operate simply through computers or elaborate electronic circuits, but through employees making deci-

Modifying Employee Behavior

sions. Every organization has its pattern of decision-making behaviors. These patterns are influenced by the values of top management, the leadership practices of managers, the reward system used to motivate employees, and informal group rules. Any change in an organization, whether it's introduced through a new structural design or a training program, basically is trying to get employees to change their behavior and ground rules for relating to one another. For the change to be successful, these new behaviors must be evident throughout the entire organization. In the final analysis, all organizational efforts must take account of the fact that people are being called on to do things differently.

We see the problems of organizational change as twofold. First, organizations must learn to adjust effectively to meet the changing demands of the external forces in the environment. Managers who see themselves as change agents and who know how to function effectively in this role clearly are among the most valuable members of the organization. Second, when we consider the problems inherent in changing employee behavior, we also need to study the processes a manager should consider when attempting to implement a change.

A MODEL FOR ORGANIZATIONAL CHANGE

Figure 18.3 presents a seven-stage overview of the total change process as it relates to organizations. Each stage is dependent on the prior one. Since successful change is likely to be greater when the manager considers each of these stages in logical order, we will explore each stage separately.

Changes in the External Environment

An organization's external environment is in a state of flux. One of the primary functions of a manager is to cope with this situation so the organization can function effectively. In Chapters 7 and 8, we noted that two major factors contribute to this state of flux: market and technological changes. In Chapters 3 and 4, we indicated how groups and government regulations can also require managers to change certain rules and regulations.

The market structure of an organization may be stable (with respect to price, materials, supplies, suppliers, customers, governmental regulations, and so forth) or unstable. Stable markets can be found in the brewing, insurance, and commercial baking industries. Within each of these industries, the products, customers, suppliers, methods of distribution, and the price are similar. Extensive advertising campaigns are carried on by firms in these industries in an attempt to differentiate products and create a demand for their products. Miller Brewing Company makes a "Lite" beer and the Joseph P.

695
A Model for
Organizational Change

18.3
A model for the
management of change

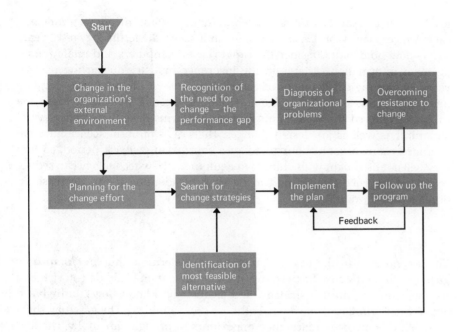

Schlitz Company sells "Light" beer. These two firms are competing for the same beer drinker, charge similar prices, negotiate with the same international union, and face similar distribution problems. Insurance premiums of the large companies, such as State Farm, Allstate, Prudential, Travelers, and Hartford, are very similar. The difference among these firms is in the service each insurance agent promises to give to the client.

Conglomerates are examples of firms facing relatively unstable markets. Gulf & Western Industries, Inc., Textron, Northwest Industries, AMF, United Technologies, and ITT are examples of firms operating in highly different markets. Gulf & Western owns Collyer Wire, Bliss Hydraulic Press, Titanium Corporation, Kayser-Roth, Schrafft's Candy, Muriel Cigars, and Paramount Pictures, among others. Each of these markets presents a unique challenge for Gulf & Western management in terms of government regulations and competitors. Kayser-Roth, which manufactures "No Nonsense" and "Supp-hose" hosiery, "Catalina" swimwear, and "Paris" belts, faces a different environment than does Paramount Pictures, producers of *The Great Gatsby*, *Chinatown*, and the television series, "Happy Days," and the "Odd Couple." The task of Gulf & Western's top management team is to integrate these diverse companies where necessary.

The second problem for the firm is technology. The rapid rate of technological change is born out by the fact that 93 percent of all scientists who ever lived are alive today. Most industries have undergone tremendous technological advances since World War II. In some industries, the technology of 20 years ago is now outdated. Consider the rapid rise of computers and related management information systems in the insurance industry during the past 20 years. Before the development of computers, most of the work was done by hand or processed on elementary accounting posting machines. Since the computer entered the picture, most insurance firms have undergone several structural as well as job-design changes. High rates of obsolescence have encouraged many organizations to adopt a short-term payback period, so that they will not be caught with outmoded equipment. New technology can reduce costs and improve quality, and to be slow in adopting it can decrease an organization's profitability.

Performance Gap   The second step in the change process is to determine the ***performance gap,*** i.e., the difference between what the organization could do (by virtue of its opportunities, market strategy, and technological know-how) and what it actually does (in taking advantage of those opportunities). The gap may show up positively in new marketing opportunities brought about by changes among consumers — or negatively by loss of market because of new competition. It may also occur when new technical breakthroughs are made. For example, American Telephone & Telegraph plans to link the Northeast corridor with a lasar-powered telecommunications system based on cable made of glass. When completed by 1984, the $79 million cable will carry up to 80,000 calls simultaneously on pulses of light rather than electrical signals. The half-inch-thick light-wave cable, consisting of hair-width strands of glass, will replace 611 miles of copper cable. Savings are expected not only in construction, but in operating costs as well.[8]

A performance gap may persist for some time before it is recognized. In fact, it may never be recognized. When recognized, however, it must also be seen to have significant consequences for the firm, if it is to be narrowed or bridged.

CASE STUDY

Ralston Purina Company*   Ralston Purina Company, under the direction of Chairman R. Hal Dean, had been showing profits from each venture it had undertaken since 1977.[9] Profits from highly successful agricultural processing operations were put into consumer product businesses — pet food, fast-food, house-

---

* This case was prepared by Alan Sweet, Cox School of Business, Southern Methodist University, Dallas, TX, 1980.

plants, and cereals. After seven consecutive record years, and a consistent 15 percent earnings growth, Ralston Purina suddenly experienced as much as a 16 percent fall in earnings in 1978–79. The main reason for this sharp decline was a combination of the company's reckless implementation and its poor execution of strategies in several areas.

The company had a huge headstart in the pet-food business, but it ignored new competition that, at one point, reduced Ralston's market share from a high of 50 percent to 38 percent in only 18 months. Their troubles started early in 1978 when other companies, such as Quaker Oats, the Liggett group, General Foods, and Carnation put big advertising dollars behind their pet-food products, such as Tender Chunks and Friskies Dinners. Ralston's decline in this area was seen clearly in the fact that the total sales volume of dry dog food *grew* 10 percent in 1978, while Ralston's sales dropped 1.5 percent.

In the fast-food industry, Ralston's Jack-in-the-Box restaurants, which offer, among other meals, hamburgers and Mexican food, expanded too late into the Midwest and Eastern markets. These markets were already saturated with competition, such as McDonald's Corp. and Pillsbury Co.'s Burger King chain. Ralston also ignored the fact that Mexican food was never popular in these regions.

In 1977, management failed to closely look at the $45 million acquisition of the Green Thumb Co., a grower and distributor of house plants. This unit's massive growing facilities in Florida and Guatemala turned out to be far more costly than expected. Green Thumb's management was riddled with problems and cash was needed to correct these. On top of that, Ralston failed to foresee a drop-off in demand for house plants.

To reduce this performance gap, Ralston Purina has implemented several new policies. First, Chairman Dean started one of the most sweeping management reorganizations in food industry history. Within a nine-month period he replaced more than a dozen top managers. He created four distinct operating groups, each with its own board of directors and headed by a corporate vice-president. It is expected that this will assure closer scrutiny of business decisions.

Second, in 1979 Ralston increased its pet-food promotion by 30 percent. It also concentrated more on products meeting the growing demand for dry and slightly moist pet food, rather than canned pet food, its major product line in the past. Third, the company sold 250 less profitable units from its 1050-unit Jack-in-the-Box chain. They will double fast-food efforts in its more successful markets of the Sunbelt and West. Fourth, the company took a $22 million write-off on the ailing Green Thumb Co., and they are now looking to sell the entire business in several pieces.

Fifth, Ralston is looking to acquire some other type of business that will brighten the short-term outlook while the pet-food and fast-food earnings take time to pick up. Ralston's highly successful agricultural business (animal feeds and soybean processing), along with its continually successful cereal business, will generate enough profits to allow Ralston to invest in these strategies that should reduce the performance gap.

Diagnosis of Organizational Problems

The change process often gets under way early in the diagnostic stage, depending on who does the diagnosis and the methods chosen for analyzing the problem areas. The objective of the diagnostic stage is for management to identify the nature and extent of the problem area(s) before taking any action. *Diagnosis should precede action.* (This may sound obvious, but it is nonetheless important. Often harassed and results-oriented managers let their impatience push them toward attempting solutions before the problem is clear.) By now, you should have recognized that most managerial problems have multiple causes. In organizations, as in life, there is seldom one, simple, obvious cause for organizational problems. Go back to the answers you gave to Mr. Schaadt. Were they simple and obvious? To aid in the identification of problems, several general questions may be asked:

1. What are the specific problems to be corrected?

2. What are the determinants of these problems?

3. What must be changed to resolve the problems?

4. What are the forces likely to work for and against change?

5. What goals or objectives are expected from the change, and how will these be measured?

The approach that management uses to diagnose the problem plays a crucial part in determining the problem(s) to be analyzed. A variety of data-gathering techniques have been used successfully — such as attitude surveys, conferences, informal interviews, and team meetings. The central concern of these approaches is to gather data that are not biased by a few dominant persons in the organization or by consultants. Conference meetings between the manager and his or her subordinates may quickly highlight technical problems.

Interpersonal problems usually involve extensive attitude surveys and/or the use of outside consultants. Attitude surveys can usually tap the feelings of the employees most effectively. This method may enable management to evaluate the organization's climate and the employees' attitudes toward pay, work, and related working conditions. Surveys should be answered anonymously so that the employees can express their genuine attitudes without the fear of reprisal from management. Because this technique can prove insightful for many potential problem areas, management should spend time in formulating the proper questions on a wide variety of work-related factors.

Managers often feel that subordinates and other managers tend to resist all changes because they can be difficult to implement. Changes are often resisted when the results are expected to be negative or uncertain. **Resistance** is any behavior that serves to maintain the status quo in the face of pressure to alter the status quo. Uncertainty may create feelings of insecurity and, therefore, opposition. Even though the public may benefit from the technological advances in the electronics field, there may be employee resistance to change. Uniroyal Inc. hoped to solve its financial woes by closing two of its five U.S. tire-building plants by the summer of 1980, but the plan met resistance from both workers and managers. To overhaul its tire manufacturing and marketing, the company is burdened with the possibility that the United Rubber Workers of America will organize one non-unionized plant.

Organizational change can succeed only if the manager understands the resistances that will be encountered from individuals and the organization. The purpose of this section is to focus on some of those resistances to change. Figure 18.4 lists some reasons why people tend to resist change.

Once an attitude has been established, a person responds to other people's suggestions within the framework of that attitude — a condition known as *selective perception*. Situations may be thought to reinforce the original attitude when actually they do not. Individuals resist the possible impact of change on their lives by reading or listening to what agrees with their present views. People resist change by conveniently forgetting things that support viewpoints they oppose. Many managers who enroll in training programs and are exposed to different managerial philosophies may do very well at discussing and answering questions about these philosophies. But they may carefully segregate in their minds the new approaches, "which of course would not work in my job," from those they are already using.

Employees will usually oppose a change unless they have requested it. Since their status, prestige, or jobs may be (or may seem to be) threatened by the change, employees must be convinced of the need for it. They must see some personal benefit to be gained before they are willing to participate in the change process.

All humans begin life *dependent* on adults. Parents sustain the life of the helpless infant and provide major satisfactions. For this reason, children tend to accept the values, attitudes, and beliefs of their parents. The adult who is highly dependent on others and lacks self-esteem is likely to resist change until significant others endorse it. When Tree-Sweet orange juice hired O. J. Simpson to promote its product, Tree-Sweet's share of the market soared from one-half of one percent to over three percent. The endorsement of a product by a sports celebrity can help overcome resistance to change — the change of trying something new.

In an organization, some workers may be highly dependent on their bosses for feedback on performance. These workers probably will not change to any new techniques or methods unless their bosses personally okay the decision and indicate to them how these changes will improve their performance. In a situation requiring cooperative behaviors — whether it is a workgroup, baseball players, or managers and employees — each person tries to develop a stable work pattern. When these stable patterns are disturbed, people experience stress or an uncomfortable feeling of pressure or dissatisfaction. Under stress, people react emotionally, and because more than one individual is involved, the reactions usually conflict with each other. People get upset and, depending on their individual characteristics, react temperamentally. Joe is angry with Bill, so he does not check with him before starting a new experimental run. Consequently, a special test that should have been conducted in the run is left out, and the whole thing has to be done over.

Resistance to Change by Organizations

Most organizations have been designed to resist innovation.[10] That is, like fully automated factories, organizations have customarily been designed to do a certain few things and do them consistently. To ensure consistency, an organization may create strong defenses against change. Some of these resistances are illustrated in Fig. 18.5.

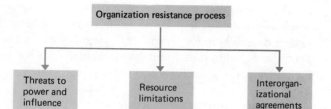

Organizations resist change primarily because they want *stability*. While this is understandable, it is a manager's key job to balance the need for stability against the need for changes. The typical bureaucratic organization narrowly defines jobs, spells out lines of authority and responsibility, and emphasizes the hierarchical flow of information and orders from the top to the bottom. It stresses discipline through the use of rewards and punishments. Novel ideas and/or new uses of resources may be perceived as threats to the internal distribution of power and status. The conservative financial policy of Sewell Avery, Chairman of the Board of Montgomery Ward, immediately after World War II ensured great financial stability. But this drive for economic stability was instrumental in Ward's decline in the merchandising field because it hindered store and merchandise expansions. Any move to change was perceived by Avery as a loss of control over his decision-making power. The goal of financial conservatism tended to discourage any new ventures by Ward's management. On the other hand, Sears, Roebuck assumed that change, in terms of opening new stores in suburban areas and adding new lines of merchandise, was needed to gain a larger share in the market. These different perspectives on stability and change enabled Sears, in 1980, to report sales about four and one-half times Ward's. Comparing A&P and Safeway shows that A&P's strategy was to concentrate in cities and not expand in the suburbs. To maintain this strategy, A&P promoted executives from within the firm. This policy worked for many years and provided A&P with management stability. But as the food store business changed, A&P had to make major organizational changes in order to survive in this highly competitive market. It remains to be seen whether these changes will be enough for the long-term survival of A&P.

Although some organizations emphasize stability, others would change if they had available the *resources* necessary to implement a change. Bethlehem Steel Corporation made a decision to close its Johnstown, Pa. operation rather than spend huge sums of money to comply with the environmental standards proposed by the state and federal governments. Only after the agencies modified their environmental regulations was Bethlehem able to continue its Johnstown operations. Of course, some would say that Bethlehem simply made a power play to get the government to make concessions. Another example is the decline in central business districts. Many firms watch their customers desert them for the greater convenience of suburban shopping centers. Yet the companies find themselves unable to raise the funds needed to provide the public parking facilities and rapid transit systems required to counter this trend.

Resource limitations obviously are not confined to organizations lacking assets. "Rich" organizations may find themselves hard put because they have invested much of their capital in fixed assets (e.g., equipment, building, land, etc.). They may be locked into the present by their assets, for those represent past costs. Companies may decide to terminate all or part of their business rather than put new money into a plant. This is exactly what U.S. Steel did in November of 1979 when it announced the permanent shutdown of 16 plants. The company said the operations were no longer profitable, and it was in the best interests of the stockholders for the company to close them. Although the employees were eligible for many benefits, the 13,000 persons thrown out of work showed much resistance to this particular change.[11]

Interorganizational agreements can create obligations on management that restrain future alternatives. Labor contracts are the most common examples, because some things that were once considered major rights of management (right to hire and fire, assignment of personnel to jobs, promotions, etc.) have now become subjects of negotiation. Labor contracts are not the only kinds of contracts that create obligations for management. Advocates of change may find their plan delayed by arrangements with competitors, commitments to suppliers, pledges to public officials in return for licenses or permits, promises to contractors, and unions. Although agreements can be ignored or violated, legal costs may be expensive, lost customers might be hesitant to buy the product again, and a declining credit rating can be disastrous.

Overcoming Resistances to Change

Not all resistance is bad. It can bring some benefits. Resistance may encourage management to reexamine its change proposals so that it can be sure they are appropriate. In this way, employees operate as a check-and-balance to ensure that management properly plans and implements the change. If reasonable employee resistance causes management to screen its proposed changes more carefully, then employees have discouraged careless management decisions.

Does it follow, then, that managers must forever expect strong resistance when they try to make changes in organizations or individuals? Our answer is no. Resistance to change will probably never cease completely, but managers can learn to succeed and to minimize the resistance by planning the change. Selected activities to overcome resistance are summarized in Fig. 18.6 and are discussed below.

18.6
Selected ways to
overcome resistance to
change
Adapted from K. Davis,
Human Behavior at Work, 6th
ed. New York: McGraw-Hill,
1981, p. 212.

- Use of group norms
- Leadership expectations
- Participation
- Communication about change
- Shared rewards

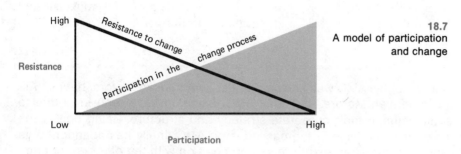

18.7
A model of participation
and change

Effective change focuses on the *group,* rather than on individuals. One's behavior is influenced by the group to which one belongs, so changes in what a group expects of a member will encourage changes in that member's behavior. The idea is to help the group join with management to encourage desired change.

Capable *leadership* reinforces a climate of psychological support for change. The leader presents change on the basis of the requirements of the situation rather than on personal grounds. Change is more likely to be successful if the leaders introducing it have high expectations of success. In other words, expectations of change may be as important as any other effort toward change.

A fundamental way to build support for change is through *participation.* It encourages employees to discuss, to communicate, to make suggestions, and to become interested in change. Participation encourages commitment to the change, rather than mere compliance with it. Commitment implies motivation to support a change and work to assure that it is carried off smoothly. As shown in Figure 18.7, as participation increases, resistance to change tends to decrease. Resistance declines because employees have less cause to resist. Their needs are being considered, so they feel more secure in a changing situation.

Communication is essential to improve the support for change. Even though a change might affect only one or two people in a work group of 10, all of them need to know about the change in order to feel secure and to maintain group cooperation. Management often does not realize that activities that help get change accepted, such as communication and group processes, usually are disrupted by change.

Shared rewards are another way to overcome resistance to change. It is only natural for employees to ask, "What's in it for me?" If they see that a change brings them losses and no gains, they can hardly be enthusiastic about it. Rewards for employees say, "Management cares. We want you to benefit from the change." Rewards also give employees a sense of progress with the change. Both financial and nonfinancial rewards are useful. Employees appreciate a pay increase or promotion, but they also appreciate emotional support, training in new skills, and recognition from management.

CASE STUDY

American Motors Corporation*

Until recently, AMC was known not just as American Motors, but as "Ailing American Motors."[12] Today AMC seems to have recovered due to some shifts in their corporate strategy and structure. Being one of the smallest companies in the car industry, AMC finally has abandoned its long-standing strategy of competing head-on with the other larger companies.

For close to 20 years, AMC was committed to the passenger car industry. This strategy was particularly successful in the early sixties, with the rise in consumer demand for small, efficient cars. Consumers' tastes changed over the years. Unfortunately, AMC's design did not change. As competitors' compact cars became more stylish and powerful, AMC's share of the market decreased. Although they developed some larger models, AMC continued to see themselves as sellers of practical, low-priced cars.

AMC's survival in the mid-seventies actually could be considered lucky. They received a boost from the oil embargo in 1974, when people again wanted energy-efficient cars. By the end of 1976, however, the AMC Hornet and Gremlin were no longer competitive; sales of the larger Matador were falling; and the Pacer, the hope of the 70s, had flopped miserably.

In 1976 AMC had the capacity to produce 450,000 automobiles but built only 332,900 and ended the year with a loss of $46 million. Jeep sales were increasing but not enough to offset car losses. The Jeep Corporation had been purchased from Kaiser in 1970, and sales had been rising each year. At the beginning of 1977, the board of AMC realized that the factors that had caused these losses were not going to disappear. They

---

* This case was prepared by Alan Sweet, Cox School of Business, Southern Methodist University, Dallas, TX, 1980. Materials were taken from *Fortune*, July 16, 1979, and from the *Dallas Morning News*, October 13, 1979.

appointed Gerald C. Meyers to chairman of the board in hopes that he could make the changes that would prevent further losses.

Under Meyers' direction, AMC began to cut back unprofitable car operations and strengthen the specialty vehicle business — the Jeep. The first task was to reduce the costly surplus in passenger cars and to expand Jeep production. During the next year and a half, AMC converted its Brampton, Ontario, plant from passenger car to Jeep production and closed down virtually all of its huge Milwaukee body plant. Car assembly operations were consolidated in one plant at Kenosha, Wisconsin. The Matador line was dropped. AMC had been planning to purchase a 2-liter, 4-cylinder engine designed by Volkswagen, but instead arranged to buy Pontiac's 2.5-liter, 4-cylinder engine. This decision trimmed capital expenditures by $50 million and gave AMC a more suitable engine.

In addition to these production changes, AMC revamped its management structure to focus more closely on operations. Management set up a supply department to coordinate the activities of quality control, new product development, and purchasing. This allowed AMC to use the more than 70 percent of its component parts brought from outside suppliers more efficiently. President W. Paul Tippett, Jr., also formed a new committee whose responsibility was to ''ride herd'' on all new projects. Had this committee existed when AMC introduced the Pacer in 1969, many of the car's problems, such as fuel economy and cost targets, could have been pinpointed earlier.

Meyers also strove to create a strong new management team. In an unprecedented move, he replaced many senior marketing executives with people from outside of the automobile industry. These new employees, who were aggressive, hard-driving opportunists, replaced employees Meyers characterized as ''slow, cautious, nervous, and sometimes even panicky.''

Under this new structure and leadership, Meyers became better able to deal with problems. For example, as soon as orders for the larger model Jeeps began lagging due to the 1979 gas shortage, AMC quickly set up a schedule for closing its Toledo, Ohio, plant. If there were no orders, plants were closed, thus saving monies formerly tied up in large inventories. AMC started new dealership promotions for the Jeep CJ. Advertisements were geared toward the fun-loving — built for fun and tough going: ''We build 'em tough because you play rough.'' These marketing slogans prevented any loss in sales, but AMC did postpone a $30 million conversion of a plant from car to Jeep production due to uncertainties of the oil crisis.

In the future, AMC plans for its jeeps to get 30 percent better gas mileage and a larger overseas market. AMC's 1979 earnings from international markets were five times what they were in 1976, and AMC is forecasting greater growth in this market. In 1978, AMC signed a partnership agreement with France's Regie Nationales Des Usines Renault. This agreement permitted AMC to sell Renaults in its dealerships, and by 1983 it hopes to be producing the "world car." In 1979, AMC moved aggressively into the production of military vehicles and light delivery trucks for the U.S. government and dropped its production of buses. In 1981, AMC planned to market its line of military vehicles overseas, where it is hoping for easier competition and higher profits.

Planning the Change Effort

If a change effort is to be effective, objectives or goals must be stated clearly before the change program is under way. Where possible, the objectives should be stated in measurable terms. The objectives should be (1) based on realistic organizational and employee needs, (2) stated clearly, and (3) consistent with the organization's policies. If an objective of a change program is to help foremen reduce machine downtime, one of the organization's tasks is to train foremen and then delegate maintenance procedures to them. If the change program cannot do this, why undertake it? Many change efforts have failed because the objectives were not stated clearly or understood by all involved.

Managers generally have used two classes of objectives, internal and external, to assess the effectiveness of an organization change program. *Internal objectives* refer to changes that occur within the individual — such as changes in attitudes, improved decision-making ability, increased motivation, and increased job satisfaction. *External objectives* — turnover, grievances, absenteeism, profits, new customers, rate of production — measure changes in behavior on the job. The external objectives attempt to measure directly how the change program affects job behavior. Changes in attitudes, for example, should be related to improved performance before the manager can call the change a success. If the objectives of the change effort are spelled out in this fashion, the sequence of learning activities can be planned, and the most appropriate change strategy can be adopted by the organization.

The Search for Change Strategies

The sixth step is to look for change strategies that management might use. An organization's direction and status are determined by internal and external forces. Successful change can be accomplished only by modifying these forces.

An organization is composed of four interrelated parts — task, structure, people, and technology, as indicated in Fig. 18.8. A change in any one part usually results in a change in one or more of the others. For example, a structural change toward the decentralization of decision-making should result in the assignment of different people to certain organizational tasks. But decentralization of decision-making probably will also change the technology for performing certain tasks, as well as the attitudes and behaviors of the employees performing those tasks. Some change strategies that are appropriate to achieve changes in each part are shown in Table 18.1. We will discuss some of these strategies in the last section of this chapter.

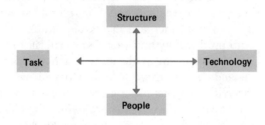

18.8
Forces in organizational change

(From H. Leavitt, "Applied Organizational Change in Industry: Structural, Technological and Humanistic Approaches," in *Handbook of Organizations,* ed. J. March, Chicago: Rand McNally, 1965, p. 1145. Used with permission.)

		18.1
		Strategies Affecting
		Changes in the
Major Emphasis	**Selected Strategies**	*Organization*
Task	Job enrichment Job simplification Team development	
Technology	Modification of production methods Modification of machinery Automation	
People	On-the-job training Management development courses Organizational development programs	
Structure	Change of position descriptions Modification of authority and responsibility relationships Modification of formal reward systems	

Adapted from H. Carlisle, *Management: Concepts and Situations,* Chicago: Science Research Associates, 1976, p. 450.

Implementing and Following the Process

The final step in the change process is to implement and follow the change over a period of time. Designing the change process so the best method can be used requires that the change be sustained over a period of time. The results of a change depend to a considerable extent on how much a manager helps his or her team members to learn and practice their newly acquired skills. The results are also affected by how much and how well the organization reinforces this learned behavior during and after the development effort.

In discussing the planning phase, we indicated that managers often use both internal and external criteria to measure the impact of the change process on the organization. The major source of feedback is the firm's information system. It is quite possible that productivity can increase while morale declines. A manager should not blindly assume that an increase in productivity means an increase in morale. Rather, the change effort should consider both productivity and morale as criteria to be evaluated.

The problem of deciding when the change process has been a success depends on the trend in improvement over a period of time. This trend has three dimensions: (1) the level of satisfaction, productivity, new product development, and market share before the change process begins; (2) the magnitude of the improvement or decline; and (3) the duration of the improvement or decline. Before the program is started, it is critical that the organization establish benchmarks that adequately measure its objectives. This should be done in the diagnostic phase of the change process. A well-designed change process also should specify the magnitude of the change expected and some time period (after the formal change process has been completed) over which the objectives will be measured.

Ideally, the manager should monitor the change process closely. This may be too costly and time-consuming, however, so managers usually measure the change process at predetermined time intervals after the program has been started. One measurement usually is taken immediately after the change. If a "people" change strategy is used, changes in attitudes, knowledge, skills, and the emotional makeup of the employees can be compared against the predetermined objectives of the change program. To avoid relying too much on only temporary changes in attitudes, another measurement of attitudes should be taken later, after the immediate effect of participating in the process has worn off. The second measure will often indicate attitudinal changes the first measure did not reveal. This is because the organization did not have the opportunity to reinforce (or try to eliminate) newly acquired employee attitudes. Participants in a human-relations training program might show an initial increase in their sensitivity to others. Unless the organization reinforces this behavior over a period of time, through salary increases and promotions, the attitudes acquired in the training program are not likely to be permanent.

In the eighth, or follow-up step, the internal objectives are related to the external ones; otherwise, faulty conclusions about the change could be reached. For example, in a large insurance company, the jobs of many of the clerks were enriched (see Chapter 13 "Motivation," for a full discussion of this). The employees indicated greater job satisfaction, but their productivity did not increase. Therefore, the manager must not conclude that the change was entirely successful because non-positive changes in performance occurred. Change-program effectiveness should not be determined only by measures of behavior or measures of performance improvement. Rather, a composite index, made up of both behavioral and performance objectives, should be used. Following up on the change process over a period of time involves measuring both objectives.

Now that we have reviewed the major processes in achieving organizational change, let's turn our attention to the strategies for achieving change and examine the various methods used to achieve change in each strategy. It might be helpful if you tried to work through our model when analyzing the methods used by managers.

STRATEGIES FOR ORGANIZATIONAL CHANGE

The strategies for changing organizations and employees that are considered in the next few pages are representative of the strategies indicated in Table 18.1. Some of the strategies have been woven into previous chapters — such as job enrichment in Chapter 13, MBO in Chapter 6, structural changes in Chapter 8 — and thus will not be discussed at length here. There is no ready-made or agreed-on formula for determining what strategies to use to change the way an organization responds to its environment or change the behavior of its employees. One key managerial concern should be the nature of the problem the organization is attempting to solve. With this in mind, we will discuss change strategies that have been used by managements.

Changing the Technology

There have always been two fundamental ways to widen business profits: by increasing demand for the product, and by reducing unit costs. During the 1960s, when new market horizons seemed boundless, corporations put much of their effort into marketing. Now corporate managers are paying increased attention to reducing costs. Changing the technology of an organization can have far-reaching effects on costs and personnel throughout the organization. Not only are the production people and costs affected by the change, but marketing, industrial engineering, and financial systems are often affected. Let's look at what happened when Corning Glass changed technologies.

CASE STUDY

Corning Glass Works

In 1880, when Thomas A. Edison asked Corning to make him up a batch of glass envelopes that he could fashion into light bulbs, glassmaking was a handicraft.[13] By 1926, a "ribbon" machine was invented to replace hand blowing, and Corning's costs dropped dramatically. Recently, Corning developed an all-electric furnace that has been responsible for further cost reductions.

Thomas MacAvoy, president of Corning, says that most of the gains have come from technology. Productivity in the glass industry has been growing at a three-percent rate throughout the 1970s, but Corning has got its productivity growth up to six percent. According to MacAvoy, "We are always trying to redesign jobs, motivate people, and whatnot, but frankly I don't think people are basically lazy and ineffective. I don't think it's possible to get them to work 20 percent harder. To get them to work smarter is different, and that involves the application of technology."

In Corning's Pressware plant, which makes laminated glass dinnerware, there is a control panel next to the long kilns in which the dinnerware is fired. Because the kiln operators will be working together rather than in separate stations, they will be able to control the flow of production much more smoothly. Further down the line, there are three sets of traffic lights hanging from the ceiling. A green light means that the line is running smoothly; amber advertises the fact that the line needs close inspection because defects were found in some dinnerware, and red is shutdown. The signals are regulated by quality-control inspectors, who used to hand-check each plate, but who now only sample. This new method has led to better quality control and much faster production.

White-collar productivity is also crucial at Corning since the company depends heavily on bright, innovative scientists and engineers. The company hopes to improve the productivity of the corporate engineering people by bringing them together under one roof in a new building. The coffee lounges will be equipped with blackboards to encourage engineers to talk out technical problems. Escalators will be installed instead of elevators to facilitate movement from floor to floor and make face-to-face communication easier.

When the company introduced its new computerized accounting system, it enabled Corning management to regularly measure productivity at each of Corning's 39 plants. This program will tell managers exactly how much productivity they are squeezing out of labor, capital, energy, and materials. These more refined productivity data should help Thomas Howitt, energy expert, control Corning's energy costs. In 1972, Corning's total energy cost was $18 million. If Corning had been operating the same way in 1978, even allowing for a substantial increase in volume, its energy bill would have been $80 million. However, because of technological innovations, its bill was only $56 million. The resulting $24 million was achieved mostly through conversion of glass melting furnaces from natural gas or oil to electric. More energy was saved by such measures as removing fluorescent bulbs in offices and watching room temperatures.

Changing Organizational Structure

Another method of attempting to improve the functioning of the organization is by changing the organization's structure. The restructuring of an organization involves changing the bases of departmentation and coordination. The reasons behind such a reorganization typically include the following:

1. The pressure of competition on margins and profits has put a premium on an efficient organizational structure. Overlapping departments have to be combined, product divisions consolidated, and marginal functions eliminated.

2. The booming international trade market has required more and more companies to change export departments to international divisions, to establish regional management groups, and to restructure the corporate staff.

3. Mergers and acquisitions have generated strong pressures for reorganization in parent companies as well as in newly acquired subsidiaries.

4. New developments in technology often require new organizational arrangements to realize their ultimate potential for improving corporate performance.

CASE STUDY

Bonanza International*

Bonanza International offers a large-scale example of a structural change. Early in 1976, the management of Bonanza, a Dallas, Texas, headquartered restaurant chain specializing in a family priced menu of steaks and hamburgers, recognized there was a problem with their company-owned stores. Bonanza had 241 company restaurants and

* This case was prepared by Joyce Crawford, Cox School of Business, Southern Methodist University, Dallas, TX, in collaboration with Mr. Robert German, Senior Vice-President for Human Resources, and Professor Mick McGill, Cox School of Business, Southern Methodist University, June 1980.

franchised an additional 350 restaurants. Company-owned restaurants were showing higher costs and lower profitability, and restaurant manager turnover was 120 people a year. The cost of replacing each manager was about $15,000. Mr. Robert German, senior vice-president for human resources, was charged by Donald Thompson, President, with redesigning the company's structure.

Donald G. Thompson, President and Chief Executive Officer of Bonanza.

Thompson and German thought there were three main reasons for turnover and cost problems. First, there was poor communication between headquarters and the field. Headquarter's directives were not acted upon by restaurant managers. The restaurant managers identified more readily with the district manager than they did with management in the home office. There were several good reasons for this: (1) All headquarter's information passed through the district managers. (2) The home office did not maintain contact with the individual restaurant manager. (3) Visits from the home office seldom were made to a local restaurant. (4) Restaurant managers had trouble visualizing just what the home office did. Communications were also hindered by the mountains of paperwork and forms the home office piled on the restaurant managers. Because the managers operated on a day-to-day basis, solving crises as they came along, there was not time to plan and respond to these memos. A typical problem involved purchasing. The home office did all the purchasing and then shipped supplies to the restaurants. This was done with no communication with the restaurant manager to find out whether they needed the items and even knew how to use them. Oftentimes the restaurant managers did not even know when they were getting a shipment of supplies.

The second problem was that the whole corporate-field relationship was poor. It was an adversary instead of cooperative one. The district office was more power-oriented than achievement-oriented. Managers throughout the organization did not seem to share the same goals.

The third problem was that individual restaurant managers complained they had no authority but were held accountable for sales. Geographical areas within the United States were divided into districts. District managers had 16 restaurant managers reporting to them, and several area managers (see Fig. 18.9). The area manager was assigned only a few stores. This meant that the area manager dropped by several times a week and conceivably more than once a day to check on the restaurant manager's performance. The restaurant managers felt more like assistants than managers because "big brother" was always around.

Before deciding on a specific structural change, Thompson and German considered four issues: (1) Personnel quality, in the home office and in the field, would not change dramatically over the short run. (2) The number and geographical spread of the restaurants would probably increase or stay the same. (3) Any reorganization would be met with suspicion and mistrust by the restaurant and district managers. (4) The reorganization should be accomplished with no increase in overhead.

District manager suggestions were solicited. Three major themes came out of these discussions. First, the restructuring should provide clear channels of communication from Dallas to the field. Second, goal and

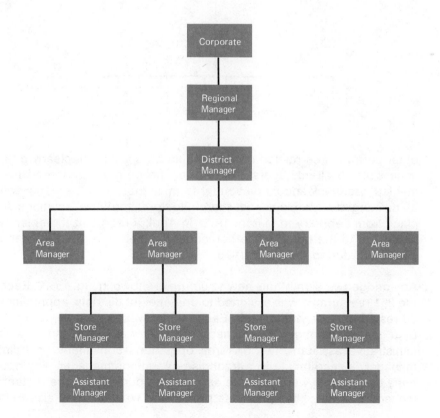

18.9
District organization chart
before 1976 change

18.10
District organization chart
after change

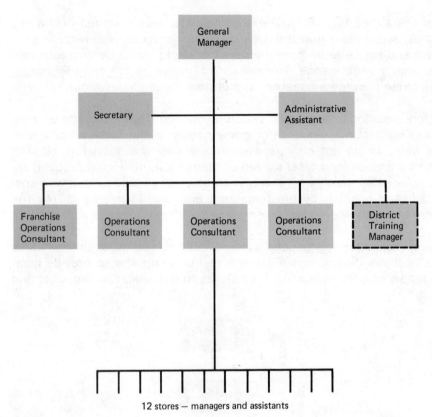

12 stores — managers and assistants

other performance-related criteria should be spelled out clearly and be accessible to all managers. Third, after the program had been implemented, feedback should be sought from all those involved. This action of defining the problem and searching for alternative solutions took place from February to March, 1976. In April, a reorganization plan was presented to the home office personnel for their approval and was implemented during the fall of 1976.

An abridged version of this new structure is shown in Fig. 18.10. Each of the 241 restaurants was assigned to one of eight districts, approximately 30 restaurants in each district. Each district was a profit center headed by a general manager. The general manager was supported by an administrative assistant, two or three operations consultants, a training manager, a secretary, and a franchise operations manager. The operations consultants were to serve as resource persons for the restaurant managers to help them increase profits and volume. They also helped the restaurant managers train new employees, handle personnel problems, and in general, maintain company policies. The absence of the area managers gave the restaurant managers more autonomy and also made them directly responsible and accountable for their restaurant's operations (e.g., hiring, firing, supplies, advertising). Three other support units were formed to help the general managers relate to Dallas. The field information unit was designed to speed up the communications and act as a link between the home office and districts. The field audit unit was responsible for seeing that the standards were upheld. The task force unit was created to facilitate the development of new products, services, policies, and procedures.

The number of people in each district was reduced from 55 to 45. This saved $165,880 in salaries and administrative overhead. It looked as though the areas that needed attention had been solved. The new structure more closely resembled that of other successful operations (e.g., McDonald's, Burger King, Taco Bell, Wendy's) and increased avenues of responsibility and authority for both district and restaurant managers.

By 1978, it was obvious many of the managers at both the district and restaurant level were dissatisfied with this new structure. Many of the managers were not trained to handle the responsibilities of finance, marketing, and personnel because these had been previously handled by the area managers. Profits started to decline and, in 1979, Mr. German recommended Bonanza sell or close all of its company owned restaurants. Today, all Bonanza restaurants are owned and operated under a franchise agreement. On Mr. German's wall now hangs this quote:

> *We trained hard — but it seemed that every time we were beginning to form up into teams we would be reorganized . . . . we tend to meet any new situation by reorganizing, and a wonderful method it can be for creating the illusion of progress while producing confusion, inefficiency, and demoralization.*
>
> Petronius, 210 B.C.

Changing Tasks

Whenever a job is changed — whether because of a new technology, an internal reorganization, or managerial whim — task redesign has taken place. When specific jobs are changed with the intent of increasing both the quality of the employees' work experience and their on-the-job productivity, it is referred to as "job enrichment." The basic strategy has been described in Chapter 13, but we shall review briefly the major points and cite two examples.

There are four unique aspects to the redesign of tasks.[13] First, job enrichment changes the basic relationship between a person and what he or she does on the job. It enables workers to break out of the "givens" in a job. Job enrichment is based on the assumption that work itself may be a very powerful influence on employee motivation, satisfaction, and productivity. Where work may be satisfying only the lower-order needs (or hygiene factors), job enrichment provides a strategy for moving toward satisfaction of higher-order needs (or motivators). Hopefully, the individual will do the work because she or he finds it interesting, challenging, and intrinsically rewarding. Second, task redesign directly changes behavior. The basic objective of job enrichment is to change the behavior of the worker in a way that gradually leads to a more positive set of attitudes about the work, the organization, and the person's own image. Because enriched jobs usually increase feelings of autonomy and personal freedom, the individual is likely to develop attitudes that are supportive of his or her new on-the-job behaviors.

Third, task redesign offers numerous opportunities for initiating other organizational changes. Technical problems are likely to develop when jobs are changed. This offers management an opportunity to refine the work. Interpersonal issues almost inevitably arise between supervisors and subordinates and sometimes among co-workers who have to relate to each other in different ways. These issues offer opportunities for developing new supervisory skills and teamwork. Finally, work redesign can humanize the organization. Job enrichment can help individuals to experience the kick that comes from doing a job well and to care about developing competence in their work. Individuals are encouraged to grow and push themselves.

CASE STUDY

Pet Foods   When plans were being developed for a new plant in the late 1960's, top management at Pet Foods decided to use behavioral science knowledge to design and manage the plant.[14] The physical design and layout of the plant, the type of management style desired, the information and feedback systems, and the compensation systems were all developed on this basis.

A key part of the plan was the development of teams. Each team (consisting of from seven to fourteen workers) was given nearly total responsibility for a significant task. A processing team and a packaging team operated during each shift. The processing team unloaded and stored materials, got materials from storage to mix them into products, and then actually produced the products. The packaging team's responsibilities included the finishing stages of the manufacturing — packaging operations, warehousing, and shipping. In addition to actually carrying out the work required to perform these tasks, team members performed many activities that had been reserved traditionally for management, e.g., solving production problems, assigning team members to jobs, screening and selecting new team members, and counseling those team members who did not meet team standards.

The basic jobs performed were designed to be as challenging as possible, and employees were encouraged to broaden their skills further in order to be able to handle even more challenging tasks. For example, each team member maintains the equipment he or she runs and housekeeps the area in which he or she works. Each team member has the responsibility for performing quality control tests and ensuring that the product meets standards. Pay increases are geared to an employee mastering an increasing number of jobs, first in the team and then in the total plant. Because there are no limits on the number of employees who can qualify for higher pay brackets, employees are encouraged to help each other out. Although not without some problems, the Topeka plant of Pet Foods appears to be profitable, and many employees are having pleasant work experiences for the first times in their lives.

Changing People

The people-oriented approach to change chiefly takes the form of various educational and developmental programs intended to improve one or more of the three basic skills that underlie managerial effectiveness – technical, human, and conceptual. As we indicated in Chapter 1, mastery of technical skills is central to understanding production methods, equipment, work processes, and techniques. Indeed, a worker may well be promoted to first-line supervision because he or she is the most technically qualified worker. To bridge the gap to middle management will require the development of human-relations skills. The employee must be able to show effective interpersonal skills, to work as a team member, and to build cooperation in a group. At the top-management level, the conceptual skill is very important. The members of the top management team must be able to see the organization as a whole and understand how the various functions fit together in relation to the firm's environment.

As we indicated in Chapter 1, these three classes of skills are not mutually exclusive. An effective manager should possess certain technical and human-relations skills as well as conceptual ones, but successful upward movement and performance require a shift in emphasis. Various programs exist for developing these three skills.

**Organization
Development**

Organization development (OD) refers to a variety of behavioral-science approaches used to move organizations toward more open and honest communication among individuals and groups.[15] Essential to organization development is the acquisition of self-critical attitudes toward present policies, procedures, and behavioral patterns. Members of the developed organization are, ideally, more open, explicit, and direct in their dealing with one another.

Organization development can be achieved by a variety of methods and techniques. Approaches to redesigning work that were described early in this chapter, and also in Chapter 13, can rightfully be called OD techniques because they enable an organization to resolve behavioral problems that are negatively affecting its overall effectiveness. The approach to organization development we will discuss is the Managerial Grid.

We wish to caution you, however, that not all activities given the label OD refer to the types of activities described in the following pages. Many industrial organizations (such as TRW Systems, Exxon, Corning Glass Works, ARCO, Mack Trucks, Frito-Lay, Southland, and Shell Oil Corporation) have OD units within their personnel departments that may or may not conduct OD sessions as we shall describe. Some of these personnel departments are involved essentially in labor planning, career planning, pensions, and other employee-related benefits.

The Managerial Grid   Since the early 1960s, the Managerial Grid has been used by nine of the 10 largest corporations in the world and has widespread application throughout the world.[16] The Grid technique assumes that it is possible for managers and the organizations of which they are members to maximize both production and concern for human values. That is, it assumes that organizational and individual goals are compatible rather than at odds.

The Grid is a graphic representation of five styles of managerial behavior. These styles are based on two key variables — concern for production, or output, and concern for people. These two variables and some of their possible combinations are shown in Fig. 18.11. The number one (1), represents minimum concern on the scale; the nine (9), maximum concern.

The lower left corner (1,1) indicates a person with minimum concern for both people and production. This managerial style is characterized by withdrawal from the organization; the manager is simply a communication link between the subordinates and higher management. Production will be limited, because it is assumed that people don't want to work and there is little reward attached to work accomplished with others.

The upper left (1,9) represents minimum concern for production and maximum concern for people. Here the manager assumes that production requirements are not compatible with the needs of people and therefore are secondary to people considerations. Human relationships are an end in themselves. It is assumed that if people are made comfortable and secure in a

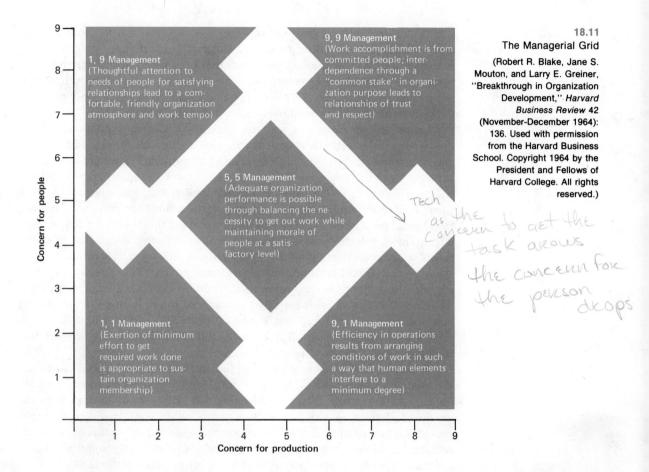

18.11
The Managerial Grid

(Robert R. Blake, Jane S. Mouton, and Larry E. Greiner, "Breakthrough in Organization Development," *Harvard Business Review* 42 (November-December 1964): 136. Used with permission from the Harvard Business School. Copyright 1964 by the President and Fellows of Harvard College. All rights reserved.)

The grid labels read:

- **1, 9 Management** (Thoughtful attention to needs of people for satisfying relationships lead to a comfortable, friendly organization atmosphere and work tempo)
- **9, 9 Management** (Work accomplishment is from committed people; interdependence through a "common stake" in organization purpose leads to relationships of trust and respect)
- **5, 5 Management** (Adequate organization performance is possible through balancing the necessity to get out work while maintaining morale of people at a satisfactory level)
- **1, 1 Management** (Exertion of minimum effort to get required work done is appropriate to sustain organization membership)
- **9, 1 Management** (Efficiency in operations results from arranging conditions of work in such a way that human elements interfere to a minimum degree)

Concern for people (vertical axis, 1–9)
Concern for production (horizontal axis, 1–9)

[handwritten note: Tech as the concern to get the task grows the concern for the person drops]

warm way, production will take care of itself. Conflict is avoided or smoothed over by not pressuring people.

The lower right corner (9,1) represents maximum concern for production and minimum concern for people. People are viewed as instruments of the task, and human interactions are minimized. This management style also assumes that people basically resist production. Unlike the 1,9 manager, however, the 9,1 manager exerts heavy pressures and controls on people to get high production.

At the center point (5,5), the management style balances the concerns for production and people. Decisions are made by compromise and guided by precedents. This management style also assumes that there is conflict between the needs of people and production. The manager resolves this conflict through splitting the difference, compromise, and similar measures.

The upper right corner (9,9) represents a high concern for both production and people. According to the Managerial Grid, it represents the ideal managerial style. This manager assumes that people are basically mature and responsible and, if given rewarding work to which they are committed, will produce at maximum level. This manager basically believes that the needs of the organization and its members are compatible.

There are six phases of grid development. The educational content of Phase 1 includes self-evaluation forms, placing oneself on the "Grid," and organizational problem-solving exercises. The problems typically attempt to simulate organizational conditions in which interpersonal behavior affects task performance. To simulate organizational life, teams of from five to nine members, representing all levels of the organization, are formed. They are responsible for developing solutions and improving their own problem-solving effectiveness. Effectiveness is measured against objective standards. After the teams have been informed of their performance, the members return to their separate rooms and critique their operational effectiveness. Weaknesses and strengths are identified and analyzed. Plans for increasing effectiveness are introduced. This process is repeated throughout the first phase, emphasizing learning through critique. Thus, Phase 1 creates the readiness to really work with the human problems of production, and is not intended to produce immediate organizational improvement.

Phases 2 and 3 concentrate on the application of behavioral-science knowledge to teamwork and intergroup development. The most common barriers to increasing team effectiveness are failure to fully communicate, improper planning, unwillingness to listen to others' opinions, and interpersonal friction. Improvement in behavioral skills is necessary to overcome these problems. In these phases, each member analyzes the climate and problems of the team and proposes solutions. Each member makes a self-evaluation of his or her job performance and that of others on the team. The team then discusses these problems and develops its own solutions. Each member of the team attends at least two team meetings, playing a subordinate's role in one meeting and a superior's role in the other. The focus is on improving relationships between groups, among people at the same level, and between superiors and subordinates. For example, although competitiveness may increase organizational effectiveness, it may also cause departmental goals to be placed ahead of more important organizational goals. A goal of these phases is to avoid the "win-lose" pattern of problem-solving and to introduce joint problem-solving activity, in which both teams benefit.

The fourth phase stresses organizational goals that require commitment at all levels of the organization. Goals discussed in this phase pertain to union-management relations, basic policy development, safety, promotions, and determining the proper structure of the organization. The specific goals to be introduced are identified by the teams. Departmental groups may also help to define goals and problems.

The final phase of the developmental process is stabilization. During this phase, the organization must be supportive of the changes brought about in the earlier phases. These changes are assessed and reinforced so that there will be no slipping back to the original condition.

The final success of Phase 5, implementation of the corporate model for effectiveness, is based on the quality and character of the achievements resulting from all of the preceding phases. At this point, behavioral theories have been understood, communication roadblocks removed, and a full understanding of and commitment to corporate excellence obtained. The manager's primary goal is to help achieve the goals established during Phase 4 and also recognize previously undefined problems.

The effectiveness of the Grid Organization Development program is open to question. Although many corporations — such as British-America Tobacco Company, Texas Instruments, Pillsbury, Charles Pfizer and Company, Union Carbide and Company, and Honeywell, among others — have participated in the Grid program, its effectiveness has not been tested rigorously. In many of the reported studies using the Grid approach, the exact causes of the changes were not reported, nor was the effect of any particular phase of the change program evaluated for its contribution to the total change. Productivity, profits, and attitudes have been shown to improve in some companies where the executives participated in the program. In these companies, more time was spent on team problem-solving, where managers became aware of the alternatives available for solving managerial problems. Similarly, subordinates have reported that their managers became more understanding of their problems. However, changes in attitudes and knowledge of behavioral concepts do not necessarily lead to positive changes in performance.[17]

SUMMARY

This chapter has focused on several universal change-related issues. One is that organization change has two objectives — adapting to the environment and changing the behavior of employees in the organization. An eight-step model for organizational change can be used to show that the firm's external environment, its internal structure, and its organizational climate need systematic analysis by a manager. The manager often is aware of the need for change because of the performance gap, or the difference between what the organization *could do* with its market opportunities and what it actually *does* with those opportunities. As in the Bonanza case, not all organization change is received warmly by employees. Change efforts may be resisted by employees and even by the entire organization. Once the reasons for resistance have been explored, management must plan the change strategy and examine the available alternative strategies.

We identified four change strategies. A *technology* strategy focuses on change in workflows, methods, materials, and information systems, as might occur in most companies. The *organizational-structure* strategy emphasizes the internal changes that are brought about by the manager who is performing his or her decisional role. In this role the manager is constantly on the lookout for new ideas and anticipating the consequences of action undertaken. *Task strategies* focus on specific job activities that have been changed to increase both the quality of the employees' work experience and their on-the-job productivity. Pet Foods used job enrichment to increase employees' job satisfactions and productivity. *People* strategies usually are directed toward improving communications and relations among individuals and groups to achieve increased organizational effectiveness. The Managerial Grid is a people-oriented strategy.

The manner by which managers diagnose problems, and how accurately they recognize the need for change, will affect the change process. The success of a change program depends largely on the current levels of dissatisfaction with the firm, support by top management for the change effort, and the correct diagnosis of the sources of resistance to the change effort. In successful programs, those directly affected by the change are generally involved in the process from the start. If change is successful, individual goals, social ties, and economic rewards may be altered. Any alteration of the steps in the change process should involve all the employees who will be affected by that alteration. Otherwise it may not be possible to accomplish the overall objectives of the change program.

KEYWORDS

external forces to change
external objectives
fire-fighting
future shock
internal objectives

managerial grid
organization development
performance gap
resistance

DISCUSSION QUESTIONS

1. Why do organizations change?

2. What are some of the external pressures faced by top management?

3. What are attributes of an organization's climate? How do these relate to change?

4. Why do organizations resist change?

5. Why do people resist change?

6. What factors influence whether or not a manager sees a performance gap?

7. Review your understanding of the change model by using it to evaluate a change that you implemented recently in your approach to getting a college degree.

8. Discuss the forces and strategy involved in determining and implementing large-scale organization changes.

9. Which step in the change process is the most difficult and most likely to be ignored by management because of its difficulty? Why?

10. What are the assumptions of organization development?

11. What are the differences between the "people" and "structural" change strategies?

12. What are the major differences between a successful and unsuccessful change program?

13. Do the five things listed under "Learning Objectives" at the beginning of this chapter.

Management Incidents and Cases

PEOPLE'S PLUMBING

People's Plumbing is a West Coast manufacturer of do-it-yourself plumbing kits sold in convenience hardware stores throughout the western United States. The products of People's Plumbing fall into four categories: toilets, sinks, faucets, and outdoor sprinklers. The company is now operating in the manner described below.

At the small production facility, workers assembling kits in each of these four areas draw from a common parts bay, where the requisite pipe joints, washers, and such are manufactured and warehoused. Each product line uses basically the same parts, although some are cut to different dimensions and specifications. It is the responsibility of the manufacturing center to plan its activities so that no product line runs short of those parts needed for kit assembly. Such shortages could cause slowdowns and in some instances force a line to shut down. From even this simplified description it is obvious that workers in the individual product lines are completely dependent on the manufacturing center.

Of the four product lines, sprinkler kits have the greatest demand and the highest profit margin, followed by the faucets, sinks, and toilet kits, in that order. Production priorities in the manufacturing center follow the same order. Since the manufacturing center gives priority to the providing of parts for the faucet and outdoor sprinkler groups, the sink and toilet production groups frequently run out of the parts they need. This leads to a great deal of intergroup competition. In some instances, production materials are stolen and there are even suspected cases of sabotage of rival product lines. Morale among workers in the low-priority product lines is very low and turnover among all employees is quite high.

In assessing the situation, management decides to solve the problem by buying additional production equipment, and a consultant is hired to do a feasibility study of such a capital investment. The equipment is purchased but the overall situation does not improve.

Questions

1. What are the problems at People's Plumbing?

2. What are some of the factors influencing the resistance to change?

3. How can these be overcome?

4. What would you recommend that the president of People's do to correct the problems you identified?

CANYON CREEK ENGINEERING

Canyon Creek Engineering, a division of American Engineering, has its main office in Plano, a suburb of Dallas, Texas. About 3000 people are currently employed at this office. The work force is equally divided between engineering groups and support groups, such as accounting, computer operations, personnel, quality and cost control, and construction. Canyon Creek is heavily committed to the design and construction of power plants of various sizes and types and requires large commitments of manpower for long periods of time to design and build a plant. It bids on contracts 10 years into the future. The division is organized under a matrix structure, whereby all performance for a project is under the direction of one project manager. The division has grown rapidly in recent years because of its ability to engineer power plants that use either coal, oil, or nuclear and solar sources of energy. Because of the demand for its products, Canyon Creek has increased the number of its personnel about 30 percent per year. This has resulted in physical crowding in the current building, necessitating the commitment to build new, larger facilities, which are about two years from completion. This overcrowding has caused frequent relocation of personnel from floor to floor, resulting in confusion and almost amusing states of chaos. Departmental lines are strong, arising from the complete isolation of project personnel from one another; even the different engineering groups are departmentally isolated from one another. All of this has led to a major duplication of effort, not only in the engineering groups but in the support groups as well.

This duplication of effort and the presence of strong departmental lines are especially obvious to one who works in the support groups. If someone in engineering design notes that a particular task has already been performed by the engineering system group, it is considered of little importance, since the regenerating of the task becomes necessary to maintain departmental autonomy. This is an indication that the departments are highly competitive and do not wish to compromise their control of any activity. The rationale is that because each project is "cost-plus" this type of activity only tends to increase profits for the entire division and is therefore encouraged by all managers.

Max Richards, manager of the computer center, has indicated that this attitude (passing everything on to the customer) has created some major problems for the computer center. For example, when the assistance of the computer center was requested by the solar engineering group, the computer center's activities were dictated to the point where the solar group was requesting programs and statistical procedures that it was unqualified to use. Max indicates that this procedure has alienated his group and most of the engineering groups. He believes that each engineering group is foolishly trying to preserve its complete control over the center's activities. Moreover, he feels that other support groups (accounting, personnel) are often extremely limited in their own activities. Since they have to perform their duties within the constraints imposed by the engineering departments, they often feel they are not doing a job from which the entire division would benefit. As a result, morale in the computer group is low, turnover is high, and people are spending most of their time griping about the problems.

Questions

1. What are the problems facing Canyon Creek Engineering? Can you draw an organizational chart?

2. Do you foresee any changes in the external environment of the division that it should be aware of?

3. What type of change strategy would you recommend?

4. What types of resistance might you find when attempting to create this change? By whom?

REFERENCES

1. M. Ways, "The era of radical change." *Fortune* **79**, 1964, 113.

2. A. Toffler, *Future Shock.* New York: Random House, 1970.

3. C. Varkonyi, "Computer Checkout Debuts in Coopersburg." *Centre Daily Times*, December 27, 1976.

4. "Changing Consumer Preferences." *Business Week*, November 19, 1979, 52ff.

5. *Business Week*, February 4, 1980, 38.

6. *Business Week*, January 29, 1979, 37.

7. *Time*, October 8, 1979, 30; *Business Week*, February 4, 1980, 38.

8. *Business Week*, February 4, 1980, 38.

9. *Business Week*, September 10, 1979, 112ff; *Wall Street Journal*, July 13, 1979, 3; June 26, 2; and June 6, 1.

10. G. Zaltman, R. Duncan, and J. Holbeck, *Strategies for Planned Change.* New York: Wiley Interscience, 1977, pp. 94–103.

11. *Dallas Morning News*, November 28, 1979, 16.

12. *Fortune*, July 16, 1979, and *Dallas Morning News*, October 13, 1979.

13. E. Meadows, "How three companies increased their productivity." *Fortune*, March 10, 1980, 93–101.

14. R. Walton, "Work Innovations in the United States." *Harvard Business Review* **57,** 1979, 88–98.

15. E. Huse, *Organization Development and Change.* St. Paul, MN: West Publishing Company, 1980.

16. R. Blake and J. Mouton, *The Managerial Grid.* Houston, TX: Gulf, 1965.

17. A. Filley, R. House, and S. Kerr, *Managerial Process and Organizational Behavior.* Glenview, IL: Scott Foresman, 1976, pp. 505–506.

Chapter 19

CHALLENGES TO MANAGEMENT IN THE 1980s

After reading this chapter, you should be able to:

1. Describe the three stages of organizational growth.

2. Identify the problems of a multinational organization.

3. Describe changes in values.

4. Identify the basic changes in the make-up of the workforce.

5. Explain why Honda has been successful while the overall automotive market was declining.

6. Explain how the role of the federal government will affect organizations in the 1980s.

PREVIEW CASE

Standard Oil of Ohio*

In 1969 the Standard Oil Company of Ohio (SOHIO) and six other large oil companies, who would later form the ALYESKA Pipeline Service Company, began what was eventually to become the largest business venture ever undertaken by private enterprise. The eight hundred mile pipeline was planned to eventually carry 1.2 million barrels of crude oil a day from Alaska's North Slope to the Port of Valdez on its south coast. The original plan called for the oil to be transported by tanker to the California coast, where it would be unloaded and either refined or moved through a pipeline system to refineries lying east of the Rocky Mountains. These refineries have the greatest shortage of crude oil and represent 65 percent of the industry's total refining capacity.

SOHIO executives originally estimated that the Trans-Alaska Pipeline System (TAPS) would be completed by 1973 and would cost approximately $900 million. By mid-1977 TAPS was finally completed at a cost of more than $9 billion, ten times the original estimate. There were many reasons for the increased cost. Because of environmental and other concerns, construction of the pipeline was delayed until it was specifically authorized by Congress in 1973, after the Arab oil embargo. Because of increased equipment costs, the size of the line was doubled. There were endless hassles with regulatory bodies, delays due to weather, technical foul-ups, and accidents. An important cost factor was the need to protect the fragile Arctic environment — including the caribou and moose migration patterns and the fish streams.

Financing was hard to get, partly because of the uncertainties of the project and partly because it was not clear where the oil would actually go. A number of major institutional investors chose not to participate in the TAPS financing. Some investors were concerned about the risk that the government would not permit Alaskan crude oil to compete with the world oil in the marketplace and thus would limit the rate of return the oil companies could pay their investors.

When the pipeline finally opened in 1977, the destination of the oil it would carry was still uncertain. There was a glut of oil on the West Coast, and permits to build a new terminal and connecting links to existing pipelines were still not available. Alternatives included selling the oil to Japan or shipping it to the Gulf Coast by tanker through the Panama Canal, which would be more expensive than a pipeline.

In Alaska, there appeared to be evidence that many environmental concerns were justified. There were reports that ALYESKA had frequently violated state and federal environmental rules agreed to when the right-of-way lease agreement was signed in 1974. Apparently, the pipeline took priority over the environment. For example, nearly 40 percent of the moose and caribou crossings built in 1975 were reported to be too low or wrongly located. Reports of environmental damage include erosion of tundra, water pollution resulting from improperly run sewage treatment plants, massive oil spills at construction sites, damage to fish spawning beds, and blocked fish streams. Some problems had been corrected, but it was too early to know just how permanent and serious the overall environmental impact would be, especially on wildlife and fish.[1]

The Trans-Alaskan Pipeline System is a good example of the types of problems that will face managers of the 1980s. This chapter will suggest that challenges to management will arise from three general areas: organizationally related forces (e.g., growth and technology); people-related forces (e.g., values and workforce composition); and politically related forces (e.g., governmental regulation and international competition). You will be spending more and more of your time trying to handle these challenges.

**MANAGING IN THE
CHANGING WORLD**

The world is changing continually — politically, socially, and technologically — and these changes seem to have accelerated in recent years. Alfred P. Sloan, past president of General Motors, has said, "To deliberately stop growing is to suffocate." What Sloan is telling us is that if managements are to survive in an ever-changing world, they must be aware of the changes taking place in the business world. Although the exact meaning of "change" is hazy, certainly increases in the sheer size of an organization may be one indicator that change has taken place. The hospital that has added beds, nurses, or patients treated per year apparently is growing. Kodak Company's introduction of an instant automatic camera similar to Polaroid's, coupled with extensive advertising campaigns and active research and development programs, may indicate that Kodak is changing and growing. Other companies with extraordinary growth are the franchises (such as McDonald's, Pizza Hut, Midas Muffler, Burger King, Kentucky Fried Chicken, Holiday Inn, and Radio Shack) and the conglomerates (Gulf & Western, United Technologies, Transamerica). A **conglomerate** is a company that runs several companies in unrelated industries.

**Expansion of
Organizations**

One of the most relevant considerations for tomorrow's managers is the expansion of most organizations. Organizations of today are larger than those of yesterday, and tomorrow's organizations will be even larger. As organizations grow, they require different managerial practices and structures. Let's look at how the Coca-Cola Company grew through various changes.

CASE STUDY

Coca-Cola*

When the Coca-Cola Company was first formed in 1892, the drink had already been sold at drugstore soda fountains, originally as a headache remedy, since 1886.[2] Asa G. Candler, first president of the new company, planned to continue selling the drink only at soda fountains. Benjamin Thomas, a southern lawyer serving as chief clerk in the office of the Assistant Army Quartermaster during the Spanish-American War, had noticed the brisk sales of bottled carbonated pineapple drinks to American soldiers stationed in Cuba. Thomas presented the idea of selling bottled Coke to Candler, but Candler was not interested. Candler sold the exclusive rights to distribute bottled Coca-Cola in the United States to Thomas and his partner for one dollar.

---

* Adapted from M. Hooper, *The Coca-Cola Company*, unpublished manuscript, Edwin L. Cox School of Business, Southern Methodist University, Dallas, TX, 1980, and correspondence from A. Vitale, Corporate Communications Department, The Coca-Cola Company, March 1981.

Thomas and his partner realized that they personally could not establish bottling plants throughout the entire country. They subcontracted the exclusive right to bottle Coke to franchise managers in different regions.

As the sale of Coke skyrocketed, Candler began to realize the value of the franchising system and started repurchasing the bottling rights. In 1919, the Candler interests sold The Coca-Cola Company to Atlanta banker Ernest Woodruff and an investor group he had organized. In the mid-1920s the Company moved into the international market, exporting syrup concentrate to be processed overseas. Today, Coke issues all franchises, and the business has grown to the point where sales exceed $4 billion annually and with operations in more than 150 countries.

When Thomas and his partner initiated the franchise system, they probably had no idea of what a clever organizational scheme they had devised. The *franchiser (The Coca-Cola Company) licenses others (franchisees) to sell its products.* Usually each franchisee pays an initial fee and yearly sums for the right to use the trade name and to get managerial and financial help. In return, franchisees can be sure of getting a standardized product from the parent company. The major advantage for the franchiser is that a franchise can be withdrawn if the performance slips or the rules and regulations established by the parent company are not followed. According to Paul Austin, former chairman of the board for The Coca-Cola Company, when a franchise is in the hands of competent and motivated managers, it is the greatest distribution system there is for a large corporation.

The Coca-Cola Company divides the world into three parts, with an executive vice-president in charge of each. One part includes operations in the United States and Central and South America. Another involves Europe, Africa, Southeast Asia, and the Indian subcontinent. The third is Canada, the Pacific, and the Far East. In the United States, there are 16 syrup distribution outlets geographically organized to serve the 1500 bottling plants. This organizational structure has not changed much since 1923.

The Coca-Cola Company has maintained its number-one position by being a good community citizen, studying the market, and diversifying into other product lines. The Company strongly encourages bottlers to show interest in their community by working on hospital drives, sponsoring little league teams, and by joining the local Chamber of Commerce and other local community groups. From its start, the Company has been associated with religious institutions and has used its earnings

AFTER
EXERCISE
DRINK
DELICIOUS *Coca-Cola* REFRESHING

5¢ AT ALL FOUNTS 5¢
AND SOLD IN BOTTLES

A 1905 magazine
advertisement for
Coca-Cola.

Photo courtesy of The
Coca-Cola Company.

to further develop Emory University, a Methodist college in Atlanta.
Rarely is Coke advertised as a mixer for rum and bourbon.

The Coca-Cola Company also has been innovative and quick to recognize changes in the market. For the past 20 years the United States has had a bountiful supply of consumers between the ages of 13 and 24. Today, there are nearly 49 million people in this age group. These are the lifeblood of the soft-drink industry. On the average, each person in this age group drinks 823 cans or bottles of soft drinks a year, while the average for all age groups is only 547. During the 1980s, however, there will be four million fewer in the 13–24 age group, and this means a potential decline of 3.3 billion units, if the ratio of consumption by age groups remains unchanged. Since the Company generates 95 percent of its revenues from its drinks, it has begun to diversify into other product lines. It purchased Taylor & Great Western Wines, Minute Maid, Maryland Club Coffee, Snow-Crop, Butter-Nut, and Aqua-Chem, a division that designs and manufactures equipment for desalting sea water.

Growth is a consequence of success. If a business earns a profit and makes the proper strategic choices, then growth is possible. As organizations grow, they go through certain obvious **growth stages:**[3] the number of employees increases along with other resources; activities and functions increase in size, scope, and number; management problems grow in scale and complexity. We can analyze how The Coca-Cola Company has expanded by examining the characteristics of company growth listed in Table 19.1.

Stages of Growth

In Stage 1, the first problem is determining the specific niche in the market the organization is to fill. If this is done properly, the organization can survive. The central function of management is to bring people with different skills and abilities together to get the work done. All employees work for the individual who founded the company. Control systems are simple and highly personal. The structure of the organization is relatively informal, with few written rules and procedures. Most decisions are made on an ad-hoc basis, with little formal strategic planning, such as Candler selling Thomas the exclusive U.S. rights to bottle Coke for one dollar.

Stage 2 presents different problems, and the managerial approach to solve them is different. This stage usually means the Company has a steadily growing, or perhaps diversified, product line and a growing market for its products. Managing for survival is not necessary. After 1906 Candler saw a tremendous demand for Coke. He saw the success of the franchise management system begun by Thomas. Coke was being sold throughout the United States. With the repurchase of the bottlers from Thomas and his partner, Candler no longer knew the intimate details of the organization. A second-level of management was needed as the organization required specialists in marketing, financing, production, purchasing, and personnel. The control function changed from being rather personal to one being carried out through the establishment of policies and rules.

Planning also changed. Rather than immediate and ad-hoc planning that characterized The Coca-Cola Company's first stage, planning was now more formalized. Long-range plans were needed. This implementation was done through the specialists in the management hierarchy.

At Stage 3, the problems shift again. The major problem is allocation of resources between multiple product lines (Taylor and Great Western Wines, Aqua-Chem, etc.) serving a varied set of customers in different countries. Dealing in the multinational market requires decisions and strategies considerably different from those made when the Company was operating only in the United States. For example, when The Coca-Cola Company gave an Israeli firm a franchise to bottle Coke in Israel,

19.1 Managing Different-Sized Companies

Characteristics of Company Growth

Organization characteristic	Patterns of the first stage	Patterns of the second stage	Patterns of the third stage
Major problem	Survival	Management of growth	Allocation and control of resources
Product line	Single	Single product in multiple geographical markets	Multiple product lines; multiple geographical markets
Distribution	One channel	One set of channels	Multiple channels
Organization structure	Little or no formal structure, a 'one-man' show	Specialization based on function	Specialization based on product-market relationships
Level of management	Two	At least three	At least four
Control systems	Personal control of both strategic and operating decisions and survival in marketplace	Personal control of strategic decisions, with increasing delegation of operating decisions	Profit centers, with delegation of product-market decisions to businesses, and 'results' oriented
Strategic choice	Needs of founders vs. needs of company	Breadth of product-line market-share objective	Entry and exit from industries; rate of growth; allocation of resources by industry
President's job	Direct supervision of employees	Managing specialized managers	Managing generalist managers

Adapted from J. Child, *Organization: A Guide to Problems and Practice.* London: Harper & Row, Ltd., 1977, pp. 150–151; and H. Mintzberg, *The Structuring of Organizations.* Englewood Cliffs, NJ: Prentice-Hall, 1979, pp. 242–248.

Coke was boycotted in Arab countries. Since the Company also owns Aqua-Chem, more was at stake because Saudi Arabia planned to spend several billion dollars desalting water over the next few years. What should the Company have done? India posed a different problem. The Indian government insisted that multinationals transfer some knowledge and ownership to Indian firms. The Coca-Cola Company refused to reveal its secret formula to any firm, and this decision meant losses in the potentially lucrative Indian market.

The structure of the Company has changed from a functional to product form. Different product lines now are profit centers, responsible for marketing, manufacturing and distribution of their own products. With permission from top management, managers of these product lines can purchase other firms that fit the business strategy. To coordinate these diverse product lines, planning is now highly formalized. Planning departments are established in each product line to assist both top management of the product line and The Coca-Cola Company's managers at headquarters. Policies and procedures are established by management at headquarters to maintain common practices among the various product line groups.

Change in Goals

Changes in organizational growth have caused firms to shift their goals. The goals of hospitals, for example, have undergone a steady transformation. In earlier times, a hospital's goal was to care for the poor and sick who could not afford private medical assistance. During the last century, hospitals changed this goal to place greater emphasis on preventive treatment. Today the objectives of hospitals typically emphasize quality care, the coordination of various activities of the physician and hospital staff, and the recruitment of physicians oriented to hospital practice. Hospitals also have expanded their range of influence by undertaking to maintain optimum health-care service for all people in the community rather than simply the care of individual patients. Similarly, the modern prison has expanded its scope to include not only activities related to prisoner confinement, but the training and rehabilitation of prisoners as well.

**THE
MULTINATIONAL
CORPORATION**

As we discussed in Chapter 4, development of the multinational corporation has significantly changed the operation of many companies. A *multinational corporation* is one with its headquarters in one nation but its operations in many countries.[4] These corporations came into existence during the 1960s, when it became profitable for American firms, such as IBM, Singer Company, Colgate-Palmolive, Heinz, and Hoover, to cross international boundaries. Approximately 6000 American corporations currently operate in foreign countries, and virtually every large corporation has overseas operations. Corning Glass Works, for example, has plants in Mexico, France, Japan, India, Brazil, and Italy. In the past few years, Volkswagen and several Japanese firms have opened plants in the United States.

Multinational corporations have expanded for many reasons, including:

1. An expanding world population desiring a higher standard of living.

2. High transportation costs prohibiting the long-distance shipping of many products.

3. The easier establishment of new markets which offset domestic markets saturated with a product.

4. International laws facilitating world trade.

5. Increased world demand and higher personal incomes.

Foreign operations can create major headaches for the multinational firm. John Deere & Company, a farm machinery manufacturer with sales of more than $1 billion and more than 5200 dealers, expanded into the European market in 1964.[5] Subsequently, Deere built factories in France, Argentina, Germany, Spain, Mexico, Africa, Venezuela, Brazil, and Japan. While Deere's share of the market is estimated to be around $150 million annually, the move into the international market has not been without problems. For instance, in France, government-owned Renault dominates the market and is satisfied to break even and create jobs. In Argentina, currency inflation took a big toll, resulting in an $11.6 million loss in 1979. In Japan, Deere had to strike up a partnership with Yanmar Diesel to build small tractors because of high tariffs on imported machinery. To keep its international dealers abreast of the latest developments, the company spent close to $3 million in September 1979 to bring all 1400 of its foreign dealers and 1600 of their staff to the company headquarters in Moline, Illinois. In groups of 350, dealers were shuffled between sprawling farms and presentations at headquarters in French, Spanish, German, and English. Early in 1980, Deere took trainloads of new farm equipment through the European countryside to introduce farmers to their new line of tractors.

CHANGES IN VALUES   Daniel Yankelovich, president of Yankelovich, Skelley, and White, Inc., a public opinion research firm specializing in probing changes in basic values of Americans, says the productivity of the American worker is declining.[6] He sees the major factor contributing to this decline as a changing American attitude toward work, while also recognizing changes in the economic, political and legal system of the United States. In the 1960s, 50 percent of the workers he surveyed throughout the United States saw work as a source of personal fulfillment. Today, only 25 percent agree with this view. In the 1960s, 58 percent agreed with the statement, "Hard work always pays off." Today, only 43 percent agree with it. Today, only 13 percent of the workforce sees work as more meaningful than leisure.

Many managements have continued to stick by the conventional wisdom that to make an organization successful, capital investment, technology, and management systems are more important than people. But the American workforce is seeing a growing mismatch between incentives and motivations. Values and attitudes have changed faster. If management is to increase worker productivity, it will have to find new ways to balance this mismatch. Managers need to find an incentive system consistent with the workers' new values and attitudes toward work.

There are four major "old incentives" which organizations have used in the past to motivate workers. These four, according to Yankelovich, are (1) fear, (2) a reliance on automation to minimize the human factor, (3) money, and (4) the desire to do a good job. Unfortunately, there are limitations to these "old incentives." First, workers today are not as fearful of losing their jobs because unemployment compensation and other benefits act as a financial cushion. As more and more households have two wage-earners, the loss of one wage-earner is not as drastic. A job loss no longer strikes masculinity as it once did. Second, many companies (e.g., Ford, General Motors) saw automation, or minimization of the human element, as one way to increase productivity. However, since about 70 percent of the workforce is in some service industry, intangibles, such as dedication, caring, and responsibility for doing a real service, can be achieved only when people are motivated to work.

Third, in inflationary periods, pay raises do not make a very effective incentive. With inflation near or in double-digit figures, many companies cannot give employees big enough raises to counteract inflation, let alone reward them by merit increases.

Fourth, the **work ethic,** or the desire to do a good job, is something the worker brings — or does not bring — into the workplace. It is not something that can be created on the job. Management can no longer assume, as it did in the past, that workers will have this work ethic when they enter the organization.

Yankelovich divides the population into two groups. The first group consists of workers still motivated effectively by the old incentives. The mismatch between the incentives and these workers' values and attitudes is not severe. About 56 percent of the workforce fall into this group. This group is divided into three subgroups: (1) the poor and older workers who look at work as a habit — traditionalists who accept the guidelines and enjoy their job security;

(2) the positively work-oriented, who are close to management's ideal of hard workers, who are committed to work, who "work for pleasure" — and of whom only one-third are under 34 years of age; and (3) the real "go-getters" who are motivated by money and by getting ahead. For them there is no mismatch, and seven out of 10 are under 35.

The second major group is made up primarily of workers who cannot be motivated by the old incentives. This group is divided into two subgroups. The first subgroup consists of people who are "turned off." They are the least educated, the lowest earners, and the largest proportion of blue-collar workers. Their American Dream has "unraveled." They seek pleasure, live for today; they want a diversion from boredom. The other subgroup consists of the youngest workers. They are well-educated, white-collar, middle management who have strong needs for self-actualizing and achievement. They are not finding satisfaction in their work, so they turn away, looking for other outlets — leisure and hobbies. Not all members of the workforce have the same motivations, and, therefore, no single incentive system can motivate the full spectrum of today's workers. The key to effective incentive systems of the future must be "pluralism." Because the values of workers are so divergent, a "cafeteria" type of incentive system will have to be adopted. A **cafeteria incentive** system permits employees to choose what they want from among a list of incentives. Some new incentives include the following:

1. Innovative and ingenious ways of using time. Not only flexitime, but also vacations, sabbaticals, informal schedules, and other ways of using time and flexibilities in a wide range.

2. Leisure and health opportunities to build up the body and mind.

3. Customized feedback mechanisms on achievement — a way for the individual to determine how well he or she is doing.

4. Making the working world a major part of the social world of the employee — providing the opportunity to practice one's lifestyle.

5. For the "turned-off" group — providing variety and constant change that can lead to stimulation.

6. For the new young breed of creative workers — more responsibility as an incentive.

**CHANGES IN
WORKFORCE
COMPOSITION**

The strain on the United States workforce exerted by several forces in the 1960s and 1970s will ease considerably in the 1980s.[7] Much of the turbulence in the 70s — crowds of young people job hunting, unemployment rates fluctuating, and women besieging the employment agencies — probably will subside in the 1980s. However, we will have a continuous labor force problem related to minorities, as well as more immigrants — both legal and illegal — entering the U.S. job market. In order to achieve maximum productivity in the 1980s, managers must recognize the changes (as well as the continuing patterns), the reasons for them, and their ramifications in the labor market.

The Baby Boom

It is becoming clear how much the "baby boom" after World War II affected us during the 1970s. From 1946 to 1962 the population of the United States grew by 45 million, a figure never approached in a like period. Since those years, these people have been moving through society with profound effects. These new citizens overloaded educational institutions, introduced society to the problems of the youth culture (higher juvenile delinquency and crime rates) and boosted national unemployment averages. In the 1980s, however, these problems will moderate as the decline of 15- to 24-year-olds continues. By 1990, the most populous single segment of society will be between the ages of 25 and 44. Through the 1980s, the present society will be "maturing."

The most pervasive consequence of the growth and maturation of America will be the associated changes taking place in the labor force. The greatest number of new entrants in the 70s had come from the ranks of the young. Since they had a long search for jobs, and switched jobs more than other workers, teen-agers forced up the unemployment rate. But the labor force of the 1980s is not going to have to absorb new job seekers in numbers anywhere near those of the 1970s. This tapering off of new job seekers will lead to a more mature workforce in the 80s. By 1990, if population trends continue as expected, seasoned workers in the prime of their working lives (between the ages of 25 and 54) will constitute about 70 percent of the labor force.

**Women in the
Workforce**

The problems associated with so many young people coming of working age were aggravated during the 1970s by an accompanying phenomenon, the enormous influx of women into the job market. From 1960 to 1978, 19 million women joined the labor forces, accounting for 60 percent of the growth. In 1980, 51 percent of all women age 16 and over, a proportion once considered unthinkable, were out in the labor force. Another surprise is the degree to which married women have entered the job market. Twenty-three million wives work outside the home — 16 million with children under 18; six million with children under six.

In 1980 there were over 29 million women of age 20 or older working full time. Of these, about 2.4 million were holding managerial or administrative jobs. There has been a definite rise in the proportion of women managers in the workforce. For example, of the 975,000 accountants in 1978, just over 30 percent were women, and of the 99,000 computer specialists, 23 percent were women. The number of women in these professions has increased about 15 percent over the last five years. There are professions where women still dominate: over 80 percent in the teaching field, 80 percent of the librarians, 93 percent of the nurses, and 70 percent of the physical therapists.[8] There are other professions in which women have shown some increase since 1972: judges and lawyers from 4 percent to over 9 percent; life and physical scientists from 10 percent to 18 percent, and personnel and labor relations from 31 percent to 44 percent.

Money probably best explains this influx of women into the workforce. To bring their family's standard of living up to anticipations, wives have entered the job market. More subtle economic arguments are advanced to explain why married women work. One is that there are no comparable rewards, such as pay increases, for working in the home. Wages may permit the family to purchase more labor-saving devices, more meals out, and domestic help. A hidden cost is that a wife may go to the labor market to fulfill an immediate need and become "entrapped" in the labor force. Another possible explanation is that since birth control gave women the option to defer having children, or not to have children at all, those who choose to work outside the home have time to do so. Changing social attitudes allow women the freedom to choose something besides homemaking, and better education has also contributed to the higher likelihood that women would join the workforce.

This increase of women in the workforce may continue in the 1980s, but the rate will slow. Otherwise, they would soon pass the participation rates for men, a highly unlikely development. This stabilization, like the decrease in the number of youth entering the market, should help decrease the unemployment rate. The rising level of women's education also promises to improve the labor force's quality. More employed women than men have high school diplomas. However, many more working men than women have completed four years of college, and that is where an important shift is taking place. In 1958, 35 percent of the college population was women; today they are half of it. The trend has been for younger and more educated women to replace older and less educated men.

The economy, society, and the workforce in the 1980s will see other changes, as well. The proportion of "senior citizens" in the population will remain constant during the 1980s, at about 11 to 12 percent. If fertility rates stay low, there will be fewer infants in relation to the number of adults. There will be more workers with fewer people dependent upon them.

The trouble for minority groups in the labor force is likely to persist. The blacks' fertility rates remain higher than the whites'. As black teenagers entered the workforce in the 1970s, they were disadvantaged by the numbers of white women and teenagers. As those black groups grow older through the 1980s, most will take their disadvantaged positions along with them.

There may be another problem in the 1980s when the time comes for minority managers to move up the corporate ladder. There may be some conflict for higher-level, higher-paying jobs then because of the number of qualified competitors for those jobs. The fact is that more and more professionally educated college graduates will find fewer and fewer positions available. This could force them into lower-level management positions, a factor that could mean that their expectations will be unfilled.

The influx of immigrants has increased in recent years. Between May and June in 1980, for example, more than 100,000 people fled Castro's regime in Cuba to find homes and work in the United States. Besides these legal immigrants, illegal immigration is full of problems and unanswered questions, the most basic of which is "How many are there?" They are likely to displace some U.S. teenage workers. But as the number of teenagers decreases in the 1980s, the unskilled labor the immigrants usually supply may be a blessing in disguise for some industries.

Many business firms have responded voluntarily to the challenge of the *National Alliance of Businessmen* (NAB) to reduce barriers to employment. The NAB was formed in 1968 by President Lyndon B. Johnson to combat structural unemployment among the nation's hard-to-employ. Using a "community chest" type of drive, quotas for cities were established. Each city was canvassed by the NAB, which called on businesses to pledge a specific number of jobs. In particular, it asked each business to review and modify its hiring policies so it would take on hard-core applicants. During 1978 and 1979, 456,000 workers were placed in permanent jobs, and this was 22 percent more than the target amount.[9]

Ruben F. Mettler, chairman during this 18-month time span, feels the way to stop unemployment is to expand the jobs in the private sector. Toward this end, he worked to persuade business persons to find volunteers in their community who would commit time and resources to the training and hiring of the chronically unemployed. He said that the main reason for any resistance he encountered was due to certain demotivating factors coming from Washington. One such factor is the red tape involved in keeping up with the financing of a venture. Another is that coordinating local programs from Washington is difficult because the programs are sent out without knowledge of each community's specific needs.

Despite these problem areas the NAB has been considered quite a success. In New York City, approximately 50 percent of Consolidated Edison's new employees are Puerto Rican or black. The Bank of America in California increased its minority-group personnel from 11 percent in 1965 to 22 percent by mid-1970. The federal government, through the Department of Labor, has tried to help firms hire the hard-core unemployed by awarding subsidy contracts to them.

**Temporary
Employees**

Until World War II, there were very few temporary employees. By contrast, approximately three to four million people worked as temporaries during 1980.[10] Virtually every company now uses temporaries, with a typical firm purchasing nearly 250 days of temporary office help per year. Temporary help has become a $2.5 billion-a-year industry. Most of the jobs that temporary employees fill are clerical, and most of the temporary employees are women. For example, International Transportation hires clerical employees who are bilingual and places them in organizations where the use of two languages is essential. Salespower, a division of Manpower, furnishes salespersons on a temporary basis. Kelly Services and Typing Service guarantee their temporaries a full week of work so their customers are assured of service at any time.

Who is drawn to this type of work? Some individuals want temporary work because a permanent job would be inconvenient or impossible for them. Others like it because it provides freedom of movement, a continually changing environment, flexibility in work hours, and the opportunity to meet other people and make more friends. According to several large surveys, temporary workers report that they have very little interest in becoming full-time employees.

Why do firms hire temporary employees? One major advantage of using temporaries is that the hiring firm is not responsible for fringe benefits (such as life and health insurance, vacation time, stock bonuses, and discounts at company shops). Another attraction is that the firm can attempt to hire a temporary as a regular employee, if he or she performs well. Conversely, there is no problem of terminating a temporary employee who is performing unsatisfactorily. Temporary employees are often used to fill in for full-time employees who are ill or on leave, to aid the firm during peak periods (as when the postal service hires college students during the Christmas rush), or to handle special jobs. The major disadvantage of hiring the temporary employee is training and orientation. If the job is complex, it is often wasteful to provide the needed training to a short-time worker.

**The White-Collar
Workforce**

At present, the number of professional and technical workers is increasing faster than any other type, with an estimated increase of 50 percent between 1968 and 1980. The number of service workers and salespersons also is increasing more rapidly than is the number of craftsmen and foremen, factory workers, and farm workers. There also has been a corresponding change in the educational levels of workers. It has been estimated that by the mid-1980s most adults will have completed high school and attended some sort of college. There is likely to be a rapid growth of junior colleges, whose goal is to provide continuing education for many individuals.

United States firms are facing increased foreign competition, especially in the automobile, electronics, and steel industries. Other products, such as cameras, sewing machines, shoes, radios, toys, and television sets, are facing similar stiff competition. The rapidly improving quality of some of these goods, together with lower prices, have made competition difficult for some domestic firms. Since World War II, foreign competitors have been able to build modern plants and use the latest management techniques and practices to be innovative and keep prices low. Probably the industry hit hardest by foreign competition has been the automotive industry. Early in 1981 the big three (GM, Ford, and Chrysler) all reported that sales were down about 30 percent. More than 290,000 automobile workers were laid off. In 1980, more than 700 dealerships went bankrupt.[11] The only U.S. auto manufacturer to report a slight increase in sales in 1979–1980 was American Motors. Since the U.S. economy also was in a recession, it would be foolish to attribute all these problems to foreign competition. However, most imports did not suffer a sharp decline in sales. Honda has been able to increase sales each year it has competed in the U.S. market, so let's look at their management strategy.

CASE STUDY

Honda

As a $4.5 billion manufacturer, Honda has enjoyed tremendous growth during the last decade in the U.S. market.[12] Honda makes only subcompacts that offer outstanding gas mileage. During these times of short gasoline supplies and high prices, the demand in the United States for the Honda has far exceeded the supply. Honda marketing officials say they offer a superior product with many appealing features. Honda cars are equipped with front-wheel drive. The engine, mounted sideways, runs smoothly and quietly. They also have independent suspension, which permits them to take bumps better than most small cars. *Consumer Reports* gives the Honda Accord high marks for quality, craftsmanship, and attention to detail. For example, a coin box is standard in the dashboard to keep loose change for toll roads. Honda jumped from eleventh among foreign importers in 1972 to third in 1979, trailing only Toyota Motor and Nissan Motor (which makes Datsuns). U.S. sales increased from 20,500 units in 1972 to about 315,000 in 1979, and Honda executives say they could sell 500,000 if they had that many available. The demand is such that some dealers have sold Hondas at $1000 above list price, and customers are willing to wait months for cars. No importer has sold half a million cars since 1973, when Volkswagen did it.

Supplying many more cars to the United States is out of the question for the time being. Honda's production capacity is just too small. The company currently has just two automobile plants, both in Japan, with a combined capacity of fewer than 800,000 cars per year. The United States already gets 40 percent of the production (Japan gets only 30 percent). Allocating any more to the U.S. would seriously damage Honda's distribution system to the other 90 foreign country markets. In 1980, Honda pushed its capacity to more than 800,000 of which 355,000 were promised for export to the United States. Toyota and Nissan, considerably larger companies than Honda, can adjust more readily to the swelling U.S. demand and have taken away customers.

The need for a new plant seemed justified economically. Honda management preferred to build the plant in Japan, but land was too costly, and Honda's management was aware of the political values of Americans. In 1979 and 1980, senators, representatives, and strong labor-union leaders pressed Congress for legislation that would impose restrictions on imports from Japan. Honda management read these trends and decided to build its new plant on 260 acres in Marysville, Ohio. Honda also decided, like Volkswagen when it opened its plant in New Staton, Pennsylvania, not to import any foreign laborers to work the plant.

Honda also has established an American-based export operation, called Honda International Trading Corporation. It ships American goods to Japan aboard giant car-carrying vessels that bring Honda vehicles to U.S. ports. Honda says this helps the U.S. balance-of-payment problems. But the export company's volume is only about $120 million annually, compared with the $2 billion worth of cars, motorcycles, lawnmowers, and other products Honda sells here.

Honda officials admit they are worried about the plant in Ohio. They wonder whether American workmanship can match Japanese standards. They are concerned about the availability, and again the quality, of parts and components in the United States. They are alarmed by the high labor costs caused by American labor unions. In 1981 the average hourly compensation for an auto worker was $20.45 in the United States, $9.12 in Italy, and $10.75 in Japan. Honda's management believes that American workers, for the most part, are not interested in productivity.

Today the functions and responsibilities of most managers are influenced greatly by governmental regulation and the social and political forces that led to increased regulation. Because managers have to base their decisions, in part, on what they anticipate the future will be, it is important that they have accurate forecasts about the trend of government-corporate relations. A number of pro-business think-tanks, such as the American Enterprise Institute, Hoover Institution, Institute for Contemporary Studies, and the Heritage Foundation, have produced numerous studies that indicate several major problem areas managers in the 1980s will face.[13] We realize that some of these were discussed at length in Chapter 3 and shall present only a summary here.

**GOVERNMENT–
CORPORATE
RELATIONS**

The federal government will continue to play an active role in reducing pollution and in conserving resources. The Environmental Protection Agency (EPA) estimates that during the 1980s, businesses will spend $215 billion to clean up the air, water, and noise pollutants in our society.[14] The government will spend another $56 billion in that effort. Who will pay? The government will raise its share through taxation. Businesses will raise their money from customers in the form of higher prices and possibly lower dividends to stockholders. The questions remain: What are reasonable costs? How clean is clean? For example, the federal fund which pays for cleaning up oil and chemical spills was about broke in April 1980. In 1979 alone, the Mexican oil well that spilled millions of gallons of oil on the Texas shoreline, the kerosene spill that threatened water supplies in Northern Virginia, and the Love Canal problem in Niagara Falls, New York, cost the U.S. government $31.5 million. The Love Canal incident, where nearly 700 families were driven from their homes by a leaking World War II-era chemical dump, caused Congress to rethink legislation that it needs to pass to give the public a minimal amount of protection against companies dumping pollutants and chemicals.[15]

U.S. Steel, Republic Steel, and Youngstown Sheet and Tube were dumping 160 tons of oil, grease, and cyanide into the Mahoning River each day. When the EPA ordered the companies to clean up the river, the companies said they did not have the money to conform to the EPA demands. If EPA required them to clean up the river, they would close the mills. The people living in the

**The Natural
Environment and
Resources**

area decided that having a polluted river was better than not having jobs. In 1979, however, because of continuous EPA pressure and foreign competition, some of those mills were closed.

Employment

The federal government will expand its role in employment through the introduction of such measures as indexing the minimum wage to the cost of living, instituting manpower planning, guaranteeing employment for employees who lose their jobs because of foreign competition, and establishing a national health policy. The Occupational Safety and Health Administration (OSHA) has had a profound effect on workers' safety and health, especially in the construction, extraction (coal mining, oil exploration, salt mining), and chemical industries.[16] For example, after vinyl chloride (which forms an important compound in plastics materials) was declared potentially cancer-causing as a result of industry and government studies, American Cyanamid, Hercules, DuPont, Borden, and other chemical firms took steps to prevent workers from coming into contact with this material.

Companies also are using their employees to write to their elected representatives in support of company policies. For example, Rockwell International Corporation provided preprinted postcards to employees so they could petition Congress in support of the B-1 bomber in 1977. Rockwell was the primary bidder for the production of the B-1. During 1980, most of the major oil companies used company newsletters, pep-talks over company intercoms, and fliers on bulletin boards to urge employees to send Congress the message that the "windfall" profits tax would unjustly hurt oil companies. Similarly, the United Auto Workers (UAW) organized a campaign in 1979 to obtain support for Chrysler's federal loan guarantees. With the U.S. automobile industry in a slump, the UAW actively campaigned for and got employee support.[17]

**Corporate
Governance**

Federal government involvement in corporate governance will be expanded, particularly in the areas of social responsibility, disclosure of corporate information, and protection of individual worker rights. While extreme interference is unlikely, the special interests of political-action committees will be closely examined. In 1979, 141,898 companies contributed some $152 million to trade associations to act as intermediaries between themselves and the federal government.[18] For example, the members of the American Footwear Industry Association were able to influence legislation limiting the number of shoes imported from Taiwan and Korea.

Given the increasing involvement of business in politics, regulatory bodies like the Securities and Exchange Commission are using trends in the country to foster democracy in the corporation. Some of the key trends are:

- The growing desire of labor unions for a voice in governance via pension funds and bank deposits.
- Surging state and local attempts to restrict corporate relocation of plants. Rising demand for outside representatives on boards of directors.
- Increasing stockholder criticism of executive salaries.
- Growing pressure on universities, for ideological purposes, to declare their stock holdings in companies.

The business community is aware of these trends, and most major corporations now have offices in Washington, D.C. for the primary purpose of lobbying. For example, General Motors' Washington office has grown from three people to 28 in the past 10 years. Arthur Anderson, a major accounting firm, has expanded its Washington office staff from 25 people to over 400 during the last 10 years.

**Government
Regulations**

Federal regulation of business will continue to be important, but important changes have already taken place in several industries, notably in the automobile and transportation industries. The backbone of the American enterprise system has always been to foster competition among corporations. Congress has aided Chrysler Corporation financially to maintain the competitiveness and jobs of that industry. The deregulation of the airline, trucking, and railroad industries also has opened the way to a new competitive spirit between lines. A look at how the government has intervened in the railroad industry[19] will illustrate some of these points.

CASE STUDY

**U.S. Railroad
Industry**

During the 1970s, the wisest managers in the railroad industry decided that the best way to run the business was to get out of it, or more practically, to sidetrack their railroads in favor of other diversified investments. A new attitude began to emerge in the 1980s however, and for the first time in decades, transportation experts were speculating that a freight-rail renaissance was at hand. The reasons for the optimism stemmed partly from the demand, due to shortages of foreign oil, for railroads to carry greater amounts of coal. More importantly, federal regulators finally were attempting to apply some economic logic to the freight-rail system, particularly in the long-neglected western half of the United States. "The opportunity is here" said Transportation Secretary Neil Goldschmidt, "to come out with a rational system."

Signs of this new antiregulatory ethic were everywhere. Congress considered deregulation bills to give railroads more freedom in setting freight rates and to abandon little-used routes. Even the Interstate Commerce Commission (ICC) promoted cost-saving mergers that could shrink the total number of carriers. On Wall Street, rail stocks were fast becoming investor favorites.

For all the apparent progress, huge problems remain. The rail system itself is still a mess; there are 190,000 miles of track in place, nearly as many as when the railroads had a virtual monopoly on American transportation. Trucks now carry huge chunks of traffic that once rode the rails, and 67 percent of the freight that railroads do get moves over just 20 percent of the track. As much as 60,000 miles of track, nearly one-third the national system, could be abandoned with little loss in efficiency. The railroads' inability to abandon profitless routes because of government regulations is a major reason for the industry's miserable profit record in recent years. From 1970 through 1979, the average railroad earned shareholders just three percent a year on their investment.

Congress has been leaning toward railroad reform ever since airline deregulation proved so successful, and mounting problems of the Midwestern carriers have accelerated the agenda. The Rock Island and Milwaukee Road railways had expected to be taken over by Union Pacific and Burlington Northern, respectively, and had avoided spending money to maintain their tracks and equipment. Milwaukee Road never did work out a deal, and by the time ICC approved the UP-Rock Island deal, 12 years had passed and the Rock Island line was in such poor condition that UP backed out. The Rock Island slid into bankruptcy in 1976, and the Milwaukee followed two years later.

In the past, the government would have insisted on yet another reorganization of the "sick" railroads, preserving all their routes to maintain service. In early 1980, both the regulators and courts were taking an approach leaning heavily toward free enterprise. All 7500 miles of Rock Island track, for instance, will be sold to other railroads or abandoned. The Federal Railroad Administration also had recommended that the Milwaukee Road either sell or abandon 6400 miles of track. The deregulation bills being considered in Congress would give the railroads the right to establish their own rates.

A possible merger of the Union Pacific and the Missouri Pacific, assisted by regulators, could ultimately lead to a series of transcontinental mergers. According to John P. Fishwick, president of the prosperous Norfolk and Western, ''Getting down to four, five, or six railroads is the only opportunity for the railroads to reduce costs substantially.''

Before they can even contemplate going coast-to-coast with an efficient system, serious problems will have to be solved. For example, the regulators still must deal with other ailing carriers after the Rock Island and Milwaukee Road cases have been resolved. Economic trends and government sentiment seem to be running in the railroad industry's favor, and the prospects for a real revival look good.

SUMMARY

In this chapter, we discussed some of the important factors that will pose challenges for you as managers in the 1980s. Some of these challenges will require organizations to structure themselves differently and managers to change their internal operating rules, regulations, assumptions about their employees, and styles of leadership. This chapter focused only on the external factors managers must learn to handle.

Business organizations have changed quickly in the past decade. With the rise of the conglomerate type of organization, corporate growth and expansion occurred rapidly. When Pepsico acquired Pizza Hut, Taco Bell and Frito-Lay, it put itself in a good position to sell products to members of the World War II baby boom entering their thirties and forties. It also enabled Pepsico to become the fourth-largest fast-food concern in the United States. Organizational growth progresses in stages. The first stage is concerned with survival, the second stage with permanent growth, and the third with allocation and control of resources between product lines. As organizations expand, internal management structures, control systems, and strategies change. Increased foreign competition and the formation of multinational companies represent further challenges for managers.

The effective manager is aware that changes have been taking place in the composition of the workforce and its values. The proportion of women and minorities entering the workforce has increased steadily. Most employees no longer believe that "hard work pays off," and the manager must develop new kinds of incentives to motivate workers.

One of the most important requirements for tomorrow's managers is to learn to live with the federal government. Obviously, the government business environment is immensely complex. It is in part a function of the growth of government and, to some extent, a result of the growing and conflicting expectations of the public. Through the enactment of rules and regulations, the government has had an impact on managerial decisions with respect to the use of natural resources, employment, and governance.

KEYWORDS

cafeteria incentive sysytems *multinational corporation*
conglomerate *national alliance of businessmen*
franchiser *temporary employees*
growth stages *work ethic*

DISCUSSION
QUESTIONS

1. Why are organizations growing in size?

2. What are the three states of growth that usually occur as organizations expand?

3. Why are changing values important to managers?

4. Why has it become more important now than in the past for managers to take the environment of their organizations into account when making plans and decisions?

5. Why do people seek temporary work?

6. In what way has foreign competition changed the way of doing business for many U.S. firms?

7. How has the government affected the decision-making processes of managers? In what areas?

8. In general, how is American business viewed by the general public? Provide examples.

9. Describe two major problems that often face multinational companies.

Management Incidents and Cases

TULSA MOTOR
INN*

Mr. Jim Baggett had heard about Oklahoma's penal reform plans. One phase of the plan involved the establishment of prisoner prerelease centers in both Tulsa and Oklahoma City. This idea seemed to make sense in some ways; the cost of rehabilitating a man might be lowered, and the percentage of parolees who made the transition from tax-using regimented prisoner to useful tax-paying citizen might be increased.

* This case was prepared by James C. Johnson and Howard A. Thompson of the University of Tulsa as the basis for class discussion and not to illustrate either effective or ineffective handling of an administrative situation. Expenses involved in developing this case were funded by the Office of Research, The University of Tulsa. Presented at the Case Workshop of the Southern Case Writers Association and Intercollegiate Case Clearing House, Soldiers Field, Boston, MA 02163. All rights reserved to the contributors. Printed in the U.S.A. Used with permission.

But as Jim scanned the newspaper that morning, his attitude toward one particular prisoner prerelease center (PRC) began to change. The headline catching his eye read: TULSA MOTEL TO BECOME PRISONER PRERELEASE CENTER. The article went on to explain the state had entered into a long-term lease with the owners of a mismanaged and floundering motel to use that facility as the Tulsa PRC. Another PRC was to be located in Oklahoma City. The most important information in the article to Jim, however, was the location of the PRC motel. It was *next door*, not 50 yards away from his own motel, the Tulsa Motor Inn.

The Baggetts had acquired the Tulsa Motor Inn 18 months prior to the PRC announcement. After successfully managing a motel in the Oklahoma City area, they had purchased one in Tulsa, which at the time was also mismanaged and losing money. Jim carefully planned and financed its remodeling and renaming under a nationally franchised motel chain. After investing $1,250,000 and a year and a half of hard work, the operation was beginning to show promise of success. "And now the state wants to locate 20 to 30 parolees within 50 yards of my guests, dozens of new cars, vacation-enlarged billfolds, and dressed-for-the-pool swimmers!" The thought brought with it a vision of empty rooms, forced room-rate reductions, and higher overhead stemming from new security precautions.

During the last 12 months the Tulsa Motor Inn had grossed $197,000, permitting a net profit before taxes of $41,000. Although he considered this to be less than half of its potential profitability, assuming occupancy percentages continued to improve, Baggett believed the Motor Inn to be "on target" according to his forecast nearly two years earlier. The PRC, however, was definitely not part of the "game plan." He had little doubt but the excellent repeat business with commercial travelers (sales representatives), now believed to constitute about one-half of total revenue, would shift to a "safer" location once the prisoners were known to be 50 yards away. An earlier advantage of being located near an expressway within 15 minutes of downtown Tulsa while still out of the congested part of the city now seemed almost a disadvantage.

Baggett's business associates counseled him to seek an injunction to prevent the state from locating an "undesirable" facility next door. He, with his son, a management major at the University of Tulsa, had been wrestling with questions of social responsibility, environmental pollution, and the like only a few weeks ago. He was very much in favor of business committing itself to the pursuit of these goals and ideas. But if he failed to act quickly against the state's announced plan for the new PRC, Baggett was certain this could mean a severe financial reversal for the Motor Inn.

What counsel would you give Baggett?

Two broad types of travelers are customers of the Tulsa Motor Inn, transient or through travelers and business travelers making frequent trips to Tulsa. In terms of room-occupancy percentages, the business traveler is slightly more important. This is true except during the summer months when through travelers are most numerous. Through travelers, however, are most important in terms of annual gross rental income. During the only full calendar year of operational experience under the present management, 56.8 percent of gross rental income was from through travelers and 43.2 percent from business travelers. Multiple occupancy among through-traveler customers creates a total gross rental income greater than that received from the more numerous business traveler rentals.

Average monthly room occupancy increased from about 30 percent at the time of purchase to 60.2 percent last year.

At the present the Tulsa Motor Inn enjoys a fine reputation with its repeat customers, the business travelers. Comments such as "clean," "well-managed," "best beds in town," and "best motel for your money in the area" are frequently filled in on rating cards left in their rooms by business travelers.

Among business travelers "previous experience" was a strong factor influencing the choice of the Tulsa Motor Inn. Approximately 72 percent indicated that this was the reason which drew them back to Tulsa Motor Inn whenever they were in the Tulsa area. Other business travelers volunteered the information that they had only recently started staying at the Tulsa Motor Inn as a result of advice from other salesmen. Such indicators as these suggest that the present business volume at the Tulsa Motor Inn is healthy and growing, especially among this customer group.

CENTRAL
EXPRESSWAY
INSURANCE
COMPANY

To forestall action by the Department of Health, Education, and Welfare because of the lack of women in its managerial ranks, the Central Expressway Insurance Company of Tucker, Georgia, decided to recruit a woman MBA student to fill a recent vacancy in its research division. The requirements for the job were an MBA (with a major emphasis in finance), at least two years of proven managerial experience, and proven capability in the insurance field. After an exhaustive search, Joyce Nichols was chosen. She had graduated with distinction from a local university. Nichols had previously been employed as a broker in a highly respected Atlanta banking firm. Central Expressway was able to hire her only after Peter Bennett, her potential immediate boss, assured her of equal opportunity on all levels.

At the end of the third month on the job, Nichols privately acknowledged her frustrations with the company. She began reviewing the activities of the previous three months in an attempt to determine the basis for her negative attitude and what she would say to Bennett.

The first day on the job, the entire office welcomed her. When Nichols suggested they all go out to lunch, Graham Clark, a division manager, told her, "We all brown-bag it to avoid the lines in the local restaurants." Nichols decided to brown-bag it. She was surprised therefore when at noon the following day, Graham opened his office door and urged, "come on, you guys, let's research our brown bags — Frank, you and Rich get the coffee while Mick and I get the ice cream, and don't forget that Alan wants double cream in his coffee." Since Nichols' name wasn't called, she decided, after some thought, to eat alone in her office. Joyce didn't want to eat with the secretaries and clerks, although she knew she would be welcomed. This lunch routine became established.

Only once during her three months had her colleagues invited her to join them for coffee. She noticed that the men in the office seemed to plan social activities for both after work and the weekends, but she was never asked to join them. She decided that although she had okay relationships with them at work, perhaps being single was one reason that she had little in common with them outside of work.

Nichols' specific assignments were low-level ones that required only infrequent attention by Bennett. The major portion of her time was spent on the cost allocations project. Cost allocation is a major computer system that will, when completed, provide complete accident information on each of the company's customers. All records of accidents were pooled for analysis. Her job was to develop customer profiles to pinpoint potential high-risk customers for the company. Since accident reports had been filed by hand, Nichols anticipated the usual problems of employee resistance to a new computer system. She, therefore, had begun some system orientation classes for the personnel involved. Nichols had determined that the existing personnel, with training, would be adequate to effectively use and run the new system. No personnel displacement would be necessary.

Nichols was in the final stages of debugging the system with Roger Lotta, the programmer assigned to her. When she took the first run of the test data in to Bennett, he expressed complete surprise. He admitted, "I can't believe that cost allocation has gotten off the ground. This system has been knocking around for three years. In fact, Clark has just sent this memo to headquarters indicating that we should write the entire project off. I guess we'll have to start thinking about getting some money for funding this project."

Nichols was shocked and disappointed at his reaction. She went back to her office and prepared her resignation letter. Before she left the office that day, she put her resignation letter on Bennett's desk. He was shocked and asked her to reconsider, but she refused. Nichols told Bennett the office wasn't ready for a woman manager and the attitudes and behaviors of her co-workers made her situation intolerable.

Bennett was bothered by her comments and thought about them during the Sunday afternoon football game on TV. The first thing Monday morning, he called the personnel department and asked them to survey the entire managerial staff's attitudes on women. The personnel department gave each managerial employee the questionnaire included here.

The personnel department informed Bennett that his staff's score was a 54, indicating that most of his staff had negative attitudes about women as managers.

The Women As Managers Scale (WAMS)

Instructions

The following items are an attempt to assess the attitudes people have about women in business. The best answer to each statement is your *personal opinion*. The statements cover many different and opposing points of view; you may find yourself agreeing strongly with some of the statements, disagreeing just as strongly with others, and perhaps uncertain about others. Whether you agree or disagree with any statement, you can be sure that many people feel the same way you do.

Rating scale

1 = Strongly disagree
2 = Disagree
3 = Slightly disagree
4 = Neither disagree nor agree
5 = Slightly agree
6 = Agree
7 = Strongly agree

Using the numbers from 1 to 7 on the rating scale to the right, mark your personal opinion about each statement in the blank that immediately precedes it. Remember, give your *personal opinion* according to how much you agree or disagree with each item. Please respond to all 21 items. Thank you.

_____ **1.** It is desirable for women rather than men to have a job that requires responsibility.

_____ **2.** Women have the objectivity required to evaluate business situations properly.

_____ **3.** Challenging work is equally as important to men as it is to women.

_____ **4.** Men and women should be given equal opportunity for participation in management training programs.

_____ 5. Women have the capability to acquire the necessary skills to be successful managers.

_____ 6. On the average, women managers are as capable of contributing to an organization's overall goals as are men.

_____ 7. It is acceptable for women to assume leadership roles as often as men.

_____ 8. The business community should, some day, accept women in key managerial positions.

_____ 9. Society should regard work by female managers as valuable as work by male managers.

_____ 10. It is acceptable for women to compete with men for top executive positions.

_____ 11. The possibility of pregnancy does not make women less desirable employees than men.

_____ 12. Women would no more allow their emotions to influence their managerial behavior than would men.

_____ 13. Problems associated with menstruation should not make women less desirable than men as employees.

_____ 14. To be a successful executive, a woman does not have to sacrifice some of her femininity.

_____ 15. On the average, a woman who stays at home all the time with her children is as good a mother as a woman who works outside the home at least half-time.

_____ 16. Women are as capable of learning mathematical and mechanical skills as are men.

_____ 17. Women are ambitious enough to be successful in the business world.

_____ 18. Women can be assertive in business situations that demand it.

_____ 19. Women possess the self-confidence required of a good leader.

_____ 20. Women are competitive enough to be successful in the business world.

_____ 21. Women can be aggressive in business situations that demand it.

Adapted from J. Terborg, L. Peters, D. Ilgen, and F. Smith, "Organizational and Personal Correlates of Attitudes Toward Women as Managers," *Academy of Management Journal* **20** (1977): p. 93. Used with permission. The higher your score, the more favorable your attitude toward women as managers.

Questions   **1.** Take the questionnaire yourself. How did you score? What does this mean to you?

2. What do the results tell Bennett about Nichols' problems?

3. How can Central Expressway Insurance attract and motivate women to stay with them?

4. How can Bennett explain to the district manager of HEW why Nichols quit?

FINANCIAL
SYSTEMS, INC.*
Financial Systems, Inc., of Houston, Texas, had begun operations in the check processing business in November of 1973 when its current president, Mr. Earl Roberts, agreed to join the firm on a full-time basis. Prior to that time, Mr. Roberts had been acting as a consultant to the firm. In that capacity, he assisted management in arranging for a series of small loans that were needed to maintain operations. Up until this time, the company had been attempting, with little success, to develop and market check-processing equipment for the commercial banking industry. No sales had actually been made because the product design efforts had encountered serious technical problems.

When asked why he had agreed to join the firm, Mr. Roberts replied that "Even though the future for Financial Systems, Inc. was very uncertain in 1973, I felt that the technical problems with the product could be solved and I felt certain that a good market existed for a product of this type if we could just get into production and begin selling."

By the end of 1974, after scrapping the original product design and starting with a new approach, the engineering staff had developed a product that could be manufactured. Several of the units had been sold by Mr. Roberts toward the end of 1974 and had been shipped to customers. Revenues totaled $13,000 and $209,000 for 1973 and 1974 respectively. The initial success of the product in the customers' installations indicated that the new design was a good one and that a substantial market existed.

Early in 1974, it became apparent that the company would need new outside financing for the expansion of marketing, manufacturing, and engineering efforts. Private investors were approached by Mr. Roberts and were persuaded to invest a total of approximately $300,000 for which they received stock and warrants. With these new funds, a staff of three key managers

---

* This case was prepared by Grahame Clark, Cox School of Business, Southern Methodist University, Dallas, TX, 1981, under the direction of John W. Slocum, Jr.

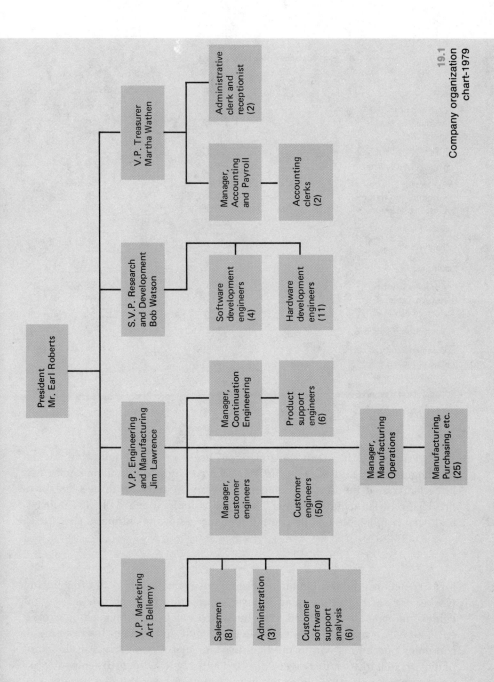

19.1
Company organization chart—1979

19.2   Balance Sheet (000's)

Assets	1980	1973
Cash and near cash	$1531	$ 21
Accounts receivable	2419	16
Inventories	970	15
Prepaid expenses	76	3
Total current assets	4996	55
Equipment	1586	59
Furniture and fixtures	103	8
Less: Depreciation	(233)	(2)
Total Fixed Assets	1456	65
Total Assets	$6452	$ 120
Liabilities		
Accounts payable	$1100	$ 82
Notes payable	50	44
Accrued liabilities	1035	21
Total current liabilities	2185	147
Common equity at par	26	26
Paid-in-surplus	1271	318
Retained earnings	2970	(371)
Total Liabilities and Equity	$6452	$ 120

were recruited to head up the functional areas of Marketing, Manufacturing/Engineering, and Accounting. These three individuals, along with Mr. Roberts, formed the initial management team. In 1980, all three were Vice-Presidents of Financial Systems. These individuals, along with Mr. Roberts, had been responsible for the growth and success of the company (Fig. 19.2).

**Marketing
Organization**

Mr. Art Bellamy joined Financial Systems in February of 1974 after having worked for several years as an industry marketing manager for a large facilities management firm. Although he lacked extensive direct selling experience, he was a tireless, dynamic individual with an excellent background in computer operations within the banking industry. Upon arrival at the company, Mr. Bellamy's efforts were directed entirely to selling. His sales success was impressive. In 1975, with the introduction of a second new product, he began to recruit a small staff of salespersons, and by 1979 he had hired a staff of eight. Each salesperson was experienced at the time they were hired and each was assigned a specific geographic territory. The salespersons lived in their territories and communicated with Mr. Bellamy and others at the home office primarily by telephone. A secretary served as a communications link between the individual salespersons, Mr. Bellamy, and the home office staff. In addition she typed correspondence and prepared trip itineraries. All official company correspondence and sales proposals were prepared at the home office and mailed to users and prospective customers. This was necessary since the salespersons did not have typing facilities and because Mr. Bellamy approved all customer and prospect communications. As a result, the salespersons spent a great deal of time dictating and reviewing proposal contents by telephone prior to finalization by Bellamy.

The Marketing V.P. kept a very heavy travel schedule since he felt that "Whenever one of my salespeople has an account that is ready to sign a contract, I want to be there. I want to be certain that nothing goes wrong at the last minute, and also I am the only person, except Mr. Roberts, who can negotiate contract terms with a customer."

In addition to salespeople, Mr. Bellamy had a home office staff of six software specialists. They were scheduled by Mr. Bellamy to customers' facilities to assist in equipment-related operational problems. Reporting also to the Marketing V.P. were two Administrative Assistants. They prepared equipment demonstrations, scheduled trade-show acitivities, and maintained contract and customer records. Contract review and signing, as well as equipment shipment schedules, were the direct responsibility of Mr. Bellamy.

Markets Served

Financial Systems' primary marketplace is the domestic commercial banking industry. Specificially, the firm manufactures, markets, and supports automated computer-based systems and associated supplies for check processing. Current and planned future products are directed at fulfilling the needs of the 500 largest U.S. banks whose check-processing centers, either directly for their own customers or indirectly through correspondent relationships with smaller area banks, process a major portion of the estimated 40 billion checks written annually in the United States. Check volume is forecast to grow at an annual rate of from five to seven percent through the 1980s and would approach 55 billion annually by 1985.

In addition to processing checks, there are many other document-processing applications within banks that can be addressed by the company's products. These applications include return items (checks that cannot be processed due to insufficient funds, closed accounts, invalid signature, etc.), lockbox remittance processing, and bank card drafts (Mastercard, Visa, etc.), in addition to others. Each of these represent a major market for the company.

In marketing new products, the firm tries to take advantage of the needs of its present customer base, the upward compatibility between its current and new products, and its in-depth knowledge of the banking and document-processing industries. Planned new products will complement the existing product line and extend the market within commercial banking.

Outside the commercial banking industry, only a few customers currently have Financial Systems' equipment installed. However, document-processing applications that are compatible with the company's products offer significant potential in the insurance, energy utility, retail credit, and government markets.

Market Potential

Since 1973, when the company began actively marketing its products, penetration into the commercial banking market and acceptance of the company's products have progressed rapidly. Continued growth in the volume of checks has been forecast (55 billion by 1985) by industry sources, assuring a large and growing market for present and future products. The additional applications within commercial banking and the ongoing sales of equipment supplies significantly extend potential for current products to a total of more than $150 million over the next five years. One large bank initially installed eight systems for check processing and now has a total of 31 installed, processing a variety of applications.

The new banking products, which will be availble for delivery in late 1980, combine to provide additional potential over the next five years of approximately $200 million. These new systems represent a significant technological advance over equipment that is presently available from other firms and has reached its maximum level of effectiveness for most banks. The new technology will provide for significant gains in cost reduction, processing time, accuracy, and for new products and services that banks may then offer to both commercial and individual customers.

Competition

Companies with whom Financial Systems, Inc. competes in the commercial banking industry are the large data-processing firms such as Burroughs, NCR, and IBM. However, Financial Systems has successfully segmented the market by addressing applications where its present products offer clear operational (e.g., speed, accuracy, etc.) and financial advantages (e.g. lower product cost) over those of competitors. These applications are traditionally labor intensive clerical functions that lend themselves to automation, yet are small enough to avoid the concentrated attention of the large firms.

The versatility of the company's products in meeting a variety of processing needs, in addition to the primary application for which the systems are purchased, has been a key element to Financial Systems' success. Operational and financial gains that are available to customers in addition to the in-depth expertise and service orientation of the sales and support staff provide a significant competitive advantage in the selected market segments. Future products have been similarly targeted at market segments where they can enjoy price and operational advantages.

Manufacturing/Engineering

Mr. Jim Lawrence, Vice-President of Manufacturing and Engineering, is one of the original group of key employees who joined Financial Systems in 1974. Previously, he had been a division manager for a medium sized instrument company, and was responsible for engineering, research, and manufacturing. A quiet, low-key individual, Mr. Lawrence relied on procedures, rules and regulations, structures, and job definitions, rather than dynamic personal leadership, to manage his department. He preferred to give only broad, general advice to his managers, and to allow them to make their own decisions within their defined area of responsibility.

Manufacturing operations are limited in scope and require only 25 employees. Most major components for the company's products are bought from outside vendors under long-term purchase agreements. However, some components and sub-units are assembled in Houston, and are shipped directly to the customer's facility along with those parts purchased from outside suppliers. Final system configuration and check-out is performed at the customer's facility. A customer engineering department, consisting of 50 service engineers reporting to Mr. Lawrence (see Fig. 19.1), is responsible for the final assembly and checkout of equipment, and for the ongoing maintenance for all equipment that has been sold. Equipment maintenance is provided to each customer under a renewable one-year contract. Prior to 1979, maintenance had been provided by a third-party contractor. During the past year Mr. Lawrence had been given the responsibility for organizing, staffing, and managing the conversion to the present maintenance system. According to Mr. Roberts, he handled this new responsibility very well.

A small continuation engineering group also reports to Mr. Lawrence. Its function is to provide technical support to the manufacturing assembly and the customer engineering groups. The staff is comprised of senior engineers with broad-based experience who design engineering solutions to technical problems on short notice and provide minor product improvements and/or modifications necessary to meet unique customer requirements. They are also responsible for maintaining engineering standards and documentation as well as providing the technical interface to outside vendors.

Finance

Financial Systems is a privately held corporation whose stock is owned by a small group of institutional and individual investors. These investors are very active in the management of the company either as members of the board of directors or as corporate officers. The total amount of invested capital is slightly more than $1 million (see Fig 19.2). Since early 1978, growth has been entirely financed with internally generated funds.

The Finance and Accounting Department employs four people whose primary functions include accounts payable, accounts receivable, payroll, and preparation of quarterly and annual statements. Ms. Martha Wathen, another of the original group of employees, has the responsibility for the finance department. Before joining the company, Ms. Wathen had performed accounting services for small companies in the local area. Although she had no formal training in accounting or finance, she had been an assistant to the chief financial officer of a medium-sized computer firm and had gained practical experience before joining Financial Systems. Mr. Roberts had also served as a financial officer in the past and participated in setting financial policy for the firm.

Research and Development

Early in 1979, Financial Systems acquired, by merger, a small firm that was actively involved in the development of a very advanced bank data-processing system. According to Mr. Roberts, the merger extends the company's product line. The owner and president of the acquired firm, Mr. Bob Watson, and a small group of very capable development engineers now comprise Financial Systems' Research and Development Department. Prior to the merger, the product development activities had been the responsibility of the engineering/manufacturing group headed by Mr. Lawrence. These two groups now share some resources, such as test equipment and technicians, often resulting in conflict over assignment of resources and priorities.

As a result of the merger, Mr. Watson became the major stockholder in Financial Systems, a Senior Vice-President and member of the board of directors. Having earned both an engineering degree and an MBA, and as a result of his experience as a founder of an electronics firm, he was well qualified in both the technical and business aspects of the company's operations.

The rapid growth of the company caused some internal stress and inefficiencies that concerned Mr. Roberts. He felt that the product strategy Financial Systems had adopted, the acceptance of the company's products in the marketplace, and the growing size of the market, all indicated that continued rapid growth was possible. Sales of $25 million with profits of $6 million were forecast for 1980 and were expected to grow to $100 million and $30 million by 1985. Further, the board of directors was considering a public offering of the company's stock sometime in 1980. The president was very much involved in analyzing the structure, strategy, and personnel requirements necessary to ensure that the company was capable of meeting the demands of continued rapid growth. Additionally, he wanted to position the company for a public offering if one were made.

Roberts was involved on a day-to-day basis in the management of each functional department. Recently, he had had several lengthy conversations with Art Bellamy regarding the need to hire subordinate managers and also the need to allow the individual salesmen more flexibility and discretion in their jobs. He felt these actions were necessary since it was clear to him that Bellamy was having problems maintaining control over growing marketing operations, and that many of the more experienced salesmen were unhappy with Bellamy's management style. These ideas had met with strong resistance from Bellamy who felt that their past success was a result of his direct involvement in all sales activity. Their conversations tended to digress into conflicts existing between marketing and finance or manufacturing over such things as control over product shipping schedules, commission payments, or other operating decisions which Bellamy felt he should participate in. The problem was compounded by his heavy travel schedule.

Because Roberts' efforts were needed in these areas, his time was being consumed more and more with these day-to-day activities. He was concerned that the corporate management functions were being neglected. Further, the department managers were used to operating in a "hands-on" role and were not able to give adequate attention to planning.

1. Identify the transition that is taking place in the life cycle of the company. What are the causes of the conflicts between functional groups and within marketing?

2. What action(s) should Roberts take regarding the organization structure? What would be the likely short- and long-term effects?

3. How would you implement your recommendations if you were in Roberts' position? How would you feel about making changes to the organization if you were Roberts?

REFERENCES

1. E. Huse, *The Modern Manager.* St. Paul, MN: West Publishing Company, 1979, pp. 446–447.

2. M. Hooper, *The Coca-Cola Company.* Unpublished manuscript, Edwin L. Cox School of Business, Southern Methodist University, Dallas, TX, 1980.

3. A. Filley and R. Aldag, "Organizational Growth and Types: Lessons From Small Institutions." In *Research in Organizational Behavior.* L. Cummings and B. Staw, (eds). Greenwich, CT: JAI Press, Inc., 1980, pp. 279–320; W. Shanklin, "Strategic Business Planning: Yesterday, Today, and Tomorrow." *Business Horizons* **22,** 5, 1979, 7–14.

4. J. Daniels, L. Radebaugh, and E. Orgram, *International Business: Environments and Operations.* Reading, MA: Addison-Wesley, 1980.

5. B. Tamarkin, "The Country Slicker." *Forbes*, January 21, 1980, 39–44.

6. D. Yankelovich, "Changing Values." *Industry Week*, August 6, 1979, 60ff. Also see entire issue of *Journal of Contemporary Business* **8,** 4, 1979; J. Beck, "Firms consider new 'cafeteria' benefit plans." *Dallas Times Herald*, April 14, 1980, b-1ff; and S. Ronen, *Flexible Working Hours.* New York: McGraw Hill, 1981.

7. W. Guzzardi, "Changing the Mix of the Workforce." *Fortune*, November 5, 1979, 92–106; J. Rosow, "Changing Attitudes to Work and Life Styles." *Journal of Contemporary Business* **8,** 4, 1979, 5–18.

8. *Bureau of Labor Statistics*, December 1979.

9. *Industry Week*, October 29, 1979, 48.

10. Mr. James Casale, Vice-President, Public Relations, Manpower, Inc., Chicago, IL, 1980. Also see the excellent discussion by S. Ronen, *Flexible Working Hours.* New York: McGraw-Hill, 1981.

11. *Dallas Morning News*, April 10, 1980, B-1.

12. A. Louis, "Honda." *Fortune*, July 30, 1979, 92–99.

13. J. Fleming, "A Possible Future of Government-Corporate Relations." *Business Horizons* **22,** 6, 1979, pp. 43–47 and M. Weidenbaum, "The True Obligation of the Business Firm to Society," *Public Affairs Review* **2,** 1981, 50–53.

14. K. Phillips, "Twelve Political Problems Facing American Business." *Business and Public Affairs* **1,** 13, 1979.

15. *Dallas Times Herald,* April 16, 1980, A-6.

16. B. Mathis and J. Jackson, *Personnel: Contemporary Perspectives and Applications.* St. Paul, MN: West Publishing Company, 1979, pp. 398–408; B. Rosen and T. Jerdee, "Coping with Affirmative Action Backlash." *Business Horizons* **22,** 4, 1979, 15–20.

17. *Business Week,* March 10, 1980, 132–133.

18. *Business Week,* April 17, 1979, 109–110; W. Boulton, "Government Control: Business Strikes Back." *Business Horizons* **22,** 4, 1979, pp. 61–66.

19. *Newsweek,* February 25, 1980, 63ff.

GLOSSARY

Abilities   Individual characteristics that can affect the ability to perform a task, e.g., intellectual capacity, manual skills, and personality traits.

Accountability   A person's obligation to carry out responsibilities and be answerable for decisions and activities.

Action plan   The detailed steps and resources needed for implementing departmental or individual objectives.

Activites   What individuals do to or with others or with inanimate objects, e.g., machines and tools.

Administrative management   A management school of thought that focuses on the similarities of managers performing their basic functions of organizing, planning, and controlling. This school is associated with Henry Fayol's belief that a manager's success is not due to personal qualities, but to the methods used.

Affiliation needs   The need for friendship, love, and belongingness.

Ambiguous situation   A high degree of uncertainty about the nature of the problem, the goals to be pursued, and the environment surrounding the decision structure.

Authority   The right to make a decision. A manager's authority is limited by the organization's policies and procedures.

Autocratic leader   A leadership style characterized by orders or commands. The commands are generally obeyed in order to avoid punishment.

Automation   Processes that are primarily self-regulating and capable of operating independently in a wide range of conditions.

G-1

√ ***Autonomy*** The degree to which a job provides substantial freedom and independence, and allows the individual to use his or her own judgment in scheduling work and determining the procedures to be used in carrying out the task(s).

Avoidance style The tendency to withdraw from or remain neutral in conflict situations.

Bargaining strategy The negotiation of an agreement between two or more organizations or individuals about the exchange of goods, services, or expected behaviors.

Behavioral school A school of management thought that focuses on helping managers deal more effectively with the "people side" of their organization. It highlights the importance of a manager's leadership style and group dynamics.

Behavioral-science approach The viewpoint that the organization's success depends on people. The emphasis is on the development of the manager's human skills.

Beliefs about causation Amount of agreement or disagreement between two or more managers as to the means that should be used to reach their goals.

Bounded rationality The tendency of managers to: (1) set less than optimal goals (satisfice); (2) engage in a limited search of alternatives; and (3) have inadequate information about — and control over — the factors influencing the outcomes of their decisions.

√ ***Brainstorming*** A method designed to encourage and support the free flow of ideas with all critical judgments suspended.

Break-even model Shows the basic relationships among units produced (output), dollars of sales revenue, and the levels of costs and profits for an entire firm or a product line.

Break-even point The point at which total costs equal total sales.

Budgeting The process of determining and assigning the resources required to reach objectives.

Budgets These define and link proposed expenditures with desired future objectives.

Bureaucracy A system of management characterized by rules and regulations, a clearly outlined hierarchy, division of labor, impersonal relationships among members, and rigid criteria of promotion and selection.

Cafeteria incentive systems   Under this plan, an employee selects from a number of incentive options to meet individual needs. Options include flexitime, customized fringe-benefit packages, and more responsibility.

Capital   The money, machinery, equipment, buildings, and other assets of the organization.

Capital budgeting   The financial planning for allocating resources to major tangible projects often requiring a time horizon beyond one year.

Cause-and-effect diagram   A graphic method to aid the decision-maker in identifying factors that influence a problem or goals, as well as the effects resulting from these factors.

Centralization   The extent to which responsibility and authority in an organization reside with top management. A minimal amount of authority is delegated to subordinates.

Certainty   The decision situation in which the individual has complete knowledge and information regarding the nature of the problem, the possible alternatives, and the results from each.

Changing environment   An environment in which changing products, technological innovation, and changing competition create an ongoing need for organizations to adapt their structures.

Channel   In the communication process, this is the style of transmission. It can take the form of oral or written communication.

Charismatic authority   Occurs when subordinates voluntarily comply with the leader because of the extraordinary personal capacities, strengths, or powers they perceive in him or her.

Classical school   The identifiable school of management thought. It focuses on managers and how they should plan and direct the efforts of employees toward the accomplishment of organizational goals. Its branches include bureaucracy, scientific management, and administrative management.

Clout   The influence that some managers have over decisions. This influence or "pull" is derived from the manager's location in the formal and informal systems of the organization. Clout enables the manager to deliver valued rewards to subordinates.

Coalition strategy   The combination of two or more organizations to obtain common goals and increase their influence over their environment.

Coercive power   The ability of a person or group to administer punishments to others.

Collaborative situation   What occurs when there is a high-integrative and low-distributive relationship.

Collaborative style   The tendency to identify underlying causes, openly share information, and search out an alternative considered to be mutually beneficial.

Collectivism   When individuals are submerged by the groups they belong to, ranging from the family to the total society.

Communication   The process by which information is exchanged with other people.

Compromise style   The tendency to sacrifice one's own position by seeking a middle ground through the splitting of differences.

Conceptual skills   The ability to see the organization as a whole and to understand how the parts of the organization depend on one another. This skill is particularly important to top-level managers.

Conglomerate   An organization comprising two or more companies that produce unrelated products.

Consensus   When problems and alternatives are identified, discussed, and modified until agreement on one solution is reached.

Contingency approach   This approach suggests that the effectiveness of various managerial styles should vary according to the situation. Management styles should be consistent with the tasks, individuals, and external environments facing the organization.

Contingency planning   Identifying alternative future possibilities and developing a plan of action for each of them.

Continuous-process technology   The ongoing flow of activities for transforming inputs into outputs, with virtually all physical activities being perfomed by machines.

Control   Process by which a person, group, or organization consciously determines or influences what another person, group, or organization will do.

Cooptation strategy   What is being practiced when the organization formally brings individuals (who represent external publics) into its managerial decision-making groups.

Corrective control   Mechanisms designed to return the individual, department, or organization to some predetermined condition.

Corrective model of control   The process of detecting and correcting deviations from preestablished goals or standards.

Cosmopolitans Managers, scientists, and engineers who identify with professional groups outside of the organization. They may have different norms and values from those stated by the organization.

Creativity Applied imagination.

Critical psychological states According to the Hackman-Oldham Job-Enrichment Model, these states are: experienced meaningfulness, experienced responsibility, and knowledge of results. These states are critical in affecting motivations and satisfactions of employees on the job.

Critical path The longest time path through a PERT network.

Cross impact analysis A technique for examining all possible pairings of events.

Cyclical forecast Changes in market demand that are primarily a result of general economic conditions.

Decentralization The degree to which responsibility and authority are pushed downard to lower-level managers in the organization.

Decision tree A model that identified the relationships among future decision strategies, possible states of nature, and present decision strategies.

Decisional roles The roles of entrepreneur, resource allocator, disturbance handler, and negotiator. A manager who takes on these roles plays a key part in the decision-making system of the organization.

Decoding The process by which receivers interpret messages and translate them into meaningful thoughts or feelings for themselves. It is affected by the receiver's past experiences, intelligence, personality, and expectations.

Defend-and-hold strategy Investment and marketing efforts designed to maintain sales and profit levels from a particular service or product.

Delphi technique A method for securing the consensus of experts on their predictions for the future or assessment of current needs.

Democratic leader A leader who allows group discussions in the decision-making process.

Departmentation The process of grouping or joining together jobs on some common basis to perform tasks; typically by function, product, place, or customer.

Deviant A group member who does not follow the standards of behavior established by the group.

Distributive variable The degree to which one or more goals of each of the individuals or groups in an organization are perceived as incompatible.

Divest-and-exit-strategy Efforts designed to eliminate a product or service line by selling or discontinuing it.

Division of labor The method of dividing a task into specialized parts, with employees doing different subtasks so that they may efficiently perform the task.

Domestic instability Subversion, rebellion, and turmoil within a nation.

Downward channel Used by management for sending orders, directives, goals, policies, memorandums, etc. to employees at lower levels in the organization.

Economic climate The degree of market and financial risks associated with investments.

Emotions Feelings that people have toward others.

Encoding The process of translating thoughts or feelings into understandable messages.

Esteem needs Maslow's fourth set of human needs. Esteem needs include personal feelings of achievement or self-worth, and recognition or respect from others.

Ethical-moral value orientation The tendency of an individual to respond to highly important concepts as "right."

Executive-dominated strategy A focus of top management on managing the portfolio of firms under its control.

Expectancy The perceived probability that if a person puts forth effort in task-related activities, he or she will be able to attain the desired performance level. Part of the Expectancy theory of motivation.

Expectancy theory A motivational theory based on the idea that people choose behaviors that they see leading to outcomes that satisfy their needs.

Expected value The weighted average outcome for each strategy.

Experienced meaningfulness A psychological state in the Hackman-Oldham job-enrichment model that refers to the degree to which work is viewed as important, valuable, and worthwhile.

Experienced responsibility A psychological state in the Hackman-Oldham job-enrichment model that refers to the extent to which a person feels responsible and accountable for the work being performed.

Expert power A person's level of knowledge and skills.

Exponential smoothing model A method for estimating moving averages by adjusting them through a weighted difference of the actual demand and the past forecast.

External forces to change Organizations may change in order to adapt to changes in the external environment, e.g., technological innovation, market changes, changes in legal requirements, and/or pressure from outside groups.

External objectives The means by which managers attempt to measure the effects of a change program on job behavior, e.g., turnover, profits, grievances, absenteeism, rate of production.

External system The second part of Homans' model representing the "givens" that existed before the group was formed.

Extrapolation The projection into the future of some tendency from the past or present.

Extrinsic factors Job-related rewards that include supervision, working conditions, salary, status, job security, and fringe benefits. These are rewards a person receives from sources other than the work itself.

Feedback Knowledge about performance that a person obtains from the job itself, friends, or supervision.

Fiedler's model A model of leadership which specifies that a group's performance is contingent on the motivation system of the leader and the degree to which the leader has control and influence in a particular situation. This model utilizes the Least Preferred Co-worker scale to measure leadership style.

Fire fighting Management's response to problems by making small changes as needed instead of developing a program of planned change.

First-line managers The lowest level of managers in the hierarchy. They are responsible for the actual production of goods and services, and serve as a link between the managers and non-managers.

Fixed costs Those costs that remain constant regardless of the number of units produced.

Fixed-order period model A method for determining the number of items to be ordered at fixed time intervals up to a predetermined maximum level.

Fixed-order quantity model A method for determining the standard number of items to be ordered when the inventory reaches a predetermined level.

Focal person The individual who receives the role expectations from the role senders.

Forcing style   The tendency to use coercive and reward power to dominate the other party by suppressing differences and requiring the adoption of one's own position.

Forecasting   Predicting, projecting, or estimating future events or conditions in the organization's environment.

Foreign conflict   The degree to which a nation shows hostility toward other nations.

Formal channel   The flow of information that follows the hierarchical structure of the organization. There are three kinds of formal channels: downward, upward, and horizontal.

Formal group   One which has goals and activities related directly to the achievement of stated organizational goals.

Francisher   An individual or company that licenses others to sell its products or services.

Functional foremanship   The division of labor at the foreman level suggested by Frederick Taylor. It involves splitting the task of the foreman into eight areas and having each worker report to several foremen.

Functional manager   A manager who is responsible for a specialized area of operations, such as accounting, personnel, finance, marketing, or production.

Future shock   What happens when the types of changes and the rapidity of change overpower the individual's ability to successfully adapt.

General manager   A manager who is responsible for more than one specialized area, such as a company or plant. People from various functions report to this type of manager.

Goals   Results to be obtained.

Group   Two or more individuals who come into personal, meaningful, and purposeful contact on a relatively continuing basis.

Group coalition   Two or more individuals who band together to maintain or increase their outcomes (such as money, free time, etc.) relative to another person or group.

Grow-and-penetrate strategy   Active investment and marketing efforts designed to increase the size and sales of the firm.

Growth-need strength   A feature of the Hackman-Oldham job-enrichment model that refers to the individual's desire for personal accomplishments and learning on the job.

Growth stages   The three stages organizations move through to experience success: survival, management of growth, and allocation and control of resources.

Hackman-Oldham job-enrichment model   A model that focuses on certain job characteristics that lead to critical psychlogical states for the worker. These states affect personal and work outcomes, which are moderated by employee growth-need strengths.

Harvest strategy   Investment and marketing efforts designed to draw excess cash and profits generated from a particular product or service line for use elsewhere.

Hawthorne effect   The tendency of people who are being observed to react differently than they would if they did not know they were being observed. This phenomenon was identified by Mayo in the Hawthorne experiments.

Hawthorne experiments   These studies, which began the human-relations movement, were conducted by researchers from Harvard University at the Chicago plant of Western Electric. The experiments involved changing the working conditions to determine whether they increased productivity. The conclusion pointed to a need for further understanding of human relations.

Horizontal channel   Information that flows across lines of communication. It can be classified as either a formal or informal channel.

Human relations   A school of management thought that stresses the social needs of the employees, and how the social environment of the organization influences the quality and quantity of the work produced.

Human-relations skills   These are the skills that a manager needs in order to lead, motivate, manage conflict, and work with others. These skills are vital no matter what level of management a manager is in.

Hygienes   In Herzberg's two-factor theory, the extrinsic sources of motivation (e.g., company policy and administration, supervision, working conditions, co-workers, salary, and job security) that influence the degree of job dissatisfaction.

Impersonality   The idea that all employees are subject to the same rules and regulations, and are thus saved from the personal whims of the manager.

Individual characteristics   The interests, values, attitudes, and needs that workers bring to the job.

Informal channel   Organizational communication that does not follow the lines of the formal organization, but is spread by employees talking. Often known as the "grapevine."

Informal group   One which develops out of the day-to-day activities, inter-actions, and sentiments of the members for the purpose of meeting their own needs.

Informational roles   Roles of monitor, disseminator, and company spoke-sperson.

In-process inventory   Those goods which are partially completed and will have additional labor and materials added to obtain a finished good.

Innovation-dominated strategy   A focus of key managers on the creation and/or implementation of new technologies, products, or services.

Inspiration strategy   The use of imitation, intuition, feelings, or creativity.

Instrumental leadership   A style characterized by managers who plan, organize, control, and coordinate the activities of subordinates to reach de-partmental or group goals.

Instrumentality   The perceived probability that a level of performance will lead to desired outcomes. Part of the expectancy approach to motivation.

Integrative variable   The degree to which one or more goals of different individuals or groups are perceived as compatible.

Interactions   The starting actions and following reactions between two or more individuals.

Interest group   Two or more individuals who perceive themselves as having common objectives that can be best achieved through united action.

Intergroup conflict   Differences and clashes between groups, departments or divisions within an organization.

Internal objectives   The means by which managers assess the effective-ness of an organizational change program based on a change in attitudes, increased motivation, and/or job satisfaction.

Internal system   The activities, interactions, sentiments, and norms of in-formal groups in Homans' systems model.

International corporation   One with business interests in different coun-tries, often focusing on the import or export of goods and services.

Interpersonal conflict   Disagreements over policies, practices, or plans; and emotional issues involving negative feelings between two or more indi-viduals.

Interpersonal roles   A manager's roles as figurehead, leader, and liaison that arise directly from the manager's formal authority and involve basic in-terpersonal relationships.

Interrole conflict Role pressures associated with membership in one group or organization that are in conflict with those stemming from membership in other groups or organizations.

Intersender role conflict When pressures from one role sender are perceived as being incompatible with pressures from one or more other role senders.

Intrinsic rewards Rewards that come directly from performing the task, such as the opportunity to perform meaningful work, complete cycles of work, see finished products, carry out complete visible cycles of activities, and receive feedback on performance.

Intuition The use of hunches, images, insights, or thoughts that often spontaneously surface to the individual's awareness.

Inventory The amount of inputs or outputs kept on hand.

Inventory costs The expenses associated with maintaining an inventory.

Job characteristics The characteristics of a worker's task, e.g., variety of work, responsibility for completing task, and knowledge of results.

Job enrichment A job design strategy for giving workers more recognition and a feeling of greater personal achievement by providing them with more challenge, responsibility, and authority.

Judgment strategy The use of personal beliefs and experiences for choosing among alternatives and deciding how the selected alternative should be implemented.

Knowledge of results In the Hackman-Oldham job-enrichment model, feedback (information) received by the worker on how well or poorly he or she is performing the task.

Labor The human resources (employees) in the organization.

Laissez-faire leadership A leadership style which allows the group total freedom. The leader exerts a minimal amount of influence.

Lead time The amount of time between the placement of an order and the actual receipt of that order by the purchaser.

Leader-member relations Proposed by Fiedler, this refers to the leader's feeling of being accepted by the group. It is the most important influence on a leader's effectiveness.

Leader power position The extent to which the leader has legitimate, coercive, and reward power to influence subordinates.

Leadership The ability of one person to influence the behavior of another toward the accomplishment of certain goals.

Least-preferred co-worker (LPC) The motivational system or behavioral preferences of the leader. High-LPC leaders are relations-oriented; low-LPC leaders are task-oriented.

Legitimate power A manager's formal authority based on his or her position in the hierarchy.

Line A function in which managers and employees are directly involved in the production of the final product or service that the organization produces. In a university, the faculty members are line managers.

Lobbying strategy Attempting to influence decisions of an administrative or legislative branch of government through persuasion and the provision of information.

Locals Managers and professionals who have an inside-the-organization orientation. They tend to be loyal to the organization's norms and values.

Low-interdependency situation When there is both a low-distributive and low-integrative relationship.

Management The process of getting things done through other people. People, technology, and other resources are combined and coordinated to achieve organizational goals

Management by objectives (MBO) A process, system, and philosophy of management that can serve as both a planning aid and way of organizational life which requires a manager to set forth goals to be achieved in each area.

Management functions The activities that a manager must perform for the organization to reach its goals, e.g., organize, plan, command, coordinate, and control.

Management strategies The dominant thrusts of key managers for implementing the various marketing/investment strategies.

Managerial grid An organizational change approach that assumes that managers should be both people- and production-centered.

Managers Individuals who are responsible for helping the organization reach its goals.

Marketing-dominated strategy A focus of key managers on "managing" the consumer.

Mass-production technology The manufacture of large volumes of identical or similar goods through assembly line techniques.

Materials   The physical items that are directly used or transformed to create the desired outputs.

Matrix   An organization that employs a multiple authority structure. This design represents a compromise between functional and product departmentation. In this arrangement, special program managers have authority to supervise and temporarily request subordinates from functional departments.

Means-goal staircase   Systematically linking the goals of lower-level units or individuals with those of higher-level units or individuals.

Measurement   The means used to assess the amount or degree of specific characteristics.

Measuring by attribute   The assessment of characteristics that must fall within specified upper and lower limits.

Measuring by variable   The assessment of characteristics for which there are specific standards.

Mechanistic system   An organization that is usually centralized, relies very little on employee participation, and emphasizes the development and use of rules and regulations.

Message   Part of the communication process that contains the verbal and nonverbal symbols representing the information that we want to send to receivers.

Middle-managers   These are on a level between top and first-line management. They receive broad, overall strategies from top managers and translate them into specific action programs that can be implemented by first-line managers.

Mitchell's planning law   "He who allows detailed trivia to smother clarity of purpose shall suffer the flames of hell."

Mixed conflict situation   When there is both a highly distributive and highly integrative relationship.

Motivation   An inner state that causes, channels, and sustains people's behavior.

Motivators   In Herzberg's two-factor theory of motivation, those job-related factors, which, if present, operate to build a high level of achievement and performance, e.g., work itself, recognition, advancement, responsibility, and growth.

Moving averages model   A method for smoothing or reducing the effects of random variations in market demand data.

Multinational corporation   One in which: (1) the key managers try to take a worldwide view in assessing problems and opportunities in the environment; (2) there are one or more subsidiaries operating in several countries; and (3) there is a natural willingness to consider a variety of locations in the world to make sales, obtain resources, and produce goods.

National Alliance of Businessmen A coalition of business firms founded in 1968 to combat structural unemployment among the nation's hard-to-employ by reducing the barriers to their employment.

Needs An individual want or desire. Maslow suggested that human needs are arranged in a hierarchy. Basic needs must be met before attempting to satisfy higher-order needs.

Negotiation A process in which two or more individuals or groups, who have both common goals and conflicting goals, put forth and discuss proposals concerning terms of a possible agreement.

Negotiation strategy The use of bargaining and compromise to adjust the goals of decision-makers so they can reach agreement.

Nenko system The general pattern of human resource management commonly used in large-scale Japanese organizations.

Network A diagram of the sequence of activities that must be performed to complete a project.

Nodes. Usually represented by circles, squares, and rectangles which make up the skeleton of the decision tree.

Nominal group technique A structured group meeting designed to stimulate creative decision-making where the participants lack agreement or there is incomplete knowledge concerning the nature of the problem.

Nonverbal communication All those messages that are not communicated with words, e.g., body language, space, appearance.

Normative decision models The various step-by-step procedures that prescribe how managers should make decisions to reach their goals.

Norms The standards of behavior widely shared and enforced by members of the group.

Objective probabilities The decision situation in which the individual can determine, with relative certainty, the likelihood that each state of nature will occur.

Operatinal planning The detailed means of implementing the broader goals and strategies that have already been determined.

Operations management The production process of transforming inputs (resources) into desired outputs (goods or services).

Organic system An organization design having a decentralized authority structure, flexible jobs and procedures, team leadership, and few hierarchical levels.

Organization A system that coordinates people, jobs, financial resources, and managerial practices to achieve goals.

Organization chart A graphic representation of organizational structure.

Organization definition The answers to the following types of questions: (1) Who are we? (2) What do we want to become? and (3) What are our basic goals?

Organization development The name given to a variety of behavioral science techniques directed toward moving organizations toward more open and honest communication among individuals and groups.

Organization goals The general directions and areas in which accomplishments are desired.

Organization structure The formally defined framework of task and authority relationships.

Organizational change An attempt by management to improve the overall performance of individuals, groups, and the organization by changing the organization's structure, technology, task, or people.

Organizational characteristics Those dimensions of the organization that influence managers' motivation to perform. These include structure, rewards, and workers' view of the job.

Organizational politics The use of power by individuals or interest groups to increase or protect (1) their control over resources and (2) their authority to decide and control the objectives being sought in the use of these resources.

Organizational socialization The formal or informal attempts to "mold" employees into having certain desired attitudes and ways of dealing with others and their jobs.

Organizing function All managerial activity that results in the design of the formal structure.

Osborn technique A procedure designed to encourage unconventional, intuitive, and freewheeling thinking.

Outcome The "payoff" that can be expected for each possible combination of strategy and state of nature.

Outputs The goods, services, wastes, or other possible results of the transformation process.

Participative leadership   Leadership style characterized by the sharing of information, power, and influence between superiors and subordinates.

Path   The sequence of events and activities that should be followed over the course of a project.

Path-goal model   A contingency leadership model that emphasizes the influence of leadership on subordinate goals and the paths to these goals. This model uses supportive and instrumental leadership styles depending on the situation and the needs of the subordinates.

Payoff-matrix   A two-dimensional list of figures or symbols arranged in rows and columns that identifies the possible states of nature, probabilities, and outcomes (payoffs) associated with each strategy (alternative).

Perceived effort-rewards   A characteristic of the Porter-Lawler Model that refers to a person's expectations that rewards depend on given amounts of effort.

Perceived equitable rewards   The amount of rewards people feel they should receive as the result of their performance.

Perception   The selection and organization of a message into a meaningful experience for a person.

Performance   The level of work achieved by the individual.

Performance gap   The difference between what the organization could do by virtue of its opportunities, and what it actually does in taking advantage of those opportunities.

Person-role conflict   When incompatibilities arise between the pressures of the focal person's role(s) and his or her own needs, attitudes, values, or abilities.

Physiological needs   The lowest level of needs in Maslow's hierarchy of needs; includes food, water, air, and shelter.

Planning   The formal process of making decisions that are intended to affect the future.

Policy   A guide for carrying out action.

Political climate   The degreee to which a government is likely to swing to the far left or far right.

Political risk   The probability of occurrence of some political event that will change the profitability of a given investment.

Political strategies   The general approaches used by firms in dealing with important and powerful components in the environment.

Political system   The components in a business firm's environment that can influence its decisions, survival, or growth.

Porter-Lawler model   An extension of the expectancy theory that draws together individual, job, and organizational characteristics to describe the motivational process.

Power   The ability to limit choices.

Pragmatic value orientation   The individual's tendency to respond to highly important concepts as "successful."

Preferences about goals   The degree of agreement or disagreement between two or more managers as to the goals that should be pursued.

Preventive control   Mechanisms designed to minimize the need for corrective action.

Principle of selectivity   The principle that in any series of elements to be controlled, a small fraction (in terms of the number of elements) always accounts for a large portion of the results.

Probability   The likelihood that each state of nature will occur.

Product/service life cycle   The market phases for most products and services.

Production-dominated strategy   The focus of key decision-makers on manufacturing and processing know-how.

Profits   The excess of total dollar sales over total dollar costs associated with certain levels of production.

Program Evaluation and Review Technique (PERT)   A special type of visual flow diagram for planning and controlling nonrecurring projects or programs.

Quality circle   A forum of workers and managers that meet on a regular basis to discuss product-quality improvement.

Quality control   Processes for assuring that outputs meet certain predetermined standards.

Quantitative school   A school of management that develops mathematical models to simulate problems that managers cannot handle by intuition or experience. This decision-making tool is particularly valuable in the areas of planning and operations management.

Random demand   A change in market demand that has no pattern and cannot be forecasted.

Rational-legal authority An authority structure based on law. Supervisors are obeyed because of the individual's position in the organization's hierarchy.

Rationality The process of making decisions that serve to maximize the firm's goals.

Rebuild strategy Investment and marketing efforts designed to increase or exceed sales, profits, or market share levels that were held at an earlier time.

Receiver The person who gets the sender's message in the communication process.

Referent power The desire of one individual or group to identify with or be like another person or group.

Regression analysis model A method by which knowledge of one (independent) variable can be used to estimate the second (dependent) variable.

Regulations Means of controlling and coordinating the decision-making behavior of all employees by having them follow rules.

Relationship-motivated leadership That shown by a leader who is motivated to seek strong emotional ties with co-workers.

Representation strategy Encouraging or requiring members of one organization to form or join other groups or organizations.

Resistance Any behavior that serves to maintain the status quo in the face of pressure to change.

Responsibility Performance areas in which a person or department has the obligation to perform assigned activities to produce results.

Reward The outcomes or benefits desired by the individual.

Reward power The ability of a person or group to provide varying amounts and types of benefits to others.

Risk The decision situation in which the individual can define the nature of the problem, the possible alternatives, and the probability of each alternative leading to the desired results.

Risk-taker One who is willing to take chances and may aggressively seek out chancy situations which offer the possibility of significant payoffs.

Robot A reprogrammable, multifunctional manipulator designed to move material, parts, tools, or specialized devices through variable programmed motions for the performance of a variety of tasks.

Role A group of related activities carried out by an individual.

Role conflict What occurs when an individual must cope with two or more sets of incompatible pressures.

Role episode When one or more role senders attempt to influence the behavior of a focal person, and the focal person attempts to influence the future expectations of the role sender(s).

Role perceptions The kind of activities that people believe they should perform if they want to perform their job successfully.

Role senders Members of the role set who communicate expectations to the focal person.

Role Set The collection of roles directly targeted to the activities of an individual.

Routine strategy Well-established procedures or computational techniques that can be followed systematically to arrive at a decision.

Rule A specific course of action or conduct that must be followed.

Satisfaction The difference between what a person receives and the amount that person feels he or she should receive.

Satisficing An individual who does not set an optimum goal in a decision problem, but instead establishes a very limited range of goals that would be acceptable.

Scalar principle The chain of direct authority relationships from managers to subordinates throughout the organization. Every employee should know his or her area of responsibility, and report to only one superior.

Scenario A potential sequence of events and processes in a particular area of interest during a certain time period.

Scheduling The creation of a timetable to show when certain things should occur or be done.

Scientific management A perspective of management developed by Taylor that attempts to precisely define all aspects of the worker-machine relationship. In the process, it utilizes time-and-motion studies and functional foremen to yield the "one best way" to do the job.

Seasonal forecast Changes in market demand that depend primarily on the time of year.

Security needs The need for safety, stability, and absence from pain, threat, or illness. These needs must be met before higher needs in Maslow's hierarchy can be met.

Self-actualization needs Self-fulfillment, or the realization of one's potential. This need is the highest in Maslow's hierarchy of needs.

Self-satisfaction value orientation In which the individual tends to respond to highly important concepts as "pleasant."

Semantics The study of how words are used and what meanings they convey.

Sender The source or initiator of information in the communication process.

Sentiments Day-to-day feelings (such as anger, happiness, sadness) as well as deeper feelings (such as trust, openness, and freedom).

Simulation models Methods by which the performance of the whole organization or just one of its departments may be used to forecast the effects on performance of possible changes in the environment and/or decisons by management.

Skill variety The degree to which a person must perform a number of different activities to complete a job. It involves the use of a number of skills and talents.

Smoothing style The tendency to minimize or suppress the open recognition of real or perceived differences, while emphasizing common interests in conflict situations.

Social audit A systematic study of the social peformance of a business.

Social behaviors Actions such as joking, laughing, rewarding others, and agreeing with others.

Social responsibility Corporate behavior that is consistent with current social norms, values, and the performance expectations of society.

Social specialists Individuals who show a great deal of feeling and support for others.

Social structure The pattern of sentiments, activities, and interactions among group members.

Socialization The attempt to indoctrinate people in beliefs or values consistent with the interests of the organization or the broader society.

Span of control The number of people reporting to a single superior.

Stability The objective of creating a sense of predictability, control, and certainty in the organization.

Stable environment   An environment which is characterized by relatively small changes in technology and customers that have a minimal impact on the internal operations of the organization.

Staff   Employees who advise and assist line managers and employees, but who are not directly engaged in the production of the final good or service.

Standards   The criteria for evaluating the activities undertaken by an individual or group against a level of performance.

Stars   Individuals who are active, effective group members and exhibit a variety of behaviors.

States of nature   Those conditions beyond the control of decison-makers that can influence the results of their decisions.

Status   A social ranking within a group assigned on the basis of position in the group or on individual characteristics.

Strategic business unit   A division or company within an organization that typically provides related products or services to a particular market.

Strategic planning   The process of (1) analyzing the environment; (2) defining the nature of the organization; (3) formulating basic goals; and (4) identifying, evaluating, and selecting the fundamental courses of action for the organization.

Strategies   The patterns of important decisions that (1) guide the organization in its environment; (2) influence the structure and processes of the organization; and (3) centrally affect the profitability, growth, and survival of the organization.

Stress   The physiological and/or psychological conditions an individual may experience in response to potentially harmful external events or situations.

Subjective probability   A decision situation in which an individual can determine the likelihood of each possible state of nature based on his or her judgments and beliefs.

Suboptimization   When the maximization of one goal reduces the overall level of goal attainment for the whole individual or organization.

Superordinate goals   Shared goals of groups that can be achieved only through cooperation.

Supportive leadership   The style of managers who consider the needs of their subordinates — their well-being, status, and comfort. These leaders seek to create a friendly and pleasant working climate for employees.

Systems approach   An approach to management that emphasizes the interdependence between departments in the organization.

Task behaviors   Actions such as giving suggestions, providing information, analyzing problems, evaluating alternatives, and making decisions.

Task dependency   The situation in which one group or individual must rely on another group or individual for services, information, or goods.

Task environment   All those factors and forces external to the organization that are important to managerial decision-making.

Task identity   A job in which completion of the whole task is required; an identifiable piece of work. That is, doing from beginning to end a job that has a visible outcome.

Task interdependency   The extent to which two groups or individuals rely on each other for service, information, and goods to accomplish their own goals.

Task-motivated leadership   That in which the manager tends to describe his or her least preferred co-worker in an unfavorable light. This leader is task-controlling, managing, and less concerned with the human relations aspects of the job.

Task significance   The degree to which the job has a substantial impact on the lives or work of others in the company.

Task structure   The extent to which the task is simple (routine) or complex (nonroutine). An important contingency in both Fiedler's and House's models of leadership.

Technical skill   The ability to perform specific kinds of activities in a specialized field. This skill is particularly important for first-level managers.

Technical specialists   Group members who show a great deal of concern with task-related problems and use their expertise to solve them.

Temporary employees   Nonpermanent members of an organization's workforce who often do clerical work.

Theory X   A managerial philosphy that assumes that employees dislike to work, are motivated basically by money and fringe benefits, and must be closely controlled.

Theory Y   A managerial philosophy that assumes workers are motivated to achieve organizational goals and are self-directed adults.

Time-and-motion studies   The measurement of all movements made by the worker in order to eliminate those movements that do not lead to increased productivity. An objective of these studies is to make the job highly routine and efficient.

Top managers Managers who are responsible for the overall operations of the organization.

Traditional approach A body of knowledge managers can use to create order and stability within an organization. Its emphasis is on formal management processes, e.g., organizing, planning, controlling, and decison-making.

Trait approach The assumption that leaders differ from other people in specific physical, social, personality, and personal traits. The approach relies on research that relates these classes of traits to leader-success criteria.

Transformation Conversion of inputs, through a production process, to create outputs.

Trend forecast The long-term changes in market demand.

Turbulent environment A complex, changing, and erratic environment.

Two-factor theory Frederick Herzberg's theory of motivation based on two separate components — satisfiers (motivators) and dissatisfiers (hygienes).

Uncertainty The decision situation in which the individual cannot assign subjective probabilities to each of the possible states of nature.

Underchosen Participants who are uncommitted to the group and tend to show interest only in their personal needs.

Unit-small batch technology The custom manufacturing of indiviudal items.

Unity of command A management principle that recommends that a subordinate have only one superior to report to.

Upward channel A subordinate's major means of communicating information to a supervisor. It provides feedback to management.

Value A basic concept that has considerable importance and meaning to the individual and is relatively stable over time.

Value system The sum of an individual's or group's values that normally fits into a pattern of relative importance and meaning.

Variable costs Those costs that tend to vary with changes in the number of units produced.

Vroom-Yetton model A contingency model of leadership that focuses on the degree of participation leaders should use in reaching a decision. The diagnosis of situational factors determines the degree of participation required.

Win-lose conflict situation   Occurs when there is a high-distributive and low-integrative relationship.

Workplace politics   Occur when organization members intentionally seek selfish goals that conflict with those of others in the organization.

Work ethic   The desire to do a good job that is brought with the worker into the workplace.

Work outcomes   The result of the worker's critical psychological states in the Hackman-Oldham job-enrichment model. Includes high internal work motivation, high quality work performance, high satisfaction with the work, and low absenteeism and turnover.

Zero-base budgeting   (ZBB) A system of justifying each activity and program in terms of efficiency, effectiveness, and organizational priorities, and treating each one as if it were entirely new.

AUTHOR INDEX

SUBJECT INDEX